# The Complete Frances Harper

# The Complete Frances Harper

Frances Ellen Watkins Harper

MINT EDITIONS

*The Complete Frances Harper* contains work first published from 1845–1892.

This edition published by Mint Editions 2021.

ISBN 9781513218557 | E-ISBN 9781513217550

Published by Mint Editions®

 MINT
EDITIONS

minteditionbooks.com

Publishing Director: Jennifer Newens
Design & Production: Rachel Lopez Metzger
Project Manager: Micaela Clark
Typesetting: Westchester Publishing Services

# Contents

NOVELS

MINNIE'S SACRIFICE

## Shadows Uplifted

# Note from the Publisher

The Complete Frances Harper is a collection of Frances Harper's best work—her poetry, speeches, stories and novels—a reflection of one of the most prolific and influential Black women writers of the 19th century.

M. Clark
Berkeley, CA

POEMS

# FOREST LEAVES

# ETHIOPIA

Yes, Ethiopia, yet shall stretch
Her bleeding hands abroad,
Her cry of agony shall reach
The burning throne of God.

The tyrant's yoke from off her neck,
His fetters from her soul,
The mighty hand of God shall break,
And spurn their vile control.

Redeem'd from dust and freed from chains
Her sons shall lift their eyes,
From cloud capt hills and verdant plains
Shall shouts of triumph rise.

Upon her dark despairing brow
Shall play a smile of peace,
For God hath bent unto her woe
And bade her sorrows cease.

'Neath sheltering vines and stately palms,
Shall laughing children play,
And aged sires with joyous psalms,
Shall gladden every day.

Secure by night, and blest by day
Shall pass her happy hours,
Nor human tigers hunt for prey
Within her peaceful bowers.

Then Ethiopia, stretch, Oh stretch
Thy bleeding hands abroad,
Thy cry of agony shall reach
And find redress from God.

# The Soul

Bring forth the balance, let the weights be gold,
We'd know the worth of a deathless soul;
Bring rubies and jems from every mine,
With the wealth of ocean, land and clime.

Bring the joys of the glad green earth,
Its playful smiles and careless mirth;
The dews of youth, and flushes of health,
Bring! Oh bring! the wide world's wealth.

Bring the rich radiant gems of thought
From the mines and deeps of knowledge brought;
Bring glowing words and ponderous lore,
Search heaven and earth's arcana o'er.

Bring the fairest, brightest rolls of fame,
Unwritten with a deed of guilt or shame;
Bring honor's guerdon, and victory's crown,
Robes of pride, and laurels of renown.

We've brought the wealth of every mine,
We've ransack'd ocean, land clime,
And caught the joyous smiles away
From the prattling babe to the sire grey.

We've brought the names of the noble dead
With those who in their footsteps tread;
Here are wreaths of pride and gems of thought
From the battle field and study brought.

Heap high the gems, pile up the gold,
Heavy's the weight of a deathless soul;
Make room for all the wealth of earth,
Its honors, joys, and careless mirth.

Leave me a niche for the rolls of fame
For precious indeed is a spotless name,
For the wreaths, the robes and gems of thought,
Let an empty place in the scale be sought.

With care we've adjusted balance and scale,
Futile our efforts we've seen them fail;
Lighter than dust is the wealth of earth
Weigh'd in the scales with immortal worth.

Could we drag the sun from its golden car
To lay in this balance with ev'ry star,
T'would darken the day and obscure the night,
But the weight of the balance would still be light.

# "He Knoweth Not That the Dead Are There"

In yonder halls reclining
Are forms surpassing fair,
And brilliant lights are shining,
But, Oh! the dead are there.

There's music, song and dance,
There is banishment of care,
And mirth in every glance,
But still the dead are there.

Like the asp's seductive venom
Hid 'neath flowerets fair,
This charnal house concealeth
The dead that slumber there.

'Neath that flow of song and laughter
Runs the current of despair,
But the simple sons of pleasure
Know not the dead are there.

They'll shudder, start and tremble,
They'll weep in wild despair,
When the solemn truth breaks on them
That the dead, the dead are there.

They who've scoff'd at ev'ry warning,
Who've turn'd from ev'ry prayer,
Shall learn in bitter anguish
That the dead, the dead are there.

# THAT BLESSED HOPE

Oh touch it not that hope so blest
Which cheers the fainting heart,
And points it to the coming rest
Where sorrow has no part.

Tear from heart each worldly prop,
Unbind each earthly string;
But to this blest and glorious hope,
Oh let my spirit cling.

It cheer'd amid the days of old
Each holy patriarch's breast,
It was an anchor to their souls,
Upon it let me rest.

When wand'ring in the dens and caves,
In goat and sheep skins drest,
Apeel'd and scatter'd people learn'd
To know this hope was blest.

Help me to love this blessed hope;
My heart's a fragile thing;
Will you not nerve and bear it up
Around this hope to cling.

Help amid this world of strife
To long for Christ to reign,
That when he brings the crown of life
I may that crown obtain.

# Yearnings For Home

Oh let me go I'm weary here
And fevers scorch my brain,
I long to feel my native air
Breathe o'er each burning vein.

I long once more to see
My home among the distant hills,
To breathe amid the melody
Of murmering brooks and rills.

My home is where eternal snow
Round threat'ning craters sleep,
Where streamlets murmer soft and low
And playful cascades leap.

Tis where glad scenes shall meet
My weary, longing eye;
Where rocks and Alpine forests greet
The bright cerulean sky.

Your scenes are bright I know,
But there my mother pray'd,
Her cot is lowly, but I go
To die beneath its shade.

For, Oh I know she'll cling
'Round me her treasur'd long,
My sisters too will sing
Each lov'd familiar song.

They'll soothe my fever'd brow,
As in departed hours,
And spread around my dying couch
The brightest, fairest flowers.

Then let me go I'm weary here
And fevers scorch my brain,
I long to feel my native air,
Breathe o'er each burning vein.

# Farewell, My Heart is Beating

Farewell, my heart is beating
With feelings sad and wild,
I've strove to hide its heaving
And 'mid my tears to smile.

This heart the lone and trusting,
Hath twin'd itself to thee;
And now when almost bursting,
Say, must it sever'd be.

When other brows for mine
Were alter'd, cold and strange,
I clasp'd my yearning heart to thine
And never found it chang'd.

This heart when almost breaking
Has leaned upon thy breast,
But when again 'tis aching
On thine it may not rest.

Oh clasp me closely ere we part
But breathe no sad farewell;
We can't be sever'd while thy heart
Retains o'er mine its spell.

# HAMAN AND MORDECAI

He stood at Persia's Palace gate
And vassal round him bow'd,
Upon his brow was written hate
And he heeded not the crowd.

He heeded not the vassal throng
Whose praises rent the air,
His bosom shook with rage and scorn
For Mordecai stood there.

When ev'ry satrap bow'd
To him of noble blood,
Amid that servile crowd
One form unbending stood.

And as he gaz'd upon that form,
Dark flash'd his angry eye,
'Twas as the light'ning ere the storm
Hath swept in fury by.

On noble Mordecai alone,
He scorn'd to lay his hand;
But sought an edict from the throne
'Gainst all the captive band.

For full of pride and wrath
To his fell purpose true,
He vow'd that from his path
Should perish ev'ry Jew.

Then woman's voice arose
In deep impassion'd prayer,
Her fragile heart grew strong
'Twas the nervings of despair.

The king in mercy heard
Her pleading and her prayer
His heart with pity stirr'd,
And he resolved to spare.

And Haman met the fate
He'd for Mordecai decreed,
And from his cruel hate
The captive Jews are freed.

# LET ME LOVE THEE

Let me love thee I have known
The agony deception brings,
And tho' my riven heart is lone
It fondly clasps and firmly clings.

Oh! let me love thee, I have seen
Hope's fairest blossoms fail,
Have felt my life a mournful dream
And this world a tearful vale.

Oh! let me love thee, I have felt
Deep yearnings for a kindly heart,
When joy would thrill or sorrow melt
Some kindred soul to bear a part.

Let me love thee, yet Oh! yet
Breathe not distrust around my heart,
The lov'd, the cherish may forget
And act a cold and faithless part.

Let me love thee, I have press'd
Sadly my aching heart and brow,
But banish'd ne'er from each recess
The thirst of love that fills them now.

Let me love thee, let my breast
Closely round thee entwine,
And hide within its deep recess
True constant love like thine.

# Ruth and Naomi

Turn my daughters full of woe,
Is my heart so sad and lone,
Leave me, children, I would go
To my lov'd and distant home.

From my bosom death has torn,
Husband, children, all my stay;
Left me not a single one
For my life's declining day.

Want and wo surround my way,
Grief and famine where I tread;
In my native land they say
God is giving Jacob bread.

Naomi ceased, her daughters wept,
Their yearning hearts were fill'd,
Falling upon her wither'd neck
Their grief in tears distill'd.

Like rain upon a blighted tree
The tears of Orpah fell,
Kissing the pale and quiv'ring lip,
She breath'd her sad farewell.

But Ruth stood up, on her brow
There lay a heavenly calm,
And from her lips came soft and low
Words like a holy charm.

I will not leave thee, on thy brow
Are lines of sorrow, age and care,
Thy form is bent, thy step is slow,
Thy bosom stricken, lone and sear.

Thy failing lamp is growing dim,
It's flame is flick'ring past,
I will not leave thee withering,
'Neath stern affliction's blast.

When thy heart and home were glad,
I freely shar'd thy joyous lot
And now that heart is lone and sad,
Cease to entreat I'll leave thee not.

Oh if a lofty palace proud
Thy future home shall be,
Where sycophants around thee crowd
I'll share that home with thee.

And if on earth the humblest spot
Thy future home shall prove,
I'll bring into thy lowly cot
The wealth of woman's love.

However drear, earth has no lot
My spirit shrinks to share with thee,
Then mother, dear entreat me not
To turn from following after thee.

Go where thou wilt my steps are there,
Our path in life is one,
Thou hast no lot I will not share
Till life itself be done.

My country and home for thee
I freely, willingly resign;
Thy people shall my people be,
Thy God he shall be mine.

Then mother, dear, entreat me not
To turn from following thee,
My heart is mov'd to share thy lot
What e'er that lot may be.

# "Bible Defence of Slavery"

Take sackcloth of the darkest dye
And shroud the pulpits round,
Servants of him that cannot lie
Sit mourning on the ground.

Let holy horror blanche each cheek,
Pale ev'ry brow with fears,
And rocks and stones if ye could speak
Ye well might melt to tears.

Let sorrow breathe in ev'ry tone
And grief in ev'ry strain ye raise,
Insult not heaven's majestic throne
With the mockery of praise.

A man whose light should be
The guide of age and youth,
Brings to the shrine of slavery
The sacrifice of truth.

For the fiercest wrongs that ever rose
Since Sodom's fearful cry,
The word of life has been unclos'd
To give your God the lie.

An infidel could do no more
To hide his country's guilty blot,
Than spread God's holy record o'er
The loathesome leprous spot.

Oh, when ye pray for heathen lands,
And plead for dark benighted shores,
Remember slavery's cruel hands
Make heathens at your doors.

FRANCES ELLEN WATKINS HARPER

# To a Missionary

Joy, joy! unto the heathen,
Unfurl each snowy sail,
And waft the breath of prayer
On ev'ry breeze and gale.

Spread, spread your sails with mercy
As you plough the trackless,
And at your stern and helm
Shall God a vigil keep.

You're freighted with rich blessings,
You've glorious things to tell,
Your tidings are salvation,
Your theme Immanuel.

Heathen minds by sin degraded,
Captives 'neath the tempter's sway,
Shall from their moral vision
Have the darkness chas'd away.

'Neath bamboo hut and palm tree
Shall prayer like incense rise,
An oblation pure and holy
To the God of earth and skies.

He who from the fiery pillar
Guided once a pilgrim train,
Shall protect you by his power
As you sweep across the main.

More faithful than the needle
Pointing constant to the pole,
Shall the God of love be with you
When the darkest tempests roll.

God speed you on your journey,
May his presence and his power
Be your stay in grief and trial
And the joy of every hour.

## "I Thirst"

I thirst, but earth cannot allay
The fever coursing thro' my veins,
The healing stream is far away,
It flows thro' Salem's glorious plains

The murmers of its crystal flow
Break ever o'er this world of strife,
My heart is weary let me go
To bathe it in the stream of life.

For a worn and weary heart
Hath bath'd in this pure stream,
And felt its griefs and cares depart
Like some forgotten dream.

# THE DYING CHRISTIAN

The light was faintly streaming
Within a darken'd room,
Where a woman, faint and feeble
Was sinking to the tomb.

"The silver cord" was loosened,
We knew that she must die,
We read the mournful token
In the dimness of her eye.

We read it in the radiance
That lit her pallid cheek,
And the quivering of the feeble lip
Too faint its joys to speak.

We read in the glorious flash
Of strange unearthy light,
That ever and non would dash
The dimness from her sight.

And in the thoughts of living fire
Learn'd from God's encamping band,
Her words seem'd like a holy lyre
Tun'd in the spirit land.

Meet, oh meet me in the kingdom,
Said our lov'd and dying one,
I long to be with Jesus,
I am going, going home.

Like a child oppress'd with slumber
She calmly sank to rest,
With her trust in the Redeemer
And her head upon his breast.

She faded from our vision
Like a thing of love and light,
But we feel she lives forever
A spirit pure and bright.

# A Dream

I had a dream, a varied dream,
A dream of joy and dread;
Before me rose the judgement scene
For God had raised the dead.

Oh for an angel's hand to paint
The glories of that day,
When God did gather home each saint
And wipe their tears away.

Each waiting one lifted his head
Rejoic'd to see him nigh,
And earth cast out her sainted dead
To meet him in the sky.

Before his white and burning throne
A countless throng did stand;
Whilst Christ confess'd his own,
Whose names were on his hand.

I had a dream, a varied dream,
A dream of joy and dread;
Before me rose the judgment scene
For God had rais'd the dead.

Oh for an angel's hand to paint
The terrors of that day,
When God in vengeance for his saints
Girded himself with wrath to slay.

But, oh the terror, grief, and dread,
Tongue can't describe or pen portray;
When from their graves arose the dead,
Guilty to meet the judgment day.

As sudden as the lightning's flash
Across the sky doth sweep,
Earth's kingdom's were in pieces dash'd,
And waken'd from their guilty sleep.

I heard the agonizing cry,
Ye rocks and mountains on us fall,
And hide us from the Judge's eye,
But rocks and mounts fled from the call.

I saw the guilty ruin'd host
Standing before the burning throne,
The ruin'd, lost forever lost,
Whom God in wrath refus'd to own.

# The Felon's Dream

He slept, but oh, it was not calm,
As in the days of infancy;
When sleep is nature's tender balm
To hearts from sorrow free.

He dream'd that fetters bound him fast,
He pin'd for liberty;
It seem'd deliverance came at last
And he from bonds were free.

In thought he journey'd where
Familiar voices rose,
Where not a brow was dim with care,
Or bosom heav'd with woes.

Around him press'd a happy band;
His wife and child drew near;
He felt the pressure of the hand,
And dried each falling tear.

His tender mother cast aside
The tears that dim'd her eye;
His father saw him as the pride
Of brighter days gone by.

He saw his wife around him cling,
He heard her breathe his name;
Oh! woman's love's a precious thing,
A pure undying flame.

His brethren wept for manly pride,
May bend to woman's tears;
Then welcom'd round their fireside
The playmate of departed years.

His gentle sister fair and mild
Around him closely press'd,
She clasp'd his hand and smil'd
Then wept upon his breast.

All, all were glad around that hearth,
They hop'd his wanderings o'er;
That weary of the strange cold earth
He'd roam from them no more.

'Twas but a dream, 'twas fancy's flight
It mock'd his yearning heart;
It made his bosom feel its blight,
It probed him like a dart.

A prison held his fettered limbs,
Confinement was his lot,
No kindred voice rose to cheer,
He seem'd by friends and all forgot.

# A Dialogue

### Enquirer

Who hath a balm that will impart,
Strength to the fainting heart and brow;
I've look'd upon earth, and many a heart
Weary and wasting with woe.

### Riches

I've heaps, I've heaps of shining dust,
I've gems from every mine;
Bid the weary spirit learn to trust
In gold that glitters, and gems that shine.

### Enquirer

Oh! vain were the hopes of that heart,
Sighing its sorrows should cease,
That would search mid rubies and gems,
For the priceless pearl of peace.

### Fame

I've wreaths, I've wreaths for the fever'd brow,
They're bright, and my name is fame;
Will not the heart forget its woe,
When I write it a deathless name?

### Enquirer

No! your wreaths and laurels rare,
Would blanche and pale on a brow unblest;
While the heart, remindful of its care,
Would ache and throb with the same unrest.

### Pleasure

Oh! I am queen of a laughing train,
The lightsome, the gay and glad;
I've a nectar cup for every pain,
They drink and forget to be sad.

### Enquirer

But I have seen the cheek all pale,
When life was fading from the heart;
'Twas then I saw thy nectar fail,
I watch'd and saw thy smiles depart.

### Religion

Oh! I am from the land of light,
My home is the world on high;
But I with the sons of night,
And bid their darkness fly.

I have no heaps of shining dust,
No gems from every mine;
But gifts to beautify the just,
On the brow of the pure to shine.

I have no wreaths of fading fame;
No records of decaying worth;
But God's remembrance and a name,
That can't be written in the earth.

When pleasure's smiles shall all depart,
Her nectar but increase the thirst,
I'll point the fever'd brow and heart,
To crystal founts that freshly burst.

# Enquirer

Thy words do brighter hopes impart,
Than pleasure, wealth or fame;
Thou hast balm for the wounded heart,
Tell me, kind stranger, thy name.

My name and my nature is love;
God only wise, formed the plan
That mission'd me down from above,
As the guide and the solace of man.

Then I tell the fever'd brow and heart,
Thou'st balm for its wounds, and peace for its strife,
And the guerdon's which thou dost impart,
Are the pearl of peace and the crown of life.

# CRUCIFIXION

The shadows of morning empurpled with light,
Bent o'er Judea, all lovely and bright;
The zephyr just risen, stole o'er the lea,
And dimpled the cheeks of river and sea.

On that bright morn, a clamor was heard,
The footsteps of men whose passions were stirred;
The voice of wrath, of tumult and strife,
'Twas the bloodthirsty cry of innocent life.

I gaz'd on their victim, on his pale brow,
'Mid beamings of love, were shadows of woe;
And his eyes, mid reproach and with'ring scorn,
Seemed like a star bending o'er a dark storm.

Tho' pale was his cheek, and ashy his brow,
By sorrow and anguish his spirit bent low;
Yet calm 'mid the fierce and cruel he stood,
Who, like beasts of the forests were eager for blood.

And this was the multitude fickle and vain,
Who hail'd him in triumph, as coming to reign;
Incited by priests, insatiate they stood,
Their cry was his life, their clamor his blood.

When dying earth drew round her form,
A mantle as dark as the vest of a storm,
Nature grew sad, earth trembled and shrank,
Astonish'd as Jesus the dire cup drank.

# AN ACROSTIC

Angels bright that hover o'er thee,
Deem thee an object of their care;
Ever watchful they surround thee,
Lending aid when danger's near.

May this life, thus guarded, sister,
Always feel thy Saviour near;
Render him thy heart's devotion—
Trust his goodness, seek his care;
In these vales of grief and sorrow,
Nought shall harm while God is near.

# For She Said If I May But Touch of His Clothes I Shall Be Whole

Life to her no brightness brought,
Pale and sorrow'd was her brow,
Till a bright and joyous thought,
Lit the darkness of her woe.

Long had sickness on her prayed;
Strength from every nerve had gone;
Skill and art could give no aid,
Thus her weary life passed on.

Like a sad and mornful dream,
Daily felt she life depart;
Hourly knew the vital stream,
Left the fountains of her heart.

He who'd lull'd the storm to rest,
Cleans'd the lepers, raised the dead;
Whilst a crowd around him prest
Near that suffering one did tread.

Nerv'd by blended hope and fear,
Reason'd thus her anxious heart,—
If to touch him I draw near,
All my suffering shall depart.

While the crowd around him stand,
I will touch, the sufferer said,—
Forth she reach'd her timid hand,
As she touch'd, her sickness fled.

"Who hath touch'd me." Jesus cried,
Virtue from my body's gone; From
the crowd a voice replied, Why
inquire, thousands throng.

Faint with fear thro' ev'ry limb,
Yet too grateful to deny;
Tremblingly, she knelt to him,
"Lord," she answered, "It was I."

Kindly, gently, Jesus said,
Words like balm unto her soul,
Peace upon her life be shed,
Child, thy faith has made thee whole.

# The Presentiment

There's something strangely thrills my breast,
And fills it with a deep unrest,—
It is not grief, it is not pain,
Nor wish to live the past again.

'Tis something which I scarce can tell,
And yet I know, and feel it well;
Thro' ev'ry vein it seems to run,
And whispers life will soon be done.

It comes in accents soft and low,
Like bright streamlets crystal flow,
It whispers, lingers round my heart,
And tells me I must soon depart.

I felt it when the glow of life
Was warm upon my cheek,
In mornful cadence to my heart,
It solemnly did speak.

I felt it when a fearful strife
Was preying on my heart,
It told me from the cares of life,
I quickly must depart.

I felt it when my cheek grew pale,
By cares I could'nt repress;
It whisper'd to my wearried soul,
This earth is not your rest.

POEMS ON MISCELLANEOUS SUBJECTS

# The Syrophenician Woman

Joy to my bosom! rest to my fear!
Judea's prophet draweth near!
Joy to my bosom! peace to my heart!
Sickness and sorrow before him depart!

Rack'd with agony and pain,
Writhing long, my child has lain;
Now the prophet draweth near,
All our griefs shall disappear.

"Lord!" she cried, with mournful breath,
"Save! Oh, save my child from death!"
But as though she was unheard,
Jesus answered not a word.

With a purpose naught could move.
And the zeal of woman's love,
Down she knelt in anguish wild—
"Master! Save, Oh I save my child!"

"'Tis not meet," the Savior said,
"Thus, to waste the children's bread;
I am only sent to seek
Israel's lost and scattered sheep."

"True," she said, "Oh gracious Lord!
True and faithful is thy word;
But the humblest, meanest, may
Eat the crumbs they cast away."

"Woman," said the' astonish'd Lord,
"Be it even as thy word I
By thy faith that knows no fail,
Thou hast ask'd, and shalt prevail."

# THE SLAVE MOTHER

Heard you that shriek? It rose
    So wildly on the air,
It seemed as if a burden'd heart
    Was breaking in despair.

Saw you those hands so sadly clasped—
    The bowed and feeble head—
The shuddering of that fragile form—
    That look of grief and dread?

Saw you the sad, imploring eye?
    Its every glance was pain,
As if a storm of agony
    Were sweeping through the brain.

She is a mother pale with fear,
    Her boy clings to her side,
And in her kirtle vainly tries
    His trembling form to hide.

He is not hers, although she bore
    For him a mother's pains;
He is not hers, although her blood
    Is coursing through his veins!

He is not hers, for cruel hands
    May rudely tear apart
The only wreath of household love
    That binds her breaking heart.

His love has been a joyous light
    That o'er her pathway smiled,
A fountain gushing ever new,
    Amid life's desert wild.

FRANCES ELLEN WATKINS HARPER

His lightest word has been a tone
        Of music round her heart.
Their lives a streamlet blent in one—
        Oh, Father I must they part?

They tear him from her circling arms,
        Her last and fond embrace:—
Oh! never more may her sad eyes
        Gaze on his mournful face.

No marvel, then, these bitter shrieks
        Disturb the listening air;
She is a mother, and her heart
        Is breaking in despair.

# BIBLE DEFENCE OF SLAVERY

Take sackcloth of the darkest dye,
And shroud the pulpits round!
Servants of him that cannot lie,
Sit mourning on the ground.

Let holy horror blanch each cheek,
Pale every brow with fears;
And rocks and stones, if ye could speak,
Ye well might melt to tears!

Let sorrow breathe in every tone,
In every strain ye raise;
Insult not God's majestic throne
With the' mockery of praise.

A "reverend" man, whose light should be
The guide of age and youth,
Brings to the shrine of Slavery
The sacrifice of truth!

For the direst wrong by man imposed,
Since Sodom's fearful cry.
The word of life has been unclos'd.
To give your God the lie.

Oh, I when ye pray for heathen lands.
And plead for their dark shores,
Remember Slavery's cruel hands
Make heathens at your doors!

# Eliza Harris

Like a fawn from the arrow, startled and wild,
A woman swept by us, bearing a child;
In her eye was the night of a settled despair.
And her brow was o'ershaded with anguish and care.

She was nearing the river—in reaching the brink.
She heeded no danger, she paused not to think!
For she is a mother—her child is a slave—
And she'll give him his freedom or find him a grave!

T'was a vision to haunt us, that innocent face—
So pale in its aspect, so fair in its grace;
As the tramp of the horse and the hay of the hound,
With the fetters that gall, were trailing the ground!

She was nerv'd by despair, and strengthened by woe,
As she leap'd o'er the chasms that yawn'd from below;
Death howl'd in the tempest, and rav'd in the blast,
But she heard not the sound till the danger was past.

Oh! how shall I speak of my proud country's shame?
Of the stains on her glory, how give them their name?
How say that her banner in mockery waves—
Her "star-spangled banner"—o'er millions of slaves?

How say that the lawless may torture and chase
A woman whose crime is the hue of her face?
How the depths of the forest may echo around
With the shrieks of despair, and the bay of the hound?

With her step on the ice, and her arm on her child,
The danger was fearful, the pathway was wild;
But, aided by Heaven, she gained a free shore,
Where the friends of humanity open'd their door.

So fragile and lovely, so fearfully pale,
Like a lily that bends to the breath of the gale,
Save the heave of her breast, and the sway of her hair.
You'd have thought her a statue of fear and despair.

In agony close to her bosom she press'd
The life of her hearty the child of her breast:—
Oh! love from its tenderness gathering might,
Had strengthen'd er soul for the dangers of flight.

But she's free!—yes, free from the land where the slave
From the hand of oppression must rest in the grave;
Where bondage and torture, where scourges and chains,
Have plac'd on our banner indelible stains.

The bloodhounds have miss'd the scent of her way;
The hunter is rifled and foil'd of his prey;
Fierce jargon and cursing, with clanking of chains,
Make sounds of strange discord on Liberty's plains.

With the rapture of love and fullness of bliss,
She plac'd on his brow a mother's fond kiss:—
Oh! poverty, danger and death she can brave,
For the child of her love is no longer a slave!

# ETHIOPIA

Yes! Ethiopia yet shall stretch
Her bleeding hands abroad;
Her cry of agony shall reach
The burning throne of God.

The tyrant's yoke from off her neck.
His fetters from her soul,
The mighty hand of God shall break,
And spurn the base control.

Redeemed from dust and freed from chains.
Her sons shall lift their eyes;
From cloud-capt hills and verdant plains
Shall shouts of triumph rise.

Upon her dark, despairing brow.
Shall play a smile of peace;
For God shall bend unto her wo,
And bid her sorrows cease.

'Neath sheltering vines and stately palms
Shall laughing children play,
And aged sires with joyous psalms
Shall gladden every day.

Secure by night, and blest by day,
Shall pass her hoppy hours;
Nor human tigers hunt for prey
Within her peaceful bowers.

Then, Ethiopia! stretch, oh! stretch
Thy bleeding hands abroad;
Thy cry of agony shall reach
And find redress from God.

# The Drunkard's Child

He stood beside his dying child,
With a dim and bloodshot eye;
They'd won him from the haunts of vice
To see his first-born die.
He came with a slow and staggering tread,
A vague, unmeaning stare,
And, reeling, clasped the clammy hand,
So deathly pale and fair.

In a dark and gloomy chamber,
Life ebbing fast away.
On a coarse and wretched pallet,
The dying sufferer lay:
A smile of recognition
Lit up the glazing eye;
"I'm very glad," it seemed to say,
"You've come to see me die."

That smile reached to his callous heart,
Its sealed fountains stirred;
He tried to speak, but on his lips
Faltered and died each word.
And burning tears like rain
Poured down his bloated face.
Where guilt, remorse and shame
Had scathed, and left their trace.

"My father!" said the dying child,
(His Voice was faint and low,)
"Oh! clasp me closely to your heart.
And kiss me ere I go.
Bright angels beckon me away,
To the holy city fair—
Oh! tell me, father, ere I go,
Say, will you meet me there?"

He clasped him to his throbbing heart,
"I will! I will!" he said;
His pleading ceased—the father held
His first-born and his dead!
The marble brow, with golden curls.
Lay lifeless on his breast;
Like sunbeams on the distant clouds
Which line the gorgeous west.

# The Slave Auction

The sale began—young girls were there,
Defenceless in their wretchedness,
Whose stifled sobs of deep despair
Revealed their anguish and distress.

And mothers stood, with streaming eyes,
And saw their dearest children sold;
Unheeded rose their bitter cries.
While tyrants bartered them for gold.

And woman, with her love and truth—
For these in sable forms may dwell—
Gaz'd on the husband of her youth,
With anguish none may paint or tell.

And men, whose sole crime was their hue,
The impress of their Maker's hand,
And frail and shrinking children, too,
Were gathered in that mournful band.

Ye who have laid your lov'd to rest.
And wept above their lifeless clay,
Know not the anguish of that breast.
Whose lov'd are rudely torn away.

Ye may not know how desolate
Are bosoms rudely forced to part.
And how a dull and heavy weight
Will press the life-drops from the heart.

# THE REVEL

"He knoweth not that the dead are there."

In yonder halls reclining
Are forms surpassing fair,
And brilliant lights are shining,
But, oh! the dead are there!

There's music, song and dance,
There's banishment of care,
And mirth in every glance.
But, oh! the dead are there!

The wine cup's sparkling glow
Blends with the viands rare.
There is revelry and show.
But still, the dead are there!

'Neath that flow of song and mirth.
Runs the current of despair.
But the simple sons of earth
Know not the dead are there!

They'll shudder, start and tremble,
They'll weep in wild despair.
When the solemn truth breaks on them,
That the dead, the dead, are there!

# That Blessed Hope

Oh! crush it not, that hope so blest,
Which cheers the fainting heart,
And points it to the coming rest.
Where sorrow has no part.

Tear from my heart each worldly prop.
Unbind each earthly string.
But to this blest and glorious hope,
Oh! let my spirit cling.

It cheered, amid the days of old.
Each holy patriarch's breast;
It was an anchor to their souls.
Upon it let me rest.

When wandering in dens and caves,
In sheep and goat skins dressed,
A peel'd and scattered people learned.
To know this hope was blest

Help me, amid this world of strife.
To long for Christ to reign,
That when He brings the crown of lift,
I may that crown obtain.

# The Dying Christian

The light was faintly streaming
Within a darkened room,
Where a woman, faint and feeble.
Was sinking to the tomb.

The silver cord was loosened,
We knew that she must die;
We read the mournful token
In the dimness of her eye.

We read it in the radiance
That lit her pallid cheek,
And the quivering of the feeble lip,
Too faint its joys to speak.

Like a child oppressed with slumber,
She calmly sank to rest.
With her trust in the Redeemer,
And her head upon His breast.

She faded from our vision.
Like a thing of love and light;
But we feel she lives forever,
A spirit pure and bright.

# Report

I Heard, my young friend,
You were seeking a wife,
A woman to make
Your companion for life.

Now, if you are seeking
A wife for your youth.
Let this be your aim, then—
Seek a woman of truth.

She may not have talents.
With greatness combined,
Her gifts may be humble,
Of person and mind:

But if she be constant.
And gentle, and true.
Believe me, my friend.
She's the woman for you!

Oh! wed not for beauty,
Though fair is the prize;
It may pall when you grasp it,
And fade in your eyes.

Let gold not allure you.
Let wealth not attract;
With a house full of treasure,
A woman may lack.

Let her habits be frugal,
Her hands not afraid
To work in her household,
Or follow her trade.

Let her language be modest.
Her actions discreet;
Her manners refined,
And free from deceit.

Now, if such you should find,
In your journey through life.
Just open your mind,
And make her your wife.

# Advice to the Girls

Nay, do not blush! I only heard
You had a wish to marry;
I thought I'd speak a friendly word,
So just one moment tarry.

Wed not a man whose merit lies
In things of outward show,
In raven hair or flashing eyes,
That please your fancy so.

But marry tee who's good and kind,
And free from all pretence;
Who, if without a gifted mind.
At least has common sense.

# Saved By Faith

*"She said, if I may but touch his clothes, I shall be whole."*

Life to her no brightness brought.
Pale and stricken was her brow.
Till a bright and joyous thought
Lit the darkness of her woe.

Long had sickness on her preyed,
Strength from every nerve had gone;
Skill and art could give no aid:
Thus, her weary life passed on.

Like a sad and mournful dream,
Daily felt she life depart.
Hourly knew the vital stream
Left the fountain of her heart.

He who lull'd the storm to rest,
Cleans'd the lepers, rais'd the dead,
Whilst a crowd around him pressed,
Near that suffering one did tread.

Nerv'd by blended hope and fear,
Reasoned thus her anxious heart:
"If to touch him I draw near,
All my suffering shall depart.

While the crowd around him stand,
I will touch," the sufferer said;
Forth she reached her timid hand—
As she touched, her sickness fled.

"Who hath touched me?" Jesus cried;
"Virtue from my body's gone."
From the crowd a voice replied,
"Why inquire in such a throng?"

Faint with fear through every limb,
Yet too grateful to deny.
Tremblingly she knelt to him,
"Lord!" she answered, "it was I!"

Kindly, gently, Jesus said—
Words like balm unto her soul—
"Peace upon thy life be shed!
Child! thy faith hath made thee whole!"

# Died of Starvation

They forced him into prison,
  Because he begged for bread;
"My wife is starving—dying!"
  In vain the poor man plead.[1]

They forced him into prison,
  Strong bars enclosed the walls,
While the rich and proud were feasting
  Within their sumptuous halls.

He'd striven long with anguish.
  Had wrestled with despair;
But his weary heart was breaking
  'Neath its crushing load of care.

And he prayed them in that prison,
  "Oh, let me seek my wife!"
For he knew that want was feeding,
  On the remnant of her life.

That night his wife lay moaning
  Upon her bed in pain;
Hunger gnawing at her vitals,
  Fever scorching through her brain.

She wondered at his tarrying,
  He was not wont to stay;
Mid hunger, pain and watching.
  The moments waned away.

Sadly crouching by the embers,
  Her famished children lay;
And she longed to gaze upon them.
  As her spirit passed away.

---

1. See this case, as touchingly related, in *Oliver Twist* by Dickens.

But the embers were too feeble,
She could not see each face.
So she clasped her arms around them—
'Twas their mother's last embrace.

They loosed him from his prison.
As a felon from his chain;
Though his strength was hunger bitter,
He sought his home again.

Just as her spirit lingered
On Time's receding shore.
She heard his welcome footstep
On the threshold of the door.

He was faint and spirit-broken.
But, rousing from despair,
He clasped her icy fingers,
As she breathed her dying prayer.

With a gentle smile and blessing,
Her spirit winged its flight,
As the room, in all its glory.
Bathed the world in dazzling light.

There was weeping, bitter weeping.
In the chamber of the dead.
For well the stricken husband knew
She had died for want of bread.

# A Mother's Heroism

"When the noble mother of Lovejoy heard of her son's death, she said, 'It is well! I had rather he should die so than desert his principles.'"

The murmurs of a distant strife
Fell on a mother's ear;
Her son had yielded up his life,
Mid scenes of wrath and fear.

They told her how he'd spent his breath
In pleading for the dumb,
And how the glorious martyr wreath
Her child had nobly won.

They told her of his courage high.
Mid brutal force and might;
How he had nerved himself to die,
In battling for the right.

It seemed as if a fearful storm
Swept wildly round her soul;
A moment, and her fragile form
Bent 'neath its fierce control.

From lip and brow the color fled—
But light flashed to her eye:
"'T is well! 't is well!" the mother said,
"That thus my child should die."

"'T is well that, to his latest breath,
He plead for liberty;
Truth nerved him for the hour of death,
And taught him how to die."

"It taught him how to cast aside
Earth's honors and renown;
To trample on her fame and pride.
And win a martyr's crown."

# The Fugitive's Wife

It was my sad and weary lot
To toil in slavery;
But one thing cheered my lowly cot–
My husband was with me.

One evening, as our children played
Around our cabin door,
I noticed on his brow a shade
I'd never seen before;

And in his eyes a gloomy night
Of anguish and despair;—
I gazed upon their troubled light,
To read the meaning there.

He strained me to his heaving heart—
My own beat wild with fear;
I knew not, but I sadly felt
There must be evil near.

He vainly strove to cast aside
The tears that fell like rain:—
Too frail, indeed, is manly pride,
To strive with grief and pain.

Again he clasped me to his breast,
And said that we must part:
I tried to speak—but, oh! it seemed
An arrow reached my heart.

"Bear not," I cried, "unto your grave.
The yoke you've borne from birth;
No longer live a helpless slave.
The meanest thing on earth!"

FRANCES ELLEN WATKINS HARPER

# The Contrast

They scorned her for her sinning.
Spoke harshly of her fall.
Nor lent the hand of mercy
To break her hated thrall.

The dews of meek repentance
Stood in her downcast eye:
Would no one heed her anguish?
All pass her coldly by?

From the cold, averted glances
Of each reproachful eye,
She turned aside, heart-broken,
And laid her down to die.

And where was he, who sullied
Her once unspotted name;
Who lured her from life's brightness
To agony and shame?

Who left her on Life's billows,
A wrecked and ruined thing;
Who brought the winter of despair
Upon Hope's blooming spring?

Through the halls of wealth and fashion.
In gaiety and pride.
He was leading to the altar
A fair and lovely bride!

None scorned him for his sinning,
Few saw it through his gold;
His crimes were only foibles.
And these were gently told.

Before him rose a vision,
A maid of beauty rare;
Then a pale, heart-broken woman,
The image of despair.

Next came a sad procession,
With many a sob and tear;
A widow'd, childless mother
Totter'd by an humble bier.

The vision quickly faded,
The sad, unwelcome sight;
But his lip forgot its laughter,
And his eye its careless light

A moment, and the flood-gates
Of memory opened wide;
And remorseful recollection
Flowed like a lava tide.

That widow's wail of anguish
Seemed strangely blending there,
And mid the soft lights floated
That image of despair.

# The Prodigal's Return

He came—a wanderer—years of sin
Had blanched his blooming cheek,
Telling a tale of strife within.
That words might vainly speak.

His feet were bare, his garments torn,
His brow was deadly white;
His heart was bleeding, crushed and worn.
His soul had felt a blight.

His father saw him; pity swept
And yearn'd through every vein;
He ran and clasp'd his child, and wept,
Murm'ring, "He lives again!"

"Father, I've come, but not to claim
Aught from thy love or grace;
I come, a child of guilt and shame.
To beg a servant's place."

"Enough! Enough!" the father said,
"Bring robes of princely cost!"—
The past with all its shadows fled,
For now was found the lost.

"Put shoes upon my poor child's feet.
With rings his hand adorn,
And bid my house his coming greet
With music, dance and song."

Oh, Savior! mid this world of strife.
When wayward here we roam.
Conduct us to the paths of life,
And guide us safely home.

Then in thy holy courts above,
Thy praise our lips shall sound,
While angels join our song of love,
That we, the lost, are found!

# Eva's Farewell

Farewell, father! I am dying,
Going to the "glory land,"
Where the sun is ever shining.
And the zephyr's ever bland;

Where the living fountains flowing.
Quench the pining spirit's thirst;
Where the tree of life is growing.
Where the crystal fountains burst.

Father! hear that music holy
Floating from the spirit land!
At the pearly gates of glory.
Radiant angels waiting stand.

Father! kiss your dearest Eva,
Press her cold and clammy hand.
Ere the glittering hosts receive her,
Welcome to their cherub band.

# FREE LABOR

I wear an easy garment,
    O'er it no toiling slave
Wept tears of hopeless anguish,
    In his passage to the grave.
And from its ample folds
    Shall rise no cry to God,
Upon its warp and woof shall be
    No stain of tears and blood.
Oh, lightly shall it press my form,
    Unladened with a sigh,
I shall not 'mid its rustling hear,
    Some sad despairing cry.
This fabric is too light to bear
    The weight of bondsmen's tears,
I shall not in its texture trace
    The agony of years.
Too light to bear a smother'd sigh,
    From some lorn woman's heart,
Whose only wreath of household love
    Is rudely torn apart.
Then lightly shall it press my form,
    Unburden'd by a sigh;
And from its seams and folds shall rise,
    No voice to pierce the sky,
And witness at the throne of God,
    In language deep and strong,
That I have nerv'd Oppression's hand,
    For deeds of guilt and wrong.

FRANCES ELLEN WATKINS HARPER

# Bury Me in a Free Land

Make me a grave where'er you will,
In a lowly plain, or a lofty hill;
Make it among earth's humblest graves,
But not in a land where men are slaves.

I could not rest if around my grave
I heard the steps of a trembling slave;
His shadow above my silent tomb
Would make it a place of fearful gloom.

I could not rest if I heard the tread
Of a coffle gang to the shambles led,
And the mother's shriek of wild despair
Rise like a curse on the trembling air.

I could not sleep if I saw the lash
Drinking her blood at each fearful gash,
And I saw her babes torn from her breast,
Like trembling doves from their parent nest.

I'd shudder and start if I heard the bay
Of bloodhounds seizing their human prey,
And I heard the captive plead in vain
As they bound afresh his galling chain.

If I saw young girls from their mother's arms
Bartered and sold for their youthful charms,
My eye would flash with a mournful flame,
My death-paled cheek grow red with shame.

I would sleep, dear friends, where bloated might
Can rob no man of his dearest right;
My rest shall be calm in any grave
Where none can call his brother a slave.

I ask no monument, proud and high,
To arrest the gaze of the passers-by;
All that my yearning spirit craves,
Is bury me not in a land of slaves.

SKETCHES OF SOUTHERN LIFE

# Aunt Chloe

I Remember, well remember,
    That dark and dreadful day,
When they whispered to me, "Chloe,
    Your children's sold away!"

It seemed as if a bullet
    Had shot me through and through,
And I felt as if my heart-strings
    Was breaking right in two.

And I says to cousin Milly,
    "There must be some mistake;
Where's Mistus?" "In the great house crying—
    Crying like her heart would break."

"And the lawyer's there with Mistus;
    Says he's come to 'ministrate,
'Cause when master died he just left
    Heap of debt on the estate."

"And I thought 'twould do you good
    To bid your boys good-bye—
To kiss them both and shake their hands,
    And have a hearty cry."

"Oh! Chloe, I knows how you feel,
    'Cause I'se been through it all;
I thought my poor old heart would break,
    When master sold my Saul."

Just then I heard the footsteps
    Of my children at the door,
And I rose right up to meet them,
    But I fell upon the floor.

And I heard poor Jakey saying,
    "Oh, mammy, don't you cry!"
And I felt my children kiss me
    And bid me, both, good-bye.

Then I had a mighty sorrow,
    Though I nursed it all alone;
But I wasted to a shadow,
    And turned to skin and bone.

But one day dear uncle Jacob
    (In heaven he's now a saint)
Said, "Your poor heart is in the fire,
    But child you must not faint."

Then I said to uncle Jacob,
    If I was good like you,
When the heavy trouble dashed me
    I'd know just what to do.

Then he said to me, "Poor Chloe,
    The way is open wide:"
And he told me of the Saviour,
    And the fountain in His side.

Then he said "Just take your burden
    To the blessed Master's feet;
I takes all my troubles, Chloe,
    Right unto the mercy-seat."

His words waked up my courage,
    And I began to pray,
And I felt my heavy burden
    Rolling like a stone away.

And a something seemed to tell me,
    You will see your boys again—
And that hope was like a poultice
    Spread upon a dreadful pain.

And it often seemed to whisper,
 Chloe, trust and never fear;
You'll get justice in the kingdom,
 If you do not get it here.

# The Deliverance

Master only left old Mistus
    One bright and handsome boy;
But she fairly doted on him,
    He was her pride and joy.

We all liked Mister Thomas,
    He was so kind at heart;
And when the young folkes got in scrapes,
    He always took their part.

He kept right on that very way
    Till he got big and tall,
And old Mistus used to chide him,
    And say he'd spile us all.

But somehow the farm did prosper
    When he took things in hand;
And though all the servants liked him,
    He made them understand.

One evening Mister Thomas said,
    "Just bring my easy shoes:
I am going to sit by mother,
    And read her up the news."

Soon I heard him tell old Mistus
    "We're bound to have a fight;
But we'll whip the Yankees, mother,
    We'll whip them sure as night!"

Then I saw old Mistus tremble;
    She gasped and held her breath;
And she looked on Mister Thomas
    With a face as pale as death.

"They are firing on Fort Sumpter;
    Oh! I wish that I was there!—
Why, dear mother! what's the matter?
    You're the picture of despair."

"I was thinking, dearest Thomas,
    'Twould break my very heart
If a fierce and dreadful battle
    Should tear our lives apart."

"None but cowards, dearest mother,
    Would skulk unto the rear,
When the tyrant's hand is shaking
    All the heart is holding dear."

I felt sorry for old Mistus;
    She got too full to speak;
But I saw the great big tear-drops
    A running down her cheek.

Mister Thomas too was troubled
    With choosing on that night,
Betwixt staying with his mother
    And joining in the fight.

Soon down into the village came
    A call for volunteers;
Mistus gave up Mister Thomas,
    With many sighs and tears.

His uniform was real handsome;
    He looked so brave and strong;
But somehow I couldn't help thinking
    His fighting must be wrong.

Though the house was very lonesome,
    I thought 'twould all come right,
For I felt somehow or other
    We was mixed up in that fight.

And I said to Uncle Jacob,
    "Now old Mistus feels the sting,
For this parting with your children
    Is a mighty dreadful thing."

"Never mind," said Uncle Jacob,
    "Just wait and watch and pray,
For I feel right sure and certain,
    Slavery's bound to pass away;"

"Because" I asked the Spirit,
    "If God is good and just,
How it happened that the masters
    Did grind us to the dust."

"And something reasoned right inside,
    Such should not always be;
And you could not beat it out my head,
    The Spirit spoke to me."

And his dear old eyes would brighten,
    And his lips put on a smile,
Saying, "Pick up faith and courage,
    And just wait a little while."

Mistus prayed up in the parlor,
    That the Secesh all might win;
We were praying in the cabins,
    Wanting freedom to begin.

Mister Thomas wrote to Mistus,
    Telling 'bout the Bull's Run fight,
That his troops had whipped the Yankees
    And put them all to flight.

Mistus' eyes did fairly glisten;
    She laughed and praised the South,
But I thought some day she'd laugh
    On tother side her mouth.

I used to watch old Mistus' face,
    And when it looked quite long
I would say to Cousin Milly,
    The battle's going wrong;

Not for us, but for the Rebels.—
    My heart 'would fairly skip,
When Uncle Jacob used to say,
    "The North is bound to whip."

And let the fight go as it would—
    Let North or South prevail—
He always kept his courage up,
    And never let it fail.

And he often used to tell us,
    "Children, don't forget to pray;
For the darkest time of morning
    Is just 'fore the break of day."

Well, one morning bright and early
    We heard the fife and drum,
And the booming of the cannon—
    The Yankee troops had come.

When the word ran through the village,
    The colored folks are free—
In the kitchens and the cabins
    We held a jubilee.

When they told us Mister Lincoln
    Said that slavery was dead,
We just poured our prayers and blessings
    Upon his precious head.

We just laughed, and danced, and shouted,
    And prayed, and sang, and cried,
And we thought dear Uncle Jacob
    Would fairly crack his side.

But when old Mistus heard it,
    She groaned and hardly spoke;
When she had to lose her servants,
    Her heart was almost broke.

'Twas a sight to see our people
    Going out, the troops to meet,
Almost dancing to the music,
    And marching down the street.

After years of pain and parting,
    Our chains was broke in two,
And we was so mighty happy,
    We didn't know what to do.

But we soon got used to freedom,
    Though the way at first was rough;
But we weathered through the tempest,
    For slavery made us tough.

But we had one awful sorrow,
    It almost turned my head,
When a mean and wicked cretur
    Shot Mister Lincoln dead.

'Twas a dreadful solemn morning,
    I just staggered on my feet;
And the women they were crying
    And screaming in the street.

But if many prayers and blessings
    Could bear him to the throne,
I should think when Mister Lincoln died,
    That heaven just got its own.

Then we had another President,—
    What do you call his name?
Well, if the colored folks forget him
    They wouldn't be much to blame.

We thought he'd be the Moses
    Of all the colored race;
But when the Rebels pressed us hard
    He never showed his face.

But something must have happened him,
    Right curi's I'll be bound,
'Cause I heard 'em talking 'bout a circle
    That he was swinging round.

But everything will pass away—
    He went like time and tide—
And when the next election came
    They let poor Andy slide.

But now we have a President,
    And if I was a man
I'd vote for him for breaking up
    The wicked Ku-Klux Klan.

And if any man should ask me
    If I would sell my vote,
I'd tell him I was not the one
    To change and turn my coat;

If freedom seem'd a little rough
    I'd weather through the gale;
And as to buying up my vote,
    I hadn't it for sale.

I do not think I'd ever be
    As slack as Jonas Handy;
Because I heard he sold his vote
    For just three sticks of candy.

But when John Thomas Reeder brought
    His wife some flour and meat,
And told her he had sold his vote
    For something good to eat,

You ought to seen Aunt Kitty raise,
    And heard her blaze away;
She gave the meat and flour a toss,
    And said they should not stay.

And I should think he felt quite cheap
    For voting the wrong side;
And when Aunt Kitty scolded him,
    He just stood up and cried.

But the worst fooled man I ever saw,
    Was when poor David Rand
Sold out for flour and sugar;
    The sugar was mixed with sand.

I'll tell you how the thing got out;
    His wife had company,
And she thought the sand was sugar,
    And served it up for tea.

When David sipped and sipped the tea,
    Somehow it didn't taste right;
I guess when he found he was sipping sand,
    He was made enough to fight.

The sugar looked so nice and white—
    It was spread some inches deep—
But underneath was a lot of sand;
    Such sugar is mighty cheap.

You'd laughed to seen Lucinda Grange
    Upon her husband's track;
When he sold his vote for rations
    She made him take 'em back.

Day after day did Milly Green
    Just follow after Joe,
And told him if he voted wrong
    To take his rags and go.

I think that Curnel Johnson said
    His side had won the day,
Had not we women radicals
    Just got right in the way.

And yet I would not have you think
    That all our men are shabby;
But 'tis said in every flock of sheep
    There will be one that's scabby.

I've heard, before election came
    They tried to buy John Slade;
But he gave them all to understand
    That he wasn't in that trade.

And we've got lots of other men
    Who rally round the cause,
And go for holding up the hands
    That gave us equal laws

Who know their freedom cost too much
    Of blood and pain and treasure,
For them to fool away their votes
    For profit or for pleasure.

# Aunt Chloe's Politics

Of course, I don't know very much
    About these politics,
But I think that some who run 'em,
    Do mighty ugly tricks.

I've seen 'em honey-fugle round,
    And talk so awful sweet,
That you'd think them full of kindness,
    As an egg is full of meat.

Now I don't believe in looking
    Honest people in the face,
And saying when you're doing wrong,
    That "I haven't sold my race."

When we want to school our children,
    If the money isn't there,
Whether black or white have took it,
    The loss we all must share.

And this buying up each other
    Is something worse than mean,
Though I thinks a heap of voting,
    I go for voting clean.

# Learning to Read

Very soon the Yankee teachers
    Came down and set up school;
But, oh! how the Rebs did hate it,—
    It was agin' their rule.

Our masters always tried to hide
    Book learning from our eyes;
Knowledge didn't agree with slavery—
    'Twould make us all too wise.

But some of us would try to steal
    A little from the book,
And put the words together,
    And learn by hook or crook.

I remember Uncle Caldwell,
    Who took pot liquor fat
And greased the pages of his book,
    And hid it in his hat.

And had his master ever seen
    The leaves upon his head,
He'd have thought them greasy papers,
    But nothing to be read.

And there was Mr. Turner's Ben,
    Who heard the children spell,
And picked the words right up by heart,
    And learned to read 'em well.

Well, the Northern folks kept sending
    The Yankee teachers down;
And they stood right up and helped us,
    Though Rebs did sneer and frown.

And, I longed to read my Bible,
 For precious words it said;
But when I begun to learn it,
 Folks just shook their heads,

And said there is no use trying,
 Oh! Chloe, you're too late;
But as I was rising sixty,
 I had no time to wait.

So I got a pair of glasses,
 And straight to work I went,
And never stopped till I could read
 The hymns and Testament.

Then I got a little cabin
 A place to call my own—
And I felt as independent
 As the queen upon her throne.

# Church Building

Uncle Jacob often told us,
    Since freedom blessed our race
We ought all to come together
    And build a meeting place.

So we pinched, and scraped, and spared,
    A little here and there:
Though our wages was but scanty,
    The church did get a share.

And, when the house was finished,
    Uncle Jacob came to pray;
He was looking mighty feeble,
    And his head was awful gray.

But his voice rang like a trumpet;
    His eyes looked bright and young;
And it seemed a mighty power
    Was resting on his tongue.

And he gave us all his blessing—
    'Twas parting words he said,
For soon we got the message
    The dear old man was dead.

But I believe he's in the kingdom,
    For when we shook his hand
He said, "Children, you must meet me
    Right in the promised land;

For when I'm done a moiling
    And toiling here below,
Through the gate into the city
    Straightway I hope to go."

# The Reunion

Well, one morning real early
    I was going down the street,
And I heard a stranger asking
    For Missis Chloe Fleet.

There was something in his voice
    That made me feel quite shaky,
And when I looked right in his face,
    Who should it be but Jakey!

I grasped him tight, and took him home—
    What gladness filled my cup!
And I laughed, and just rolled over,
    And laughed, and just give up.

"Where have you been? O Jakey, dear!
    Why didn't you come before?
Oh! when you children went away
    My heart was awful sore."

"Why, mammy, I've been on your hunt
    Since ever I've been free,
And I have heard from brother Ben,—
    He's down in Tennessee."

"He wrote me that he had a wife."
    "And children?" "Yes, he's three."
"You married, too?" "Oh no, indeed,
    I thought I'd first get free."

"Then, Jakey, you will stay with me,
    And comfort my poor heart;
Old Mistus got no power now
    To tear us both apart."

"I'm richer now than Mistus,
    Because I have got my son;
And Mister Thomas he is dead,
    And she's got nary one."

"You must write to brother Benny
    That he must come this fall,
And we'll make the cabin bigger,
    And that will hold us all."

"Tell him I want to see 'em all
    Before my life do cease:
And then, like good old Simeon,
    I hope to die in peace."

# "I Thirst"

I Thirst, but earth cannot allay
    The fever coursing through my veins,
The healing stream is far away—
    It flows through Salem's lovely plains.

The murmurs of its crystal flow
    Break ever o'er this world of strife;
My heart is weary, let me go,
    To bathe it in the stream of life;

For many worn and weary hearts
    Have bathed in this pure healing stream,
And felt their griefs and cares depart,
    E'en like some sad forgotten dream.

## Second Voice

"The Word is nigh thee, even in thy heart."

Say not, within thy weary heart,
    Who shall ascend above,
To bring unto thy fever'd lips
    The fount of joy and love.

Nor do thou seek to vainly delve
    Where death's pale angels tread,
To hear the murmur of its flow
    Around the silent dead.

Within, in thee is one living fount,
    Fed from the springs above;
There quench thy thirst till thou shalt bathe
    In God's own sea of love.

FRANCES ELLEN WATKINS HARPER

# The Dying Queen

"I would meet death awake."

THE strength that bore her on for years
    Was ebbing fast away,
And o'er the pale and life-worn face,
    Death's solemn shadows lay.

With tender love and gentle care,
    Friends gathered round her bed,
And for her sake each footfall hushed
    The echoes of its tread.

They knew the restlessness of death
    Through every nerve did creep,
And carefully they tried to lull
    The dying Queen to sleep.

In vain she felt Death's icy hand
    Her failing heart-strings shake;
And, rousing up, she firmly said,
    "I'd meet my God awake."

Awake, I've met the battle's shock,
    And born the cares of state;
Nor shall I take your lethean cup,
    And slumber at death's gate.

Did I not watch with eyes alert,
    The path where foes did tend;
And shall I veil my eyes with sleep,
    To meet my God and friend?

Nay, rather from my weary lids,
    This heavy slumber shake,
That I may pass the mystic vale,
    And meet my God awake.

# THE JEWISH GRANDFATHER'S STORY

Come, gather around me, children,
    And a story I will tell.
How we builded the beautiful temple—
    The temple we love so well.

I must date my story backward
    To a distant age and land,
When God did break our fathers' chains
    By his mighty outstretched hand

Our fathers were strangers and captives,
    Where the ancient Nile doth flow;
Smitten by cruel taskmasters,
    And burdened by toil and woe.

As a shepherd, to pasture green
    Doth lead with care his sheep,
So God divided the great Red Sea,
    And led them through the deep.

You've seen me plant a tender vine,
    And guard it with patient care,
Till its roots struck in the mellow earth,
    And it drank the light and air.

So God did plant our chosen race,
    As a vine in this fair land;
And we grew and spread a fruitful tree,
    The planting of his right hand.

The time would fail strove I to tell,
    All the story of our race—
Of our grand old leader, Moses,
    And Joshua in his place,

     FRANCES ELLEN WATKINS HARPER

Of all our rulers and judges,
　　From Joshua unto Saul,
Over whose doomed and guilty head
　　Fell ruin and death's dark pall.

Of valiant Jepthath, whose brave heart
　　With sudden grief did bow,
When his daughter came with dance and song
　　Unconscious of his vow.

Of Gideon, lifting up his voice
　　To him who rules the sky,
And wringing out his well drenched fleece,
　　When all around was dry.

How Deborah, neath her spreading palms,
　　A judge in Israel rose,
And wrested victory from the hands
　　Of Jacob's heathen foes.

Of Samuel, an upright judge.
　　The last who ruled our tribes,
Whose noble life and cleanly hands,
　　Were pure and free from bribes.

Of David, with his checkered life
　　Our tuneful minstrel king,
Who breathed in sadness and delight,
　　The psalms we love to sing.

Of Solomon, whose wandering heart,
　　From Jacob's God did stray,
And cast the richest gifts of life,
　　In pleasure's cup away.

How aged men advised his son,
　　But found him weak and vain,
Until the kingdom from his hands
　　Was rudely rent in twain.

Oh! sin and strife are fearful things,
    They widen as they go,
And leave behind them shades of death,
    And open gates of woe.

A trail of guilt, a gloomy line,
    Ran through our nation's life,
And wicked kings provoked our God,
    And sin and woe were rife.

At length, there came a day of doom—
    A day of grief and dread;
When judgment like a fearful storm
    Swept o'er our country's head.

And we were captives many years,
    Where Babel's stream doth flow;
With harps unstrung, on willows hung,
    We wept in silent woe.

We could not sing the old, sweet songs,
    Our captors asked to hear;
Our hearts were full, how could we sing
    The songs to us so dear?

As one who dreams a mournful dream,
    Which fades, as wanes the night,
So God did change our gloomy lot
    From darkness into light.

Belshazzar in his regal halls,
    A sumptuous feast did hold;
He praised his gods and drank his wine
    From sacred cups of gold.

When dance and song and revelry
    Had filled with mirth each hall,
Belshazzar raised his eyes and saw
    A writing on the wall.

FRANCES ELLEN WATKINS HARPER

He saw, and horror blanched his cheek,
    His lips were white with fear;
To read the words he quickly called
    For wise men, far and near.

But baffled seers, with anxious doubt
    Stood silent in the room,
When Daniel came, a captive youth,
    And read the words of doom.

That night, within his regal hall,
    Belshazzar lifeless lay;
The Persians grasped his fallen crown,
    And with the Mede held sway.

Darius came, and Daniel rose
    A man of high renown;
But wicked courtiers schemed and planned
    To drag the prophet down.

They came as men who wished to place
    Great honors on their king—
With flattering lips and oily words,
    Desired a certain thing.

They knew that Daniel, day by day
    Towards Salem turned his face,
And asked the king to sign a law
    His hands might not erase.

That till one moon had waned away,
    No cherished wish or thing
Should any ask of men or Gods,
    Unless it were the king.

But Daniel, full of holy trust,
    His windows opened wide,
Regardless of the king's command,
    Unto his God he cried.

They brought him forth that he might be
    The hungry lion's meat,
Awe struck, the lions turned away
    And crouched anear his feet.

The God he served was strong to save
    His servant in the den;
The fate devised for Daniel's life
    O'er took those scheming men.

And Cyrus came, a gracious king,
    And gave the blest command,
That we, the scattered Jews, should build
    Anew our fallen land.

The men who hated Juda's weal
    Were filled with bitter rage,
And 'gainst the progress of our work
    Did evil men engage.

Sanballat tried to hinder us,
    And Gashmu uttered lies,
But like a thing of joy and light,
    We saw our temple rise.

And from the tower of Hananeel
    Unto the corner gate,
We built the wall and did restore
    The places desolate.

Some mocked us as we labored on
    And scoffingly did say,
"If but a fox climb on the wall,
    Their work will give away."

But Nehemiah wrought in hope,
    Though heathen foes did frown
"My work is great," he firmly said,
    "And I cannot come down."

And when Shemai counselled him
    The temple door to close,
To hide, lest he should fall a prey
    Unto his cruel foes.

Strong in his faith, he answered, "No,
    He would oppose the tide,
Should such as he from danger flee,
    And in the temple hide?"

We wrought in earnest faith and hope
    Until we built the wall,
And then, unto a joyful feast
    Did priest and people call.

We came to dedicate the wall
    With sacrifice and joy—
A happy throng, from aged sire
    Unto the fair-haired boy.

Our lips so used to mournful songs,
    Did joyous laughter fill,
And strong men wept with sacred joy
    To stand on Zion's hill.

Mid scoffing foes and evil men,
    We built our city blest,
And 'neath our sheltering vines and palms
    Today in peace we rest.

# Out in the Cold

Out in the cold mid the dreary night,
Under the eaves of homes so bright:
Snowflakes falling o'er mother's grave
Will no one rescue, no one save?

A child left out in the dark and cold,
A lamb not sheltered in any fold,
Hearing the wolves of hunger bark,
Out in the cold! and out in the dark

Missing tonight the charming bliss,
That lies in the mother's good-night kiss;
And hearing no loving father's prayer,
For blessings his children all may share.

Creeping away to some wretched den,
To sleep mid the curses of drunken men
And women, not as God has made,
Wrecked and ruined, wronged and betrayed.

Church of the Lord reach out thy arm,
And shield the hapless one from harm;
Where the waves of sin are dashing wild
Rescue and save the drifting child.

Wash from her life guilt's turbid foam,
In the fair haven of a home;
Tenderly lead the motherless girl
Up to the gates of purest pearl.

The wandering feet which else had strayed,
From thorny paths may yet be stayed;
And a crimson track through the cold dark night
May exchange to a line of loving light.

# Save the Boys

Like Dives in the deeps of Hell
I cannot break this fearful spell,
Nor quench the fires I've madly nursed,
Nor cool this dreadful raging thirst.
Take back your pledge—ye come too late!
Ye cannot save me from my fate,
Nor bring me back departed joys;
But ye can try to save the boys.

Ye bid me break my fiery chain,
Arise and be a man again,
When every street with snares is spread,
And nets of sin where'er I tread.
No; I must reap as I did sow.
The seeds of sin bring crops of woe;
But with my latest breath I'll crave
That ye will try the boys to save.

These bloodshot eyes were once so bright;
This sin-crushed heart was glad and light;
But by the wine-cup's ruddy glow
I traced a path to shame and woe.
A captive to my galling chain,
I've tried to rise, but tried in vain—
The cup allures and then destroys.
Oh! from its thraldom save the boys.

Take from your streets those traps of hell
Into whose gilded snares I fell.
Oh! freemen, from these foul decoys
Arise, and vote to save the boys.
Oh ye who license men to trade
In draughts that charm and then degrade,
Before ye hear the cry, Too late,
Oh, save the boys from my sad fate.

# Nothing and Something

It is nothing to me, the beauty said,
With a careless toss of her pretty head;
The man is weak if he can't refrain
From the cup you say is fraught with pain.
It was something to her in after years;
When her eyes were drenched with burning tears,
And she watched in lonely grief and dread,
And startled to hear a staggering tread.

It is nothing to me, the mother said;
I have no fear that my boy will tread
In the downward path of sin and shame,
And crush my heart and darken his name.
It was something to her when that only son
From the path of right was early won,
And madly cast in the flowing bowl
A ruined body and sin-wrecked soul.

It is nothing to me, the young man cried:
In his eye was a flash of scorn and pride;
I heed not the dreadful things ye tell:
I can rule myself I know full well.
It was something to him when in prison he lay
The victim of drink, life ebbing away;
And thought of his wretched child and wife,
And the mournful wreck of his wasted life.

It is nothing to me, the merchant said,
As over his ledger he bent his head;
I'm busy today with tare and tret,
And I have no time to fume and fret.
It was something to him when over the wire
A message came from a funeral pyre—
A drunken conductor had wrecked a train,
And his wife and child were among the slain.

FRANCES ELLEN WATKINS HARPER

It is nothing to me, the voter said,
The party's loss is my greatest dread;
Then gave his vote for the liquor trade,
Though hearts were crushed and drunkards made.
It was something to him in after life,
When his daughter became a drunkard's wife
And her hungry children cried for bread,
And trembled to hear their father's tread.

Is it nothing for us to idly sleep
While the cohorts of death their vigils keep?
To gather the young and thoughtless in
And grind in our midst a grist of sin?
It is something, yes, all, for us to stand
Clasping by faith our Saviour's hand;
To learn to labor, live and fight
On the side of God and changeless light.

# WANDERER'S RETURN

My home is so glad, my heart is so light,
My wandering boy has returned tonight.
He is blighted and bruised, I know, by sin,
But I am so glad to welcome him in.

The child of my tenderest love and care
Has broken away from the tempter's snare;
Tonight my heart is o'erflowing with joy,
I have found again my wandering boy.

My heart has been wrung with a thousand fears,
Mine eyes have been drenched with the bitterest tears;
Like shadows that fade are my past alarms,
My boy is enclasped in his mother's arms.

The streets were not safe for my darling child;
Where sin with its evil attractions smiled.
But his wandering feet have ceased to roam,
And tonight my wayward boy is at home—

At home with the mother that loves him best,
With the hearts that have ached with sad unrest,
With the hearts that are thrilling with untold joy
Because we have found our wandering boy.

In that wretched man so haggard and wild
I only behold my returning child,
And the blissful tears from my eyes that start
Are the overflow of a happy heart.

I have trodden the streets in lonely grief,
I have sought in prayer for my sole relief;
But the depths of my heart tonight are stirred,
I know that the mother's prayer has been heard.

FRANCES ELLEN WATKINS HARPER

If the mother-love be so strong and great
For her child, sin-weary and desolate,
Oh what must the love of the Father be
For souls who have wandered like you and me!

# "Fishers of Men"

I had a dream, a varied dream:
    Before my ravished sight
The city of my Lord arose,
    With all its love and light.

The music of a myriad harps
    Flowed out with sweet accord;
And saints were casting down their crowns
    In homage to our Lord.

My heart leaped up with untold joy;
    Life's toil and pain were o'er;
My weary feet at last had found
    The bright and restful shore.

Just as I reached the gates of light,
    Ready to enter in,
From earth arose a fearful cry
    Of sorrow and of sin.

I turned, and saw behind me surge
    A wild and stormy sea;
And drowning men were reaching out
    Imploring hands to me.

And ev'ry lip was blanched with dread
    And moaning for relief;
The music of the golden harps
    Grew fainter for their grief.

Let me return, I quickly said,
    Close to the pearly gate;
My work is with these wretched ones,
    So wrecked and desolate.

An angel smiled and gently said:
    This is the gate of life,
Wilt thou return to earth's sad scenes,
    Its weariness and strife,

To comfort hearts that sigh and break,
    To dry the falling tear,
Wilt thou forego the music sweet
    Entrancing now thy ear?

I must return, I firmly said,
    The strugglers in that sea
Shall not reach out beseeching hands
    In vain for help to me.

I turned to go; but as I turned
    The gloomy sea grew bright,
And from my heart there seemed to flow
    Ten thousand cords of light.

And sin-wrecked men, with eager hands,
    Did grasp each golden cord;
And with my heart I drew them on
    To see my gracious Lord.

Again I stood beside the gate.
    My heart was glad and free;
For with me stood a rescued throng
    The Lord had given me.

# Signing the Pledge

Do you see this cup—this tempting cup—
    Its sparkle and its glow?
I tell you this cup has brought to me
    A world of shame and woe.

Do you see that woman sad and wan?
    One day with joy and pride,
With orange blossoms in her hair,
    I claimed her as my bride.

And vowed that I would faithful prove
    Till death our lives should part;
I've drenched her soul with floods of grief,
    And almost crushed her heart.

Do you see that gray-haired mother bend
    Beneath her weight of years?
I've filled that aged mother's eyes
    With many bitter tears.

Year after year for me she prays,
    And tries her child to save;
I've almost brought her gray hairs down
    In sorrow to the grave.

Do you see that boy whose wistful eyes
    Are gazing on my face?
I've overshadowed his young life
    With sorrow and disgrace.

He used to greet me with a smile,
    His heart was light and glad;
I've seen him tremble at my voice,
    I've made that heart so sad.

Do you see this pledge I've signed tonight?
    My mother, wife, and boy
Shall read my purpose on that pledge
    And smile through tears of joy.

To know this night, this very night,
    I cast the wine-cup down,
And from the dust of a sinful life
    Lift up my manhood's crown.

The faded face of my young wife
    With roses yet shall bloom,
And joy shall light my mother's eyes
    On the margin of the tomb.

I have vowed tonight my only boy,
    With brow so fair and mile,
Shall not be taunted on the streets,
    And called a drunkard's child.

Never again shall that young face
    Whiten with grief and dread,
Because I've madly staggered home
    And sold for drink his bread.

This strong right arm unnerved by rum
    Shall battle with my fate;
And peace and comfort crown the home
    By drink made desolate.

Like a drowning man, tempest-tossed,
    Clings to a rocky ledge,
With trembling hands I've learned to grasp
    The gospel and the pledge.

A captive bounding from my chain,
    I've rent each hateful band,
And by the help of grace divine
    A victor hope to stand.

LIGHT BEYOND THE DARKNESS

# A Fairer Hope, a Brighter Morn

From the peaceful heights of a higher life
I heard your maddening cry of strife
It quivered with anguish, wrath and pain,
Like a demon struggling with his chain.
A chain of evil, heavy and strong,
Rusted with ages of fearful wrong.
Encrusted with blood and burning tears.
The chain I had worn and dragged for years.
It clasped ray limbs, but it bound your heart.
And formed of your life a fearful part
You sowed the wind, but could not control
The tempest wild of a guilty soul.
You saw me stand with my broken chain
Forged in the furnace of fiery pain.
You saw my children around me stand
Lovingly clasping my unbound hand.
But you remembered my blood and tears
'Mid the weary wasting flight of years.
You thought of the rice swamps, lone and dank,
When my heart in hopeless anguish sank.
You thought of your fields with harvest white,
Where I toiled in paiu from morn till night
You thought of the days you bought and sold
The children I loved, for paltry gold.
You thought of our shrieks that rent the air—
Our moans of anguish and deep despair;
With chattering teeth and paling face,
You thought of your nation's deep disgrace,
You wove from your fears a fearful fate
To spring from your seeds of scorn and hate
You imagined the saddest, wildest thing,
That time, with revenges fierce, could bring
The cry you thought from a Voodoo breast
Was the echo of your soul's unrest;
When thoughts too sad for fruitless tears
Loomed like the ghosts of avenging years.

Oh, prophet of evil, could not your voice
In our new hopes and freedom rejoice?
'Mid the light which streams around our way
Was there naught to see but an evil day?
Nothing but vengeance, wrath and hate,
And the serpent coils of an evil fate—
A fate that shall crush and drag you down;
A doom that shall press like an iron crown?
A fate that shall crisp and curl your hair
And darken your faces now so fair.
And send through your veins like a poisoned flood
The hated stream of the Negro's blood?
A fate to madden the heart and brain
You've peopled with phantoms of dread and pain,
And fancies wild of your daughter's shriek
With Congo kisses upon her cheek?
Beyond the mist of your gloomy fears,
I see the promise of brighter years.
Through the dark I see their golden hem
And my heart gives out its glad amen.
The banner of Christ was your sacred trust.
But you trailed that banner in the dust,
And mockingly told us amid our pain
The hand of your God had forged our chain.
We stumbled and groped through the dreary night
Till our fingers touched God's robe of light;
And we knew He heard, from his lofty throne,
Our saddest cries and faintest moan.
The cross you have covered with sin and shame
We'll bear aloft in Christ's holy name.
Oh, never again may its folds be furled
While sorrow and sin enshroud our world
God, to whose fingers thrills each heart beat,
Has not sent us to walk with aimless feet,
To cower and crouch, with bated breath
From margins of life to shores of death.
Higher and better than hate for hate.
Like the scorpion fangs that desolate,
Is the hope of a brighter, fairer morn

FRANCES ELLEN WATKINS HARPER

And a peace and a love that shall yet be born;
When the Negro shall hold an honored place,
The friend and helper of every race;
His mission to build and not destroy.
And gladden the world with love and joy.

# Our Hero

Onward to her destination,
O'er the stream the Hannah sped,
When a cry of consternation
Smote and chilled our hearts with dread.
Wildly leaping, madly sweeping,
All relentless in their sway,
Like a band of cruel demons.
Flames were closing 'round our way.
Oh! the horror of those moments;
Flames above and waves below.
Oh! the agony of ages
Crowded in one hour of woe.
Fainter grew our hearts with anguish
In that hour with peril rife,
When we saw the pilot flying,
Terror-stricken, for his life.
Then a man uprose before us—
We had once despised his race—
But we saw a lofty purpose
Lighting up his darkened face.
While the flames were madly roaring,
With a courage grand and high,
Forth he rushed unto our rescue,
Strong to suffer, brave to die.
Helplessly the boat was drifting,
Death was staring in each face,
When he grasped the fallen rudder.
Took the pilot's vacant place.
Could he save us? Would he save us
All his hope of life give o'er
Could he hold that fated vessel
Till she reached the nearer shore
All our hopes and fears were centred
'Round his strong, unfaltering hand;
If he failed us we must perish,
Perish just in sight of land.

FRANCES ELLEN WATKINS HARPER

Breathlessly we watched and waited
While the flames were raging fast
When our anguish changed to rapture—
We were saved, yes, saved at last.
Never strains of sweetest music
Brought to us more welcome sound
Than the grating of that steamer
When her keel had touched the ground.
But our faithful martyr hero
Through a fiery pathway trod,
Till he laid his valiant spirit
On the hosom of his God.
Fame has never crowned a hero
On the crimson fields of strife,
Grander, nobler, than that pilot
Yielding up for us his life.

ATLANTA OFFERING

# MY MOTHER'S KISSES

My mother's kiss, my mother's kiss,
I feel its impress now;
As in the bright and happy days
She pressed it on my brow.
You say it is a fancied thing
Within my memory fraught;
To me it has a sacred place—
The treasure house of thought.
Again, I feel her fingers glide
Amid my clustering hair;
I see the love-light in her eyes,
When all my life was fair.
Again, I hear her gentle voice
In warning or in love.
How precious was the faith that taught
My soul of things above.
The music of her voice is stilled,
Her lips are paled in death.
As precious pearls I'll clasp her words
Until my latest breath.
The world has scattered round my path
Honor and wealth and fame;
But naught so precious as the thoughts
That gather round her name.
And friends have placed upon my brow
The laurels of renown;
But she first taught me how to wear
My manhood as a crown.
My hair is silvered o'er with age,
I'm longing to depart;
To clasp again my mother's hand,
And be a child at heart.
To roam with her the glory-land
Where saints and angels greet;
To cast our crowns with songs of love
At our Redeemer's feet.

# A Grain of Sand

Do you see this grain of sand
Lying loosely in my hand?
Do you know to me it brought
Just a simple loving thought?
When one gazes night by night
On the glorious stars of light,
Oh how little seems the span
Measured round the life of man.
Oh! how fleeting are his years
With their smiles and their tears;
Can it be that God does care
For such atoms as we are?
Then outspake this grain of sand
"I was fashioned by His hand
In the star lit realms of space
I was made to have a place."
"Should the ocean flood the world,
Were its mountains 'gainst me hurled,
All the force they could employ
Wouldn't a single grain destroy;
And if I, a thing so light,
Have a place within His sight;
You are linked unto his throne
Cannot live nor die alone.
In the everlasting arms
Mid life's dangers and alarms
Let calm trust your spirit fill;
Know He's God, and then be still."
Trustingly I raised my head
Hearing what the atom said;
Knowing man is greater far
Than the brightest sun or star.

FRANCES ELLEN WATKINS HARPER

# THE CROCUSES

They heard the South wind sighing
A murmur of the rain;
And they knew that Earth was longing
To see them all again.
While the snow-drops still were sleeping
Beneath the silent sod;
They felt their new life pulsing
Within the dark, cold clod.
Not a daffodil nor daisy
Had dared to raise its head;
Not a fairhaired dandelion
Peeped timid from its bed;
Though a tremor of the winter
Did shivering through them run;
Yet they lifted up their foreheads
To greet the vernal sun.
And the sunbeams gave them welcome,
As did the morning air—
And scattered o'er their simple robes
Rich tints of beauty rare.
Soon a host of lovely flowers
From vales and woodland burst;
But in all that fair procession
The crocuses were first.
First to weave for Earth a chaplet
To crown her dear old head;
And to beautify the pathway
Where winter-still did tread.
And their loved and white haired mother
Smiled sweetly 'neath the touch,
When she knew her faithful children
Were loving her so much.

# The Present Age

Say not the age is hard and cold—
I think it brave and grand;
When men of diverse sects and creeds
Are clasping hand in hand.
The Parsee from his sacred fires
Beside the Christian kneels;
And clearer light to Islam's eyes
The word of Christ reveals.
The Brahmin from his distant home
Brings thoughts of ancient lore;
The Bhuddist breaking bonds of caste
Divides mankind no more.
The meek-eyed sons of far Cathay
Are welcome round the board;
Not greed, nor malice drives away
These children of our Lord.
And Judah from whose trusted hands
Came oracles divine;
Now sits with those around whose hearts
The light of God doth shine.
Japan unbars her long sealed gates
From islands far away;
Her sons are lifting up their eyes
To greet the coming day.
The Indian child from forests wild
Has learned to read and pray;
The tomahawk and scalping knife
From him have passed away.
From centuries of servile toil
The Negro finds release,
And builds the fanes of prayer and praise
Unto the God of Peace.
England and Russia face to face
With Central Asia meet;
And on the far Pacific coast,
Chinese and natives greet.

FRANCES ELLEN WATKINS HARPER

Crusaders once with sword and shield
The Holy Land to save;
From Moslem hands did strive to clutch
The dear Redeemer's grave.

A battle greater, grander far
Is for the present age;
A crusade for the rights of man
To brighten history's page.

Where labor faints and bows her head,
And want consorts with crime;
Or men grown faithless sadly say
That evil is the time.

There is the field, the vantage ground
For every earnest heart;
To side with justice, truth and right
And act a noble part.

To save from ignorance and vice
The poorest, humblest child;
To make our age the fairest one
On which the sun has smiled;

To plant the roots of coming years
In mercy, love and truth;
And bid our weary, saddened earth
Again renew her youth.

Oh! earnest hearts! toil on in hope,
'Till darkness shrinks from light;
To fill the earth with peace and joy,
Let youth and age unite;

To stay the floods of sin and shame
That sweep from shore to shore;
And furl the banners stained with blood,
'Till war shall be no more.

Blame not the age, nor think it full
Of evil and unrest;
But say of every other age,
"This one shall be the best."

The age to brighten every path
By sin and sorrow trod;
For loving hearts to usher in
The commonwealth of God.

# Dedication Poem

Dedication Poem on the reception of the annex to the home for aged colored people, from the bequest of Mr. Edward T. Parker.

Outcast from her home in Syria
In the lonely, dreary wild;
Heavy hearted, sorrow stricken,
Sat a mother and her child.
There was not a voice to cheer her
Not a soul to share her fate;
She was weary, he was fainting,—
And life seemed so desolate.
Far away in sunny Egypt
Was lone Hagar's native land;
Where the Nile in kingly bounty
Scatters bread throughout the land.
In the tents of princely Abram
She for years had found a home;
Till the stern decree of Sarah
Sent her forth the wild to roam.
Hour by hour she journeyed onward
From the shelter of their tent,
Till her footsteps slowly faltered
And the water all was spent;
Then she veiled her face in sorrow,
Feared her child would die of thirst;
Till her eyes with tears so holden
Saw a sparkling fountain burst.
Oh! how happy was that mother,
What a soothing of her pain;
When she saw her child reviving,
Life rejoicing through each vein
Does not life repeat this story,
Tell it over day by day?
Of the fountains of refreshment
Ever springing by our way.
Here is one by which we gather,

On this bright and happy day,
Just to bask beside a fountain
Making gladder life's highway.
Bringing unto hearts now aged
Who have borne life's burdens long,
Such a gift of love and mercy
As deserves our sweetest song.
Such a gift that even heaven
May rejoice with us below,
If the pure and holy angels
Join us in our joy and woe.
May the memory of the giver
In this home where age may rest,
Float like fragrance through the ages,
Ever blessing, ever blest.
When the gates of pearl are opened
May we there this friend behold,
Drink with him from living fountains,
Walk with him the streets of gold.
When life's shattered cords of music
Shall again be sweetly sung;
Then our hearts with life immortal,
Shall be young, forever young.

# A DOUBLE STANDARD

Do you blame me that I loved him?
If when standing all alone
I cried for bread a careless world
Pressed to my lips a stone.
Do you blame me that I loved him,
That my heart beat glad and free,
When he told me in the sweetest tones
He loved but only me?
Can you blame me that I did not see
Beneath his burning kiss
The serpent's wiles, nor even hear
The deadly adder hiss?
Can you blame me that my heart grew cold
That the tempted, tempter turned;
When he was feted and caressed
And I was coldly spurned?
Would you blame him, when you draw from me
Your dainty robes aside,
If he with gilded baits should claim
Your fairest as his bride?
Would you blame the world if it should press
On him a civic crown;
And see me struggling in the depth
Then harshly press me down?
Crime has no sex and yet today
I wear the brand of shame;
Whilst he amid the gay and proud
Still bears an honored name.
Can you blame me if I've learned to think
Your hate of vice a sham,
When you so coldly crushed me down
And then excused the man?
Would you blame me if tomorrow
The coroner should say,
A wretched girl, outcast, forlorn,
Has thrown her life away?

Yes, blame me for my downward course,
But oh! remember well,
Within your homes you press the hand
That led me down to hell.
I'm glad God's ways are not our ways,
He does not see as man;
Within His love I know there's room
For those whom others ban.
I think before His great white throne,
His throne of spotless light,
That whited sepulchres shall wear
The hue-of endless night.
That I who fell, and he who sinned,
Shall reap as we have sown;
That each the burden of his loss
Must bear and bear alone.
No golden weights can turn the scale
Of justice in His sight;
And what is wrong in woman's life
In man's cannot be right.

FRANCES ELLEN WATKINS HARPER

# THE DYING BONDMAN

Life was trembling, faintly trembling
On the bondman's latest breath,
And he felt the chilling pressure
Of the cold, hard hand of Death.

He had been an African chieftain,
Worn his manhood as a crown;
But upon the field of battle
Had been fiercely stricken down.

He had longed to gain his freedom,
Waited, watched and hoped in vain,
Till his life was slowly ebbing—
Almost broken was his chain.

By his bedside stood the master,
Gazing on the dying one,
Knowing by the dull grey shadows
That life's sands were almost run.

"Master," said the dying bondman,
"Home and friends I soon shall see;
But before I reach my country,
Master write that I am free;"

"For the spirits of my fathers
Would shrink back from me in pride,
If I told them at our greeting
I a slave had lived and died;—"

"Give to me the precious token,
That my kindred dead may see—
Master! write it, write it quickly!
Master! write that I am free!"

At his earnest plea the master
Wrote for him the glad release,
O'er his wan and wasted features
Flitted one sweet smile of peace.

Eagerly he grasped the writing;
"I am free!" at last he said.
Backward fell upon the pillow,
He was free among the dead.

# "A Little Child Shall Lead Them"

Only a little scrap of blue
Preserved with loving care,
But earth has not a brilliant hue
To me more bright and fair.
Strong drink, like a raging demon,
Laid on my heart his hand,
When my darling joined with others
The Loyal Legion band.
But mystic angels called away
My loved and precious child,
And o'er life's dark and stormy way
Swept waves of anguish wild.
This badge of the Loyal Legion
We placed upon her breast,
As she lay in her little coffin
Taking her last sweet rest.
To wear that badge as a token
She earnestly did crave,
So we laid it on her bosom
To wear it in the grave.
Where sorrow would never reach her
Nor harsh words smite her ear;
Nor her eyes in death dimmed slumber
Would ever shed a tear.
"What means this badge?" said her father,
Whom we had tried to save;
Who said, when we told her story,
"Don't put it in the grave."
We took the badge from her bosom
And laid it on a chair;
And men by drink deluded
Knelt by that badge in prayer.
And vowed in that hour of sorrow
From drink they would abstain;
And this little badge became the wedge
Which broke their galling chain.

FRANCES ELLEN WATKINS HARPER

And lifted the gloomy shadows
That overspread my life,
And flooding my home with gladness,
Made me a happy wife.
And this is why this scrap of blue
Is precious in my sight;
It changed my sad and gloomy home
From darkness into light.

# The Sparrow's Fall

Too frail to soar—a feeble thing—
It fell to earth with fluttering wing;
But God, who watches over all,
Beheld that little sparrow's fall.
'Twas not a bird with plumage gay,
Filling the air with its morning lay;
'Twas not an eagle bold and strong,
Borne on the tempest's wing along.
Only a brown and weesome thing,
With drooping head and listless wing;
It could not drift beyond His sight
Who marshals the splendid stars of night.
Its dying chirp fell on His ears,
Who tunes the music of the spheres,
Who hears the hungry lion's call,
And spreads a table for us all.
Its mission of song at last is done,
No more will it greet the rising sun;
That tiny bird has found a rest
More calm than its mother's downy breast.
Oh, restless heart, learn thou to trust
In God, so tender, strong and just;
In whose love and mercy everywhere
His humblest children have a share.
If in love He numbers ev'ry hair,
Whether the strands be dark or fair,
Shall we not learn to calmly rest,
Like children, on our Father's breast?

FRANCES ELLEN WATKINS HARPER

# God Bless Our Native Land

God bless our native land,
Land of the newly free,
Oh may she ever stand
For truth and liberty.
God bless our native land,
Where sleep our kindred dead,
Let peace at thy command
Above their graves be shed.
God help our native land,
Bring surcease to her strife,
And shower from thy hand
A more abundant life.
God bless our native land,
Her homes and children bless,
Oh may she ever stand
For truth and righteousness.

# DANDELIONS

Welcome children of the Spring,
In your garbs of green and gold,
Lifting up your sun-crowned heads
On the verdant plain and wold.
As a bright and joyous troop
From the breast of earth ye came
Fair and lovely are your cheeks,
With sun-kisses all aflame.
In the dusty streets and lanes,
Where the lowly children play,
There as gentle friends ye smile,
Making brighter life's highway.
Dewdrops and the morning sun,
Weave your garments fair and bright,
And we welcome you today
As the children of the light.
Children of the earth and sun,
We are slow to understand
All the richness of the gifts
Flowing from our Father's hand.
Were our vision clearer far,
In this sin-dimmed world of ours,
Would we not more thankful be
For the love that sends us flowers?
Welcome, early visitants,
With your sun-crowned golden hair
With your message to our hearts
Of our Father's loving care.

# THE BUILDING

"Build me a house," said the Master,
"But not on the shifting sand,
 Mid the wreck and roar of tempests,
 A house that will firmly stand.
"I will bring thee windows of agates,
 And gates of carbuncles bright,
 And thy fairest courts and portals
 Shall be filled with love and light.
"Thou shalt build with fadeless rubies,
 All fashioned around the throne,
 A house that shall last forever,
 With Christ as the cornerstone.
"It shall be a royal mansion,
 A fair and beautiful thing,
 It will be the presence-chamber
 Of thy Saviour, Lord and King.
"Thy house shall be bound with pinions
 To mansions of rest above,
 But grace shall forge all the fetters
 With the links and cords of love.
"Thou shalt be free in this mansion
 From sorrow and pain of heart,
 For the peace of God shall enter,
 And never again depart."

# Home, Sweet Home

Sharers of a common country,
They had met in deadly strife;
Men who should have been as brothers
Madly sought each other's life.
In the silence of the even,
When the cannon's lips were dumb,
'Thoughts of home and all its loved ones
To the soldier's heart would come.
On the margin of a river,
'Mid the evening's dews and damps,
Could be heard the sounds of music
Rising from two hostile camps.
One was singing of its section
Down in Dixie, Dixie's land,
And the other of the banner
Waved so long from strand to strand.
In the land where Dixie's ensign
Floated o'er the hopeful slave,
Rose the song that freedom's banner,
Starry-lighted, long might wave.
From the fields of strife and carnage,
Gentle thoughts began to roam,
And a tender strain of music
Rose with words of "Home, Sweet Home."
Then the hearts of strong men melted,
For amid our grief and sin
Still remains that "touch of nature,"
Telling us we all are kin.
In one grand but gentle chorus,
Floating to the starry dome,
Came the words that brought them nearer,
Words that told of "Home, Sweet Home."
For awhile, all strife forgotten,
They were only brothers then,
Joining in the sweet old chorus,
Not as soldiers, but as men.

Men whose hearts would flow together,
Though apart their feet might roam,
Found a tie they could not sever,
In the mem'ry of each home.
Never may the steps of carnage
Shake our land from shore to shore,
But may mother, home and Heaven,
Be our watchwords evermore.

# The Pure in Heart Shall See God

They shall see Him in the crimson flush
Of morning's early light,
In the drapery of sunset,
Around the couch of night.
When the clouds drop down their fatness,
In late and early rain,
They shall see His glorious footprints
On valley, hill and plain.
They shall see Him when the cyclone
Breathes terror through the land;
They shall see Him 'mid the murmurs
Of zephyrs soft and bland.
They shall see Him when the lips of health,
Breath vigor through each nerve,
When pestilence clasps hands with death,
His purposes to serve.
They shall see Him when the trembling earth
Is rocking to and fro;
They shall see Him in the order
The seasons come and go.
They shall see Him when the storms of war
Sweep wildly through the land;
When peace descends like gentle dew
They still shall see His hand.
They shall see Him in the city
Of gems and pearls of light,
They shall see Him in his beauty,
And walk with Him in white.
To living founts their feet shall tend,
And Christ shall be their guide,
Beloved of God, their rest shall be
In safety by His side.

# He "Had Not Where to Lay His Head"

The conies had their hiding-place,
The wily fox with stealthy tread
A covert found, but Christ, the Lord,
Had not a place to lay his head.
The eagle had an eyrie home,
The blithesome bird its quiet rest,
But not the humblest spot on earth
Was by the Son of God possessed.
Princes and kings had palaces,
With grandeur could adorn each tomb,
For Him who came with love and life,
They had no home, they gave no room.
The hands whose touch sent thrills of joy
Through nerves unstrung and palsied frame,
The feet that travelled for our need,
Were nailed unto the cross of shame.
How dare I murmur at my lot,
Or talk of sorrow, pain and loss,
When Christ was in a manger laid,
And died in anguish on the cross.
That homeless one beheld beyond
His lonely agonizing pain,
A love outflowing from His heart,
That all the wandering world would gain.

# Go Work in My Vineyard

Go work in my vineyard, said the Lord,
And gather the bruised grain;
But the reapers had left the stubble bare,
And I trod the soil in pain.
The fields of my Lord are wide and broad,
He has pastures fair and green,
And vineyards that drink the golden light
Which flows from the sun's bright sheen.
I heard the joy of the reapers' song,
As they gathered golden grain;
Then wearily turned unto my task,
With a lonely sense of pain.
Sadly I turned from the sun's fierce glare.
And sought the quiet shade,
And over my dim and weary eyes
Sleep's peaceful fingers strayed.
I dreamed I joined with a restless throng,
Eager for pleasure and gain;
But ever and anon a stumbler fell,
And uttered a cry of pain.
But the eager crowd still hurried on,
Too busy to pause or heed,
When a voice rang sadly through my soul,
You must staunch these wounds that bleed.
My hands were weak, but I reached them out
To feebler ones than mine,
And over the shadows of my life
Stole the light of a peace divine.
Oh! then my task was a sacred thing,
How precious it grew in my eyes!
'Twas mine to gather the bruised grain
For the "Lord of Paradise."
And when the reapers shall lay their grain
On the floors of golden light,
I feel that mine with its broken sheaves
Shall be precious in His sight.

FRANCES ELLEN WATKINS HARPER

Though thorns may often pierce my feet,
And the shadows still abide,
The mists will vanish before His smile,
There will be light at eventide.

# Renewal of Strength

The prison-house in which I live
Is falling to decay,
But God renews my spirit's strength,
Within these walls of clay.
For me a dimness slowly creeps
Around earth's fairest light,
But heaven grows clearer to my view,
And fairer to my sight.
It may be earth's sweet harmonies
Are duller to my ear,
But music from my Father's house
Begins to float more near.
Then let the pillars of my home
Crumble and fall away;
Lo, God's dear love within my soul
Renews it day by day.

FRANCES ELLEN WATKINS HARPER

# JAMIE'S PUZZLE

There was grief within our household
Because of a vacant chair.
Our mother, so loved and precious,
No longer was sitting there.
Our hearts grew heavy with sorrow,
Our eyes with tears were blind,
And little Jamie was wondering,
Why we were left behind.
We had told our little darling,
Of the land of love and light,
Of the saints all crowned with glory,
And enrobed in spotless white.
We said that our precious mother,
Had gone to that land so fair,
To dwell with beautiful angels,
And to be forever there.
But the child was sorely puzzled,
Why dear grandmamma should go
To dwell in a stranger city,
When her children loved her so.
But again the mystic angel
Came with swift and silent tread,
And our sister, Jamie's mother,
Was enrolled among the dead.
To us the mystery deepened,
To Jamie it seemed more clear;
Grandma, he said, must be lonesome,
And mamma has gone to her.
But the question lies unanswered
In our little Jamie's mind,
Why she should go to our mother,
And leave her children behind;
To dwell in that lovely city,
From all that was dear to part,
From children who loved to nestle
So closely around her heart.

Dear child, like you, we are puzzled,
With problems that still remain;
But think in the great hereafter
Their meaning will all be plain.

# TRUTH

A rock, for ages, stern and high,
Stood frowning 'gainst the earth and sky,
And never bowed his haughty crest
When angry storms around him prest.
Morn, springing from the arms of night,
Had often bathed his brow with light,
And kissed the shadows from his face
With tender love and gentle grace.
Day, pausing at the gates of rest,
Smiled on him from the distant West,
And from her throne the dark-browed Night
Threw round his path her softest light.
And yet he stood unmoved and proud,
Nor love, nor wrath, his spirit bowed;
He bared his brow to every blast
And scorned the tempest as it passed.
One day a tiny, humble seed—
The keenest eye would hardly heed—
Fell trembling at that stern rock's base,
And found a lowly hiding-place.
A ray of light, and drop of dew,
Came with a message, kind and true;
They told her of the world so bright,
Its love, its joy, and rosy light,
And lured her from her hiding-place,
To gaze upon earth's glorious face.
So, peeping timid from the ground,
She clasped the ancient rock around,
And climbing up with childish grace,
She held him with a close embrace;
Her clinging was a thing of dread;
Where'er she touched a fissure spread,
And he who'd breasted many a storm
Stood frowning there, a mangled-form;
A Truth, dropped in the silent earth,
May seem a thing of little worth,

'Till, spreading round some mighty wrong,
It saps its pillars proud and strong,
And o'er the fallen ruin weaves
The brightest blooms and fairest leaves.

# DEATH OF THE OLD SEA KING

Twas a fearful night—the tempest raved
With loud and wrathful pride,
The storm-king harnessed his lightning steeds,
And rode on the raging tide.
The sea-king lay on his bed of death,
Pale mourners around him bent;
They knew the wild and fitful life
Of their chief was almost spent.
His ear was growing dull in death
When the angry storm he heard,
The sluggish blood in the old man's veins
With sudden vigor stirred.
"I hear them call," cried the dying man,
His eyes grew full of light;
"Now bring me here my warrior robes,
My sword and armor bright."
"In the tempest's lull I heard a voice,
I knew 'twas Odin's call.
The Valkyrs are gathering round my bed
To lead me unto his hall."
"Bear me unto my noblest ship,
Light up a funeral pyre;
I'll walk to the palace of the braves
Through a path of flame and fire."
Oh! wild and bright was the stormy light
That flashed from the old man's eye,
As they bore him from the couch of death
To his battle-ship to die,
And lit with many a mournful torch
The sea-king's dying bed,
And like a banner fair and bright
The flames around him spread.
But they heard no cry of anguish
Break through that fiery wall,
With rigid brow and silent lips
He was seeking Odin's hall.

Through a path of fearful splendor,
While strong men held their breath,
The brave old man went boldly forth
And calmly talked with death.

# Save the Boys

Like Dives in the deeps of Hell
I cannot break this fearful spell,
Nor quench the fires I've madly nursed,
Nor cool this dreadful raging thirst.
Take back your pledge—ye come too late!
Ye cannot save me from my fate,
Nor bring me back departed joys;
But ye can try to save the boys.
Ye bid me break my fiery chain,
Arise and be a man again,
When every street with snares is spread,
And nets of sin where'er I tread.
No; I must reap as I did sow.
The seeds of sin bring crops of woe;
But with my latest breath I'll crave
That ye will try the boys to save.
These bloodshot eyes were once so bright;
This sin-crushed heart was glad and light;
But by the wine-cup's ruddy glow
I traced a path to shame and woe.
A captive to my galling chain,
I've tried to rise, but tried in vain—
The cup allures and then destroys.
Oh! from its thraldom save the boys.
Take from your streets those traps of hell
Into whose gilded snares I fell.
Oh! freemen, from these foul decoys
Arise, and vote to save the boys.
Oh, ye who license men to trade
In draughts that charm and then degrade,
Before ye hear the cry, Too late,
Oh, save the boys from my sad fate.

# Nothing and Something

It is nothing to me, the beauty said,
With a careless toss of her pretty head;
The man is weak if he can't refrain
From the cup you say is fraught with pain.
It was something to her in after years,
When her eyes were drenched with burning tears,
And she watched in lonely grief and dread,
And startled to hear a staggering tread.
It is nothing to me, the mother said;
I have no fear that my boy will tread
In the downward path of sin and shame,
And crush my heart and darken his name.
It was something to her when that only son
From the path of right was early won,
And madly cast in the flowing bowl
A ruined body and sin-wrecked soul.
It is nothing to me, the young man cried:
In his eye was a flash of scorn and pride;
I heed not the dreadful things ye tell:
I can rule myself I know full well.
It was something to him when in prison he lay
The victim of drink, life ebbing away;
And thought of his wretched child and wife,
And the mournful wreck of his wasted life.
It is nothing to me, the merchant said,
As over his ledger he bent his head;
I'm busy today with tare and tret,
And I have no time to fume and fret.
It was something to him when over the wire
A message came from a funeral pyre—
A drunken conductor had wrecked a train,
And his wife and child were among the slain.
It is nothing to me, the voter said,
The party's loss is my greatest dread;
Then gave his vote for the liquor trade,
Though hearts were crushed and drunkards made.

FRANCES ELLEN WATKINS HARPER

It was something to him in after life,
When his daughter became a drunkard's wife
And her hungry children cried for bread,
And trembled to hear their father's tread.
Is it nothing for us to idly sleep
While the cohorts of death their vigils keep?
To gather the young and thoughtless in,
And grind in our midst a grist of sin?
It is something, yes, all, for us to stand
Clasping by faith our Saviour's hand;
To learn to labor, live and fight
On the side of God and changeless light.

# VASHTI

She leaned her head upon her hand
And heard the King's decree—
"My lords are feasting in my halls;
Bid Vashti come to me.

"I've shown the treasures of my house,
My costly jewels rare,
But with the glory of her eyes
No rubies can compare.

"Adorn'd and crown'd I'd have her come,
With all her queenly grace,
And, 'mid my lords and mighty men,
Unveil her lovely face.

"Each gem that sparkles in my crown,
Or glitters on my throne,
Grows poor and pale when she appears,
My beautiful, my own!"

All waiting stood the chamberlains
To hear the Queen's reply.
They saw her cheek grow deathly pale,
But light flash'd to her eye:

"Go, tell the King," she proudly said,
"That I am Persia's Queen,
And by his crowds of merry men
I never will be seen.

"I'll take the crown from off my head
And tread it 'neath my feet,
Before their rude and careless gaze
My shrinking eyes shall meet.

"A queen unveil'd before the crowd!—
Upon each lip my name!—
Why, Persia's women all. would blush
And weep for Vashti's shame!

"Go back!" she cried, and waved her hand,
And grief was in her eye:
"Go, tell the King," she sadly said,
"That I would rather die."

FRANCES ELLEN WATKINS HARPER

They brought her message to the King;
Dark flash'd his angry eye;
'Twas as the lightning ere the storm
Hath swept in fury by.
Then bitterly outspoke the King,
Through purple lips of wrath—
"What shall be done to her who dares
To cross your monarch's path?"
Then spake his wily counsellors—
"O King of this fair land!
From distant Ind to Ethiop,
All bow to thy command.
"But if, before thy servants' eyes,
This thing they plainly see,
That Vashti doth not heed thy will
Nor yield herself to thee,
"The women, restive 'neath our rule,
Would learn to scorn our name,
And from her deed to us would come
Reproach and burning shame.
"Then, gracious King, sign with thy hand
This stern but just decree,
That Vashti lay aside her crown,
Thy Queen no more to be."
She heard again the King's command,
And left her high estate;
Strong in her earnest womanhood,
She calmly met her fate,
And left the palace of the King,
Proud of her spotless name—
A woman who could bend to grief,
But would not bow to shame.

# Thank God for Little Children

Thank God for little children,
Bright flowers by earth's wayside,
The dancing, joyous lifeboats
Upon life's stormy tide.
Thank God for little children;
When our skies are cold and gray,
They come as sunshine to our hearts,
And charm our cares away.
I almost think the angels,
Who tend life's garden fair,
Drop down the sweet wild blossoms
That bloom around us here.
It seems a breath of heaven
Round many a cradle lies,
And every little baby
Brings a message from the skies.
Dear mothers, guard these jewels,
As sacred offerings meet,
A wealth of household treasures
To lay at Jesus' feet.

# The Martyr of Alabama

The following news item appeared in the newspapers throughout the country, issue of December 27th, 1894:

Tim Thompson, a little negro boy, was asked to dance for the amusement of some white toughs. He refused, saying he was a church member. One of the men knocked him down with a club and then danced upon his prostrate form. He then shot the boy in the hip. The boy is dead; his murderer is still at large.

He lifted up his pleading eyes,
And scanned each cruel face,
Where cold and brutal cowardice
Had left its evil trace.
It was when tender memories
Round Beth'lem's manger lay,
And mothers told their little ones
Of Jesu's natal day.
And of the Magi from the East
Who came their gifts to bring,
And bow in rev'rence at the feet
Of Salem's new-born King.
And how the herald angels sang
The choral song of peace,
That war should close his wrathful lips,
And strife and carnage cease.
At such an hour men well may hush
Their discord and their strife,
And o'er that manger clasp their hands
With gifts to brighten life.
Alas! that in our favored land,
That cruelty and crime
Should cast their shadows o'er a day,
The fairest pearl of time.
A dark-browed boy had drawn anear
A band of savage men,
Just as a hapless lamb might stray
Into a tiger's den.

Cruel and dull, they saw in him
For sport an evil chance,
And then demanded of the child
To give to them a dance.
"Come dance for us," the rough men said;
"I can't," the child replied,
"I cannot for the dear Lord's sake,
Who for my sins once died."
Tho' they were strong and he was weak,
He wouldn't his Lord deny.
His life lay in their cruel hands,
But he for Christ could die.
Heard they aright? Did that brave child
Their mandates dare resist?
Did he against their stern commands
Have courage to resist?
Then recklessly a man arose,
And dealt a fearful blow.
He crushed the portals of that life,
And laid the brave child low.
And trampled on his prostrate form,
As on a broken toy;
Then danced with careless, brutal feet,
Upon the murdered boy.
Christians! behold that martyred child!
His blood cries from the ground;
Before the sleepless eye of God,
He shows each gaping wound.
Oh! Church of Christ arise! arise!
Lest crimson stain thy hand,
When God shall inquisition make
For blood shed in the land.
Take sackcloth of the darkest hue,
And shroud the pulpits round;
Servants of him who cannot lie
Sit mourning on the ground.
Let holy horror blanch each brow,
Pale every cheek with fears,
And rocks and stones, if ye could speak,

FRANCES ELLEN WATKINS HARPER

Ye well might melt to tears.
Through every fane send forth a cry,
Of sorrow and regret,
Nor in an hour of careless ease
Thy brother's wrongs forget.
Veil not thine eyes, nor close thy lips,
Nor speak with bated breath;
This evil shall not always last,—
The end of it is death.
Avert the doom that crime must bring
Upon a guilty land;
Strong in the strength that God supplies,
For truth and justice stand.
For Christless men, with reckless hands,
Are sowing round thy path
The tempests wild that yet shall break
In whirlwinds of God's wrath.

# The Night of Death

Twas a night of dreadful horror,—
Death was sweeping through the land;
And the wings of dark destruction
Were outstretched from strand to strand.
Strong men's hearts grew faint with terror,
As the tempest and the waves
Wrecked their homes and swept them downward,
Suddenly to yawning graves.
'Mid the wastes of ruined households,
And the tempest's wild alarms,
Stood a terror-stricken mother
With a child within her arms.
Other children huddled 'round her,
Each one nestling in her heart;
Swift in thought and swift in action,
She at least from one must part.
Then she said unto her daughter,
"Strive to save one child from death."
"Which one?" said the anxious daughter,
As she stood with bated breath.
Oh! the anguish of that mother;
What despair was in her eye!
All her little ones were precious;
Which one should she leave to die?
Then outspake the brother Bennie:
"I will take the little one."
"No," exclaimed the anxious mother;
"No, my child, it can't be done."
"See! my boy, the waves are rising,
Save yourself and leave the child!"
"I will trust in Christ," he answered;
Grasped the little one and smiled.
Through the roar of wind and waters
Ever and anon she cried;
But throughout the night of terror
Never Bennie's voice replied.

FRANCES ELLEN WATKINS HARPER

But above the waves' wild surging
He had found a safe retreat,
As if God had sent an angel,
Just to guide his wandering feet.
When the storm had spent its fury,
And the sea gave up its dead,
She was mourning for her loved ones,
Lost amid that night of dread.
While her head was bowed in anguish,
On her ear there fell a voice,
Bringing surcease to her sorrow,
Bidding all her heart rejoice.
"Didn't I tell you true?" said Bennie,
And his eyes were full of light,
"When I told you God would help me
Through the dark and dreadful night?"
And he placed the little darling
Safe within his mother's arms,
Feeling Christ had been his guardian,
'Mid the dangers and alarms.
Oh! for faith so firm and precious,
In the darkest, saddest night,
Till life's gloom-encircled shadows
Fade in everlasting light.
And upon the mount of vision
We our loved and lost shall greet,
With earth's wildest storms behind us,
And its cares beneath our feet.

# Mother's Treasures

Two little children sit by my side,
I call them Lily and Daffodil;
I gaze on them with a mother's pride,
One is Edna, the other is Will.
Both have eyes of starry light,
And laughing lips o'er teeth of pearl.
I would not change for a diadem
My noble boy and darling girl.
Tonight my heart o'erflows with joy;
I hold them as a sacred trust;
I fain would hide them in my heart,
Safe from tarnish of moth and rust.
What should I ask for my dear boy?
The richest gifts of wealth or fame?
What for my girl? A loving heart
And a fair and a spotless name?
What for my boy? That he should stand
A pillar of strength to the state?
What for my girl? That she should be
The friend of the poor and desolate?
I do not ask they shall never tread
With weary feet the paths of pain.
I ask that in the darkest hour
They may faithful and true remain.
I only ask their lives may be
Pure as gems in the gates of pearl,
Lives to brighten and bless the world—
This I ask for my boy and girl.
I ask to clasp their hands again
'Mid the holy hosts of heaven,
Enraptured say: "I am here, oh! God,
And the children Thou hast given."

FRANCES ELLEN WATKINS HARPER

# THE REFINER'S GOLD

He stood before my heart's closed door,
And asked to enter in;
But I had barred the passage o'er
By unbelief and sin.
He came with nail-prints in his hands,
To set my spirit free;
With wounded feet he trod a path
To come and sup with me.
He found me poor and brought me gold,
The fire of love had tried,
And garments whitened by his blood,
My wretchedness to hide.
The glare of life had dimmed my
Its glamour was too bright.
He came with ointment in his hands
To heal my darkened sight.
He knew my heart was tempest-tossed,
By care and pain oppressed;
He whispered to my burdened heart,
Come unto me and rest.
He found me weary, faint and worn,
On barren mountains cold;
With love's constraint he drew me on,
To shelter in his fold.
Oh! foolish heart, how slow wert thou
To welcome thy dear guest,
To change thy weariness and care
For comfort, peace and rest.
Close to his side, oh! may I stay,
Just to behold his face,
Till I shall wear within my soul
The image of his grace.
The grace that changes hearts of stone
To tenderness and love,
And bids us run with willing feet
Unto his courts above.

# A Story of Rebellion

The treacherous sands had caught our boat,
And held it with a strong embrace
And death at our imprisoned crew
Was sternly looking face to face.
With anxious hearts, but failing strength,
We strove to push the boat from shore;
But all in vain, for there we lay
With bated breath and useless oar.
Around us in a fearful storm
The fiery hail fell thick and fast;
And we engirded by the sand,
Could not return the dreadful blast.
When one arose upon whose brow
The ardent sun had left his trace;
A noble purpose strong and high
Uplighting all his dusky face.
Perchance within that fateful hour
The wrongs of ages thronged apace;
But with it came the glorious hope
Of swift deliverance to his race.
Of galling chains asunder rent,
Of severed hearts again made one,
Of freedom crowning all the land
Through battles gained and victories won.
"Some one," our hero firmly said,
"Must die to get us out of this;"
Then leaped upon the strand and bared
His bosom to the bullets' hiss.
"But ye are soldiers, and can fight,
May win in battles yet unfought;
I have no offering but my life,
And if they kill me it is nought."
With steady hands he grasped the boat,
And boldly pushed it from the shore;
Then fell by rebel bullets pierced,
His life work grandly, nobly o'er.

FRANCES ELLEN WATKINS HARPER

Our boat was rescued from the sands
And launched in safety on the tide;
But he our comrade good and grand,
In our defence had bravely died.

# Burial of Sarah

He stood before the sons of Heth,
And bowed his sorrowing head;
"I've come," he said, "to buy a place
Where I may lay my dead."
"I am a stranger in your land,
My home has lost its light;
Grant me a place where I may lay
My dead away from sight."
Then tenderly the sons of Heth
Gazed on the mourner's face,
And said, "Oh, Prince, amid our dead,
Choose thou her resting-place."
"The sepulchres of those we love,
We place at thy command;
Against the plea thy grief hath made
We close not heart nor hand."
The patriarch rose and bowed his head,
And said, "One place I crave;
'Tis at the end of Ephron's field,
And called Machpelah's cave."
"Entreat him that he sell to me
For her last sleep that cave;
I do not ask for her I loved
The freedom of a grave."
The son of Zohar answered him,
"Hearken, my lord, to me;
Before our sons, the field and cave
I freely give to thee."
"I will not take it as a gift,"
The grand old man then said;
"I pray thee let me buy the place
Where I may lay my dead."
And with the promise in his heart,
His seed should own that land,
He gave the shekels for the field
He took from Ephron's hand.

FRANCES ELLEN WATKINS HARPER

And saw afar the glorious day
tis chosen seed should tread,
The soil where he in sorrow lay
His loved and cherished dead.

# Going Fast

She came from the East a fair, young bride,
With a light and a bounding heart,
To find in the distant West a home
With her husband to make a start.
He builded his cabin far away,
Where the prairie flower bloomed wild;
Her love made lighter all his toil,
And joy and hope around him smiled.
She plied her hands to life's homely tasks,
And helped to build his fortunes up;
While joy and grief, like bitter and sweet,
Were mingled and mixed in her cup.
He sowed in his fields of golden grain,
All the strength of his manly prime;
Nor music of birds, nor brooks, nor bees,
Was as sweet as the dollar's chime.
She toiled and waited through weary years
For the fortune that came at length;
But toil and care and hope deferred,
Had stolen and wasted her strength.
The cabin changed to a stately home,
Rich carpets were hushing her tread;
But light was fading from her eye,
And the bloom from her cheek had fled.
Her husband was adding field to field,
And new wealth to his golden store;
And little thought the shadow of death
Was entering in at his door.
Slower and heavier grew her step,
While his gold and his gains increased;
But his proud domain had not the charm
Of her humble home in the East.
He had no line to sound the depths
Of her tears repressed and unshed;
Nor dreamed 'mid plenty a human heart
Could be starving, but not for bread.

FRANCES ELLEN WATKINS HARPER

Within her eye was a restless light,
And a yearning that never ceased,
A longing to see the dear old home
She had left in the distant East.
A longing to clasp her mother's hand,
And nestle close to her heart,
And to feel the heavy cares of life
Like the sun-kissed shadows depart.
The hungry heart was stilled at last;
Its restless, baffled yearning ceased.
A lonely man sat by the bier
Of a corpse that was going East.

# The Hermit's Sacrifice

From Rome's palaces and villas
Gaily issued forth a throng;
From her humbler habitations
Moved a human tide along.
Haughty dames and blooming maidens,
Men who knew not mercy's sway,
Thronged into the Coliseum
On that Roman holiday.
From the lonely wilds of Asia,
From her jungles far away,
From the distant torrid regions,
Rome had gathered beasts of prey.
Lions restless, roaring, rampant,
Tigers with their stealthy tread,
Leopards bright, and fierce, and fiery,
Met in conflict wild and dread.
Fierce and fearful was the carnage
Of the maddened beasts of prey,
As they fought and rent each other
Urged by men more fierce than they.
Till like muffled thunders breaking
On a vast and distant shore,
Fainter grew the yells of tigers,
And the lions' dreadful roar.
On the crimson-stained arena
Lay the victims of the fight;
Eyes which once had glared with anguish,
Lost in death their baleful light.
Then uprose the gladiators
Armed for conflict unto death,
Waiting for the prefect's signal,
Cold and stern with bated breath.
"Ave Caesar, morituri,
Te, salutant," rose the cry
From the lips of men ill-fated,
Doomed to suffer and to die.

FRANCES ELLEN WATKINS HARPER

Then began the dreadful contest,
Lives like chaff were thrown away,
Rome with all her pride and power
Butchered for a holiday.
Eagerly the crowd were waiting,
Loud the clashing sabres rang,
When between the gladiators
All unarmed a hermit sprang.
"Cease your bloodshed," cried the hermit,
"On this carnage place your ban;"
But with flashing swords they answered,
"Back unto your place, old man."
From their path the gladiators
Thrust the strange intruder back,
Who between their hosts advancing
Calmly parried their attack.
All undaunted by their weapons,
Stood the old heroic man;
While a maddened cry of anger
Through the vast assembly ran.
"Down with him," cried out the people,
As with thumbs unbent they glared,
Till the prefect gave the signal
That his life should not be spared.
Men grew wild with wrathful passion,
When his fearless words were said
Cruelly they fiercely showered
Stones on his devoted head.
Bruised and bleeding fell the hermit,
Victor in that hour of strife;
Gaining in his death a triumph
That he could not win in life.
Had he uttered on the forum
Struggling thoughts within him born,
Men had jeered his words as madness,
But his deed they could not scorn.
Not in vain had been his courage,
Nor for naught his daring deed;
From his grave his mangled body

Did for wretched captives plead.
From that hour Rome, grown more thoughtful,
Ceased her sport in human gore;
And into her Coliseum
Gladiators came no more.

# SONGS FOR THE PEOPLE

Let me make the songs for the people,
Songs for the old and young;
Songs to stir like a battle-cry
Wherever they are sung.
Not for the clashing of sabres,
For carnage nor for strife;
But songs to thrill the hearts of men
With more abundant life.
Let me make the songs for the weary,
Amid life's fever and fret,
Till hearts shall relax their tension,
And careworn brows forget.
Let me sing for little children,
Before their footsteps stray,
Sweet anthems of love and duty,
To float o'er life's highway.
I would sing for the poor and aged,
When shadows dim their sight;
Of the bright and restful mansions,
Where there shall be no night.
Our world, so worn and weary,
Needs music, pure and strong,
To hush the jangle and discords
Of sorrow, pain, and wrong.
Music to soothe all its sorrow,
Till war and crime shall cease;
And the hearts of men grown tender
Girdle the world with peace.

SPEECHES

# Liberty for Slaves

C ould we trace the record of every human heart, the aspirations of every immortal soul, perhaps we would find no man so imbruted and degraded that we could not trace the word liberty either written in living characters upon the soul or hidden away in some nook or corner of the heart. The law of liberty is the law of God, and is antecedent to all human legislation. It existed in the mind of Deity when He hung the first world upon its orbit and gave it liberty to gather light from the central sun.

Some people say, set the slaves free. Did you ever think, if the slaves were free, they would steal everything they could lay their hands on from now till the day of their death—that they would steal more than two thousand millions of dollars? Ask Maryland, with her tens of thousands of slaves, if she is not prepared for freedom, and hear her answer: "I help supply the coffee-gangs of the South." Ask Virginia, with her hundreds of thousands of slaves, if she is not weary with her merchandise of blood and anxious to shake the gory traffic from her hands, and hear her reply: "Though fertility has covered my soil, through a genial sky bends over my hills and vales, though I hold in my hand a wealth of water-power enough to turn the spindles to clothe the world, yet, with all these advantages, on of my chief staples has been the sons and daughters I send to the human market and human shambles." Ask the farther South, and all the cotton-growing States chime in, "We have need of fresh supplies to fill the ranks of those whose lives have gone out in unrequited toil on our distant plantations."

A hundred thousand new-born babes are annually added to the victims of slavery; twenty thousand lives are annually sacrificed on the plantations of the South. Such a sight should send a thrill of horror through the nerves of civilization and impel the heart of humanity to lofty deeds. So it might, if men had not found out a fearful alchemy by which this blood can be transformed into gold. Instead of listening to the cry of agony, they listen to the ring of dollars and stoop down to pick up the coin.

But a few months since a man escaped from bondage and found a temporary shelter almost beneath the shadow of Bunker Hill. Had that man stood upon the deck of an Austrian ship, beneath the shadow of the house of the Hapsburgs, he would have found protection. Had he been wrecked upon an island or colony of Great Britain, the waves of the tempest-lashed ocean would have washed him deliverance. Had he landed upon the territory of vine-encircled France and a Frenchman had reduced him to a thing and brought him here beneath the protection of our institutions and our laws, for such a nefarious deed that Frenchman would have lost his citizenship in France. Beneath the feebler light which glimmers from the Koran, the Bey of Tunis would have granted him freedom in his own dominions. Beside the ancient pyramids of Egypt he would have found liberty, for the soil laved by the glorious Nile is now consecrated to freedom. But from Boston harbour, made memorable by the infusion of three-penny taxed tea, Boston in its proximity to the plains of Lexington and Concord, Boston almost beneath the shadow of Bunker Hill and almost in sight of Plymouth Rock, he is thrust back from liberty and manhood and reconverted into a chattel. You have heard that, down South, they keep bloodhounds to hunt slaves. Ye bloodhounds, go back to your kennels; when you fail to catch the flying fugitive, when his stealthy tread is heard in the place where the bones of the revolutionary sires repose, the ready North is base enough to do your shameful service.

Slavery is mean, because it tramples on the feeble and weak. A man comes with his affidavits from the South and hurries me before a commissioner; upon that evidence ex parte and alone he hitches me to the car of slavery and trails my womanhood in the dust. I stand at the threshold of the Supreme Court and ask for justice, simple justice. Upon my tortured heart is thrown the mocking words, "You are a negro; you have no rights which white men are bound to respect"! Had it been my lot to have lived beneath the Crescent instead of the Cross, had injustice and violence been heaped upon my head as a Mohammedan woman, as a member of a common faith, I might have demanded justice and been listened to by the Pasha, the Bey or the Vizier; but when I come here to ask for justice, me tell me, "We have no higher law than the Constitution."

But I will not dwell on the dark side of the picture. God is on the side of freedom; and any cause that has God on its side, I care not how much it may be trampled upon, how much it may be trailed in the dust, is sure to triumph. The message of Jesus Christ is on the side of freedom, "I come to preach deliverance to the captives, the opening of the prison doors to them that are bound." The truest and noblest hearts in the land are on the side of freedom. They may be hissed at by slavery's minions, their names cast out as evil, their characters branded with fanaticism, but O, "to side with Truth is noble when we share her humble crust Ere the cause bring fame and profit and it's prosperous to be just."

May I not, in conclusion, ask every honest, noble heart, every seeker after truth and justice, if they will not also be on the side of freedom. Will you not resolve that you will abate neither heart nor hope till you hear the death-knell of human bondage sounded, and over the black ocean of slavery shall be heard a song, more exulting than the song of Miriam when it floated o'er Egypt's dark sea, the requiem of Egypt's ruined hosts and the anthem of the deliverance of Israel's captive people?

# We Are All Bound Up Together

I feel I am something of a novice upon this platform. Born of a race whose inheritance has been outrage and wrong, most of my life had been spent in battling against those wrongs. But I did not feel as keenly as others, that I had these rights, in common with other women, which are now demanded. About two years ago, I stood within the shadows of my home. A great sorrow had fallen upon my life. My husband had died suddenly, leaving me a widow, with four children, one my own, and the others stepchildren. I tried to keep my children together. But my husband died in debt; and before he had been in his grave three months, the administrator had swept the very milk-crocks and wash tubs from my hands. I was a farmer's wife and made butter for the Columbus market; but what could I do, when they had swept all away? They left me one thing—and that was a looking glass! Had I died instead of my husband, how different would have been the result! By this time he would have had another wife, it is likely; and no administrator would have gone into his house, broken up his home, and sold his bed, and taken away his means of support.

I took my children in my arms, and went out to seek my living. While I was gone, a neighbor to whom I had once lent five dollars, went before a magistrate and Swore that he believed I was a non-resident, and laid an attachment on my very bed. And I went back to Ohio with my orphan children in my arms, without a single feather bed in this wide world, that was not in the custody of the law. I say, then, that justice is not fulfilled so long as woman is unequal before the law.

We are all bound up together in one great bundle of humanity, and society cannot trample on the weakest and feeblest of its members without receiving the curse in its own soul. You tried that in the case of the Negro. You pressed him down for two centuries; and in so doing you crippled the moral strength and paralyzed the spiritual energies of the white men of the country. When the hands of the black were fettered, white men were deprived of the liberty of speech and the freedom of the press. Society cannot afford to neglect the enlightenment of any class of its members. At the South, the legislation of the country was in behalf of the rich slaveholders, while the poor white man was neglected. What is the consequence today? From that very class of neglected poor white men, comes the man who stands today, with his hand upon the

FRANCES ELLEN WATKINS HARPER

helm of the nation. He fails to catch the watchword of the hour, and throws himself, the incarnation of meanness, across the pathway of the nation. My objection to Andrew Johnson is not that he has been a poor white man; my objection is that he keeps "poor whits" all the way through. That is the trouble with him.

This grand and glorious revolution which has commenced, will fail to reach its climax of success, until throughout the length and brea(d)th of the American Republic, the nation shall be so color-blind, as to know no man by the color of his skin or the curl of his hair. It will then have no privileged class, trampling upon and outraging the unprivileged classes, but will be then one great privileged nation, whose privilege will be to produce the loftiest manhood and womanhood that humanity can attain.

I do not believe that giving the woman the ballot is immediately going to cure all the ills of life. I do not believe that white women are dew-drops just exhaled from the skies. I think that like men they may be divided into three classes, the good, the bad, and the indifferent. The good would vote according to their convictions and principles; the bad, as dictated by preju(d)ice or malice; and the indifferent will vote on the strongest side of the question, with the winning party.

You white women speak here of rights. I speak of wrongs. I, as a colored woman, have had in this country an education which has made me feel as if I were in the situation of Ishmael, my hand against every man, and every man's hand against me. Let me go tomorrow morning and take my seat in one of your street cars—I do not know that they will do it in New York, but they will in Philadelphia—and the conductor will put up his hand and stop the car rather than let me ride.

Going from Washington to Baltimore this Spring, they put me in the smoking car. Aye, in the capital of the nation, where the black man consecrated himself to the nation's defence, faithful when the white man was faithless, they put me in the smoking car! They did it once; but the next time they tried it, they failed; for I would not go in. I felt the fight in me; but I don't want to have to fight all the time. Today I am puzzled where to make my home. I would like to make it in Philadelphia, near my own friends and relations. But if I want to ride in the streets of Philadelphia, they send me to ride on the platform with the driver. Have women nothing to do with this? Not long since, a colored woman took her seat in an Eleventh Street car in Philadelphia, and the conductor stopped the car, and told the rest of the passengers to get out, and left the car with her in it alone, when they took it back to the station. One day I took my seat in a car, and the conductor came to me and told me to take another seat. I just screamed "murder." The man said if I was black I ought to behave myself. I knew that if he was white he was not behaving himself. Are there not wrongs to be righted?

In advocating the cause of the colored man, since the Dred Scott decision, I have sometimes said I thought the nation had touched bottom. But let me tell you there is a depth of infamy lower than that. It is when the nation, standing upon the threshold of a great peril, reached out its hands to a feebler race, and asked that race to help it, and when the peril was over, said, You are good enough for soldiers, but not good enough for citizens. . .

We have a woman in our country who has received the name of "Moses," not by lying about it, but by acting it out—a woman who has gone down into the Egypt of slavery and brought out hundreds of our people into liberty. The last time I saw that woman, her hands were swollen. That woman who had led one of Montgomery's most successful expeditions, who was brave enough and secretive enough to act as a scout for the American army, had her hands all swollen from a conflict with a brutal conductor, who undertook to eject her from her place. That woman, whose courage and bravery won a recognition from our army and from every black man in the land, is excluded from every thoroughfare of travel. Talk of giving women the ballot-box? Go on. It is a normal school, and the white women of this country need it. While there exists this brutal element in society which tramples upon the feeble and treads down the weak, I tell you that if there is any class of people who need to be lifted out of their airy nothings and selfishness, it is the white women of America.

# THE GREAT PROBLEM TO BE SOLVED

Ladies and Gentlemen: The great problem to be solved by the American people, if I understand it, is this: Whether or not there is strength enough in democracy, virtue enough in our civilization, and power enough in our religion to have mercy and deal justly with four millions of people but lately translated from the old oligarchy of slavery to the new commonwealth of freedom; and upon the right solution of this question depends in a large measure the future strength, progress and durability of our nation. The most important question before us colored people is not simply what the Democratic party may do against us or the Republican party do for us; but what are we going to do for ourselves? What shall we do toward developing our character, adding our quota to the civilization and strength of the country, diversifying our industry, and practicing those lordly virtues that conquer success and turn the world's dread laugh into admiring recognition? The white race has yet work to do in making practical the political axiom of equal rights and the Christian idea of human brotherhood; but while I lift mine eyes to the future I would not ungratefully ignore the past. One hundred years ago and Africa was the privileged hunting ground to Europe and America, and the flag of different nations hung a sign of death on the coasts of Congo and Guinea, and for years unbroken silence had hung around the horrors of the African slave trade. Since then Great Britain and other nations have wiped the bloody traffic from their hands and shaken the gory merchandise from their fingers, and the brand of piracy has been placed upon the African slave trade. Less than fifty years ago mob violence belched out its wrath against the men who dared to arraign the slave holder before the bar of conscience and Christendom. Instead of golden showers upon his head, he who garrisoned the front had a halter around his neck. Since, if I may borrow the idea, the nation has caught the old inspiration from his lips and written it in the new organic world. Less than twenty five years ago slavery clasped hands with King Cotton, and said slavery fights and cotton conquers for American slavery. Since then slavery is dead, the colored man has exchanged the fetters on his wrist for the ballot in his hand. Freedom is king, and Cotton a subject.

It may not seem to be a gracious thing to mingle complaint in a season of general rejoicing. It may appear like the ancient Egyptians seating a corpse at their festal board to avenge the Americans for their shortcomings when so much has been accomplished. And yet, with all the victories and triumphs which freedom and justice have won in this country, I do not believe there is another civilized nation under heaven where there are half as many people who have been brutally and shamefully murdered, with or without impunity, as in this Republic within the last ten years. And who cares? Where is the public opinion that has scorched with red hot indignation the cowardly murderers of Vicksburg and Louisiana? Sheridan lifts up the veil from Southern society, and behind it is the smell of blood and our bones scattered at the grave's mouth; murdered people; a White League with its "covenant of death and agreement with hell." And who cares? What city pauses one hour to drop a pitying tear over these mangled corpses, or has forged against the perpetrator one thunderbolt of furious protest? But let there be a supposed or real invasion of Southern rights by our soldiers, and our great commercial emporium will rally its forces from the old man in his classic shades, to clasp hands with "dead rabbits" and "plug uglies" in protesting against military interference. What we need today in the onward march of humanity is a public sentiment in favor of common justice and simple mercy. We have a civilization which has produced grand and magnificent results, diffused knowledge, overthrown slavery, made constant conquests over nature, and built up a wonderful material property. But two things are wanting in American civilization a keener and deeper, broader and tenderer sense of justice; a sense of humanity, which shall crystallize into the life of the nation the sentiment that justice, simple justice, is the right, not simply of the strong and powerful, but of the weakest and feeblest of all God's children; a deeper and broader humanity, which will teach men to look upon their feeble brethren not as vermin to be crushed out, or beasts of burden to be bridled and bitten, but as the children of the living God; of that God whose may earnestly hope is in perfect wisdom and in perfect love working for the best good of all. Ethnologists may differ about the origin of the human race. Huxley may search for it in protoplasm, and Darwin send for the missing links, but there is one thing of which we may rest assured that we all come from the living God and that He is the common Father. The nation that has no reverence for man is also lacking in reverence for God and need to be instructed.

As fellow citizens, leaving out all humanitarian views as a mere matter of political economy it is better to have the colored race a living force animated and strengthened by self reliance and self respect, than a stagnant mass, degraded and self condemned. Instead of the North relaxing its efforts to defuse education in the South, it behooves us for our national life to throw into the South all the healthful reconstructing influences we can command.

Our work in this country is grandly constructive. Some races have come into this world and overthrown and destroyed. But if it is glory to destroy, it is happiness to save; and oh, what a noble work there is before our nation! Where is there a young man who would consent to lead an aimless life when there are such glorious opportunities before him? Before our young men is another battle not a battle of flashing swords and clashing steel, but a moral warfare, a battle against ignorance, poverty and low social condition. In physical warfare the keenest swords may be blunted and the loudest batteries hushed; but in the great conflict of moral and spiritual progress your weapons shall be brighter for their service and better for their use. In fighting truly and nobly for others you win the victory for yourselves.

Give power and significance to your life, and in the great work of upbuilding there is room for woman's work and woman's heart. Oh, that our hearts were alive and our vision quickened, to see the grandeur of the work that lies before. We have some culture among us, but I think our culture lacks enthusiasm. We need a deep earnestness and a lofty unselfishness to round out our lives. It is the inner life that develops the outer, and if we are in earnest the precious things lie all around our feet, and we need not waste our strength in striving after the dim and unattainable. Women, in your golden youth; mother, binding around your heart all the precious ties of life, let no magnificence of culture, or amplitude of fortune, or refinement of sensibilities, repel you from helping the weaker and less favored. If you have ampler gifts, hold them as larger opportunities with which you can benefit others. Oh, it is better to feel that the weaker and feebler our race the closer we will cling to them, than it is to isolate ourselves from them in selfish, or careless unconcern, saying there is a lion without. Inviting you to this work I do not promise you fair sailing and unclouded skies. You may meet with coolness where you expect sympathy; disappointment where you feel sure of success; isolation and loneliness instead of heart support and cooperation. But if your lives are based and built upon these divine certitudes, which are the only enduring strength of humanity, then whatever defeat and discomfiture may overshadow your plans or frustrate your schemes, for a life that is in harmony with God and sympathy for man there is no such word as fail. And in conclusion, permit me to say, let no misfortunes crush you, no hostility of enemies or failure of friends discourage you. Apparent failure may hold in its rough shell the germs of a success that will blossom in time, and bear fruit throughout eternity. What seemed to be a failure around the Cross of Calvary and in the garden has been the grandest recorded success.

# Enlightened Motherhood: An Address

Before the Brooklyn Literary Society,
November 15th, 1892

It is nearly thirty years since an emancipated people stood on the threshold of a new era, facing an uncertain future—a legally un married race, to be taught the sacredness of the marriage relation; an ignorant people, to be taught to read the hook of the Christian law and to learn to comprehend more fully the claims of the gospel of the Christ of Calvary. A homeless race, to be gathered into homes of peaceful security and to he instructed how to plant around their firesides the strongest batteries against the sins that degrade and the race vices that demoralize. A race unversed in the science of government and unskilled in the just administration of law, to be translated from the old oligarchy of slavery into the new common wealth of freedom, and to whose men came the right to exchange the fetters on their wrists for the ballots in their right hands—a ballot which, if not vitiated by fraud or restrained by intimidation, counts just as much as that of the most talented and influential man in the land.

While politicians may stumble on the barren mountain of fretful controversy, and men, lacking faith in God and the invisible forces which make for righteousness, may shrink from the unsolved problems of the hour, into the hands of Christian women comes the opportunity of serving the ever blessed Christ, by ministering to His little ones and striving to make their homes the brightest spots on earth and the fairest types of heaven. The school may instruct and the church may teach, but the home is an institution older than the church and antedates school, and that is the place where children should be trained for useful citizenship on earth and a hope of holy companionship in heaven.

Every mother should endeavor to be a true artist. I do not mean by this that every woman should be a painter, sculptor, musician, poet, or writer, but the artist who will write on the tablet of childish innocence thoughts she will not blush to see read in the light of eternity and printed amid the archives of heaven, that the young may learn to wear them as amulets around their hearts and throw them as bulwarks around their lives, and that in the hour of temptation and trial the voices from home may linger around their paths as angels of guidance, around their steps, and be incentives to deeds of high and holy worth.

The home may be a humble spot, where there are no velvet carpets to hush your tread, no magnificence to surround your way, nor costly creations of painter's art or sculptor's skill to please your conceptions or gratify your tastes; but what are the costliest gifts of fortune when placed in the balance with the confiding love of dear children or the true devotion of a noble and manly husband whose heart can safely trust in his wife? You may place upon the brow of a true wife and mother the greenest laurels; you may crowd her hands with civic honors; but, after all, to her there will be no place like home, and the crown of her mother hood will be more precious than the diadem of a queen.

As marriage is the mother of homes, it is important that the duties and responsibilities of this relation should be understood before it is entered on. A mistake made here may run through every avenue of the future, cast its shadow over all our coming years, and enter the lives of those whom we should shield with our love and defend with our care. We may be versed in ancient lore and modern learning, may be able to trace the path of worlds that roll in light and power on high, and to tell when comets shall cast their trail over our evening skies. We may understand the laws of stratification well enough to judge where lies the vein of silver and where nature has hidden her virgin gold. We may be able to tell the story of departed nations and conquering chieftains who have added pages of tears and blood to the world's history; but our education is deficient if we are perfectly ignorant how to guide the little feet that are springing up so gladly in our path, and to see in undeveloped possibilities gold more fine than the pavements of heaven and gems more precious than the foundations of the holy city. Marriage should not be a blind rushing together of tastes and fancies, a mere union of fortunes or an affair of convenience. It should be a "tie that only love and truth should weave and nothing but death should part."

Marriage between two youthful and loving hearts means the laying the foundation stones of a new home, and the woman who helps erect that home should be careful not to build it above the reeling brain of a drunkard or the weakened fibre of a debauchee.

If it be folly for a merchant to send an argosy, laden with the richest treasures, at midnight on a moonless sea, without a rudder, compass, or guide, is it not madness for' a woman to trust her future happiness, and the welfare of the dear children who may yet nestle in her arms and make music and sunshine around her fireside, in the unsteady hands of a characterless man, too lacking in self-respect and self-control to hold

FRANCES ELLEN WATKINS HARPER

the helm and rudder of his own life; who drifts where he ought to steer, and only lasts when he ought to live?

The moment the crown of motherhood falls on the brow of a young wife, God gives her a new interest in the welfare of the home and the good of society. If hitherto she had been content to trip through life a lighthearted girl, or to tread amid the halls of wealth and fashion the gayest of the gay, life holds for her now a high and noble service. She must be more than the child of pleasure or the devotee of fashion. Her work is grandly constructive. A helpless and ignorant babe lies smiling in her arms. God has trusted her with a child, and it is her privilege to help that child develop the most precious thing a man or woman can possess on earth, and that is a good character. Moth may devour our finest garments, fire may consume and floods destroy our fairest homes, rust may gather on our silver and tarnish our gold, but there is an asbestos that no fire can destroy, a treasure which shall be richer for its service and better for its use, and that is a good character.

But the question arises, What constitutes an enlightened motherhood I do not pretend that I will give you an exhaustive analysis of all that a mother should learn and of all she should teach. In the Christian scriptures the story is told of a mother of whom it was said: "From henceforth all nations shall call her blessed." While, in these days of religious unrest, criticism, and investigation, numbers are ready to relegate this story to the limbo of myth and fiction; whether that story be regarded as fact or fiction, there are lessons in it which we could not take into our lives without its making life higher, better, and more grandly significant. It is the teaching of a divine overshadowing and a touching self-surrender which still floats down the ages, fragrant with the aroma of a sweet submission. "The handmaid of the Lord, be it done unto me according to Thy word."

We read that Christ left us an example that we should tread in His footsteps; but does not the majority of the Christian world hold it as a sacred creed that the first print of His feet in the flesh began in the days of His antenatal life; and is not the same spirit in the world now which was there when our Lord made His advent among us, bone of our bone and flesh of our flesh; and do we not need the incarnation of God's love and light in our hearts as much now as it was ever needed in any preceding generation? Do we not need to hold it as a sacred thing, amid sorrow, pain, and wrong, that only through the love of God are human hearts made strong? And has not every prospective mother the right to ask for the overshadowing of the same spirit, that her child may be one of whom it may be truly said, "Of such is the kingdom of heaven," and all his life he shall be lent to the Lord Had all the mothers of this present generation dwelt beneath the shadow of the Almighty, would it have been possible for slavery to have cursed us with its crimes, or intemperance degraded us with its vices? Would the social evil still have power to send to our streets women whose laughter is sadder than their tears, and over whose wasted lives death draws the curtains of the grave and silently hides their sin and shame? Are there not women, respectable women, who feel that it would wring their hearts with untold anguish, and bring their gray hairs in sorrow to the grave, if their daughters should trail the robes of their womanhood in the dust, yet who would say of their sons, if they were trampling their manhood down and fettering their souls with cords of vice, "O, well, boys will be boys, and young men will sow their wild oats."

I hold that no woman loves social purity as it deserves to be loved and valued, if she cares for the purity of her daughters and not her sons who would gather her dainty robes from contact with the fallen woman and yet greet with smiling lips and clasp with warm and welcoming hands the author of her wrong and ruin. How many mothers today shrink from a double standard for society which can ostracise the woman and condone the offense of the man? How many mothers say within their hearts, I intend to teach my boy to be as pure in his life, as chaste in his conversation, as the young girl who sits at my side encircled in the warm clasp of loving arms? How many mothers strive to have their boys shun the gilded saloon as they would the den of a deadly serpent Not the mother who thoughtlessly sends her child to the saloon for a beverage to make merry with her friends. How many mothers teach their boys to shrink in horror from the fascinations of women, not as God made them, but as sin has degraded them?

Tonight, if you and I could walk through the wards of various hospitals at home and abroad, perhaps we would find hundreds, it may be thousands, of young men awaiting death as physical wrecks, having burned the candle of their lives at both ends. Were we to bend over their dying couches with pitying glances, and question them of their lives, perhaps numbers of them could tell you sad stories of careless words from thoughtless lips, that tainted their imaginations and sent their virus through their lives; of young eyes, above which God has made the heavens so eloquent with His praise, and the earth around so poetic with His ideas, turning from the splendor of the magnificent sunsets or glorious early dawns, and finding allurement in the dreadful fascinations of sin, or learning to gloat over impure pictures and vile literature. Then, later on, perhaps many of them could say, "The first time I went to a house where there were revelry and song, and the dead were there and I knew it not, I went with men who were older than myself; men, who should have showed me how to avoid the pitfalls which lie in the path of the young, the tempted, and inexperienced, taught me to gather the flowers of sin that blossom around the borders of hell."

Suppose we dared to question a little further, not from idle curiosity, but for the sake of getting, from the dying, object lessons for the living, and say, "God gave you, an ignorant child, into the hands of a mother. Did she never warn you of your dangers and teach you how to avoid them?" How many could truthfully say, "My mother was wise enough to teach me and faithful enough to warn me." If the cholera or yellow-fever were raging in any part of this city, and to enter that section meant peril to health and life, what mother would permit her child to walk carelessly through a district where pestilence was breathing its bane upon the morning air and distilling its poison upon the midnight dews? And yet, when boys go from the fireside into the arena of life, how many ever go there forewarned and forearmed against the soft seductions of vice, against moral conditions which are worse than "fever, plague and palsy, and madness *all* combined?"

Among the things I would present for the enlightenment of mothers are attention to the laws of heredity and environment. Mrs. Winslow, in a paper on social purity, speaks of a package of letters she had received from a young man of talent, good education, and a strong desire to live a pure and useful life. In boyhood he ignorantly ruined his health, and, when he resolved to rise above his depressed condition, his own folly, his heredity and environment, weighed him down like an incubus. His appeals, she says, are most touching. He says: "If you cannot help me, what can I do? My mother cursed me with illegitimacy and hereditary insanity. I have left only the alternative of suicide or madness." A fearful legacy! For stolen money and slandered character we may make reparation, but the opportunity of putting the right stamp on an antenatal life, if once gone, is gone forever; and there never was an angel of God, however bright, terrible, or strong he may be who was ever strong enough to roll away the stone from the grave of a dead opportunity.

In the annals of this State may be found a record of six generations of debased manhood and womanhood, and prominent among them stands the name of Margaret, the mother of criminals. She is reported as having five sisters, the greater number of whom trailed the robes of their womanhood in the dust, and became fallen women. Some time since, their posterity was traced out, and five hundred and forty persons are represented as sharing the blood of these unfortunate women; and it is remarkable, as well as very sad, to see the lines of debasement and weakness, vice and crime, which are displayed in their record. In the generation of Margaret, fifty percent, of the women were placed among the fallen, and in all the generations succeeding, including only those of twelve years of age and over, to the extent of fifty percent; and of this trail of weakness there were three families in the sixth generation who had six children sent to the house of refuge. Out of seven hundred and nine members of this family, nearly one-ninth have been criminals, and nearly one-tenth paupers; twenty-two had acquired property, and eight had lost property nearly one-seventh were illegitimate, and one sister was the mother of distinctively pauperized lines.

Or, take another line of thought. Would it not be well for us women to introduce into all of our literary circles, for the purpose of gaining knowledge, topics on this subject of heredity and the influence of good and bad conditions upon the home life of the race, and study this subject in the light of science for our own and the benefit of others? For instance, may we not seriously ask the question, Can a mother or father be an habitual tippler, or break God's law of social purity, and yet impart to their children, at the same time, abundant physical vitality and strong moral fibre? Can a father dash away the reins of moral restraint, and, at the same time, impart strong will-power to his offspring?

A generation since, there lived in a Western city a wealthy English gentleman who was what is called a high liver. He drank his toddy in the morning, washed down his lunch with champagne, and finished a bottle of port for dinner, though he complained that the heavy wines here did not agree with him, owing to the climate. He died of gout at fifty years, leaving four sons. One of them became an epileptic, two died from drinking. Called good fellows, generous, witty, honorable young men, but before middle age miserable sots. The oldest of the brothers was a man of fixed habits, occupying a leading place in the community, from his keen intelligence, integrity, and irreproachable morals. He watched over his brothers, laid them in their graves, and never ceased to denounce

FRANCES ELLEN WATKINS HARPER

the vice which had ruined them; and when he was long past middle age, financial trouble threw him into a low, nervous condition, for which wine was prescribed. He drank but one bottle. Shortly after, his affairs were righted and his health and spirits returned, but it was observed that once or twice a year he mysteriously disappeared for a month or six weeks. Nor wife, nor children, nor even his partner, knew where he went; but at last, when he was old and gray headed, his wife was telegraphed from an obscure neighboring village, where she found him dying of *mania a potu*. He had been in the habit of hiding there when the desire for liquor became maddening, and when there he drank like a brute.

May Wright Sewall, president of the Woman's National Council, writing of disinherited children, tells of a country school where health and joyousnesss and purity were the rule, vulgarity and coarseness the exception, and morbid and mysterious manners quite unknown. There came one morning, in her childhood, two little girls, sisters, of ten and twelve years. They were comfortably dressed. At the noon day meal their baskets opened to an abundant and appetizing lunch. But they were not like other children. They had thin, pinched faces, with vulgar mouths, and a sidelong look from their always downcast eyes which made her shudder; and skin, so wrinkled and yellow, that her childish fears fancied them to be witches' children. They held themselves aloof from all the rest. For two or three years they sat in the same places in that quiet school doing very little work, but, not being disorderly, they were allowed to stay. One day, when my father had visited the school, as we walked home together, I questioned him as to what made Annie and Minnie so different from all the other little girls at the school, and the grave man answered: Before they were born their father sold their birthright, and they must feed on pottage all their lives. She felt that an undefined mystery hovered around their blighted lives. She knew, she says, that they were blighted, as the simplest child knows the withered leaf of November from the glowing green of May, and she questioned no more, half conscious that the mystery was sin and that knowledge of it would be sinful too.

But we turn from these sad pictures to brighter pages in the great books of human life. To Benjamin West saying: "My mother's kiss made me a painter." To John Randolph saying, "I should have been an atheist, if it had not been for one recollection, and that was the memory of the time when my departed mother used to take my little hands in hers and sank me on my knees to say: 'Our Father, who art in heaven.' Amid the cold of an Arctic expedition, Adam Isles found sickness had settled on part of his comrades, and the request came to him, "I think from one of the officers of the ship, saying: Isles, for God's sake, take some spirits, or we will be lost." Then the memory of the dear mother came back, and looking the entreaty in the face, he said, "I promised my mother I would not do it, and I wouldn't do it if I die in the ice."

I would ask, in conclusion, is there a branch of the human race in the Western Hemisphere which has greater need of the inspiring and uplifting influences that can flow out of the lives and examples of the truly enlightened than ourselves? Mothers who can teach their sons not to love pleasure or fear death; mothers who can teach their children to embrace every opportunity, employ every power, and use every means to build up a future to contrast with the old sad past. Men may boast of the aristocracy of blood; they may glory in the aristocracy of talent, and be proud of the aristocracy of wealth, but there is an aristocracy which must ever outrank them all, and that is the aristocracy of character.

The work of the mothers of our race is grandly constructive. It is for us to build above the wreck and ruin of the past more stately temples of thought and action. Some races have been overthrown, dashed in pieces, and destroyed but today the world is needing, fainting, for something better than the results of arrogance, aggressiveness, and indomitable power. We need mothers who are capable of being character builders, patient, loving, strong, and true, whose homes will be an uplifting power in the race. This is one of the greatest needs of the hour. No race can afford to neglect the enlightenment of its mothers. If you would have a clergy without virtue or morality, a manhood without honor, and a womanhood frivolous, mocking, and ignorant, neglect the education of your daughters. But if, on the other hand, you would have strong men, virtuous women, and good homes, then enlighten your women, so that they may be able to bless their homes by the purity of their lives, the tenderness of their hearts, and the strength of their intellects. From schools and colleges your children may come well versed in ancient lore and modern learning, but it is for us to learn and teach, within the shadow of our own homes, the highest and best of all sciences, the science of a true life. When the last lay of the minstrel shall die upon his ashy lips, and the sweetest numbers of the poet cease to charm his death-dulled ear; when the eye of the astronomer shall be too dim to mark the path of worlds that roll in light and power on high; and when all our earthly knowledge has performed for us its mission, and we are ready to lay aside our environments as garments we have outworn and outgrown if we have learned the science of a true life, we may rest assured that this acquirement will go with us through the valley and shadow of death, only to grow lighter and brighter through the eternities.

# Woman's Political Future

If before sin had cast its deepest shadows or sorrow had distilled its bitterest tears, it was true that it was not good for man to be alone, it is no less true, since the shadows have deepened and life's sorrows have increased, that the world has need of all the spiritual aid that woman can give for the social advancement and moral development of the human race. The tendency of the present age, with its restlessness, religious upheavals, failures, blunders, and crimes, is toward broader freedom, an increase of knowledge, the emancipation of thought, and a recognition of the brotherhood of man; in this movement woman, as the companion of man, must be a sharer. So close is the bond between man and woman that you cannot raise one without lifting the other. The world cannot move without woman's sharing in the movement, and to help give a right impetus to that movement is woman's highest privilege.

If the fifteenth century discovered America to the Old World, the nineteenth is discovering woman to herself. Little did Columbus imagine, when the New World broke upon his vision like a lovely gem in the coronet of the universe, the glorious possibilities of a land where the sun should be our engraver, the winged lightning our messenger, and steam our beast of burden. But as mind is more than matter, and the highest ideal always the true real, so to woman comes the opportunity to strive for richer and grander discoveries than ever gladdened the eye of the Genoese mariner.

Not the opportunity of discovering new worlds, but that of filling this old world with fairer and higher aims than the greed of gold and the lust of power, is hers. Through weary, wasting years men have destroyed, dashed in pieces, and overthrown, but today we stand on the threshold of woman's era, and woman's work is grandly constructive. In her hand are possibilities whose use or abuse must tell upon the political life of the nation, and send their influence for good or evil across the track of unborn ages.

As the saffron tints and crimson flushes of morn herald the coming day, so the social and political advancement which woman has already gained bears the promise of the rising of the full-orbed sun of emancipation. The result will be not to make home less happy, but society more holy; yet I do not think the mere extension of the ballot a panacea for all the ills of our national life. What we need today is not simply more voters, but better voters. Today there are red-handed men in our republic, who walk unwhipped of justice, who richly deserve to exchange the ballot of the freeman for the wristlets of the felon; brutal and cowardly men, who torture, burn, and lynch their fellow-men, men whose defenselessness should be their best defense and their weakness an ensign of protection. More than the changing of institutions we need the development of a national conscience, and the upbuilding of national character. Men may boast of the aristocracy of blood, may glory in the aristocracy of talent, and be proud of the aristocracy of wealth, but there is one aristocracy which must ever outrank them all, and that is the aristocracy of character; and it is the women of a country who help to mold its character, and to influence if not determine its destiny; and in the political future of our nation woman will not have done what she could if she does not endeavor to have our republic stand foremost among the nations of the earth, wearing sobriety as a crown and righteousness as a garment and a girdle. In coming into her political estate woman will find a mass of illiteracy to be dispelled. If knowledge is power, ignorance is also power. The power that educates wickedness may manipulate and dash against the pillars of any state when they are undermined and honeycombed by injustice.

I envy neither the heart nor the head of any legislator who has been born to an inheritance of privileges, who has behind him ages of education, dominion, civilization, and Christianity, if he stands opposed to the passage of a national education bill, whose purpose is to secure education to the children of those who were born under the shadow of institutions which made it a crime to read.

Today women hold in their hands influence and opportunity, and with these they have already opened doors which have been closed to others. By opening doors of labor woman has become a rival claimant for at least some of the wealth monopolized by her stronger brother. In the home she is the priestess, in society the queen, in literature she is a power, in legislative halls law-makers have responded to her appeals, and for her sake have humanized and liberalized their laws. The press has felt the impress of her hand. In the pews of the church she constitutes the majority; the pulpit has welcomed her, and in the school, she has the blessed privilege of teaching children and youth. To her is apparently coming the added responsibility of political power; and what she now possesses should only be the means of preparing her to use the coming power for the glory of God and the good of mankind; for power without righteousness is one of the most dangerous forces in the world.

Political life in our country has plowed in muddy channels, and needs the infusion of clearer and cleaner waters. I am not sure that women are naturally so much better than men that they will clear the stream by the virtue of their womanhood; it is not through sex but through character that the best influence of women upon the life of the nation must be exerted.

I do not believe in unrestricted and universal suffrage for either men or women. I believe in moral and educational tests. I do not believe that the most ignorant and brutal man is better prepared to add value to the strength and durability of the government than the most cultured, upright, and intelligent woman. I do not think that willful ignorance should swamp earnest intelligence at the ballot-box, nor that educated wickedness, violence, and fraud should cancel the votes of honest men. The unsteady hands of a drunkard cannot cast the ballot of a freeman. The hands of lynchers are too red with blood to determine the political character of the government for even four short years. The ballot in the hands of woman means power added to influence. How well she will use that power I cannot foretell. Great evils stare us in the face that need to be throttled by the combined power of an upright manhood and an enlightened womanhood; and I know that no nation can gain its full measure of enlightenment and happiness if one-half of it is free and the other half is fettered. China compressed the feet of her women and thereby retarded the steps of her men. The elements of a nation's weakness must ever be found at the hearthstone.

More than the increase of wealth, the power of armies, and the strength of fleets is the need of good homes, of good fathers, and good mothers.

The life of a Roman citizen was in danger in ancient Palestine, and men had bound themselves with a vow that they would eat nothing until they had killed the Apostle Paul. Pagan Rome threw around that imperiled life a bulwark of living clay consisting of four hundred and seventy human hearts, and Paul was saved. Surely the life of the humblest American citizen should be as well protected in America as that of a Roman citizen was in heathen Rome. A wrong done to the weak should be an insult to the strong. Woman coming into her kingdom will find enthroned three great evils, for whose overthrow she should be as strong in a love of justice and humanity as the warrior is

FRANCES ELLEN WATKINS HARPER

in his might. She will find intemperance sending its flood of shame, and death, and sorrow to the homes of men, a fretting leprosy in our politics, and a blighting curse in our social life; the social evil sending to our streets women whose laughter is sadder than their tears, who slide from the paths of sin and shame to the friendly shelter of the grave; and lawlessness enacting in our republic deeds over which angels might weep, if heaven knows sympathy.

How can any woman send petitions to Russia against the horrors of Siberian prisons if, ages after the Inquisition has ceased to devise its tortures, she has not done all she could by influence, tongue, and pen to keep men from making bonfires of the bodies of real or supposed criminals?

O women of America! into your hands God has pressed one of the sublimest opportunities that ever came into the hands of the women of any race or people. It is yours to create a healthy public sentiment; to demand justice, simple justice, as the right of every race; to brand with everlasting infamy the lawless and brutal cowardice that lynches, burns, and tortures your own countrymen.

To grapple with the evils which threaten to undermine the strength of the nation and to lay magazines of powder under the cribs of future generations is no child's play.

Let the hearts of the women of the world respond to the song of the herald angels of peace on earth and good will to men. Let them throb as one heart unified by the grand and holy purpose of uplifting the human race, and humanity will breathe freer, and the world grow brighter. With such a purpose Eden would spring up in our path, and Paradise be around our way.

NOVELS

MINNIE'S SACRIFICE

# I

Miriam sat in her lowly cabin, painfully rocking her body to and fro; for a great sorrow had fallen upon her life. She had been the mother of three children, two had died in their infancy, and now her last, her loved and only child was gone, but not like the rest, who had passed away almost as soon as their little feet had touched the threshold of existence. She had been entangled in the mazes of sin and sorrow; and her sun had gone down in darkness. It was the old story. Agnes, fair, young and beautiful, had been a slave, with no power to protect herself from the highest insults that brutality could offer to innocence. Bound hand and foot by that system, which has since gone down in wrath, and blood, and tears, she had fallen a victim to the wiles and power of her master; and the result was the introduction of a child of shame into a world of sin and suffering; for herself an early grave; and for her mother a desolate and breaking heart.

While Miriam was sitting down hopelessly beneath the shadow of her mighty grief, gazing ever and anon on the pale dead face, which seemed to bear in its sad but gentle expression, an appeal from earth to heaven, some of the slaves would hurry in, and looking upon the fair young face, would drop a word of pity for the weeping mother, and then hurry on to their appointed tasks. All day long Miriam sat alone with her dead, except when these kindly interruptions broke upon the monotony of her sorrow.

In the afternoon, Camilla, the only daughter of her master, entered her cabin, and throwing her arms around her neck exclaimed, "Oh! Mammy, I am so sorry I didn't know Agnes was dead. I've been on a visit to Mr. Le Grange's plantation, and I've just got back this afternoon, and as soon as I heard that Agnes was dead I hurried to see you. I would not even wait for my dinner. Oh! how sweet she looks," said Camilla, bending over the corpse, "just as natural as life. When did she die?"

"This morning, my poor, dear darling!" And another burst of anguish relieved the overcharged heart.

"Oh! Mammy, don't cry, I am so sorry; but what is this?" said she, as the little bundle of flannel began to stir.

"That is poor Agnes' baby."

"Agnes' baby? Why, I didn't know that Agnes had a baby. Do let me see it?"

Tenderly the grandmother unfolded the wrappings, and presented the little stranger. He was a beautiful babe, whose golden hair, bright blue eyes and fair complexion showed no trace of the outcast blood in his veins.

"Oh, how beautiful!" said Camilla; "surely this can't be Agnes' baby. He is just as white as I am, and his eyes—what a beautiful blue—and his hair, why it is really lovely."

"He is very pretty, Miss, but after all he is only a slave."

A slave. She had heard that word before; but somehow, when applied to that fair child, it grated harshly on her ear; and she said, "Well, I think it is a shame for him to be a slave, when he is just as white as anybody. Now, Mammy," said she, throwing off her hat, and looking soberly into the fire, "if I had my way, he should never be a slave."

"And why can't you have your way? I'm sure master humors you in everything."

"I know that; Pa does everything I wish him to do; but I don't know how I could manage about this. If his mother were living, I would beg Pa to set them both free, and send them North; but his mother is gone; and, Mammy, we couldn't spare you. And besides, it is so cold in the North, you would freeze to death, and yet, I can't bear the thought of his being a slave. I wonder," said she, musing to herself, "I wonder if I couldn't save him from being a slave. Now I have it," she said, rising hastily, her face aglow with pleasurable excitement. "I was reading yesterday a beautiful story in the Bible about a wicked king, who wanted to kill all the little boys of a people who were enslaved in his land, and how his mother hid her child by the side of a river, and that the king's daughter found him and saved his life. It was a fine story; and I read it till I cried. Now I mean to do something like that good princess. I am going to ask Pa, to let me take him to the house, and have a nurse for him, and bring him up like a white child, and never let him know that he is colored."

Miriam shook her head doubtfully; and Camilla, looking disappointed, said, "Don't you like my plan?"

"Laws, honey, it would be fustrate, but your Pa wouldn't hear to it."

"Yes, he would, Mammy, because I'll tell him I've set my heart upon it, and won't be satisfied if he don't consent. I know if I set my heart upon it, he won't refuse me, because he always said he hates to see me fret. Why, Mammy, he bought me two thousand dollars worth of jewelry when we were in New York, just because I took a fancy to a diamond set which I saw at Tiffany's. Anyhow, I am going to ask him."

Eager and anxious to carry out her plan, Camilla left the cabin to find her father. He was seated in his library, reading Homer. He looked up, as her light step fell upon the threshold, and said playfully, "What is your wish, my princess? Tell me, if it is the half of my kingdom."

Encouraged by his manner, she drew near, perched upon his knee, and said; "Now, you must keep your word, Pa. I have a request to make, but you must first promise me that you will grant it."

"But I don't know what it is. I can't tell. You might want me to put my head in the fire."

"Oh no, Pa, you know I don't!"

"Well, you might wish me to run for Congress."

"Oh no, Pa, I know that you hate politics."

"Well, darling, what is your request?"

"No; tell me first that you will grant it. Now, don't tease me, Pa; say yes, and I will tell you."

"Well, yes; if it is anything in reason."

"Well, it is in reason, let me tell you, Pa. Today, after I came home, I asked Annette where was Agnes, and she told me she was dead. Oh I was so sorry; and so before I got my dinner I hastened to Mammy's cabin, and found poor Mammy almost heart-broken, and Agnes lying dead, but looking just as natural as life."

"She was dead, but had left one of the dearest little babies I ever saw. Why, Pa, he is just as white as we are; and I told Mammy so, but she said it didn't matter; 'he is a poor slave, just like the rest of us.' Now, Pa, I don't want Agnes' baby to be a slave. Can't you keep him from growing up a slave?"

"How am I to do that, my little Abolitionist?"

"No, Pa, I am not an Abolitionist. I heard some of them talk when I was in New York, and I think they are horrid creatures; but, Pa, this child is so white, nobody would ever know that he had one drop of Negro blood in his veins. Couldn't we take him out of that cabin, and make all the servants promise that they would never breathe a word about his being colored, and let me bring him up as a white child?"

"Well," said Mr. Le Croix, bursting into a hearty laugh, "that is a capital joke; my little dewdrop talk of bringing up a child! Why, darling, you would tire of him in a week."

"Oh no, Pa, I wouldn't! Just try me; if it is only for a week."

"Why, Sunbeam, it is impossible. Who ever heard of such a thing as a Negro being palmed upon society as a white person?"

"Negro! Pa, he is just as white as you are, and his eyes are as blue as mine."

"Still he belongs to the Negro race; and one drop of that blood in his veins curses all the rest. I would grant you anything in reason, but this is not to be thought of. Were I to do so I would immediately lose caste among all the planters in the neighborhood; I would be set down as an Abolitionist, and singled out for insult and injury. Ask me anything, Camilla, but that."

"Oh, Pa, what do you care about social position? You never hunt, nor entertain company, nor take any part in politics. You shut yourself up in your library, year after year, and pore over your musty books, and hardly any one knows whether you are dead or alive. And I am sure that we could hide the secret of his birth, and pass him off as the orphan child of one of our friends, and that will be the truth; for Agnes was our friend; at least I know she was mine."

"Well, I'll see about it; now, get down, and let me finish reading this chapter."

The next day Camilla went again to the cabin of Miriam; but the overseer had set her to a task in the field, and Agnes' baby was left to the care of an aged woman who was too old to work in the fields, but not being entirely past service, she was appointed as one of the nurses for the babies and young children, while their mothers were working in the fields.

Camilla, feeling an unusual interest in the child, went to the overseer, and demanded that Miriam should be released from her tasks, and permitted to attend the child.

In vain the overseer plead the pressure for hands, and the busy season. Camilla said it did not matter, she wanted Miriam, and she would have her; and he, feeling that it was to his interest to please the little lady, had Miriam sent from the field to Camilla.

"Mammy, I want you to come to the house. I want you to come and be my Mammy. Agnes is dead; your husband is gone, and I want you to come and bring the baby to the house, and I am going to get him some beautiful dresses, and some lovely coral I saw in New Orleans, and I am going to dress him so handsomely, that I believe Pa will feel just as I do, and think it a shame that such a beautiful child should be a slave."

Camilla went home, and told her father what she had done. And he, willing to compromise with her, readily consented; and in a day or two the child and his grandmother were comfortably ensconced in their new quarters.

The winter passed; the weeks ripened into months, and the months into years, and the child under the pleasant dispensations of love and kindness grew to be a fine, healthy, and handsome boy.

One day, when Mr. Le Croix was in one of his most genial moods, Camilla again introduced the subject which she had concealed, but not abandoned.

"Now, father, I do think it is a shame for this child to be a slave, when he is just as white as anybody; I am sure we could move away from here to France, and you could adopt him as your son, and no one would know anything of his birth and parentage. He is so beautiful, I would like him for my brother; and he looks like us anyhow."

Le Croix flushed deep at these words, and he looked keenly into his daughter's face; but her gaze was so open, her expression so frank and artless, he could not think that her words had any covert meaning in reference to the paternity of the child; but to save that child from being a slave, and to hide his origin was with her a pet scheme; and, to use her own words, "she had set her heart upon it."

# II

M r. Bernard Le Croix was the only son of a Spanish lady, and a French gentleman, who were married in Hayti a few months before the revolution, which gave freedom to the Island, and made Hayti an independent nation.

His father, foreseeing the storm which was overshadowing the land, contrived to escape, bringing with him a large amount of personal property; and preferring a climate similar to his own, he bought a plantation on Red river, and largely stocked it with slaves. Only one child blessed their union; Bernard Le Croix, who grew up sensitive, shy and retiring, with a taste for solitude and literary pursuits.

During the troubles in Hayti, his uncle and only daughter escaped from the Island, leaving every thing behind except the clothing upon their persons, and a few jewels they had hastily collected. Broken in spirits, feeble in health, Louis Le Croix reached Louisiana, only to die in his brother's arms and to leave his orphan daughter to his care. She was about ten years old and Bernard was twelve, and in their childhood was commenced a friendship which ripened into love and marriage. Bernard's father and mother lived long enough to see their first and only grandchild, and then died, leaving their son a large baronial estate, 500 slaves, and a vast amount of money.

Passionately fond of literature, aesthetic in his tastes, he devoted himself to poetry and the ancient classics; filled his home with the finest paintings and the most beautiful statuary, and had his gardens laid out in the most exquisite manner. And into that beautiful home he brought his young and lovely bride; but in that fair house where velvet carpets hushed her tread, and magnificence surrounded her path, she drooped and faded. Day by day her cheek grew paler, her footsteps slower, until she passed away like a thing of love and light, and left her heart-broken husband and a child of six summers to mourn her loss.

Bernard, ever shy and sensitive, grew more so after the death of his wife. He sought no society; seemed to lose all interest in politics; and secluded himself in his library till he had almost passed from the recollection of his nearest neighbors. He superintended the education of his daughter, because he could not bear the thought of being separated from her. And she, seeing very little of society, and reading only from the best authors, both ancient and modern, was growing up with very little knowledge of the world, except what she learned from books.

Without any female relatives to guide her, she had no other associates than the servants of her household, and the family of Mr. Le Grange. Her mother's nurse and favorite servant had taken the charge of her after her death, and Agnes had been her nurse and companion.

Camilla, although (adored?) and petted by every one, and knowing no law but her own will, was still a very lovely child. Her father, wrapped in his literary pursuits, had left the entire control of his plantation to overseers, in whom he trusted almost implicitly. And many a tale of wrong and sorrow came to the ear of Camilla; for these simple-minded people had learned to love her, and to trust in her as an angel of mercy. Often would she interfere in their behalf, and tell the story of their wrongs to her father. And at her instance, more than one overseer had been turned away; which, coming to the ears of others, made them cautious how they offended the little lady, for young as she was they soon learned that she had great influence with her ease-loving father, who would comply with almost any fancy or request rather than see her unhappy or fretting.

And Camilla, knowing her power, insisted that Agnes' child should be raised as a white child, and the secret of his birth effectually concealed. At first, Mr. Le Croix thought it was a passing whim that she would soon forget; that the child would amuse and interest her for awhile; and then she would tire of him as she had of other things; such as her birds, her squirrel, and even her Shetland pony. But when he found that instead of her intention being a passing whim it was a settled purpose, he made up his mind to accede to her wishes.

His plan was to take the child North, to have him educated, and then adopt him as his son. And in fact the plan rather suited him; for then he could care for him as a son, without acknowledging the relationship. And being a member of two nations having a Latin basis, he did not feel the same pride of race and contempt and repulsion for weaker races which characterizes the proud and imperious Anglo-Saxon.

The next Summer Mr. Le Croix took a journey to the North, taking Louis and Camilla with him. He found a very pleasant family school in New England; and having made suitable arrangements, he left Louis in the care of the matron, whose kindness and attentions soon won the child's heart; and before he left the North, Louis seemed perfectly contented with his new home.

Camilla was delighted with her tour; the constant companion of her father, she visited with him every place of amusement or interest they could find. She was much pleased with the factories; and watched with curious eyes the intelligent faces of the operatives, as they plied with ready fingers their daily tasks. Sometimes she would contrast their appearance with the laborers she had seen wending their way into their lowly huts; and then her face would grow sober even to sadness. A puzzled expression would flit over her countenance, as if she were trying to solve a problem which was inexplicable to her.

One day on the hunt for some new excitement, her father passed down Tremont St., and saw advertised, in large letters, on the entrance to Tremont Temple, "Anti Slavery Meeting;" and never having been in such a place before he entered, impelled by a natural curiosity to hear what could be said against a system in which he had been involved from his earliest recollections, without taking the pains to examine it.

The first speaker was a colored man. This rather surprised him. He had been accustomed to colored men all the days of his life; and as such, he had known some of them to be intelligent, shrewd, and wide awake; but this was a new experience. The man had been a slave, and recounted in burning words the wrongs which had been heaped upon him. He told that he had been a husband and a father: that his wife had possessed (for a slave) the "fatal gift of beauty;" that a trader, from whose presence her soul had recoiled with loathing, had marked her as his prey. Then he told how he had knelt at his master's feet, and implored him not to sell her, but it was all in vain. The trader was rich in sin-cursed gold; and he was poor and weak. He next attempted to describe his feelings when he saw his wife and children standing on the auction block; and heard the coarse jests of the spectators, and the fierce competition of the bidders.

The speaker made a deep impression upon the minds of the audience; and even Le Croix, who had been accustomed to slavery all his life, felt a sense of guilt passing over him for his complicity in the system; whilst Camilla grew red and pale by turns, and clutching her little hands nervously together, said, "Father, let us go home."

Le Croix saw the deep emotion on his daughter's face, and the nervous twitchings of her lips, and regretted that he had introduced her to such an exciting scene.

When they were seated in their private parlor, Le Croix said: "Birdie, I am sorry that we attended that meeting this morning. I didn't believe a word that nigger said; and yet these people all drank it down as if every word were gospel truth. They are a set of fanatics, calculated to keep the nation in hot water. I hope that you will never enter such a place again. Did you believe one word that negro said?"

"Why, yes, Pa, I did, because our Isaac used to tell me just such a story as that. If I had shut my eyes, I could have imagined that it was Isaac telling his story."

"Isaac! What business had Isaac telling you any such stories?"

"Oh, Pa, don't get angry with Isaac. It wasn't his fault; it was mine.

"You know when you brought him home to drive the carriage, he used to look so sorrowful, and I said to him one day, Isaac, what makes you so sad? Why don't you laugh and talk, like Jerry and Sam?

"And he said, 'Oh Missus, I can't! Ise got a mighty heap of trouble on my mind.' And he looked so down-hearted when he said this, I wanted to know what was the matter; but he said, 'It won't do, for a little lady like you to know the troubles of we poor creatures,' but one day, when Sam came home from New Orleans he brought him a letter from his wife, and he really seemed to be overjoyed, and he kissed the letter, and put it in his bosom, and I never saw him look half so happy before. So the next day when I asked him to get the pony ready, he asked me if I wouldn't read it for him. He said he had been trying to make it out, but somehow he could not get the hang of the words, and so I sat down and read it to him. Then he told me about his wife, how beautiful she was; and how a trader, a real mean man, wanted to buy her, and that he had begged his master not to sell her; but it was no use. She had to go; but he was glad of one thing; the trader was dead, and his wife had got a place in the city with a very nice lady, and he hoped to see her when he went to New Orleans. Pa, I wonder how slavery came to be. I should hate to belong to anybody, wouldn't you, Pa?"

"Why, yes, darling, but then the negroes are contented, and wouldn't take their freedom, if you would give it to them."

"I don't know about that, Pa; there was Mr. Le Grange's Peter. Mr. Le Grange used to dress him so fine and treat him so well that he thought no one would ever tempt Peter to leave him; and he came North with him every year for three or four summers, and he always made out that he was afraid of the abolitionists—bobolitionists he used to call them—and Mr. Le Grange just believed that Peter was in earnest, and somehow he got Mrs. Le Grange to bring his wife North to wait on her. And when they both got here, they both left; and Mrs. Le Grange had to wait on herself, until she got another servant. She told me she had got enough of the North, and never wanted to see it again so long as she lived; that she wouldn't have taken three thousand dollars for them."

"Well, darling, they would have never left, if these meddlesome abolitionists hadn't put it in their heads; but, darling, don't bother your brain about such matters. See what I have bought you this morning," said he, handing her a necklace of the purest pearls; "here, darling, is a birth-day present for you." Camilla took the necklace, and gazing absently upon it said, "I can't understand it."

"What is it, my little philosopher, that you can't understand?"

"Pa, I can't understand slavery; that man made me think it was something very bad. Do you think it can be right?"

Le Croix's face flushed suddenly, and he bit his lip, but said nothing, and commenced reading the paper.

"Why don't you answer me, Pa?" Le Croix's brow grew darker, but he tried to conceal his vexation, and quietly said, "Darling, never mind. Don't puzzle your little head about matters you cannot understand, and which our wisest statesmen cannot solve."

Camilla said no more, but a new train of thought had been awakened. She had lived so much among the slaves, and had heard so many tales of sorrow breathed confidentially into her ears, that she had unconsciously imbibed their view of the matter; and without comprehending the injustice of the system, she had learned to view it from their standpoint of observation.

What she had seen of slavery in the South had awakened her sympathy and compassion. What she had heard of it in the North had aroused her sense of justice. She had seen the old system under a new light. The good seed was planted, which was yet to yield its harvest of blessed deeds.

# III

"W hat is the matter?" said St. Pierre Le Grange, as he entered suddenly the sitting-room of his wife, Georgietta Le Grange, and saw her cutting off the curls from the head of little girl about five years old, the child of a favorite slave.

"Matter enough!" said the angry wife, her cheeks red with excitement and her eyes half blinded with tears of vexation. "This child shan't stay here; and if she does, she shall never again be taken for mine."

"Who took her for yours? What has happened that has brought about all this excitement?"

"Just wait a minute," said Georgietta, trying to frame her excitement into words.

"Yesterday I invited the Le Fevres and the Le Counts, and a Northern lady they had stopping with Mrs. Le Fevre, to dine with us. Today I told Ellen to have the servants all cleaned up, and looking as well as possible; and so I distributed around more than a dozen turbans, for I wanted Mrs. King to see how much better and happier our negroes looked here than they do when they are free in the North, and what should Ellen do but dress up her little minx in her best clothes, and curl her hair and let her run around in the front yard."

"So she overdid the thing," said Le Grange, beginning to comprehend the trouble.

"Yes, she did, but she will never do it again," exclaimed Mrs. Le Grange, her dark eyes flashing defiantly.

Le Grange bit his lip, but said nothing. He saw the storm that was brewing, and about to fall on the head of the hapless child and mother, and thought that he would do nothing to increase it.

"When Mrs. Le Fevre," continued Georgietta, "alighted from the carriage, she noticed the child, and calling the attention of the whole party to her, said, 'Oh, how beautiful she is! The very image of her father.' 'Mrs. Le Grange,' said she, after passing the compliments of the day, 'I congratulate you on having such a beautiful child. She is the very image of her father. And how large she is for her age.' Just then Marie came to the door and said 'She's not my sister, that is Ellen's child.' I saw the gentlemen exchange glances, and the young ladies screw up their mouths to hide their merriment, while Mrs. Le Fevre, with all her obtuseness, seemed to comprehend the blunder, and she said,

'Child, you must excuse me, for my poor old eyes are getting so good for nothing I can hardly tell one person from the other.' I blundered some kind of answer, I hardly know what I said. I was almost ready to die with vexation; but this shall never happen again."

"What are you going to do?"

"You see what I have begun to do. I am going to have all this curling business broken up, and I am going to have her dressed in domestic, like the other little niggers. I'll let Ellen know that I am mistress here; and as soon as a trader comes along I mean to sell her. I want a new set of pearls anyhow."

Le Grange made no reply. He was fond of the child, but knowing what a termagant his wife was, he thought that silence like discretion was the better part of valor, and hastily beat a retreat from her presence.

"Take these curls and throw them away," said Mrs. Le Grange to Sally, her waiting-maid. "Move quick, and take this child into the kitchen, and don't let me see her in the front yard again. Do you hear what I say?" said Georgiette in a sharp, shrill tone. "Don't you let me see that child in the front yard again. Here, before you go, darken this room, and let me see if I can get any rest. I am so nervous, I am almost ready to fly."

Sally did as she was bidden; and taking the child to the kitchen, exclaimed to Milly, the cook, "Hi! Oh! there's been high times upstairs today."

"What's the matter?" said Milly, wiping the dough from her hands, and turning her face to Sally.

"Oh! Missus mad 'bout Ellen's child. She's mad as a March hare. See how she's cut all her hair off."

"A debil," said Milly. "What did she do dat for? She is allers up to some debilment. What did that poor innercence child do to her? I wonder what she'll get at next!"

"I don't know, but today when Mrs. Le Ferre come'd here she kissed the child, and said it was the very image of its father, and Missus just looked mad enough to run her through."

Milly, in spite of her indignation could not help laughing. "Well, that's a good joke. I guess Missus' high as ninety. What did Massa say?"

"He neber said a word; he looked like he'd been stealin' a sheep; and Missus she jist cut up high, and said she was going to keep her hair cut short, and have her dressed in domestic, and kept in the kitchen, and when she got a good chance she meant to sell her, for she wanted a new

FRANCES ELLEN WATKINS HARPER

set of pearls anyhow. Massa neber said beans. I jist b'lieve he's feared of her. She's sich a mity piece. I spect some night the debil will come and fly way wid her. I hope so anyhow."

To which not very pious wish Milly replied, "I am fraid there is no such good luck. Nothin' don't s'prise me that Miss Georgiette does 'cause she's a chip off the old block. Her mother's poor niggers used to be cut up and slashed all the time; for she was a horse at the mill. De debil was in dat woman big as a sheep. Dere was Nancy, my fellow servant; somehow she got a spite agin Nancy's husban', said he shouldn't come dere any more. Pore Nancy, her and Andy war libing together in dar nice little cabin, and Nancy did keep ebery ting shinin' like a new pin, 'cause she would work so hard when she was done her task for Missus. But one day Missus got de debil in her, and sayed Andy shouldn't come der any more, and she jist had all Nancy's tings took out de cabin and shut it up, and made her come and sleep in de house. Pore Nancy, she cried as if her heart would break right in two; and she says why does you take my husban' from me? and Missus said I did it to please my own self, and den Nancy kneeled at her feet and said, 'Missus I'll get up before day and set up till twelve or one o'clock at night and work for you, but please don't take me from my husban'. An' what do you think ole Missus did? Why she jist up wid her foot and kicked Nancy in de mouf, and knocked out two of her teef. I seed her do it wid my own blessed eyes. An' I sed to myself de debil will never git his own till he gits you. Well she did worry dat pore cretur almost to death. She used to make her sleep in the room wid her chillen, and locked de door ebery night, and Sundays she'd lebe some one to watch her, she was so fraid she'd git to see her husban'. An' dis Miss Georgiette is de very moral of her Ma, and she's jist as big as a spitfire."

"Hush," said Milly, "here comes Jane. Don't say no more 'bout Missus, cause she's real white people's nigger, and tells all she knows, and what she don't."

# IV

I am really sorry, Ellen, but I can't help it. Georgiette has taken a dislike to the child, and there is no living in peace with her unless I sell the child or take it away."

"Oh! Mr. St. Pierre, you would not sell that child when it is your own flesh and blood?" Le Grange winced under these words.

"No, Ellen, I'll never consent to sell the child, but it won't do for her to stay here. I've made up my mind to send her North, and have her educated."

"And then I'll never see my darling any more."

"But, Ellen, that is better than having her here to be knocked around by Georgiette, and if I die to be sold as a slave. It is the best thing I can do,—hang old Mrs. Le Fevre's tongue; but I guess it would have come out some time or the other. I just tell you what I'll do, Ellen. I'll take the child down to New Orleans, and make out to Georgiette that I am going to sell her, but instead of that, I'll get a friend of mine who is going to Pennsylvania to take her with him, and have her boarded there, and educated. Nobody need know anything about her being colored. I'd send you both, Ellen, but, to tell you the truth, the plantation is running down, and the crops are so short this year I can't afford it; but when times get better, I'll send you up there and tell you where you can find her."

"Well, Mr. St. Pierre, that is better than having Missus knocking her around or selling her to one of those old mean nigger traders, and never having a chance to see my darling no more. But, Mr. St. Pierre, before you take her away won't you please give me her likeness? Maybe I won't know her when I see her again."

Le Grange consented, and when he went to the city again he told his wife he was going to sell the child.

"I am glad of it," said Georgiette. "I would have her mother sold, but we can't spare her; she is so handy with her needle, and does all the cutting out on the place."

## Le Grange's Plan

"The whole fact is this Joe, I am in an awkward fix. I have got myself into a scrape, and I want you to help me out of it. You were good at such things when we were at College, and I want you to try your hand again."

FRANCES ELLEN WATKINS HARPER

"Well, what's the difficulty now?"

"Well, it is rather a serious one. I have got a child on my hands, and I don't know what to do with it."

"Whose child is it?"

"Now, that's just where the difficulty lies. It is the child of one of my girls, but it looks so much like me, that my wife don't want it on the place. I am too hard up just now to take the child and her mother, North, and take care of them there. And to tell you the truth I am too humane to have the child sold here as a slave. Now in a word do you think that among your Abolitionist friends in the North you could find any one who would raise the child and bring it up like a white child."

"I don't know about that St. Pierre. There are a number of our people in the North, who do two things. They hate slavery and hate negroes. They feel like the woman who in writing to her husband said, they say (or don't say) that absence conquers love; for the longer you stay away the better I love you. But then I know some who, I believe, are really sincere, and who would do anything to help the colored people. I think I know two or three families who would be willing to take the child, and do a good part by her. If you say so, I will write to a friend whom I have now in mind, and if they will consent I will take the child with me when I go North, provided I can do it without having it discovered that she is colored, for it would put me in an awkward fix to have it known that I took a colored child away with me."

"Oh, never fear," said St. Pierre, slapping his friend on the shoulder. "The child is whiter than you are, and you know you can pass for white."

True to his promise, Josiah Collins wrote to a Quaker friend, whom he knew in Pennsylvania, and told him the particulars of the child's history, and the wishes of her father, and the compensation he would give. In a few days he received a favorable response in which the friend told him he was glad to have the privilege of rescuing one of that fated race from a doom more cruel than the grave; that the compensation was no object; that they had lost their only child, and hoped that she would in a measure fill the void in their hearts.

Highly gratified with the kind letter of the friend, Le Grange gave the child into the charge of Josiah Collins, and putting a check for five hundred dollars in his hand, parted with them at the (station).

He went back into the country, and told his wife that he had found a trader, who thought the child so beautiful, and that he had bought her to raise as a fancy girl, and had given him five hundred dollars for her. "And here," said he, handing her a set of beautiful pearls, "is my peace offering."

Georgette's eyes glistened as she entertwined the pearls amid the wealth of her raven hair, and clasped them upon her beautifully rounded arms.

What mattered it to her if every jewel cost a heart throb, and if the whole set were bought with the price of blood? They suited her style of beauty, and she cared not what they cost. Proud, imperious, and selfish, she knew no law but her own will; no gratification but the enjoyment of her own desires.

Passing from the boudoir of his wife, he sought the room where Ellen sat, busily cutting and arranging the clothing for the field hands, and gazing furtively around he said, "here is Minnie's likeness. I have managed all right." "Thank Heaven!" said the sad hearted mother, as she paused to dry her tears, and then resumed her needle. "Anything is better—than Slavery."

# V

B efore I proceed any further with my story, let me tell the reader something of the Le Granges, whom I have so unceremoniously introduced.

Le Grange, like Le Croix, was of French and Spanish descent, and his father had also been a Haytian refugee. But there the similitude ends; unlike Le Croix, he had grown up a gay and reckless young man, fond of sports, and living an aimless life.

His father had on his plantation a beautiful quadroon girl, named Ellen, whom he had bought in Richmond because she begged him to buy her when he had bought her mother, who had been recommended to him as a first-rate cook. They had been servants in what was called one of the first families of Virginia, and had been treated by their mistress with more kindness and consideration than generally fell to the lot of persons in their condition. As long as she lived, they had been well fed and well clothed, and except the deprivation of their freedom, had known but few of the hardships so incident to slave life; but a reverse had fallen upon them.

Their mistress had intended to set them free, but, dying suddenly, she had failed to carry out her intention. Her property fell into the hands of distant heirs, who sold it all, and divided it among themselves. Ellen and her mother were put up at auction, when a kindly looking old Frenchman bought the mother. Ellen stood trembling by; but, when she saw her mother's new master, she started forth, and kneeling at his feet, she begged him to buy her. The mother joined in and said, "Do, Massa, and I'll serve you faithful day and night; there is a heap of work in these old bones yet."

Mr. Le Grange told her to be quiet, and he would buy her. And, true to his word, although the bidding ran high, and the competition was fierce, he bought her; and the next day, he started with them for his plantation on Red River.

His son, Louis, had just graduated, and was spending the winter at home, in just that mood of which it is said that Satan finds some mischief for idle hands to do. Milly, who knew the wiles of the world better than Ellen, tried to keep her as much as possible out of his way; but her caution was all in vain. She saw her child engulfed, as thousands of her race had been.

Mrs. Le Grange, when she became apprised of the condition of things, grew very angry; but, instead of venting her indignation upon the head of her offending son, she poured out the vials of her wrath upon the defenseless girl. She made up her mind to sell her off the place, and picked the opportunity, while her son was absent, to send her to a trader's pen in the city. When Louis came home, he found Milly looking very sullen and distressed, and her eyes red with weeping.

"What is the matter?" said Louis.

"Matter enough," said Milly. "Missus done gone and sold Ellen."

"Sold Ellen! Why, how did that happen?"

"Why, she found out all about her, and said she should not stay on the place another day, and so she sent her down to Orleans to the nigger traders, and my heart's most broke," and Milly sat down, wiping her tears with her apron.

"Never mind, Milly," said Louis, "I'll go down to New Orleans and bring her back. Mother sha'n't do as she pleases with me, as if I were a boy, and must always be tied to her apron string. I've got some money of my own, and I mean to find Ellen if I have to look all over the country."

He entered the dining room, and saw his mother seated at the tea table, looking as bland and pleasant as a Spring morning, and asked, "Where is Ellen?"

The smile died from her lips, and she answered, curtly, "She is out of *your* reach (?). I've sold her."

"But where have you sold her?"

"Out of your reach, and that is all I am going to tell you."

Louis, without saying another word went out to the coachman, and asked what time the cars left the station.

"Ten minutes to nine."

"Can you take me there in time to reach the train? I want to go to the city tonight."

"Dunno, massa; my best horse is lame, and what—"

"Never mind your excuse; here," said he, throwing him a dollar, "hitch up as quick as possible, and take me there without any 'buts' or 'ifs.'"

"All right, massa," said Sam, grinning with delight. "I'll have you over there in short order."

The carriage harnessed, Samuel found no difficulty with his horses, and reached the depot almost a half hour before the time.

Louis arrived in the city after midnight, and the next day he devoted to hunting for Ellen. He searched through different slave pens, inquired of all the traders, until at last, ready to abandon his search in hopelessness, he heard of a private jail in the suburbs of the city. Nothing daunted by his failure, he found the place and Ellen also.

The trader eyed him keenly, and saw from his manner that he was in earnest about having the girl.

"She is not for sale in this city. Whoever buys her must give me a pledge to take her out of this city. That was the bargain I made with her mistress. She made me promise her that I would sell her to no one in the vicinity of the city. In fact, she wanted me to sell her out of the way of her son. His mother said she had dedicated him to the Blessed Virgin, and I reckon she wanted to keep him out of the way of temptation. Now what will you give me for her?"

"Will you take a thousand for her?"

"Now you ain't saying nothing," said the trader, shutting one eye, and spitting on the floor.

"How will twelve hundred do?"

"It won't do at all, not for such a fancy article as that. I'd rather keep her for myself than sell her at such a low figure. Why, just look at her! Why, she's pretty as a picture! Look at that neck, and her shoulders. See how she carries her head! And look at that splendid head of hair. Why some of our nabobs would give three thousand dollars; but I'll tell you what I'll do, I'll let you have her for two thousand dollars; fancy article is cheap at that."

Louis demurred, but the trader was inexorable, and rather than let the opportunity to rescue Ellen from him escape he paid the exorbitant price, and had her brought to his hotel. His next work was to get a house for Ellen, and have her taken there, installed as his mistress. He then went back to the plantation as if nothing had happened, and his mother soon thought he was reconciled about the loss of Ellen. Only Milly knew his secret, and she kept it as a secret thing.

"I've got some pleasant news for you, Louis," said Mrs. Le Grange, one day to her son: "your uncle and cousin are coming down from Virginia, and I want you to be all attention to your cousin, for she is very rich. She has a fortune in her right, which was left her by her grandmother, and besides she will have another one at her father's death, added, to which they say, she is a very beautiful girl."

Great preparations were made for the expected guests. Georgiette was Mrs. Le Grange's brother's child, and having been separated from him for more than fifteen years she was full of joyful anticipations, when he apprised her of his intention of visiting her in company with his daughter. At length the welcome day arrived, and Mrs. Le Grange stood arranging her jewels and ribbons to receive the guests.

"You are welcome to Louisiana," said she, removing Georgiette's shawl, and tenderly kissing her, "and you too, brother," she said, as Mr. Monteith followed his daughter. "How beautiful Georgiette has grown since I saw her. Why darling you look charming! I'm afraid I shan't be able to keep you long for some of the beaux will surely run away with you." "My son," said Mrs. Le Grange, introducing Louis, who just then entered the door.

Louis bowed very low, and expressed his pleasure in seeing them; and hoped they would have a happy time, and that nothing should be wanting on his part, to make it so. Very pleasantly passed the time away; Georgiette was in high and charming spirits; and many a pleasant ride and delightful saunter she took with her cousin through the woods, or in visiting other plantations. She was very popular among the planters' sons; admired by the young men, but feared and envied by the girls.

And thus the hours passed in a whirl of pleasurable excitement, until Louis actually imagined himself in love with her, and found himself one pleasant afternoon offering her his hand and heart.

She blushed and sighed, and referred him to her papa; and in a few weeks they were engaged.

At length the time of their departure came; and Louis, after accompanying them to New Orleans, returned to make ready for the wedding. His father made him a present of a large plantation, which he stocked from his own purse, with three hundred slaves; and installed Ellen there as housekeeper till the arrival of the new mistress.

# VI

T hee is welcome to S.," said the cheerful voice of Thomas Carpenter, as Josiah Collins alighted, bringing with him his charge; "and is this the little child thee wrote me about? I am heartily glad thee has rescued her from that dreadful system!"

"Anna," said he, turning to his wife, who had just entered the room, "here is our friend, Josiah Collins, and the little girl I told thee about."

"I am glad thee has come," said Anna, "sit down and make thyself at home. And this is the little girl thee wrote Thomas about. She is a beautiful child," continued Anna, gazing admiringly at the child. "I hope she will be contented. Does she fret about her mother?"

"Not much; she would sometimes ask, 'where is mamma?' But the ladies in the cars were very kind to her, and she was quite at home with them. I told them I was taking her North; that I thought the North would better agree with her; and that it was not convenient for her mother to come on just now. I was really amused with the attention she received from the Southern ladies; knowing how they would have shrunk from such offices if they had known that one drop of the outcast blood ran in her veins."

"Why, Josiah," said Anna, "I have always heard that there was more prejudice against the colored people in the North than in the South. There is a difference in the manifestations of this feeling, but I do not think there is as much prejudice here as there. (Here?) we have a prejudice which is (formed from?) traditional ideas. We see in many parts of the North a very few of the colored people, and our impressions of them have received their coloring more or less from what the slaveholders have said of them."

"We have been taught that they are idle, improvident, and unfitted for freedom, and incapable of progression; and when we see them in the cities we see them overshadowed by wealth, enterprise, and activity, so that our unfavorable impressions are too often confirmed. Still if one of that class rises above this low mental condition, we know that there are many who are willing to give such a one a healthy recognition."

"I know that there are those that have great obstacles to overcome, but I think that while Southerners may have more personal likings for certain favorite servants, they have stronger prejudices than even we have, or if they have no more than we have, they have more self-restraint, and show it more virulently."

"But I (think?) they do not seem to have any horror of personal contact."

"Of course not; constant familiarity with the race has worn away all sense of physical repulsion but there is a prejudice which ought to be an American feeling; it is a prejudice against their rising in the scale of humanity. A prejudice which virtually says you are down, and I mean to keep you down. As a servant I tolerate you; you are useful as you are valuable, but rise one step in the scale of being, and I am ready to put you down. I see this in the treatment that the free colored people receive in parts of the South; they seem to me to be the outcasts of an outcast race. They are denied the right to walk in certain public places accessible to every class unless they go as nurses, and are forbidden to assemble in evening meetings, and forced to be in the house unless they have passes, by an early hour in the night, and in fact they are hampered or hemmed in on every side; subject to insults from any rude, coarse or brutal white, and in case of outrages, denied their testimony. Prejudiced as we are in Pennsylvania, we do not go that far."

"But, Josiah, we have much to blush for in Pennsylvania; colored people are denied the privilege of riding in our street cars. Only last week when I was in Philadelphia I saw a very decent-looking colored woman with a child, who looked too feeble to walk, and the child too heavy for her to carry. She beckoned to a conductor, but he swept by and took no more heed of her than if she had been a dog. There was a young lady sitting in the car, who remarked to her mother, as a very filthy-looking white man entered, 'See, they will let that filthy creature ride and prohibit a decent respectable colored person!' The mother quietly assented.

"From her dress I took her to be a Quakeress, for she had a lovely dress of dove-colored silk. The young lady had scarcely uttered the words when a young man who sat next the mother deliberately arose, and beckoned to the man with the sooty clothes to take his seat; but fortunately for the Quakeress, a lady who was sitting next her daughter arose just at that moment, and left the seat, and the old man without noticing the manoeuvre passed over to the other side, and thus avoided the contact. I was amused, however, about one thing; for the young man who gave up his seat was compelled to ride about a mile standing."

"Served him right," said Thomas Carpenter; "it was a very

contemptible action, to attempt to punish the hardihood of the young lady by attempting to soil her mother's dress; and yet little souls who feel a morbid satisfaction in trampling on the weak, always sink themselves in the scale of manhood."

While this conversation was going on, the tea bell rang, and Josiah and his little charge sat down to a well supplied table; for the Friends, though plain and economical, are no enemies to good living.

Anna had brought the high-chair in which their own darling had sat a few months before, when she had made gladness and sunshine around her parent's path.

There was a tender light in the eye of the Quakeress as she dusted the chair, and sat Minnie at the table.

"Do you think," said Thomas, addressing Josiah, "that we will ever outgrow this wicked, miserable prejudice?"

"Oh, yes, but it must be the work of time. Both races have their work to do. The colored man must outgrow his old condition of things, and thus create around him a new class of associations. This generation has known him as a being landless, poor, and ignorant. One of the most important things for him to do is to acquire land. He will never gain his full measure of strength until (like Anteus) he touches the earth. And I think here is the great fault, or misfortune of the race; they seem to me to readily accept their situation, and not to let their industrial aspirations rise high enough. I wish they had more of the earth hunger that characterizes the German, or the concentration of purpose which we see in the Jews."

"I think," said Thomas, "that the Jews and Negroes have one thing in common, and that is their power of endurance. They, like the negro, have lived upon an idea, and that is the hope of a deliverer yet to come; but I think this characteristic more strongly developed in the Jews than in the Negroes."

"Doubtless it is, but their origin and history have been different. The Jews have a common ancestry and grand traditions, that have left alive their pride of race. 'We have Abraham to our father,' they said, when their necks were bowed beneath the Roman yoke."

"But I do not think the negro can trace with certainty his origin back to any of the older civilizations, and here for more than two hundred years his history has been a record of blood and tears, of ignorance, degradation, and slavery. And when nominally free, prejudice has assigned him the lowest positions and the humblest situations. I have not much hope of their progress while they are enslaved in the South."

"Well, Josiah, I have faith enough in the ultimate triumph of our principles to believe that slavery will bite the dust before long."

"I don't know, friend Carpenter; for the system is very strongly rooted and grounded in the institutions of the land, and has entrenched itself in the strongholds of Church and State, fashion, custom, and social life. And yet when I was in the South, I saw on every hand a growing differentiation towards the Government."

"Do you know, Josiah, that I have more hope from the madness and folly of the South than I have from the wisdom and virtue of the North? I have read too 'whom the gods would destroy they first make mad.'"

# VII

Ten years have elapsed since Minnie came to brighten the home of Thomas Carpenter, and although within the heart of Anna there is a spot forever green and sacred to the memory of her only child, yet Minnie holds an undivided place in their affections.

There is only one subject which is to them a source of concern. It is the connection of Minnie with the colored race. Not that they love her less on account of the blood that is in her veins, but they dread the effect its discovery would have upon the pleasant social circle with which she is surrounded, and also the fear that the revelation would be painful to her.

They know that she is Anti-Slavery in her principles. They have been careful to instil into her young mind a reverence for humanity, and to recognize beneath all externals, whether of condition or color, the human soul all written over with the handmarks of divinity and the common claims of humanity.

She has known for years that their home has been one of the stations of the underground railroad. And the Anti-Slavery lecturer, whether white or colored, has always been among the welcomed guests of her home. Still they shrink from the effect the knowledge would have on her mind. They know she is willing to work for the colored race; but they could not divine what it cost her to work with them.

"It seems to me, Anna, that we ought to reveal to Minnie the fact of her connection with the colored race. I am afraid that she will learn in some way that will rudely shock her; whereas we might break it to her in the tenderest manner. Every time a fugitive comes I dread that our darling will be recognized."

"Nay, Thomas; thy fears have made thee over sensitive. Who would imagine he saw in this bright and radiant girl of fifteen the little five-year-old child we took to our hearts and home? I never feel any difference between her and the whitest child in the village as far as prejudice is concerned. And if every body in the village knew her origin I would love her just as much as I ever did, for she is a dear good child."

"Well, dear, if you think it is best to keep it a secret, I will not interfere. But we must not forget that Minnie will soon be a young lady; that she is very beautiful, and even now she begins to attract admiration. I do not think it would be right for us to let her marry a white man without letting her know the prejudices of society, and giving her a chance to explain to him the conditions of things."

"Yes," said Anna, "that is true; I have heard that traces of that blood will sometimes reappear even in grandchildren, when it has not been detected in the first. And to guard against difficulty which might arise from such a course, I think it is better to apprise her of the facts in the case."

"It is time enough for that. I want her to finish her education before she thinks of marrying, and I am getting her ready to go to Philadelphia, where she will find an excellent school as I have heard it very highly spoken of. She is young and happy, trouble will come time enough, let me not hasten its advent."

But if time has only strewed the path of Minnie with flowers, and ripened the promised beauty of her childhood, it has borne a heavy hand upon the destiny of the La Croix family.

La Croix is dead; but before his death he took the precaution to have Louis emancipated, and then made him a joint heir with his daughter. The will he entrusted to the care of Camilla; but the deed of emancipation he placed in the hands of Miriam, saying, "Here are your free papers, and here are Louis'. There is nothing in this world sure but death; and it is well to be on the safe side. Some one might be curious enough to search out his history; and if there should be no legal claim to his freedom, he might be robbed of both his liberty and his inheritance; so keep these papers, and if ever the hour comes when you or he should need them, you must show me."

Miriam did as she was bidden; but her heart was lighter when she knew that freedom had come so near her and Louis.

Le Croix, before his death, had sold the greater part of his slaves, and invested the money in Northern bonds and good Northern securities. Camilla had married a gentleman from the North, and is living very happily upon the old plantation. She does not keep an overseer, and tries to do all in her power to ameliorate the condition of her slaves; still she is not satisfied with the system, and is trying to prepare her slaves for freedom, by inducing them to form, as much as possible, habits of self-reliance, and self-restraint, which they will need in the freedom which she has determined they shall enjoy as soon as she can arrange her affairs to that effect. But she also has to proceed with a great deal of caution.

The South is in a state of agitation and (foment?). The air is laden

FRANCES ELLEN WATKINS HARPER

with rumors of a (rising?) conflict between the North and the South, and any want of allegiance to Southern opinions is punished either as a crime if the offender is a man, or with social ostracism and insult if a woman.

The South in the palmy days of her pride and power would never tolerate any heresy to her creed, whose formula of statement might have been written we believe in the divine right of the Master, to take advantage of the weakness, ignorance, and poverty of the slave; that might makes right, and that success belongs to the strongest arm.

Some of her former friends were beginning to eye her with coldness and suspicion because she would not join in their fanatical hatred of the North and because she would profess her devotion to the old flag, while they were ready to spit upon and trample it under foot.

Her adopted brother was still in the North, and strange to say he did not share her feelings; his sympathies were with the South, and although he was too young to take any leading part in the events there about to transpire, yet year after year when he spent his vacations at home, he attended the hustings and political meetings, and there he learned to consider the sentiment, "My country right or wrong," as a proper maxim for political action.

This difference in their sentiments did not produce the least estrangement between them; only Camilla regretted to see Louis ready to raise his hand against the freedom of his mother's race, although he was perfectly unconscious of his connection with it, for the conflict which was then brewing between the North and the South was in fact a struggle between despotism and idea; between freedom on one side and slavery on the other.

# VIII

C ommencement over, what are you going to do with yourself?"
"I don't know; loaf around, I suppose."

"Why don't you go to Newport?"

"Don't want to; got tired of it last year."

"Saratoga?"

"A perfect bore!"

"Niagara?"

"Been there twice."

"A pedestrian tour to the White Mountains?"

"Haven't got energy enough."

"What will you do?"

"Stay at home and fight mosquitoes."

"Very pleasant employment. I don't envy you, but I can tell you something better than that."

"What is it?" said his companion, yawning.

"Come, go home with me."

"Go home with you! Where is that, and what is the attraction?"

"Well, let me see, it is situated in one of the most beautiful valleys of Western Pennsylvania, our village is environed by the most lovely hills, and nestling among the trees, with its simple churches and unpretending homes of quiet beauty and good taste, it is one of the most pleasant and picturesque places I ever saw. And, besides, as you love to hunt and fish, we have one of the finest streams of trout, and some of the most excellent game in the woods."

"Is that all?"

"Why, isn't that enough? You must be rather hard to please this morning."

"Think so?"

"Yes, but I have not told you the crowning attraction."

"What is it?"

"Oh, one of the most beautiful girls I ever saw! We call her the lily of the valley."

"Describe her."

"I can't. It would be like attempting to paint a sun beam or doing what no painter has ever done, sketch a rainbow."

"You are very poetical this morning, but I want you to do as our President sometimes tells us, proceed from the abstract to the concrete."

"Well, let me begin: she has the most beautiful little feet. I never see her stepping along without thinking of Cinderella and the glass slipper. As to eyes, they are either dark brown or black, I don't know which; but I do know they are beautiful; and her hair, well, she generally wears that plain in deference to the wishes of her Quaker friends, but sometimes in the most beautiful ripples of golden brown I ever saw."

"That will do, now tell me who she is? You spoke of her Quaker friends. Is she not their daughter?"

"No, there seems to be some mystery about her history. About ten years ago, my father brought her to Josiah Carpenter's but he's always been reticent about her, in fact I never took the pains to inquire. She's a great favorite in the village, and everybody says she is as beautiful as she is good, and vice versa."

"Well, I'd like to see this paragon of yours. I believe I'll go."

"Well, let us get ready."

"When do you start?"

"Tomorrow."

"All right. I'll be on hand." And with these words the two friends parted to meet again the next day at the railroad station.

The first of the speakers is the son of Josiah Collins, and his friend is Louis Le Croix, Camilla's adopted brother. He is somewhat changed within the last ten years. Time has touched the golden wealth of his curls with a beautiful deep auburn, and the rich full tones of his voice tell that departed is written upon his childhood.

He is strongly Southern in his feelings, but having been educated in the North, whilst he is an enthusiast in defense of his section, as he calls the South, he is neither coarse and brutal in actions, nor fanatical in his devotion to slavery. He thinks the Negroes are doing well enough in slavery, if the Abolitionists would only let matters rest, and he feels a sense of honor in defending the South. She is his mother, he says, and that man is an ingrate who will not stand by his mother and defend her when she is in peril.

He and Charles Collins are fast friends, but (on the subject of slavery they are entirely opposed?). And so on that point they have agreed to disagree. They often have animated and exciting discussions, but they (pass?) and Josiah and Louis are just as friendly as they were before.

There were two arrivals the next evening in the (quiet?) village of S. One was Charles Collins, the other his Southern friend, who was received with the warmest welcome, and soon found himself at home in the pleasant society of his friend's family. The evening was enlivened with social chat and music, until ten o'clock, when Josiah gathered his children and having read the Bible in a deeply impressive manner, breathed one of the most simple and fervent prayers he had ever heard.

While they were bending at prayer in this pleasant home, a shabby looking man came walking slowly and wearily into the village. He gazed cautiously around and looked anxiously in the street as though he were looking for some one, but did not like to trust his business to every one.

At length he saw an elderly man, dressed in plain clothes, and a broad brim hat, and drawing near he spoke to him in a low and hesitating voice, and asked if he knew a Mr. Thomas Carpenter.

"My name is Carpenter," said the friend, "come with me."

There was something in the voice, and manner of the friend that *assured* the stranger. His whole manner changed. A peaceful expression stole over his dark, sad face, and the drooping limbs seemed to be aroused by a new infusion of energy.

"Come in," said Thomas, as he reached his door, "come in, thee's welcome to stop and rest with us."

"Anna," said Thomas, his face beaming with kindness, "I've brought thee a guest. Here is another passenger by the Underground Railroad."

"I'm sure thee's welcome," said Anna, handing him a chair, "sit down, thee looks very tired. Where did thee come from?"

Moses, that was the fugitive's name, hesitated a moment.

"Oh, never fear, thee's among friends; thee need not be afraid to tell all about thyself."

Moses then told them that he had come from Kentucky.

"And how did thee escape?"

He said, "I walked from Lexington to Covington."

"Why, that was almost one hundred miles, and did thee walk all that way?"

"Yes, sir," said he, "I hid by day, and walked by night."

"Did no one interrupt?"

"Yes, one man said to me, 'Where's your pass?' I suppose I must have grown desperate, for I raised my fists and said dem's my passes; and he let me alone. I don't know whether he was friendly or scared, but he let me alone."

"And how then?"

"When I come to Covington I found that I could not come across the river without a pass, but I watched my chance, and hid myself on a boat, and I got across. I'd heard of you down home."

"How did you?"

"Oh, we's got some few friends dere, but we allers promise not to tell."

Anna and Thomas smiled at his reticence, which had grown into a habit.

"Were you badly treated?"

"Not so bad as some, but I allers wanted my freedom, I did."

"Well, we will not talk about thee any more; if thee walked all that distance thee must be very tired and we'll let thee rest. There's thy bed. I hope thee'll have a good night's rest, and feel better in the morning."

"Thankee marm," said Moses, "you's mighty good."

"Oh no, but I always like to do my duty by my fellow men! Now, be quiet, and get a good night's sleep. Thee looks excited. Thee mustn't be uneasy. Thee's among friends."

A flood of emotions crept over the bosom of Moses when his kind friends left the room. Was this freedom, and was this the long wished for North? and were these the Abolitionists of whom he had heard so much in the South? They who would allure the colored people from their homes in the South and then leave them to freeze and starve in the North? He had heard all his life that the slaveholders were the friends of the South, and the language of his soul had been, "If these are my friends, save me from my foes." He had lived all his life among the white people of the South, and had been owned by several masters, but he did not know that there was so much kindness among the white race, till he had rested in a Northern home, and among Northern people.

Here kindness encouraged his path, and in that peaceful home every voice that fell upon his ear was full of tenderness and sympathy. True, there were rough, coarse, brutal men even in that village, who for a few dollars or to prove their devotion to the South, would have readily remanded him to his master, but he was not aware of that. And so when he sank to his rest a sense of peace and safety stole over him, and his sleep was as calm and peaceful as the slumber of a child.

The next morning he looked refreshed, but still his strength was wasted by his great physical exertion and mental excitement; and Thomas thought he had better rest a few days till he grew stronger and better prepared to travel; for Thomas noticed that he was nervous, starting at the sound of every noise, and often turning his head to the door with an anxious, frightened look.

Thomas would have gladly given him shelter and work, and given him just wages, but he dared not do so. He was an American citizen it is true, but at that time slavery reigned over the North and ruled over the South, and he had not the power under the law of the land to give domicile, and break his bread to that poor, hunted and flying man; for even then they were hunting in the South and sending out their human bloodhounds to search for him in the North.

Throughout the length and breadth of the land, from the summit of the rainbow-crowned Niagara to the swollen waters of the Mexican Gulf; from the golden gates of sunrise to the gorgeous portals of departing day, there was not a hill so high, a forest so secluded, a glen so sequestered, nor mountain so steep, that he knew he could not be tracked and hailed in the name of the general government.

"What's the news, friend Carpenter? any new arrivals?" said Josiah Collins in a low voice to Thomas.

"Yes, a very interesting case; can't you come over?"

"Yes, after breakfast. By the way, you must be a little more cautious than usual. Charley came home last night, and brought a young friend with him from college. I think from his conversation that he is either a Southerner himself, or in deep sympathy with the South."

Both men spoke in low tones, for although they were Northerners, they were talking about a subject on which they were compelled to speak with bated breaths.

After breakfast Josiah came over, but Moses seemed so heavy and over wearied that they did not care to disturb him. There was a look of dejection and intense sadness on the thin worn face, and a hungry look in the mournful eyes, as if his soul had been starving for kindness and sympathy. Sometimes he would forget his situation, and speak hopefully of the future, but still there was a weariness that he could not shake off, a languor that seemed to pervade every nerve and muscle.

Thomas thought it was the natural reaction of the deep excitement, through which he just passed, that the tension of his nerves had been too great, but that a few days rest and quiet would restore him to his normal condition; but that hope soon died away.

The tension, excitement, and consequent exhaustion had been too much. Reason tottered on its throne, and he became a raving maniac; in his moments of delirium he would imagine that he was escaping from slavery; that the pursuers were upon his back; that they had caught him, and were rebinding him about to take him back to slavery, and then it was heartrending to hear him beg, and plead to be carried to Thomas Carpenter's.

He would reach out his emaciated hands, and say "Carry me to Mr. Carpenter's, that good man's house," for that name which had become more precious to him than a household to his soul, still lingered amid shattered cells. But the delirium spent its force, and through the tempests of his bosom the light of reason came back.

One night he slept more soundly than usual; and on the next morning his faithful friends saw from the expression of his countenance and the light in his eyes that his reason had returned. They sent for their family physician, a man in whose honor they could confide. All that careful nursing and medical skill could do was done, but it was in vain; his strength was wasted; the silver cord was loosed, and the golden bowl was broken; his life was fast ebbing away. Like a tempest tossed mariner dying in sight of land, so he passing away from earth, found the precious, longed for, and dearly bought prize was just before, but his hand was too feeble to grasp, his arms too powerless to hold it.

His friends saw from the expression of his face that he had something to say; and they bent down to catch the last words of the departing spirit.

"I am dying," he said, "but I am thankful that I have come this near to freedom."

He attempted to say no more, the death rattles sounded in his throat; the shadows that never deceive flitted o'er his face, and he was dead. His spirit gone back to God, another witness against the giant crime of the land.

Josiah came again to see him, and entered the room just as the released spirit winged its flight. Silently he uncovered him as if paying that reverence to the broken casket which death exacts for his meanest subjects. With tenderness and respect they prepared the body for the grave, followed him to the silent tomb, and left him to his dreamless sleep.

# IX

Friend Carpenter, I have brought a friend to see you. He is a real hot-headed Southerner, and I have been trying to convert him, but have been almost ready to give it up as a hopeless task. I thought as you are so much better posted than I am on the subject, *you* might be able to convert him from the error of his ways. He is a first-rate fellow, my College chum. He has only one fault, he will defend Slavery. Cure him of that, and I think he will be as near perfect as young men generally are."

Friend Carpenter smiled at this good-natured rally, and said, "It takes time for all things. Perhaps your friend is not so incorrigible as you think he is."

"I don't know," said Charley, "but here he is; he can speak for himself."

"Oh the system is well enough of itself, but like other things, it is liable to abuse."

"I think, my young friend," said Thomas, "thee has never examined the system by the rule of impartial justice, which tells us to do to all men as we would have them do to us. If thee had, thee would not talk of the abuses of Slavery, when the system is an abuse itself. I am afraid thee has never gauged the depth of its wickedness. Thy face looks too honest and frank to defend this system from conviction. Has thee ever examined it?"

"Why, no, I have always been used to it."

Louis, who liked the honest bluntness of the Quaker, would have willingly prolonged the conversation, simply for the sake of the argument, but just then Minnie entered, holding in her hand a bunch of flowers, and started to show them to her father, before she perceived that any company was in the room.

"Oh father," said she, "see what I have brought you!" when her eye fell upon the visitors, and a bright flush overspread her cheek, lending it additional beauty.

Charles immediately arose, and giving her his hand, introduced her to his friend.

"I am glad to see you, Minnie; you are looking so well this summer," said Charles, gazing on her with unfeigned admiration.

"I am glad you think so," said she, with charming frankness.

Some business having called friend Carpenter from the room, the young people had a pleasant time to themselves, talking of books, poetry, and the current literature of the day, although being students, their acquaintance with these things was somewhat limited. By the time they were ready to go, Thomas had re-entered the room and bidding them good-bye, cordially invited them to return again.

"What do you think of her?" said Charles to his friend.

"Beautiful as a dream. The half had not been told. Her *acquaintance* pays me for my trip; yes, I would like to become better acquainted with her; there was such a charming simplicity about her, and such unaffected grace that I am really delighted with her. How is it that you have never fallen in love with her?"

"Oh, I have left that for you; but in fact we have almost grown together, played with each other when we were children, until she appears like one of our family, and to marry her would be like marrying my own sister."

"How does thee like Charles' friend?" said Minnie, to her adopted father.

Thomas spoke slowly and deliberately, and said, "He impresses me rather favorably. I think there's the making of a man in him. But I hear that he is pro-slavery."

"Yes, he is, but I think that is simply the result of former associations and surroundings. I do not believe that he has looked deeper than the surface of Slavery; he is quite young yet; his reflective faculties are hardly fully awakened. I believe the time will come, when he will see it in its true light, and if he joins our ranks he will be an important accession to our cause. I have great hopes of him. He seems to be generous, kind-hearted, and full of good impulses, and I believe there are grand possibilities in his nature. How do you like him?"

"Oh, I was much pleased with him. We had a very pleasant time together."

In a few days, Charles and Louis called again. Minnie was crocheting, and her adopted mother was occupied with sewing; while Thomas engaged them in conversation, the subject being the impending conflict; Louis, taking a decided stand in favor of the South, and Thomas being equally strong in his defense of the North.

The conversation was very animated, but temperate; and when they parted, each felt confident of the rightfulness of his position.

"Come, again," said Thomas, as they were leaving; "we can't see eye to eye, but I like to have thee come."

Louis was very much pleased with the invitation, for it gave him opportunity to see Minnie, and sometimes she would smile, or say a word or two when the discussion was beginning to verge on the borders of excitement.

The time to return to College was drawing near, and Louis longed to tell her how dear she was to him, but he never met her alone. She was so young he did not like to ask the privilege of writing to her; and yet he felt when he left the village, that it would afford him great satisfaction to hear from her. He once hinted to Friend Carpenter that he would like to hear from his family, and that if he was too busy perhaps Miss Minnie might find time to drop a line, but Thomas did not take the hint, so the matter ended; he hoping in the meantime to meet her again, and renew their very pleasant acquaintance.

# X

(Text missing.)

# XI

I s Minnie not well?" said Thomas Carpenter, entering one morning, the pleasant room, where Anna was labelling some preserves. "She seems to be so drooping, and scarcely eats anything."

"I don't know. I have not heard her complain; perhaps she is a little tired and jaded from her journey; and then I think she studies too much. She spends most of her time in her room, and since I think of it, she does appear more quiet than usual; but I have been so busy about my preserves that I have not noticed her particularly."

"Anna," said Thomas suddenly, after a moment's pause, "does thee think that there is any attachment between Louis and Minnie? He was very attentive to her when we were in Boston."

"Why, Thomas, I have never thought anything about it. Minnie always seems so much like a child that I never get her associated in my mind with courtship and marriage. I suppose I ought to though," said Anna, with the faintest sigh.

"Anna, I think that something is preying on that child's mind, and mother, thee knows that you women understand how to manage these things better than we men do, and I wish thee would find out what is the matter with the child. Try to find out if there is anything between her and Louis, and if there is, by all means we must let her know about herself; it is a duty we owe her and him."

"Well, Thomas, if we must we must; but I shrink from it. Here she comes. Now I'll leave in a few minutes, and then thee can tell her; perhaps thee can do it better than I can."

"What makes thee look so serious?" said Thomas, as Minnie entered the room.

"Do I, father?"

"Yes, thee looks sober as a Judge. What has happened to disturb thee?"

"Nothing in particular; only I was down to Mr. Hickman's this morning, and they have a colored woman stopping with them. She is a very interesting and intelligent woman, and she was telling us part of her history, and it was very interesting, but, mother, I do think it is a dreadful thing to be a colored person in this country; how I should suffer if I knew that I was hated and despised for what I couldn't help. Oh, it must be dreadful to be colored."

FRANCES ELLEN WATKINS HARPER

"Oh, don't talk so, Minnie, God never makes any mistakes."

"I know that, mother; but, mother, it must be hard to be forced to ride in smoking cars; to be insulted in the different thoroughfares of travel; to be denied access to public resorts in some places,—such as lectures, theatres, concerts, and even have a particular seat assigned in the churches, and sometimes feel you were an object of pity even to your best friends. I know that Mrs. Heston felt so when she was telling her story, for when Mrs. Hickman said, 'Well, Sarah, I really pity you,' I saw her dark eyes flash, and she has really beautiful eyes, as she said, 'it is not pity we want, it is justice.'"

"In the first place, mother, she is a widow, with five children. She had six. One died in the army,—and she had some business in Washington connected with him. She says she was born in Virginia, and had one little girl there, but as she could not bear the idea of her child growing up in ignorance, she left the South and went to Albany. Her husband was a barber, and was doing a good business there. She was living in a very good neighborhood, and sent her child to the nearest district school.

"After her little girl had been there awhile, her teacher told her she must go home and not come there any more, and sent her mother a note; the child did not know what she had done; she had been attentive to her lessons, and had not behaved amiss, and she was puzzled to know why she was turned out of school.

"'Oh! I hated to tell Mrs. Heston,' said the teacher; 'but the child insisted, and I knew that it must come sooner or later. And so, said she, I told her it was because she was colored.'

"'Is that all.' Poor child, she didn't know, that, in that fact lay whole volumes of insult, outrage, and violence. I made up my mind, she continued, that I would leave the place, and when my husband came home, I said, 'Heston, let us leave this place; let us go farther west. I hear that we can have our child educated there, just the same as any other child.' At first my husband demurred, for we were doing a good business; but I said, let us go, if we have to live on potatoes and salt.

"True, it was some pecuniary loss; but I never regretted it, although I have been pretty near the potatoes and salt. My husband died, but I kept my children together, and stood over the wash-tub day after day to keep them at school. My oldest daughter graduated at the High School, and was quite a favorite with the teachers. One term there was a vacancy in her room, caused by the resignation of one of the assistant teachers, and the first teacher had the privilege of selecting her assistants from the graduates of the High School, their appointment, of course, being subject to the decision of the Commissioner of Public Schools.

"'Her teacher having heard that she was connected by blood with one of the first families of Virginia, told the Commissioner that she had chosen an Assistant, a young lady of high qualifications, and as she understood, a descendant of Patrick Henry.

"'Ah, indeed,' said the Commissioner, 'I didn't know that we had one of that family among us. By all means employ her;' but as she was about to leave, she said: 'I forgot to tell you one thing, she is colored.'

"A sudden change came over him, and he said: 'Do you think I would have you walk down the street with a colored woman? Of course not. I'll never give my consent to *that*.' And there the matter ended. And then she made us feel so indignant when she told us that on her way to Washington to get her son's pension, she stopped in Philadelphia, and the conductor tried to make her leave the car, and because she would not, he ran the car off the track."

"Oh, father," said she, turning to Thomas, "how wicked and cruel this prejudice. Oh, how I should hate to be colored!"

Anna and Thomas exchanged mournful glances. Their hearts were too full; and as Minnie left the room, Thomas said, "Not now, Anna. Not just yet." And so Minnie was permitted to return again to school with the secret untold.

"Minnie, darling, what are you doing? moping as usual over your books? Come, it is Saturday morning, and you have worked hard enough for one week; got all good marks; so now just put up that Virgil, and come go out with me."

"Where do you wish to go?" said Minnie, to her light-hearted friend, Carrie Wise.

"I want to go out shopping. Pa has just sent me twenty dollars, and you know a girl and her money are soon parted."

"What do you wish to get?"

"Well, I want a pair of gloves, some worsted to match this fringe, and a lot of things. Come, won't you go?"

"Oh, I don't know, I didn't intend going out this morning."

"Well, never mind if you didn't, just say you will go. Where's your hat and mantle?" said Carrie, going to her wardrobe.

"Well, just wait till I fix my hair; it won't take long."

"Oh, Minnie, do let me fix it for you! If ever I have to work for my living, I shall be a hair-dresser. I believe it is the only thing that I have any talent for."

"What an idea! But do, Minnie, won't you, let me arrange your hair? You always wear it so plain, and I do believe it would curl beautifully. May I, Minnie?"

"Why yes."

So Carrie sat down, and in a short time, she had beautifully arranged Minnie's hair with a profusion of curls.

"Do you know what I was thinking?" said Carrie, gazing admiringly upon her friend. "You look so much like a picture I have seen of yours in your father's album. He was showing me a number of pictures which represent you at different ages, and the one I refer to, he said was our Minnie when she was five years old. Now let me put on your hat. And let me kiss you for you look so pretty?"

"Oh, Carrie, what an idea! You are so full of nonsense. Which way will we go first?"

"First down to Carruther's. I saw a beautiful collar there I liked so much; and then let us go down to Mrs. Barguay's. I want to show you a love of a bonnet, one of the sweetest little things in ribbon, lace, and flowers I ever saw."

Equipped for the journey the two friends sauntered down the street; as they were coming out of a store, Carrie stopped for a moment to speak to a very dear friend of her mother's, and Minnie passed on.

As she went slowly on, loitering for her friend, she saw a woman approaching her from the opposite side of the street. There was something in her look and manner which arrested the attention of Minnie. She was a tall, slender woman about thirty five years old, with a pale, care-worn face—a face which told that sorrow had pressed her more than years. A few threads of silver mingled with the wealth of her raven hair, and her face, though wearing a sad and weary expression, still showed traces of great beauty.

As soon as her eyes fell on Minnie, she raised her hands in sudden wonder, and clasping her in her arms, exclaimed: "Heaven is merciful! I have found you, at last, my dear, darling, long-lost child. Minnie, is this you, and have I found you at last?"

Minnie trembled from head to foot; a deadly pallor overspread her cheek, and she stood still as if rooted to the ground in silent amazement, while the woman stood anxiously watching her as if her future were hanging on the decision of her lips.

"Who are you? and where did you come from?" said Minnie, as soon as she gained her breath.

"I came from Louisiana. Oh, I can't be mistaken. I have longed for you, and prayed for you, and now I have found you."

Just then, Carrie, who had finished speaking with her friend, seeing Minnie and the strange woman talking together, exclaimed, "What is the matter?"

Noticing the agitation of her friend, "Who is this woman, and what has she said to you?"

"She says that she is my mother, my long-lost mother."

"Why, Minnie, what nonsense! She can't be your mother. Why don't you see she is colored?"

"Where do you live?" said Minnie, without appearing to notice the words of Carrie.

"I don't live anywhere. I just came here yesterday with some of the Union soldiers."

"Come with me then, and I will show you a place to stop."

"Why, Minnie, you are not going to walk down the street with that Nig—colored woman; if you are, please excuse me. My business calls me another way."

And without any more ceremony Carrie and Minnie parted. Silently she walked by the side of the stranger, a thousand thoughts revolving in her mind. Was this the solution of the mystery which enshrouded her young life? Did she indeed belong to that doomed and hated race, and must she share the cruel treatment which bitter, relentless prejudice had assigned them?

Thomas Carpenter and Anna were stopping in P., at the house of relatives who knew Minnie's history, but who had never made any difference in their treatment of her on that account.

"Is father and mother at home?" said Minnie to the servant, who opened the door. She answered in the affirmative.

"Tell them to come into the parlor, they are wanted immediately."

"Sit down," said Minnie to the stranger, handing her a chair, "and wait till father comes."

Anna and Thomas soon entered the room, and Minnie approaching them said, "Father, this woman met me on the street today, and says she is my mother. You know all about my history. Tell me if there is any truth in this story."

"I don't know, Minnie, I never saw thy mother."

"But question her, father, and see if there is any truth in what she says; but tell me first, father, am I white or colored?"

"Minnie, I believe there is a small portion of colored blood in thy veins."

"It is enough," said Minnie, drawing closer to the strange woman. "What makes you think that I am your child?"

"By this," said she, taking a miniature from her bosom. "By this, which I carried next to my heart for more than twelve years, and never have been without it a single day or night."

Thomas looked upon the miniature; it was an exact likeness of Minnie when she first came to them, and although she had grown and changed since the likeness was taken, there was too close a resemblance between it and one which had been taken soon after she came, for him to doubt that Minnie was the original of that likeness.

Thomas questioned the woman very closely, but her history and narrative corresponded so well with what he had heard of Minnie's mother, that he could not for a moment doubt that this was she, and as such he was willing to give her the shelter of his home, till he could make other arrangements.

"But why," said Anna, somewhat grieved at the shock, that Minnie had received, "did thee startle her by so suddenly claiming her in the street? Would it not have been better for thee to have waited and found out where she lived, and then discovered thyself to her?"

"I'spect it would, 'Mam," said Ellen, very meekly and sorrowfully, "but when I saw her and heard the young lady say, Minnie, wait a minute, I forgot everything but that this was my long-lost child. I am sorry if I did any harm, but I was so glad I could not help it. My heart was so hungry for my child."

"Yes, yes," said Anna sadly, "I understand thee; it was the voice of nature."

Minnie was too nervous and excited to return to her school that day; the next morning she had a very high fever, and Thomas concluded it would be better to take her home and have her mother accompany her.

And so on Monday morning Anna and Thomas left P., taking Minnie and her mother along.

Once again in her pleasant home, surrounded by the tenderest care (for her mother watched over her with the utmost solicitude) the violence of her fever abated, but it was succeeded by a low nervous affection which while it produced no pain yet it slowly unstrung her vitality.

Ellen hovered around her pillow as if she begrudged every moment that called her from her daughter's side, and never seemed so well contented as when she was performing for her some office of love and tenderness. A skilful nurse, she knew how to prepare the most delicate viands to tempt the failing appetite, and she had the exquisite pleasure of seeing her care and attention rewarded by the returning health and strength of her child.

One morning as she grew stronger, and was able to sit in her chair, she turned her eyes tenderly towards Ellen and said, "Mother, come and sit near me and let me hold your hand."

"Mother," Oh how welcome was that word. Ellen's eyes filled with sudden tears.

"Mother," she said, "It comes back to me like a dream. I have a faint recollection of having seen you before, but it is so long I can scarcely remember it. Tell me all about myself and how I came to leave you. I always thought that there was some mystery about me, but I never knew what it was before, but now I understand it."

"Darling," said the mother, "you had better wait till you get a little stronger, and then I will tell you all."

"Very well," said Minnie, "you have been so good to me and I am beginning to love you so much."

It was touching to see the ripening love between those two long-suffering ones. Ellen would comb Minnie's hair, and do for her every office in her power. Still Minnie continued feeble. The suffering occasioned by her refusal of Louis; the hard study and deep excitement through which she had passed told sadly upon her constitution; but she was young, and having a large share of recuperative power she slowly came back to health and strength, and when the spring opened Thomas decided that she should return again to her school in P.

# XII

Let us now return to Carrie Wise, whom we left parting with Minnie.

"Where is Minnie?" said two of her schoolmates, who observed that Carrie had come home alone.

"Oh," said she, "one of the strangest things I ever heard of happened!"

"Well, what was it?" said the girls; and by this time they had joined another group of girls.

"Why this morning, Minnie and I walked out shopping, and just as I came out of Carruthers' I met an old friend of mother's, and stopped to speak with her, and I said 'Minnie, just wait a minute.'"

"She passed on, and left me talking with Mrs. Jackson. When I joined her, I found a colored woman talking to her, and she was trembling from head to foot, and just as pale as a ghost; and I said, 'Why, Minnie, what is the matter?'"

"She gasped for breath, and I thought she was going to faint, and I got real scared. And what do you think Minnie said?"

"Why," she said, "Carrie, this woman says she's my mother!"

"Her mother!" cried a half dozen voices. "Why you said she was colored!"

"Well, so she was. She was quite light, but I knew she was colored."

"How did you know? Maybe she was only a very dark-complexioned white woman."

"Oh no, she wasn't, I know white people from colored, I've seen enough of them."

"A colored woman! well that is very strange; but do tell us what Minnie said."

"She asked her where she came from, and where she lived. She said she came in yesterday with the Union soldiers, and that she had come from Louisiana, and then Minnie told her to come with her, and she would find a place for her to stop."

"And did she leave you in the street to walk with a Nigger?" said a coarse, rough-looking girl.

"Yes, and so I left her. I wasn't going to walk down the street with them!"

"Well, did I ever?" said a pale and interesting-looking girl.

"That is just as strange as a romance I have been reading!"

"Well, they say truth is stranger than fiction. A deceitful thing to try to pass for white when she is colored! If she comes back to this school I shan't stay!" said the coarse rough girl, twirling her gold pencil. "I ain't a going to sit alongside of niggers."

"How you talk! I don't see that if the woman is Minnie's mother, and *is* colored, it makes any difference in her. I am sure it does not to me," said one of Minnie's friends.

"Well, it does to me," said another; "you may put yourself on an equality with niggers, but I won't." "And I neither," chimed in another voice. "There are plenty of colored schools; let her go to them."

"Oh, girls, I think it real cruel the way you talk!"

"How would you like any one to treat you so?" "Can't help it, I ain't a coming to school with a nigger." "She is just as good as you are, Mary Patuck, and a great deal smarter." "I don't care, she's a nigger, and that's enough for me."

And so the sentiment of the school was divided. Some were in favor of treating her just as well as usual, and others felt like complaining to their parents that a Negro was in school.

At last the news reached the teacher, and he, poor, weak, and vacillating man, had not manhood enough to defend her, but acted according to the prejudices of society, and wrote Thomas a note telling him that circumstances made it desirable that she should not again come to school.

In the meantime the news had reached their quiet little village, and of course it offered food for gossip; it was discussed over tea-tables and in the sewing circle. Some concluded that Thomas should have brought her up among the colored people, and others that he did perfectly right.

Still there was a change in Minnie's social relations. Some were just as kind as ever. Others grew distant, and some avoided having anything to say to her, and stopped visiting the house. Anna and Thomas, although superior people, were human, and could not help feeling the difference, but some business of importance connected with the death of a relative called Thomas abroad, and he made up his mind that he would take Anna and Minnie with him, hoping that the voyage and change of scene would be beneficial to his little girl, as he still called Minnie, and so on a bright and beautiful morning in the spring of '62 he left the country for a journey to England and the Continent.

Let us now return to Louis Le Croix, whom we left disappointed and wounded by Minnie's refusal. After he left her he entered his room, and sat for a long time in silent thought; at last he rose, and walked to the window and stood with his hands clenched, and his finely chiseled lips firmly set as if he had bound his whole soul to some great resolve—a resolve which he would accomplish, let it cost what it might.

And so he had; for he had made up in his mind within the last two hours that he would join the Confederacy. "That live or die, sink or swim, survive or perish," he would unite his fortunes to her destiny.

His next step then was to plan how he could reach Louisiana; he felt confident that if he could get as far as Louisville he could manage to get into Tennessee, and from thence to Louisiana.

And so nothing daunted by difficulties and dangers, he set out on his journey, and being aided by rebels on his way in a few weeks he reached the old plantation on Red River; he found his sister and Miriam there both glad to see him.

Camilla's husband was in Charleston, some of the slaves had deserted to the Union ranks, but the greater portion she still retained with her.

Miriam was delighted to see Louis, and seemed never weary of admiring his handsome face and manly form. And Louis, who had never known any other mother seemed really gratified by her little kindnesses and attention; but of course the pleasant and quiet monotony of home did not suit the restless and disquieted spirit of Louis. All the young men around here were in the army or deeply interested in its success.

There was a call for more volunteers, and a new company was to be raised in that locality. Louis immediately joined, and turned his trained intellect to the study of military tactics; day and night he was absorbed in this occupation, and soon, although Minnie was not forgotten, the enthusiasm of his young life gathered around the Confederate cause.

He did not give himself much time to reflect. Thought was painful to him, and he continued to live in a whirl of excitement.

News of battle, tidings of victory and defeats, the situation of the armies, and the hopes and fears that clustered around those fearful days of struggle made the staple of conversation.

Louis rapidly rose in favor with the young volunteers, and was chosen captain of a company who were permitted to drill and stay from the front as a reserve corps, ready to be summoned at any moment.

# XIII

Miriam and Camilla watched with anguish Louis' devotion to the Confederation, and many sorrowful conversations they had about it.

At last one day Miriam said, "Miss Camilla, I can stand it no longer;—that boy is going to lift his hand agin his own people, and I can't stand it no longer; I'se got to tell him all about it. I just think I'd bust in two if I didn't tell him."

"Well, Mammy," said Camilla, "I'd rather he should know it than that he should go against his country and raise his hand against the dear old flag."

"It's not the flag nor the country I care for," said Miriam, "but it is that one of my own flesh and blood should jine with these secesh agin his own people."

"Well, Miriam, if you get a chance you can tell him."

"Get a chance, Miss Camilla, I'se bound to get that."

Louis was somewhat reticent about his plans; for he knew that Camilla was a strong Union woman; that she not only loved the flag, but she had taught her two boys to do the same; but he understood from headquarters that his company was to march in a week, and although on that subject there was no common sympathy between them, yet he felt that he must acquaint her with his plans, and bid her and Miriam good-bye.

So one morning he came in looking somewhat flushed and excited, and said: "Sister, we have got our marching orders; we leave on Thursday, and I have only three days to be with you. I am sorry that I have seen so little of you, but my country calls me, and when she is in danger it is no time for me to seek for either ease or pleasure."

"Your country! Louis," said Miriam, her face paling and flushing by turns. "Where is your country?"

"Here," said he, somewhat angrily, "in Louisiana."

"My country," said Camilla, "is the whole Union. Yes, Louis," said she, "your country is in danger, but not from the Abolitionists in the North, but from the rebels and traitors in the South."

"Rebels and traitors!" said Louis, in a tone like one who felt the harsh grating of the words.

"Whom do you mean?"

FRANCES ELLEN WATKINS HARPER

"I mean," said she, "the ambitious, reckless men who have brought about this state of things. The men who are stabbing their country in their madness and folly; who are crowding our graves and darkening our homes; who are dragging our young men, men like you, who should be the pride and hope of our country, into the jaws of ruin and death."

Louis looked surprised and angry; he had never seen Camilla under such deep excitement. Her words had touched his pride and roused his anger; but suppressing his feelings he answered her coolly, "Camilla, I am old enough to do my own thinking. We had better drop this subject; it is not pleasant to either of us."

"Louis," said she, her whole manner changing from deep excitement to profound grief, "Oh, Louis, it will never do for you to go! Oh, no, you must not!"

"And why not?"

"Because,"—and she hesitated. Just then Miriam took up the unfinished sentence,"—because to join the secesh is to raise your hands agin your own race."

"My own race?" and Louis laughed scornfully. "I think you are talking more wildly than Camilla. What do you mean, Miriam?"

"I mean," said she, stung by his scornful words, "I mean that you, Louis Le Croix, white as you look, are colored, and that you are my own daughter's child, and if it had not been for Miss Camilla, who's been such an angel to you, that you would have been a slave today, and then you wouldn't have been a Confederate."

At these words a look of horror and anguish passed over the face of Le Croix, and he turned to Camilla, but she was deadly pale, and trembling like an aspen leaf; but her eyes were dry and tearless.

"Camilla," said he, turning fiercely to his adopted sister, "Tell me, is there any truth in these words? You are as pale as death, and trembling like a leaf,—tell me if there is any truth in these words," turning and fixing his eyes on Miriam, who stood like some ancient prophetess, her lips pronouncing some fearful doom, while she watched in breathless anguish the effect upon the fated victim.

"Yes, Louis," said Camilla, in a voice almost choked by emotion. "Yes, Louis, it is all true."

"But how is this that I never heard it before? Before I believe this tale I must have some proof, clear as daylight. Bring me proofs."

"Here they are," said Miriam, drawing from her pocket the free papers she had been carrying about her person for several days.

Louis grasped them nervously, hastily read them, and then more slowly, like one who might read a sentence of death to see if there was one word or sentence on which he might hang a hope of reprieve.

Camilla watched him anxiously, but silently, and when he had finished, he covered his bowed face with his hands as he said with a deep groan, "It is true, too true. I see it all. I can never raise my hand against my mother's race."

He arose like one in a dream, walked slowly to the door and left the room.

"It was a painful task," said Camilla, with a sigh of relief, as if a burden had fallen from her soul.

"Yes," said Miriam, "but not so bad as to see him fighting agin his own color. I'd rather follow him to his grave than see him join that miserable secesh crew."

"Yes," said Camilla, "It was better than letting him go."

When Louis left the room a thousand conflicting thoughts passed through his mind. He felt as a mariner at midnight on a moonless sea, who suddenly, when the storm is brewing, finds that he has lost his compass and his chart.

# XIV

Where was he steering; and now, the course of his life was changed, what kind of future must he make for himself?

Had it been in time of peace, he could have easily decided, as he had a large amount of money in the North, which his father left him when he came of age.

He would have no difficulty as to choosing the means of living; for he was well supplied, as far as that was concerned; but here was a most unpleasant dilemma in which he had placed himself.

Convinced that he was allied to the Negro race, his whole soul rose up against the idea of laying one straw in its way; if he belonged to the race he would not join its oppressors. And yet his whole sympathy had been so completely with them, that he felt that he had no feeling in common with the North.

And as to the colored people, of course it never entered his mind to join their ranks, and ally himself to them; he had always regarded them as inferior; and this sudden and unwelcome revelation had not changed the whole tenor of his thoughts and opinions.

But what he had to do must be done quickly; for in less than three days his company would start for the front. To desert was to face death; to remain was to wed dishonor. He surveyed the situation calmly and bravely, and then resolved that he would face the perils of re-capture rather than the contempt of his own soul.

While he was deciding, he heard Camilla's step in the passage; he opened the door, and beckoned her to a seat, and said, very calmly, "I have been weighing the whole matter in my mind, and I have concluded to leave the South."

"How can you do it?" said Camilla. "I tremble lest you should be discovered. Oh slavery! what a curse. Our fathers sowed the wind, and we are reaping the whirlwind! What," continued she, as if speaking to herself, "What are your plans? Have you any?"

"None, except to disguise myself and escape."

"When?"

"As soon as possible."

"Suppose I call Miriam. She can help you. Shall I?"

"Yes."

Camilla called Miriam, and after a few moments consultation it was decided that Louis should escape that night, and that Miriam should prepare whatever was needed for his hasty flight.

"Don't trust your secret to any white person," said Miriam, "but if you meet any of the colored people, just tell them that you is for the Linkum soldiers, and it will be all right; we don't know all about this war, but we feels somehow we's all mixed up in it."

And so with many prayers and blessings from Miriam, and sad farewells from Camilla, he left his home to enter upon that perilous flight, the whole current of his life changed.

It was in the early part of Winter; but the air was just as pleasant as early Spring in that climate. Louis walked all that night, guiding himself northward at night by the light of the stars and a little pocket compass, Camilla had just given him before starting, and avoiding the public roads during the day.

And thus he travelled for two days, when his lunch was exhausted, his lips parched with thirst, and his strength began to fail.

Just in this hour of extremity he saw seated by the corner of a fence a very black and homely-looking woman; there was something so gloomy and sullen in her countenance that he felt repelled by its morose expression. Still he needed food, and was very weary, and drawing near he asked her if she would give him anything to eat.

"Ain't got nothing. De sojers done been here, and eat all up."

Louis drew near and whispered a few words in her ear, and immediately a change passed over her whole countenance. The sullen expression turned to a look of tenderness and concern. The harsh tones of her voice actually grew mellow, and rising up in haste she almost sprang over the fence, and said, "I'se been looking for you, if you's Northman you's mighty welcome," and she set before him her humble store of provisions.

"Do you know," said Louis, "where I will find the Lincoln soldiers, or where the secesh are encamped?"

"No," said she "but my old man's mighty smart, and he'll find out; you come wid me."

Nothing doubting he went, and found the husband ready to do anything in his power to help him.

"You's better not go any furder today. I'll get you a place to hide where nobody can't find you, and then I'll pump Massa 'bout the sojers."

FRANCES ELLEN WATKINS HARPER

True to his word, he contrived to find out whether the soldiers were near.

"Massa," said he, scratching his head, and looking quite sober, "Massa, hadn't I better hide the mules? Oh I's 'fraid the Linkum sojers will come take 'em, cause dey gobbles up ebery ting dey lays dere hans on, jis like geese. I yerd dey was coming; mus' I hide de mules?"

"No, Sam, the scalawags are more than a hundred miles away; they are near Natchez."

"Well, maybe, t'was our own Fedrate soldiers."

"No, Sam, our nearest soldiers are at Baton Rouge."

"All right Massa. I don't want to lose all dem fine mules."

As soon as it was convenient Sam gave Louis the desired information. "Here," said Sam, when Louis was ready to start again, "is something to break your fast, and if you goes dis way you musn't let de white folks know what you's up to, but you trust dis," said he, laying his hand on his own dark skin.

His new friend went with him several miles, and pointing him out the way left him to pursue his journey onward. The next person he met with was a colored man, who bowed and smiled, and took off his hat.

Louis returned the bow, and was passing on when he said, "Massa, 'scuse me for speakin' to you, but dem secesh been hunting all day for a 'serter, him captin dey say."

Louis turned pale, but bracing his nerves he said, "Where are they?"

"Dey's in the house; is you he?"

"I am a Union man," Louis said, "and am trying to reach the Lincoln soldiers."

"Den," said the man, "if dat am de fac I's got a place for you; come with me," and Louis having learned to trust the colored people followed him to a place of safety.

Soon it was noised abroad that another deserter had been seen in that neighborhood, but the colored man would not reveal the whereabouts of Louis. His master beat him severely, but he would let neither threats nor torture wring the secret from his lips.

Louis saw the faithfulness of that man, and he thought with shame of his former position to the race from whom such unswerving devotion could spring. The hunt proving ineffectual, Louis after the search and excitement had subsided resumed his journey Northward, meeting with first one act of kindness and then another.

One day he had a narrow escape from the bloodhounds. He had trusted his secret to a colored man who, faithful like the rest, was directing him on his way when deep ominous sounds fell on their ears. The colored man knew that sound too well; he knew something of the nature of bloodhounds, and how to throw them off the track.

So hastily opening his pen-knife he cut his own feet so that the blood from them might deepen the scent on one track, and throw them off from Louis's path.

It was a brave deed, and nobly done, and Louis began to feel that he had never known them, and then how vividly came into his mind the words of Dr. Charming: "After all we may be trampling on one of the best branches of the human race." Here were men and women too who had been trampled on for ages ready to break to him their bread, aye share with him their scanty store.

One had taken the shoes from his feet and almost forced him to take them. What was it impelled these people? What was the Union to them, and who were Lincoln's soldiers that they should be so ready to gravitate to the Union army and bring the most reliable information to the American General?

Was it not the hope of freedom which they were binding as amulets around their hearts? They as a race had lived in a measure upon an idea; it was the hope of a deliverance yet to come. Faith in God had underlain the life of the race, and was it strange if when even some of our politicians did not or could not read the signs of the times aright these people with deeper intuitions understood the war better than they did.

But at last Louis got beyond the borders of the confederacy, and stood once more on free soil, appreciating that section as he had never done before.

# XV

(Text missing.)

A nd I," said Minnie, "will help you pay it."

And so their young hearts had met at last, and with the approval and hearty consent of Anna, Minnie and Louis were married.

It was decided that Minnie should spend the winter in Southern France, and then in the spring they returned to America. On their arrival they found the war still raging, and Louis was ready and anxious to benefit that race to whom he felt he owed his life, and with whom he was connected by lineage.

He had plenty of money, a liberal education, and could have chosen a life of ease, but he was too ardent in his temperament, too decided in his character, not to feel an interest in the great events which were then transpiring in the country.

He made the acquaintance of some Anti-Slavery friends, and listened with avidity to their doctrines; he attended a number of war meetings, and caught the enthusiasm which inspired the young men who were coming from valley, hill, and plain to fill up the broken ranks of the Union army.

Minnie, educated in peace principles, could not conscientiously encourage him, and yet when she saw how the liberty of a whole race was trembling in the balance she could not help wishing (success?) to the army, nor find it in her heart to dissuade him from going.

Others had given their loved and cherished ones to camp and field. The son of a dear friend had said to his mother, "I know I shall be killed, but I go to free the slave." His presentiment had been met, for he had been brought home in his shroud.

Another dear friend had said, "I have drawn my sword, and it shall never sleep in its scabbard till the nation is free!" And she had heard that summer of '64 how bravely the colored soldiers had stood at Fort Wagner, when the storms of death were sweeping through the darkened sky. How they summoned the world to see the grandeur of their courage and the daring of their prowess.

How Corny had held with unyielding hand the nation's flag, and even when he was wounded still held it in his grasp, and crawling from the scene of action exclaimed, "I only did my duty, the old flag, I didn't let it trail on the ground."

And she felt on reading it with tearful eyes, that if she belonged to that race they had not shamed her by their want of courage; and so when Louis came to her and told her his intention, she would not attempt to oppose him, and when he was ready to depart, with many prayers, and sad farewells, she gave him up to fight the battles of freedom, for such it was to him, who went with every nerve in his right arm tingling to strike a blow for liberty.

Hitherto Louis had known the race by their tenderness and compassion, but the war gave him an opportunity to become acquainted with men brave to do, brave to dare, and brave to die.

A colored man was the hero of one of the most tender, touching, and tragic incidents of the war. A number of soldiers were in a boat exposed to the fire of the rebels; on board was a colored man who had not enrolled as a soldier, though his soul was full of sublime valor. The bullets hissed and split the water, and the rowers tried to get out of their reach, but all their efforts were in vain; the treacherous mud had caught the boat, and some one must peril life and limb to shove that boat into the water. And this man, the member of a doomed, a fated race, who had been trodden down for ages, comprehending the danger, said, "Some one must die to get us out of this, and it mout's well be me as anybody; you are soldiers, and you can fight. If they kill me it is nothing."

And with these words he arose, gave the boat a push, received a number of bullets, and died within two days after.

Louis acquitted himself bravely, and rapidly rose in favor with his superior officers. To him the place of danger was the post of duty. He often received letters from Minnie, but they were always hopeful; for she had learned to look on the bright side of everything.

She tried to beguile him with the news of the neighborhood, and to inspire him with bright hopes for the future; that future in which they should clasp hands again and find their duty and their pleasure in living for the welfare and happiness of *our* race, as Minnie would often say.

A race upon whose brows God had poured the chrism of a new era—a race newly anointed with freedom.

Oh, how the enthusiasm of her young soul gathered around that work! She felt it was no mean nor common privilege to be the pioneer of a new civilization. If he who makes two blades of grass grow where only one flourished before is a benefactor of the human race, how much higher and holier must his or her work be who dispenses light, instead of darkness, knowledge, instead of ignorance, and over the ruins of the slave-pen and auction-block erects institutions of learning.

She would say in her letters to Louis that the South will never be rightly conquered until another army should take the field, and that must be an army of civilizers; the army of the pen, and not the sword. Not the destroyers of towns and cities, but the builders of machines and factories; the organizers of peaceful industry and honorable labor; and as soon as she possibly could she intended to join that great army.

Sometimes Louis would shake his head doubtfully, and tell her that the South was a very sad place to live in, and would be for years, and, while he was willing to bear toil and privation in the cause he had learned to love, yet he shrank from exposing her to the social ostracism which she must bear whether she identified herself with the colored race or not.

However, her brave young heart never failed her, but kept true to its purpose to join that noble band who left the sunshine of their homes to help build up a new South on the basis of a higher and better civilization.

Louis remained with the army till Lee had surrendered. The storm-cloud of battle had passed away, and the thunders of contending batteries no longer crashed and vibrated on the air.

And then he returned to Minnie, who still lived with Thomas Carpenter. Very tender and joyous was their greeting. Louis thought he would rest awhile and then arrange his affairs to return to the South. In this plan he was heartily seconded by Minnie.

Thomas and Anna were sorry to part with her, but they knew that life was not made for a holiday of ease and luxury, and so they had no words of discouragement for them. If duty called them to the South it was right that they should go; and so they would not throw themselves across the purpose of their souls.

# XVII

Before he located, Louis concluded to visit the old homestead, and to present his beautiful young bride to his grandmother and Camilla.

He knew his adopted sister too well to fear that Minnie would fail to receive from her the warmest welcome, and so with eager heart he took passage on one of the Mississippi boats to New Orleans, intending to stop in the city a few days, and send word to Camilla; but just as he was passing from the levee to the hotel, he caught a glimpse of Camilla walking down the street, and stopping the carriage, he alighted, and spoke to her. She immediately recognized him, although his handsome face had become somewhat bronzed by exposure in camp and field.

"Do not go to the hotel," she said, "you are heartily welcome, come home with me."

"But my wife is along."

"Never mind, she's just as welcome as you are."

"But, like myself, she is colored."

"It does not matter. I should not think of your going to a hotel, while I have a home in the city."

Camilla following, wondering how she would like the young wife. She had great kindness and compassion for the race, but as far as social equality was concerned, though she had her strong personal likings, yet, except with Louis, neither custom nor education had reconciled her to the maintenance of any equal, social relations with them.

"My wife," said Louis, introducing Camilla to Minnie. Camilla immediately reached out her hand to the young wife, and gave her a cordial greeting, and they soon fell into a pleasant and animated conversation. Mutually they were attracted to each other, and when they reached their destination, Minnie had begun to feel quite at home with Camilla.

"How is Aunt Miriam, or rather, my grandmother?" said Louis.

"She is well, and often wonders what has become of her poor boy; but she always has persisted in believing that she would see you again, and I know her dear old eyes will run over with gladness. But things have changed very much since we parted. We have passed through the fire since I saw you, and our troubles are not over yet; but we are hoping for better days. But we are at home. Let us alight."

And Louis and Minnie were ushered into a home whose quiet and refined beauty were very pleasant to the eye, for Camilla had inherited from her father his aesthetic tastes; had made her home and its surroundings models of loveliness. Half a dozen varieties of the sweetest and brightest roses clambered up the walls and arrayed them with a garb of rare beauty. Jessamines breathed their fragrance on the air; magnolias reared their stately heads and gladdened the eye with the exquisite beauty of their flowers.

"This is an unexpected pleasure," said Camilla, removing Minnie's bonnet, and gazing with unfeigned admiration upon her girlish face, "but really some one must enjoy this pleasure besides myself."

Camilla rang the bell; a bright, smiling girl of about ten years appeared. "Tell Miriam," she said, "to come; that her boy Louis is here."

Miriam appeared immediately, and throwing her arms around his neck, gave vent to her feelings in a burst of joy. "I always said you'd come back. I's prayed for you night and day, and I always believed I'd see you afore I died, and now my word's come true. There's nothing like having faith."

"Here's my wife," said Louis, turning to Minnie.

"Your wife; is you married, honey? Well I hopes you'll have a good time."

Minnie came forward and gave her hand to Miriam, as Louis said, "This is my grandmother."

A look of proud satisfaction passed over the old woman's face, and a sudden joy lit up her eyes at these words of pleasant recognition.

"Ah, my child," said Miriam, "We's had a mighty heap of trouble since you left. Them miserable secesh searched the house all over for you, when you was gone, and they was mighty sassy; but we didn't mind that, so they didn't ketch you. How did you get along? We was dreadfully uneasy about you?"

Louis then told them of the kindness of the colored people, his thrilling adventures, and hair-breadth escapes, and unfolded to them his plans for the future.

Camilla listened with deep interest, and turning to Minnie, who had left the peaceful sunshine of her mother's home to dwell in the midst of that rough and rude state of society, she said, "I cannot help feeling sad to see you exposing yourself to the dangers that lay around your path. The few Southern women who have been faithful to the flag have had a sad experience since the war. We have been ostracized and abused, and often our husbands have been brutally murdered, in a number of instances when they were faithful to the dear old flag. A friend of mine, who was an angel of mercy to the Union prisoners, dressing their wounds and carrying them relief, had a dear son, who always kept a Union flag at home, which he regarded with almost religious devotion. This made him a marked boy in the community, and during the war he was so cruelly beaten, by some young rebels, that he never recovered, and colored women who would wend their way under the darkness and cover of night to aid our suffering soldiers, were in danger of being flogged, if detected, and I understand that one did receive 75 lashes for such an offence, and I heard of another who was shot down like a dog, for giving bread to a prisoner, who said, 'Mammy, I am starving.' I think, (but I have no right to dictate to you) had I been you, and my home in the North, that I would have preferred staying there, where, to say the least, you could have had pleasanter social relations. You and Louis are nearer the white race than the colored. Why should you prefer the one to the other?"

"Because," said Minnie, "the prejudices of society are so strong against the people with whom I am connected on my mother's side, that I could not associate with white people on equal terms, without concealing my origin, and that I scorned to do. The first years of my life passed without my knowing that I was connected with the colored race; but when it was revealed to me by mother, who suddenly claimed me, at first I shrank from the social ostracism to which that knowledge doomed me, and it was some time before I was reconciled to the change. Oh, there are lessons of life that we never learn in the bowers of ease. They must be learned in the fire. For months life seemed to me a dull, sad thing, and for a while I did not care whether I lived or died, the sunshine had suddenly faded from my path, and the future looked so dark and cheerless. But now, when I look back upon those days of gloom and suffering, I think they were among the most fruitful of my life, for in those days of pain and sorrow my resolution was formed to join the fortunes of my mother's race, and I resolved to brighten her old age with a joy, with a gladness she had never known in her youth. And how could I have done that had I left her unrecognized and palmed myself upon society as a white woman? And to tell you the truth, having passed most of my life in white society, I did not feel that the advantages of that society would have ever paid me for the loss of my self-respect, by passing as white, when I knew that I was colored;

when I knew that any society, however cultivated, wealthy or refined, would not be a social gain to me, if my color and not my character must be my passport of admission. So, when I found out that I was colored, I made up my mind that I would neither be pitied nor patronized by my former friends; but that I would live out my own individuality and do for my race, as a colored woman, what I never could accomplish as a white woman."

"I think I understand you," said Camilla; "and although I tremble for you in the present state, yet you cannot do better than live out the earnest purpose of your life. I feel that we owe a great debt to the colored race, and I would aid and not hinder any hand that is ready to help do the needed work. I have felt for many years that slavery was wrong, and I am glad, from the bottom of my heart, that it has at last been destroyed. And what are your plans, Louis?"

"We are going to open a school, and devote our lives to the upbuilding of the future race. I intend entering into some plan to facilitate the freedmen in obtaining homes of their own. I want to see this newly enfranchised race adding its quota to the civilization of the land. I believe there is power and capacity, only let it have room for exercise and development. We demand no social equality, no supremacy of power. All we ask is that the American people will take their Christless, Godless prejudices out of the way, and give us a chance to grow, an opportunity to accept life, not merely as a matter of ease and indulgence, but of struggle, conquest, and achievement."

"Yes," said Camilla, "what you want and what the nation should be just enough to grant you is fair play."

"Yes, that is what we want; to be known by our character, and not by our color; to be permitted to take whatever position in society we are fitted to fill. We do not want to be bolstered and propped up on the one hand, nor to be crushed and trampled down on the other."

"Well, Louis, I think that we are coming to that. No, I cannot feel that all this baptism of fire and blood through which we have passed has been in vain. Slavery, as an institution, has been destroyed. Slavery, as an idea, still lives, but I believe that we shall outgrow this spirit of caste and proscription which still tarnishes our civilization, both North and South."

# XVIII

After spending a few weeks with Camilla, Louis resolved to settle in the town of L——n, and as soon as he had chosen his home and made arrangements for the future, he sent for Ellen, and in a few days she joined her dear children, as she called Louis and Minnie. Very pleasant were the relations between Minnie and the newly freed people.

She had found her work, and they had found their friend. She did not content herself with teaching them mere knowledge of books. She felt that if the race would grow in the right direction, it must plant the roots of progress under the hearthstone. She had learned from Anna those womanly arts that give beauty, strength and grace to the fireside, and it was her earnest desire to teach them how to make their homes bright and happy.

Louis, too, with his practical turn of mind, used his influence in teaching them to be saving and industrious, and to turn their attention towards becoming land owners. He attended their political meetings, not to array class against class, nor to inflame the passions of either side. He wanted the vote of the colored people not to express the old hates and animosities of the plantation, but the new community of interests arising from freedom.

For awhile the aspect of things looked hopeful. The Reconstruction Act, by placing the vote in the hands of the colored man, had given him a new position. There was a lull in Southern violence. It was a great change from the fetters on his wrist to the ballot in his right hand, and the uniform testimony of the colored people was, "We are treated better than we were before."

Some of the rebels indulged in the hope that their former slaves would vote for them, but they were learning the power of combination, and having no political past, they were radical by position, and when Southern State after State rolled up its majorities on the radical side, then the vials of wrath were poured upon the heads of the colored people, and the courage and heroism which might have gained them recognition, perhaps, among heathens, made them more obnoxious here.

Still Louis and Minnie kept on their labors of love; their inner lives daily growing stronger and broader, for they learned to lean upon a strength greater than their own; and some of the most beautiful lessons of faith and trust they had ever learned, they were taught in the lowly cabins of these newly freed people.

Often would Minnie enter these humble homes and listen patiently to the old story of wrong and suffering. Sympathizing with their lot, she would give them counsel and help when needed. When she was leaving they would look after her wistfully, and say,

"She mighty good; we's low down, but she feels for we."

And thus day after day of that earnest life was spent in deeds and words of love and kindness.

But let us enter their pleasant home. Louis has just returned from a journey to the city, and has brought with him the latest Northern papers. He is looking rather sober, and Minnie, ready to detect the least change of his countenance, is at his side.

"What is the matter?" Minnie asked, in a tone of deep concern.

"I am really discouraged."

"What about?"

"Look here," said he, handing her the *New York Tribune*. "State after State has rolled up a majority against negro suffrage. I have been trying to persuade our people to vote the Republican ticket, but today, I feel like blushing for the party. They are weakening our hands and strengthening those of the rebels."

"But, Louis, they were not Republicans who gave these majorities against us."

"But, darling, if large numbers of these Republicans stayed at home, and let the election go by default, the result was just the same. Now every rebel can throw it in our teeth and say, 'See your great Republican party; they refuse to let the negro vote with them, but they force him upon us. They don't do it out of regard to the negro, but only to spite us.' I don't think, Minnie, that I am much given to gloomy forebodings, but I see from the temper and actions of these rebels, that they are encouraged and emboldened by these tidings from the North, and today they are turning people out of work for voting the radical ticket. A while ago they tried flattery and cajolery. You could hear it on almost every side—'We are the best friends of the colored people.' Appeals were made to the memories of the past; how they hunted and played together, and searched for birds' nests in the rotten peach trees, and when the colored people were not to be caught by such chaff, some were trying to force them into submission by intimidation and starvation."

Just then a knock was heard at the door, and a dark man entered.

FRANCES ELLEN WATKINS HARPER

There was nothing in his appearance that showed any connection with the white race. There was a tone of hopefulness in his speech, though his face wore a somewhat anxious expression.

"Good morning, Mr. Jackson," said Louis, for, in deference to their feelings he had dropped the "aunt" and "uncle" of bygone days.

"Good morning," replied the man, while a pleasant smile flitted over his countenance.

"How does the world use you?" said Louis.

"Well, times are rather bilious with me, but I am beginning to pick up a little. I get a few boots and shoes to mend. I always used to go to the mountains, and get plenty of work to do; but this year they wouldn't give me the situation because I had joined the radicals."

"What a shame," said Louis; "these men who have always had their rights of citizenship, seem to know so little of the claims of justice and humanity, that they are ready to brow-beat and intimidate these people for voting according to their best interests. And what saddens me most is to see so many people of the North clasping hands with these rebels and traitors, and to hear it repeated that these people are too ignorant to vote."

"Ignorant as they are," said Minnie, "during the war they knew more than their masters; for they knew how to be true to their country, when their masters were false to it, and rallied around the flag, when they were trampling it under foot, and riddling it with bullets."

"Ah!" said uncle Richard, "I knows them of old. Last week some of them offered me $500 if I would desert my party; but I wasn't going to forsake my people. I have been in purty tight places this year. One night when I come home my little girl said to me, 'Daddy, dere ain't no bread in de house.' Now, that jist got me, but I begun to pray, and the next day I found a quarter of a dollar, and then some of my colored friends said it wouldn't do to let uncle Jack starve, and they made me up seventy-five cents. My wife sometimes gets out of heart, but she don't see very far off."

"I wish," said Louis, after Mr. Jackson had left, "that some of our Northern men would only see the heroism of that simple-minded man. Here he stands facing an uncertain future, no longer young in years, stripped by slavery, his wife not in full sympathy with him, and yet with what courage he refused the bribe."

"Yes," said Minnie, "$500 means a great deal for a man landless and poor, with no assured support for the future. It means a comfortable fire when the blasts of winter are roving around your home; it means bread for the little ones, and medicine for the sick child, and little start in life."

"But on the other hand," said Louis, "it meant betrayal of the interests of his race, and I honor the faithfulness which shook his hands from receiving the bribe and clasping hands politically with his life-long oppressors. And I asked myself the question while he was telling his story, which hand was the better custodian of the ballot, the white hand that offered the bribe or the black one that refused it. I think the time will come when some of the Anglo Saxon race will blush to remember that when they were trailing the banner of freedom in the dust black men were grasping it with earnest hands, bearing it aloft amid persecution, pain, and death."

"Louis" said Minnie very seriously, "I think the nation makes one great mistake in settling this question of suffrage. It seems to me that everything gets settled on a partial basis. When they are reconstructing the government why not lay the whole foundation anew, and base the right of suffrage not on the claims of service or sex, but on the broader basis of our common humanity."

"Because, Minnie, we are not prepared for it. This hour belongs to the negro."

"But, Louis, is it not the negro woman's hour also? Has she not as many rights and claims as the negro man?"

"Well, perhaps she has, but, darling, you cannot better the condition of the colored men without helping the colored women. What elevates him helps her."

"All that may be true, but I cannot recognize that the negro man is the only one who has pressing claims at this hour. Today our government needs woman's conscience as well as man's judgment. And while I would not throw a straw in the way of the colored man, even though I know that he would vote against me as soon as he gets his vote, yet I do think that woman should have some power to defend herself from oppression, and equal laws as if she were a man."

"But, really, I should not like to see you wending your way through rough and brawling mobs to the polls."

"Because these mobs are rough and coarse I would have women vote. I would soften the asperity of the mobs, and bring into our politics a deeper and broader humanity. When I see intemperance send its floods of ruin and shame to the homes of men, and pass by the grog-shops that are constantly grinding out their fearful grist of poverty, ruin and death,

I long for the hour when woman's vote will be levelled against these charnel houses; and have, I hope, the power to close them throughout the length and breadth of the land."

"Why darling," said Louis, gazing admiringly upon the earnest enthusiasm lighting up her face, "I shall begin to believe that you are a strong-minded woman."

"Surely, you would not have me a weak-minded woman in these hours of trial."

"But, darling, I did not think that you were such an advocate for women's voting."

"I think, Louis, that basing our rights on the ground of our common humanity is the only true foundation for national peace and durability. If you would have the government strong and enduring you should entrench it in the hearts of both the men and women of the land."

"I think you are right in that remark," said Louis. And thus their evenings were enlivened by pleasant and interesting conversations upon the topics of the day.

Once when a union friend was spending an evening at their home Louis entered, looking somewhat animated, and Minnie ever ready to detect his moods and feelings, wanted to know what had happened.

"Oh, I have been to a wedding since I left home."

"And pray who was married?"

"Guess."

"I don't know whom to guess. One of our friends?"

"Yes."

"Was it Mr. Welland?"

"Yes."

"And who did he marry? Is she a Northern woman, and a staunch unionist?"

"Well, I can't imagine who she can be."

"Why he married Miss Henson, who sent you those beautiful flowers."

"Why, Louis, is it possible? Why she is a colored woman."

"I know."

"But how came he to marry her?"

"For the same reason I married you, because he loved her?"

"Well," said the union man, who sat quietly listening, "I am willing to give to the colored people every right that I possess myself, but as to intermarrying with them, I am not prepared for that."

"I think," said Louis, "that marrying and social equality among the races will simply regulate itself. I do not think under the present condition of things that there will be any general intermarrying of the races, but this idea of rooted antagonism of races to me is all moonshine. I believe that what you call the instincts of race are only the prejudices which are the result of custom and education, and if there is any instinct in the matter it is rather the instinct of nature to make a Semi-tropical race in a Semi-tropical climate. Welland told me that he had met his wife when she was a slave, that he loved her then, and would have bought her had it been in his power, but now that freedom had come to her he was glad to have the privilege of making her his wife. He is an Englishman by birth and he intends taking her home with him to England when a favorable opportunity presents itself. And that is far more honorable and manly than living together after the old order of things. I think," said Louis facing the floor "that a cruel wrong was done to Minnie and myself when life was given to us under conditions that doomed us to hopeless slavery, and from which we were rescued only by good fortune. I have heard some colored persons boasting of the white blood, but I always feel like blushing for mine. Much as my father did for me he could never atone for giving me life under the conditions he did."

"Never mind," said Minnie, "it all turned out for the best."

"Yes, Darling," said Louis, growing calmer, "for it gave me you. And that was life's compensation. But the question of the intermingling of the races in marriage is one that scarcely interests this question. The question that presses upon us with the most fearful distinctness is how can we make life secure in the South. I sometimes feel as if the very air was busting with bayonets. There is no law here but the revolver. There must be a screw loose somewhere, and this government that taxes its men in peace and drafts them in war, ought to be wise enough to know its citizens and strong enough to protect them."

# XIX

B ut the pleasant home-life of Louis and Minnie was destined to be rudely broken up. He began to receive threats and anonymous letters, such as these: "Louis Lecroix, you are a doomed man. We are determined to tolerate no scalawags, nor carpetbaggers among us. Beware, the sacred serpent has hissed."

But Louis, brave and resolute, kept on the even tenor of his way, although he never left his home without some forebodings that he tried in vain to cast off. But his young wife being less in contact with the brutal elements of society in that sin-cursed region, did not comprehend the danger as Louis did, and yet she could not help feeling anxious for her husband's safety.

They never parted without her looking after him with a sigh, and then turning to her school, or whatever work or reading she had on her hand, she would strive to suppress her heart's forebodings. But the storm about to burst and to darken forever the sunshine of that home was destined to fall on that fair young head.

Imperative business called Louis from home for one night. Minnie stood at the door and said, "Louis, I hate to have you go. I have been feeling so badly here lately, as if something was going to happen. Come home as soon as you can."

"I will, darling," he said, kissing her tenderly again and again. "I do feel rather loath to leave you, but death is every where, always lurking in ambush. A man may escape from an earthquake to be strangled by a hair. So, darling, keep in good spirits till I come."

Minnie stood at the door watching him till he was out of sight, and then turning to her mother with a sigh, she said, "What a wretched state of society. When he goes I never feel easy till he returns. I do wish we had a government under which our lives would be just as safe as they were in Pennsylvania."

Ellen felt very anxious, but she tried to hide her disquietude and keep Minnie's spirits from sinking, and so she said, "This is a hard country. We colored people have seen our hard times here."

"But, mother, don't you sometimes feel bitter towards these people, who have treated you so unkindly?"

"No, Minnie; I used to, but I don't now. God says we must forgive, and if we don't forgive, He won't forgive."

"But, mother, how did you get to feeling so?"

"Why, honey, I used to suffer until my heart was almost ready to burst, but I learned to cast my burden on the Lord, and then my misery all passed away. My burden fell off at the foot of the cross, and I felt that my feet were planted on a rock."

"How wonderful," said Minnie, "is this faith! How real it is to them! How near some of these suffering people have drawn to God!"

"Yes," said Ellen, "Mrs. Sumpter had a colored woman, to whom they were real mean and cruel, and one day they whipped her and beat her on her feet to keep her from running away; but she made up her mind to leave, and so she packed up her clothes to run away. But before she started, I believe she kneeled down and prayed, and asked what she should do, and something reasoned with her and said, 'Stand still and see what I am going to do for you,' and so she unpacked her clothes and stayed, and now the best part of it was this, Milly's son had been away, and he came back and brought with him money enough to buy his mother; for he had been out begging money to buy her, and so Milly got free, and she was mighty glad that she had stayed, because when he'd come back, if she had been gone, he would not have known where to find her."

"Well, it is wonderful. Somehow these people have passed through the darkness and laid their hands on God's robe of love and light, and have been sustained. It seems to me that some things they see clearer through their tears."

"Mother," said Minnie, "As it is Saturday I will visit some of my scholars."

"Well, Minnie, I would; you look troubled, and may be you'll feel better."

"Yes, Mother, I often feel strengthened after visiting some of these good old souls, and getting glimpses into their inner life. I sometimes ask them, after listening to the story of their past wrongs, what has sustained you? What has kept you up? And the almost invariable answer has been the power of God. Some of these poor old souls, who have been turned adrift to shift for themselves, don't live by bread alone; they live by bread and faith in God. I asked one of them a few days since, Are you not afraid of starving? and the answer was, Not while God lives."

After Minnie left, she visited a number of lowly cabins. The first one she entered was the home of an industrious couple who were just making a start in life. The room in which Minnie was, had no window-lights, only an aperture that supplied them with light, but also admitted the cold.

"Why don't you have window-lights?" said Minnie.

"Oh we must crawl before we walk;" and yet even in this humble home they had taken two orphan children of their race, and were giving them food and shelter. And this kindness to the orphans of their race Minnie found to be a very praiseworthy practice among some of those people who were not poorer than themselves.

The next cabin she entered was very neat, though it bore evidences of poverty. The woman, in referring to the past, told her how her child had been taken away when it was about two years old, and how she had lost all trace of him, and would not know him if he stood in her presence.

"How did you feel?" said Minnie.

"I felt as I was going to my grave, but I thought if I wouldn't get justice here, I would get it in another world."

"My husband," said another, "asked if God is a just God, how would sich as slavery be, and something answered and said, 'sich shan't always be,' and you couldn't beat it out of my husband's head that the Spirit didn't speak to him."

And thus the morning waned away, and Minnie returned calmer than when she had left. A holy peace stole over her mind. She felt that for high and low, rich and poor, there was a common refuge. That there was no corner so dark that the light of heaven could not shine through, and that these people in their ignorance and simplicity had learned to look upon God as a friend coming near to them in their sorrows, and taking cognizance of their wants and woes.

Minnie loved to listen to these beautiful stories of faith and trust. To her they were grand inspirations to faith and duty. Sometimes Minnie would think, when listening to some dear aged saint, I can't teach these people religion, I must learn from them.

Refreshed and strengthened she returned home and began to work upon a dress for a destitute and orphaned child, and when night came she retired quite early, being somewhat wearied with her day's work.

During his absence Louis had been among the freedmen in a new settlement where he had lately established a school, where, notwithstanding all their disadvantages, he was pleased to see evidences of growth and progress.

There was an earnestness and growing manliness that commanded his respect. They were beginning to learn the power of combination, and gave but little heed to the cajoling words, "We are your best friends."

"Don't you think," Louis said to an intelligent freedman, "that the rebels are your best friends?"

"I'll think so when I lose my senses."

"But you are ignorant," Louis said to another one. "How will you know whom to vote for?"

"Well if I don't, I know how not to vote for a rebel."

"How do you know you didn't vote for a rebel?" said Louis to another one who came from one of the most benighted districts.

"I voted for one of my own color," as if treason and a black skin were incompatible.

In the evening Louis called the people together, and talked with them, trying to keep them from being discouraged, for the times were evil, and the days were very gloomy. The impeachment had failed. State after State in the North had voted against enfranchising the colored man in their midst. The spirit of the lost cause revived, murders multiplied. The Ku Klux spread terror and death around. Every item of Northern meanness to the colored people in their midst was a message of hope to the rebel element of the South, which had only changed. Ballot and bullet had failed, but another resort was found in secret assassination. Men advocating equal rights did so at the peril of their lives, for violence and murder were rampant in the land. Oh those dark and weary days when politicians were flattering for place and murdered Union men were sleeping in their bloody shrouds. Louis' courage did not desert him, and he tried to nerve the hearts of those that were sinking with fear in those days of gloom and terror. His advice to the people was, "Defend your firesides if they are invaded, live as peaceably as you can, spare no pains to educate your children, be saving and industrious, try to get land under your feet and homes over your heads. My faith is very strong in political parties, but, as the world has outgrown other forms of wrong, I believe that it will outgrow this also. We must trust and hope for better things." What else could he say? And yet there were times when his words seemed to him almost like bitter mockery. Here was outrage upon outrage committed upon these people, and to tell them to hope and wait for better times, but seemed like speaking hollow words. Oh he longed for a central administration strong enough to put down violence and misrule in the South. If Johnson was clasping hands with rebels and traitors was there no power in Congress to give, at least, security to life? Must they wait till murder was organized into an institution, and life and property were at the mercy of the mob? And, if so, would not such a government be a farce, and such a civilization a failure?

With these reflections passing through his mind he fell asleep, but his slumber was restless and disturbed. He dreamed (but it seemed so plain to him, that he thought it was hardly a dream,) that Minnie came to his side and pressed her lips to his, but they were very pale and very cold. He reached out his hand to clasp her, but she was gone, but as she vanished he heard her say, "My husband."

Restless and uneasy he arose; there was a strange feeling around his soul, a great sinking and depression of his spirits. He could not account for his feelings. He arose and walked the floor and looked up at the heavens, but the night was very bright and beautiful, still he could not shake off his strange and sad forebodings, and as soon as it was light he started for home.

# XX

I n the afternoon when the body had been prepared for the grave, the sorrowing friends gathered around, tearfully noting the look of peace and rest which had stolen over the pale, dead face, when all traces of the death agony had passed away by the contraction of the muscles.

"That is just the way she looked yesterday," said a sad-eyed woman, whose face showed traces of a deep "and fearful sorrow."

Louis drew near, for he was eager to hear any word that told him of Minnie before death had robbed her of life, and him of peace. He came near enough to hear, but not to interrupt the conversation.

"She was at my house yesterday, trying to comfort me, when I was telling her how these Secesh used to *cruelize* us."

"I was telling her about my poor daughter Amy, and what a sprightly, pert piece she was, and how dem awful Secesh took my poor chile and hung'd her."

"Hung'd? Aunt Susan, Oh how was dat?" said half a dozen voices.

"Well, you see it was jist dis way. My darter Amy was a mighty nice chile, and Massa could truss her wid any ting. So when de Linkum Sogers had gone through dis place, Massa got her to move some of his tings over to another place. Now when Amy seed de sojers had cum'd through she was mighty glad, and she said in a kine of childish way, 'I'se so glad, I'm gwine to marry a Linkum soger, and set up house-keeping for myself.' I don't spect she wer in arnest 'bout marrying de sojer, but she did want her freedom. Well, no body couldn't blame her for dat, for freedom's a mighty good thing."

"I don't like it, I jist loves it," said one of Aunt Sue's auditors.

"And I does too, 'cause I'd rather live on bread and water than be back again in de old place, but go on, Aunt Susan."

"Well, when she said dat, dat miserable old Heston—"

"Heston, I know dat wretch, I bound de debil's waiting for him now, got his pitch fork all ready."

"Well, he had my poor girl tookened up, and poor chile, she was beat shameful, and den dey had her up before der sogers and had her tried for saying 'cendiary words, and den dey had my poor girl hung'd." And the poor old woman bowed her head and rocked her body to and fro.

"Well," she continued after a moment's pause, "I was telling dat

FRANCES ELLEN WATKINS HARPER

sweet angel dere my trouble, and she was mighty sorry, and sat dere and cried, and den she said, 'Mrs. Thomas, I hope in a better world dat you'll see a joy according to all the days wherein you have seen sorrow!' Bless her sweet heart, she's got in de shining gate afore me, but I bound to meet her on de sunny banks of deliberance.

"And she was at my house yesterday," said another. "She cum'd to see if I wanted any ting, and I tell'd her I would like to hab a little flannel, 'cause I had the rheumatiz so bad, and she said I should hab it. Den she asked me if I didn't like freedom best. I told her I would rather live in a corn crib, and so I would. It is hard getting along, but I hopes for better times. And den she took down de Bible, and read wid dat sweet voice of hers, about de eagle stirring up her nest, and den she said when de old eagle wanted her young to fly she broked up de nest, and de little eagles didn't known what was de matter, but some how dey didn't feel so cumfertable, 'cause de little twigs and sticks stuck in 'em, and den dey would work dere wings, and dat was de way she said we must do; de ole nest of slavery was broke up, but she said we mus'n't get discouraged, but we must plume our wings for higher flying. Oh she did tell it so purty. I wish I could say it like she did, it did my heart so much good. Poor thing, she done gone and folded her wing in de hebenly mansion. I wish I was 'long side of her, but I'se bound to meet her, 'cause I'm gwine to set out afresh for heben and 'ternal glory."

And thus did these stricken children of sorrow unconsciously comfort the desolate and almost breaking heart of Louis Lacroix. And their words of love and hope were like rays of light shimmering amid the gloomy shadows that overhung his suddenly darkened life.

Surely, thought Louis, if the blessings and tears of the poor and needy and the prayers of him who was ready to perish would crystalize a path to the glory-land, then Minnie's exit from earth must have been over a bridge of light, above whose radiant arches hovering angels would delight to bend.

While these thoughts were passing through his mind, a knock was heard at the door, and Louis rose to open it, and then he saw a sight which shook all his gathered firmness to tears. Headed by the eldest of Minnie's scholars came a procession of children, each one bearing a bunch of fairest and brightest flowers to spread around the couch of their beloved teacher. Some kissed her, and others threw themselves beside the corpse and wept bitter, burning tears. All shared in Louis' grief, for all had lost a dear, good friend and loving instructor.

Louis summoned all the energies of his soul to bear his mournful loss. It was his task to bow to the Chastener, and let his loved one go, feeling that when he had laid her in the earth that he left her there in the hope of a better resurrection.

Life with its solemn responsibilities still met him; its earnest duties still confronted him, and, though he sometimes felt like a weary watcher at the gates of death, longing to catch a glimpse of her shining robes and the radiant light of her glorified face, yet her knew it was his work to labor and to wait.

Sorrow and danger still surrounded his way, and he felt his soul more strongly drawn out than ever to share the fortunes of the colored race. He felt there were grand possibilities stored up in their future. The name of the negro had been associated with slavery, ignorance and poverty, and he determined as far as his influence could be exerted to lift that name from the dust of the centuries and place it among the most honored names in the history of the human race.

He still remained in the South, for Minnie's grave had made the South to him a sacred place, a place in which to labor and to wait until peace like bright dew should descend where carnage had spread ruin around, and freedom and justice, like glorified angels, should reign triumphant where violence and slavery had held their fearful carnival of shame and crime for ages. Earnestly he set himself to bring around the hour when

> *Peace, white-robed and pure, should move*
> *O'er rifts of ruin deep and wide,*
> *When her hands should span with lasting love*
> *The chasms rent by hate and pride.*

And he was blessed in his labors of love and faith.

# CONCLUSION

And now, in conclusion, may I not ask the indulgence of my readers for a few moments, simply to say that Louis and Minnie are only ideal beings, touched here and there with a coloring from real life?

But while I confess (not wishing to mis-represent the most lawless of the Ku-Klux) that Minnie has only lived and died in my imagination, may I not modestly ask that the lesson of Minnie shall have its place among the educational ideas for the advancement of our race?

The greatest want of our people, if I understand our wants aright, is not simply wealth, nor genius, nor mere intelligence, but live men, and earnest, lovely women, whose lives shall represent not a "stagnant mass, but a living force."

We have wealth among us, but how much of it is ever spent in building up the future of the race? in encouraging talent, and developing genius? We have intelligence, but how much do we add to the reservoir of the world's thought? We have genius among us, but how much can it rely upon the colored race for support?

Take even the *Christian Recorder*; where are the graduates from colleges and high school whose pens and brains lend beauty, strength, grace and culture to its pages?

If, when their school days are over, the last composition shall have been given at the examination, will not the disused faculties revenge themselves by rusting? If I could say it without being officious and intrusive, I would say to some who are about to graduate this year, do not feel that your education is finished, when the diploma of your institution is in your hands. Look upon the knowledge you have gained only as a stepping stone to a future, which you are determined shall grandly contrast with the past.

While some of the authors of the present day have been weaving their stories about white men marrying beautiful quadroon girls, who, in so doing were lost to us socially, I conceived of one of that same class to whom I gave a higher, holier destiny; a life of lofty self-sacrifice and beautiful self-consecration, finished at the post of duty, and rounded off with the fiery crown of martyrdom, a circlet which ever changes into a diadem of glory.

The lesson of Minnie's sacrifice is this, that it is braver to suffer with one's own branch of the human race,—to feel, that the weaker and the more despised they are, the closer we will cling to them, for the sake of helping them, than to attempt to creep out of all identity with them in their feebleness, for the sake of mere personal advantages, and to do this at the expense of self-respect, and a true manhood, and a truly dignified womanhood, that with whatever gifts we possess, whether they be genius, culture, wealth or social position, we can best serve the interests of our race by a generous and loving diffusion, than by a narrow and selfish isolation which, after all, is only one type of the barbarous and anti-social state.

SOWING AND REAPING

# I

I hear that John Andrews has given up his saloon; and a foolish thing it was. He was doing a splendid business. What could have induced him?"

"They say that his wife was bitterly opposed to the business. I don't know, but I think it quite likely. She has never seemed happy since John has kept saloon."

"Well, I would never let any woman lead me by the nose. I would let her know that as the living comes by me, the way of getting it is my affair, not hers, as long as she is well provided for."

"All men are not alike, and I confess that I value the peace and happiness of my home more than anything else; and I would not like to engage in any business which I knew was a source of constant pain to my wife."

"But, what right has a woman to complain, if she has every thing she wants. I would let her know pretty soon who holds the reins, if I had such an unreasonable creature to deal with. I think as much of my wife as any man, but I want her to know her place, and I know mine."

"What do you call her place?"

"I call her place staying at home and attending to her own affairs. Were I a laboring man I would never want my wife to take in work. When a woman has too much on hand, something has to be neglected. Now I always furnish my wife with sufficient help and supply every want but how I get the living, and where I go, and what company I keep, is my own business, and I would not allow the best woman in the world to interfere. I have often heard women say that they did not care what their husbands did, so that they provided for them; and I think such conclusions are very sensible."

"Well, John, I do not think so. I think a woman must be very selfish, if all she cares for her husband is, to have a good provider. I think her husband's honor and welfare should be as dear to her as her own; and no true woman and wife can be indifferent to the moral welfare of her husband. Neither man nor woman can live by bread alone in the highest and best sense of the term."

"Now Paul, don't go to preaching. You have always got some moon struck theories, some wild, visionary and impracticable ideas, which would work first rate, if men were angels and earth a paradise. Now don't be so serious, old fellow; but you know on this religion business, you and I always part company. You are always up in the clouds, while I am trying to invest in a few acres, or town lots of solid *terra firma*."

"And would your hold on earthly possessions, be less firm because you looked beyond the seen to the unseen?"

"I think it would, if I let conscience interfere constantly, with every business transaction I undertook. Now last week you lost $500 fair and square, because you would not foreclose that mortgage on Smith's property. I told you that 'business is business,' and that while I pitied the poor man, I would not have risked my money that way, but you said that conscience would not let you; that while other creditors were gathering like hungry vultures around the poor man, you would not join with them, and that you did not believe in striking a man when he is down. Now Paul, as a business man, if you want to succeed, you have got to look at business in a practical, common sense way. Smith is dead, and where is your money now?"

"Apparently lost; but the time may come when I shall feel that it was one of the best investments I ever made. Stranger things than that have happened. I confess that I felt the loss and it has somewhat cramped my business. Yet if it was to do over again, I don't think that I would act differently, and when I believe that Smith's death was hurried on by anxiety and business troubles, while I regret the loss of my money, I am thankful that I did not press my claim."

"Sour grapes, but you are right to put the best face on matters."

"No, if it were to do over again, I never would push a struggling man to the wall when he was making a desperate fight for his wife and little ones."

"Well! Paul, we are both young men just commencing life, and my motto is to look out for Number 1, and you—"

"Oh! I believe in lending a helping hand."

"So do I, when I can make every corner out to my advantage. I believe in every man looking out for himself."

You will see by the dialogue, that the characters I here introduce are the antipodes of each other. They had both been pupils in the same school, and in after life, being engaged as grocers, they frequently met and renewed their acquaintance. They were both established in business, having passed the threshold of that important event, "Setting out in life." As far as their outward life was concerned, they were acquaintances; but to each other's inner life they were strangers. John Anderson has a fine robust constitution, good intellectual abilities, and superior business faculties. He is eager, keen and alert, and if there is one article of faith that moulds and colors all his life more than anything else, it is a firm and unfaltering belief in the "main chance." He has made up his mind to be rich, and his highest ideal of existence may be expressed in four words—*getting on in life*. To this object, he is ready to sacrifice time, talent, energy and every faculty, which he possesses. Nay, he will go farther; he will spend honor, conscience and manhood, in an eager search for gold. He will change his heart into a ledger on which he will write *tare* and *tret*, loss and gain, exchange and barter, and he will succeed, as worldly men count success. He will add house to house; he will encompass the means of luxury; his purse will be plethoric but, oh, how poverty stricken his soul will be. Costly viands will please his taste, but unappeased hunger will gnaw at his soul. Amid the blasts of winter he will have the warmth of Calcutta in his home; and the health of the ocean and the breezes of the mountains shall fan his brow, amid the heats of summer, but there will be a coolness in his soul that no breath of summer can ever dispel; a fever in his spirit that no frozen confection can ever allay; he shall be rich in lands and houses, but fear of loss and a sense of poverty will poison the fountains of his life; and unless he repent, he shall go out into the eternities a pauper and a bankrupt.

Paul Clifford, whom we have also introduced to you, was the only son of a widow, whose young life had been overshadowed by the curse of intemperance. Her husband, a man of splendid abilities and magnificent culture, had fallen a victim to the wine cup. With true womanly devotion she had clung to him in the darkest hours, until death had broken his hold in life, and he was laid away the wreck of his former self in a drunkard's grave. Gathering up the remains of what had been an ample fortune, she installed herself in an humble and unpretending home in the suburbs of the city of B., and there with loving solicitude she had watched over and superintended the education of her only son. He was a promising boy, full of life and vivacity, having inherited much of the careless joyousness of his father's temperament; and although he was the light and joy of his home, yet his mother sometimes felt as if her heart was contracting with a spasm of agony, when she remembered that it was through that same geniality of disposition and wonderful fascination of manner, the tempter had woven his meshes for her husband, and that the qualities that made him so desirable at home, made him equally so to his jovial, careless, inexperienced companions. Fearful that the appetite for strong drink might have been transmitted to her child as a fatal legacy of sin, she sedulously endeavored to develop within him self control, feeling that the lack of it is a prolific cause of misery and crime, and she spared no pains to create within his mind a horror of intemperance, and when he was old enough to understand the nature of a vow, she knelt with him in earnest prayer, and pledging him to eternal enmity against everything that would intoxicate, whether fermented or distilled. In the morning she sowed the seed which she hoped would blossom in time, and bear fruit throughout eternity.

# II

## The Decision

I hear Belle," said Jeanette Roland addressing her cousin Belle Gordon, "that you have refused an excellent offer of marriage."

"Who said so?"

"Aunt Emma."

"I am very sorry that Ma told you, I think such things should be kept sacred from comment, and I think the woman is wanting in refinement and delicacy of feeling who makes the rejection of a lover a theme for conversation."

"Now you dear little prude I had no idea that you would take it so seriously but Aunt Emma was so disappointed and spoke of the rejected suitor in such glowing terms, and said that you had sacrificed a splendid opportunity because of some squeamish notions on the subject of temperance, and so of course, my dear cousin, it was just like me to let my curiosity overstep the bounds of prudence, and inquire why you rejected Mr. Romaine."

"Because I could not trust him."

"Couldn't trust him? Why Belle you are a greater enigma than ever. Why not?"

"Because I feel that the hands of a moderate drinker are not steady enough to hold my future happiness."

"Was that all? Why I breathe again, we girls would have to refuse almost every young man in our set, were we to take that stand."

"And suppose you were, would that be any greater misfortune than to be the wives of drunkards."

"I don't see the least danger. Ma has wine at her entertainments, and I have often handed it to young gentlemen, and I don't see the least harm in it. On last New Year's day we had more than fifty callers. Ma and I handed wine, to every one of them." "Oh I do wish people would abandon that pernicious custom of handing around wine on New Year's day. I do think it is a dangerous and reprehensible thing."

"Wherein lies the danger? Of course I do not approve of young men drinking in bar rooms and saloons, but I cannot see any harm in handing round wine at social gatherings. Not to do so would seem so odd."

"It is said Jeanette, 'He is a slave who does not be, in the right with two or three.' It is better, wiser far to stand alone in our integrity than to join with the multitude in doing wrong. You say while you do not approve of young men drinking in bar rooms and saloons, that you have no objection to their drinking beneath the shadow of their homes, why do you object to their drinking in saloons, and bar rooms?"

"Because it is vulgar. Oh! I think these bar rooms are horrid places. I would walk squares out of my way to keep from passing them." "And I object to intemperance not simply because I think it is vulgar but because I know it is wicked; and Jeanette I have a young brother for whose welfare I am constantly trembling; but I am not afraid that he will take his first glass of wine in a fashionable saloon, or flashy gin palace, but I do dread his entrance into what you call 'our set.' I fear that my brother has received as an inheritance a temperament which will be easily excited by stimulants, that an appetite for liquor once a awakened will be hard to subdue, and I am so fearful, that at some social gathering, a thoughtless girl will hand him a glass of wine, and that the first glass will be like adding fuel to a smouldering fire."

"Oh Belle do stop, what a train of horrors you can conjure out of an innocent glass of wine."

"Anything can be innocent that sparkles to betray, that charms at first, but later will bite like an adder and sting like a serpent."

"Really! Belle, if you keep on at this rate you will be a monomaniac on the temperance question. However I do not think Mr. Romaine will feel highly complimented to know that you refused him because you dreaded he might become a drunkard. You surely did not tell him so."

"Yes I did, and I do not think that I would have been a true friend to him, had I not done so."

"Oh! Belle, I never could have had the courage to have told him so."

"Why not?"

"I would have dreaded hurting his feelings. Were you not afraid of offending him?"

"I certainly shrank from the pain which I knew I must inflict, but because I valued his welfare more than my own feelings, I was constrained to be faithful to him. I told him that he was drifting where he ought steer, that instead of holding the helm and rudder of his young life, he was floating down the stream, and unless he stood firmly on the side of temperance, that I never would clasp hands will him for life."

"But Belle, perhaps you have done him more harm than good; may be you could have effected his reformation by consenting to marrying him."

"Jeanette, were I the wife of a drunken man I do not think there is any depth of degradation that I would not fathom with my love and pity in trying to save him. I believe I would cling to him, if even his own mother shrank from him. But I never would consent to marry any man, whom I knew to be unsteady in his principles and a moderate drinker. If his love for me and respect for himself were not strong enough to reform him before marriage, I should despair of effecting it afterwards, and with me in such a case discretion would be the better part of valor."

"And so you have given Mr. Romaine a release?"

"Yes, he is free."

"And I think you have thrown away a splendid opportunity."

"I don't think so, the risk was too perilous. Oh Jeanette, I know by mournful and bitter experience what it means to dwell beneath the shadow of a home cursed by intemperance. I know what it is to see that shadow deepen into the darkness of a drunkard's grave, and I dare not run the fearful risk."

"And yet Belle this has cost you a great deal, I can see it in the wanness of your face, in your eyes which in spite of yourself, are filled with sudden tears, I know from the intonations of your voice that you are suffering intensely."

"Yes Jeanette, I confess, it was like tearing up the roots of my life to look at this question fairly and squarely in the face, and to say, no; but I must learn to suffer and be strong, I am deeply pained, it is true, but I do not regret the steps I have taken. The man who claims my love and allegiance, must be a victor and not a slave. The reeling brain of a drunkard is not a safe foundation on which to build up a new home."

"Well Belle, you may be right, but I think I would have risked it. I don't think because Mr. Romaine drinks occasionally that I would have given him up. Oh young men will sow their wild oats."

"And as we sow, so must we reap, and as to saying about young men sowing their wild oats, I think it is full of pernicious license. A young man has no more right to sow his wild oats than a young woman. God never made one code of ethics for a man and another for a woman. And it is the duty of all true women to demand of men the same standard of morality that they do of woman."

"Ah Belle that is very fine in theory, but you would find it rather difficult, if you tried to reduce your theory to practice."

"All that may be true, but the difficulty of a duty is not a valid excuse for its non performance."

"My dear cousin it is not my role to be a reformer. I take things as I find them and drift along the tide of circumstances."

"And is that your highest ideal of life? Why Jeanette such a life is not worth living."

"Whether it is or not, I am living it and I rather enjoy it. Your vexing problems of life never disturb me. I do not think I am called to turn this great world 'right side up with care,' and so I float along singing as I go,

> *"I'd be a butterfly born in a bower*
> *Kissing every rose that is pleasant and sweet,*
> *I'd never languish for wealth or for power*
> *I'd never sigh to have slaves at my feet."*

"Such a life would never suit me, life must mean to me more than ease, luxury and indulgence, it must mean aspiration and consecration, endeavor and achievement."

"Well, Belle, should we live twenty years longer, I would like to meet you and see by comparing notes which of us shall have gathered the most sunshine or shadow from life."

"Yes Jeanette we will meet in less than twenty years, but before then your glad light eyes will be dim with tears, and the easy path you have striven to walk will be thickly strewn with thorn; and whether you deserve it or not, life will have for you a mournful earnestness, but notwithstanding all your frivolity and flippancy there is fine gold in your character, which the fire of affliction only will reveal."

# III

(Text missing.)

# IV

H ow is business?"

"Very dull, I am losing terribly."

"Any prospect of times brightening?"

"I don't see my way out clear; but I hope there will be a change for the better. Confidence has been greatly shaken, men of business have grown exceedingly timid about investing and there is a general depression in every department of trade and business."

"Now Paul will you listen to reason and common sense? I have a proposition to make. I am about to embark in a profitable business, and I know that it will pay better than anything else I could undertake in these times. Men will buy liquor if they have not got money for other things. I am going to open a first class saloon, and club-house, on M. Street, and if you will join with me we can make a splendid thing of it. Why just see how well off Joe Harden is since he set up in the business; and what airs he does put on! I know when he was not worth fifty dollars, and kept a little low groggery on the corner of L. and S. Streets, but he is out of that now—keeps a first class *Cafe*, and owns a block of houses. Now Paul, here is a splendid chance for you; business is dull, and now accept this opening. Of course I mean to keep a first class saloon. I don't intend to tolerate loafing, or disorderly conduct, or to sell to drunken men. In fact, I shall put up my scale of prices so that you need fear no annoyance from rough, low, boisterous men who don't know how to behave themselves. What say you, Paul?"

"I say, no! I wouldn't engage in such a business, not if it paid me a hundred thousand dollars a year. I think these first class saloons are just as great a curse to the community as the low groggeries, and I look upon them as the fountain heads of the low groggeries. The man who begins to drink in the well lighted and splendidly furnished saloon is in danger of finishing in the lowest dens of vice and shame."

"As you please," said John Anderson stiffly, "I thought that as business is dull that I would show you a chance, that would yield you a handsome profit; but if you refuse, there is no harm done. I know young men who would jump at the chance."

You may think it strange that knowing Paul Clifford as John Anderson did, that he should propose to him an interest in a drinking saloon; but John Anderson was a man who was almost destitute of faith in human goodness. His motto was that "every man has his price," and as business was fairly dull, and Paul was somewhat cramped for want of capital, he thought a good business investment would be the price for Paul Clifford's conscientious scruples.

"Anderson," said Paul looking him calmly in the face, "you may call me visionary and impracticable; but I am determined however poor I may be, never to engage in any business on which I cannot ask God's blessing. And John I am sorry from the bottom of my heart, that you have concluded to give up your grocery and keep a saloon. You cannot keep that saloon without sending a flood of demoralizing influence over the community. Your profit will be the loss of others. Young men will form in that saloon habits which will curse and overshadow all their lives. Husbands and fathers will waste their time and money, and confirm themselves in habits which will bring misery, crime, and degradation; and the fearful outcome of your business will be broken hearted wives, neglected children, outcast men, blighted characters and worse than wasted lives. No not for the wealth of the Indies, would I engage in such a ruinous business, and I am thankful today that I had a dear sainted mother who taught me that it was better to have my hands clear than to have them full. How often would she lay her dear hands upon my head, and clasp my hands in hers and say, 'Paul, I want you to live so that you can always feel that there is no eye before whose glance you will shrink, no voice from whose tones your heart will quail, because your hands are not clean, or your record not pure,' and I feel glad today that the precepts and example of that dear mother have given tone and coloring to my life; and though she has been in her grave for many years, her memory and her words are still to me an ever present inspiration."

"Yes Paul; I remember your mother. I wish! Oh well there is no use wishing. But if all Christians were like her, I would have more faith in their religion."

"But John the failure of others is no excuse for our own derelictions."

"Well, I suppose not. It is said, the way Jerusalem was kept clean, every man swept before his own door. And so you will not engage in the business?"

"No John, no money I would earn would be the least inducement."

"How foolish," said John Anderson to himself as they parted. "There is a young man who might succeed splendidly if he would only give up some of his old fashioned notions, and launch out into life as if he had some common sense. If business remains as it is, I think he will find out before long that he has got to shut his eyes and swallow down a great many things he don't like."

After the refusal of Paul Clifford, John soon found a young man of facile conscience who was willing to join with him in a conspiracy of sin against the peace, happiness and welfare of the community. And he spared neither pains nor expense to make his saloon attractive to what he called, "the young bloods of the city," and by these he meant young men whose parents were wealthy, and whose sons had more leisure and spending money than was good for them. He succeeded in fitting up a magnificent palace of sin. Night after night till morning flashed the orient, eager and anxious men sat over the gaming table watching the turn of a card, or the throw of a dice. Sparkling champaign, or ruby-tinted wine were served in beautiful and costly glasses. Rich divans and easy chairs invited weary men to seek repose from unnatural excitement. Occasionally women entered that saloon, but they were women not as God had made them, but as sin had debased them. Women whose costly jewels and magnificent robes were the livery of sin, the outside garnishing of moral death; the flush upon whose cheek, was not the flush of happiness, and the light in their eyes was not the sparkle of innocent joy,—women whose laughter was sadder than their tears, and who were dead while they lived. In that house were wine, and mirth, and revelry, "but the dead were there," men dead to virtue, true honor and rectitude, who walked the streets as other men, laughed, chatted, bought, sold, exchanged and bartered, but whose souls were encased in living tombs, bodies that were dead to righteousness but alive to sin. Like a spider weaving its meshes around the unwary fly, John Anderson wove his network of sin around the young men that entered his saloon. Before they entered there, it was pleasant to see the supple vigor and radiant health that were manifested in the poise of their bodies, the lightness of their eyes, the freshness of their lips and the bloom upon their cheeks. But Oh! it was so sad to see how soon the manly gait would change to the drunkard's stagger. To see eyes once bright with intelligence growing vacant and confused and giving place to the drunkard's leer. In many cases lassitude supplanted vigor, and sickness overmastered health. But the saddest thing was the fearful power that appetite had gained over its victims, and though nature lifted her signals of distress, and sent her warnings through weakened nerves and disturbed functions, and although they were wasting money, time, talents, and health, ruining their characters, and alienating their friends, and bringing untold agony to hearts that loved them and yearned over their defections, yet the fascination grew stronger and ever and anon the grave opened at their feet; and disguise it as loving friends might, the seeds of death had been nourished by the fiery waters of alcohol.

# V

(Text missing.)

# VI

For a few days the most engrossing topic in A.P. was what shall I wear, and what will you wear. There was an amount of shopping to be done, and dressmakers to be consulted and employed before the great event of the season came off. At length the important evening arrived and in the home of Mr. Glossop, a wealthy and retired whiskey dealer, there was a brilliant array of wealth and fashion. Could all the misery his liquor had caused been turned into blood, there would have been enough to have oozed in great drops from every marble ornament or beautiful piece of frescoe that adorned his home, for that home with its beautiful surroundings and costly furniture was the price of blood, but the glamor of his wealth was in the eyes of his guests; and they came to be amused and entertained and not to moralize on his ill-gotten wealth.

The wine flowed out in unstinted measures and some of the women so forgot themselves as to attempt to rival the men in drinking. The barrier being thrown down Charles drank freely, till his tones began to thicken, and his eye to grow muddled, and he sat down near Jeanette and tried to converse; but he was too much under the influence of liquor to hold a sensible and coherent conversation.

"Oh! Charley you naughty boy, that wine has got into your head and you don't know what you are talking about."

"Well, Miss Jenny, I b'lieve you're 'bout half-right, my head does feel funny."

"I shouldn't wonder; mine feels rather dizzy, and Miss Thomas has gone home with a sick headache, and I know what her headaches mean," said Jeanette significantly.

"My head," said Mary Gladstone, "really feels as big as a bucket."

"And I feel real dizzy," said another.

"And so do I," said another, "I feel as if I could hardly stand, I feel awful weak."

"Why girls, you! are all, all, tipsy, now just own right up, and be done with it," said Charles Romaine.

"Why Charlie you are as good as a wizard, I believe we have all got too much wine aboard: but we are not as bad as the girls of B.S., for they succeeded in out drinking the men. I heard the men drank eight bottles of wine, and that they drank sixteen."

Alas for these young people they were sporting upon the verge of a precipice, but its slippery edge was concealed by flowers. They were playing with the firebrands of death and thought they were Roman-candles and harmless rockets.

"Good morning Belle," said Jeanette Roland to her cousin Belle as she entered her cousin's sitting-room the morning after the party and found Jeanette lounging languidly upon the sofa.

"Good morning. It is a lovely day, why are you not out enjoying the fresh air? Can't you put on your things and go shopping with me? I think you have excellent taste and I often want to consult it."

"Well after all then I am of some account in your eyes."

"Of course you are; who said you were not(?)"

"Oh! nobody only I had an idea that you thought that I was as useless as a canary bird."

"I don't think that a canary bird is at all a useless thing. It charms our ears with its song, and pleases our eye with its beauty, and I am a firm believer in the utility of beauty—but can you, or rather will you not go with me?"

"Oh Belle I would, but I am as sleepy as a cat."

"What's the matter?"

"I was up so late last night at Mrs. Glossop's party; but really it was a splendid affair, everything was in the richest profusion, and their house is magnificently furnished. Oh Belle I wish you could have been there."

"I don't; there are two classes of people with whom I never wish to associate, or number as my especial friends, and they are rum sellers and slave holders."

"Oh! well, Mr. Glossop is not in the business now and what is the use of talking about the past; don't be always remembering a man's sins against him."

"Would you say the same of a successful pirate who could fare sumptuously from the effects of his piracy?"

"No I would not; but Belle the cases is not at all parallel."

"Not entirely. One commits his crime against society within the pale of the law, the other commits his outside. They are both criminals against the welfare of humanity. One murders the body, and the other stabs the soul. If I knew that Mr. Glossop was sorry for having been a liquor dealer and was bringing forth fruits meet for repentance, I would be among the first to hail his reformation with heartfelt satisfaction;

FRANCES ELLEN WATKINS HARPER

but when I hear that while he no longer sells liquor, that he constantly offers it to his guests, I feel that he should rather sit down in sackcloth and ashes than fireside at sumptuous feasts, obtained by liquor selling. When crime is sanctioned by law, and upheld by custom and fashion, it assumes its most dangerous phase; and there is often a fearful fascination in the sin that is environed by success."

"Oh! Belle do stop. I really think that you will go crazy on the subject of temperance. I think you must have written these lines that I have picked up somewhere; let me see what they are,—

> *"Tell me not that I hate the bowl,*
> *Hate is a feeble word."*

"No Jeanette, I did not write them, but I have felt all the writer has so nervously expressed. In my own sorrow-darkened home, and over my poor father's grave, I learned to hate liquor in any form with all the intensity of my nature."

"Well, it was a good thing you were not at Mrs. Glossop's last night, for some of our heads were rather dizzy, and I know that Mr. Romaine was out of gear. Now Belle! don't look so shocked and pained; I am sorry I told you."

"Yes, I am very sorry. I had great hopes that Mr. Romaine had entirely given up drinking, and I was greatly pained when I saw him take a glass of wine at your solicitation. Jeanette I think Mr. Romaine feels a newly awakened interest in you, and I know that you possess great influence over him. I saw it that night when he hesitated, when you first asked him to drink, and I was so sorry to see that influence. Oh Jeanette instead of being his temptress, try and be the angel that keeps his steps. If Mr. Romaine ever becomes a drunkard and goes down to a drunkard's grave, I cannot help feeling that a large measure of the guilt will cling to your shirts."

"Oh Belle, do stop, or you will give me the horrors. Pa takes wine every day at his dinner and I don't see that he is any worse off for it. If Charles Romaine can't govern himself, I can't see how I am to blame for it."

"I think you are to blame for this Jeanette: (and pardon me if I speak plainly). When Charles Romaine was trying to abstain, you tempted him to break his resolution, and he drank to please you. I wouldn't have done so for my right hand."

"They say old coals are easily kindled, and I shall be somewhat chary about receiving attention from him, if you feel so deeply upon the subject."

"Jeanette you entirely misapprehend me. Because I have ceased to regard Mr. Romaine as a lover, does not hinder me from feeling for him as a friend. And because I am his friend and yours also, I take the liberty to remonstrate against your offering him wine at your entertainments."

"Well Belle, I can't see the harm in it, I don't believe there was another soul who refused except you and Mr. Freeman, and you are so straightlaced, and he is rather green, just fresh from the country, it won't take him long to get citified."

"Citified or countrified, I couldn't help admiring his strength of principle which stood firm in the midst of temptation and would not yield to the blandishments of the hour. And so you will not go out with me this morning?"

"Oh! No Belle, I am too tired. Won't you excuse me?"

"Certainly, but I must go. Good morning."

"What a strange creature my cousin Belle is," said Jeanette, to herself as Miss Gordon left the room. "She will never be like any one else. I don't think she will ever get over my offering Mr. Romaine that glass of wine, I wish she hadn't seen it, but I'll try and forget her and go to sleep."

But Jeanette was not destined to have the whole morning for an unbroken sleep. Soon after Bell's departure the bell rang and Charles Romaine was announced, and weary as Jeanette was, she was too much interested in his society to refuse him; and arraying herself in a very tasteful and becoming manner, she went down to receive him in the parlor.

# VII

Very pleasant was the reception Jeanette Roland gave Mr. Romaine. There was no reproof upon her lips nor implied censure in her manner. True he had been disguised by liquor or to use a softer phrase, had taken too much wine. But others had done the same and treated it as a merry escapade, and why should she be so particular? Belle Gordon would have acted very differently but then she was not Belle, and in this instance she did not wish to imitate her. Belle was so odd, and had become very unpopular, and besides she wished to be very very pleasant to Mr. Romaine. He was handsome, agreeable and wealthy, and she found it more congenial to her taste to clasp hands with him and float down stream together, than help him breast the current of his wrong tendencies, and stand firmly on the rock of principle.

"You are looking very sweet, but rather pensive this morning," said Mr. Romaine, noticing a shadow on the bright and beautiful face of Jeanette, whose color had deepened by the plain remarks of her cousin Belle. "What is the matter?"

"Oh nothing much, only my cousin Belle has been here this morning, and she has been putting me on the stool of repentance."

"Why! what have you been doing that was naughty?"

"Oh! she was perfectly horror-stricken when I told her about the wine we drank and Mrs. Glossop's party. I wish I had not said a word to her about it."

"What did she say?"

"Oh she thought it was awful, the way we were going on. She made me feel that I died (*sic*) something dreadful when I offered you a glass of wine at Ma's silver wedding. I don't believe Belle ever sees a glass of wine, without thinking of murder, suicide and a drunkard's grave."

"But we are not afraid of those dreadful things, are we Jeanette?"

"Of course not, but somehow Belle always makes me feel uncomfortable, when she begins to talk on temperance. She says she is terribly in earnest, and I think she is."

"Miss Gordon and I were great friends once," said Charles Romaine, as a shadow flitted over his face, and a slight sigh escaped his lips.

"Were you? Why didn't you remain so?"

"Because she was too good for me."

"That is a very sorry reason."

"But it is true. I think Miss Gordon is an excellent young lady, but she and I wouldn't agree on the temperance question. The man who marries her has got to toe the mark. She ought to be a minister's wife."

"I expect she will be an old maid."

"I don't know, but if I were to marry her, I should prepare myself to go to Church every Sunday morning and to stay home in the afternoon and repeat my catechism."

"I would like to see you under her discipline."

"It would come hard on a fellow, but I might go farther and fare worse."

"And so you and Belle were great friends, once?"

"Yes, but as we could not agree on the total abstinence question, we parted company."

"How so? Did you part as lovers part?"

*She with a wronged and broken heart?*
*And you, rejoicing you were free,*
*Glad to regain you liberty?*

"Not at all. She gave me the mitten and I had to take it."

"Were you very sorry?"

"Yes, till I met you."

"Oh! Mr. Romaine," said Jeanette blushing and dropping her eyes.

"Why not? I think I have found in your society an ample compensation for the loss of Miss Gordon."

"But I think Belle is better than I am. I sometimes wish I was half so good."

"You are good enough for me; Belle is very good, but somehow her goodness makes a fellow uncomfortable. She is what I call distressingly good; one doesn't want to be treated like a wild beast in a menagerie, and to be every now and then stirred up with a long stick."

"What a comparison!"

"Well it is a fact; when a fellow's been busy all day pouring over Coke and Blackstone, or casting up wearisome rows of figures, and seeks a young lady's society in the evening, he wants to enjoy himself, to bathe in the sunshine of her smiles, and not to be lectured about his shortcomings. I tell you, Jeanette, it comes hard on a fellow."

"You want some one to smooth the wrinkles out of the brow of care, and not to add fresh ones."

"Yes, and I hope it will be my fortune to have a fair soft hand like his," said Mr. Romaine, slightly pressing Jeanette's hand to perform the welcome and agreeable task.

"Belle's hand would be firmer than mine for the talk."

"It is not the strong hand, but the tender hand I want in a woman."

"But Belle is very kind; she did it all for your own good."

"Of course she did; my father used to say so when I was a boy, and he corrected me; but it didn't make me enjoy the correction."

"It is said our best friends are those who show us our faults, and teach us how to correct them."

"My best friend is a dear, sweet girl who sits by my side, who always welcomes me with a smile, and beguiles me so with her conversation, that I take no note of the hours until the striking of the clock warns me it is time to leave; and I should ask no higher happiness than to be permitted to pass all the remaining hours of my life at her side. Can I dare to hope for such a happy fortune?"

A bright flush overspread the cheek of Jeanette Roland; there was a sparkle of joy in her eyes as she seemed intently examining the flowers on her mother's carpet, and she gently referred him to Papa for an answer. In due time Mr. Roland was interviewed, his consent obtained, and Jeanette Roland and Charles Romaine were affianced lovers.

"Girls, have you heard the news?" said Miss Tabitha Jones, a pleasant and wealthy spinster, to a number of young girls who were seated at her tea table.

"No! what is it?"

"I hear Mr. Romaine is to be married next spring."

"To whom?"

"Jeanette Roland."

"Well! I do declare; I thought he was engaged to Belle Gordon."

"I thought so too, but it is said that she refused him, but I don't believe it; I don't believe that she had a chance."

"Well I do."

"Why did she refuse him?"

"Because he would occasionally take too much wine."

"But he is not a drunkard."

"But she dreads that he will be."

"Well! I think it is perfectly ridiculous. I gave Belle credit for more common sense. I think he was one of the most eligible gentlemen in our set. Wealthy, handsome and agreeable. What could have possessed Belle? I think he is perfectly splendid."

"Yes said another girl, I think Belle stood very much in her own light. She is not rich, and if she would marry him she could have everything heart could wish. What a silly girl! You wouldn't catch me throwing away such a chance."

"I think," said Miss Tabitha, "that instead of Miss Gordon's being a silly girl, that she has acted both sensibly and honorably in refusing to marry a man she could not love. No woman should give her hand where she cannot yield her heart."

"But Miss Tabitha, the strangest thing to me is, that I really believe that Belle Gordon cares more for Mr. Romaine than she does for any one else; her face was a perfect study that night at Mrs. Roland's party."

"How so?"

"They say that after Miss Gordon requested Mr. Romaine, that for a while he scrupulously abstained from taking even a glass of wine. At several entertainments, he adhered to this purpose but on the evening of Mrs. Roland's silver wedding Jeanette succeeded in persuading him to take a glass, in honor of the occasion. I watched Belle's face and it was a perfect study, every nerve seemed quivering with intense anxiety. Once I think she reached out her hand unconsciously as if to snatch away the glass, and when at last he yielded I saw the light fade from her eyes, a deadly pallor overspread her cheek, and I thought at one time she was about to faint, but she did not, and only laid her head upon her side as if to allay a sudden spasm of agony."

FRANCES ELLEN WATKINS HARPER

# VIII

P aul Clifford sat at his ledger with a perplexed and anxious look. It was near two o'clock and his note was in bank. If he could not raise five hundred dollars by three o'clock, that note would be protested. Money was exceedingly hard to raise, and he was about despairing. Once he thought of applying to John Anderson, but he said to himself, "No, I will not touch his money, for it is the price of blood," for he did not wish to owe gratitude where he did not feel respect. It was now five minutes past two o'clock and in less than an hour his note would be protested unless relief came from some unexpected quarter.

"Is Mr. Clifford in?" said a full manly voice. Paul, suddenly roused from his painful reflections, answered, "Yes, come in. Good morning sir, what can I do for you this morning?"

"I have come to see you on business."

"I am at your service," said Paul.

"Do you remember," said the young man, "of having aided an unfortunate friend more than a dozen years since by lending him five hundred dollars?"

"Yes, I remember he was an old friend of mine, a school-mate of my father's, Charles Smith."

"Well I am his son, and I have come to liquidate my father's debt. Here is the money with interest for twelve years."

Paul's heart gave a sudden bound of joy. Strong man as he was a mist gathered in his eyes as he reached out his hand to receive the thrice welcome sum. He looked at the clock, it was just fifteen minutes to three.

"Will you walk with me to the bank or wait till I return?"

"I will wait," said James Smith, taking up the morning paper.

"You are just in time, Mr. Clifford," said the banker smiling and bowing as Paul entered, "I was afraid your note would be protested; but it is all right."

"Yes," said Paul, "the money market is very tight, but I think I shall weather the storm."

"I hope so, you may have to struggle hard for awhile to keep your head above the water; but you must take it for your motto that there is no such word as 'fail.'"

"Thank you, good morning."

"Well Mr. Smith," said Paul when he returned, "your father and mine were boys together. He was several years younger than my father, and a great favorite in our family among the young folks. About twelve years since when I had just commenced business, I lent him five hundred dollars, and when his business troubles became complicated I refused to foreclose a mortgage which I had on his home. An acquaintance of mine sneered at my lack of business keenness, and predicted that my money would be totally lost, when I told him perhaps it was the best investment I ever made." He smiled incredulously and said, "I would rather see it than hear of it: but I will say that in all my business career I never received any money that came so opportune as this. It reminds me of the stories that I have read in fairy books. People so often fail in paying their own debts, it seems almost a mystery to me that you should pay a debt contracted by your father when you were but a boy."

"The clue to this mystery has been the blessed influence of my sainted mother;" and a flush of satisfaction mantled his cheek as he referred to her.

"After my father's death my mother was very poor. When she looked into the drawer there were only sixty cents in money. Of course, he had some personal property, but it was not immediately available like money, but through the help of kind friends she was enabled to give him a respectable funeral. Like many other women in her condition of life, she had been brought up in entire ignorance of managing any other business, than that which belonged to her household. For years she had been shielded in the warm clasp of loving arms, but now she had to bare her breast to the storm and be father and mother both to her little ones. My father as you know died in debt, and he was hardly in his grave when his creditors were upon her track. I have often heard her speak in the most grateful manner of your forbearance and kindness to her in her hour of trouble. My mother went to see my father's principal creditor and asked him only to give her a little time to straighten out the tangled threads of her business, but he was inexorable, and said that he had waited and lost by it. Very soon he had an administrator appointed by the court, who in about two months took the business in his hands; and my mother was left to struggle along with her little ones, and face an uncertain future. These were dark days but we managed to live through them. I have often heard her say that she lived by faith and not sight, that poverty had its compensations, that there was something

FRANCES ELLEN WATKINS HARPER

very sweet in a life of simple trust, to her, God was not some far off and unapproachable force in the universe, the unconscious Creator of all consciousness, the unperceiving author of all perception, but a Friend and a Father coming near to her in sorrows, taking cognizance of her grief, and gently smoothing her path in life. But it was not only by precept that she taught us; her life was a living epistle. One morning as the winter was advancing I heard her say she hoped she would be able to get a nice woolen shawl, as hers was getting worse for wear. Shortly after I went out into the street and found a roll of money lying at my feet. Oh I remember it as well as if it had just occurred. How my heart bounded with joy. 'Here,' I said to myself, 'is money enough to buy mother a shawl and bonnet. Oh I am so glad,' and hurrying home I laid it in her lap and said with boyish glee, 'Hurrah for your new shawl; look what I found in the street.'"

"What is it my son?" she said.

"Why here is money enough to buy you a new shawl and bonnet too." It seems as if I see her now, as she looked, when she laid it aside, and said—

"But James, it is not ours?"

"Not ours, mother, why I found it in the street!"

"Still it is not ours."

"Why mother ain't you going to keep it?"

"No my son, I shall go down to the *Clarion* office and advertise it."

"But mother why not wait till it is advertised?"

"And what then?"

"If there is no owner for it, then we can keep it."

"James" she said calmly and sadly, "I am very sorry to see you so ready to use what is not your own. I should not feel that I was dealing justly, if I kept this money without endeavoring to find the owner."

"I confess that I was rather chopfallen at her decision, but in a few days after advertising we found the rightful owner. She was a very poor woman who had saved by dint of hard labor the sum of twenty dollars, and was on her way to pay the doctor who had attended her during a spell of rheumatic fever, when she lost the money and had not one dollar left to pay for advertising and being disheartened, she had given up all hope of finding it, when she happened to see it advertised in the paper. She was very grateful to my mother for restoring the money and offered her some compensation, but she refused to take it, saying she had only done her duty, and would have been ashamed of herself had she not done so. Her conduct on this occasion made an impression on my mind that has never been erased. When I grew older she explained to me about my father's affairs, and uncancelled debts, and I resolved that I would liquidate every just claim against him, and take from his memory even the shadow of a reproach. To this end I have labored late and early; today I have paid the last claim against him, and I am a free man."

"But how came you to find me and pay me today?" "I was purchasing in Jones & Brother's store, when you came in to borrow money, and I heard Jones tell his younger brother that he was so sorry that he could not help you, and feared that you would be ruined."

"Who is he?" said I, "for out West I had lost track of you."

"He is Paul Clifford, a friend of your father's. Can you help him? He is perfectly reliable. We would trust him with ten thousand dollars if we had it. Can you do anything for him? we will go his security, he is a fine fellow and we hate to see him go under."

"Yes" said I, "he was one of my father's creditors and I have often heard my mother speak of his generosity to her little ones, and I am glad that I have the privilege of helping him. I immediately went to the bank had a note cashed and I am very glad if I have been of any special service to you."

"You certainly have been, and I feel that a heavy load had been lifted from my heart."

Years ago Paul Clifford sowed the seeds of kindness and they were yielding him a harvest of satisfaction.

# IX

## BELLE GORDON

B elle Gordon was a Christian; she had learned or tried to realize
what is meant by the apostle Paul when he said, "Ye are bought
with a price." To her those words meant the obligation she was under to
her heavenly Father, for the goodness and mercy that had surrounded
her life, for the patience that had borne with her errors and sins, and
above all for the gift of his dear Son, the ever blessed Christ. Faith to
her was not a rich traditional inheritance, a set of formulated opinions,
received without investigation, and adopted without reflection. She
could not believe because others did, and however plausible or popular a
thing might be she was too conscientious to say she believed it if she did
not, and when she became serious on the subject of religion it was like
entering into a wilderness of doubt and distress. She had been taught to
look upon God, more as the great and dreadful God, than as the tender
loving Father of his human children, and so strong was the power of
association, that she found it hard to believe that God is good, and yet
until she could believe this there seemed to be no resting place for her
soul; but in course of time the shadows were lifted from her life. Faith
took the place of doubting, and in the precious promises of the Bible
she felt that her soul had found a safe and sure anchorage. If others
believed because they had never doubted, she believed because she
had doubted and her doubts had been dispelled by the rays of heaven,
and believing, she had entered into rest. Feeling that she was bought
with a price, she realized that she was not her own, but the captive of
Divine Love, and that her talents were not given her to hide beneath
a bushel or to use for merely selfish enjoyments. That her time was
not her own to be frittered away by the demands of fashion or to be
spent in unavailing regrets. Every reform which had for its object the
lessening of human misery, or the increase of human happiness, found
in her an earnest ally. On the subject of temperance she was terribly in
earnest. Every fiber of her heart responded to its onward movement.
There was no hut or den where human beings congregated that she
felt was too vile or too repulsive to enter, if by so doing she could help
lift some fallen soul out of the depths of sin and degradation. While

some doubted the soundness of her religious opinions, none doubted the orthodoxy of her life. Little children in darkened homes smiled as the sunlight of her presence came over their paths; reformed men looked upon her as a loving counsellor and faithful friend and sister; women wretched and sorrowful, dragged down from love and light, by the intemperance of their husbands, brought to her their heavy burdens, and by her sympathy and tender consideration she helped them bear them. She was not rich in this world's goods, but she was affluent in tenderness, sympathy, and love, and out of the fullness of her heart, she was a real minister of mercy among the poor and degraded. Believing that the inner life developed the outer, she considered the poor, and strove to awaken within them self-reliance, and self-control, feeling that one of the surest ways to render people helpless or dangerous is to crush out their self-respect and self-reliance. She thought it one of the greatest privileges of her life to be permitted to scatter flowers by the wayside of life. Other women might write beautiful poems; she did more. She made her life a thing of brightness and beauty.

"Do you think she will die?" said Belle Gordon, bending tenderly over a pale and fainting woman, whose face in spite of its attenuation showed traces of great beauty.

"Not if she is properly cared for; she has fainted from exhaustion brought on by overwork and want of proper food." Tears gathered in the eyes of Belle Gordon as she lifted the beautiful head upon her lap and chafed the pale hands to bring back warmth and circulation.

"Let her be removed to her home as soon as possible," said the doctor. "The air is too heavy and damp for her."

"I wonder where she lives," said Belle thoughtfully, scanning her face, as the features began to show returning animation.

"Round the corner," said an urchin, "she's Joe Cough's wife. I seed her going down the street with a great big bundle, and Mam said, she looked like she was going to topple over."

"Where is her husband?"

"I don't know, I 'spec he's down to Jim Green's saloon."

"What does he do?"

"He don't do nothing, but Mam says she works awful hard. Come this way," said he with a quickness gathered by his constant contact with street life.

Up two flights of rickety stairs they carried the wasted form of Mary

FRANCES ELLEN WATKINS HARPER

Gough, and laid her tenderly upon a clean but very poor bed. In spite of her extreme poverty there was an air of neatness in the desolate room. Belle looked around and found an old tea pot in which there were a few leaves. There were some dry crusts in the cupboard, while two little children crouched by the embers in the grate, and cried for the mother. Belle soon found a few coals in an old basin with which she replenished the fire, and covering up the sick woman as carefully as she could, stepped into the nearest grocery and replenished her basket with some of good the things of life.

"Is it not too heavy for you(r) might?" said Paul Clifford from whose grocery Belle had bought her supplies.

"Can I not send them home for you?"

"No I don't want them sent home. They are for a poor woman and her suffering children, who live about a square from here in Lear's Court." Paul stood thoughtfully a moment before handing her the basket, and said—"That court has a very bad reputation; had I not better accompany you? I hope you will not consider my offer as an intrusion, but I do not think it is safe for you to venture there alone."

"If you think it is not safe I will accept of your company; but I never thought of danger for myself in the presence of that fainting woman and her hungry children. Do you know her? Her name is Mrs. Gough." "I think I do. If it is the person I mean, I remember her when she was as lighthearted and happy a girl as I ever saw, but she married against her parents' consent, a worthless fellow named Joe Gough, and in a short time she disappeared from the village and I suppose she has come home, broken in health and broken in spirit."

"And I am afraid she has come home to die. Are her parents still alive?"

"Yes, but her father never forgave her. Her mother I believe would take her to her heart as readily as she ever did, but her husband has an iron will and she has got to submit to him."

"Where do they live?"

"At No 200 Rouen St. but here we are at the door." Paul carried the basket up stairs, and sat down quietly, while Belle prepared some refreshing tea and toast for the feeble mother; and some bread and milk for the hungry children.

"What shall I do?" said Belle looking tenderly upon the wan face, "I hate to leave her alone and yet I confess I do not prefer spending the night here."

"Of course not," said Paul looking thoughtfully into the flickering fire of the grate.

"Oh! I have it now; I know a very respectable woman who occasionally cleans out my store. Just wait a few moments, and I think I can find her," said Paul Clifford turning to the door. In a short time he returned bringing with him a pleasant looking woman whose face in spite of the poverty of her dress had a look of genuine refinement which comes not so much from mingling with people of culture as from the culture of her own moral and spiritual nature. She had learned to "look up and not to look down." To lend a helping hand wherever she felt it was needed. Her life was spent in humble usefulness. She was poor in this world's goods, but rich in faith and good works. No poor person who asked her for bread ever went away empty. Sometimes people would say, "I wouldn't give him a mouthful; he is not worthy," and then she would say in the tenderest and sweetest manner:

"Suppose our heavenly Father only gave to us because we are worthy; what would any of us have?" I know she once said of a miserable sot with whom she shared her scanty food, that he is a wretched creature, but I wanted to get at his heart, and the best way to it was through his stomach. I never like to preach religion to hungry people. There is something very beautiful about the charity of the poor, they give not as the rich of their abundance, but of their limited earnings, gifts which when given in a right spirit bring a blessing with them.

# X

## Mary Gough

I think," said Paul Clifford to Miss Gordon, "that I have found just the person that will suit you, and if you accept I will be pleased to see you safe home." Belle thanked the young grocer, and gratefully accepted his company.

Belle returned the next day to see her protege and found her getting along comfortably although she could not help seeing it was sorrow more than disease that was sapping her life, and drying up the feeble streams of existence.

"How do you feel this morning?" said Belle laying her hand tenderly upon her forehead.

"Better, much better," she replied with an attempt at cheerfulness in her voice. "I am so glad, that Mother Graham is here. It is like letting the sunshine into these gloomy rooms to have her around. It all seems like a dream to me, I remember carrying a large bundle of work to the store, that my employer spoke harshly to me and talked of cutting down my wages. I also remember turning into the street, my eyes almost blinded with tears, and that I felt a dizziness in my head. The next I remember was seeing a lady feeding my children, and a gentleman coming in with Aunty Graham."

"Yes," said Belle, "fortunately after I had seen you, I met with Mr. Clifford who rendered me every necessary assistance. His presence was very opportune," just then Belle turned her eyes toward the door and saw Mr. Clifford standing on the threshold.

"Ah," said he smiling and advancing "this time the old adage has failed, which says that listeners never hear any good of themselves; for without intending to act the part of an eavesdropper, I heard myself pleasantly complimented."

"No more than you deserve," said Belle smiling and blushing, as she gave him her hand in a very frank and pleasant manner. "Mrs. Gough is much better this morning and is very grateful to you for your kindness."

"Mine," said Mr. Clifford "if you, will call it so, was only the result of an accident. Still I am very glad if I have been of any service, and you are perfectly welcome to make demands upon me that will add to Mrs. Cough's comfort."

"Thank you, I am very glad she has found a friend in you. It is such a blessed privilege to be able to help others less fortunate than ourselves."

"It certainly is."

"Just a moment," said Belle, as the voice of Mrs. Gough fell faintly on her ear.

"What is it, dear?" said Belle bending down to catch her words. "Who is that gentleman? His face and voice seem familiar."

"It is Mr. Clifford."

"Paul Clifford?"

"Yes. Do you know him?"

"Yes, I knew him years ago when I was young and happy; but it seems an age since. Oh, isn't it a dreadful thing, to be a drunkard's wife?"

"Yes it is, but would you like to speak to Mr. Clifford?"

"Yes! Mam, I would."

"Mr. Clifford," said Belle, "Mrs. Gough would like to speak with you."

"Do you not know me?" said Mary, looking anxiously into his face.

"I recognized you as soon as you moved into the neighborhood."

"I am very glad. I feared that I was so changed that my own dear mother would hardly recognize me. Don't you think she would pity and forgive me, if she saw what a mournful wretch I am?"

"Yes, I think she has long forgiven you and longs to take you to her heart as warmly as she ever did."

"And my father?"

"I believe he would receive you, but I don't think he would be willing to recognize your husband. You know he is very set in his ways."

"Mr. Clifford, I feel that my days are numbered and that my span of life will soon be done; but while I live I feel it my duty to cling to my demented husband, and to do all I can to turn him from the error of his ways. But I do so wish that my poor children could have my mother's care, when I am gone. If I were satisfied on that score, I would die content."

"Do not talk of dying," said Belle taking the pale thin hand in hers. "You must try and live for your children's sake. When you get strong I think I can find you some work among my friends. There is Mrs. Roberts, she often gives out work and I think I will apply to her."

"Mrs. James Roberts on St. James St. near 16th?"

"Yes! do you know her?"

"Yes," said Mrs. Gough closing her eyes wearily, "I know her and have worked for her."

"I think she is an excellent woman, I remember one morning we were talking together on religious experience, and about women speaking in class and conference meetings. I said I did not think I should like to constantly relate my experience in public, there was often such a lack of assurance of faith about me that I shrank from holding up my inner life to inspection; and she replied that she would always say that she loved Jesus, and I thought Oh, how I would like to have her experience. What rest and peace I would have if I could feel that I was always in harmony with Him."

"Miss Belle I hope you will not be offended with me, for I am very ignorant about these matters; but there was something about Mrs. Roberts dealings with us poor working people, that did seem to me not to be just what I think religion calls for. I found her a very hard person to deal with; she wanted so much work for so little money."

"But, Mrs. Gough, the times are very hard; and the rich feel it as well as the poor."

"But not so much. It curtails them in their luxuries, and us in our necessities; perhaps I shouldn't mention, but after my husband had become a confirmed drunkard, and all hope had died out of my heart, I hadn't time to sit down and brood helplessly over my misery. I had to struggle for my children and if possible keep the wolf from the door; and besides food and clothing, I wanted to keep my children in a respectable neighborhood, and my whole soul rose up in revolt against the idea of bringing them up where their eyes and ears would be constantly smitten by improper sights and sounds. While I was worrying over my situation and feeling that my health was failing under the terrible pressure of care and overwork, Mrs. Roberts brought me work; 'What will you do this for,' she said, displaying one of the articles she wanted made. I replied, 'One dollar and twenty-five cents,' and I knew the work well worth it. 'I can get it done for one dollar,' she replied, 'and I am not willing to give any more.' What could I do? I was out of work, my health was poor, and my children clutching at my heart strings for bread; and so I took it at her price. It was very unprofitable, but it was better than nothing."

"Why that is very strange. I know she pays her dressmaker handsomely."

"That is because her dressmaker is in a situation to dictate her own terms; but while she would pay her a large sum for dressmaking, she would screw and pinch a five-cent piece from one who hadn't power to resist her demands. I have seen people save twenty-five or fifty cents in dealing with poor people, who would squander ten times as much on some luxury of the table or wardrobe. I often find that meanness and extravagance go hand in hand."

"Yes, that is true, still Mrs. Gough, I think people often act like Mrs. Roberts more from want of thought than want of heart. It was an old charge brought against the Israelite, 'My people doth not consider.'"

"WHAT IS THE MATTER, MY dear?" said Belle a few mornings after this conversation as she approached the bedside of Mary Gough, "I thought you were getting along so nicely, and that with proper care you would be on your feet in a few days, but this morning you look so feeble, and seem so nervous and depressed. Do tell me what has happened and what has become of your beautiful hair; oh you had such a wealth of tresses, I really loved to toy with them. Was your head so painful that the doctor ordered them to be cut?"

"Oh, no," she said burying her face in the pillow and breaking into a paroxysm of tears. "Oh, Miss Belle, how can I tell you," she replied recovering from her sudden outburst of sorrow.

"Why, what is it darling? I am at a loss to know what has become of your beautiful hair."

With gentle womanly tact Belle saw that the loss of her hair was a subject replete with bitter anguish, and turning to the children she took them in her lap and interested and amused them by telling beautiful fairy stories. In a short time Mary's composure returned, and she said, "Miss Belle, I can now tell you how I lost my hair. Last night my husband, or the wreck of what was once my husband, came home. His eyes were wild and bloodshot; his face was pale and haggard, his gait uneven, and his hand trembling. I have seen him suffering from *Manipaotu* and dreaded lest he should have a returning of it. Mrs. Graham had just stepped out, and there was no one here but myself and children. He held in his hand a pair of shears, and approached my bedside. I was ready to faint with terror, when he exclaimed, 'Mary I must have liquor or I shall go wild,' he caught my hair in his hand; I was too feeble to resist, and in a few minutes he had cut every lock from my head, and left it just as you see it."

"Oh, what a pity, and what a shame."

"Oh, Miss Gordon do you think the men who make our laws ever stop to consider the misery, crime and destruction that flow out of the liquor traffic? I have done all I could to induce him to abstain, and he has abstained several months at a time and then suddenly like a flash of lightning the temptation returns and all his resolutions are scattered like chaff before the wind. I have been blamed for living with him, but Miss Belle were you to see him in his moments of remorse, and hear his bitter self reproach, and his earnest resolutions to reform, you would as soon leave a drowning man to struggle alone in the water as to forsake him in his weakness when every one else has turned against him, and if I can be the means of saving him, the joy for his redemption will counterbalance all that I have suffered as a drunkard's wife."

# XI

(Text missing.)

# XII

(Text missing.)

# XIII

## John Anderson's Saloon

*"The end of these things is death."*

W hy do you mix that liquor with such care and give it to that child? You know he is not going to pay you for it?"

"I am making an investment."

"How so?"

"Why you see that boy's parents are very rich, and in course of time he will be one of my customers."

"Well! John Anderson as old a sinner as I am, I wouldn't do such a thing for my right hand."

"What's the harm? You are one of my best customers, did liquor ever harm you?"

"Yes it does harm me, and when I see young men beginning to drink, I feel like crying out, 'Young man you are in danger, don't put your feet in the terrible flood, for ten to one you will be swamped.'"

"Well! this is the best joke of the season: Tom Cary preaching temperance. When do you expect to join the Crusade? But, Oh! talk is cheap."

"Cheap or dear, John Anderson, when I saw you giving liquor to that innocent boy, I couldn't help thinking of my poor Charley. He was just such a bright child as that, with beautiful brown eyes, and a fine forehead. Ah that boy had a mind; he was always ahead in his studies. But once when he was about twelve years old, I let him go on a travelling tour with his uncle. He was so agreeable and wide awake, his uncle liked to have him for company; but it was a dear trip to my poor Charley. During this journey they stopped at a hotel, and my brother gave him a glass of wine. Better for my dear boy had he given him a glass of strychnine. That one glass awakened within him a dreadful craving. It raged like a hungry fire. I talked to him, his mother pled with him, but it was no use, liquor was his master, and when he couldn't get liquor I've known him to break into his pantry to get our burning fluid to assuage his thirst. Sometimes he would be sober for several weeks at a time, and then our hopes would brighten that Charley would be himself again, and then in an hour all our hopes would be dashed to the ground. It seemed as if a spell was upon him. He married a dear good girl, who was as true as steel, but all her entreaties for him to give up drinking were like beating the air. He drank, and drank, until he drank himself into the grave."

By this time two or three loungers had gathered around John Anderson and Thomas Gary, and one of them said, "Mr. Gary you have had sad experience, why don't you give up drinking yourself?"

"Give it up! because I can't. Today I would give one half of my farm if I could pass by this saloon and not feel that I wanted to come in. No, I feel that I am a slave. There was a time when I could have broken my chain, but it is too late now, and I say young men take warning by me and don't make slaves and fools of yourselves."

"Now, Tom Cary," said John Anderson, "it is time for you to dry up, we have had enough of this foolishness, if you can't govern yourself, the more's the pity for you."

Just then the newsboy came along crying: *"Evening Mail. All about the dreadful murder! John Coots and James Loraine. Last edition. Buy a paper, Sir! Here's your last edition, all 'bout the dreadful murder".*

"John Coots," said several voices all at once, "Why he's been here a half dozen times today."

"I've drank with him," said one, "at that bar twice since noon. He had a strange look out of his eyes; and I heard him mutter something to himself."

"Yes," said another, "I heard him say he was going to kill somebody, 'one or the other's got to die,' what does the paper say?"

"Love, Jealousy, And Murder."

"The old story," said Anderson, looking somewhat relieved, "A woman's at the bottom of it."

"And liquor," said Tom Cary, "is at the top of it."

"I wish you would keep a civil tongue in your head," said Anderson, scowling at Cary.

"Oh! never mind; Tom, will have his say. He's got a knack of speaking out in meeting."

"And a very disagreeable knack it is."

"Oh never mind about Tom, read about the murder, and tend to Tom some other time."

Eagerly and excitedly they read the dreadful news. A woman, frail and vicious, was at the bottom; a woman that neither of those men would have married as a gracious gift, was the guilty cause of one murder, and when the law would take its course, two deaths would lie at her door. Oh, the folly of some men, who, instead of striving to make home a thing of beauty, strength and grace, wander into forbidden pastures, and reap for themselves harvests of misery and disgrace. And all for what? Because of the allurements of some idle, vain and sinful woman who has armed herself against the peace, the purity and the progress of the fireside. Such women are the dry rot in the social fabric; they dig in the dark beneath the foundation stones of the home. Young men enter their houses, and over the mirror of their lives, comes the shadow of pollution. Companionship with them unprepares them for the pure, simple joys of a happy and virtuous home; a place which should be the best school for the affections; one of the fairest spots on earth and one of the brightest types of heaven. Such a home as this, may exist without wealth, luxury or display; but it cannot exist without the essential elements of purity, love and truth.

The story was read, and then came the various comments.

"Oh, it was dreadful," said one. "Mr. Loraine belongs to one of the first families in the town; and what a cut it will be to them, not simply that he has been murdered, but murdered where he was—in the house of Lizzie Wilson. I knew her before she left husband and took to evil courses."

"Oh, what a pity, I expect it will almost kill his wife, poor thing, I pity her from the bottom of my heart."

"Why what's the matter Harry Richards? You look as white as a sheet, and you are all of a tremor."

"I've just come from the coroner's inquest, had to be one of the witnesses. I am afraid it will go hard with Coots."

"Why? What was the verdict of the jury?"

"They brought in a verdict of death by killing at the hands of John Coots."

"Were you present at the murder?"

"Yes."

"How did it happen?"

"Why you see John had been spending his money very freely on Lizzie Wilson, and he took it into his head because Loraine had made her some costly presents, that she had treated him rather coolly and wanted to ship him, and so he got dreadfully put out with Loraine and made some bitter threats against him. But I don't believe he would have done the deed if he had been sober, but he's been on a spree for several

FRANCES ELLEN WATKINS HARPER

days and he was half crazy when he did it. Oh it was heartrending to see Loraine's wife when they brought him home a corpse. She gave an awful shriek and fell to the floor, stiff as a poker; and his poor little children, it made my heart bleed to look at them; and his poor old mother. I am afraid it will be the death of her."

In a large city with its varied interests, one event rapidly chases the other. Life-boats are stranded on the shores of time, pitiful wrecks of humanity are dashed amid the rocks and reefs of existence. Old faces disappear and new ones take their places and the stream of life ever hurries on to empty where death's waters meet.

At the next sitting of the Court John Coots was arraigned, tried, and convicted of murder in the first degree. His lawyer tried to bring in a plea of emotional insanity but failed. If insane he was insane through the influence of strong drink. It was proven that he had made fierce threats against the life of Loraine, and the liquor in which he had so freely indulged had served to fire his brain and nerve his hand to carry out his wicked intent; and so the jury brought in its verdict, and he was sentenced to be executed, which sentence was duly performed and that closed another act of the sad drama. Intemperance and Sensuality had clasped hands together, and beneath their cruel fostering the gallows had borne its dreadful fruit of death. The light of one home had been quenched in gloom and guilt. A husband had broken over the barriers that God placed around the path of marital love, and his sun had gone down at mid-day. The sun which should have gilded the horizon of life and lent it additional charms, had gone down in darkness, yes, set behind the shadow of a thousand clouds. Innocent and unoffending childhood was robbed of a father's care, and a once happy wife, and joyful mother sat down in her widow's weeds with the mantle of a gloomier sorrow around her heart. And all for what? Oh who will justify the ways of God to man? Who will impress upon the mind of youth with its impulsiveness that it is a privilege as well as a duty to present the body to God, as a living sacrifice holy and acceptable in his sight. That God gives man no law that is not for his best advantage, and that the interests of humanity, and the laws of purity and self-denial all lie in the same direction, and the man who does not take care of his body must fail to take the best care of his soul; for the body should be temple for God's holy spirit and the instrument to do his work, and we have no right to defile the one or blunt the other and thus render ourselves unfit for the Master's service.

# XIV

Belle Gordon's indignation was thoroughly aroused by hearing Mary Gough's story about the loss of her hair, and she made up her mind that when she saw Joe Gough she would give him a very plain talking.

"I would like to see your husband; I would just like to tell him what I think about his conduct."

"Oh," said Mary, her pale cheek growing whiter with apprehension; "That's his footsteps now, Miss Belle don't say anything to him, Joe's as good and kind a man as I ever saw when he is sober, but sometimes he is really ugly when he has been drinking."

Just then the door was opened, and Joe Gough entered, or rather all that remained of the once witty, talented and handsome Josiah Gough. His face was pale and haggard, and growing premature by age, his wealth of raven hair was unkempt and hung in tangled locks over his forehead, his hand was unsteady and trembling from extreme nervousness, but he was sober enough to comprehend the situation, and to feel a deep sense of remorse and shame, when he gazed upon the weary head from whence he had bereft its magnificent covering.

"Here Mary," said he approaching the bed, "I've brought you a present; I only had four cents, and I thought this would please you, I know you women are so fond of jew-gaws," and he handed (her) a pair of sleeve buttons.

"Thank you," said she, as a faint smile illuminated her pallid cheek. "This," she said turning to Miss Gordon, "is my husband, Josiah Gough."

"Good morning, Mr. Gough," said Belle bowing politely and extending her hand. Joe returned the salutation very courteously and very quietly, sitting down by the bedside, made some remarks about the dampness of the weather. Mary lay very quiet, looking pitifully upon the mour(n)ful wretch at her side, who seemed to regard her and her friend with intense interest. It seemed from his countenance that remorse and shame were rousing up his better nature. Once he rose as if to go—stood irresolutely for a moment, and then sitting down by the bedside, clasped her thin pale hand in his with a caressing motion, and said, "Mary you've had a hard time, but I hope there are better days in store for us, don't get out of heart," and there was a moisture in his eyes in which for a moment beamed a tender, loving light. Belle immediately felt her indignation changing to pity. Surely she thought within herself, this man is worth saving—There is still love and tenderness within him, notwithstanding all his self-ruin, he reminds me of an expression I have picked up somewhere about "Old Oak," holding the young fibres at its heart, I will appeal to that better nature, I will use it as a lever to lift him from the depths into which he has fallen. While she was thinking of the best way to approach him, and how to reach that heart into whose hidden depths she had so unexpectedly glanced, he arose and bending over his wife imprinted upon her lips a kiss in which remorse and shame seemed struggling for expression, and left the room.

"Mother Graham," said Belle, "a happy thought has just struck me, Couldn't we induce Mr. Gough to attend the meeting of the Reform Club? Mr. R.N. speaks tonight and he has been meeting with glorious success as a Temperance Reformer, hundreds of men, many of them confirmed drunkards, have joined, and he is doing a remarkable work, he does not wait for the drunkards to come to him, he goes to them, and wins them by his personal sympathy, and it is wonderful the good he has done, I do wish he would go."

"I wish so too," said Martha Graham.

"If he should not return while I am here will you invite him to attend? Perhaps Mrs. Gough can spare you an hour or two this evening to accompany him."

"That I would gladly do, I think it would do me more good than all the medicines you could give me, to see my poor husband himself once more. Before he took to drinking, I was so happy, but it seems as if since then I have suffered sorrow by the spoonful. Oh the misery that this drink causes. I do hope these reform clubs will be the means of shutting up every saloon in the place, for just as long as one of them is open he is in danger."

"Yes," said Belle, "what we need is not simply to stop the men from drinking, but to keep the temptation out of their way."

"Joe," said Mary, "belongs to a good family, he has a first-rate education, is a fine penman, and a good bookkeeper, but this dreadful drink has thrown him out of some of the best situations in the town where we were living."

"Oh what a pity, I heard Mr. Clifford say that his business was increasing so that he wanted a good clerk and salesman to help him, that he was overworked and crippled for want of sufficient help. Maybe if your husband would sign the pledge, Mr. Clifford would give him a trial, but it is growing late and I must go. I would liked to have seen your husband before I left, and have given him a personal invitation, but you and Mother Graham can invite him for me, so good bye, keep up a good heart, you know where to cast your burden."

Just as Miss Gordon reached the landing, she saw Joe Gough standing at the outer door and laying her hand gently upon his shoulder, exclaimed, "Oh Mr. Gough, I am so glad to see you again, I wanted to invite you to attend a temperance meeting tonight at Amory Hall. Will you go?"

"Well I don't like to promise," he replied, looking down upon his seedy coat and dilapidated shoes.

"Never mind your wardrobe," said Miss Gordon divining his thoughts. "The soul is more than raiment, 'the world has room for another man and I want you to fill the place.'"

"Well," said he, "I'll come."

"Very well, I expect to be there and will look for you. Come early and bring Mother Graham."

"Mrs. Gough can spare her an hour or two this evening, I think your wife is suffering more from exhaustion and debility than anything else."

"Yes poor Mary has had a hard time, but it shan't be always so. As soon as I get work I mean to take her out of this," said he looking disdainfully at the wretched tenement house, with its broken shutters and look of general decay.

"WHY MOTHER GRAHAM IS (THE) meeting over? You must have had a fine time, you just look delighted. Did Joe go in with you, and where is he now?"

"Yes, he went with me, listened to the speeches, and joined the club, I saw him do it with my own eyes, Oh, we had a glorious time!"

"Oh I am so glad," said Mary, her eyes filling with sudden tears. "I do hope he will keep his pledge!"

"I hope so too, and I hope he will get something to do. Mr. Clifford was there when he signed, and Miss Belle was saying today that he wanted a clerk that would be a first r(at)e place for Joe, if he will only keep his pledge. Mr. Clifford is an active temperance man, and I believe would help to keep Joe straight."

"I hope he'll get the place, but Mother Graham, tell me all about the meeting, you don't know how happy I am."

"Don't I deary? Have I been through it all, but it seems as if I had passed through suffering into peace, but never mind Mother Graham's past troubles, let me tell you about the meeting."

"At these meetings quite a number of people speak, just as we went in one of the speakers was telling his experience, and what a terrible struggle he had to overcome the power of appetite. Now when he felt the fearful craving coming over him he would walk the carpet till he had actually worn it threadbare; but that he had been converted and found grace to help him in time of need, and how he had gone out and tried to reform others and had seen the work prosper in his hand. I watched Joe's face, it seemed lit up with earnestness and hope, as if that man had brought him a message of deliverance; then after the meeting came the signing of the pledge and joining the reform club, and it would have done you good to see the men that joined."

"Do you remember Thomas Allison?"

"Yes, poor fellow, and I think if any man ever inherited drunkenness, he did, for his father and his mother were drunkards before him."

"Well, he joined and they have made him president of the club."

"Well did I ever! But tell me all about Joe."

"When the speaking was over, Joe sat still and thoughtful as if making up his mind, when Miss Gordon came to him and asked him to join, he stopped a minute to button his coat and went right straight up and had his name put down, but oh how the people did clap and shout. Well as Joe was one of the last to sign, the red ribbons they use for badges was all gone and Joe looked so sorry, he said he wanted to take a piece of ribbon home to let his wife know that he belonged to the Reform Club, Miss Gordon heard him, and she had a piece of black lace and red ribbon twisted together around her throat and she separated the lace from the ribbon and tied it in his button-hole, so his Mary would see it. Oh Miss Belle did look so sweet and Mr. Clifford never took his eyes off her. I think he admires her very much."

"I don't see how he can help it, she is one of the dearest—sweetest, ladies I ever saw, she never seemed to say by her actions, 'I am doing so much for you poor people' and you can't be too thankful."

"Not she, and between you and I, and the gate-post, I think that will be a match."

"I think it would make a splendid one, but hush, I hear some persons coming."

The door opened and Paul Clifford, Joe Gough, and Belle Gordon entered.

"Here Mrs. Gough," said Paul Clifford, "as we children used to say. Here's your husband safe and sound, and I will add, a member of our reformed club and we have come to congratulate you upon the event."

"My dear friends, I am very thankful to you for your great kindness, I don't think I shall ever be able to repay you."

"Don't be uneasy darling," said Belle, "we are getting our pay as we go along, we don't think the cause of humanity owes us anything." "Yes," said Joe seating himself by the bed side with an air of intense gratification. "Here is my badge, I did not want to leave the meeting without having this to show you."

"This evening," said Mrs. Gough smiling through her tears, "reminds me of a little temperance song I learned when a child, I think it commenced with these words:

> *"And are you sure the news is true?*
> *Are you sure my John has joined?*
> *I can't believe the happy news,*
> *And leave my fears behind,*
> *If John has joined and drinks no more,*
> *The happiest wife am I*
> *That ever swept a cabin floor,*
> *Or sung a lullaby.*

"That's just the way I feel tonight, I haven't been so happy before for years."

"And I hope," said Mr. Clifford, "that you will have many happy days and nights in the future."

"And I hope so too," said Joe, shaking hands with Paul and Belle as they rose to go.

Mr. Clifford accompanied Belle to her door, and as they parted she said, "This is a glorious work in which it is our privilege to clasp hands."

"It is and I hope," but as the words rose to his lips, he looked into the face of Belle, and it was so radiant with intelligent tenderness and joy, that she seemed to him almost like a glorified saint, a being too precious high and good for common household uses, and so the remainder of the sentence died upon his lips and he held his peace.

# XV

"I have resolved to dissolve partnership with Charles," said Augustine Romaine to his wife, the next morning after his son's return from the Champaign supper at John Anderson's.

"Oh! no you are not in earnest, are you? You seem suddenly to have lost all patience with Charlie."

"Yes I have, and I have made up my mind that I am not going to let him hang like a millstone on our business. No, if he will go down, I am determined he shall not drag me down with him. See what a hurt it would be to us, to have it said, 'Don't trust your case with the Romaine's for the Junior member of that firm is a confirmed drunkard.'"

"Well, Augustine you ought to know best, but it seems like casting him off, to dissolve partnership with him."

"I can't help it, if he persists in his downward course he must take the consequences. Charles has had every advantage; when other young lawyers have had to battle year after year with obscurity and poverty, he entered into a business that was already established and flourishing. What other men were struggling for, he found ready made to his hand, and if he chooses to throw away every advantage and make a complete wreck of himself, I can't help it."

"Oh! it does seem so dreadful, I wonder what will become of my poor boy?"

"Now, mother I want you to look at this thing in the light of reason and common sense. I am not turning Charles out of the house. He is not poor, though the way he is going on he will be. You know his grandfather has left him a large estate out West, which is constantly increasing in value. Now what I mean to do is to give Charles a chance to set up for himself as attorney, wherever he pleases. Throwing him on his own resources, with a sense of responsibility, may be the best thing for him; but in the present state of things I do not think it advisable to continue our business relations together. For more than twenty-five years our firm has stood foremost at the bar. Ever since my brother and I commenced business together our reputation has been unspotted and I mean to keep it so, if I have to cut off my right hand."

Mrs. Romaine gazed upon the stern sad face of her husband, and felt by the determination of his manner that it was useless to entreat or reason with him to change his purpose; and so with a heavy heart, and eyes drooping with unshed tears, she left the room.

"John," said Mr. Romaine to the waiter, "tell Charles I wish to see him before I go down to the office." Just then Charles entered the room and bade good morning to his father.

"Good morning," replied his father, rather coldly, and for a moment there was an awkward silence.

"Charles," said Mr. Romaine, "after having witnessed the scene of last night, I have come to the conclusion to dissolve the partnership between us."

"Just as you please," said Charles in a tone of cold indifference that irritated his father; but he maintained his self-control.

"I am sorry that you will persist in your downward course; but if you are determined to throw yourself away I have made up my mind to cut loose from you. I noticed last week when you were getting out the briefs in that Sumpter case, you were not yourself, and several times lately you have made me hang my head in the court room. I am sorry, very sorry," and a touch of deep emotion gave a tone of tenderness to the closing sentence. There was a slight huskiness in Charles' voice, as he replied, "Whenever the articles of dissolution are made out I am ready to sign."

"They shall be ready by tomorrow."

"All right, I will sign them."

"And what then?"

"Set up for myself, the world is wide enough for us both."

After Mr. Romaine had left the room, Charles sat, burying his head in his hands and indulging bitter thoughts toward his father. "Today," he said to himself, "he resolved to cut loose from me apparently forgetting that it was from his hands, and at his table I received my first glass of wine. He prides himself on his power of self-control, and after all what does it amount to? It simply means this, that he has an iron constitution, and can drink five times as much as I can without showing its effects, and today if Mr. R.N. would ask him to sign the total-abstinence pledge, he wouldn't hear to it. Yes I am ready to sign any articles he will bring, even if it is to sign never to enter this house, or see his face; but my mother—poor mother, I am sorry for her sake."

Just then his mother entered the room.

"My son."

"Mother."

"Just what I feared has come to pass. I have dreaded more than anything else this collision with your father."

"Now mother don't be so serious about this matter. Father's law office does not take in the whole world. I shall either set up for myself in A.P., or go West."

"Oh! don't talk of going away, I think I should die of anxiety if you were away."

"Well, as I passed down the street yesterday I saw there was an office to let in Frazier's new block, and I think I will engage it and put out my sign. How will that suit you?"

"Anything, or anywhere, Charlie, so you are near me. And Charlie don't be too stout with your father, he was very much out of temper when you came home last night, but be calm; it will blow over in a few days, don't add fuel to the fire. And you know that you and Miss Roland are to be married in two weeks, and I do wish that things might remain as they are, at least till after the wedding. Separation just now might give rise to some very unpleasant talk, and I would rather if you and your father can put off this dissolution, that you will consent to let things remain as they are for a few weeks longer. When your father comes home I will put the case to him, and have the thing delayed. Just now Charles I dread the consequences of a separation."

"Well, Mother, just as you please; perhaps the publication of the articles of dissolution in the paper might complicate matters."

When Mr. Romaine returned home, his wrath was somewhat mollified, and Mrs. Romaine having taken care to prepare his favorite dishes for dinner, took the opportunity when he had dined to entreat him to delay the intended separation till after the wedding, to which he very graciously consented.

AGAIN THERE WAS A MERRY gathering at the home of Jeanette Roland. It was her wedding night, and she was about to clasp hands for life with Charles Romaine. True to her idea of taking things as she found them, she had consented to be his wife without demanding of him any reformation from the habit which was growing so fearfully upon him. His wealth and position in society like charity covered a multitude of sins. At times Jeanette felt misgivings about the step she was about to take, but she put back the thoughts like unwelcome intruders, and like the Ostrich, hiding her head in the sand, instead of avoiding the danger, she shut her eyes to its fearful reality. That night the wine flowed out like a purple flood; but the men and women who drank were people of culture, wealth and position, and did not seem to think it was just as disgraceful or more so to drink in excess in magnificently furnished parlors, as it was in low Barrooms or miserable dens where vice and poverty are huddled together. And if the weary children of hunger and hard toil instead of seeking sleep as nature's sweet restorer, sought to stimulate their flagging energies in the enticing cup, they with the advantages of wealth, culture and refinement could not plead the excuses of extreme wretchedness, or hard and unremitting drudgery.

"How beautiful, very beautiful," fell like a pleasant ripple upon the ear of Jeanette Roland, as she approached the altar, beneath her wreath of orange blossoms, while her bridal veil floated like a cloud of lovely mist from her fair young head. The vows were spoken, the bridal ring placed upon her finger, and amid a train of congratulating friends, she returned home where a sumptuous feast awaited them.

"Don't talk so loud, but I think Belle Gordon acted wisely when she refused Mr. Romaine," said Mrs. Gladstone, one of the guests.

"Do you, indeed? Why Charles Romaine, is the only son of Mr. Romaine, and besides being the heir he has lately received a large legacy from his grandfather's estate. I think Jeanette has made a splendid match. I hope my girls will do as well."

"I hope on the other hand that my girls will never marry unless they do better."

"Why how you talk! What's the matter with Mr. Romaine?"

"Look at him now," said Mrs. Fallard joining in the conversation. "This is his wedding night and yet you can plainly see he is under the influence of wine. Look at those eyes, don't you know how beautiful and clear they are when he is sober, and how very interesting he is in conversation. Now look at him, see how muddled his eye is—but he is approaching—listen to his utterance, don't you notice how thick it is? Now if on his wedding night, he can not abstain, I have very grave fears for Jeanette's future."

"Perhaps you are both right, but I never looked at things in that light before, and I know that a magnificent fortune can melt like snow in the hands of a drunken man."

"I wish you much joy," rang out a dozen voices, as Jeanette approached them. "Oh Jeanette, you just look splendid! and Mr. Romaine, oh he is so handsome." "Oh Jeanette what's to hinder you from being so happy?" "But where is Mr. Romaine? we have missed him for some time." "I don't know, let me seek my husband." "Isn't that a mouthful?" said Jeanette laughingly disengaging herself from the merry group, as an undefined sense of apprehension swept over her. Was it a presentiment of coming danger? An unspoken prophecy to be verified by bitter tears, and lonely fear that seemed for a moment to turn life's sweetness into bitterness and gall. In the midst of a noisy group, in the dining room, she found Charles drinking the wine as it gave its color aright in the cup. She saw the deep flush upon his cheek, and the cloudiness of his eye, and for the first time upon that bridal night she felt a shiver of fear as the veil was suddenly lifted before her unwilling eye; and half reluctantly she said to herself, "Suppose after all my cousin Belle was right."

# XVI

G ood morning! Mr. Clifford," said Joe Gough, entering the store of Paul Clifford, the next day after he joined the Reform Club. "I have heard that you wanted some one to help you, and I am ready to do anything to make an honest living."

"I am very sorry," said Paul, "but I have just engaged a young man belonging to our Club to come this morning."

Joe looked sad, but not discouraged, and said, "Mr. Clifford, I want to turn over a new leaf in my life, but everyone does not know that. Do you know of any situation I can get? I have been a book-keeper and a salesman in the town of C., where I once lived, but I am willing to begin almost anywhere on the ladder of life, and make it a stepping-stone to something better."

There was a tone of earnestness in his voice, and an air of determination, in his manner that favorably impressed Paul Clifford and he replied,—

"I was thinking of a friend of mine who wants a helping hand; but it may not be, after all, the kind of work you prefer. He wants a porter, but as you say you want to make your position a stepping-stone to something better, if you make up your mind to do your level best, the way may open before you in some more congenial and unexpected quarter. Wait a few minutes, and I will give you a line to him. No! I can do better than that; he is a member of our Club, and I will see him myself; but before you do, had we better not go to the barber's?"

"I would like to," said Joe, "but I haven't—"

"Haven't the money?"

"Yes, Mr. Clifford, that's the fact, I am not able to pay even for a shave. Oh! what a fool I have been."

"Oh! well never mind, let the dead past, bury its dead. The future is before you, try and redeem that. If you accept it, I will lend you a few dollars. I believe in lending a helping hand. So come with me to the barber's and I'll make it all right, you can pay me when you are able, but here we are at the door, let us go in."

They entered, and in a few moments Joe's face was under the manipulating care of the barber.

"Fix this so," said Joe to the barber, giving him directions how to cut his mustache.

Paul was somewhat amused, and yet in that simple act, he saw a return of self-respect, and was glad to see its slightest manifestations, and it was pleasant to witness the satisfaction with which Joe beheld himself in the glass, as he exclaimed, "Why Mary would hardly know me!"

"Suppose now, we go to the tailor's and get some new rigging?"

"Mr. Clifford," said Joe hesitatingly, "you are very kind, but I don't know when I shall be able to pay you, and—"

"Oh! never mind, when you are able I will send my bill. It will help you in looking for a place to go decently dressed. So let us go into the store and get a new suit."

They entered a clothing store and in a few moments Joe was dressed in a new suit which made him look almost like another person.

"Now, we are ready," said Paul, "appearances are not so much against you."

"Good morning Mr. Tennant," said Paul to the proprietor of a large store. "I heard last night that you wanted help in your store and I have brought you Mr. Gough, who is willing to take any situation you will give him, and I will add, he is a member of our Reform Club."

Mr. Tennant looked thoughtfully a moment, and replied, "I have only one vacancy, and I do not think it would suit your friend. My porter died yesterday and that is the only situation which I can offer him at present."

"I will accept it," said Joe, "if you will give it to me, I am willing to do anything to make an honest living for my family."

"Well you can come tomorrow, or stop now and begin."

"All right," said Joe with a promptness that pleased his employer, and Joe was installed in the first day's regular work he had had for months.

"What! sitting up sewing?" said Belle Gordon entering the neat room where Mrs. Gough was rejuvenating a dress for her older daughter. "Why you look like another woman, your cheeks are getting plump, your eyes are brightening, and you look so happy."

"I feel just like I look, Miss Gordon. Joe has grown so steady, he gets constant work, and he is providing so well for us all, and he won't hear to me taking again that slop-shop work. He says all he wants me to do, is to get well, and take care of the home and children. But you look rather pale, have you been sick?"

"Yes, I have been rather unwell for several weeks, and the doctor has ordered among other things that I should have a plentiful supply of fresh air, so tomorrow as there is to be a free excursion, and I am on the Committee, I think if nothing prevents, I shall go. Perhaps you would like to go?"

"Yes, if Joe will consent, but—"

"But, what?"

"Well Joe has pretty high notions, and I think he may object, because it is receiving charity. I can't blame him for it, but Joe has a right smart of pride that way."

"No! I don't blame him, I rather admire his spirit of self-reliance, and I wouldn't lay the weight of my smallest finger upon his self-respect to repress it; still I would like to see your Mamy, and Hatty, have a chance to get out into the woods, and have what I call a good time. I think I can have it so arranged that you can go with me, and serve as one of the Committee on refreshments, and your services would be an ample compensation for your entertainment."

"Well if you put it in that light, I think Joe would be willing for me to go."

"I will leave the matter there, and when your husband comes home you can consult him and send me word. And so you are getting along nicely?"

"Oh! yes indeed, splendidly. Just look here, this is Joe's present," and Mary held up with both hands a beautifully embossed and illustrated Bible. "This was my birth-day present. Oh! Miss Belle, Joe seems to me like another man. Last night we went to a conference and prayer-meeting, and Joe spoke. Did you know he had joined the church?"

"No! when did that happen?"

"Last week."

"Has he become religious?"

"Well I think Joe's trying to do the best he can. He said last night in meeting that he felt like a new man, and if they didn't believe he had religion to ask his wife."

"And suppose they had asked you, what would you have said?"

"I would have said I believe Joe's a changed man, and I hope he will hold out faithful. And Miss Belle I want to be a Christian, but there are some things about religion I can't understand. People often used to talk to me about getting religion, and getting ready to die. Religion somehow got associated in my mind with sorrow and death, but it seems to me since I have known you and Mr. Clifford the thing looks different. I got it associated with something else besides the pall, the hearse, and weeping mourners. You have made me feel that it is as beautiful and valuable for life as it is necessary for death. And yet there are some things I can't understand. Miss Belle will you be shocked if I tell you something which has often puzzled me?"

"I don't know, I hope you have nothing very shocking to tell me."

"Well perhaps it is, and maybe I had better not say it."

"But you have raised my curiosity, and woman like I want to hear it."

"Now don't be shocked, but let me ask you, if you really believe that God is good?"

"Yes I do, and to doubt it would be to unmoor my soul from love, from peace, and rest. It seems to me to believe that must be the first resting place for my soul, and I feel that with me

> "To doubt would be disloyalty
> To falter would be sin.

"But my dear I have been puzzled just as you have, and can say,—

> "I have wandered in mazes dark and distressing
> I've had not a cheering ray my spirit to bless,
> Cheerless unbelief held my laboring soul in grief."

"And what then?"

> "I then turned to the Gospel that taught me to pray
> And trust in the living word from folly away.

"And it was here my spirit found a resting place, and I feel that in believing I have entered into rest."

"Ah!" said Mary to herself when Belle was gone, "there is something so restful and yet inspiring in her words. I wish I had her faith."

# XVII

I am sorry, very sorry," said Belle Gordon, as a shadow of deep distress flitted over her pale sad face. She was usually cheerful and serene in her manner; but now it seemed as if the very depths of her soul had been stirred by some mournful and bitter memory. "Your question was so unexpected and—"

"And what!" said Paul in a tone of sad expectancy, "so unwelcome?"

"It was so sudden, I was not prepared for it."

"I do not," said Paul, "ask an immediate reply. Give yourself ample time for consideration."

"Mr. Clifford," said Belle, her voice gathering firmness as she proceeded, "while all the relations of life demand that there should be entire truthfulness between us and our fellow creatures, I think we should be especially sincere and candid in our dealings with each other on this question of marriage, a question not only as affecting our own welfare but that of others, a relation which may throw its sunshine or shadow over the track of unborn ages. Permit me now to say to you, that there is no gentleman of my acquaintance whom I esteem more highly than yourself; but when you ask me for my heart and hand, I almost feel as if I had no heart to give; and you know it would be wrong to give my hand where I could not place my heart."

"But would it be impossible for you to return my affection?" "I don't know, but I am only living out my (vow) of truthfulness when I say to you, I feel as if I had been undone for love. You tell that in offering your hand that you bring me a heart unhackneyed in the arts of love, that my heart is the first and only shrine on which you have ever laid the wealth of your affections. I cannot say the same in reply. I have had my bright and beautiful day dream, but it has faded, and I have learned what is the hardest of all lessons for a woman to learn. I have learned to live without love."

"Oh no," said Paul, "not to live without love. In darkened homes how many grateful hearts rejoice to hear your footsteps on the threshold. I have seen the eyes of young Arabs of the street grow brighter as you approached and say, 'That's my lady, she comes to see my mam when she's sick.' And I have seen little girls in the street quicken their face to catch a loving smile from their dear Sunday school teacher. Oh Miss Belle instead of living without love, I think you are surrounded with a cordon of loving hearts."

"Yes, and I appreciate them—but this is not the love to which I refer. I mean a love which is mine, as anything else on earth is mine, a love precious, enduring and strong, which brings hope and joy and sunshine over one's path in life. A love which commands my allegiance and demands my respect. This is the love I have learned to do without, and perhaps the poor and needy had learned to love me less, had this love surrounded me more."

"Miss Belle, perhaps I was presumptuous, to have asked a return of the earnest affection I have for you; but I had hoped that you would give the question some consideration; and may I not hope that you will think kindly of my proposal? Oh Miss Gordon, ever since the death of my sainted mother, I have had in my mind's eye the ideal of a woman nobly planned, beautiful, intellectual, true and affectionate, and you have filled out that ideal in all its loveliest proportions, and I hope that my desire will not be like reaching out to some bright particular star and wishing to win it. It seems to me," he said with increasing earnestness, "whatever obstacle may be in the way, I would go through fire and water to remove it."

"I am sorry," said Belle as if speaking to herself, and her face had an absent look about it, as if instead of being interested in the living present she was grouping amid the ashes of the dead past. At length she said, "Mr. Clifford, permit me to say in the first place, let there be truth between us. If my heart seems callous and indifferent to your love, believe me it is warm to esteem and value you as a friend, I might almost say as a brother, for in sympathy of feeling and congeniality of disposition you are nearer to me than my own brother; but I do not think were I so inclined that it would be advisable for me to accept your hand without letting you know something of my past history. I told you a few moments since that I had my day dream. Permit me to tell you, for I think you are entitled to my confidence. The object of that day dream was Charles Romaine."

"Charles Romaine!" and there was a tone of wonder in the voice, and a puzzled look on the face of Paul Clifford.

"Yes! Charles Romaine, not as you know him now, with the marks of dissipation on his once handsome face, but Charles Romaine, as I knew him when he stood upon the threshold of early manhood, the very incarnation of beauty, strength and grace. Not Charles Romaine with the blurred and bloated countenance, the staggering gait, the confused and vacant eye; but Charles Romaine as a young, handsome and talented lawyer, the pride of our village, the hope of his father and the joy of his mother; before whom the future was opening full of rich and rare promises. Need I tell you that when he sought my hand in preference to all the other girls in our village, that I gave him what I never can give to another, the first, deep love of my girlish heart. For nearly a whole year I wore his betrothal ring upon my finger, when I saw to my utter anguish and dismay that he was fast becoming a drunkard. Oh! Mr. Clifford if I could have saved him I would have taken blood from every vein and strength from every nerve. We met frequently at entertainments. I noticed time after time, the effects of the wine he had imbibed, upon his manner and conversation. At first I shrank from remonstrating with him, until the burden lay so heavy on my heart that I felt I must speak out, let the consequences be what they might. And so one evening I told him plainly and seriously my fears about his future. He laughed lightly and said my fears were unfounded; that I was nervous and giving away to idle fancies; that his father always had wine at the table, and that he had never seen him under the influence of liquor. Silenced, but not convinced, I watched his course with painful solicitude. All remonstrances on my part seemed thrown away; he always had the precedent of his father to plead in reply to my earnest entreaties. At last when remonstrances and entreaties seemed to be all in vain, I resolved to break the engagement. It may have been a harsh and hard alternative, but I would not give my hand where my respect could not follow. It may be that I thought too much of my own happiness, but I felt that marriage must be for me positive misery or positive happiness, and I feared that if I married a man so lacking in self-control as to become a common drunkard, that when I ceased to love and respect him, I should be constantly tempted to hate and despise him. I think one of the saddest fates that can befall a woman is to be tied for life to a miserable bloated wreck of humanity. There may be some women with broad generous hearts, and great charity, strong enough to lift such men out of the depths, but I had no such faith in my strength and so I gave him back his ring. He accepted it, but we parted as friends. For awhile after our engagement was broken, we occasionally met at the houses of our mutual friends in social gatherings and I noticed with intense satisfaction that whenever wine was offered he scrupulously abstained from ever tasting a drop, though I think at times his self-control was severely tested. Oh! what hope revived in my heart. Here I said to myself is compensation for all I have suffered, if by it he shall be restored to manhood usefulness and society, and learn to make his life not a thing of careless ease and sensuous indulgence, but of noble struggle and high and holy endeavor. But while I was picturing out for him a magnificent future, imagining the lofty triumphs of his intellect—an intellect grand in its achievements and glorious in its possibilities, my beautiful daydream was rudely broken up, and vanished away like the rays of sunset mingling with the shadows of night. My Aunt Mrs. Roland, celebrated her silver-wedding and my cousin's birth-day by giving a large entertainment; and among other things she had a plentiful supply of wine. Mr. Romaine had lately made the acquaintance of my cousin Jeanette Roland. She was both beautiful in person and fascinating in her manners, and thoughtlessly she held a glass of wine in her hand and asked Mr. Romaine if he would not honor the occasion, by drinking her mother's health. For a moment he hesitated, his cheek paled and flushed alternately, he looked irresolute. While I watched him in silent anguish it seemed as if the agony of years was compressed in a few moments. I tried to catch his eye but failed, and with a slight tremor in his hand he lifted the glass to his lips and drank. I do not think I would have felt greater anguish had I seen him suddenly drowned in sight of land. Oh! Mr. Clifford that night comes before me so vividly, it seems as if I am living it all over again. I do not think Mr. Romaine has ever recovered from the reawakening of his appetite. He has since married Jeanette. I meet her occasionally. She has a beautiful home, dresses magnificently, and has a retinue of servants; and yet I fancy she is not happy. That somewhere hidden out of sight there is a worm eating at the core of her life. She has a way of dropping her eyes and an absent look about her that I do not fully understand, but it seems to me that I miss the old elasticity of her spirits, the merry ring of her voice, the pleasant thrills of girlish laughter, and though she never confesses it to me I doubt that Jeanette is happy. And with this sad experience in the past can you blame me if I am slow, very slow to let the broken tendrils of my heart entwine again?"

"Miss Belle," said Paul Clifford catching eagerly at the smallest straw of hope, "if you can not give me the first love of a fresh young life, I am content with the rich aftermath of your maturer years, and ask from life no higher prize; may I not hope for that?"

"I will think on it but for the present let us change the subject."

"Do you think Jeanette is happy? She seems so different from what she used to be," said Miss Tabitha Jones to several friends who were spending the evening with her.

"Happy!" replied Mary Gladstone, "don't see what's to hinder her from being happy. She has everything that heart can wish. I was down to her house yesterday, and she has just moved in her new home. It has all the modern improvements, and everything is in excellent taste. Her furniture is of the latest style, and I think it is really superb."

"Yes," said her sister, "and she dresses magnificently. Last week she showed me a most beautiful set of jewelry, and a camel's hair shawl, and I believe it is real camel's hair. I think you could almost run it through a ring. If I had all she has, I think I should be as happy as the days are long. I don't believe I would let a wave of trouble roll across my peaceful breast."

"Oh! Annette," said Mrs. Gladstone, "don't speak so extravagantly, and I don't like to hear you quote those lines for such an occasion."

"Why not mother? Where's the harm?"

"That hymn has been associated in my mind with my earliest religious impressions and experience, and I don't like to see you lift it out of its sacred associations, for such a trifling occasion."

"Oh mother you are so strict. I shall never be able to keep time with you, but I do think, if I was off as Jeanette, that I would be as blithe and happy as a lark, and instead of that she seems to be constantly drooping and fading."

"Annette," said Mrs. Gladstone, "I knew a woman who possesses more than Jeanette does, and yet she died of starvation."

"Died of starvation! Why, when, and where did that happen? and what became of her husband?"

"He is in society, caressed and ed on by the young girls of his set and I have seen a number of managing mammas to whom I have imagined he would not be an objectionable son-in-law."

"Do I know him mother?"

"No! and I hope you never will."

"Well mother I would like to know how he starved his wife to death and yet escaped the law."

"The law helped him."

"Oh mother!" said both girls opening their eyes in genuine astonishment.

"I thought," said Mary Gladstone, "it was the province of the law to protect women, I was just telling Miss Basanquet yesterday, when she was talking about woman's suffrage that I had as many rights as I wanted and that I was willing to let my father and brothers do all the voting for me."

"Forgetting my dear, that there are millions of women who haven't such fathers and brothers as you have. No my dear, when you examine the matter, a little more closely, you will find there are some painful inequalities in the law for women."

"But mother, I do think it would be a dreadful thing for women to vote Oh! just think of women being hustled and crowded at the polls by rude men, their breaths reeking with whiskey and tobacco, the very air heavy with their oaths. And then they have the polls at public houses. Oh mother, I never want to see the day when women vote."

"Well I do, because we have one of the kindest and best fathers and husbands and good brothers, who would not permit the winds of heaven to visit us too roughly, there is no reason we should throw ourselves between the sunshine and our less fortunate sisters who shiver in the blast."

"But mother, I don't see how voting would help us, I am sure we have influence I have often heard papa say that you were the first to awaken him to a sense of the enormity of slavery. Now mother if we women would use our influence with our fathers, brothers, husbands, and sons, could we not have everything we want."

"No, my dear we could not, with all our influence we never could have the same sense of responsibility which flows from the possession of power. I want women to possess power as well as influence, I want every Christian woman as she passes by a grogshop or liquor saloon, to feel that she has on her heart a burden of responsibility for its existence, I hold my dear that a nation as well as an individual should have a conscience, and on this liquor question there is room for woman's conscience not merely as a persuasive influence but as an enlightened and aggressive power."

"Well Ma I think you would make a first class stump speaker. I expect when women vote we shall be constantly having calls, for the gifted, and talented Mrs. Gladstone to speak on the duties and perils of the hour."

"And I would do it, I would go among my sister women and try to persuade them to use their vote as a moral lever, not to make home less happy, but society more holy. I would have good and sensible women, grave in manner, and cultured in intellect, attend the primary meetings and bring their moral influence and political power to frown down corruption, chicanery, and low cunning."

"But mother just think if women went to the polls how many vicious ones would go?"

"I hope and believe for the honor of our sex that the vicious women of the community are never in the majority, that for one woman whose feet turn aside from the paths of rectitude that there are thousands of feet that never stray into forbidden paths, and today I believe there is virtue enough in society to confront its vice, and intelligence enough to grapple with its ignorance."

# XVIII

Why Mrs. Gladstone," said Miss Tabitha, "you are as zealous as a new convert to the cause of woman suffrage. We single women who are constantly taxed without being represented, know what it is to see ignorance and corruption striking hands together and voting away our money for whatever purposes they choose. I pay as large a tax as many of the men in A.P., and yet cannot say who shall assess my property for a single year."

"And there is another thing," said Mrs. Gladstone, "ought to be brought to the consideration of the men, and it is this. They refuse to let us vote and yet fail to protect our homes from the ravages of rum. My young friend, whom I said died of starvation; foolishly married a dissipated man who happened to be rich and handsome. She was gentle, loving, sensitive to a fault. He was querulous, fault-finding and irritable, because his nervous system was constantly unstrung by liquor. She lacked tenderness, sympathy and heart support, and at last faded and died, not starvation of the body, but a trophy of the soul, and when I say the law helped, I mean it licensed the places that kept the temptation ever in his way. And I fear, that is the secret of Jeanette's faded looks, and unhappy bearing."

No Jeanette was not happy. Night after night would she pace the floor of her splendidly furnished chamber waiting and watching for her husband's footsteps. She and his friends had hoped that her influence would be strong enough to win him away from his boon companions, that his home and beautiful bride would present superior attractions to Anderson's saloon, his gambling pool, and champaign suppers, and for a while they did, but soon the novelty wore off, and Jeanette found out to her great grief that her power to bind him to the simple attractions of home were as futile as a role of cobwebs to moor a ship to the shore, when it has drifted out and is dashing among the breakers. He had learned to live an element of excitement, and to depend upon artificial stimulation, until it seemed as if the very blood in his veins grew sluggish fictitious excitement was removed. His father, hopeless of his future, had dissolved partnership with him, and for months there had been no communication between them; and Jeanette saw with agony and dismay that his life was being wrecked upon the broad sea of sin and shame.

"Where is his father? The child can't live. It is one of the worst cases of croup I have had this year, why didn't you send for me sooner? Where is his father? It is now just twelve o'clock, time for all respectable men to be in the house," said the bluff but kind hearted family doctor looking tenderly upon Jeanette's little boy who lay gasping for breath in the last stages of croup.

"Oh! I don't know," said Jeanette her face crimsoning beneath the doctor's searching glance. "I suppose he is down to Anderson's."

"Anderson's!" said the doctor in a tone of hearty indignation, "what business has he there, and his child dying here?"

"But doctor, he didn't know, the child had fever when he went out, but neither of us thought much of it till I was awakened by his strange and unnatural breathing. I sent for you as soon as I could rouse the servants." "Well rouse them again, and tell them to go down to Anderson's and tell your husband that his child is dying."

"Oh! no not dying doctor, you surely don't mean it." "Yes Jeanette," said the old family doctor, tenderly and sadly, "I can do nothing for him, let me take him in my arms and rest you. Dear little darling, he will be saved from the evils to come."

Just as his life was trembling on its frailest chords, and its delicate machinery almost wound up, Charles Romaine returned, sober enough to take in the situation. He strode up to the dying child, took the clammy hands in his, and said in a tone of bitter anguish, "Charlie, don't you know papa? Wouldn't you speak one little word to papa?" But it was too late, the shadows that never deceive flitted over the pale beauty of the marble brow, the waxen lid closed over the once bright and laughing eye, and the cold grave for its rest had won the child.

# XIX

(Text missing.)

# XX

If riches could bring happiness, John Anderson should be a happy man; and yet he is far from being happy. He has succeeded in making money, but failed in every thing else. But let us enter his home. As you open the parlor door your feet sink in the rich and beautiful carpet. Exquisite statuary, and superbly framed pictures greet your eye and you are ready to exclaim, "Oh! how lovely." Here are the beautiful conceptions of painters' art and sculptors' skill. It is a home of wealth, luxury and display, but not of love, refinement and culture. Years since, before John Anderson came to live in the city of A.P. he had formed an attachment for an excellent young lady who taught school in his native village, and they were engaged to be married; but after coming to the city and forming new associations, visions of wealth dazzled his brain, and unsettled his mind, till the idea of love in a cottage grew distasteful to him. He had seen men with no more ability than himself who had come to the city almost pennyless, and who had grown rich in a few years, and he made up his mind that if possible he would do two things, acquire wealth and live an easy life, and he thought the easiest way to accomplish both ends was to open up a gorgeous palace of sin and entice into his meshes the unwary, the inexperienced, and the misguided slaves of appetite. For awhile after he left his native village, he wrote almost constantly to his betrothed; but as new objects and interests engaged his attention, his letters became colder and less frequent, until they finally ceased and the engagement was broken. At first the blow fell heavily upon the heart of his affianced, but she was too sensible to fade away and die the victim of unrequited love, and in after years when she had thrown her whole soul into the temperance cause, and consecrated her life to the work of uplifting fallen humanity, she learned to be thankful that it was not her lot to be united to a man who stood as a barrier across the path of human progress and would have been a weight to her instead of wings. Released from his engagement, he entered into an alliance (for that is the better name for a marriage) which was not a union of hearts, or intercommunion of kindred souls; but only an affair of convenience; in a word he married for money a woman, who was no longer young in years, nor beautiful in person, nor amiable in temper. But she was rich, and her money like charity covered a multitude of faults, and as soon as he saw the golden bait he caught at it, and they were married, for he was willing to do almost any thing for

FRANCES ELLEN WATKINS HARPER

money, except work hard for it. It was a marriage however that brought no happiness to either party. Mrs. Anderson was an illy educated, self willed, narrow minded (woman), full of airs and pretensions, the only daughter of a man who had laid the foundation of his wealth by keeping a low groggery, and dying had left her his only heir. John Anderson was selfish and grasping. He loved money, and she loved display, and their home was often the scene of the most pitiful contentions about money matters. Harsh words and bitter recriminations were almost common household usages. The children brought up in this unhealthy atmosphere naturally took sides with their mother and their home was literally a house divided against itself. The foolish conduct of the mother inspired the children with disrespect for their father, who failed to support the authority of his wife as the mother and mistress of the home. As her sons grew older they often sought attractions in questionable places, away from the sombre influences of their fireside, and the daughters as soon as they stood upon the verge of early womanhood learned to look upon marriage as an escape valve from domestic discomforts; and in that beautiful home with all its costly surroundings, and sumptuous furniture, there was always something wanting, there was always a lack of tenderness, sympathy and mutual esteem.

"I can't afford it," said John Anderson, to his wife who had been asking for money for a trip to a fashionable watering place. "You will have to spend the summer elsewhere."

"Can't afford it! What nonsense; is not it as much to your interest as mine to carry the girls around and give them a chance?"

"A chance for what?"

"Why to see something of the world. You don't know what may happen. That English Earl was very attentive last night to Sophronia at Mrs. Jessap's ball."

"An English Count? who is he? and where did he spring from?"

"Why he's from England, and is said to be the only son and heir of a very rich nobleman."

"I don't believe it, I don't believe he is an Earl any more than I am."

"That's just like you, always throw cold water on every thing I say"

"It is no such thing, but I don't believe in picking up strangers and putting them into my bosom; it is not all gold that glitters."

"I know that, but how soon can you let me have some money? I want to go out this afternoon and do some shopping and engage the semptress."

"I tell you, Annette, I have not the money to spare; the money market is very tight, and I have very heavy bills to meet this month."

"The money market tight! why it has been tight ever since I have been married."

"Well you may believe it or not, just as you choose, but I tell you this crusading has made quite a hole in my business."

"Now John Anderson, tell that to somebody that don't know. I don't believe this crusading has laid a finger's weight upon your business."

"Yes it has, and if you read the papers you would find that it has even affected the revenue of the state and you will have to retrench somewhere."

"Well, I'll retrench somewhere. I think we are paying our servants too high wages any how. Mrs. Shenflint gets twice as much work done for the same money. I'll retrench, John Anderson, but I want you to remember that I did not marry you empty handed."

"I don't think I shall be apt to forget it in a hurry while I have such a gentle reminder at hand," he replied sarcastically.

"And I suppose you would not have married me if I had had no money."

"No, I would not," said John Anderson thoroughly exasperated, "and I would have been a fool if I had."

These bitter words spoken in a heat of passion were calculated to work disastrously in that sin darkened home.

For some time she had been suspecting that her money had been the chief inducement which led him to seek her hand, and now her worse suspicions were confirmed, and the last thread of confidence was severed.

"I should not have said it," said Anderson to himself, "but the woman is so provoking and unreasonable. I suppose she will have a fit of sulks for a month and never be done brooding over those foolish words"; and Anderson sighed as if he were an ill used man. He had married for money, and he had got what he bargained for; love, confidence, and mutual esteem were not sought in the contract and these do not necessarily come of themselves.

"Well, the best I can do is to give her what money she wants and be done with it."

"Is not in her room?"

"No sir and her bed has not been rumpled."

"Where in the world can she be?"

"I don't know, but here is a note she left."

"What does she say? read it Annette."

"She says she feels that you were unjust to the Earl and that she hopes you will forgive her the steps she has taken, but by the time the letter reaches you she expects to be the Countess of Clarendon."

"Poor foolish girl, you see what comes of taking a stranger to your bosom and making so much of him."

"That's just like you, John Anderson, every thing that goes wrong is blamed on me. I almost wish I was dead."

"I wish so too," thought Anderson but he concluded it was prudent to keep the wish to himself.

John Anderson had no faith whatever in the pretensions of his new son-in-law, but his vain and foolish wife on the other hand was elated at the dazzling prospects of her daughter, and often in her imagination visited the palatial residence of "My Son, the Earl," and was graciously received in society as the mother of the Countess of Clarendon. She was also highly gratified at the supposed effect of Sophronia's marriage upon a certain clique who had been too exclusive to admit her in their set. Should not those Gladstone girls be ready to snag themselves? and there was that Mary Talbot, did every thing she could to attract his attention but it was no go. My little Sophronia came along and took the rag off the bush. I guess they will almost die with envy. If he had waited for her father's consent we might have waited till the end of the chapter; but I took the responsibility on my shoulders and the thing is done. My daughter, the Countess of Clarendon. I like the ring of the words; but dear me here's the morning mail, and a letter from the Countess, but what does it mean?"

"Come to me, I am in great trouble."

In quick response to the appeal Mrs. Anderson took the first train to New York and found her daughter in great distress. The "Earl" had been arrested for forgery and stealing, and darker suspicions were hinted against him. He had been a body servant to a nobleman who had been travelling for his health and who had died by a lonely farmhouse where he had gone for fresh air and quiet, and his servant had seized upon his effects and letters of introduction, and passed himself off as the original Earl, and imitating his handwriting had obtained large remittances, for which he was arrested, tried and sent to prison, and thus ended the enchanting dream of "My daughter the Countess of Clarendon."

# XXI

I cannot ensure your life a single hour, unless you quit business. You are liable to be stricken with paralysis at any moment, if once subject to the (least) excitement. Can't you trust your business in the hands of your sons?"

"Doctor," said John Anderson, "I have only two boys. My oldest went West several years ago, and never writes to us unless he wants something, and as to Frank, if I would put the concern into his hands, he would drink himself into the grave in less than a month. The whole fact is this, my children are the curse of my life," and there was bitterness in the tone of John Anderson as he uttered these words of fearful sorrow.

"Well," said the doctor, "you must have rest and quiet or I will not answer for the consequences."

"Rest and quiet!" said John Anderson to himself, "I don't see how I am to get it, with such a wife as I have always worrying and bothering me about something." "Mr. Anderson," said one of the servants, "Mrs. Anderson says please come, as quick as possible into Mr. Frank's room."

"What's the matter now!"

"I don't know, but Mr. Frank's acting mightily queer; he thinks there are snakes and lizards crawling over him."

"He's got the horrors, just what I expected. Tell me about rest and quiet! I'll be there in a minute. Oh what's the matter? I feel strange," said Anderson falling back on the bed suddenly stricken with paralysis. While in another room lay his younger son a victim to delirium tremens, and dying in fearful agony. The curse that John Anderson had sent to other homes had come back darkened with the shadow of death to brood over his own habitation. His son is dying, but he has no word of hope to cheer the parting spirit as it passed out into the eternity, for him the darkness of the tomb, is not gilded with the glory of the resurrection.

The best medical skill has been summoned to the aid of John Anderson, but neither art, nor skill can bind anew the broken threads of life. The chamber in which he is confined is a marvel of decoration, light streams into his home through panes of beautifully stained glass. Pillows of the softest down are placed beneath his head, beautiful cushions lie at his feet that will never take another step on the errands of sin, but no appliances of wealth can give peace to his guilty conscience.

He looks back upon the past and the retrospect is a worse than wasted life; and when the future looms up before him he shrinks back from the contemplation, for the sins of the past throw their shadow over the future. He has houses, money and land, but he is a pauper in his soul, and a bankrupt in his character. In his eager selfish grasp for gold, he has shriveled his intellect and hardened and dried up his heart, and in so doing he has cut himself off from the richest sources of human enjoyment. He has wasted life's best opportunities, and there never was an angel, however bright, terrible and strong, that ever had power to roll away the stone from the grave of a dead opportunity, and what John Anderson has lost in time, he can never make up in eternity. He has formed no taste for reading, and thus has cut himself off from the glorious companionship of the good, the great, and the wise of all ages. He has been selfish, mean and grasping, and the blessing of the poor and needy never fall as benedictions on his weary head; and in that beautiful home with disease and death clutching at his heartstrings, he has wealth that he cannot enjoy, luxuries that pall upon his taste, and magnificence that can never satisfy the restless craving of his soul. His life has been a wretched failure. He neglected his children to amass the ways of iniquity, and their coldness and indifference pierce him like poisoned arrows. Marriage has brought him money, but not the sweet, tender ministrations of loving wifely care, and so he lives on starving in the midst of plenty; dying of thirst, with life's sweetest fountains eluding his grasp.

Charles Romaine is sleeping in a drunkard's grave. After the death of his boy there was a decided change in him. Night after night he tore himself away from John Anderson's saloon, and struggled with the monster that had enslaved him, and for awhile victory seemed to be perching on the banner of his resolution. Another child took the place of the first born, and the dead, and hope and joy began to blossom around Jeanette's path. His mother who had never ceased to visit the house marked the change with great satisfaction and prevailed upon his father to invite Charles and Jeanette to a New Year's dinner (only a family gathering). Jeanette being unwell excused herself from going, and Charles went alone. Jeanette felt a fearful foreboding when she saw him leaving the door, and said to herself, "I hope his father will not offer him wine. I am so afraid that something will happen to him, and yet I hated to persuade him not to go. His mother might think I was averse to his reconciliation with his father."

"It looks very natural to have Charles with us again," said Mrs. Ro(maine) looking fondly on her son.

"Yes, it seems like old times, when I always had my seat next to yours."

"And I hope," said his father, "it will never be vacant so long again."

The dinner hour passed on enlivened by social chat and pleasant reminiscences, and there was nothing to mar the harmony of the occasion. Mrs. Romaine had been careful to keep everything from the table that would be apt to awaken the old appetite for liquor, but after dinner Mr. Romaine invited Charles into the library to smoke. "Here," said he, handing him a cigar, "is one of the finest brands I have smoked lately, and by the way here is some rare old wine, more than 25 years old, which was sent to me yesterday by an old friend and college class mate of mine. Let me pour you out a glass." Charles suddenly became agitated, but as his father's back was turned to him, pouring out the wine, he did not notice the sudden paling of his cheek, and the hesitation of his manner. And Charles checking back his scruples took the glass and drained it, to the bottom.

There is a fable, that a certain king once permitted the devil to kiss his shoulder, and out of those shoulders sprang two serpents that in the fury of their hunger aimed at his head and tried to get at his brain. He tried to extricate himself from their terrible power. He tore at them with his fingers and found that it was his own flesh that he was lacerating. Dormant but not dead was the appetite for strong drink in Charles Romaine, and that one glass awakened the serpent coiled up in his flesh. He went out from his father's house with a newly awakened appetite clamoring and raging for strong drink. Every saloon he passed adding intensity to his craving. At last his appetite overmastered him and he almost rushed into a saloon, and waited impatiently till he was served. Every nerve seemed to be quivering with excitement, restlessness; and there was a look of wild despairing anguish on his face, as he clutched the glass to allay the terrible craving of his system. He drank till his head was giddy, and his gait was staggering, and then started for home. He entered the gate and slipped on the ice, and being too intoxicated to rise or comprehend his situation, he lay helpless in the dark and cold, until there crept over him that sleep from which there is no awakening, and when morning had broken in all its glory, Charles Romaine had drifted out of life, slain by the wine which at (last) had "bitten like an adder and stung like a serpent." Jeanette had waited and watched through the small hours of the night, till nature o'erwearied had sought

FRANCES ELLEN WATKINS HARPER

repose in sleep and rising very early in the morning, she had gone to the front door to look down the street for his coming when the first object that met her gaze was the lifeless form of her husband. One wild and bitter shriek rent the air, and she fell fainting on the frozen corpse. Her friends gathered round her, all that love and tenderness could do was done for the wretched wife, but nothing could erase from her mind one agonizing sorrow, it was the memory of her fatal triumph over his good resolution years ago at her mother's silver wedding. Carelessly she had sowed the seeds of transgression whose fearful yield was a harvest of bitter misery. Mrs. Clifford came to her in her hour of trial, and tried to comfort and sustain the heart-stricken woman; who had tried to take life easy, but found it terribly hard, and she has measurably succeeded. In the home of her cousin she is trying to bear the burden of her life as well as she can. Her eye never lights up with joy. The bloom and flush have left her careworn face. Tears from her eyes long used to weeping have blenched the coloring of her life existence, and she is passing through life with the shadow of the grave upon her desolate heart.

Joe Gough has been true to his pledge, plenty and comfort have taken the place of poverty and pain. He continued his membership with the church of his choice and Mary is also striving to live a new life, and to be the ministering angel that keeps his steps, and he feels that in answer to prayer, his appetite for strong drink has been taken away.

Life with Mrs. Clifford has become a thing of brightness and beauty, and when children sprang up in her path making gladness and sunshine around her home, she was a wife and tender mother, fond but not foolish; firm in her household government, but not stern and unsympathising in her manner. The faithful friend and companion of her daughters, she won their confidence by her loving care and tender caution. She taught them to come to her in their hours of perplexity and trial and to keep no secrets from her sympathising heart. She taught her sons to be as upright in their lives and as pure in their conversation as she would have her daughters, recognizing for each only one code of morals and one law of spiritual life, and in course of time she saw her daughters ripening into such a beautiful womanhood, and her sons entering the arena of life not with the simplicity which is ignorant of danger and evil, but with the sterling integrity which baffles the darts of temptation with the panoply of principle and the armor of uprightness. Unconsciously she elevated the tone of society in which she moved by a life which was a beautiful and earnest expression of patient continuance in well doing. Paul Clifford's life has been a grand success, not in the mere accumulation of wealth, but in the enrichment of his moral and spiritual nature. He is still ever ready to lend a helping hand. He has not lived merely for wealth and enjoyment, but happiness, lasting and true springs up in his soul as naturally as a flower leaps into blossoms, and whether he is loved or hated, honored or forgotten, he constantly endeavors to make the world better by his example and gladdened by his presence feeling that if every one would be faithful to duty that even here, Eden would spring up in our path, and Paradise be around our way.

TRIAL AND TRIUMPH

# I

O h, that child! She is the very torment of my life. I have been the mother of six children, and all of them put together, never gave me as much trouble as that girl. I don't know what will ever become of her."

"What is the matter now, Aunt Susan? What has Annette been doing?"

"Doing! She is always doing something; everlastingly getting herself into trouble with some of the neighbors. She is the most mischievous and hard-headed child I ever saw."

"Well what has she been doing this morning which has so upset you?"

"Why, I sent her to the grocery to have the oil can filled, and after she came back she had not been in the house five minutes before there came such an uproar from Mrs. Larkins', my next door neighbor, that I thought her house was on fire, but—"

"Instead of that her tongue was on fire, and I know what that means."

"Yes, that's just it, and I don't wonder. That little minx sitting up there in the corner looking so innocent, stopped to pour oil on her clean steps. Now you know yourself what an aggravating thing that must have been."

"Yes, it must have been, especially as Mrs. Larkins is such a nice housekeeper and takes such pride in having everything neat and nice about her. How did you fix up matters with her."

"I have not fixed them up at all. Mrs. Larkins only knows one cure for bad children, and that is beating them, and she always blames me for spoiling Annette, but I hardly know what to do with her. I've scolded and scolded till my tongue is tired, whipping don't seem to do her a bit of good, and I hate to put her out among strangers for fear that they will not treat her right, for after all she is very near to me. She is my poor, dead Lucy's child. Sometimes when I get so angry with her that I feel as though I could almost shake the life out of her, the thought of her dying mother comes back to me and it seems to me as if I could see her eyes looking so wistfully on the child and turning so trustingly to me and saying, 'Mother, when I am gone won't you take care of Annette, and try to keep her with you?' And then all the anger dies out of me. Poor child! I don't know what is going to become of her when my head is laid low. I'm afraid she is born for trouble. Nobody will ever put up with her as I do. She has such an unhappy disposition. She is not like any of my children ever were."

"Yes. I've often noticed that she does seem different from other children. She never seems light-hearted and happy."

"Yes, that is so. She reminds me so of poor Lucy before she was born. She even moans in her sleep like she used to do. It was a dark day when Frank Miller entered my home and Lucy became so taken up with him. It seemed to me as if my poor girl just worshiped him. I did not feel that he was all right, and I tried to warn my dear child of danger, but what could an old woman like me do against him with his handsome looks and oily tongue."

"Yes," said her neighbor soothingly, "you have had a sad time, but still we cannot recall the dead past, and it is the living present with which we have to deal. Annette needs wise guidance, a firm hand and a loving heart to deal with her. To spoil her at home is only to prepare her for misery abroad."

"I am afraid that I am not equal to the task."

"If any man lack wisdom we are taught to ask it of One who giveth liberally to all men and upbraideth none. There would be so much less stumbling if we looked earnestly within for 'the light which lighteth every man that cometh into the world.'"

"Well," said Mrs. Harcourt, Annette's grandmother, "there is one thing about Annette that I like. She is very attentive to her books. If you want to keep that child out of mischief just put a book in her hand; but then she has her living to get and she can't get it by nursing her hands and reading books. She has got to work like the rest of us."

"But why not give her a good education? Doors are open to her which were closed against us. This is a day of light and knowledge. I don't know much myself, but I mean to give my girls a chance. I don't believe in saying, let my children do as I have done, when I think some of us have done poorly enough digging and delving from morning till night. I don't believe the good Lord ever sent anybody into his light and beautiful world to be nothing but a drudge, and I just think it is because some take it so easy that others, who will do, have to take it so hard."

"It always makes my blood boil," said a maiden lady who was present, "to see a great hulk of a man shambling around complaining of hard times, and that he can't get work, when his wife is just working herself down to the grave to keep up the family." I asked Mrs. Johnson, who just lives in the wash tub and is the main stay of her family, what would her husband do if she were to die? and she said, 'get another wife.' Now, I just think she has spoiled that man and if she dies first, I hope that he will never find another woman to tread in her footsteps. He ought to have me to deal with. When he got through with me he would never want to laze around another woman."

"I don't think he ever would," said Mrs. Harcourt, while a gleam of humor sparkled in her eye. Her neighbor was a maiden lady who always knew how to manage other people's husbands, but had never succeeded in getting one of her own, and not having any children herself understood perfectly well how to rate other people's.

Just then a knock was heard at the door and Mr. Thomas, Annette's former school teacher, entered the room. After an exchange of courtesies he asked, "How does Annette come on with her new teacher?"

"I have not heard any complaint," said Mrs. Harcourt. "At first Mrs. Joseph's girl did not want to sit with Annette, but she soon got over it when she saw how well the other girls treated Annette and how pleasant the teacher was to her. Mr. Scott, who has been so friendly to us, told us not to mind her; that her mother had been an ignorant servant girl, who had married a man with a little money; that she was still ignorant, loud and (dressy?) and liked to put on airs. The nearer the beggar the greater the prejudice."

"I think it is true," said Mr. Thomas. "If you apply those words, not to condition, but human souls, for none but beggarly souls would despise a man because of circumstances over which he had no control; noble, large-hearted men and women are never scornful. Contempt and ridicule are the weapons of weak souls. I am glad however, that Annette is getting on so well. I hope that she will graduate at the head of her class, with high honors."

"What's the use of giving her so much education? there are no openings for her here, and if she gets married she won't want it," and Mrs. Harcourt sighed as she finished her sentence.

Mr. Thomas looked grave for a moment and then his face relaxed into a smile. "Well, really, Mrs. Harcourt, that is not very complimentary to us young men; do we have no need of intelligent and well educated wives? I think our race needs educated mothers for the home more than we do trained teachers for the school room. Not that I would ignore or speak lightly of the value of good colored teachers nor suggest as a race, that we can well afford to do without them; but today, if it were left to my decision, whether the education of the race should be placed in the hands of the school teacher or the mothers and there was no other alternative, I should, by all means, decide for the education of the race through its motherhood rather than through its teachers."

"But we poor mothers had no chance. We could not teach our children."

"I think you could teach some of them more than they wish to learn; but I must go now; at some other time we will talk on this subject."

# II

O h, Annette!" said Mrs. Harcourt, turning to her granddaughter after Mr. Thomas had left the door; "What makes you so naughty? Why did you pour that oil on Mrs. Larkin's steps; didn't you know it was wrong?"

Annette stood silent looking like a guilty culprit.

"Why don't you answer me; what makes you behave so bad?"

"I don't know, grandma, I 'specs I did it for the devil. The preacher said the devil makes people do bad things."

"The preacher didn't say any such thing; he said the devil tempts people to be bad, but you are not to mind every thing the devil tells you to do, if you do, you will get yourself into a lot of trouble."

"Well, grandma, Mrs. Larkins is so mean and cross and she is always telling tales on me and I just did it for fun."

"Well, that is very poor fun. You deserve a good whipping, and I've a great mind to give it to you now."

"Why don't she let me alone; she is all the time trying to get you to beat me. She's a spiteful old thing anyhow. I don't like her, and I know she don't like me."

"Hush Annette, you must not talk that way of any one so much older than yourself. When I was a child I wouldn't have talked that way about any old person. Don't let me hear you talk that way again. You will never rest till I give you a good whipping."

"Yes ma'm," said Annette very demurely.

"Oh, Annette!" said her grandmother with a sudden burst of feeling. "You do give me so much trouble. You give me more worry than all my six children put together; but there is always one scabby sheep in the flock and you will be that one. Now get ready for school and don't let me hear any more complaints about you; I am not going to let you worry me to death."

Annette took up her bonnet and glided quietly out of the door, glad to receive instead of the threatened whipping a liberal amount of talk, and yet the words struck deeper than blows. Her own grandmother had prophesied evil things of her. She was to be the scabby sheep of the flock. The memory of the blows upon her body might have passed soon away after the pain and irritation of the infliction were over, but that inconsiderate prophecy struck deep into her heart and left its impress upon her unfolding life. Without intending it, Mrs. Harcourt had struck a blow at the child's self-respect; one of the things which she should have strengthened, even if it was "ready to die." Annette had entered life sadly handicapped. She was the deserted child of a selfish and unprincipled man and a young mother whose giddiness and lack of self-control had caused her to trail the robes of her womanhood in the dust. With such an ante-natal history how much she needed judicious, but tender, loving guidance. In that restless, sensitive and impulsive child was the germ of a useful woman with a warm, loving heart, ready to respond to human suffering, capable of being faithful in friendship and devoted in love. Before that young life with its sad inheritance seemed to lay a future of trial, and how much, humanly speaking, seemed to depend upon the right training of that life and the development within her of self-control, self-reliance and self-respect. There was no mother's heart for her to nestle upon in her hours of discouragement and perplexity; no father's strong, loving arms to shelter and defend her; no sister to brighten her life with joyous companionship, and no brother to champion her through the early and impossible period of ripening womanhood. Her grandmother was kind to her, but not very tender and loving. Her struggle to keep the wolf from the door had absorbed her life, and although she was neither hard nor old, yet she was not demonstrative in her affections, and to her a restless child was an enigma she did not know how to solve. If the child were hungry or cold she could understand physical wants, but for the hunger of the heart she had neither sympathy nor comprehension. Fortunately Annette had found a friend who understood her better than her grandmother, and who, looking beneath the perverseness of the child, saw in her rich possibilities, and would often speak encouragingly to her. Annette early developed a love for literature and poetry and would sometimes try to make rhymes and string verses together and really Mrs. Lasette thought that she had talent or even poetic genius and ardently wished that it might be cultivated and rightly directed; but it never entered the minds of her grandmother and aunts that in their humble home was a rarely gifted soul destined to make music which would set young hearts to thrilling with higher hopes and loftier aspirations.

Mrs. Lasette had been her teacher before she married. After she became a wife and mother, instead of becoming entirely absorbed in a round of household cares and duties, the moment the crown of motherhood fell upon her, as she often said, she had poured a new interest into the welfare of her race. With these feelings she soon became known as a friend and helper in the community in which she lived. Young girls learned to look to her for council and encouragement amid the different passages of their (lives?) sometimes with blushing cheeks they whispered in to her ears tender secrets they did not always bring to their near relatives, and young men about to choose their life work, often came to consult her and to all her heart was responsive. With this feeling of confidence in her judgment, Mr. Thomas had entered her home after leaving Mrs. Harcourt's, educating himself for a teacher. He had spent several years in the acquisition of knowledge and was proving himself an acceptable and conscientious teacher, when the change came which deprived him of his school, by blending his pupils in the different ward schools of the city. Public opinion which moves slowly, had advanced far enough to admit the colored children into the different schools, irrespective of color, but it was not prepared, except in a few places to admit the colored teachers as instructors in the schools. "What are you going to do next?" inquired Mrs. Lasette of Mr. Thomas as he seated himself somewhat wearily by the fire. "I hardly know, I am all at sea, but I am going to be like the runaway slave who, when asked, 'Where is your pass?' raised his fist and said 'Dem is my passes,' and if 'I don't see an opening I will make one.'"

"Why don't you go into the ministry? When Mr. Pugh failed in his examination he turned his attention to the ministry, and it is said that he is succeeding admirably."

"Mrs. Lasette, I was brought up to respect the institutions of religion, and not to lay rash hands on sacred things, and while I believe that every man should preach Christ by an upright life, and chaste conversation, yet I think one of the surest ways to injure a Church, and to make the pulpit lose its power over the rising generation, is for men without a true calling, or requisite qualifications to enter the ministry because they have failed in some other avocation and find in preaching an open door to success."

"But they often succeed."

"How?"

"Why by getting into good churches, increasing their congregations and paying off large church debts." "And is that necessarily success? We need in the Church men who can be more than financiers and who can attract large congregations. We need earnest thoughtful Christly men, who will be more anxious to create and develop moral earnestness than to excite transient emotions. Now there is Rev. Mr. Lamson who was educated in R. College. I have heard him preach to, as I thought, an honest, well meaning, but an ignorant congregation, and instead of lifting them to more rational forms of worship, he tried to imitate them and made a complete failure. He even tried to moan as they do in worship but it didn't come out natural."

"Of course it did not. These dear old people whose moaning during service, seems even now so pitiful and weird, I think learned to mourn out in prayers, thoughts and feelings wrung from their agonizing hearts, which they did not dare express when they were forced to have their meetings under the surveillance of a white man."

"It is because I consider the ministry the highest and most sacred calling, that I cannot, nay I dare not, rush into it unless I feel impelled by the strongest and holiest motives."

"You are right and I think just such men as you ought to be in the ministry."

"Are you calling me?" "I wish it were in my power." "I am glad that it is not, I think there are more in the ministry now than magnify their calling."

"But Mr. Thomas are you not looking on the dark side of the question? you must judge of the sun, not by its spots, but by its brightness."

"Oh I did not mean to say that the ministry is crowded with unworthy men, who love the fleece more than the flock. I believe that there are in the ministry a large number who are the salt of the earth and whose life work bears witness to their fitness. But unfortunately there are men who seem so lacking in reverence for God, by their free handling of sacred things; now I think one of the great wants of our people is more reverence for God who is above us, and respect for the man who is beside us, and I do hope that our next minister will be a good man, of active brain, warm heart and Christly sympathies, who will be among us a living, moral, and spiritual force, and who will be willing to teach us on the Bible plan of 'line upon line, precept upon precept, here a little there a little.'"

"I hope he will be; it is said that brother Lomax our new minister is an excellent young man."

"Well I hope that we will not fail to receive him as an apostle and try to hold up his hands."

"I hope so. I think that to be called of God to be an ambassador for

Christ, to help him build the kingdom of righteousness, love and peace, amid the misery, sin and strife, is the highest and most blessed position that a man can hold, and because I esteem the calling so highly I would not rush into it unless I felt divinely commissioned."

# III

M rs. Harcourt was a Southern woman by birth, who belonged to that class of colored people whose freedom consisted chiefly in not being the chattels of the dominant race—a class to whom little was given and from whom much was required. She was naturally bright and intelligent, but had come up in a day when the very book of the Christian's law was to her a sealed volume; but if she had not been educated through the aid of school books and blackboards, she had obtained that culture of manners and behavior which comes through contact with well-bred people, close observation and a sense of self-respect and self-reliance, and when deprived of her husband's help by an untimely death, she took up the burden of life bravely and always tried to keep up what she called "a stiff upper lip." Feeling the cramping of Southern life, she became restive under the privations and indignities which were heaped upon free persons of color, and at length she and her husband broke up their home and sold out at a pecuniary sacrifice to come North, where they could breathe free air and have educational privileges for their children. But while she was strong and healthy her husband, whose health was not very firm, soon succumbed to the change of climate and new modes of living and left Mrs. Harcourt a stranger and widow in a strange land with six children dependent on her for bread and shelter: but during her short sojourn in the North she had enlisted the sympathy and respect of kind friends, who came to her relief and helped her to help herself, the very best assistance they could bestow upon her. Capable and efficient, she found no difficulty in getting work for herself and older children, who were able to add their quota to the support of the family by running errands, doing odd jobs for the neighbors and helping their mother between school hours. Nor did she lay all the household burdens on the shoulders of the girls and leave her boys to the mercy of the pavement; she tried to make her home happy and taught them all to have a share in adding to its sunshine. "It makes boys selfish," she would say, "to have their sisters do all the work and let the boys go scot-free. I don't believe there would be so many trifling men if the boys were trained to be more helpful at home and to feel more for their mothers and sisters." All this was very well for the peace and sunshine of that home, but as the children advanced in life the question came to her with painful emphasis—"What can I do for the future of my

FRANCES ELLEN WATKINS HARPER

boys and girls?" She was not anxious to have them all professional men and school teachers and government clerks, but she wanted each one to have some trade or calling by which a respectable and comfortable living could be made; but first she consulted their tastes and inclinations. Her youngest boy was very fond of horses, but instead of keeping him in the city, where he was in danger of getting too intimate with horse jockeys and stable boys, she found a place for him with an excellent farmer, who, seeing the tastes of the boy, took great interest in teaching him how to raise stock and he became a skillful farmer. Her second son showed that he had some mechanical skill and ingenuity and she succeeded in getting him a situation with a first-class carpenter, and spared no pains to have him well instructed in all the branches of carpentry, and would often say to him, "John, don't do any sham work if you are going to be a carpenter; be thorough in every thing you do and try to be the best carpenter in A.P., and if you do your work better than others, you won't have to be all the time going around advertising yourself; somebody will find out what you can do and give you work." Her oldest son was passionately fond of books and she helped him through school till he was able to become a school teacher. But as the young man was high spirited and ambitious, he resolved that he would make his school teaching a stepping stone to a more congenial employment. He studied medicine and graduated with M.D., but as it takes a young doctor some time to gain the confidence of an old community, he continued after his graduation to teach and obtained a certificate to practice medicine. Without being forced to look to his mother for assistance, while the confidence of his community was slowly growing, he depended on the school for his living and looked to the future for his success as a physician.

For the girls, because they were colored, there were but few avenues open, but they all took in sewing and were excellent seamstresses, except Lucy, who had gone from home to teach school in a distant city as there were no openings of the kind for her at her own home.

Mrs. Harcourt was very proud of her children and had unbounded confidence in them. She was high-spirited and self-respecting and it never seemed to enter her mind that any evil might befall the children that would bring sorrow and shame to her home; but nevertheless it came and Lucy, her youngest child, the pet and pride of the household returned home with a great sorrow tugging at her heart and a shadow on her misguided life. It was the old story of woman's weakness and folly and man's perfidy and desertion. Poor child, how wretched she was till "peace bound up her bleeding heart," and even then the arrow had pierced too deep for healing. Sorrow had wasted her strength and laid the foundation of disease and an early death. Religion brought balm to the wounded spirit, but no renewed vigor to the wasted frame and in a short time she fell a victim to consumption, leaving Annette to the care of her mother. It was so pitiful to see the sorrow on the dear old face as she would nestle the wronged and disinherited child to her heart and would say so mournfully, "Oh, I never, never expected this!"

Although Annette had come into the family an unbidden and unwelcome guest, associated with the saddest experience of her grandmother's life, yet somehow the baby fingers had wound themselves around the tendrils of her heart and the child had found a shelter in the warm clasp of loving arms. To her, Annette was a new charge, an increased burden; but burden to be defended by her love and guarded by her care. All her other children had married and left her, and in her lowly home this young child with infantile sweetness, beguiled many a lonely hour. She loved Lucy and that was Lucy's child.

> *But where was he who sullied*
> *Her once unspotted name;*
> *Who lured her from life's brightness*
> *To agony and shame?*

Did society, which closed its doors against Lucy and left her to struggle as best she might out of the depth into which she had fallen, pour any righteous wrath upon his guilty head? Did it demand that he should at least bring forth some fruit meet for repentance by at least helping Mrs. Harcourt to raise the unfortunate child? Not so. He left that poor old grandmother to struggle with her failing strength, not only to bear her own burden, but the one he had so wickedly imposed upon her. He had left A.P. before Lucy's death and gone to the Pacific coast where he became wealthy through liquor selling, speculation, gambling and other disreputable means, and returned with gold enough to hide a multitude of sins, and then fair women permitted and even courted his society. Mothers with marriageable daughters condoned his offences against morality and said, "oh, well, young men will sow their wild oats; it is no use to be too straight laced." But there were a few thoughtful mothers old fashioned enough to believe that the law of purity is as binding upon the man as the woman, and who, under no conditions, would invite him to associate with their daughters. Women who tried to teach their sons to be worthy of the love and esteem of good women by being as chaste in their conversation and as pure in their lives as their young daughters who sat at their side sheltered in their pleasant and peaceful homes. One of the first things that Frank Miller did after he returned to A.P. was to open a large and elegantly furnished saloon and restaurant. The license to keep such a place was very high, and men said that to pay it he resorted to very questionable means, that his place was a resort for gamblers, and that he employed a young man to guard the entrance of his saloon from any sudden invasion of the police by giving a signal without if he saw any of them approaching, and other things were whispered of his saloon which showed it to be a far more dangerous place for the tempted, unwary and inexperienced feet of the young men of A.P., than any low groggery in the whole city. Young men who would have scorned to enter the lowest dens of vice, felt at home in his gilded palace of sin. Beautiful pictures adorned the walls, light streamed into the room through finely stained glass windows, women, not as God had made them, but as sin had debased them, came there to spend the evening in the mazy dance, or to sit with partners in sin and feast at luxurious tables. Politicians came there to concoct their plans for coming campaigns, to fix their slates and to devise means for grasping with eager hands the spoils of government. Young men anxious for places in the gift of the government found that winking at Frank Miller's vices and conforming to the demoralizing customs of his place were passports to political favors, and lacking moral stamina, hushed their consciences and became partakers of his sins. Men talked in private of his vices, and drank his liquors and smoked his cigars in public. His place was a snare to their souls. "The dead were there but they knew it not." He built a beautiful home and furnished it magnificently, and some said that the woman who married him would do well, as if it were possible for any woman to marry well who linked her destinies to a wicked, selfish and base man, whose business was a constant menace to the peace, the purity and progress of society. I believe it was Milton who said that the purity of a man should be more splendid than the purity of a woman, basing his idea upon the declaration, "The head of the woman is the man, and the head of the man is Jesus Christ." Surely if man occupies this high rank in the creation of God he should ever be the true friend and helper of woman and not, as he too often proves, her falsest friend and basest enemy.

# IV

A nnette," said Mrs. Harcourt one morning early, "I want you to stir your stumps today; I am going to have company this evening and I want you to help me to get everything in apple pie order."

"Who is coming, grandma?"

"Mr. Thomas and Mrs. Lasette."

"Mrs. Lasette!" Annette's eyes brightened. "I hope she will come; she is just as sweet as a peach and I do love her ever so much; and who else?"

"Brother Lomax, the minister who preached last Sunday and gave us such a good sermon."

"Is he coming, too?" Annette opened her eyes with pleased surprise. "Oh, I hope he will come, he's so nice."

"What do you know about him?"

"Why, grandmother, I understood everything that he said, and I felt that I wanted to be good just like he told us, and I went and asked aunt 'Liza how people got religion. She had been to camp-meeting and seen people getting religion, and I wanted her to tell me all about it for I wanted to get it too."

"What did she tell you?"

"She told me that people went down to the mourner's bench and prayed and then they would get up and shout and say they had religion, and that was all she knew about it."

"You went to the wrong one when you went to your aunt 'Liza. And what did you do after she told you?"

"Why, I went down in the garden and prayed and I got up and shouted, but I didn't get any religion. I guess I didn't try right."

"I guess you didn't if I judge by your actions. When you get older you will know more about it."

"But, grandma, Aunt 'Liza is older than I am, why don't she know?"

"Because she don't try; she's got her head too full of dress and dancing and nonsense."

Grandmother Harcourt did not have very much faith in what she called children's religion, and here was a human soul crying out in the darkness; but she did not understand the cry, nor look for the "perfecting of praise out of the mouths of babes and sucklings," not discerning the emotions of that young spirit, she let the opportunity slip for rightly impressing that young soul. She depended too much on the church and too little on the training of the home. For while the church can teach and the school instruct, the home is the place to train innocent and impressible childhood for useful citizenship on earth and a hope of holy companionship in heaven; and every Christian should strive to have "her one of the provinces of God's kingdom," where she can plant her strongest batteries against the ramparts of folly, sin and vice.

"Who else is coming, grandma?"

"Why, of course I must invite Mrs. Larkins; it would never do to leave her out."

Annette shrugged her shoulders, a scowl came over her face and she said:

"I hope she won't come."

"I expect she will and when she comes I want you to behave yourself and don't roll up your eyes at her and giggle at her and make ugly speeches. She told me that you made mouths at her yesterday, and that when Mr. Ross was whipping his horse you said you knew some one whom you wished was getting that beating, and she said that she just believed you meant her. How was that, Annette? If I were like you I would be all the time keeping this neighborhood in hot water."

Annette looked rather crestfallen and said, "I did make mouths at her house as I came by, but I didn't know that she saw me."

"Yes she did, and you had better mind how you cut your cards with her."

Annette finding the conversation was taking a rather disagreeable turn suddenly remembered that she had something to do in the yard and ceased to prolong the dialogue. If the truth must be confessed, Annette was not a very earnest candidate for saintship, and annoying her next door neighbor was one of her favorite amusements.

Grandma Harcourt lived in a secluded court, which was shut in on every side but one from the main streets, and her environments were not of the most pleasant and congenial kind. The neighbors, generally speaking, belonged to neither the best nor worst class of colored people. The court was too fully enclosed to be a thoroughfare of travel, but it was a place in which women could sit at their doors and talk to one another from each side of the court. Women who had no scruples about drinking as much beer, and sometimes stronger drinks, as they could absorb, and some of the men said that the women drank more than men, and under the besotting influence of beer and even stronger drinks, a fearful amount of gossiping, news-carrying and tattling went on, which often resulted in quarrels and contentions, which, while it never resulted in blood, sadly lowered the tone of social life. It was the arena of wordy strife in which angry tongues were the only weapons of warfare, and poor little Annette was fast learning their modes of battle. But there was one thing against which grandmother Harcourt set her face like flint, and that was sending children to saloons for beer, and once she flamed out with righteous indignation when one of her neighbors, in her absence, sent Annette to a saloon to buy her some beer. She told her in emphatic terms she must never do so again, that she wanted her girl to grow up a respectable woman, and that she ought to be ashamed of herself, not only to be guzzling beer like a toper, but to send anybody's child to a saloon to come in contact with the kind of men who frequented such places, and that any women who sent their children to such places were training their boys to be drunkards and their girls to be street-walkers. "I am poor," she said, "but I mean to keep my credit up and if you and I live in this neighborhood a hundred years you must never do that thing again."

Her neighbor looked dazed and tried to stammer out an apology, but she never sent Annette to a beer saloon again, and in course of time she became a good temperance woman herself, influenced by the faithfulness of grandmother Harcourt.

The court in which Mrs. Harcourt lived was not a very desirable place, but, on account of her color, eligible houses could not always be obtained, and however decent, quiet or respectable she might appear on applying for a house, she was often met with the rebuff, "We don't rent to colored people," and men who virtually assigned her race the lowest place and humblest positions could talk so glibly of the degradation of the Negro while by their Christless and inhuman prejudice they were helping add to their low social condition. In the midst of her unfavorable environments Mrs. Harcourt kept her home neat and tidy; sent Annette to school constantly and tried to keep her out of mischief, but there was moral contagion in the social atmosphere of Tennis Court and Annette too often succumbed to its influence; but Annette was young and liked the company of young girls and it seemed cruel to confine the child's whole life to the home and schoolhouse and give her no chance to be merry and playful with girls of her own age. So now and then grandmother Harcourt would let her spend a little time with some of the neighbors' girls but from the questions that Annette often asked her grandmother and the conversations she sometimes repeated Mrs. Harcourt feared that she was learning things which should only be taught by faithful mothers in hours of sacred and tender confidence, and she determined, even if it gave offence to her neighbors, that she would choose among her own friends, companions for her granddaughter and not leave all her social future to chance. In this she was heartily aided by Mrs. Lasette, who made it a point to hold in that neighborhood, mothers' meetings and try to teach mothers, who in the dark days of slavery had no bolts nor bars strong enough to keep out the invader from scattering their children like leaves in wintry weather, how to build up light and happy homes under the new dispensation of freedom. To her it was a labor of love and she found her reward in the peace and love which flowed into the soul and the improved condition of society. In lowly homes where she visited, her presence was a benediction and an inspiration. Women careless in their household and slatternly in their dress grew more careful in the keeping of their homes and the arrangement of their attire. Women of the better class of their own race, coming among them awakened their self-respect. Prejudice and pride of race had separated them from their white neighbors and the more cultured of their race had shrunk from them in their ignorance, poverty and low social condition and they were left, in a great measure, to themselves—ostracised by the whites on the one side and socially isolated from the more cultured of their race on the other hand. The law took little or no cognizance of them unless they were presented at its bar as criminals; but if they were neither criminals nor paupers they might fester in their vices and perpetuate their social condition. Who understood or cared to minister to their deepest needs or greatest wants? It was just here where the tender, thoughtful love of a warm-hearted and intelligent woman was needed. To her it was a labor of love, but it was not all fair sailing. She sometimes met with coldness and distrust where she had expected kindness and confidence; lack of sympathy where she had hoped to find ready and willing cooperation; but she knew that if her life was in harmony with God and Christly sympathy with man; for such a life there was no such word as fail.

# V

B y dint of energy and perseverance grandmother Harcourt had succeeded in getting everything in order when her guests began to arrive. She had just put the finishing touches upon her well-spread table and was reviewing it with an expression of pleasure and satisfaction. And now while the guests are quietly taking their seats let me introduce you to them.

Mr. Thomas came bringing with him the young minister, Rev. Mr. Lomax, whose sermon had so interested and edified Mrs. Harcourt the previous Sunday. Mrs. Lasette, looking bright and happy, came with her daughter, and Mrs. Larkins entered arrayed in her best attire, looking starched and prim, as if she had made it the great business of her life to take care of her dignity and to think about herself. Mrs. Larkins, though for years a member of church, had not learned that it was unchristian to be narrow and selfish. She was strict in her attendance at church and gave freely to its support; but somehow with all her attention to the forms of religion, one missed its warm and vivifying influence from her life, and in the loving clasp of a helping hand, in the tender beam of a sympathizing glance, weary-hearted mothers and wives never came to her with their heartaches and confided to her their troubles. Little children either shrank from her or grew quiet in her presence. What was missing from her life was the magnetism of love. She had become so absorbed in herself that she forgot everybody else and thought more of her rights than her duties. The difference between Mrs. Lasette and Mrs. Larkins was this, that in passing through life one scattered sunshine and the other cast shadows over her path. Mrs. Lasette was a fine conversationalist. She regarded speech as one of heaven's best gifts, and thought that conversation should be made one of the finest arts, and used to subserve the highest and best purposes of life, and always regretted when it was permitted to degenerate into gossip and backbiting. Harsh judgment she always tried to modify, often saying in doubtful cases, "Had we not better suspend our judgments? Truly we do not like people to think the worst of us and it is not fulfilling the law of love to think the worst of them. Do you not know that if we wish to dwell in his tabernacle we are not to entertain a reproach against our neighbor, nor to back-bite with our lips and I do not think there is a sin which more easily besets society than this." "Speech," she would say, "is

FRANCES ELLEN WATKINS HARPER

a gift so replete with rich and joyous possibilities," and she always tried to raise the tone of conversation at home and abroad. Of her it might be emphatically said, "She opened her mouth with wisdom and in her lips was the law of kindness."

The young minister, Rev. Mr. Lomax, was an earnest, devout and gifted young man. Born in the midst of poverty, with the shadows of slavery encircling his early life, he had pushed his way upward in the world, "toiling while others slept." His father was dead. While living he had done what he could to improve the condition of his family, and had, it was thought, overworked himself in the struggle to educate and support his children. He was a kind and indulgent father and when his son had made excellent progress in his studies, he gave him two presents so dear to his boyish heart—a gun and a watch. But the hour came when the loving hands were closed over the quiet breast, and the widowed wife found herself unable to provide the respectable funeral she desired to give him. Thomas then came bravely and tenderly to her relief. He sold his watch and gun to defray the funeral expenses of his father. He was a good son to his aged mother, and became the staff of her declining years. With an earnest purpose in his soul, and feeling that knowledge is power, he applied himself with diligence to his studies, passed through college, and feeling within his soul a commission to teach and help others to develop within themselves the love of nature, he entered the ministry, bringing into it an enthusiasm for humanity and love of Christ, which lit up his life and made him a moral and spiritual force in the community. He had several advantageous offers to labor in other parts of the country, but for the sake of being true to the heavenly vision, which showed him the needs of his people and his adaptation to their wants, he chose, not the most lucrative, but the most needed work which was offered him with

> *A joy to find in every station,*
> *Something still to do or bear.*

He had seen many things in the life of the people with whom he was identified which gave him intense pain, but instead of constantly censuring and finding fault with their inconsistencies of conscience, he strove to live so blamelessly before them that he would show them by example a more excellent way and "criticise by creation." To him religion was a reasonable service and he wished it to influence their conduct as well as sway their emotions. Believing that right thinking is connected with right living, he taught them to be conservative without being bigoted, and liberal without being morally indifferent and careless in their modes of thought. He wanted them to be able to give a reason for the faith that was in them and that faith to be rooted and grounded in love. He was young, hopeful, and enthusiastic and life was opening before him full of hope and promise.

"It has been a beautiful day," said Mrs. Lasette, seating herself beside Mrs. Larkins, who always waited to be approached and was ever ready to think that some one was slighting her or ignoring her presence.

"It has been a fine day, but I think it will rain soon; I judge by my corn."

"Oh! I think the weather is just perfect. The sun set gloriously this evening and the sky was the brightest blue."

"I think the day was what I call a weather breeder. Whenever you see such days this time of year, you may look out for falling weather. I (expect?) that it will snow soon."

"How that child grows," said Mrs. Larkins, as Annette entered the room.

"Ill weeds grow apace; she has nothing else to do. That girl is going to give her grandmother a great deal of trouble."

"Oh! I do not think so."

"Well, I do, and I told her grandmother so one day, but she did not thank me for it."

"No, I suppose not."

"I didn't do it for thanks; I did it just to give her a piece of my mind about that girl. She is the most mischievous and worrisome child I ever saw. The partition between our houses is very thin and many a time when I want to finish my morning sleep or take an afternoon nap, if Mrs. Harcourt is not at home, Annette will sing and recite at the top of her voice and run up and down the stairs as if a regiment of soldiers were after her."

"Annette is quite young, full of life and brimful of mischief, and girls of that age I have heard likened to persimmons before they are ripe; if you attempt to eat them they will pucker your mouth, but if you wait till the first frost touches them they are delicious. Have patience with the child, act kindly towards her, she may be slow in developing womanly sense, but I think that Annette has within her the making of a fine woman."

"Do you know what Annette wants?"

"Yes, I know what she wants; but what do you think she wants?"

"She wants kissing."

"I'd kiss her with a switch if she were mine."

"I do not think it wise to whip a child of her age."

"I'd whip her if she were as big as a house."

"I do not find it necessary with my Laura; it is sufficient to deter her from doing anything if she knows that I do not approve of it. I have tried to establish perfect confidence between us. I do not think my daughter keeps a secret from me. I think many young persons go astray because their parents have failed to strengthen their characters and to forewarn and forearm them against the temptations and dangers that surround their paths. How goes the battle?" said Mrs. Lasette, turning to Mr. Thomas.

"I am still at sea, and the tide has not yet turned in my favor. Of course, I feel the change; it has taken my life out of its accustomed channel, but I am optimist enough to hope that even this change will result in greater good to the greatest number. I think one of our great wants is the diversification of our industries, and I do not believe it would be wise for the parents to relax their endeavors to give their children the best education in their power. We cannot tell what a race can do till it utters and expresses itself, and I know that there is an amount of brain among us which can and should be utilized in other directions than teaching school or seeking for clerkships. Mr. Clarkson had a very intelligent daughter whom he wished to fit for some other employment than that of a school teacher. He had her trained for a physician. She went to B., studied faithfully, graduated at the head of her class and received the highest medal for her attainments, thus proving herself a living argument of the capability in her race. Her friend, Miss Young, had artistic talent, and learned wood carving. She developed exquisite taste and has become a fine artist in that branch of industry. A female school teacher's work in the public schools is apt to be limited to her single life, but a woman who becomes proficient in a useful trade or business, builds up for herself a wall of defense against the invasions of want and privation whether she is married or single. I think that every woman, and man too, should be prepared for the reverses of fortune by being taught how to do some one thing thoroughly so as to be able to be a worker in the world's service, and not a pensioner upon its bounty. And for this end it does not become us as a race to despise any honest labor which lifts us above pauperism and dependence. I am pleased to see our people having industrial fairs. I believe in giving due honor to all honest labor, in covering idleness with shame, and crowning labor with respect."

# VI

For awhile Mrs. Harcourt was busy in preparing the supper, to which they all did ample justice. In her white apron, faultless neck handkerchief and nicely fitting, but plain dress, Mrs. Harcourt looked the impersonation of contented happiness. Sorrow had left deep furrows upon her kindly face, but for awhile the shadows seemed to have been lifted from her life and she was the pleasant hostess, forgetting her own sorrows in contributing to the enjoyment of others. Supper being over, her guests resumed their conversation.

"You do not look upon the mixing of the schools as being necessarily disadvantageous to our people," said the minister.

"That," said Mr. Thomas, "is just in accordance to the way we adapt ourselves to the change. If we are to remain in this country as a component part of the nation, I cannot fail to regard with interest any step which tends toward our unification with all the other branches of the human race in this Western Hemisphere."

"Although," said Mrs. Lasette, "I have been educating my daughter and have felt very sorry when I have witnessed the disappointment of parents who have fitted their children for teachers and have seen door after door closed against them, I cannot help regarding the mixing of the schools as at least one step in a right direction."

"But Mrs. Lasette," said the minister, "as we are educated by other means than school books and blackboards, such as the stimulus of hope, the incentives of self-respect and the consensus of public opinion, will it not add to the depression of the race if our children are made to feel that, however well educated they may be or exemplary as pupils, the color of their skin must debar them from entering avenues which are freely opened to the young girls of every other nationality."

Mr. Thomas replied, "In considering this question, which is so much broader than a mere local question, I have tried to look beyond the life of the individual to the life of the race, and I find that it is through obstacles overcome, suffering endured and the tests of trial that strength is obtained, courage manifested and character developed. We are now passing through a crucial period in our race history and what we so much need is moral earnestness, strength of character and purpose to guide us through the rocks and shoals on which so many life barques have been stranded and wrecked."

"Yes," said Mrs. Lasette, "I believe that we are capable of being more than light-hearted children of the tropics and I want our young people to gain more persistence in their characters, perseverance in their efforts and that esprit de corps, which shall animate us with higher, nobler and holier purpose in the future than we have ever known in the past; and while I am sorry for the parents who, for their children's sake, have fought against the entailed ignorance of the ages with such humble weapons as the washboard, flat iron and scrubbing brush, and who have gathered the crumbs from the humblest departments of labor, still I feel with Mr. Thomas that the mixing of the schools is a stride in the march of the nation, only we must learn how to keep step in the progress of the centuries."

"I do not think that I fully comprehend you," Mr. Lomax replied.

"Let me explain. I live in the 19th Ward. In that Ward are not a half dozen colored children. When my husband bought the land we were more than a mile from the business part of the city, but we were poor and the land was very cheap and my husband said that paying rent was like putting money in a sinking fund; so he resolved, even if it put us to a little disadvantage, that he would buy the tract of land where we now live. Before he did so, he called together a number of his acquaintances, pointed out to them the tract of land and told them how they might join with him in planting a small hamlet for themselves; but except the few colored neighbors we now have, no one else would join with us. Some said it was too far from their work, others that they did not wish to live among many colored people, and some suspected my husband of trying either to take the advantage of them, or of agrandising himself at their expense, and I have now dear friends who might have been living comfortably in their own homes, who, today, are crowded in tenement houses or renting in narrow alleys and little streets."

"That's true," said Mrs. Larkins, "I am one of them. I wanted my husband to take up with your husband's offer, but he was one of those men who knew it all and he never seemed to think it possible that any colored man could see any clearer than he did. I knew your husband's head was level and I tried to persuade Mr. Larkins to take up with his offer, but he would not hear to it; said he knew his own business best, and shut me up by telling me that he was not going to let any woman rule over him; and here I am today, Larkins gone and his poor old widow scuffing night and day to keep soul and body together; but there are some men you couldn't beat anything into their heads, not if you took a sledge hammer. Poor fellow, he is gone now and I ought not to say anything agin him, but if he had minded me, I would have had a home over my head and some land under my feet; but it is no use to grieve over spilled milk. When he was living if I said, yes, he was always sure to say, no. One day I said to him when he was opposing me, the way we live is like the old saying, 'Pull Dick and pull devil,' and what do you think he said?"

"I don't know, I'm sure, what was it?"

"Why, he just looked at me and smiled and said, 'I am Dick.' Of course he meant that I was the other fellow."

"But," said Mrs. Lasette, "this is a digression from our subject. What I meant to say is this, that in our Ward is an excellent school house with a half score of well equipped and efficient teachers. The former colored school house was a dingy looking building about a mile and a half away with only one young school teacher, who had, it is true, passed a creditable examination. Now, when my daughter saw that the children of all other nationalities, it mattered not how low and debasing might be their environments, could enter the school for which her father paid taxes, and that she was forced either to stay at home or to go through all weathers to an ungraded school, in a poorly ventilated and unevenly heated room, would not such public inequality burn into her soul the idea of race-inferiority? And this is why I look upon the mixed school as a right step in the right direction."

"Taking this view of the matter I see the pertinence of your position on this subject. Do you know," continued Mr. Lomax, his face lighting up with a fine enthusiasm, "that I am full of hope for the future of our people?"

"That's more than I am," said Mrs. Larkins very coldly. "When you have summered and wintered them as I have, you will change your tune."

"Oh, I hope not," he replied with an accent of distress in his voice. "You may think me a dreamer and enthusiast, but with all our faults I firmly believe that the Negro belongs to one of the best branches of the human race, and that he has a high and holy mission in the great drama of life. I do not think our God is a purposeless Being, but his ways are not as our ways are, and his thoughts are not our thoughts, and I dare not say 'Had I his wisdom or he my love,' the condition of humanity would be better. I prefer thinking that in the crucible of pain and apparent disaster, that we are held by the hand of a loving Father who is doing for us all, the best he can to fit us for companionship with him in the eternities, and with John G. Whittier, I feel:

> *Amid the maddening maze of things*
> *When tossed by storm and flood,*
> *To one fixed stake my spirit clings*
> *I know that God is good.*

"I once questioned and doubted, but now I have learned to love and trust in 'Him whom the heavens must receive till the time of the restitution of all things.' By this trust I do not mean a lazy leaning on Providence to do for us what we have ability to do for ourselves. I think that our people need more to be taught how to live than to be constantly warned to get ready to die. As Brother Thomas said, we are now passing through a crucial period of our history and what we need is life—more abundant life in every fibre of our souls; life which will manifest itself in moral earnestness, vigor of purpose, strength of character and spiritual progression."

"I do hope," said Mr. Thomas, "that as you are among us, you will impart some of your earnestness and enthusiasm to our young people."

"As I am a new comer here, and it is said that the people of A.P., are very sensitive to criticism, though very critical themselves and rather set and conservative in their ways, I hope that I shall have the benefit of your experience in aiding me to do all I can to help the people among whom my lot is cast."

"You are perfectly welcome to any aid I can give you. Just now some of us are interested in getting our people out of these wretched alleys and crowded tenement houses into the larger, freer air of the country. We want our young men to help us fight the battle against poverty, ignorance, degradation, and the cold, proud scorn of society. Before our public lands are all appropriated, I want our young men and women to get homesteads, and to be willing to endure privations in order to place our means of subsistence on a less precarious basis. The land is a basis of power, and like Anteus in the myth, we will never have our full measure of material strength till we touch the earth as owners of the soil. And when we get the land we must have patience and perseverance enough to hold it."

"In one of our Western States is a city which suggests the idea of Aladdin's wonderful lamp. Where that city now stands was once the homestead of a colored man who came from Virginia and obtained it under the homestead law. That man has since been working as a servant for a man who lives on 80 acres of his former section, and who has plotted the rest for the city of C."

"How did he lose it?"

"When he came from the South the country was new and female labor in great demand. His wife could earn $1.50 a day, and instead of moving on his land, he remained about forty miles away, till he had forfeited his claim, and it fell into the hands of the present proprietor. Since then our foresight has been developing and some months since in travelling in that same State, I met a woman whose husband had taken up a piece of land and was bringing it under cultivation. She and her children remained in town where they could all get work, and transmit him help and in a few years, I expect, they will be comfortably situated in a home owned by their united efforts."

# VII

What next? was the question Mr. Thomas was revolving in his mind, when a knock was heard at his door, and he saw standing on the threshold, one of his former pupils.

"Well, Charley, how does the world use you? Everything going on swimmingly?"

"Oh, no indeed. I have lost my situation."

"How is that? You were getting on so well. Mr. Hazleton seemed to be perfectly satisfied with you, and I thought that you were quite a favorite in the establishment. How was it that you lost your place?"

"I lost it through the meanness of Mr. Mahler."

"Mr. Mahler, our Superintendent of public schools?"

"Yes, it was through him that I lost my situation."

"Why, what could you have done to offend him?"

"Nothing at all; I never had an unpleasant word with him in my life."

"Do explain yourself. I cannot see why he should have used any influence to deprive you of your situation."

"He had it in his power to do me a mean, low-life trick, and he did it, and I hope to see the day when I will be even with him," said the lad, with a flashing eye, while an angry flush mantled his cheek.

"Do any of the family deal at Mr. Hazleton's store? Perhaps you gave some of them offence through neglect or thoughtlessness in dealing with them."

"It was nothing of the kind. Mr. Mahler knew me and my mother. He knew her because she taught under him, and of course saw me often enough to know that I was her son, and so last week when he saw me in the store, I noticed that he looked very closely at me, and that in a few moments after he was in conversation with Mr. Hazleton. He asked him, 'if he employed a nigger for a cashier?' He replied, 'Of course not.' 'Well,' he said, 'you have one now.' After that they came down to the desk where I was casting up my accounts and Mr. Mahler asked, 'Is Mrs. Cooper your mother?' I answered, 'yes sir.' Of course I would not deny my mother. 'Isn't your name Charley?' and again I answered, yes; I could have resorted to concealment, but I would not lie for a piece of bread, and yet for mother's sake I sorely needed the place.

"What did Mr. Hazleton say?"

"Nothing, only I thought he looked at me a little embarrassed, just as any half-decent man might when he was about to do a mean and cruel thing. But that afternoon I lost my place. Mr. Hazleton said to me when the store was about to close, that he had no further use for me. Not discouraged, I found another place; but I believe that my evil genius found me out and that through him I was again ousted from that situation and now I am at my wits end."

"But, Charley, were you not sailing under false colors?"

"I do not think so, Mr. Thompson. I saw in the window an advertisement, 'A boy wanted.' They did not say what color the boy must be and I applied for the situation and did my work as faithfully as I knew how. Mr. Hazleton seemed to be perfectly satisfied with my work and as he did not seek to know the antecedents of my family I did not see fit to thrust them gratuitously upon him. You know the hard struggle my poor mother has had to get along, how the saloon has cursed and darkened our home and I was glad to get anything to do by which I could honestly earn a dollar and help her keep the wolf from the door, and I tried to do my level best, but it made no difference; as soon as it was known that I had Negro blood in my veins door after door was closed against me; not that I was not honest, industrious, obliging and steady, but simply because of the blood in my veins."

"I admit," said Mr. Thomas, trying to repress his indignation and speak calmly, "that it was a hard thing to be treated so for a cause over which you had not the least control, but, Charley, you must try to pick up courage."

"Oh, it seems to me that my courage has all oozed out. I think that I will go away; maybe I can find work somewhere else. Had I been a convict from a prison there are Christian women here who would have been glad to have reached me out a helping hand and hailed my return to a life of honest industry as a blessed crowning of their labors of love; while I, who am neither a pauper nor felon, am turned from place after place because I belong to a race on whom Christendom bestowed the curse of slavery and under whose shadow has flourished Christless and inhuman caste prejudice. So I think that I had better go and start life afresh."

"No, Charley, don't go away. I know you could pass as a white man; but, Charley, don't you know that to do so you must separate from your kindred and virtually ignore your mother? A mother, who, for your sake, would, I believe, take blood from every vein and strength from every nerve if it were necessary. If you pass into the white basis your mother can never be a guest in your home without betraying your origin; you cannot visit her openly and crown her with the respect she so well deserves without divulging the secret of your birth; and Charley, by doing so I do not think it possible that however rich or strong or influential you may be as a white man, that you can be as noble and as true a man as you will be if you stand in your lot without compromise or concealment, and feel that the feebler your mother's race is the closer you will cling to it. Charley, you have lately joined the church; your mission in the world is not to seek to be rich and strong, but because there is so much sin and misery in the world by it is to clasp the hand of Christ through faith and try to make the world better by your influence and gladder and brighter by your presence."

"Mr. Thomas I try to be, and I hope I am a Christian, but if these prejudices are consistent with Christianity then I must confess that I do not understand it, and if it is I do not want it. Are these people Christians who open the doors of charitable institutions to sinners who are white and close them against the same class who are black? I do not call such people good patriots, let alone clear-sighted Christians. Why, they act as if God had done wrong in making a man black, and that they have never forgiven him and had become reconciled to the workmanship of his hands."

"Charley, you are excited just now, and I think that you are making the same mistake that better educated men than you have done. You are putting Christianity and its abuses together. I do think, notwithstanding all its perversions, and all the rubbish which has gathered around its simplicity and beauty, that Christianity is the world's best religion. I know that Christ has been wounded in what should have been the house of his friends; that the banner of his religion which is broad enough to float over the wide world with all its sin and misery, has been drenched with the blood of persecution, trampled in the mire of slavery and stained by the dust of caste proscription; but I believe that men are beginning more fully to comprehend the claims of the gospel of Jesus Christ. I am not afraid of what men call infidelity. I hold the faith which I profess, to be too true, too sacred and precious to be disturbed by every wave of wind and doubt. Amid all the religious upheavals of the Nineteenth Century, I believe God is at the helm, that there are petrifactions of creed and dogma that are to (be) broken up, not by mere intellectual speculations, but by the greater solvent of the constraining love of Christ, and it is for this that I am praying, longing and waiting. Let schoolmen dispute and contend, the faith for which I most ardently long and earnestly contend, is a faith which works by love and purifies the soul."

"Mr. Thomas, I believe that there is something real about your religion, but some of these white Christians do puzzle me awfully. Oh, I think that I will go. I am sick and tired of the place. Everything seems to be against me."

"No, Charley; stay for your mother's sake. I know a noble and generous man who is brave enough to face a vitiated public opinion, and rich enough to afford himself the luxury of a good conscience. I shall tell him your story and try to interest him in your behalf. Will you stay?"

"I certainly will if he will give me any chance to get my living and help my mother."

"It has been said that everything has two handles, and if you take it by the wrong handle it will be too hard to hold."

"I should like to know which is the right handle to this prejudice against color."

"I do not think that there is prejudice against color in this country."

"No prejudice against color!" said Charley Cooper, opening his eyes with sudden wonder. "What was it that dogged my steps and shut door after door against me? Wasn't that prejudice against color?"

"Whose color, Charley? Surely not yours, for you are whiter than several of Mr. Hazleton's clerks. Do you see in your case it was not prejudice against color?"

"What was it, then?"

"It was the information that you were connected by blood with a once enslaved and despised people on whom society had placed its ban, and to whom slavery and a low social condition had given a heritage of scorn, and as soon as he found out that you were connected with that race, he had neither the manliness nor the moral courage to say, the boy is capable and efficient. I see no cause why he should be dismissed for the crimes of his white ancestors. I heard an eminent speaker once say that some people would sing, 'I can smile at Satan's rage, and face a frowning world,' when they hadn't courage enough to face their next door neighbor on a moral question."

"I think that must be the case with Mr. Hazleton."

"I once used to despise such men. I have since learned to pity them."

"I don't see what you find to pity in Mr. Hazleton, unless it is his meanness."

"Well, I pity him for that. I think there never was slave more cowed under the whip of his master than he is under the lash of public opinion. The Negro was not the only one whom slavery subdued to the pliancy of submission. Men fettered the slave and cramped their own souls, denied him knowledge and then darkened their own spiritual insight, and the Negro, poor and despised as he was, laid his hands upon American civilization and has helped to mould its character. It is God's law. As ye sow, so shall ye reap, and men cannot sow avarice and oppression without reaping the harvest of retribution. It is a dangerous thing to gather

*The flowers of sin that blossom*
*Around the borders of hell."*

# VIII

I never want to go to that school again," said Annette entering Mrs. Lasette's sitting room, throwing down her books on the table and looking as if she were ready to burst into tears.

"What is the matter now, my dear child? You seem to be all out of sorts."

"I've had a fuss with that Mary Joseph."

"Mary Joseph, the saloon-keeper's daughter?"

"Yes."

"How did it happen?"

"Yesterday in changing seats, the teacher put us together according to the first letter in our last names. You know that I, comes next to J; but there wasn't a girl in the room whose name begins with I, and so as J comes next, she put Mary Joseph and myself together."

"Ireland and Africa, and they were not ready for annexation?"

"No, and never will be, I hope."

"Never is a long day, Annette, but go on with your story."

"Well, after the teacher put her in the seat next to me she began to wriggle and squirm and I asked her if anything was biting her, because if there was, I did not want it to get on me."

"Oh, Annette, what a girl you are; why did you notice her? What did she say?"

"She said if there was, it must have got there since the teacher put her on that seat, and it must have come from me."

"Well, Mary Joseph knows how to scratch as well as you do."

"Yes, she is a real scratch cat."

"And what are you, my dear; a pattern saint?"

"No," said Annette, as the ruefulness of her face relaxed into a smile, "but that isn't all; when I went to eat my lunch, she said she wasn't used to eating with niggers. Then I asked her if her mother didn't eat with the pigs in the old country, and she said that she would rather eat with them than to eat with me, and then she called me a nigger and I called her a poor white mick."

"Oh, Annette, I am so sorry; I am afraid that trouble may come out of this fuss, and then it is so wrong and unlady-like for you to be quarrelling that way. Do you know how old you are?"

"I am almost fourteen years old."

"Where was the teacher all this time? Did she know anything about it?"

"No; she was out of the room part of the time, but I don't think she likes colored people, because last week when Joe Smith was cutting up in school, she made him get up and sit alongside of me to punish him."

"She should not have done so, but I don't suppose she thought for one moment how it looked."

"I don't know, but when I told grandma about it, Mrs. Larkins was in the room, and she said if she had done a child of hers so, she would have gone there and sauced her head off; but grandma said that she would not notice it; that the easiest way is the best."

"I think that your grandmother was right; but what did Joe say?"

He said that the teacher didn't spite him; that he would as lieve sit by me as any girl in school, and that he liked girls."

"A little scamp."

"He says he likes girls because they are so jolly."

"But tell me all about Mary Joseph."

"Well, a mean old thing, she went and told her horrid old father, and just as I was coming along he took hold of my arm and said he had heard that I had called his daughter, Miss Mary Joseph, a poor white mick and that if I did it again he would give me a good thrashing, and that for two pins he would do it then."

"What next?"

"I guess I felt like Mrs. Larkins does when she says her Guinea gets up. My Guinea was up but I was afraid to show it. Oh, but I do hate these Irish. I don't like them for anything. Grandmother says that an Irishman is only a negro turned wrong side out, and I told her so yesterday morning when she was fussing with me."

"Say, rather, when we were fussing together; I don't think the fault was all on her side."

"But, Mrs. Lasette, she had no business calling me a nigger."

"Of course not; but would you have liked it (any) better if she had called you a negro?"

"No; I don't want her to call me anything of the kind, neither negro nor nigger. She shan't even call me black."

"But, Annette, are you not black?"

"I don't care if I am, she shan't call me so."

"But suppose you were to say to Miss Joseph, 'How white your face

FRANCES ELLEN WATKINS HARPER

is,' do you suppose she would get angry because you said that she looked white?"

"No, of course not."

"But suppose you met her hurrying to school, and you said to her, how red and rosy you look this morning, would that make her angry?"

"I don't suppose that it would."

"But suppose she would say to you, 'Annette, how black your face is this morning,' how would you feel?"

"I should feel like slapping her."

"Why so; do you think because Miss Joseph—"

"Don't call her Miss, she is so mean and hateful."

"But that don't hinder her from being Miss Joseph; If she is rude and coarse, that is no reason why I should not have good manners."

"Oh, Mrs. Lasette you are too sweet for anything. I wish I was like you."

"Never mind my sweetness; that is not to the point. Will you listen to me, my dear?"

"Of course I will. I could listen to you all night."

"Well, if it were not for signs there's no mistaking I should think you had a lot of Irish blood in your veins, and had kissed the blarney stone."

"No I haven't and if I had I would try to let—"

"Hush, my child; how you do rattle on. Do you think because Miss Joseph is white that she is any better than you are."

"No, of course not."

"But don't you think that she can see and hear a little better than you can?"

"Why, no; what makes you ask such a funny question?"

"Never mind, just answer me a few more questions. Don't you think if you and she had got to fighting that she would have whipped you because she is white?"

"Why, of course not. Didn't she try to get the ruler out of my hand and didn't because I was stronger."

"But don't you think she is smarter than you are and gets her lessons better."

"Now you are shouting."

"Why, Annette, where in the world did you get that slang?"

"Why, Mrs. Lasette, I hear the boys saying it in the street, and the girls in Tennis Court all say it, too. Is there any harm in it?"

"It is slang, my child, and a young lady should never use slang. Don't use it in private and you will not be apt to use it in public. However humble or poor a person may be, there is no use in being coarse and unrefined."

"But what harm is there in it?"

"I don't say that there is any, but I don't think it nice for young ladies to pick up all sorts of phrases in the street and bring them into the home. The words may be innocent in themselves, but they may not have the best associations, and it is safer not to use them. But let us return to Miss Joseph. You do not think that she can see or hear any better than you can, learn her lessons any quicker than you can, and when it comes to a trial of strength that she is stronger than you are, now let me ask you one more question. Who made Miss Joseph?"

"Why, the Lord, of course."

"And who made you?"

"He made me, too."

"Are you sure that you did not make yourself?"

"Why, of course not," said Annette with an accent of wonder in her voice.

"Does God ever make any mistakes?"

"Why, no!"

"Then if any one calls you black, why should you get angry? You say it would not make Miss Joseph angry to say she looked white, or red and rosy."

"I don't know; I know I don't like it and it makes me mad."

"Now, let me explain the reason why it makes you angry to be called black. Suppose I were to burn my hand in that stove, what would I have on my hand?"

"A sore place."

"If it were your hand, what would you do?"

"I would put something on it, wrap it up to keep from getting cold into it and try to get it well as soon as I could."

"Well, that would be a very sensible way of dealing with it. In this country, Annette, color has been made a sore place; it has been associated with slavery, poverty and ignorance. You cannot change your color, but you can try to change the association connected with our complexions. Did slavery force a man to be servile and submissive? Learn to hold up your head and respect yourself. Don't notice Mary Joseph's taunts; if she says things to tease you don't you let her see that she has succeeded. Learn to act as if you realized that you were born into this world the child of the Ruler of the universe, that this is his world and that you have as much right in it as she has. I think it was Gilbert Haven, a Bishop of the Methodist Episcopal Church, a man for whose tombstone I do not think America has any marble too white or any laurel too green, who saw on his travels a statue of Cleopatra, which suggested to him this thought, 'I am black, but comely, the sun has looked down upon me, but I will make you who despise me feel that I am your superior,' and, Annette, I want you to be so noble, true and pure that if everybody should hate you, that no one could despise you. No, Annette, if Miss Joseph ever attempts to quarrel with you don't put yourself on the same level by quarreling with her. I knew her parents when they were very poor; when a half dozen of them slept in one room. He has made money by selling liquor; he is now doing business in one of the most valuable pieces of property I see in East L street. He has been a curse, and his saloon a nuisance in that street. He has gone up in property and even political influence, but oh, how many poor souls have gone down, slain by strong drink and debauchery."

# IX

True to his word, Mr. Thomas applied to Mr. Hastings, the merchant, of whom he had spoken to his young friend. He went to his counting-room and asked for a private interview, which was readily granted. They had kindred intellectual and literary tastes and this established between them a free masonry of mind which took no account of racial differences.

"I have a favor to ask," said Mr. Thomas, "can you spare me a few moments?"

"I am at your service," Mr. Hasting replied, "what can I do for you?"

"I have," he said, "a young friend who is honest and industrious and competent to fill the place of clerk or cashier in your store. He has been a cashier for Hazleton & Co., and while there gave entire satisfaction."

"Why did he leave?"

"I cannot say, because he was guilty of a skin not colored like your own, but because a report was brought to Mr. Hazleton that he had Negro blood in his veins."

"And what then?"

"He summarily dismissed him."

"What a shame!"

"Yes, it was a shame, but this pride of caste dwarfs men's moral perception so that it prepares them to do a number of contemptible things which, under other circumstances, they would scorn to do."

"Yes, it is so, and I am sorry to see it."

"There are men, Mr. Hastings, who would grow hotly indignant if you would say that they are not gentlemen who would treat a Negro in a manner which would not be recognized as fair, even by ruffians of the ring, for, I believe, it is their code of honor not to strike a man when he is down; but with respect to the colored man, it seems to be a settled policy with some not only to push him down, but to strike him when he is down. But I must go; I came to ask a favor and it is not right to trespass on your time."

"No; sit still. I have a little leisure I can give you. My fall trade has not opened yet and I am not busy. I see and deplore these things of which you complain, but what can be done to help it?"

"Mr. Hastings, you see them, and I feel them, and I fear that I am growing morbid over them, and not only myself, but other educated men of my race, and that, I think, is a thing to be deprecated. Between the white people and the colored people of this country there is a unanimity of interest and I know that our interests and duties all lie in one direction. Can men corrupt and intimidate voters in the South without a reflex influence being felt in the North? Is not the depression of labor in the South a matter of interest to the North? You may protect yourself from what you call the pauper of Europe, but you will not be equally able to defend yourself from the depressed laborer of the new South, and as an American citizen, I dread any turn of the screw which will lower the rate of wages here; and I like to feel as an American citizen that whatever concerns the nation concerns me. But I feel that this prejudice against my race compresses my soul, narrows my political horizon and makes me feel that I am an alien in the land of my birth. It meets me in the church, it confronts me in business and I feel its influence in almost every avenue of my life."

"I wish, Mr. Thomas, that some of the men who are writing and talking about the Negro problem would only come in contact with the thoughtful men of your race. I think it would greatly modify their views."

"Yes, you know us as your servants. The law takes cognizance of our crimes. Your charitable institutions of our poverty, but what do any of you know of our best and most thoughtful men and women? When we write how many of you ever read our books and papers or give yourselves any trouble to come near us as friends and help us? Even some of your professed Christians are trying to set us apart as if we were social lepers."

"You draw a dark picture. I confess that I feel pained at the condition of affairs in the South, but what can we do in the South?"

"Set the South a better example. But I am hindering you in your business."

"Not at all. I want to see things from the same standpoint that you do."

"Put yourself then in my place. You start both North and South from the premise that we are an inferior race and as such you have treated us. Has not the consensus of public opinion said for ages, 'No valor redeems our race, no social advancement nor individual development wipes off the ban which clings to us'; that our place is on the lowest round of the social ladder; that at least, in part of the country we are too low for the equal administrations of religion and the same dispensations of charity and a fair chance in the race of life?"

"You bring a heavy verdict against us. I hardly think that it can be sustained. Whatever our motives may have been, we have been able to effect in a few years a wonderful change in the condition of the Negro. He has freedom and enfranchisement and with these two great rights he must work out his social redemption and political solution. If his means of education have been limited, a better day is dawning upon him. Doors once closed against him in the South are now freely opened to him, and I do not think that there ever was a people who freed their slaves who have given as much for their education as we have, and my only hope is that the moral life of the race will keep pace with its intellectual growth. You tell me to put myself in your place. I think if I were a colored young man that I would develop every faculty and use every power which God had given me for the improvement and development of my race. And who among us would be so blind and foolish as to attempt to keep down an enlightened people who were determined to rise in the scale of character and condition? No, Mr. Thomas, while you blame us for our transgressions and shortcomings, do not fail to do all you can to rouse up all the latent energies of your young men to do their part worthily as American citizens and to add their quota to the strength and progress of the nation."

"I am conscious of the truth and pertinence of your remarks, but bear with me just a few moments while I give an illustration of what I mean."

"Speak on, I am all attention. The subject you bring before me is of too vital importance to be constantly ignored."

"I have a friend who is presiding elder in the A.M.E. Church and his wife, I think, is capable of being a social and intellectual accession in any neighborhood in which they might live. He rented a house in the city of L. and being of a fair complexion I suppose the lessee rented to him without having a suspicion of his race connection. When it was ascertained that he and his family were colored, he was ordered to leave, and this man, holding among the ministers of that city the position of ambassador for Christ, was ordered out of the house on account of the complexion of his family. Was there not a screw loose in the religious sentiment of that city which made such an act possible? A friend of mine who does mission work in your city, some time since, found a young woman in the slums and applied at the door of a midnight mission for fallen women, and asked if colored girls could be received, and was curtly answered, 'no.' For her in that mission there was no room. The love of Christ constrained no hand to strive to rescue her from the depths of degradation. The poor thing went from bad to worse till at last, wrecked and blighted, she went down to an early grave the victim of strong drink. That same lady found on her mission a white girl; seeing a human soul adrift, regardless of color, she went, in company with some others, to that same mission with the poor castaway; to her the door was opened without delay and ready admittance granted. But I might go on reciting such instances until you would be weary of hearing and I of relating them; but I appeal to you as a patriot and Christian, is it not fearfully unwise to keep alive in freedom the old animosities of slavery? Today the Negro shares citizenship with you. He is not arraying himself against your social order; his hands are not dripping with dynamite, nor is he waving in your face the crimson banners of anarchy, but he is increasing in numbers and growing in intelligence, and is it not madness and folly to subject him to social and public inequalities, which are calculated to form and keep alive a hatred of race as a reaction against pride of caste?"

"Mr. Thomas, you have given me a new view of the matter. To tell you the truth, we have so long looked upon the colored man as a pliable and submissive being that we have never learned to look at any hatred on his part as an element of danger, and yet I should be sorry to know that by our Southern supineness we were thoughtlessly helping create a black Ireland in our Gulf States, that in case the fires of anarchy should ever sweep through our land, that a discontented and disaffected people in our midst might be as so much fuel to fire."

"But really I have been forgetting my errand. Have you any opening in your store for my young friend?"

"I have only one vacancy, and that is the place of a utility man."

"What are the duties of that position?"

"Almost anything that comes to hand; tying up bundles, looking after the mails, scattering advertisements. A factotum whose work lies here, there and everywhere."

"I am confident that he will accept the situation and render you faithful service."

"Well, then send him around tomorrow and if there is anything in him I may be able to do better by him when the fall trade opens."

And so Charley Cooper was fortunate enough in his hour of perplexity to find a helping hand to tide him over a difficult passage in his life. Gratefully and faithfully did he serve Mr. Hastings, who never regretted the hour when he gave the struggling boy such timely assistance. The discipline of the life through which he was passing as the main stay of his mother, matured his mind and imparted to it a thoughtfulness past his years. Instead of wasting his time in idle and pernicious pleasure, he learned how to use his surplus dollar and how to spend his leisure hours, and this knowledge told upon his life and character. He was not very popular in society. Young men with cigars in their mouths and the perfume of liquor on their breaths, shrugged their shoulders and called him a milksop because he preferred the church and Sunday school to the liquor saloon and gambling dens. The society of P. was cut up and divided into little sets and coteries; there was an amount of intelligence among them, but it ran in narrow grooves and scarcely one intellect seemed to tower above the other, and if it did, no people knew better how to ignore a rising mind than the society people of A.P. If the literary aspirant did not happen to be of their set. As to talent, many of them were pleasant and brilliant conversationalists, but in the world of letters scarcely any of them were known or recognized outside of their set. They had leisure, a little money and some ability, but they lacked the perseverance and self-denial necessary to enable them to add to the great resources of natural thought. They had narrowed their minds to the dimensions of their set and were unprepared to take expansive views of life and duty. They took life as a holiday and the lack of noble purposes and high and holy aims left its impress upon their souls and deprived them of that joy and strength which should have crowned their existence and given to their lives its "highest excellence and beauty."

# X

Two years have elapsed since we left Annette recounting her school grievances to Mrs. Lasette. She has begun to feel the social contempt which society has heaped upon the colored people, but she has determined not to succumb to it. There is force in the character of that fiery, impetuous and impulsive girl, and her school experience is bringing it out. She has been bending all her mental energies to compete for the highest prize at the commencement of her school, from which she expects to graduate in a few weeks. The treatment of the saloon-keeper's daughter, and that of other girls of her ilk, has stung her into strength. She feels that however despised her people may be, that a monopoly of brains has not been given to the white race. Mr. Thomas has encouraged her efforts, and taught her to believe that not only is her own honor at stake as a student, but that as a representative of her branch of the human race, she is on the eve of winning, or losing, not only for herself, but for others. This view of the matter increases her determination and rouses up all the latent energies of her nature, and she labors day and night to be a living argument of the capability in her race. For other girls who will graduate in that school, there will be open doors, and unclosed avenues, while she knows that the color of her skin will bar against her the doors of workshops, factories and school rooms, and yet Mr. Thomas, knowing all the discouragements around her path, has done what he could to keep her interest in her studies from flagging. He knows that she has fine abilities, but that they must be disciplined by trial and endeavor before her life can be rounded by success and triumph. He has seen several of her early attempts at versification; pleased and even delighted with them, he has shown them to a few of his most intellectual friends. Eager and earnest for the elevation of the colored people, he has been pained at the coldness with which they have been received.

"I do not call that poetry," said one of the most intelligent women of A.P.

"Neither do I see anything remarkable about her," said another.

"I did not," said Mr. Thomas, "bring you the effusions of an acknowledged poet, but I think that the girl has fine ability, which needs encouragement and recognition."

But his friends could not see it; they were very charry of their admiration, lest their judgment should be found at fault, and then it was so much easier to criticise than it was to heartily admire; and they knew it seemed safer to show their superior intelligence by dwelling on the defects, which would necessarily have an amount of crudeness in them than to look beneath the defects for the suggestions of beauty, strength and grace which Mr. Thomas saw in these unripe, but promising effusions. It seemed perfectly absurd with the surroundings of Tennis Court to expect anything grand or beautiful (to) develop in its midst; but with Annette, poetry was a passion born in her soul, and it was as natural for her to speak in tropes and figures as it was for others to talk in plain, common prose. Mr. Thomas called her "our inveterate poet," and encouraged her, but the literary aspirants took scarcely any interest in the girl whom they left to struggle on as best she might. In her own home she was doomed to meet with lack of encouragement and appreciation from her relatives and grandmother's friends. One day her aunt, Eliza Hanson, was spending the day with her mother, and Annette showed her some of her verses and said to her, "that is one of my best pieces."

"Oh, you have a number of best pieces," said her aunt, carelessly. "Can you cook a beefsteak?"

"I suppose I could if I tried."

"Well, you had better try than to be trying to string verses together. You seem to think that there must be something very great about you. I know where you want to get. You want to get among the upper tens, but you haven't got style enough about you for that."

"That's just what I tell her," said her grandmother. "She's got too many airs for a girl in her condition. She talks about writing a book, and she is always trying to make up what she calls poetry. I expect that she will go crazy some of these days. She is all the time talking to herself, and I just think it is a sin for her to be so much taken up with her poetry."

"You had better put her to work; had she not better go out to service?"

"No, I am going to let her graduate first."

"What's the use of it? When she's through, if she wants to teach, she will have to go away."

"Yes, I know that, but Mrs. Lasette has persuaded me to let Annette graduate, and I have promised that I would do so, and besides I think to take Annette from school just now would almost break her heart."

"Well, mother, that is just like you; you will work yourself almost to death to keep Annette in school, and when she is through what good will it do her?"

"Maybe something will turn up that you don't see just now. When a good thing turns up if a person ain't ready for it they can't take hold of it."

"Well, I hope a good husband will turn up for my Alice."

"But maybe the good husband won't turn up for Annette."

"That is well said, for they tell me that Annette is not very popular, and that some of the girls are all the time making fun of her."

"Well, they had better make fun of themselves and their own bad manners. Annette is poor and has no father to stand by her, and I cannot entertain like some of their parents can, but Annette, with all her faults, is as good as any of them. Talk about the prejudice of the white people, I think there is just as much prejudice among some colored as there is among them, only we do not get the same chance to show it; we are most too mixed up and dependent on one another for that." Just then Mrs. Lasette entered the room and Mrs. Hanson, addressing her, said, "We were just discussing Annette's prospects. Mother wants to keep Annette at school till she graduates, but I think she knows enough now to teach a country school and it is no use for mother to be working as she does to keep Annette in school for the sake of letting her graduate. There are lots of girls in A.P. better off than she who have never graduated, and I don't see that mother can afford to keep Annette at school any longer."

"But, Eliza, Annette is company for me and she does help about the house."

"I don't think much of her help; always when I come home she has a book stuck under her nose."

"Annette," said Mrs. Lasette, "is a favorite of mine; I have always a warm place in my heart for her, and I really want to see the child do well. In my judgment I do not think it advisable to take her from school before she graduates. If Annette were indifferent about her lessons and showed no aptitude for improvement I should say as she does not appreciate education enough to study diligently and has not aspiration enough to keep up with her class, find out what she is best fitted for and let her be instructed in that calling for which she is best adapted."

"I think," said Mrs. Hanson, "you all do wrong in puffing up Annette with the idea that she is something extra. You think, Mrs. Lasette, that there is something wonderful about Annette, but I can't see it, and I hear a lot of people say she hasn't got good sense."

"They do not understand the child."

"They all say that she is very odd and queer and often goes out into the street as if she never saw a looking glass. Why, Mrs. Miller's daughter just laughed till she was tired at the way Annette was dressed when she went to call on an acquaintance of hers. Why, Annette just makes herself a perfect laughing stock."

"Well, I think Mary Miller might have found better employment than laughing at her company."

"Now, let me tell you, Mary Miller don't take her for company, and that very evening Annette was at my house, just next door, and when Mary Miller went to church she never asked her to go along with her, although she belongs to the same church."

"I am sorry to say it," said grandmother Harcourt, "but your Alice hardly ever comes to see Annette, and never asks her to go anywhere with her, but may be in the long run Annette will come out better than some who now look down upon her. It is a long road that has no turn and Annette is like a singed cat; she is better than she looks."

"I think," said Mrs. Lasette, "while Annette is very bright and intelligent as a pupil, she has been rather slow in developing in some other directions. She lacks tact, is straightforward to bluntness and has not any style about her and little or no idea of company manners, but she is never coarse nor rude. I never knew her to read a book whose author I would blush to name, and I never heard her engage in any conversation I would shrink to hear repeated. I don't think there is a girl of purer lips in A.P. than Annette, and I do not think your set, as you call it, has such a monopoly of either virtue or intelligence that you can afford to ridicule and depress any young soul who does not happen to come up to your social standard. Where dress and style are passports Annette may be excluded, but where brain and character count Annette will gain admittance. I fear," said Mrs. Lasette, rising to go, "that many a young girl has gone down in the very depths who might have been saved if motherly women, when they saw them unloved and lonely, had reached out to them a helping hand and encouraged them to live useful and good lives. We cry am I my sister's keeper? (I?) will not wipe the blood off our hands if through pride and selfishness we have stabbed by our neglect souls we should have helped by our kindness. I always feel for young girls who are lonely and neglected in large cities and are in danger of being ensnared by pretended sympathies and false friendship, and, today, no girl is more welcome at any social gathering than Annette."

"Mrs. Lasette," said Mrs. Hanson, "you are rich and you can do as you choose in A.P. You can set the fashion."

"No; I am not rich, but I hope that I will always be able to lend a hand to any lonely girl who is neglected, slighted and forgotten while she is trying to do right, who comes within my reach while I live in A.P. Good morning."

"Annette," said Mrs. Hanson, "has a champion who will stand by her."

"Yes," said Mrs. Harcourt, "Anna is true as steel; the kind of woman you can tie to. When my great trouble came, she was good as gold, and when my poor heart was almost breaking, she always had a kind word for me. I wish we had ten thousand like her."

"Well, mother, I must go, but if Annette does graduate don't let her go on the stage looking like a fright. General H's daughter has a beautiful new silk dress and a lovely hat which she got just a few weeks before her mother's death; as she has gone in black she wants to sell it, and if you say so, and will pay for it on installments, I can get if for Annette, and I think with a little alteration it would be splendid for her graduation dress."

"No; Eliza, I can't afford it."

"Why, mother, Annette will need something nice for the occasion, and it will not cost any more than what you intend to pay for her dress and hat. Why not take them?"

"Because Annette is not able to wear them. Suppose she had that one fine dress and hat, would she not want more to match with them? I don't want her to learn to dress in a style that she cannot honestly afford. I think this love of dress is the ruination of many a young girl. I think this straining after fine things when you are not able to get them, is perfectly ridiculous. I believe in cutting your coat according to your cloth. I saw Mrs. Hempstead's daughter last Sunday dressed up in a handsome light silk, and a beautiful spring hat, and if she or her mother would get sick tomorrow, they would, I suppose, soon be objects of public charity or dependent on her widowed sister, who is too proud to see her go to the poor house; and this is just the trouble with a lot of people; they not only have their own burdens to bear but somebody else's. You may call me an old fogy, but I would rather live cheap and dress plain than shirk my burdens because I had wasted when they had saved. You and John Hanson are both young and have got your health and strength, and instead of buying sealskins, and velvets and furbelows, you had better be laying up for a rainy day. You have no more need for a sealskin cloak than a cat has for a catechism. Now you do as you please, I have had my say."

# XI

It has been quite a length of time since we left Mr. Thomas and his young friend facing an uncertain future. Since then he has not only been successful in building up a good business for himself, but in opening the gates to others. His success has not inflated him with pride. Neither has he become self-abashed and isolated from others less fortunate, who need his counsel and sympathy. Generous and noble in his character, he was conservative enough to cling to the good of the past and radical enough to give hospitality to every new idea which was calculated to benefit and make life noble and better. Mr. Thomas, in laying the foundation of his education, was thoughtful enough to enter a manual labor school, where he had the double advantage of getting an education and learning a trade, through which he was enabled to rely on himself without asking aid from any one, which in itself was an education in manliness, self-respect and self-reliance, that he could not have obtained had he been the protege of the wealthiest philanthropist in the land. As he had fine mechanical skill and ingenuity, he became an excellent carpenter. But it is one thing to have a trade and another thing to have an opportunity to exercise that trade. It was a time when a number of colored churches were being erected. To build large and even magnificent churches seemed to be a ruling passion with the colored people. Their homes might be very humble, their walls bare of pictured grace, but by united efforts they could erect large and handsome churches in which they had a common possession and it was one of the grand satisfactions of freedom that they were enabled to build their own churches and carry on their own business without being interfered with, and overlooked by a class of white ecclesiastics whose presence was a reminder of their implied inferiority. The church of which Mr. Thomas was a member was about to erect a costly edifice. The trustees would probably have willingly put the work in the hands of a colored man, had there been a sufficient number to have done the work, but they did not seem to remember that white prejudice had barred the Northern workshops against the colored man, that slavery, by degrading and monopolizing labor had been the means of educating colored men in the South to be good mechanics, and that a little pains and search on their part might have brought to light colored carpenters in the South who would have done the work as efficiently as those whom they employed, but as the trustees were not very farsighted men, they did the most available thing that came to hand; they employed a white man. Mr. Thomas' pastor applied to the master builder for a place for his parishioner.

"Can you give employment to one of my members, on our church?" Rev. Mr. Lomax asked the master builder.

"I would willingly do so, but I can not."

"Why not?"

"Because my men would all rise up against it. Now, for my part, I have no prejudice against your parishioner, but my men will not work with a colored man. I would let them all go if I could get enough colored men to suit me just as well, but such is the condition of the labor market, that a man must either submit to a number of unpalatable things or run the risk of a strike and being boycotted. I think some of these men who want so much liberty for themselves have very little idea of it for other people."

After this conversation the minister told Mr. Thomas the result of his interview with the master builder, and said,

"I am very sorry; but it is as it is, and it can't be any better."

"Do you mean by that that things are always going to remain as they are?"

"I do not see any quick way out of it. This prejudice is the outgrowth of ages; it did not come in a day, nor do I expect that it will vanish in an hour."

"Nor do I; but I do not think the best way for a people to mend their pastures is to sit down and bewail their fate."

"No; we must be up and going for ourselves. White people will—"

"White people," exclaimed Mr. Thomas somewhat impatiently. "Is there not a great deal of bosh in the estimate some of us have formed of white people. We share a common human feeling, from which the same cause produces the same effect. Why am I today a social Pariah, begging for work, and refused situation after situation? My father is a wealthy Southerner; he has several other sons who are inheritors of his name and heirs of his wealth. They are educated, cultured and occupy high social positions. Had I not as good a right to be well born as any of them? And yet, through my father's crime, I was doomed to the status of a slave with its heritage of ignorance, poverty and social debasement. Talk of the heathenism of Africa, of hostile tribes warring upon each other and selling the conquered foes into the hands of white men, but

FRANCES ELLEN WATKINS HARPER

how much higher in the scale of moral progression was the white man who doomed his own child, bone of his bone, and flesh of his flesh, to a life of slavery? The heathen could plead in his defence the fortunes of war, and the hostility of an opposing tribe, but the white man who enslaved his child warred upon his hapless offspring and wrote chattel upon his condition when his hand was too feeble to hurl aside the accursed hand and recognize no other ownership but God. I once felt bitterly on this subject, and although it is impossible for my father to make full reparation for the personal wrong inflicted on me, I owe him no grudge. Hating is poor employment for any rational being, but I am not prepared to glorify him at the expense of my mother's race. She was faithful to me when he deserted me to a life of ignorance and poverty, and although three-fourths of the blood in my veins belongs to my father's face, I feel a kinship with my mother's people that I do not with his, and I will defend that race from the aspersions of the meanest Negro hater in the land. Heathenism and civilization live side by side on American soil, but all the heathenism is not on the side of the Negro. Look at slavery and kukluxism with their meanness and crimes, mormonism with its vile abominations, lynch law with its burnings and hangings, our national policy in regard to the Indians and Chinese."

"I do not think," said the minister, "that there is another civilized country in the world where men are lynched for real or supposed crimes outside of America."

"The Negro need not bow his head like a bulrush in the presence of a race whose records are as stained by crime and dishonor as theirs. Let others decry the Negro, and say hard things about him, I am not prepared to join in the chorus of depreciation."

After parting with the minister, Mr. Thomas resolved, if pluck and energy were of any avail, that he would leave no stone unturned in seeking employment. He searched the papers carefully for advertisements, walked from one workshop to the other looking for work, and was eventually met with a refusal which meant, no negro need apply. At last one day when he had tried almost every workshop in the place, he entered the establishment of Wm. C. Nell, an Englishman who had not been long enough in America to be fully saturated by its Christless and inhuman prejudices. He was willing to give Mr. Thomas work, and put tools in his hands, and while watching how deftly he handled them, he did not notice the indignant scowls on the faces of his workmen, and their murmurs of disapprobation as they uttered their dissatisfaction one to the other. At length they took off their aprons, laid down their tools and asked to be discharged from work.

"Why, what does this mean?" asked the astounded Englishman.

"It means that we will not work with a nigger."

"Why, I don't understand? what is the matter with him?"

"Why, there's nothing the matter, only he's a nigger, and we never put niggers on an equality with us, and we never will."

"But I am a stranger in this country, and I don't understand you."

"Well, he's a nigger, and we don't want niggers for nothing; would you have your daughter marry a nigger?"

"Oh, go back to your work; I never thought of such a thing. I think the Negro must be an unfortunate man, and I do not wish my daughter to marry any unfortunate man, but if you do not want to work with him I will put him by himself; there is room enough on the premises; will that suit you any better?"

"No; we won't work for a man who employs a nigger."

The builder bit his lip; he had come to America hearing that it was a land of liberty but he had found an undreamed of tyranny which had entered his workshop and controlled his choice of workmen, and as much as he deprecated the injustice, it was the dictum of a vitiated public opinion that his field of occupation should be closed against the Negro, and he felt that he was forced, either to give up his business or submit to the decree.

Mr. Thomas then thought, "my money is vanishing, school rooms and workshops are closed against me. I will not beg, and I can not resort to any questionable means for bread. I will now take any position or do any work by which I can make an honest living." Just as he was looking gloomily at the future an old school mate laid his hand upon his shoulder and said, "how do you do, old fellow? I have not seen you for a week of Sundays. What are you driving at now?"

"Oh, nothing in particular. I am looking for work."

"Well, now this is just the ticket. I have just returned from the Pacific coast and while I was there I did splendidly; everything I touched turned to gold, and now I have a good job on hand if you are not too squeamish to take it. I have just set up a tiptop restaurant and saloon, and I have some of the best merchants of the city as my customers, and I want a first rate clerk. You were always good at figures and if you will accept the place come with me right away. Since high license went into operation, I am making money hand over fist. It is just like the big fish eating up the little fish. I am doing a rushing business and I want you to do my clerking."

The first thought which rushed into Mr. Thomas' mind was, "Is thy servant a dog that he should do this thing?" but he restrained his indignation and said,

"No, Frank, I cannot accept your offer; I am a temperance man and a prohibitionist, and I would rather have my hands clean than to have them foul."

"You are a greater milksop than I gave you credit for. Here you are hunting work, and find door after door closed against you, not because you are not but because you are colored, and here am I offering you easy employment and good wages and you refuse them."

"Frank," said Mr. Thomas, "I am a poor man, but I would rather rise up early, and sit up late and eat the bread of carelessness, than to roll in wealth by keeping a liquor saloon, and I am determined that no drunkard shall ever charge me with having helped drag him down to misery, shame and death. No drunkard's wife shall ever lay the wreck of her home at my door."

"My business," said Frank Miller, "is a legitimate one; there is money in it, and I am after that. If people will drink too much and make fools of themselves I can't help it; it is none of my business, and if I don't sell to them other people will. I don't think much of a man who does not know how to govern himself, but it is no use arguing with you when you are once set in your ways; good morning."

# XII

It was a gala day in Tennis Court. Annette had passed a highly successful examination, and was to graduate from the normal school, and as a matter of course, her neighbors wanted to hear Annette "speak her piece" as they called the commencement theme, and also to see how she was going to behave before all "them people." They were, generally speaking, too unaspiring to feel envious toward any one of their race who excelled them intellectually, and so there was little or no jealousy of Annette in Tennis Court; in fact some of her neighbors felt a kind of pride in the thought that Tennis Court would turn out a girl who could stand on the same platform and graduate alongside of some of their employers' daughters. If they could not stand there themselves they were proud that one of their race could.

"I feel," said one, "like the boy when some one threatened to slap off his face who said 'you can slap off my face, but I have a big brother and you can't slap off his face;'" and strange as it may appear, Annette received more encouragement from a class of honest-hearted but ignorant and well meaning people who knew her, than she did from some of the most cultured and intelligent people of A.P. Nor was it very strange; they were living too near the poverty, ignorance and social debasement of the past to have developed much race pride, and a glowing enthusiasm in its progress and development. Although they were of African descent, they were Americans whose thoughts were too much Americanized to be wholly free from imbibing the social atmosphere with which they were in constant contact in their sphere of enjoyments. The literature they read was mostly from the hands of white men who would paint them in any colors which suited their prejudices or predilections. The religious ideas they had embraced came at first thought from the same sources, though they may have undergone modifications in passing through their channels of thought, and it must be a remarkable man or woman who thinks an age ahead of the generation in which his or her lot is cast, and who plans and works for the future on the basis of that clearer vision. Nor is it to be wondered at, if under the circumstances, some of the more cultured of A.P. thought it absurd to look for anything remarkable to come out of the black Nazareth of Tennis court. Her neighbors had an idea that Annette was very smart; that she had a great "head piece," but unless she left A.P. to teach school elsewhere, they did not see what good her education was going to do her. It wasn't going to put any meal in the barrel nor any potatoes in the bin. Even Mrs. Larkins relaxed her ancient hostility to Annette and opened her heart to present her with a basket of flowers. Annette within the last year had become very much changed in her conduct and character. She had become friendly in her manner and considerate in her behavior to Mrs. Larkins since she had entered the church, during a protracted meeting. Annette was rather crude in her religious views but here again Mrs. Lasette became her faithful friend and advisor. In dealing with a young convert she thought more was needed than getting her into the church and making her feel that the moment she rose from the altar with rejoicing on her lips, that she was a full blown christian. That, to Mrs. Lasette was the initial step in the narrow way left luminous by the bleeding feet of Christ, and what the young convert needed was to be taught how to walk worthy of her high calling, and to make her life a thing of usefulness and faithfulness to God and man, a growth in grace and in the saving knowledge of our Lord Jesus Christ. Simply attired in a dress which Mrs. Lasette thought fitted for the occasion, Annette took her seat quietly on the platform and calmly waited till her turn came. Her subject was announced: "The Mission of the Negro." It was a remarkable production for a girl of her age. At first she portrayed an African family seated beneath their bamboo huts and spreading palms; the light steps of the young men and maidens tripping to music, dance and song; their pastimes suddenly broken upon by the tramp of the merchants of flesh and blood; the capture of defenceless people suddenly surprised in the midst of their sports, the cries of distress, the crackling of flames, the cruel oaths of reckless men, eager for gold though they coined it from tears and extracted it from blood; the crowding of the slaveships, the horrors of the middle passage, the landing of the ill-fated captives were vividly related, and the sad story of ages of bondage. It seemed as if the sorrow of centuries was sobbing in her voice. Then the scene changed, and like a grand triumphal march she recounted the deliverance of the Negro, and the wondrous change which had come over his condition; the slave pen exchanged for the free school, the fetters on his wrist for the ballot in his right hand. Then her voice grew musical when she began to speak of the mission of the Negro, "His mission," she said, "is grandly constructive." Some races had been "architects of destruction," but their mission was to build over the ruins of the dead past, the most valuable thing that a man or woman could possess on earth, and that is good character. That mission should be to bless and not to curse. To lift up the banner of the Christian religion from the mire and dust into which slavery and pride of caste had trailed it, and to hold it up as an ensign of hope and deliverance to other races of the world, of whom the greater portion were not white people. It seemed as if an inspiration lit up the young face; her eye glowed with unwonted fervor; it seemed as if she had fused her whole soul into the subject, which was full of earnestness and enthusiasm. Her theme was the sensation of the hour. Men grew thoughtful and attentive, women tender and sympathetic as they heard this member of a once despised people, recount the trials and triumphs of her race, and the hopes that gathered around their future. The day before Annette graduated Mr. Thomas had met a friend of his at Mrs. Lasette's, who had lately returned from an extensive tour. He had mingled with many people and had acquired a large store of information. Mr. Thomas had invited him to accompany him to the commencement. He had expected that Annette would acquit herself creditably, but she had far exceeded his most sanguine expectations. Clarence Luzerne had come because his friend Mr. Thomas had invited him and because he and Mrs. Lasette had taken such great interest in Annette's welfare, and his curiosity was excited to see how she would acquit herself and compare with the other graduates. He did not have much faith in graduating essays. He had heard a number of such compositions at commencements which had inspired him with glowing hopes for the future of the authors, which he had never seen realized, and he had come more to gratify Mr. Thomas than to please himself. But if he came through curiosity, he remained through interest, which had become more and more absorbing as she proceeded.

"Clarence," said Mr. Thomas to his friend, noticing the deep interest he was manifesting, "Are you entranced? You appear perfectly spell-bound."

"Well, I am; I am really delighted and indebted to you for a rare and unexpected pleasure. Why, that young lady gave the finest production that I have heard this morning. I hardly think she could have written it herself. It seems wonderful that a girl of her age should have done it so well. You are a great friend of hers; now own up, are not your finger marks upon it? I wouldn't tell it out of our ranks, but I don't think she wrote that all herself."

"Who do you think wrote it for her?"

"Mrs. Lasette."

"I do not think so; Mrs. Lasette is a fine writer, but that nervous, fervid and impassioned style is so unlike hers, that I do not think she wrote one line of it, though she might have overlooked it, and made some suggestions, but even if it were so that some one else wrote it, we know that no one else delivered it, and that her delivery was excellent."

"That is so; why, she excelled all the other girls. Do you know what was the difference between her and the other girls?"

"No; what was it?" said Mr. Thomas.

"They wrote from their heads, she wrote from her heart. Annette has begun to think; she has been left a great deal to herself, and in her loneliness, she has developed a thoughtfulness past her years, and I think that a love for her race and a desire to serve it has become a growing passion in her soul; her heart has supplied her intellect."

"Ah, I think from what you say that I get the true clue to the power and pathos with which she spoke this morning and that accounts for her wonderful success."

"Yes," said Mr. Luzerne, "it is the inner life which develops the outer life, and just such young people as Annette make me more hopeful of the future of the race."

Mrs. Lasette witnessed Annette's graduation with intense interest and pleasure. Grandmother Harcourt looked the very impersonation of satisfaction as she gathered up the floral gifts, and modestly waited while Annette received the pleasant compliments of admiring friends.

At his request Mr. Thomas introduced Mr. Luzerne to Annette, who in the most gracious and affable manner, tendered to Annette his hearty congratulations which she modestly received, and for the time being all went merry as a marriage bell.

# XIII

W hat a fool he is to refuse my offer," thought the saloon-keeper. "What a pity it is," said Mr. Thomas to himself, "that a man of his education and ability should be engaged in such accursed business."

After refusing the saloonkeeper's offer Mr. Thomas found a job of work. It was not a job congenial to his feelings, but his motto was, "If I do not see an opening I will make one." After he had turned from Mr. Englishman's workshop, burning with a sense of wrong which he felt powerless to overcome, he went on the levee and looked around to see if any work might be picked up by him as a day laborer. He saw a number of men singing, joking and plying their tasks with nimble feet and apparently no other care upon their minds than meeting the demands of the present hour, and for a moment he almost envied their lightheartedness, and he thought within himself, where all men are born blind, no man misses the light. These men are contented with privileges, and I who have fitted myself for a different sphere in life, am chaffing because I am denied rights. The right to sell my labor in any workshop in this city same as the men of other nationalities, and to receive with them a fair day's wages for a fair day's work. But he was strong and healthy and he was too high spirited to sit moping at home depending upon his mother to divide with him her scanty means till something should turn up. The first thing that presented itself to him was the job of helping unload a boat which had landed at the wharf, and a hand was needed to assist in unloading her. Mr. Thomas accepted the position and went to work and labored manfully at the unaccustomed task. That being finished the merchant for whom he had done the work, hired him to labor in his warehouse. He showed himself very handy in making slight repairs when needed and being ready to turn his hand to any service out of his routine of work, hammering a nail, adjusting a disordered lock and showing a general concern in his employer's interests. One day his employer had engaged a carpenter to make him a counter, but the man instead of attending to his work had been off on a drunken spree, and neglected to do the job. The merchant, vexed at the unnecessary delay, said to Mr. Thomas in a bantering manner, "I believe you can do almost anything, couldn't you make this counter?"

Mr. Thomas answered quite modestly, "I believe I could if I had my tools."

"Tools! What do you mean by tools?"

Mr. Thomas told him how he learned to be a carpenter in the South and how he had tried so unsuccessfully in the North to get an opportunity to work at his trade until discouraged with the attempt, he had made up his mind to take whatever work came to hand till he could see farther.

The merchant immediately procured the materials and set Mr. Thomas to work, who in a short time finished the counter, and showed by his workmanship that he was an excellent carpenter. The merchant pleased with his work and satisfied with his ability, entrusted him with the erection of a warehouse and, strange as it may appear, some of those men who were too proud or foolish to work with him as a fellow laborer, were humble enough to work under him as journeymen. When he was down they were ready to kick him down. When he was up they were ready to receive his helping hand. Mr. Thomas soon reached that "tide in his affairs which taken at the flood leads on to fortune." Against the odds which were against him his pluck and perseverance prevailed, and he was enabled not only to build up a good business for himself, but also to help others, and to teach them by his own experience not to be too easily discouraged, but to trust to pluck more than luck, and learn in whatever capacity they were employed to do their work heartily as unto the Lord and not unto men.

Anxious to do what she could to benefit the community in which she lived, Mrs. Lasette threw open her parlors for the gathering together of the best thinkers and workers of the race, who choose to avail themselves of the privilege of meeting to discuss any question of vital importance to the welfare of the colored people of the nation. Knowing the entail of ignorance which slavery had left them, she could not be content by shutting up herself to mere social enjoyments within the shadow of her home. And often the words would seem to ring within her soul, "my people is destroyed for lack of knowledge," and with those words would come the question, am I doing what I can to dispel the darkness which has hung for centuries around our path? I have been blessed with privileges which were denied others; I sat 'mid the light of knowledge when some of my ill-fated sisters did not know what it was to see daylight in their cabins from one week's end to the other. Sometimes when she met with coldness and indifference where she least expected it, she would grow sad but would not yield to discouragement. Her heart was in the right place. "Freely she had received and freely she would give." It was at one of Mrs. Lasette's gatherings that Mr. Thomas met Rev. Mr. Lomax on whose church he had been refused a place, and Mr. Thurman, a tradesman who also had been ousted from his position through pride of caste and who had gone into another avocation, and also Charley Cooper, of whom we have lost sight for a number of years. He is now a steady and prosperous young man, a constant visitor at Mrs. Lasette's. Rumor says that Mrs. Lasette's bright-eyed and lovely daughter is the magnet which attracts him to their pleasant home. Rev. Lomax has also been absent for several years on other charges, but when he meets Mr. Thomas, the past flows back and the incidents of their latest interviews naturally take their place in the conversation. "It has been some time since we met," said Mr. Thomas, heartily shaking the minister's hand.

"How has life used you since last we met?" said Rev. Lomax to Mr. Thomas. "Are you well?"

"Perfectly well, I have had a varied experience since I met you, but I have no reason to complain, and I think my experience has been invaluable to me, and with this larger experience and closer observation, I feel that I am more able to help others, and that, I feel, has been one of my most valued acquirements. I sometimes think of members of our people in some directions as sheep without a shepherd, and I do wish from the bottom of my heart that I knew the best way to help them."

"You do not," said the minister, somewhat anxiously, "ignore the power of the pulpit."

"No, I do not; I only wish it had tenfold force. I wish we had ten thousand ministers like Oberlin who was not ashamed to take the lead in opening a road from Bande Roche to Strasburgh, a distance of several miles to bring his parishioners in contact with the trade and business of a neighboring village. I hope the time will come when every minister in building a church which he consecrates to the worship of God will build alongside of it or under the same roof, parish buildings or rooms to be dedicated to the special wants of our people in their peculiar condition."

"I do wish, Brother Lomax, those costly buildings which you erect will cover more needs and wants of our people than some of them do now."

"What would you have in them?"

"I would have a parish building to every church, and I would have in them an evening home for boys. I would have some persons come in and teach them different handicrafts, so as at least to give them an opportunity to be more expert in learning how to use their hands. I would have that building a well warmed and well lighted room in winter, where all should be welcome to come and get a sandwich and a warm cup of tea or coffee and a hot bowl of soup, and if the grogshops were selling liquor for five cents, I would sell the soup for three or four cents, with a roll. I would have a room reserved for such ladies as Mrs. Lasette, who are so willing to help, for the purpose of holding mother's meetings. I would try to have the church the great centre of moral, spiritual and intellectual life for the young, and try to present counter attractions to the debasing influence of the low grogshops, gambling dens and houses of ill fame."

"Part of our city (ought I confine myself to saying part of the city) has not the whole city been cursed by rum? But I now refer to a special part. I have seen church after church move out of that part of the city where the nuisance and curse were so rife, but I never, to my knowledge, heard of one of those churches offering to build a reading room and evening home for boys, or to send out paid and sustained by their efforts, a single woman to go into rum-cursed homes and teach their inmates a more excellent way. I would have in that parish building the most earnest men and women to come together and consult and counsel with each other on the best means to open for ourselves, doors which are still closed against us."

"I am sure," said the minister, "I am willing to do what I can for the temporal and spiritual welfare of our people, and in this I have the example of the great Physician who did not consider it beneath him to attend to physical maladies as well as spiritual needs, and who did not consider the synagogue too holy, nor the Sabbath day too sacred to administer to the destitute and suffering."

"I was very sorry when I found out, Brother Thomas, that I could not have you employed on my church, but I do not see what else I could have done except submit."

"That was all you could have done in that stage of the work when I applied, and I do not wish to bestow the slightest censure on you or the trustees of your church, but I think, if when you were about to build had you advertised for competent master-builders in the South, that you could have gotten enough to have built the church without having employed Mr. Hoog the master-builder. Had you been able to have gone to him and said, 'we are about to build a church and it is more convenient for us to have it done by our citizens than to send abroad for laborers. We are in communication with a colored master builder in Kentucky, who is known as an efficient workman and who would be glad to get the job, and if your men refuse to work with a colored man our only alternative will be to send for colored carpenters and put the building in their hands.' Do you think he would have refused a thirty thousand dollar job just because some of his men refused to work with colored men? I think the greater portion of his workmen would have held their prejudices in abeyance rather than let a thirty thousand dollar job slip out of their hands. Now here is another thing in which I think united effort could have effected something. Now, here is my friend Mr. Thurman; he was a saddler versed in both branches of harness making. For awhile he got steady work in a saddler's shop, but the prejudice against him was so great that his employer was forced to dismiss him. He took work home, but that did not heal the dissatisfaction, and at last he gave it up and went to well-digging. Now, there were colored men in that place who could have, as I think, invested some money in buying material and helped him, not as a charity, but as a mere business operation to set up a place for himself; he had the skill; they had the money, and had they united both perhaps today there would be a flourishing business carried on by the man who is now digging wells for a living. I do hope that some time there will be some better modes of communication between us than we now possess; that a labor bureau will be established not as a charity among us, but as a business with capable and efficient men who will try to find out the different industries that will employ men irrespective of color and advertise and find steady and reliable colored men to fill them. Colored men in the South are largely employed in raising cotton and other produce; why should there not be more openings in the South for colored men to handle the merchandize and profit by it?"

"What hinders?" said Rev. Lomax.

"I will not say what hinders, but I will say what I think you can try to do to help. Teach our young to dedicate their young lives to the noble service of devoting them to the service of our common cause; to throw away their cigars, dash down the foaming beer and sparkling wine and strive to be more like those of whom it was said, 'I write unto you, young men, because you are strong.'"

# XIV

G randmother Harcourt was failing. Annette was rising towards life's summit. Her grandmother was sinking to death's vale.

*The hours are rifting day by day*
*Strength from the walls of living clay.*

Her two children who were living in A.P. wished her to break up her home and come and live with them. They had room in their hearts and homes for her, but not for Annette. There was something in Annette's temperament with which other members of the family could not harmonize. They were not considerate enough to take into account her antenatal history, and to pity where they were so ready to condemn. Had Annette been born deficient in any of her bodily organs, they could have made allowance for her, and would have deemed it cruel to have demanded that she should have performed the same amount of labor with one hand that she could have done with both. They knew nothing of heredity, except its effects, which they were not thoughtful enough to trace back to the causes over which Annette had no control, and instead of trying to counteract them as one might strive to do in a case of inherited physical tendencies, they only aggravated, and constantly strengthened all the unlovely features in Annette's character, and Annette really seemed like an anomalous contradiction. There was a duality about her nature as if the blood of two races were mingling in her veins. To some persons Annette was loving and love-able, bright, intelligent, obliging and companionable; to others, unsociable, unamiable and repelling. Her heart was like a harp which sent out its harmonious discords in accordance with the moods of the player who touched its chords. To some who swept them it gave out tender and touching melody, to others its harshest and saddest discords. Did not the Psalmist look beneath the mechanism of the body to the constitution of the soul when he said that "We are fearfully and wonderfully made?"

But the hour came when all discussion was ended as to who was to shelter the dear old grandmother in her declining years. Mrs. Harcourt was suddenly paralyzed, and in a few days Annette stood doubly orphaned. Grandmother Harcourt's children gathered around the bedside of their dying mother. She was conscious but unable to speak. Occasionally her eyes would rest lovingly upon Annette and then turn wistfully to her children. Several times she assayed to speak, but the words died upon her lips. Her eldest son entered the room just as life was trembling on its faintest chords. She recognized him, and gathering up her remaining strength she placed his hand on Annette's, and tried again to speak. He understood her and said very tenderly,

"Mother, I will look after Annette."

All the care faded from the dear old face. Amid the shadows that never deceive flitted a smile of peace and contentment. The fading eye lit up with a sudden gaze of joy and wonder. She reached out her hand as if to meet a welcome and precious friend, and then the radiant face grew deathly pale; the outstretched hands relaxed their position, and with a smile, just such a smile as might greet a welcoming angel, her spirit passed out into the eternities, and Annette felt as she had never felt before, that she was all alone. The love that had surrounded and watched over her, born with her perverseness, and sheltered her in its warm clasp, was gone; it had faded suddenly from her vision, and left in its stead a dull and heavy pain. After the funeral, Mrs. Harcourt's children returned to the house where they quietly but earnestly discussed the question what shall be done with Annette. Mrs. Hanson's house was rather small; that is, it was rather small for Annette. She would have found room in her house if she only had room in her heart for her. She had nursed her mother through her sickness, and said with unnatural coldness, "I have got rid of one trouble and I do not want another." Another sister who lived some distance from A.P., would have taken Annette, but she knew that other members of her family would object, as they would be fearful that Annette would be an apple of discord among them. At length, her uncle Thomas decided that she should go with him. He felt that his mother had died with the assurance on her mind that he would care for Annette, and he resolved to be faithful in accepting what was to him the imposition of a new burden on his shoulders. His wife was a cold and unsympathizing woman. She was comfortably situated but did not wish that comfort invaded by her husband's relations. In household matters her husband generally deferred to her judgment, but here was no other alternative than that of taking Annette under the shadow of his home, or leaving her unprotected in the wide world, and he was too merciful and honorable to desert Annette in her saddest hour of need. Having determined that Annette should share his home, he knew that it was advisable to tell his wife about his decision, and to prepare her for Annette's coming.

"Well," said Dr. Harcourt's wife after her husband's return from the funeral, "what are you going to do with Annette?"

"She is coming here," said Dr. Harcourt quietly and firmly.

"Coming here?" said Mrs. Harcourt, looking aghast. "I think at least you might have consulted me."

"That is true, my dear, I would have gladly done so had you been present when the decision was made."

"But where are her aunts, and where was your brother, John; why didn't they take her?"

"John was at home sick with the rheumatism and sister Jane did not appear to be willing to have her come."

"I guess Jane is like I am; got enough to do to look after her own family."

"And sister Eliza said she hadn't any room."

"No room; when she has eight rooms in her house and only two children? She could have made room for her had she chosen."

"May be her husband wasn't willing."

"Oh, it is no such thing. I know John Hanson better than that; Liza is the head man of that house, and just leads him by the nose wherever she wants him to go, and besides, Mrs. Lord's daughter is there pretending to pay board, but I don't believe that she pays it one-half the time."

"She is company for Alice and they all seem very fond of her."

"I do get so sick of that girl, mambying and jambying about that family; calling Liza and her husband 'Ma and Pa,' I haven't a bit of faith in her."

"Well, I confess that I am not very much preposessed in her favor. She just puts me in mind of a pussy cat purring around you."

"Well, now as to Annette. You do not want her here?"

"Not if I can help it."

"But can't she help you to work?"

"She could if she knew how. If wishes were horses beggars might ride. Your mother made a great mistake in bringing Annette up. Annette has a good education, but when that is said, all is said."

"Why, my dear mother was an excellent housekeeper. Did she not teach Annette?"

"Your mother was out a great deal as a sick nurse, and when she went away from home she generally boarded Annette with a friend, who did not, as your mother paid her good board, exact any service from Annette, and while with her she never learned to make a loaf of bread or to cook a beefsteak, and when your mother was at home when she set Annette to do any work, if she did it awkwardly and clumsily she would take it out of her hand and do it herself rather than bother with her, and now I suppose I am to have all the bother and worry with her."

"Well my dear."

"Oh don't come dearing me, and bringing me all this trouble."

"Well my dear, I don't see how it could be helped. I could not leave Annette in the house all by herself. I couldn't afford to make myself the town's talk. May be things will turn out better than you expect. We've got children of our own, and we don't know when we are gone, how they will fare."

"That is true, but I never mean to bring my children up in such a way that they will be no use anywhere, and no one will want them."

"Well, I don't see any other way than bringing Annette here."

"Well, if I must, I must," she said with an air of despondency.

Dr. Harcourt rode over to his sister's where Annette was spending the day and brought the doubly orphaned girl to his home. As she entered the room, it seemed as though a chill struck to her heart when her Aunt bade her good morning. There was no warm pressure in the extended hand. No loving light in the cold unsympathizing eyes which seemed to stab her through and through. The children eyed her inquisitively, as if wishing to understand her status with their parents before they became sociable with her. After supper Annette's uncle went out and her aunt sat quietly and sewed till bed time, and then showed Annette to her room and left the lonely girl to herself and her great sorrow. Annette sat silent, tearless, and alone. Grief had benumbed her faculties. She had sometimes said when grandmother had scolded her that "she was growing cross and cold." But oh, what would she not have given to have had the death-created silence broken by that dear departed voice, to have felt the touch of a vanished hand, to have seen again the loving glance of the death darkened eye. But it was all over; no tears dimmed her eye, as she sat thinking so mournfully of her great sorrow, till she unfastened from her neck a little keepsake containing a lock of grandmother's hair, then all the floodgates of her soul were opened and she threw herself upon her bed and sobbed herself to sleep. In the morning she awoke with that sense of loss and dull agony which only they know, who have seen the grave close over all they have held dearest

FRANCES ELLEN WATKINS HARPER

on earth. The beautiful home of her uncle was very different from the humble apartments; here she missed all the freedom and sunshine that she had enjoyed beneath the shelter of her grandmother's roof.

"Can you sew?" said her aunt to Annette, as she laid on the table a package of handkerchiefs.

"Yes ma'm."

"Let me see how you can do this," handing her one to hem. Annette hemmed the handkerchief nicely; her aunt examined it, put it down and gave her some others to hem, but there was no word of encouragement for her, not even a pleasant, "well done." They both relapsed into silence; between them there was no pleasant interchange of thought. Annette was tolerated and endured, but she did not feel that she was loved and welcomed. It was no place to which she could invite her young friends to spend a pleasant evening. Once she invited some of her young friends to her home, but she soon found that it was a liberty which she should be careful never to repeat. Soon after Annette came to live with her aunt her aunt's mother had a social gathering and reunion of the members of her family. All Dr. Harcourt's children were invited, from the least to the greatest, but poor Annette was left behind. Mrs. Lasette, who happened in the house the evening before the entertainment, asked, "Is not Annette going?" when Mrs. Harcourt replied, very coldly, "She is not one of the family," referring to her mother's family circle.

A shadow flitted over the face of Mrs. Lasette; she thought of her own daughter and how sad it would be to have her live in such a chilly atmosphere of social repression and neglect at a period of life when there was so much danger that false friendship might spread their lures for her inexperienced feet. I will criticize, she said to herself, by creation. I, too, have some social influence, if not among the careless, wine-bibbing, ease-loving votaries of fashion, among some of the most substantial people of A.P., and as long as Annette preserves her rectitude at my house she shall be a welcome guest and into that saddened life I will bring all the sunshine that I can.

W ell mama," said Mrs. Lasette's daughter to her mother, "I cannot understand why you take so much interest in Annette. She is very unpopular. Scarcely any of the girls ever go with her, and even her cousin never calls for her to go to church or anywhere else, and I sometimes feel so sorry to see her so much by herself, and some of the girls when I went with her to the exposition, said that they wouldn't have asked her to have gone with them, that she isn't our set."

"Poor child," Mrs. Lasette replied; "I am sorry for her. I hope that you will never treat her unkindly, and I do not think if you knew the sad story connected with her life that you would ever be unkind enough to add to the burden she has been forced to bear."

"But mamma, Annette is so touchy. Her aunt says that her tear bags must lay near her eyes and that she will cry if you look at her, and that she is the strangest, oddest creature she ever saw, and I heard she did not wish her to come."

"Why, my dear child, who has been gossipping to you about your neighbors?"

"Why, Julia Thomas."

"Well, my daughter, don't talk after her; gossip is liable to degenerate into evil speaking and then I think it tends to degrade and belittle the mind to dwell on the defects and imperfections of our neighbors. Learn to dwell on the things that are just and true and of good report, but I am sorry for Annette, poor child."

"What makes her so strange, do you know?"

"Yes," said Mrs. Lasette somewhat absently.

"If you do, won't you tell me?"

Again Mrs. Lasette answered in the same absent manner.

"Why mama, what is the matter with you; you say yes to everything and yet you are not paying any attention to anything that I say. You seem like someone who hears, but does not listen; who sees, but does not look. Your face reminds me of the time when I showed you the picture of a shipwreck and you said, 'My brother's boat went down in just such a fearful storm.'"

"My dear child," said Mrs. Lasette, rousing up from a mournful reverie, "I was thinking of a wreck sadder, far sadder than the picture you showed me. It was the mournful wreck of a blighted life."

"Whose life, mama?"

"The life of Annette's (grand)mother. We were girls together and I loved her dearly," Mrs. Lasette replied as tears gathered in her eyes when she recalled one of the saddest memories of her life.

"Do tell me all about it, for I am full of curiosity."

"My child, I want this story to be more than food for your curiosity; I want it to be a lesson and a warning to you. Annette's grandmother was left to struggle as breadwinner for a half dozen children when her husband died. Then there were not as many openings for colored girls as there are now. Our chief resource was the field of domestic service, and circumstances compelled Annette's mother to live out, as we called it. In those days we did not look down upon a girl and try to ostracize her from our social life if she was forced to be a servant. If she was poor and respectable we valued her for what she was rather than for what she possessed. Of course we girls liked to dress nicely, but fine clothes was not the chief passport to our society, and yet I think on the whole that our social life would compare favorably with yours in good character, if not in intellectual attainments. Our dear old mothers were generally ignorant of books, but they did try to teach good manners and good behavior; but I do not think they saw the danger around the paths of the inexperienced with the same clearness of vision we now do. Mrs. Harcourt had unbounded confidence in her children, and as my mother thought, gave her girls too much rein in their own hands. Our mother was more strict with her daughters and when we saw Mrs. Harcourt's daughters having what we considered such good times, I used to say, 'O, I wish mother wasn't so particular!' Other girls could go unattended to excursions, moonlight drives and parties of pleasure, but we never went to any such pleasure unless we were attended by our father, brother or some trusted friend of the family. We were young and foolish then and used to chafe against her restrictions; but today, when I think of my own good and noble husband, my little bright and happy home, and my dear, loving daughter, I look back with gratitude to her thoughtful care and honor and bless her memory in her grave. Poor Lucy Harcourt was not so favored; she was pretty and attractive and had quite a number of admirers. At length she became deeply interested in a young man who came as a stranger to our city. He was a fine looking man, but there was something about him from which I instinctively shrank. My mother felt the same way and warned us to be careful how we accepted any attention from him; but poor Lucy became perfectly infatuated with him and it was rumored that they were to be shortly married. Soon after the rumor he left the city and there was a big change in Lucy's manner. I could not tell what was the matter, but my mother forbade me associating with her, and for several months I scarcely saw her, but I could hear from others that she was sadly changed. Instead of being one of the most light-hearted girls, I heard that she used to sit day after day in her mother's house and wring her hands and weep and that her mother's heart was almost broken. Friends feared that Lucy was losing her mind and might do some desperate deed, but she did not. I left about that time to teach school in a distant village, and when I returned home I heard sad tidings of poor Lucy. She was a mother, but not a wife. Her brothers had grown angry with her for tarnishing their family name, of which they were so proud; her mother's head was bowed with agony and shame. The father of Lucy's child had deserted her in her hour of trial and left her to bear her burden alone with the child like a millstone around her neck. Poor Lucy; I seldom saw her after that, but one day I met her in the Park. I went up to her and kissed her, she threw her arms around me and burst into a flood of tears. I tried to restrain her from giving such vent to her feelings. It was a lack of self-control which had placed her where she was."

"'Oh Anna!' she said, 'it does me so much good to hold your hand in mine once more. I reminds me of the days when we used to be together. Oh, what would I give to recall those days.'"

"I said to her, Lucy, you can never recall the past, but you can try to redeem the future. Try to be a faithful mother. Men may build over the wreck and ruin of their young lives a better and brighter future, why should not a woman? Let the dead past bury its dead and live in the future for the sake of your child. She seemed so grateful for what I had said. Others had treated her with scorn. Her brother Thomas had refused to speak to her; her betrayer had forsaken her; all the joyousness had faded from her life and, poor girl, I was glad that I was able to say a helpful and hopeful word to her. Mother, of course, would not let us associate with her, but she always treated her kindly when she came and did what she could to lighten the burden which was pressing her down to the grave. But, poor child, she was never again the same light-hearted girl. She grew pale and thin and in the hectic flush and faltering tread I read the death sign of early decay, and I felt that my misguided young friend was slowly dying of a broken heart. Then there came a day when we were summoned to her dying bed. Her brothers and sisters were present; all their resentment against her had vanished in the presence of death. She was their dear sister about to leave them and they bent in tearful sorrow around her couch. As one of her brothers, who was a good singer, entered the room, she asked him to sing 'Vital spark of heavenly flame.' He attempted to sing, but there were tremors in his voice and he faltered in the midst of the hymn. 'Won't you sing for your dying sister.'"

"Again he essayed to sing, but (his?) voice became choked with emotion, and he ceased, and burst into tears. Her brother Thomas who had been so hard and cold, and had refused to speak to her, now wept and sobbed like a child, but Lucy smiled as she bade them good bye, and exclaimed, 'Welcome death, the end of fear. I am prepared to die.' A sweet peace settled down on her face, and Lucy had exchanged, I hope, the sorrow and pain of life for the peace and rest of heaven, and left Annette too young to know her loss. Do you wonder then my child that I feel such an interest in Annette and that knowing as I do her antenatal history that I am ever ready to pity where others condemn, and that I want to do what I can to help round out in beauty and usefulness the character of that sinned against and disinherited child, whose restlessness and sensitiveness I trace back to causes over which she had no control."

"What became of Frank Miller? You say that when he returned to A.P. that society opened its doors to him while they were closed to Annette's mother. I don't understand it. Was he not as guilty as she was?"

"Guiltier, I think. If poor Lucy failed as a woman, she tried to be faithful as a mother, while he, faithless as a man, left her to bear her burden alone. She was frail as a woman, but he was base, mean, and selfish as a man."

"How was it that society received him so readily?"

"All did not receive him so readily, but with some his money, like charity, covered a multitude of sins. But from the depths of my heart I despised him. I had not then learned to hate the sin with all my heart, and yet the sinner love. To me he was the incarnation of social meanness and vice. And just as I felt I acted. We young folks had met at a social gathering, and were engaged in a pastime in which we occasionally clasped hands together. Some of these plays I heartily disliked, especially when there was romping and promiscuous kissing. During the play Frank Miller's hand came in contact with mine and he pressed it. I can hardly describe my feelings. It seemed as if my very veins were on fire, and that every nerve was thrilling with repulsion and indignation. Had I seen him murder Lucy and then turn with blood dripping hands to grasp mine, I do not think that I should have felt more loathing than I did when his hand clasped mine. I felt that his very touch was pollution; I immediately left the play, tore off my glove, and threw it in the fire."

"Oh, mother, how could you have done so? You are so good and gentle."

Mrs. Lasette replied, "I was not always so. I do not hate his sin any less now than I did then but I think that I have learned a Christian charity which would induce me to pluck such as he out of the fire while I hated the garments spotted by his sins. I sat down trembling with emotion. I heard a murmur of disapprobation. There was a check to the gayety of the evening. Frank Miller, bold and bad as he was looked crestfallen and uneasy. Some who appeared to be more careful of the manners of society than its morals, said that I was very rude. Others said that I was too prudish, and would be an old maid, that I was looking for perfection in young men, and would not find it. That young men sow their wild oats, and that I was more nice than wise, and that I would frighten the gentlemen away from me. I told them if the young men were so easily frightened, that I did not wish to clasp hands for life with any such timid set, and that I was determined that I would have a moral husband or none; that I was not obliged to be married, but that I was obliged to be true to my conscience. That when I married I expected to lay the foundation of a new home, and that I would never trust my future happiness in the hands of a libertine, or lay its foundations over the reeling brain of a drunkard, and I determined that I would never marry a man for whose vices I must blush, and whose crimes I must condone; that while I might bend to grief I would not bow to shame; that if I brought him character and virtue, he should give me true manhood and honor in return."

"And I think mother that you got it when you married father."

"I am satisfied that I did, and the respect and appreciation my daughter has for her father is only part of my life's reward, but it was my dear mother who taught me to distinguish between the true and the false, and although she was (not?) what you call educated, she taught me that no magnificence of fortune would atone for meanness of spirit, that without character the most wealthy and talented man is a bankrupt in soul. And she taught me how to be worthy of a true man's love."

"And I think you have succeeded splendidly."

"Thank you, my darling. But mother has become used to compliments."

# XVI

I do not think she gets any more than she deserves," said Mr. Lasette, entering the room. "She is one of whom it may be said, 'Her children arise up and call her blessed, her husband also, and he praiseth her; many daughters have done virtuously but thou excellest them all.'"

"I do not think you will say that I am excelling if I do not haste about your supper; you were not home to dinner and must be hungry by this time, and it has been said that the way to a man's heart is through his stomach."

"Oh, isn't that a libel on my sex!"

"Papa," said Laura Lasette, after her mother had left the room, "did you know Frank Miller? Mother was telling me about him but she did not finish; what became of him?"

"Now, you ask me two questions in one breath; let me answer one at a time."

"Well, papa, I am all attention."

"Do I know Frank Miller, the saloon keeper? Yes; he is connected with a turning point in my life. How so? Well, just be patient a minute and I will tell you. I was almost a stranger in A.P. when I first met your mother. It was at a social where Frank Miller was a guest. I had heard some very damaging reports concerning his reputation, but from the manner in which he was received in society, I concluded that I had been misinformed. Surely, I thought, if the man is as vicious as he has been represented, good women, while they pity him, will shrink instinctively from him, but I saw to my surprise, that with a confident and unblushing manner, he moved among what was called the elite of the place, and that instead of being withheld, attentions were lavished upon him. I had lived most of my life in a small inland town, where people were old fashioned enough to believe in honor and upright conduct, and from what I had heard of Frank Miller I was led to despise his vices and detest his character, and yet here were women whom I believed to be good and virtuous, smiling in his face, and graciously receiving his attentions. I cannot help thinking that in their case,

*"Evil is wrought by want of thought"*
*As well as want of heart.*

FRANCES ELLEN WATKINS HARPER

They were not conscious of the influence they might exert by being true to their own womanhood. Men like Frank Miller are the deadliest foes of women. One of the best and strongest safe guards of the home is the integrity of its women, and he who undermines that, strikes a fearful blow at the highest and best interests of society. Society is woman's realm and I never could understand how, if a woman really loves purity for its own worth and loveliness, she can socially tolerate men whose lives are a shame, and whose conduct in society is a blasting, withering curse."

"But, papa, tell me how you came to love my mother; but I don't see how you could have helped it."

"That's just it, my daughter. I loved her because I could not help it; and respected her because I knew that she was worthy of respect. I was present at a social gathering where Frank was a guest, and was watching your mother attentively when I saw her shrink instinctively from his touch and leave the play in which she was engaged and throw her glove in the fire. Public opinion was divided about her conduct. Some censured, others commended her, but from that hour I learned to love her, and I became her defender. Other women would tolerate Frank Miller, but here was a young and gracious girl, strong enough and brave enough to pour on the head of that guilty culprit her social disapprobation and I gloried in her courage. I resolved she should be my wife if she would accept me, which she did, and I have never regretted my choice and I think that I have had as happy a life as usually falls to the lot of mortals."

# XVII

Papa," said Laura Lasette, "all the girls have had graduating parties except Annette and myself. Would it not be nice for me to have a party and lots of fun, and then my birthday comes next week; now wouldn't it be just the thing for me to have a party?"

"It might be, darling, for you, but how would it be for me who would have to foot the bill?"

"Well, papa, could you not just give me a check like you do mama sometimes?"

"But mama knows how to use it."

"But papa, don't I know how also?"

"I have my doubts on that score, but let me refer you to your mother. She is queen of this realm, and in household matters I as a loyal subject, abide by her decisions."

"Well, I guess mama is all right on this subject."

Mrs. Lasette was perfectly willing to gratify her daughter, and it was decided to have an entertainment on Laura's birthday.

The evening of Mrs. Lasette's entertainment came bringing with it into her pleasant parlors a bright and merry throng of young people. It was more than a mere pleasure party. It was here that rising talent was encouraged, no matter how humble the garb of the possessor, and Mrs. Lasette was a model hostess who would have thought her entertainment a failure had any one gone from it smarting under a sense of social neglect. Shy and easily embarrassed Annette who was very seldom invited anywhere, found herself almost alone in that gay and chattering throng. Annette was seated next to several girls who laughed and chatted incessantly with each other without deigning to notice her. Mrs. Lasette entering the room with Mr. Luzerne whom she presented to the company, and noticing the loneliness and social isolation of Annette, gave him a seat beside her, and was greatly gratified that she had found the means to relieve the tedium of Annette's position. Mrs. Lasette had known him as a light hearted boy, full of generous impulses, with laughing eyes and a buoyant step, but he had been absent a number of years, and had developed into a handsome man with a magnificent physique, elegant in his attire, polished in his manners and brilliant in conversation. Just such a man as is desirable as a companion and valuable as a friend, staunch, honorable and true, and

FRANCES ELLEN WATKINS HARPER

it was rumored that he was quite wealthy. He was generally cheerful, but it seemed at times as if some sad memories came over him, dashing all the sunshine from his face and leaving in its stead, a sadness which it was touching to behold. Some mystery seemed to surround his life, but being reticent in reference to his past history, there was a dignity in his manner which repelled all intrusion into the secrecy over which he choose to cast a veil. Annette was not beautiful, but her face was full of expression and her manner winsome at times. Lacking social influence and social adaptation, she had been ignored in society, her faults of temper made prominent her most promising traits of character left unnoticed, but this treatment was not without some benefit to Annette. It threw her more entirely on her own resources. At first she read when she had leisure, to beguile her lonely hours, and fortunately for her, she was directed in her reading by Mrs. Lasette, who gave and lent her books, which appealed to all that was highest and best in her nature, and kindled within her a lofty enthusiasm to make her life a blessing to the world. With such an earnest purpose, she was not prepared to be a social favorite in any society whose chief amusement was gossip, and whose keenest weapon was ridicule.

Mr. Luzerne had gone to Mrs. Lasette's with the hope of meeting some of the best talent in A.P., and had come to the conclusion that there was more lulliancy than depth in the intellectual life with which he came in contact; he felt that it lacked earnestness, purpose and grand enthusiasms and he was astonished to see the social isolation of Annette, whose society had interested and delighted him, and after parting with her he found his mind constantly reverting to her and felt grateful to Mrs. Lasette for affording him a rare and charming pleasure. Annette sat alone in her humble room with a new light in her eyes and a sense of deep enjoyment flooding her soul. Never before had she met with such an interesting and congenial gentleman. He seemed to understand as scarcely as any one else had done or cared to do. In the eyes of other guests she had been treated as if too insignificant for notice, but he had loosened her lips and awakened within her a dawning sense of her own ability, which others had chilled and depressed. He had fingered the keys of her soul and they had vibrated in music to his touch. Do not smile, gentle reader, and say that she was very easily impressed, it may be that you have never known what it is to be hungry, not for bread, but for human sympathy, to live with those who were never interested in your joys, nor sympathized in your sorrows. To whom your coming gave no joy and your absence no pain. Since Annette had lost her grandmother, she had lived in an atmosphere of coldness and repression and was growing prematurely cold. Her heart was like a sealed fountain beneath whose covering the bright waters dashed and leaped in imprisoned boundary. Oh, blessed power of human love to lighten human suffering, well may we thank the giver of every good and perfect gift for the love which gladdens hearts, brightens homes and sets the solitary in the midst of families. Mr. Luzerne frequently saw Annette at the house of Mrs. Lasette and occasionally called at her uncle's, but there was an air of restraint in the social atmosphere which repressed and chilled him. In that home he missed the cordial freedom and genial companionship which he always found at Mrs. Lasette's but Annette's apparent loneliness and social isolation awakened his sympathy, and her bright intelligence and good character commanded his admiration and respect, which developed within him a deep interest for the lovely girl. He often spoke admiringly of her and never met her at church, or among her friends that he did not gladly avail himself of the opportunity of accompanying her home. Madame rumor soon got tidings of Mr. Luzerne's attentions to Annette and in a shout the tongues of the gossips of A.P. began to wag. Mrs. Larkins who had fallen heir to some money, moved out of Tennis court, and often gave pleasant little teas to her young friends, and as a well spread table was quite a social attraction in A.P., her gatherings were always well attended. After rumor had caught the news of Mr. Luzerne's interest in Annette, Mrs. Larkins had a social at her house to which she invited him, and a number of her young friends, but took pains to leave Annette out in the cold. Mr. Luzerne on hearing that Annette was slighted, refused to attend. At the supper table Annette's prospects were freely discussed.

"I expected that Mr. Luzerne would have been here this evening, but he sent an apology in which he declined to come."

"Did you invite Annette?" said Miss Croker.

"No, I did not. I got enough of her when I lived next door to her."

"Well that accounts for Mr. Luzerne's absence. They remind me of the Siamese twins; if you see one, you see the other."

"How did she get in with him?"

"She met him at Mrs. Lasette's party, and he seemed so taken up with her that for a while he had neither eyes nor ears for any one else."

"That girl, as quiet as she looks, is just as deep as the sea."

"It is not that she's so deep, but we are so shallow. Miss Booker and

Miss Croker were sitting near Annette and not noticing her, and we girls were having a good time in the corner to ourselves, and Annette was looking so lonely and embarrassed I think Mr. Luzerne just took pity on her and took especial pains to entertain her. I just think we stepped our feet into it by slighting Annette, and of course, as soon as we saw him paying attention to her, we wouldn't change and begin to make much of her."

"I don't know what he sees in Annette with her big nose and plain face."

"My father," said Laura Lasette, "says that Annette is a credit to her race and my mother is just delighted because Mr. Luzerne is attracted to her, but, girls, had we not better be careful how we talk about her? People might say that we are jealous of her and we know that we are taught that jealousy is as cruel as the grave."

"We don't see anything to be jealous about her. She is neither pretty nor stylish."

"But my mother says she is a remarkable girl," persisted Laura.

"Your mother," said Mrs. Larkins, "always had funny notions about Annette, and saw in her what nobody else did."

"Well, for my part, I hope it will be a match."

"It is easy enough for you to say so, Laura. You think it is a sure thing between you and Charley Cooper, but don't be too sure; there's many a slip between the cup and the lip."

There was a flush on Laura's cheek as she replied, "If there are a thousand slips between the cup and the lip and Charlie and I should never marry, let me tell you that I would almost as soon court another's husband as a girl's affianced lover. I can better afford to be an old maid than to do a dishonorable thing."

"Well, Laura, you are a chip off the old block; just like your mother, always ready to take Annette's part."

"I think, Mrs. Larkins, it is the finest compliment you can pay me, to tell me that I am like my dear mother."

G ood morning," said Mr. Luzerne, entering Mr. Thomas' office. "Are you busy?"

"Not very; I had just given some directions to my foreman concerning a job I have undertaken, and had just settled down to read the paper. Well how does your acquaintance with Miss Harcourt prosper? Have you popped the question yet?"

"No, not exactly; I had been thinking very seriously of the matter, but I have been somewhat shaken in my intention."

"How so," said Mr. Thomas, laying down his paper and becoming suddenly interested.

"You know that I have had an unhappy marriage which has overshadowed all my subsequent life, and I cannot help feeling very cautious how I risk, not only my own, but another's happiness in a second marriage. It is true that I have been thinking of proposing to Miss Harcourt and I do prefer her to any young lady I have ever known; but there is a depreciatory manner in which people speak of her, that sorely puzzles me. For instance, when I ask some young ladies if they know Annette, they shrug their shoulders, look significantly at each other and say, 'Oh, yes, we know her; but she don't care for anything but books; oh she is so self conceited and thinks she knows more than any one else.' But when I spoke to Mrs. Larkins about her, she said Annette makes a fine appearance, but all is not gold that glitters. By this time my curiosity was excited, and I asked, 'What is the matter with Miss Harcourt? I had no idea that people were so ready to pick at her.' She replied, 'No wonder; she is such a spitfire.'"

"Well," said Mr. Thomas, a little hotly, "if Annette is a spitfire, Mrs. Larkins is a lot of combustion. I think of all the women I know, she has the greatest genius for aggravation. I used to board with her, but as I did not wish to be talked to death I took refuge in flight."

"And so you showed the white feather that time."

"Yes, I did, and I could show it again. I don't wonder that people have nick-named her 'Aunty talk forever.' I have known Annette for years and I known that she is naturally quick tempered and impulsive, but she is not malicious and implacable and if I were going to marry tomorrow I would rather have a quick, hot-tempered woman than a cold, selfish one, who never thought or cared about anyone but herself.

Mrs. Larkins' mouth is not a prayer-book; don't be uneasy about anything she says against Annette."

Reassured by Mr. Thomas, Clarence Luzerne decided that he would ask Dr. Harcourt's permission to visit his niece, a request which was readily granted and he determined if she would consent that she should be his wife. He was wealthy, handsome and intelligent; Annette was poor and plain, but upright in character and richly endowed in intellect, and no one imagined that he would pass by the handsome and stylish girls of A.P. to bestow his affections on plain, neglected Annette. Some of the girls who knew of his friendship for Annette, but who never dreamed of its termination in marriage would say to Annette, "Speak a good word for me to Mr. Luzerne;" but Annette kept her counsel and would smile and think: I will speak a good word for myself. Very pleasant was the growing friendship between Annette and Mr. Luzerne. Together they read and discussed books and authors and agreed with wonderful unanimity, which often expressed itself in the words:

"I think as you do." Not that there was any weak compliance for the sake of agreement, but a unison of thought and feeling between them which gave a pleasurable zest to their companionship.

"Miss Annette," said Luzerne, "do you believe that matches are made in heaven?"

"I never thought anything about it."

"But have you no theory on the subject?"

"Not the least; have you?"

"Yes; I think that every human soul has its counterpart, and is never satisfied till soul has met with soul and recognized its spiritual affinity."

"Affinity! I hate the word."

"Why?"

"Because I think it has been so wrongly used, and added to the social misery of the world."

"What do you think marriage ought to be?"

"I think it should be a blending of hearts, an intercommunion of souls, a tie that only love and truth should weave, and nothing but death should part."

Luzerne listened eagerly and said, "Why, Miss Annette, you speak as if you had either loved or were using your fine imaginative powers on the subject with good effect. Have you ever loved any one?"

Annette blushed and stammered, and said, "I hardly know, but I think I have a fine idea of what love should be. I think the love of a woman for the companion of her future life should go out to him just as naturally as the waves leap to the strand, or the fire ascends to the sun."

"And this," said Luzerne, taking her hand in his, "is the way I feel towards you. Surely our souls have met at last. Annette," said he, in a voice full of emotion, "is it not so? May I not look on your hand as a precious possession, to hold till death us do part?"

"Why, Mr. Luzerne," said Annette, recovering from her surprise, "this is so sudden, I hardly know what to say. I have enjoyed your companionship and I confess have been pleased with your attentions, but I did not dream that you had any intentions beyond the enjoyment of the hour."

"No, Annette, I never seek amusement in toying with human hearts. I should deem myself a villain if I came into your house and stole your purse, and I should think myself no better if I entered the citadel of a woman's heart to steal her affections only to waste their wealth. Her stolen money I might restore, but what reparation could I make for wasted love and blighted affections? Annette, let there be truth between us. I will give you time to think on my proposal, hoping at the same time that I shall find favor in your eyes."

After Mr. Luzerne left, Annette, sat alone by the fireside, a delicious sense of happiness filling her soul with sudden joy. Could it be that this handsome and dignified man had honored her above all the girls in A.P., by laying his heart at her feet, or was it only a dream from which would come a rude awakening? Annette looked in the glass, but no stretch of imagination could make her conceive that she was beautiful in either form or feature. She turned from the glass with a faint sigh, wishing for his sake that she was as beautiful as some of the other girls in A.P., whom he had overlooked, not thinking for one moment that in loving her for what she was in intellect and character he had paid her a far greater compliment than if she had been magnificently beautiful and he had only been attracted by an exquisite form and lovely face. In a few days after Mr. Luzerne's proposal to Annette he came for the answer, to which he looked with hope and suspense.

"I am glad," he said, "to find you at home."

"Yes; all the rest of the family are out."

"Then the coast is clear for me?" There was tenderness and decision in his voice as he said, "Now, Annette, I have come for the answer which cannot fail to influence all my future life." He clasped the little hand which lay limp and passive in his own. His dark, handsome eyes

FRANCES ELLEN WATKINS HARPER

were bent eagerly upon her as if scanning every nook and corner of her soul. Her eye fell beneath his gaze, her hand trembled in his, tears of joy were springing to her eyes, but she restrained them. She withdrew her hand from his clasp; he looked pained and disappointed. "Have I been too hasty and presumptuous?"

Annette said no rather faintly, while her face was an enigma he did not know how to solve.

"Why did you release your hand and avert your eyes?"

"I felt that my will was succumbing to yours, and I want to give you an answer untrammeled and uncontrolled by your will."

Mr. Luzerne smiled, and thought what rare thoughtfulness and judgment she has evinced. How few women older than herself would have thought as quickly and as clearly, and yet she is no less womanly, although she seems so wise.

"What say you, my dear Annette, since I have released your hand. May I not hope to hold this hand as the most precious of all my earthly possessions until death us do part?"

Annette fixed her eyes upon the floor as if she were scanning the figures on the carpet. Her heart beat quickly as she timidly repeated the words, "Until death us do part," and placed her hand again in his, while an expression of love and tender trust lit up the mobile and expressive face, and Annette felt that his love was hers; the most precious thing on earth that she could call her own. The engagement being completed, the next event in the drama was preparation for the wedding. It was intended that the engagement should not be long. Together they visited different stores in purchasing supplies for their new home. How pleasant was that word to the girl, who had spent such lonely hours in the home of her uncle. To her it meant one of the brightest spots on earth and one of the fairest types of heaven. In the evening they often took pleasant strolls together or sat and chatted in a beautiful park near their future home. One evening as they sat quietly enjoying themselves Annette said, "How happened it that you preferred me to all the other girls in A. P.? There are lots of girls more stylish and better looking; what did you see in poor, plain me?" He laughingly replied:

> *"I chose you out from all the rest,*
> *The reason was I loved you best."*

"And why did you prefer me?" She answered quite archly:

*"The rose is red, the violet's blue,*
*Sugar is sweet and so are you."*

"I chose you because of your worth. When I was young, I married for beauty and I pierced my heart through with many sorrows."

"You been married?" said Annette with a tremor in her tones. "Why, I never heard of it before."

"Did not Mr. Thomas or Mrs. Lasette tell you of it? They knew it, but it is one of the saddest passages of my life, to which I scarcely ever refer. She, my wife, drifted from me, and was drowned in a freshet near Orleans."

"Oh, how dreadful, and I never knew it."

"Does it pain you?"

"No, but it astonishes me."

"Well, Annette, it is not a pleasant subject, let us talk of something else. I have not spoken of it to you before, but today, when it pressed so painfully upon my mind, it was a relief to me to tell you about it, but now darling dismiss it from your mind and let the dead past bury its dead."

Just then there came along where they were sitting a woman whose face bore traces of great beauty, but dimmed and impaired by lines of sorrow and disappointment. Just as she reached the seat where they were sitting, she threw up her hands in sudden anguish, gasped out, "Clarence! my long lost Clarence," and fell at his feet in a dead faint.

As Mr. Luzerne looked on the wretched woman lying at his feet, his face grew deathly pale. He trembled like an aspen and murmured in a bewildered tone, "has the grave restored its dead?"

But with Annette there was no time for delay. She chaffed, the rigid hands, unloosed the closely fitting dress, sent for a cab and had her conveyed as quickly as possible to the home for the homeless. Then turning to Luzerne, she said bitterly, "Mr. Luzerne, will you explain your encounter with that unfortunate woman?" She spoke as calmly as she could, for a fierce and bitter anguish was biting at her heartstrings. "What claim has that woman on you?"

"She has the claim of being my wife and until this hour I firmly believed she was in her grave." Annette lifted her eyes sadly to his; he calmly met her gaze, but there was no deception in his glance; his eyes were clear and sad and she was more puzzled than ever.

"Annette," said he, "I have only one favor to ask; let this scene be a secret between us as deep as the sea. Time will explain all. Do not judge me too harshly."

"Clarence," she said, "I have faith in you, but I do not understand you; but here is the carriage, my work at present is with this poor, unfortunate woman, whose place I was about to unconsciously supplant."

# XIX

And thus they parted. All their air castles and beautiful chambers of imagery, blown to the ground by one sad cyclone of fate. In the city of A.P., a resting place was found for the stranger who had suddenly dashed from their lips the scarcely tasted cup of happiness. Mr. Luzerne employed for her the best medical skill he could obtain. She was suffering from nervous prostration and brain fever. Annette was constant in her attentions to the sufferer, and day after day listened to her delirious ravings. Sometimes she would speak of a diamond necklace, and say so beseechingly, "Clarence, don't look at me so. You surely can't think that I am guilty. I will go away and hide myself from you. Clarence, you never loved me or you would not believe me guilty."

But at length a good constitution and careful nursing overmastered disease, and she showed signs of recovery. Annette watched over her when her wild ravings sounded in her ears like requiems for the loved and cherished dead. Between her and the happiness she had so fondly anticipated, stood that one blighted life, but she watched that life just as carefully as if it had been the dearest life on earth she knew.

One day, as Annette sat by her bedside, she surmised from the look on her face that the wandering reason of the sufferer had returned. Beckoning to Annette she said "Who are you and where am I?"

Annette answered, "I am your friend and you are with friends."

"Poor Clarence," she murmured to herself; "more sinned against than sinning."

"My dear friend," Annette said very tenderly, "you have been very ill, and I am afraid that if you do not be very quiet you will be very sick again." Annette gently smoothed her beautiful hair and tried to soothe her into quietness. Rest and careful nursing soon wrought a wondrous change in Marie Luzerne, but Annette thoughtfully refrained from all reference to her past history and waited for time to unravel the mystery she could not understand, and with this unsolved mystery the match between her and Luzerne was broken off. At length, one day when Marie's health was nearly restored, she asked for writing materials, and said, "I mean to advertise for my mother in a Southern paper. It seems like a horrid dream that all I knew or loved, even my husband, whom I deserted, believed that I was dead, till I came suddenly on him in the park with a young lady by his side. She looked like you. Was it you?"

"Yes," said Annette, as a sigh of relief came to her lips. If Clarence had wooed and won her he had not willfully deceived her. "Oh, how I would like to see him. I was wayward and young when I left him in anger. Oh, if I have sinned I have suffered; but I think that I could die content if I could only see him once more." Annette related the strange sad story to her physician, who decided that it was safe and desirable that there should be an interview between them. Luzerne visited his long lost wife and after a private interview, he called Annette to the room, who listened sadly while she told her story, which exonerated Luzerne from all intent to deceive Annette by a false marriage while she had a legal claim upon him.

"I was born," she said, "in New Orleans. My father was a Spaniard and my mother a French Creole. She was very beautiful and my father met her at a French ball and wished her for his companion for life, but as she was an intelligent girl and a devout Catholic she would not consent to live a life by which she would be denied the Sacrament of her Church; so while she could not contract a civil marriage, which would give her the legal claims of a wife, she could enter into an ecclesiastical marriage by which she would not forfeit her claim to the rights and privileges of the Church as a good Catholic. I was her only child, loved and petted by my father, and almost worshipped by my mother, and I never knew what it was to have a wish unfilled if it was in her power to gratify it. When I was about 16 I met Clarence Luzerne. People then said that I was very beautiful. You would scarcely think so now, but I suppose he thought so, too. In a short time we were married, and soon saw that we were utterly unfitted to each other; he was grave and I was gay; he was careful and industrious, I was careless and extravagant; he loved the quiet of his home and books; I loved the excitements of pleasure and the ball room, and yet I think he loved me, but it was as a father might love a wayward child whom he vainly tried to restrain. I had a cousin who had been absent from New Orleans a number of years, of whose antecedents I knew not scarcely anything. He was lively, handsome and dashing. My husband did not like his society, and objected to my associating with him. I did not care particularly for him, but I chafed against the restraint, and in sheer waywardness I continued the association. One day he brought me a beautiful diamond necklace which he said he had obtained in a distant land. I laid it aside intending to show it to my husband; in the meantime, a number of burglaries had been committed in the city of B., and among them was a diamond necklace. My heart stood still with sudden fear while I read of the account and while I was resolving what to do, my husband entered the house followed by two officers, who demanded the necklace. My husband interfered and with a large sum of money obtained my freedom from arrest. My husband was very proud of the honor of his family and blamed me for staining its record. From that day my husband seemed changed in his feelings towards me. He grew cold, distant and abstracted, and I felt that my presence was distasteful to him. I could not enter into his life and I saw that he had no sympathy with mine, and so in a fit of desperation I packed my trunk and took with me some money I had inherited from my father and left, as I said in a note, forever. I entered a convent and resolved that I would devote myself to the service of the poor and needy, for life had lost its charms for me. I had scarcely entered the convent before the yellow fever broke out and raged with fearful intensity. I was reckless of my life and engaged myself as a nurse. One day there came to our hospital a beautiful girl with a wealth of raven hair just like mine was before I became a nurse. I nursed her through a tedious illness and when she went out from the hospital, as I had an abundance of clothing, I supplied her from my wardrobe with all she needed, even to the dress she wore away. The clothing was all marked with my name. Soon after I saw in the paper that a young woman who was supposed from the marks on her clothing and the general description of her person to be myself was found drowned in a freshet. I was taken ill immediately afterwards and learned on recovering that I had been sick and delirious for several weeks. I sought for my mother, inquired about my husband, but lost all trace of them both till I suddenly came across my husband in Brightside Park. But Clarence, if you have formed other ties don't let me come between you and the sunshine. You are free to apply for a divorce; you can make the plea of willful desertion. I will not raise the least straw in your way. I will go back to the convent and spend the rest of my life in penitence and prayer. I have sinned; it is right that I should suffer." Clarence looked eagerly into the face of Annette; it was calm and peaceful, but in it he read no hope of a future reunion.

"What say you, Annette, would you blame me if I accepted this release?"

"I certainly would. She is your lawful wife. In the church of her father you pledged your faith to her, and I do not think any human law can absolve you from being faithful to your marriage vows. I do not say it lightly. I do not think any mother ever laid her first born in the grave with any more sorrow than I do today when I make my heart the sepulchre in which I bury my first and only love. This, Clarence, is the saddest trial of my life. I am sadder today than when I stood a lonely orphan over my grandmother's grave, and heard the clods fall on her coffin and stood lonely and heart-stricken in my uncle's house, and felt that I was unwelcome there. But, Clarence, the great end of life is not the attainment of happiness but the performance of duty and the development of character. The great question is not what is pleasant but what is right."

"Annette, I feel that you are right; but I am too wretched to realize the force of what you say. I only know that we must part, and that means binding my heart as a bleeding sacrifice on the altar of duty."

"Do you not know who drank the cup of human suffering to its bitter dregs before you? Arm yourself with the same mind, learn to suffer and be strong. Yes, we must part; but if we are faithful till death heaven will bring us sweeter rest." And thus they parted. If Luzerne had felt any faltering in his allegiance to duty he was too honorable and upright when that duty was plainly shown to him to weakly shrink from its performance, and as soon as his wife was able to travel he left A.P., for a home in the sunny South. After Luzerne had gone Annette thought, "I must have some active work which will engross my mind and use every faculty of my soul. I will consult with my dear friend Mrs. Lasette."

All unnerved by her great trial, Annette rang Mrs. Lasette's front door bell somewhat hesitatingly and walked wearily into the sitting-room, where she found Mrs. Lasette resting in the interval between twilight and dark. "Why Annette!" she said with pleased surprise, "I am so glad to see you. How is Clarence? I thought you would have been married before now. I have your wedding present all ready for you."

"Mrs. Lasette," Annette said, while her voice trembled with inexpressible sorrow, "it is all over."

Mrs. Lasette was lighting the lamp and had not seen Annette's face in the dusk of the evening, but she turned suddenly around at the sound of her voice and noticed the wan face so pitiful in its expression of intense suffering.

"What is the matter, my dear; have you and Luzerne had a lover's quarrel?"

"No," said Annette, sadly, and then in the ears of her sympathizing friend she poured her tale of bitter disappointment. Mrs. Lasette folded the stricken girl to her heart in tenderest manner.

"Oh, Mrs. Lasette," she said, "you make me feel how good it is for girls to have a mother."

"Annette, my brave, my noble girl, I am so glad."

"Glad of what, Mrs. Lasette?"

"Glad that you have been so true to conscience and to duty; glad that you have come through your trial like gold tried in the fiercest fire; glad that my interest in you has not been in vain, and that I have been able to see the blessed fruitage of my love and labors. And now, my dear child, what next?"

"I must have a change; I must find relief in action. I feel so weak and bruised in heart."

"A bruised reed will not break," murmured Mrs. Lasette to herself.

"Annette," said Mrs. Lasette, "this has been a fearful trial, but it must not be in vain; let it bring you more than happiness; let it bring you peace and blessedness. There is only one place for us to bring our sins and our sorrows, and that is the mercy seat. Let us both kneel there tonight and ask for grace to help in this your time of need. We are taught to cast our care upon Him for he careth for us. Come, my child, with the spirit of submission and full surrender, and consecrate your life to his service, body, soul and spirit, not as a dead offering, but a living sacrifice."

Together they mingled their prayers and tears, and when Annette rose from her knees there was a look of calmness on her face, and a deep peace had entered her soul. The strange trial was destined to bring joy and gladness and yield the peaceable fruit of righteousness in the future. Mrs. Lasette wrote to some friends in a distant Southern town where she obtained a situation for Annette as a teacher. Here she soon found work to enlist her interest and sympathy and bring out all the activity of her soul. She had found her work and the people among whom she labored had found their faithful friend.

# XX

Luzerne's failure to marry Annette and re-instatement of his wife was the sensation of the season. Some pitied Annette; others blamed Luzerne, but Annette found, as a teacher, opportunity among the freedmen to be a friend and sister to those whose advantages had been less than hers. Life had once opened before her like a fair vision enchanted with delight, but her beautiful dream had faded like sun rays mingling with the shadows of night. It was the great disappointment of her life, but she roused up her soul to bear suffering and to be true to duty, and into her soul came a joy which was her strength. Little children learned to love her, the street gamins knew her as their friend, aged women blessed the dear child as they called her, who planned for their comfort when the blasts of winter were raging around their homes. Before her great trial she had found her enjoyment more in her intellectual than spiritual life, but when every earthly prop was torn away, she learned to lean her fainting head on Christ the corner-stone and the language of her heart was "Nearer to thee, e'en though it be a cross that raiseth me." In surrendering her life she found a new life and more abundant life in every power and faculty of her soul.

Luzerne went South and found Marie's mother who had mourned her child as dead. Tenderly they watched over her, but the seeds of death were sown too deeply in her wasted frame for recovery, and she wasted away and sank into a premature grave, leaving Luzerne the peaceful satisfaction of having smoothed her passage to the grave, and lengthened with his care, her declining days. Turning from her grave he plunged into active life. It was during the days of reconstruction when tricksters and demagogues were taking advantage of the ignorance and inexperience of the newly enfranchised citizens. Honorable and upright, Luzerne preserved his integrity among the corruptions of political life. Men respected him too much to attempt to swerve him from duty for personal advantage. No bribes ever polluted his hands, nor fraud, nor political chicanery ever stained his record.

He was the friend and benefactor of his race, giving them what gold is ever too poor to buy—the benefit of a good example and a noble life, and earned for himself the sobriquet by which he was called, "honest Luzerne." And yet at times he would turn wistfully to Annette and the memory of those glad, bright days when he expected to clasp hands with her for life. At length his yearning had become insatiable and he returned to A. P.

Laura Lasette had married Charley Cooper who by patience and industry had obtained a good position in the store of a merchant who was manly enough to let it be known that he had Negro blood in his veins, but that he intended to give him a desk and place in his establishment and he told his employees that he intended to employ him, and if they were not willing to work with him they could leave. Charley was promoted just the same as others according to his merits. Time had dealt kindly with Mrs. Lasette, as he scattered his silvery crystals amid her hair, and of her it might be said,

> *Each silver hair, each wrinkle there*
> *Records some good deed done,*
> *Some flower she scattered by the way*
> *Some spark from love's bright sun.*

Mrs. Larkins had grown kinder and more considerate as the years passed by. Mr. Thomas had been happily married for several years. Annette was still in her Southern home doing what she could to teach, help and befriend those on whose chains the rust of ages had gathered. Mr. Luzerne found out Annette's location and started Southward with a fresh hope springing up in his heart.

It was a balmy day in the early spring when he reached the city where Annette was teaching. Her home was a beautiful place of fragrance and flowers. Groups of young people were gathered around their teacher listening eagerly to a beautiful story she was telling them. Elderly women were scattered in little companies listening to or relating some story of Annette's kindness to them and their children.

"I told her," said one, "that I had a vision that some one who was fair, was coming to help us. She smiled and said she was not fair. I told her she was fair to me."

"I wish she had been here fifteen years ago," said another one. "Before she came my boy was just as wild as a colt, but now he is jist as stiddy as a judge."

"I just think," said another one, "that she has been the making of my Lucy. She's just wrapped up in Miss Annette, thinks the sun rises and sets in her." Old mothers whose wants had been relieved, came with the children and younger men too, to celebrate Annette's 31st birthday.

Happy and smiling, like one who had passed through suffering into peace she stood, the beloved friend of old and young, when suddenly she heard a footstep on the veranda which sent the blood bounding in swift currents back to her heart and left her cheek very pale. It was years since she had heard the welcome rebound of that step, but it seemed as familiar to her as the voice of a loved and long lost friend, or a precious household word, and before her stood, with slightly bowed form and hair tinged with gray, Luzerne. Purified through suffering, which to him had been an evangel of good, he had come to claim the love of his spirit. He had come not to separate her from her cherished life work, but to help her in uplifting and helping those among whom her lot was cast as a holy benediction, and so after years of trial and pain, their souls had met at last, strengthened by duty, purified by that faith which works by love, and fitted for life's highest and holiest truths.

And now, in conclusion, permit me to say under the guise of fiction, I have essayed to weave a story which I hope will subserve a deeper purpose than the mere amusement of the hour, that it will quicken and invigorate human hearts and not fail to impart a lesson of usefulness and value.

SHADOWS UPLIFTED

# I

## MYSTERY OF MARKET SPEECH
## AND PRAYER-MEETING

G ood mornin', Bob; how's butter dis mornin'?"
"Fresh; just as fresh, as fresh can be."

"Oh, glory!" said the questioner, whom we shall call Thomas Anderson, although he was known among his acquaintances as Marster Anderson's Tom.

His informant regarding the condition of the market was Robert Johnson, who had been separated from his mother in his childhood and reared by his mistress as a favorite slave. She had fondled him as a pet animal, and even taught him to read. Notwithstanding their relation as mistress and slave, they had strong personal likings for each other.

Tom Anderson was the servant of a wealthy planter, who lived in the city of C——, North Carolina. This planter was quite advanced in life, but in his earlier days he had spent much of his time in talking politics in his State and National capitals in winter, and in visiting pleasure resorts and watering places in summer. His plantations were left to the care of overseers who, in their turn, employed negro drivers to aid them in the work of cultivation and discipline. But as the infirmities of age were pressing upon him he had withdrawn from active life, and given the management of his affairs into the hands of his sons. As Robert Johnson and Thomas Anderson passed homeward from the market, having bought provisions for their respective homes, they seemed to be very light-hearted and careless, chatting and joking with each other; but every now and then, after looking furtively around, one would drop into the ears of the other some news of the battle then raging between the North and South which, like two great millstones, were grinding slavery to powder.

As they passed along, they were met by another servant, who said in hurried tones, but with a glad accent in his voice:—

"Did you see de fish in de market dis mornin'? Oh, but dey war splendid, jis' as fresh, as fresh kin be."

"That's the ticket," said Robert, as a broad smile overspread his face. "I'll see you later."

"Good mornin', boys," said another servant on his way to market. "How's eggs dis mornin'?"

"Fust rate, fust rate," said Tom Anderson. "Bob's got it down fine."

"I thought so; mighty long faces at de pos'-office dis mornin'; but I'd better move 'long," and with a bright smile lighting up his face he passed on with a quickened tread.

There seemed to be an unusual interest manifested by these men in the state of the produce market, and a unanimous report of its good condition. Surely there was nothing in the primeness of the butter or the freshness of the eggs to change careless looking faces into such expressions of gratification, or to light dull eyes with such gladness. What did it mean?

During the dark days of the Rebellion, when the bondman was turning his eyes to the American flag, and learning to hail it as an ensign of deliverance, some of the shrewder slaves, coming in contact with their masters and overhearing their conversations, invented a phraseology to convey in the most unsuspected manner news to each other from the battle-field. Fragile women and helpless children were left on the plantations while their natural protectors were at the front, and yet these bondmen refrained from violence. Freedom was coming in the wake of the Union army, and while numbers deserted to join their forces, others remained at home, slept in their cabins by night and attended to their work by day; but under this apparently careless exterior there was an undercurrent of thought which escaped the cognizance of their masters. In conveying tidings of the war, if they wished to announce a victory of the Union army, they said the butter was fresh, or that the fish and eggs were in good condition. If defeat befell them, then the butter and other produce were rancid or stale.

Entering his home, Robert set his basket down. In one arm he held a bundle of papers which he had obtained from the train to sell to the boarders, who were all anxious to hear from the seat of battle. He slipped one copy out and, looking cautiously around, said to Linda, the cook, in a low voice:—

"Splendid news in the papers. Secesh routed. Yankees whipped 'em out of their boots. Papers full of it. I tell you the eggs and the butter's mighty fresh this morning."

"Oh, sho, chile," said Linda, "I can't read de newspapers, but ole Missus' face is newspaper nuff for me. I looks at her ebery mornin' wen she comes inter dis kitchen. Ef her face is long an' she walks kine o' droopy den I thinks things is gwine wrong for dem. But ef she comes out yere looking mighty pleased, an' larffin all ober her face, an' steppin' so frisky, den I knows de Secesh is gittin' de bes' ob de Yankees. Robby, honey, does you really b'lieve for good and righty dat dem Yankees is got horns?"

"Of course not."

"Well, I yered so."

"Well, you heard a mighty big whopper."

"Anyhow, Bobby, things goes mighty contrary in dis house. Ole Miss is in de parlor prayin' for de Secesh to gain de day, and we's prayin' in de cabins and kitchens for de Yankees to get de bes' ob it. But wasn't Miss Nancy glad wen dem Yankees run'd away at Bull's Run. It was nuffin but Bull's Run an' run away Yankees. How she did larff and skip 'bout de house. An' den me thinks to myself you'd better not holler till you gits out ob de woods. I specs 'fore dem Yankees gits froo you'll be larffin tother side ob your mouf. While you was gone to market ole Miss com'd out yere, her face looking as long as my arm, tellin' us all 'bout de war and saying dem Yankees whipped our folks all to pieces. And she was 'fraid dey'd all be down yere soon. I thought they couldn't come too soon for we. But I didn't tell her so."

"No, I don't expect you did."

"No, I didn't; ef you buys me for a fool you loses your money shore. She said when dey com'd down yere she wanted all de men to hide, for dey'd kill all de men, but dey wouldn't tech de women."

"It's no such thing. She's put it all wrong. Why them Yankees are our best friends."

"Dat's jis' what I thinks. Ole Miss was jis' tryin to skeer a body. An' when she war done she jis' set down and sniffled an' cried, an' I war so glad I didn't know what to do. But I had to hole in. An' I made out I war orful sorry. An' Jinny said, 'O Miss Nancy, I hope dey won't come yere.' An' she said, 'I'se jis' 'fraid dey will come down yere and gobble up eberything dey can lay dere hands on.' An' she jis' looked as ef her heart war mos' broke, an' den she went inter de house. An' when she war gone, we jis' broke loose. Jake turned somersets, and said he warnt 'fraid ob dem Yankees; he know'd which side his brad was buttered on. Dat Jake is a cuter. When he goes down ter git de letters he cuts up all kines ob shines and capers. An' to look at him skylarking dere while de folks is waitin' for dere letters, an' talkin' bout de war, yer wouldn't think dat boy had a thimbleful of sense. But Jake's listenin' all de time wid his eyes and his mouf wide open, an' ketchin' eberything he kin, an' a heap ob news he gits dat way. As to Jinny, she jis' capered and danced all ober de flore. An' I jis' had to put my han' ober her mouf to keep ole Miss from yereing her. Oh, but we did hab a good time. Boy, yer oughter been yere."

"And, Aunt Linda, what did you do?"

"Oh, honey, I war jis' ready to crack my sides larffin, jis' to see what a long face Jinny puts on wen ole Miss is talkin', an' den to see dat face wen missus' back is turned, why it's good as a circus. It's nuff to make a horse larff."

"Why, Aunt Linda, you never saw a circus?"

"No, but I'se hearn tell ob dem, and I thinks dey mus' be mighty funny. An' I know it's orful funny to see how straight Jinny's face looks wen she's almos' ready to bust, while ole Miss is frettin' and fumin' 'bout dem Yankees an' de war. But, somehow, Robby, I ralely b'lieves dat we cullud folks is mixed up in dis fight. I seed it all in a vision. An' soon as dey fired on dat fort, Uncle Dan'el says to me: 'Linda, we's gwine to git our freedom.' An' I says: 'Wat makes you think so?" An' he says: 'Dey've fired on Fort Sumter, an' de Norf is boun' to whip.'"

"I hope so," said Robert. "I think that we have a heap of friends up there."

"Well, I'm jis' gwine to keep on prayin' an' b'lievin'."

Just then the bell rang, and Robert, answering, found Mrs. Johnson suffering from a severe headache, which he thought was occasioned by her worrying over the late defeat of the Confederates. She sent him on an errand, which he executed with his usual dispatch, and returned to some work which he had to do in the kitchen. Robert was quite a favorite with Aunt Linda, and they often had confidential chats together.

"Bobby," she said, when he returned, "I thinks we ort ter hab a prayer-meetin' putty soon."

"I am in for that. Where will you have it?"

"Lem me see. Las' Sunday we had it in Gibson's woods; Sunday 'fore las', in de old cypress swamp; an' nex' Sunday we'el hab one in McCullough's woods. Las' Sunday we had a good time. I war jis' chock full an' runnin' ober. Aunt Milly's daughter's bin monin all summer, an' she's jis' come throo. We had a powerful time. Eberythin' on dat groun' was jis' alive. I tell yer, dere was a shout in de camp."

"Well, you had better look out, and not shout too much, and pray and sing too loud, because, 'fore you know, the patrollers will be on your track and break up your meetin' in a mighty big hurry, before you can say 'Jack Robinson.'"

"Oh, we looks out for dat. We's got a nice big pot, dat got cracked las' winter, but it will hole a lot o' water, an' we puts it whar we can tell it eberything. We has our own good times. An' I want you to come Sunday night an' tell all 'bout the good eggs, fish, and butter. Mark my words, Bobby, we's all gwine to git free. I seed it all in a vision, as plain as de nose on yer face."

"Well, I hope your vision will come out all right, and that the eggs will keep and the butter be fresh till we have our next meetin'."

"Now, Bob, you sen' word to Uncle Dan'el, Tom Anderson, an' de rest ob dem, to come to McCullough's woods nex' Sunday night. I want to hab a sin-killin' an' debil-dribin' time. But, boy, you'd better git out er yere. Ole Miss'll be down on yer like a scratch cat."

Although the slaves were denied unrestricted travel, and the holding of meetings without the surveillance of a white man, yet they contrived to meet by stealth and hold gatherings where they could mingle their prayers and tears, and lay plans for escaping to the Union army. Outwitting the vigilance of the patrollers and home guards, they established these meetings miles apart, extending into several States.

Sometimes their hope of deliverance was cruelly blighted by hearing of some adventurous soul who, having escaped to the Union army, had been pursued and returned again to bondage. Yet hope survived all these disasters which gathered around the fate of their unfortunate brethren, who were remanded to slavery through the undiscerning folly of those who were strengthening the hands which were dealing their deadliest blows at the heart of the Nation. But slavery had cast such a glamour over the Nation, and so warped the consciences of men, that they failed to read aright the legible transcript of Divine retribution which was written upon the shuddering earth, where the blood of God's poor children had been as water freely spilled.

# II

## Contraband of War

A few evenings after this conversation between Robert and Linda, a prayer-meeting was held. Under the cover of night a few dusky figures met by stealth in McCullough's woods.

"Howdy," said Robert, approaching Uncle Daniel, the leader of the prayer-meeting, who had preceded him but a few minutes.

"Thanks and praise; I'se all right. How is you, chile?"

"Oh, I'm all right," said Robert, smiling, and grasping Uncle Daniel's hand.

"What's de news?" exclaimed several, as they turned their faces eagerly towards Robert.

"I hear," said Robert, "that they are done sending the runaways back to their masters."

"Is dat so?" said a half dozen earnest voices. "How did you yere it?"

"I read it in the papers. And Tom told me he heard them talking about it last night, at his house. How did you hear it, Tom? Come, tell us all about it."

Tom Anderson hesitated a moment, and then said:—

"Now, boys, I'll tell you all 'bout it. But you's got to be mighty mum 'bout it. It won't do to let de cat outer de bag."

"Dat's so! But tell us wat you yered. We ain't gwine to say nuffin to nobody."

"Well," said Tom, "las' night ole Marster had company. Two big ginerals, and dey was hoppin' mad. One ob dem looked like a turkey gobbler, his face war so red. An' he sed one ob dem Yankee ginerals, I thinks dey called him Beas' Butler, sed dat de slaves dat runned away war some big name—I don't know what he called it. But it meant dat all ob we who com'd to de Yankees should be free."

"Contraband of war," said Robert, who enjoyed the distinction of being a good reader, and was pretty well posted about the war. Mrs. Johnson had taught him to read on the same principle she would have taught a pet animal amusing tricks. She had never imagined the time would come when he would use the machinery she had put in his hands to help overthrow the institution to which she was so ardently attached.

"What does it mean? Is it somethin' good for us?"

"I think," said Robert, a little vain of his superior knowledge, "it is the best kind of good. It means if two armies are fighting and the horses of one run away, the other has a right to take them. And it is just the same if a slave runs away from the Secesh to the Union lines. He is called a contraband, just the same as if he were an ox or a horse. They wouldn't send the horses back, and they won't send us back."

"Is dat so?" said Uncle Daniel, a dear old father, with a look of saintly patience on his face. "Well, chillen, what do you mean to do?"

"Go, jis' as soon as we kin git to de army," said Tom Anderson.

"What else did the generals say? And how did you come to hear them, Tom?" asked Robert Johnson.

"Well, yer see, Marster's too ole and feeble to go to de war, but his heart's in it. An' it makes him feel good all ober when dem big ginerals comes an' tells him all 'bout it. Well, I war laying out on de porch fas' asleep an' snorin' drefful hard. Oh, I war so soun' asleep dat wen Marster wanted some ice-water he had to shake me drefful hard to wake me up. An' all de time I war wide 'wake as he war."

"What did they say?" asked Robert, who was always on the lookout for news from the battle-field.

"One ob dem said, dem Yankees war talkin' of puttin' guns in our han's and settin' us all free. An' de oder said, 'Oh, sho! ef dey puts guns in dere hands dey'll soon be in our'n; and ef dey sets em free dey wouldn't know how to take keer ob demselves.'"

"Only let 'em try it," chorused a half dozen voices, "an' dey'll soon see who'll git de bes' ob de guns; an' as to taking keer ob ourselves, I specs we kin take keer ob ourselves as well as take keer ob dem."

"Yes," said Tom, "who plants de cotton and raises all de crops?"

> "'They eat the meat and give us the bones,
> Eat the cherries and give us the stones,'

"And I'm getting tired of the whole business," said Robert.

"But, Bob," said Uncle Daniel, "you've got a good owner. You don't hab to run away from bad times and wuss a comin'."

"It isn't so good, but it might be better. I ain't got nothing 'gainst my ole Miss, except she sold my mother from me. And a boy ain't nothin' without his mother. I forgive her, but I never forget her, and never expect to. But if she were the best woman on earth I would rather have my freedom than belong to her. Well, boys, here's a chance for us just as soon as the Union army gets in sight. What will you do?"

"I'se a goin," said Tom Anderson, "jis' as soon as dem Linkum soldiers gits in sight."

"An' I'se a gwine wid you, Tom," said another. "I specs my ole Marster'll feel right smart lonesome when I'se gone, but I don't keer 'bout stayin' for company's sake."

"My ole Marster's room's a heap better'n his company," said Tom Anderson, "an' I'se a goner too. Dis yer freedom's too good to be lef' behind, wen you's got a chance to git it. I won't stop to bid ole Marse good bye."

"What do you think," said Robert, turning to Uncle Daniel; "won't you go with us?"

"No, chillen, I don't blame you for gwine; but I'se gwine to stay. Slavery's done got all de marrow out ob dese poor ole bones. Ef freedom comes it won't do me much good; we ole one's will die out, but it will set you youngsters all up."

"But, Uncle Daniel, you're not too old to want your freedom?"

"I knows dat. I lubs de bery name of freedom. I'se been praying and hoping for it dese many years. An' ef I warn't boun', I would go wid you ter-morrer. I won't put a straw in your way. You boys go, and my prayers will go wid you. I can't go, it's no use. I'se gwine to stay on de ole place till Marse Robert comes back, or is brought back."

"But, Uncle Daniel," said Robert, "what's the use of praying for a thing if, when it comes, you won't take it? As much as you have been praying and talking about freedom, I thought that when the chance came you would have been one of the first to take it. Now, do tell us why you won't go with us. Ain't you willing?"

"Why, Robbie, my whole heart is wid you. But when Marse Robert went to de war, he called me into his room and said to me, 'Uncle Dan'el, I'se gwine to de war, an' I want you to look arter my wife an' chillen, an' see dat eberything goes right on de place'. An' I promised him I'd do it, an' I mus' be as good as my word. 'Cept de overseer, dere isn't a white man on de plantation, an' I hear he has to report ter-morrer or be treated as a deserter. An' der's nobody here to look arter Miss Mary an' de chillen, but myself, an' to see dat eberything goes right. I promised Marse Robert I would do it, an' I mus' be as good as my word."

"Well, what should you keer?" said Tom Anderson. "Who looked arter you when you war sole from your farder and mudder, an' neber seed dem any more, and wouldn't know dem today ef you met dem in your dish?"

"Well, dats neither yere nor dere. Marse Robert couldn't help what his father did. He war an orful mean man. But he's dead now, and gone to see 'bout it. But his wife war the nicest, sweetest lady dat eber I did see. She war no more like him dan chalk's like cheese. She used to visit de cabins, an' listen to de pore women when de overseer used to cruelize dem so bad, an' drive dem to work late and early. An' she used to sen' dem nice things when they war sick, and hab der cabins whitewashed an' lookin' like new pins, an' look arter dere chillen. Sometimes she'd try to git ole Marse to take dere part when de oberseer got too mean. But she might as well a sung hymns to a dead horse. All her putty talk war like porin water on a goose's back. He'd jis' bluff her off, an' tell her she didn't run dat plantation, and not for her to bring him any nigger news. I never thought ole Marster war good to her. I often ketched her crying, an' she'd say she had de headache, but I thought it war de heartache. 'Fore ole Marster died, she got so thin an' peaked I war 'fraid she war gwine to die; but she seed him out. He war killed by a tree fallin' on him, an' ef eber de debil got his own he got him. I seed him in a vision arter he war gone. He war hangin' up in a pit, sayin' 'Oh! oh!' wid no close on. He war allers blusterin', cussin', and swearin' at somebody. Marse Robert ain't a bit like him. He takes right arter his mother. Bad as ole Marster war, I think she jis' lob'd de groun' he walked on. Well, women's mighty curious kind of folks anyhow. I sometimes thinks de wuss you treats dem de better dey likes you."

"Well," said Tom, a little impatiently, "what's yer gwine to do? Is yer gwine wid us, ef yer gits a chance?"

"Now, jes' you hole on till I gits a chance to tell yer why I'se gwine to stay."

"Well, Uncle Daniel, let's hear it," said Robert.

"I was jes' gwine to tell yer when Tom put me out. Ole Marster died when Marse Robert war two years ole, and his pore mother when he war four. When he died, Miss Anna used to keep me 'bout her jes' like I war her shadder. I used to nuss Marse Robert jes' de same as ef I were his own fadder. I used to fix his milk, rock him to sleep, ride him on my back, an' nothin' pleased him better'n fer Uncle Dan'el to ride him piggy-back."

"Well, Uncle Daniel," said Robert, "what has that got to do with your going with us and getting your freedom?"

"Now, jes' wait a bit, and don't frustrate my mine. I seed day arter day Miss Anna war gettin' weaker and thinner, an' she looked so sweet and talked so putty, I thinks to myself, 'you ain't long for dis worl'.' And she said to me one day, 'Uncle Dan'el, when I'se gone, I want you to be good to your Marster Robert.' An' she looked so pale and weak I war almost ready to cry. I couldn't help it. She hed allers bin mighty good to me. An' I beliebs in praisin' de bridge dat carries me ober. She said, 'Uncle Dan'el, I wish you war free. Ef I had my way you shouldn't serve any one when I'm gone; but Mr. Thurston had eberything in his power when he made his will. I war tied hand and foot, and I couldn't help it.' In a little while she war gone—jis' faded away like a flower. I belieb ef dere's a saint in glory, Miss Anna's dere."

"Oh, I don't take much stock in white folks' religion," said Robert, laughing carelessly.

"The way," said Tom Anderson, "dat some of dese folks cut their cards yere, I think dey'll be as sceece in hebben as hen's teeth. I think wen some of dem preachers brings de Bible 'round an' tells us 'bout mindin our marsters and not stealin' dere tings, dat dey preach to please de white folks, an' dey frows coleness ober de meetin'."

"An' I," said Aunt Linda, "neber did belieb in dem Bible preachers. I yered one ob dem sayin' wen he war dyin', it war all dark wid him. An' de way he treated his house-girl, pore thing, I don't wonder dat it war dark wid him."

"O, I guess," said Robert, "that the Bible is all right, but some of these church folks don't get the right hang of it."

"May be dat's so," said Aunt Linda. "But I allers wanted to learn how to read. I once had a book, and tried to make out what war in it, but ebery time my mistus caught me wid a book in my hand, she used to whip my fingers. An' I couldn't see ef it war good for white folks, why it warn't good for cullud folks."

"Well," said Tom Anderson, "I belieb in de good ole-time religion. But arter dese white folks is done fussin' and beatin' de cullud folks, I don't want 'em to come talking religion to me. We used to hab on our place a real Guinea man, an' once he made ole Marse mad, an' he had him whipped. Old Marse war trying to break him in, but dat fellow war spunk to de backbone, an' when he 'gin talkin' to him 'bout savin' his soul an' gittin' to hebbin, he tole him ef he went to hebbin an' foun' he war dare, he wouldn't go in. He wouldn't stay wid any such rascal as he war."

"What became of him?" asked Robert.

"Oh, he died. But he had some quare notions 'bout religion. He thought dat when he died he would go back to his ole country. He allers kep' his ole Guinea name."

"What was it?"

"Potobombra. Do you know what he wanted Marster to do 'fore he died?" continued Anderson.

"No."

"He wanted him to gib him his free papers."

"Did he do it?"

"Ob course he did. As de poor fellow war dying an' he couldn't sell him in de oder world, he jis' wrote him de papers to yumor him. He didn't want to go back to Africa a slave. He thought if he did, his people would look down on him, an' he wanted to go back a free man. He war orful weak when Marster brought him de free papers. He jis' ris up in de bed, clutched dem in his han's, smiled, an' gasped out, 'I'se free at las'; an' fell back on de pillar, an' he war gone. Oh, but he war spunky. De oberseers, arter dey foun' out who he war, gin'rally gabe him a wide birth. I specs his father war some ole Guinea king."

"Well, chillen," said Uncle Daniel, "we's kept up dis meeting long enough. We'd better go home, and not all go one way, cause de patrollers might git us all inter trouble, an' we must try to slip home by hook or crook."

"An' when we meet again, Uncle Daniel can finish his story, an' be ready to go with us," said Robert.

"I wish," said Tom Anderson, "he would go wid us, de wuss kind."

# III

## Uncle Daniel's Story

The Union had snapped asunder because it lacked the cohesion of justice, and the Nation was destined to pass through the crucible of disaster and defeat, till she was ready to clasp hands with the negro and march abreast with him to freedom and victory.

The Union army was encamping a few miles from C——, in North Carolina. Robert, being well posted on the condition of affairs, had stealthily contrived to call a meeting in Uncle Daniel's cabin. Uncle Daniel's wife had gone to bed as a sick sister, and they held a prayer-meeting by her bedside. It was a little risky, but as Mr. Thurston did not encourage the visits of the patrollers, and heartily detested having them prying into his cabins, there was not much danger of molestation.

"Well, Uncle Daniel, we want to hear your story, and see if you have made up your mind to go with us," said Robert, after he had been seated a few minutes in Uncle Daniel's cabin.

"No, chillen, I've no objection to finishin' my story, but I ain't made up my mind to leave the place till Marse Robert gits back."

"You were telling us about Marse Robert's mother. How did you get along after she died?"

"Arter she war gone, ole Marster's folks come to look arter things. But eberything war lef' to Marse Robert, an' he wouldn't do widout me. Dat chile war allers at my heels. I couldn't stir widout him, an' when he missed me, he'd fret an' cry so I had ter stay wid him; an' wen he went to school, I had ter carry him in de mornin' and bring him home in de ebenin'. An' I learned him to hunt squirrels, an' rabbits, an' ketch fish, an' set traps for birds. I beliebs he lob'd me better dan any ob his kin'. An' he showed me how to read."

"Well," said Tom, "ef he lob'd you so much, why didn't he set you free?"

"Marse Robert tole me, ef he died fust he war gwine ter leave me free—dat I should neber sarve any one else."

"Oh, sho!" said Tom, "promises, like pie crusts, is made to be broken. I don't trust none ob dem. I'se been yere dese fifteen years, an' I'se neber foun' any troof in dem. An' I'se gwine wid dem North men soon's I gits a chance. An' ef you knowed what's good fer you, you'd go, too."

"No, Tom; I can't go. When Marster Robert went to de front, he called me to him an' said: 'Uncle Daniel,' an' he was drefful pale when he said it, 'I are gwine to de war, an' I want yer to take keer of my wife an' chillen, jis' like yer used to take keer of me wen yer called me your little boy.' Well, dat jis' got to me, an' I couldn't help cryin', to save my life."

"I specs," said Tom, "your tear bags must lie mighty close to your eyes. I wouldn't cry ef dem Yankees would make ebery one ob dem go to de front, an' stay dere foreber. Dey'd only be gittin' back what dey's been a doin' to us."

"Marster Robert war nebber bad to me. An' I beliebs in stannin' by dem dat stans by you. Arter Miss Anna died, I had great 'sponsibilities on my shoulders; but I war orful lonesome, an' thought I'd like to git a wife. But dere warn't a gal on de plantation, an' nowhere's roun', dat filled de bill. So I jis' waited, an' 'tended to Marse Robert till he war ole 'nough to go to college. Wen he went, he allers 'membered me in de letters he used to write his grandma. Wen he war gone, I war lonesomer dan eber. But, one day, I jis' seed de gal dat took de rag off de bush. Gundover had jis' brought her from de up-country. She war putty as a picture!" he exclaimed, looking fondly at his wife, who still bore traces of great beauty. "She had putty hair, putty eyes, putty mouth. She war putty all over; an' she know'd how to put on style."

"O, Daniel," said Aunt Katie, half chidingly, "how you do talk."

"Why, it's true. I 'member when you war de puttiest gal in dese diggins; when nobody could top your cotton."

"I don't," said Aunt Katie.

"Well, I do. Now, let me go on wid my story. De fust time I seed her, I sez to myself, 'Dat's de gal for me, an' I means to hab her ef I kin git her.' So I scraped 'quaintance wid her, and axed her ef she would hab me ef our marsters would let us. I warn't 'fraid 'bout Marse Robert, but I warn't quite shore 'bout Gundover. So when Marse Robert com'd home, I axed him, an' he larf'd an' said, 'All right,' an' dat he would speak to ole Gundover 'bout it. He didn't relish it bery much, but he didn't like to 'fuse Marse Robert. He wouldn't sell her, for she tended his dairy, an' war mighty handy 'bout de house. He said, I mought marry her an' come to see her wheneber Marse Robert would gib me a pass. I wanted him to sell her, but he wouldn't hear to it, so I had to put up wid what I could git. Marse Robert war mighty good to me, but ole Gundover's wife war de meanest woman dat I eber did see. She used to go out on de plantation an' boss things like a man. Arter I war married, I had a baby. It war de dearest, cutest little thing you eber did see; but, pore thing, it got sick and died. It died 'bout three o'clock; and in de mornin', Katie, habbin her cows to milk, lef her dead baby in de cabin. When she com'd back from milkin' her thirty cows, an' went to look for her pore little baby, some one had been to her cabin an' took'd de pore chile away an' put it in de groun'. Pore Katie, she didn't eben hab a chance to kiss her baby 'fore it war buried. Ole Gundover's wife has been dead thirty years, an' she didn't die a day too soon. An' my little baby has gone to glory, an' is wingin' wid the angels an' a lookin' out for us. One ob de las' things ole Gundover's wife did 'fore she died war to order a woman whipped 'cause she com'd to de field a little late when her husband war sick, an' she had stopped to tend him. Dat mornin' she war taken sick wid de fever, an' in a few days she war gone out like de snuff ob a candle. She lef' several sons, an' I specs she would almos' turn ober in her grave ef she know'd she had ten culled granchillen somewhar down in de lower kentry."

"Isn't it funny," said Robert, "how these white folks look down on colored people, an' then mix up with them?"

"Marster war away when Miss 'Liza treated my Katie so mean, an' when I tole him 'bout it, he war tearin' mad, an' went ober an' saw ole Gundover, an' foun' out he war hard up for money, an' he bought Katie and brought her home to lib wid me, and we's been a libin in clover eber sence. Marster Robert has been mighty good to me. He stood by me in my troubles, an' now his trouble's come, I'm a gwine to stan' by him. I used to think Gundover's wife war jealous ob my Katie. She war so much puttier. Gundover's wife couldn't tech my Katie wid a ten foot pole."

"But, Aunt Katie, you have had your trials," said Robert, now that Daniel had finished his story; "don't you feel bitter towards these people who are fighting to keep you in slavery?"

Aunt Katie turned her face towards the speaker. It was a thoughtful, intelligent face, saintly and calm. A face which expressed the idea of a soul which had been fearfully tempest tossed, but had passed through suffering into peace. Very touching was the look of resignation and hope which overspread her features as she replied, with the simple child-like faith which she had learned in the darkest hour, "The Lord says, we must forgive." And with her that thought, as coming from the lips of Divine Love, was enough to settle the whole question of forgiveness of injuries and love to enemies.

"Well," said Thomas Anderson, turning to Uncle Daniel, "we can't count on yer to go wid us?"

"Boys," said Uncle Daniel, and there was grief in his voice, "I'se mighty glad you hab a chance for your freedom; but, ez I tole yer, I promised Marse Robert I would stay, an' I mus' be as good as my word. Don't you youngsters stay for an ole stager like me. I'm ole an' mos' worn out. Freedom wouldn't do much for me, but I want you all to be as free as the birds; so, you chillen, take your freedom when you kin get it."

"But, Uncle Dan'el, you won't say nothin' 'bout our going, will you?" said the youngest of the company.

Uncle Daniel slowly arose. There was a mournful flash in his eye, a tremor of emotion in his voice, as he said, "Look yere, boys, de boy dat axed dat question war a new comer on dis plantation, but some ob you's bin here all ob your lives; did you eber know ob Uncle Dan'el gittin' any ob you inter trouble?"

"No, no," exclaimed a chorus of voices, "but many's de time you've held off de blows wen de oberseer got too mean, an' cruelized us too much, wen Marse Robert war away. An' wen he got back, you made him settle de oberseer's hash."

"Well, boys," said Uncle Daniel, with an air of mournful dignity, "I'se de same Uncle Dan'el I eber war. Ef any ob you wants to go, I habben't a word to say agin it. I specs dem Yankees be all right, but I knows Marse Robert, an' I don't know dem, an' I ain't a gwine ter throw away dirty water 'til I gits clean."

"Well, Uncle Ben," said Robert, addressing a stalwart man whose towering form and darkly flashing eye told that slavery had failed to put the crouch in his shoulders or general abjectness into his demeanor, "you will go with us, for sure, won't you?"

"Yes," spoke up Tom Anderson, "'cause de trader's done took your wife, an' got her for his'n now."

As Ben Tunnel looked at the speaker, a spasm of agony and anger darkened his face and distorted his features, as if the blood of some strong race were stirring with sudden vigor through his veins. He clutched his hands together, as if he were struggling with an invisible foe, and for a moment he remained silent. Then suddenly raising his head, he exclaimed, "Boys, there's not one of you loves freedom more than I do, but—"

"But what?" said Tom. "Do you think white folks is your bes' friends?"

"I'll think so when I lose my senses."

"Well, now, I don't belieb you're 'fraid, not de way I yeard you talkin' to de oberseer wen he war threatnin' to hit your mudder. He saw you meant business, an' he let her alone. But, what's to hinder you from gwine wid us?"

"My mother," he replied, in a low, firm voice. "That is the only thing that keeps me from going. If it had not been for her, I would have gone long ago. She's all I've got, an' I'm all she's got."

It was touching to see the sorrow on the strong face, to detect the pathos and indignation in his voice, as he said, "I used to love Mirandy as I love my life. I thought the sun rose and set in her. I never saw a handsomer woman than she was. But she fooled me all over the face and eyes, and took up with that hell-hound of a trader, Lukens; an' he gave her a chance to live easy, to wear fine clothes, an' be waited on like a lady. I thought at first I would go crazy, but my poor mammy did all she could to comfort me. She would tell me there were as good fish in the sea as were ever caught out of it. Many a time I've laid my poor head on her lap, when it seemed as if my brain was on fire and my heart was almost ready to burst. But in course of time I got over the worst of it; an' Mirandy is the first an' last woman that ever fooled me. But that dear old mammy of mine, I mean to stick by her as long as there is a piece of her. I can't go over to the army an' leave her behind, for if I did, an' anything should happen, I would never forgive myself."

"But couldn't you take her with you," said Robert, "the soldiers said we could bring our women."

"It isn't that. The Union army is several miles from here, an' my poor mammy is so skeery that, if I were trying to get her away and any of them Secesh would overtake us, an' begin to question us, she would get skeered almost to death, an' break down an' begin to cry, an' then the fat would be in the fire. So, while I love freedom more than a child loves its mother's milk, I've made up my mind to stay on the plantation. I wish, from the bottom of my heart, I could go. But I can't take her along with me, an' I don't want to be free and leave her behind in slavery. I was only five years old when my master and, as I believe, father, sold us both here to this lower country, an' we've been here ever since. It's no use talking, I won't leave her to be run over by everybody."

A few evenings after this interview, the Union soldiers entered the town of C——, and established their headquarters near the home of Thomas Anderson.

Out of the little company, almost every one deserted to the Union army, leaving Uncle Daniel faithful to his trust, and Ben Tunnel hushing his heart's deep aspirations for freedom in a passionate devotion to his timid and affectionate mother.

# IV

## Arrival of the Union Army

A few evenings before the stampede of Robert and his friends to the army, and as he sat alone in his room reading the latest news from the paper he had secreted, he heard a cautious tread and a low tap at his window. He opened the door quietly and whispered:—

"Anything new, Tom?"

"Yes."

"What is it? Come in."

"Well, I'se done bin seen dem Yankees, an' dere ain't a bit of troof in dem stories I'se bin yerin 'bout 'em."

"Where did you see 'em?"

"Down in de woods whar Marster tole us to hide. Yesterday ole Marse sent for me to come in de settin'-room. An' what do you think? Instead ob makin' me stan' wid my hat in my han' while he went froo a whole rigamarole, he axed me to sit down, an' he tole me he 'spected de Yankees would want us to go inter de army, an' dey would put us in front whar we'd all git killed; an' I tole him I didn't want to go, I didn't want to git all momached up. An' den he said we'd better go down in de woods an' hide. Massa Tom and Frank said we'd better go as quick as eber we could. Dey said dem Yankees would put us in dere wagons and make us haul like we war mules. Marse Tom ain't libin' at de great house jis' now. He's keepin' bachellar's hall."

"Didn't he go to the battle?"

"No; he foun' a pore white man who war hard up for money, an' he got him to go."

"But, Tom, you didn't believe these stories about the Yankees. Tom and Frank can lie as fast as horses can trot. They wanted to scare you, and keep you from going to the Union army."

"I knows dat now, but I didn't 'spect so den."

"Well, when did you see the soldiers? Where are they? And what did they say to you?"

"Dey's right down in Gundover's woods. An' de Gineral's got his headquarters almos' next door to our house."

"That near? Oh, you don't say so!"

"Yes, I do. An', oh, golly, ain't I so glad! I jis' stole yere to told you all 'bout it. Yesterday mornin' I war splittin' some wood to git my breakfas', an' I met one ob dem Yankee sogers. Well, I war so skeered, my heart flew right up in my mouf, but I made my manners to him and said, 'Good mornin', Massa.' He said, 'Good mornin'; but don't call me "massa."' Dat war de fust white man I eber seed dat didn't want ter be called 'massa,' eben ef he war as pore as Job's turkey. Den I begin to feel right sheepish, an' he axed me ef my marster war at home, an' ef he war a Reb. I tole him he hadn't gone to de war, but he war Secesh all froo, inside and outside. He war too ole to go to de war, but dat he war all de time gruntin' an' groanin', an' I 'spected he'd grunt hisself to death."

"What did he say?"

"He said he specs he'll grunt worser dan dat fore dey get froo wid him. Den he axed me ef I would hab some breakfas',' an' I said, 'No, t'ank you, sir.' 'An' I war jis' as hungry as a dorg, but I war 'feared to eat. I war 'feared he war gwine to pizen me."

"Poison you! don't you know the Yankees are our best friends?"

"Well, ef dat's so, I'se mighty glad, cause de woods is full ob dem."

"Now, Tom, I thought you had cut your eye-teeth long enough not to let them Anderson boys fool you. Tom, you must not think because a white man says a thing, it must be so, and that a colored man's word is no account 'longside of his. Tom, if ever we get our freedom, we've got to learn to trust each other and stick together if we would be a people. Somebody else can read the papers as well as Marse Tom and Frank. My ole Miss knows I can read the papers, an' she never tries to scare me with big whoppers 'bout the Yankees. She knows she can't catch ole birds with chaff, so she is just as sweet as a peach to her Bobby. But as soon as I get a chance I will play her a trick the devil never did."

"What's that?"

"I'll leave her. I ain't forgot how she sold my mother from me. Many a night I have cried myself to sleep, thinking about her, and when I get free I mean to hunt her up."

"Well, I ain't tole you all. De gemman said he war 'cruiting for de army; dat Massa Linkum hab set us all free, an' dat he wanted some more sogers to put down dem Secesh; dat we should all hab our freedom, our wages, an' some kind ob money. I couldn't call it like he did."

"Bounty money," said Robert.

"Yes, dat's jis' what he called it, bounty money. An' I said dat I war in for dat, teeth and toe-nails."

Robert Johnson's heart gave a great bound. Was that so? Had that army, with freedom emblazoned on its banners, come at last to offer them deliverance if they would accept it? Was it a bright, beautiful dream, or a blessed reality soon to be grasped by his willing hands? His heart grew buoyant with hope; the lightness of his heart gave elasticity to his step and sent the blood rejoicingly through his veins. Freedom was almost in his grasp, and the future was growing rose-tinted and rainbow-hued. All the ties which bound him to his home were as ropes of sand, now that freedom had come so near.

When the army was afar off, he had appeared to be light-hearted and content with his lot. If asked if he desired his freedom, he would have answered, very naively, that he was eating his white bread and believed in letting well enough alone; he had no intention of jumping from the frying-pan into the fire. But in the depths of his soul the love of freedom was an all-absorbing passion; only danger had taught him caution. He had heard of terrible vengeance being heaped upon the heads of some who had sought their freedom and failed in the attempt. Robert knew that he might abandon hope if he incurred the wrath of men whose overthrow was only a question of time. It would have been madness and folly for him to have attempted an insurrection against slavery, with the words of McClellan ringing in his ears: "If you rise I shall put you down with an iron hand," and with the home guards ready to quench his aspirations for freedom with bayonets and blood. What could a set of unarmed and undisciplined men do against the fearful odds which beset their path?

Robert waited eagerly and hopefully his chance to join the Union army; and was ready and willing to do anything required of him by which he could earn his freedom and prove his manhood. He conducted his plans with the greatest secrecy. A few faithful and trusted friends stood ready to desert with him when the Union army came within hailing distance. When it came, there was a stampede to its ranks of men ready to serve in any capacity, to labor in the tents, fight on the fields, or act as scouts. It was a strange sight to see these black men rallying around the Stars and Stripes, when white men were trampling them under foot and riddling them with bullets.

FRANCES ELLEN WATKINS HARPER

# V

## The Release of Iola Leroy

"Well, boys," said Robert to his trusted friends, as they gathered together at a meeting in Gundover's woods, almost under the shadow of the Union army, "how many of you are ready to join the army and fight for your freedom."

"All ob us."

"The soldiers," continued Robert, "are camped right at the edge of the town. The General has his headquarters in the heart of the town, and one of the officers told me yesterday that the President had set us all free, and that as many as wanted to join the army could come along to the camp. So I thought, boys, that I would come and tell you. Now, you can take your bag and baggage, and get out of here as soon as you choose."

"We'll be ready by daylight," said Tom. "It won't take me long to pack up," looking down at his seedy clothes, with a laugh. "I specs ole Marse'll be real lonesome when I'm gone. An' won't he be hoppin' mad when he finds I'm a goner? I specs he'll hate it like pizen."

"O, well," said Robert, "the best of friends must part. Don't let it grieve you."

"I'se gwine to take my wife an' chillen," said one of the company.

"I'se got nobody but myself," said Tom; "but dere's a mighty putty young gal dere at Marse Tom's. I wish I could git her away. Dey tells me dey's been sellin' her all ober de kentry; but dat she's a reg'lar spitfire; dey can't lead nor dribe her."

"Do you think she would go with us?" said Robert.

"I think she's jis' dying to go. Dey say dey can't do nuffin wid her. Marse Tom's got his match dis time, and I'se glad ob it. I jis' glories in her spunk."

"How did she come there?"

"Oh, Marse bought her ob de trader to keep house for him. But ef you seed dem putty white han's ob hern you'd never tink she kept her own house, let 'lone anybody else's."

"Do you think you can get her away?"

"I don't know; 'cause Marse Tom keeps her mighty close. My! but she's putty. Beautiful long hair comes way down her back; putty blue eyes, an' jis' ez white ez anybody's in dis place. I'd jis' wish you could see her yoresef. I heerd Marse Tom talkin' 'bout her las' night to his brudder; tellin' him she war mighty airish, but he meant to break her in."

An angry curse rose to the lips of Robert, but he repressed it and muttered to himself, "Graceless scamp, he ought to have his neck stretched." Then turning to Tom, said:—

"Get her, if you possibly can, but you must be mighty mum about it."

"Trus' me for dat," said Tom.

Tom was very anxious to get word to the beautiful but intractable girl who was held in durance vile by her reckless and selfish master, who had tried in vain to drag her down to his own low level of sin and shame. But all Tom's efforts were in vain. Finally he applied to the Commander of the post, who immediately gave orders for her release. The next day Tom had the satisfaction of knowing that Iola Leroy had been taken as a trembling dove from the gory vulture's nest and given a place of security. She was taken immediately to the General's headquarters. The General was much impressed by her modest demeanor, and surprised to see the refinement and beauty she possessed. Could it be possible that this young and beautiful girl had been a chattel, with no power to protect herself from the highest insults that lawless brutality could inflict upon innocent and defenseless womanhood? Could he ever again glory in his American citizenship, when any white man, no matter how coarse, cruel, or brutal, could buy or sell her for the basest purposes? Was it not true that the cause of a hapless people had become entangled with the lightnings of heaven, and dragged down retribution upon the land?

The field hospital was needing gentle, womanly ministrations, and Iola Leroy, released from the hands of her tormentors, was given a place as nurse; a position to which she adapted herself with a deep sense of relief. Tom was doubly gratified at the success of his endeavors, which had resulted in the rescue of the beautiful young girl and the discomfiture of his young master who, in the words of Tom, "was mad enough to bite his head off" (a rather difficult physical feat).

Iola, freed from her master's clutches, applied herself readily to her appointed tasks. The beautiful, girlish face was full of tender earnestness. The fresh, young voice was strangely sympathetic, as if some great sorrow had bound her heart in loving compassion to every sufferer who needed her gentle ministrations.

Tom Anderson was a man of herculean strength and remarkable

courage. But, on account of physical defects, instead of enlisting as a soldier, he was forced to remain a servant, although he felt as if every nerve in his right arm was tingling to strike a blow for freedom. He was well versed in the lay of the country, having often driven his master's cotton to market when he was a field hand. After he became a coachman, he had become acquainted with the different roads and localities of the country. Besides, he had often accompanied his young masters on their hunting and fishing expeditions. Although he could not fight in the army, he proved an invaluable helper. When tents were to be pitched, none were more ready to help than he. When burdens were to be borne, none were more willing to bend beneath them than Thomas Anderson. When the battle-field was to be searched for the wounded and dying, no hand was more tender in its ministrations of kindness than his. As a general factotum in the army, he was ever ready and willing to serve anywhere and at any time, and to gather information from every possible source which could be of any service to the Union army. As a Pagan might worship a distant star and wish to call it his own, so he loved Iola. And he never thought he could do too much for the soldiers who had rescued her and were bringing deliverance to his race.

"What do you think of Miss Iola?" Robert asked him one day, as they were talking together.

"I jis' think dat she's splendid. Las' week I had to take some of our pore boys to de hospital, an' she war dere, lookin' sweet an' putty ez an angel, a nussin' dem pore boys, an' ez good to one ez de oder. It looks to me ez ef dey ralely lob'd her shadder. She sits by 'em so patient, an' writes 'em sech nice letters to der frens, an' yit she looks so heart-broke an' pitiful, it jis' gits to me, an' makes me mos' ready to cry. I'm so glad dat Marse Tom had to gib her up. He war too mean to eat good victuals."

"He ought," said Robert, "to be made to live on herrings' heads and cold potatoes. It makes my blood boil just to think that he was going to have that lovely looking young girl whipped for his devilment. He ought to be ashamed to hold up his head among respectable people."

"I tell you, Bob, de debil will neber git his own till he gits him. When I seed how he war treating her I neber rested till I got her away. He buyed her, he said, for his housekeeper; as many gals as dere war on de plantation, why didn't he git one ob dem to keep house, an' not dat nice lookin' young lady? Her han's look ez ef she neber did a day's work in her life. One day when he com'd down to breakfas,' he chucked her under de chin, an' tried to put his arm roun' her waist. But she jis' frew it off like a chunk ob fire. She looked like a snake had bit her. Her eyes fairly spit fire. Her face got red ez blood, an' den she turned so pale I thought she war gwine to faint, but she didn't, an' I yered her say, 'I'll die fust.' I war mad 'nough to stan' on my head. I could hab tore'd him all to pieces wen he said he'd hab her whipped."

"Did he do it?"

"I don't know. But he's mean 'nough to do enythin'. Why, dey say she war sole seben times in six weeks, 'cause she's so putty, but dat she war game to de las'."

"Well, Tom," said Robert, "getting that girl away was one of the best things you ever did in your life."

"I think so, too. Not dat I specs enytin' ob it. I don't spose she would think ob an ugly chap like me; but it does me good to know dat Marse Tom ain't got her."

# VI

## ROBERT JOHNSON'S PROMOTION
## AND RELIGION

Robert Johnson, being able to meet the army requirements, was enlisted as a substitute to help fill out the quota of a Northern regiment. With his intelligence, courage, and prompt obedience, he rose from the ranks and became lieutenant of a colored company. He was daring, without being rash; prompt, but not thoughtless; firm, without being harsh. Kind and devoted to the company he drilled, he soon won the respect of his superior officers and the love of his comrades.

"Johnson," said a young officer, Captain Sybil, of Maine, who had become attached to Robert, "what is the use of your saying you're a colored man, when you are as white as I am, and as brave a man as there is among us. Why not quit this company, and take your place in the army just the same as a white man? I know your chances for promotion would be better."

"Captain, you may doubt my word, but today I would rather be a lieutenant in my company than a captain in yours."

"I don't understand you."

"Well, Captain, when a man's been colored all his life it comes a little hard for him to get white all at once. Were I to try it, I would feel like a cat in a strange garret. Captain, I think my place is where I am most needed. You do not need me in your ranks, and my company does. They are excellent fighters, but they need a leader. To silence a battery, to capture a flag, to take a fortification, they will rush into the jaws of death."

"Yes, I have often wondered at their bravery."

"Captain, these battles put them on their mettle. They have been so long taught that they are nothing and nobody, that they seem glad to prove they are something and somebody."

"But, Johnson, you do not look like them, you do not talk like them. It is a burning shame to have held such a man as you in slavery."

"I don't think it was any worse to have held me in slavery than the blackest man in the South."

"You are right, Johnson. The color of a man's skin has nothing to do with the possession of his rights."

"Now, there is Tom Anderson," said Robert, "he is just as black as black can be. He has been bought and sold like a beast, and yet there is not a braver man in all the company. I know him well. He is a noble-hearted fellow. True as steel. I love him like a brother. And I believe Tom would risk his life for me any day. He don't know anything about his father or mother. He was sold from them before he could remember. He can read a little. He used to take lessons from a white gardener in Virginia. He would go between the hours of 9 P.M. and 4 A.M. He got a book of his own, tore it up, greased the pages, and hid them in his hat. Then if his master had ever knocked his hat off he would have thought them greasy papers, and not that Tom was carrying his library on his head. I had another friend who lived near us. When he was nineteen years old he did not know how many letters there were in the ABC's. One night, when his work was done, his boss came into his cabin and saw him with a book in his hand. He threatened to give him five hundred lashes if he caught him again with a book, and said he hadn't work enough to do. He was getting out logs, and his task was ten logs a day. His employer threatened to increase it to twelve. He said it just harassed him; it set him on fire. He thought there must be something good in that book if the white man didn't want him to learn. One day he had an errand in the kitchen, and he heard one of the colored girls going over the ABC's. Here was the key to the forbidden knowledge. She had heard the white children saying them, and picked them up by heart, but did not know them by sight. He was not content with that, but sold his cap for a book and wore a cloth on his head instead. He got the sounds of the letters by heart, then cut off the bark of a tree, carved the letters on the smooth inside, and learned them. He wanted to learn how to write. He had charge of a warehouse where he had a chance to see the size and form of letters. He made the beach of the river his copybook, and thus he learned to write. Tom never got very far with his learning, but I used to get the papers and tell him all I knew about the war."

"How did you get the papers?"

"I used to have very good privileges for a slave. All of our owners were not alike. Some of them were quite clever, and others were worse than git out. I used to get the morning papers to sell to the boarders and others, and when I got them I would contrive to hide a paper, and let some of the fellow-servants know how things were going on. And our owners thought we cared nothing about what was going on."

FRANCES ELLEN WATKINS HARPER

"How was that? I thought you were not allowed to hold meetings unless a white man were present."

"That was so. But we contrived to hold secret meetings in spite of their caution. We knew whom we could trust. My ole Miss wasn't mean like some of them. She never wanted the patrollers around prowling in our cabins, and poking their noses into our business. Her husband was an awful drunkard. He ran through every cent he could lay his hands on, and she was forced to do something to keep the wolf from the door, so she set up a boarding-house. But she didn't take in Tom, Dick, and Harry. Nobody but the big bugs stopped with her. She taught me to read and write, and to cast up accounts. It was so handy for her to have some one who could figure up her accounts, and read or write a note, if she were from home and wanted the like done. She once told her cousin how I could write and figure up. And what do you think her cousin said?"

"'Pleased,' I suppose, 'to hear it.'"

"Not a bit of it. She said, if I belonged to her, she would cut off my thumbs; her husband said, 'Oh, then he couldn't pick cotton.' As to my poor thumbs, it did not seem to be taken into account what it would cost me to lose them. My ole Miss used to have a lot of books. She would let me read any one of them except a novel. She wanted to take care of my soul, but she wasn't taking care of her own."

"Wasn't she religious?"

"She went for it. I suppose she was as good as most of them. She said her prayers and went to church, but I don't know that that made her any better. I never did take much stock in white folks' religion."

"Why, Robert, I'm afraid you are something of an infidel."

"No, Captain, I believe in the real, genuine religion. I ain't got much myself, but I respect them that have. We had on our place a dear, old saint, named Aunt Kizzy. She was a happy soul. She had seen hard times, but was what I call a living epistle. I've heard her tell how her only child had been sold from her, when the man who bought herself did not want to buy her child. Poor little fellow! he was only two years old. I asked her one day how she felt when her child was taken away. 'I felt,' she said, 'as if I was going to my grave. But I knew if I couldn't get justice here, I could get it in another world.'"

"That was faith," said Captain Sybil, as if speaking to himself, "a patient waiting for death to redress the wrongs of life."

"Many a time," continued Robert, "have I heard her humming to herself in the kitchen and saying, 'I has my trials, ups and downs, but it won't allers be so. I specs one day to wing and wing wid de angels, Hallelujah! Den I specs to hear a voice sayin', "Poor ole Kizzy, she's done de bes' she kin. Go down, Gabriel, an' tote her in." Den I specs to put on my golden slippers, my long white robe, an' my starry crown, an' walk dem golden streets, Hallelujah!' I've known that dear, old soul to travel going on two miles, after her work was done, to have some one read to her. Her favorite chapter began with, 'Let not your heart be troubled, ye believe in God, believe also in Me.'"

"I have been deeply impressed," said Captain Sybil, "with the child-like faith of some of these people. I do not mean to say that they are consistent Christians, but I do think that this faith has in a measure underlain the life of the race. It has been a golden thread woven amid the sombre tissues of their lives. A ray of light shimmering amid the gloom of their condition. And what would they have been without it?"

"I don't know. But I know what she was with it. And I believe if there are any saints in glory, Aunt Kizzy is one of them."

"She is dead, then?"

"Yes, went all right, singing and rejoicing until the last, 'Troubles over, troubles over, and den my troubles will be over. We'll walk de golden streets all 'roun' in de New Jerusalem.' Now, Captain, that's the kind of religion that I want. Not that kind which could ride to church on Sundays, and talk so solemn with the minister about heaven and good things, then come home and light down on the servants like a thousand of bricks. I have no use for it. I don't believe in it. I never did and I never will. If any man wants to save my soul he ain't got to beat my body. That ain't the kind of religion I'm looking for. I ain't got a bit of use for it. Now, Captain, ain't I right?"

"Well, yes, Robert, I think you are more than half right. You ought to know my dear, old mother who lives in Maine. We have had colored company at our house, and I never saw her show the least difference between her colored and white guests. She is a Quaker preacher, and don't believe in war, but when the rest of the young men went to the front, I wanted to go also. So I thought it all over, and there seemed to be no way out of slavery except through the war. I had been taught to hate war and detest slavery. Now the time had come when I could not help the war, but I could strike a blow for freedom. So I told my mother I was going to the front, that I expected to be killed, but I went to free the slave. It went hard with her. But I thought that I ought to come, and I believe my mother's prayers are following me."

"Captain," said Robert, rising, "I am glad that I have heard your story. I think that some of these Northern soldiers do two things—hate slavery and hate niggers."

"I am afraid that is so with some of them. They would rather be whipped by Rebels than conquer with negroes. Oh, I heard a soldier," said Captain Sybil, "say, when the colored men were being enlisted, that he would break his sword and resign. But he didn't do either. After Colonel Shaw led his charge at Fort Wagner, and died in the conflict, he got bravely over his prejudices. The conduct of the colored troops there and elsewhere has done much to turn public opinion in their favor. I suppose any white soldier would rather have his black substitute receive the bullets than himself."

# VII

## Tom Anderson's Death

W here is Tom?" asked Captain Sybil; "I have not seen him for several hours."

"He's gone down the sound with some of the soldiers," replied Robert. "They wanted Tom to row them."

"I am afraid those boys will get into trouble, and the Rebs will pick them off," responded Sybil.

"O, I hope not," answered Robert.

"I hope not, too; but those boys are too venturesome."

"Tom knows the lay of the land better than any of us," said Robert. "He is the most wide-awake and gamiest man I know. I reckon when the war is over Tom will be a preacher. Did you ever hear him pray?"

"No; is he good at that?"

"First-rate," continued Robert. "It would do you good to hear him. He don't allow any cursing and swearing when he's around. And what he says is law and gospel with the boys. But he's so good-natured; and they can't get mad at him."

"Yes, Robert, there is not a man in our regiment I would sooner trust than Tom. Last night, when he brought in that wounded scout, he couldn't have been more tender if he had been a woman. How gratefully the poor fellow looked in Tom's face as he laid him down so carefully and staunched the blood which had been spurting out of him. Tom seemed to know it was an artery which had been cut, and he did just the right thing to stop the bleeding. He knew there wasn't a moment to be lost. He wasn't going to wait for the doctor. I have often heard that colored people are ungrateful, but I don't think Tom's worst enemy would say that about him."

"Captain," said Robert, with a tone of bitterness in his voice, "what had we to be grateful for? For ages of poverty, ignorance, and slavery? I think if anybody should be grateful, it is the people who have enslaved us and lived off our labor for generations. Captain, I used to know a poor old woman who couldn't bear to hear any one play on the piano."

"Is that so? Why, I always heard that colored people were a musical race."

"So we are; but that poor woman's daughter was sold, and her mistress took the money to buy a piano. Her mother could never bear to hear a sound from it."

"Poor woman!" exclaimed Captain Sybil, sympathetically; "I suppose it seemed as if the wail of her daughter was blending with the tones of the instrument. I think, Robert, there is a great deal more in the colored people than we give them credit for. Did you know Captain Sellers?"

"The officer who escaped from prison and got back to our lines?" asked Robert.

"Yes. Well, he had quite an experience in trying to escape. He came to an aged couple, who hid him in their cabin and shared their humble food with him. They gave him some corn-bread, bacon, and coffee which he thought was made of scorched bran. But he said that he never ate a meal that he relished more than the one he took with them. Just before he went they knelt down and prayed with him. It seemed as if his very hair stood on his head, their prayer was so solemn. As he was going away the man took some shingles and nailed them on his shoes to throw the bloodhounds off his track. I don't think he will ever cease to feel kindly towards colored people. I do wonder what has become of the boys? What can keep them so long?"

Just as Captain Sybil and Robert were wondering at the delay of Tom and the soldiers they heard the measured tread of men who were slowly bearing a burden. They were carrying Tom Anderson to the hospital, fearfully wounded, and nigh to death. His face was distorted, and the blood was streaming from his wounds. His respiration was faint, his pulse hurried, as if life were trembling on its frailest cords.

Robert and Captain Sybil hastened at once towards the wounded man. On Robert's face was a look of intense anguish, as he bent pityingly over his friend.

"O, this is dreadful! How did it happen?" cried Robert.

Captain Sybil, pressing anxiously forward, repeated Robert's question.

"Captain," said one of the young soldiers, advancing and saluting his superior officer, "we were all in the boat when it struck against a mud bank, and there was not strength enough among us to shove her back into the water. Just then the Rebels opened fire upon us. For awhile we lay down in the boat, but still they kept firing. Tom took in the whole situation, and said: 'Someone must die to get us out of this. I mought's well be him as any. You are soldiers and can fight. If they kill me, it is nuthin'.' So Tom leaped out to shove the boat into the water. Just then the Rebel bullets began to rain around him. He received seven or eight of them, and I'm afraid there is no hope for him."

"O, Tom, I wish you hadn't gone. O, Tom! Tom!" cried Robert, in tones of agony.

A gleam of grateful recognition passed over the drawn features of Tom, as the wail of his friend fell on his ear. He attempted to speak, but the words died upon his lips, and he became unconscious.

"Well," said Captain Sybil, "put him in one of the best wards. Give him into Miss Leroy's care. If good nursing can win him back to life, he shall not want for any care or pains that she can bestow. Send immediately for Dr. Gresham."

Robert followed his friend into the hospital, tenderly and carefully helped to lay him down, and remained awhile, gazing in silent grief upon the sufferer. Then he turned to go, leaving him in the hands of Iola, but hoping against hope that his wounds would not be fatal.

With tender devotion Iola watched her faithful friend. He recognized her when restored to consciousness, and her presence was as balm to his wounds. He smiled faintly, took her hand in his, stroked it tenderly, looked wistfully into her face, and said, "Miss Iola, I ain't long fer dis! I'se 'most home!"

"Oh, no," said Iola, "I hope that you will soon get over this trouble, and live many long and happy days."

"No, Miss Iola, it's all ober wid me. I'se gwine to glory; gwine to glory; gwine to ring dem charmin' bells. Tell all de boys to meet me in heben; dat dey mus' 'list in de hebenly war."

"O, Mr. Tom," said Iola, tenderly, "do not talk of leaving me. You are the best friend I have had since I was torn from my mother. I should be so lonely without you."

"Dere's a frien' dat sticks closer dan a brudder. He will be wid yer in de sixt' trial, an' in de sebbent' he'll not fo'sake yer."

"Yes," answered Iola, "I know that. He is all our dependence. But I can't help grieving when I see you suffering so. But, dear friend, be quiet, and try to go to sleep."

"I'll do enythin' fer yer, Miss Iola."

Tom closed his eyes and lay quiet. Tenderly and anxiously Iola watched over him as the hours waned away. The doctor came, shook his head gravely, and, turning to Iola, said, "There is no hope, but do what you can to alleviate his sufferings."

As Iola gazed upon the kind but homely features of Tom, she saw his eyes open and an unexpressed desire upon his face.

Tenderly and sadly bending over him, with tears in her dark, luminous eyes, she said, "Is there anything I can do for you?"

"Yes," said Tom, with laboring breath; "let me hole yore han', an' sing 'Ober Jordan inter glory' an' 'We'll anchor bye and bye.'"

Iola laid her hand gently in the rough palm of the dying man, and, with a tremulous voice, sang the parting hymns.

Tenderly she wiped the death damps from his dusky brow, and imprinted upon it a farewell kiss. Gratitude and affection lit up the dying eye, which seemed to be gazing into the eternities. Just then Robert entered the room, and, seating himself quietly by Tom's bedside, read the death signs in his face.

"Good-bye, Robert," said Tom, "meet me in de kingdom." Suddenly a look of recognition and rapture lit up his face, and he murmured, "Angels, bright angels, all's well, all's well!"

Slowly his hand released its pressure, a peaceful calm overspread his countenance, and without a sigh or murmur Thomas Anderson, Iola's faithful and devoted friend, passed away, leaving the world so much poorer for her than it was before. Just then Dr. Gresham, the hospital physician, came to the bedside, felt for the pulse which would never throb again, and sat down in silence by the cot.

"What do you think, Doctor," said Iola, "has he fainted?"

"No," said the doctor, "poor fellow! he is dead."

Iola bowed her head in silent sorrow, and then relieved the anguish of her heart by a flood of tears. Robert rose, and sorrowfully left the room.

Iola, with tearful eyes and aching heart, clasped the cold hands over the still breast, closed the waxen lid over the eye which had once beamed with kindness or flashed with courage, and then went back, after the burial, to her daily round of duties, feeling the sad missing of something from her life.

# VIII

## The Mystified Doctor

Colonel," said Dr. Gresham to Col. Robinson, the commander of the post, "I am perfectly mystified by Miss Leroy."

"What is the matter with her?" asked Col. Robinson. "Is she not faithful to her duties and obedient to your directions?"

"Faithful is not the word to express her tireless energy and devotion to her work," responded Dr. Gresham. "She must have been a born nurse to put such enthusiasm into her work."

"Why, Doctor, what is the matter with you? You talk like a lover."

A faint flush rose to the cheek of Dr. Gresham as he smiled, and said, "Oh! come now, Colonel, can't a man praise a woman without being in love with her?"

"Of course he can," said Col. Robinson; "but I know where such admiration is apt to lead. I've been there myself. But, Doctor, had you not better defer your love-making till you're out of the woods?"

"I assure you, Colonel, I am not thinking of love or courtship. That is the business of the drawing-room, and not of the camp. But she did mystify me last night."

"How so?" asked Col. Robinson.

"When Tom was dying," responded the doctor, "I saw that beautiful and refined young lady bend over and kiss him. When she found that he was dead, she just cried as if her heart was breaking. Well, that was a new thing to me. I can eat with colored people, walk, talk, and fight with them, but kissing them is something I don't hanker after."

"And yet you saw Miss Leroy do it?"

"Yes; and that puzzles me. She is one of the most refined and lady-like women I ever saw. I hear she is a refugee, but she does not look like the other refugees who have come to our camp. Her accent is slightly Southern, but her manner is Northern. She is self-respecting without being supercilious; quiet, without being dull. Her voice is low and sweet, yet at times there are tones of such passionate tenderness in it that you would think some great sorrow has darkened and overshadowed her life. Without being the least gloomy, her face at times is pervaded by an air of inexpressible sadness. I sometimes watch her when she is not aware that I am looking at her, and it seems as if a whole volume was depicted on her countenance. When she smiles, there is a longing in her eyes which is never satisfied. I cannot understand how a Southern lady, whose education and manners stamp her as a woman of fine culture and good breeding, could consent to occupy the position she so faithfully holds. It is a mystery I cannot solve. Can you?"

"I think I can," answered Col. Robinson.

"Will you tell me?" queried the doctor.

"Yes, on one condition."

"What is it?"

"Everlasting silence."

"I promise," said the doctor. "The secret between us shall be as deep as the sea."

"She has not requested secrecy, but at present, for her sake, I do not wish the secret revealed. Miss Leroy was a slave."

"Oh, no," said Dr. Gresham, starting to his feet, "it can't be so! A woman as white as she a slave?"

"Yes, it is so," continued the Colonel. "In these States the child follows the condition of its mother. This beautiful and accomplished girl was held by one of the worst Rebels in town. Tom told me of it and I issued orders for her release."

"Well, well! Is that so?" said Dr. Gresham, thoughtfully stroking his beard. "Wonders will never cease. Why, I was just beginning to think seriously of her."

"What's to hinder your continuing to think?" asked Col. Robinson.

"What you tell me changes the whole complexion of affairs," replied the doctor.

"If that be so I am glad I told you before you got head over heels in love."

"Yes," said Dr. Gresham, absently.

Dr. Gresham was a member of a wealthy and aristocratic family, proud of its lineage, which it could trace through generations of good blood to its ancestral isle. He had become deeply interested in Iola before he had heard her story, but after it had been revealed to him he tried to banish her from his mind; but his constant observation of her only increased his interest and admiration. The deep pathos of her story, the tenderness of her ministrations, bestowed alike on black and white, and the sad loneliness of her condition, awakened within him a desire to defend and protect her all through her future life. The fierce clashing of war had not taken all the romance out of his nature. In Iola he saw realized his ideal of the woman whom he was willing to marry. A woman, tender, strong, and courageous, and rescued only by the strong arm of his Government from a fate worse than death. She was young in years, but old in sorrow; one whom a sad destiny had changed from a light-hearted girl to a heroic woman. As he observed her, he detected an undertone of sorrow in her most cheerful words, and observed a quick flushing and sudden paling of her cheek, as if she were living over scenes that were thrilling her soul with indignation or chilling her heart with horror. As nurse and physician, Iola and Dr. Gresham were constantly thrown together. His friends sent him magazines and books, which he gladly shared with her. The hospital was a sad place. Mangled forms, stricken down in the flush of their prime and energy; pale young corpses, sacrificed on the altar of slavery, constantly drained on her sympathies. Dr. Gresham was glad to have some reading matter which might divert her mind from the memories of her mournful past, and also furnish them both with interesting themes of conversation in their moments of relaxation from the harrowing scenes through which they were constantly passing. Without any effort or consciousness on her part, his friendship ripened into love. To him her presence was a pleasure, her absence a privation; and her loneliness drew deeply upon his sympathy. He would have merited his own self-contempt if, by word or deed, he had done anything to take advantage of her situation. All the manhood and chivalry of his nature rose in her behalf, and, after carefully revolving the matter, he resolved to win her for his bride, bury her secret in his Northern home, and hide from his aristocratic relations all knowledge of her mournful past. One day he said to Iola:—

"This hospital life is telling on you. Your strength is failing, and although you possess a wonderful amount of physical endurance, you must not forget that saints have bodies and dwell in tabernacles of clay, just the same as we common mortals."

"Compliments aside," she said, smiling; "what are you driving at, Doctor?"

"I mean," he replied, "that you are running down, and if you do not quit and take some rest you will be our patient instead of our nurse. You'd better take a furlough, go North, and return after the first frost."

"Doctor, if that is your only remedy," replied Iola, "I am afraid that I am destined to die at my post. I have no special friends in the North, and no home but this in the South. I am homeless and alone."

There was something so sad, almost despairing in her tones, in the drooping of her head, and the quivering of her lip, that they stirred Dr. Gresham's heart with sudden pity, and, drawing nearer to her, he said, "Miss Leroy, you need not be all alone. Let me claim the privilege of making your life bright and happy. Iola, I have loved you ever since I have seen your devotion to our poor, sick boys. How faithfully you, a young and gracious girl, have stood at your post and performed your duties. And now I ask, will you not permit me to clasp hands with you for life? I do not ask for a hasty reply. Give yourself time to think over what I have proposed."

# IX

## Eugene Leroy and Alfred Lorraine

Nearly twenty years before the war, two young men, of French and Spanish descent, sat conversing on a large verandah which surrounded an ancient home on the Mississippi River. It was French in its style of architecture, large and rambling, with no hint of modern improvements.

The owner of the house was the only heir of a Creole planter. He had come into possession of an inheritance consisting of vast baronial estates, bank stock, and a large number of slaves. Eugene Leroy, being deprived of his parents, was left, at an early age, to the care of a distant relative, who had sent him to school and college, and who occasionally invited him to spend his vacations at his home. But Eugene generally declined his invitations, as he preferred spending his vacations at the watering places in the North, with their fashionable and not always innocent gayeties. Young, vivacious, impulsive, and undisciplined, without the restraining influence of a mother's love or the guidance of a father's hand, Leroy found himself, when his college days were over, in the dangerous position of a young man with vast possessions, abundant leisure, unsettled principles, and uncontrolled desires. He had no other object than to extract from life its most seductive draughts of ease and pleasure. His companion, who sat opposite him on the verandah, quietly smoking a cigar, was a remote cousin, a few years older than himself, the warmth of whose Southern temperament had been modified by an infusion of Northern blood.

Eugene was careless, liberal, and impatient of details, while his companion and cousin, Alfred Lorraine, was selfish, eager, keen, and alert; also hard, cold, methodical, and ever ready to grasp the main chance. Yet, notwithstanding the difference between them, they had formed a warm friendship for each other.

"Alfred," said Eugene, "I am going to be married."

Lorraine opened his eyes with sudden wonder, and exclaimed: "Well, that's the latest thing out! Who is the fortunate lady who has bound you with her silken fetters? Is it one of those beautiful Creole girls who were visiting Augustine's plantation last winter? I watched you during our visit there and thought that you could not be proof against their attractions. Which is your choice? It would puzzle me to judge between the two. They had splendid eyes, dark, luminous, and languishing; lovely complexions and magnificent hair. Both were delightful in their manners, refined and cultured, with an air of vivacity mingled with their repose of manner which was perfectly charming. As the law only allows us one, which is your choice? Miss Annette has more force than her sister, and if I could afford the luxury of a wife she would be my choice."

"Ah, Alf," said Eugene, "I see that you are a practical business man. In marrying you want a wife to assist you as an efficient plantation mistress. One who would tolerate no waste in the kitchen and no disorder in the parlor."

"Exactly so," responded Lorraine; "I am too poor to marry a mere parlor ornament. You can afford to do it; I cannot."

"Nonsense, if I were as poor as a church mouse I would marry the woman I love."

"Very fine sentiments," said Lorraine, "and were I as rich as you I would indulge in them also. You know, when my father died I had great expectations. We had always lived in good style, and I never thought for a moment he was not a rich man, but when his estate was settled I found it was greatly involved, and I was forced to face an uncertain future, with scarcely a dollar to call my own. Land, negroes, cattle, and horses all went under the hammer. The only thing I retained was the education I received at the North; that was my father's best investment, and all my stock in trade. With that only as an outfit, it would be madness for me to think of marrying one of those lovely girls. They remind me of beautiful canary birds, charming and pretty, but not fitted for the wear and tear of plantation life. Well, which is your choice?"

"Neither," replied Eugene.

"Then, is it that magnificent looking widow from New Orleans, whom we met before you had that terrible spell of sickness and to whom you appeared so devoted?"

"Not at all. I have not heard from her since that summer. She was fascinating and handsome, but fearfully high strung."

"Were you afraid of her?"

"No; but I valued my happiness too much to trust it in her hands."

"Sour grapes!" said Lorraine.

"No! but I think that slavery and the lack of outside interests are beginning to tell on the lives of our women. They lean too much on their slaves, have too much irresponsible power in their hands, are narrowed and compressed by the routine of plantation life and the lack of intellectual stimulus."

"Yes, Eugene, when I see what other women are doing in the fields of literature and art, I cannot help thinking an amount of brain power has been held in check among us. Yet I cannot abide those Northern women, with their suffrage views and abolition cant. They just shock me."

"But your mother was a Northern woman," said Eugene.

"Yes; but she got bravely over her Northern ideas. As I remember her, she was just as much a Southerner as if she had been to the manor born. She came here as a school-teacher, but soon after she came she married my father. He was easy and indulgent with his servants, and held them with a very loose rein. But my mother was firm and energetic. She made the niggers move around. No shirking nor dawdling with her. When my father died, she took matters in hand, but she only outlived him a few months. If she had lived I believe that she would have retrieved our fortune. I know that she had more executive ability than my father. He was very squeamish about selling his servants, but she would have put every one of them in her pocket before permitting them to eat her out of house and home. But whom *are* you going to marry?"

"A young lady who graduates from a Northern seminary next week," responded Eugene.

"I think you are very selfish," said Lorraine. "You might have invited a fellow to go with you to be your best man."

"The wedding is to be strictly private. The lady whom I am to marry has negro blood in her veins."

"The devil she has!" exclaimed Lorraine, starting to his feet, and looking incredulously on the face of Leroy. "Are you in earnest? Surely you must be jesting."

"I am certainly in earnest," answered Eugene Leroy. "I mean every word I say."

"Oh, it can't be possible! Are you mad?" exclaimed Lorraine.

"Never was saner in my life."

"What under heaven could have possessed you to do such a foolish thing? Where did she come from."

"Right here, on this plantation. But I have educated and manumitted her, and I intend marrying her."

"Why, Eugene, it is impossible that you can have an idea of marrying one of your slaves. Why, man, she is your property, to have and to hold to all intents and purposes. Are you not satisfied with the power and possession the law gives you?"

"No. Although the law makes her helpless in my hands, to me her defenselessness is her best defense."

"Eugene, we have known each other all of our lives, and, although I have always regarded you as eccentric, I never saw you so completely off your balance before. The idea of you, with your proud family name, your vast wealth in land and negroes, intending to marry one of them, is a mystery I cannot solve. Do explain to me why you are going to take this extremely strange and foolish step."

"You never saw Marie?"

"No; and I don't want to."

"She is very beautiful. In the North no one would suspect that she has one drop of negro blood in her veins, but here, where I am known, to marry her is to lose caste. I could live with her, and not incur much if any social opprobrium. Society would wink at the transgression, even if after she had become the mother of my children I should cast her off and send her and them to the auction block."

"Men," replied Lorraine, "would merely shrug their shoulders; women would say you had been sowing your wild oats. Your money, like charity, would cover a multitude of faults."

"But if I make her my lawful wife and recognize her children as my legitimate heirs, I subject myself to social ostracism and a senseless persecution. We Americans boast of freedom, and yet here is a woman whom I love as I never loved any other human being, but both law and public opinion debar me from following the inclination of my heart. She is beautiful, faithful, and pure, and yet all that society will tolerate is what I would scorn to do."

"But has not society the right to guard the purity of its blood by the rigid exclusion of an alien race?"

"Excluding it! How?" asked Eugene.

"By debarring it from social intercourse."

"Perhaps it has," continued Eugene, "but should not society have a greater ban for those who, by consorting with an alien race, rob their offspring of a right to their names and to an inheritance in their property, and who fix their social status among an enslaved and outcast race? Don't eye me so curiously; I am not losing my senses."

"I think you have done that already," said Lorraine. "Don't you know that if she is as fair as a lily, beautiful as a houri, and chaste as ice, that still she is a negro?"

"Oh, come now; she isn't much of a negro."

"It doesn't matter, however. One drop of negro blood in her veins curses all the rest."

"I know it," said Eugene, sadly, "but I have weighed the consequences, and am prepared to take them."

"Well, Eugene, your course is *so* singular! I do wish that you would tell me why you take this unprecedented step?"

Eugene laid aside his cigar, looked thoughtfully at Lorraine, and said, "Well, Alfred, as we are kinsmen and life-long friends, I will not resent your asking my reason for doing that which seems to you the climax of absurdity, and if you will have the patience to listen I will tell you."

"Proceed, I am all attention."

"My father died," said Eugene, "as you know, when I was too young to know his loss or feel his care and, being an only child, I was petted and spoiled. I grew up to be wayward, self-indulgent, proud, and imperious. I went from home and made many friends both at college and in foreign lands. I was well supplied with money and, never having been forced to earn it, was ignorant of its value and careless of its use. My lavish expenditures and liberal benefactions attracted to me a number of parasites, and men older than myself led me into the paths of vice, and taught me how to gather the flowers of sin which blossom around the borders of hell. In a word, I left my home unwarned and unarmed against the seductions of vice. I returned an initiated devotee to debasing pleasures. Years of my life were passed in foreign lands; years in which my soul slumbered and seemed pervaded with a moral paralysis; years, the memory of which fills my soul with sorrow and shame. I went to the capitals of the old world to see life, but in seeing life I became acquainted with death, the death of true manliness and self-respect. You look astonished; but I tell you, Alf, there is many a poor clod-hopper, on whom are the dust and grime of unremitting toil, who feels more self-respect and true manliness than many of us with our family prestige, social position, and proud ancestral halls. After I had lived abroad for years, I returned a broken-down young man, prematurely old, my constitution a perfect wreck. A life of folly and dissipation was telling fearfully upon me. My friends shrank from me in dismay. I was sick nigh unto death, and had it not been for Marie's care I am certain that I should have died. She followed me down to the borders of the grave, and won me back to life and health. I was slow in recovering and, during the time, I had ample space for reflection, and the past unrolled itself before me. I resolved, over the wreck and ruin of my past life, to build a better and brighter future. Marie had a voice of remarkable sweetness, although it lacked culture. Often when I was nervous and restless I would have her sing some of those weird and plaintive melodies which she had learned from the plantation negroes. Sometimes I encouraged her to talk, and I was surprised at the native vigor of her intellect. By degrees I became acquainted with her history. She was all alone in the world. She had no recollection of her father, but remembered being torn from her mother while clinging to her dress. The trader who bought her mother did not wish to buy her. She remembered having a brother, with whom she used to play, but she had been separated from him also, and since then had lost all trace of them. After she was sold from her mother she became the property of an excellent old lady, who seems to have been very careful to imbue her mind with good principles; a woman who loved purity, not only for her own daughters, but also for the defenseless girls in her home. I believe it was the lady's intention to have freed Marie at her death, but she died suddenly, and, the estate being involved, she was sold with it and fell into the hands of my agent. I became deeply interested in her when I heard her story, and began to pity her."

"And I suppose love sprang from pity."

"I not only pitied her, but I learned to respect her. I had met with beautiful women in the halls of wealth and fashion, both at home and abroad, but there was something in her different from all my experience of womanhood."

"I should think so," said Lorraine, with a sneer; "but I should like to know what it was."

"It was something such as I have seen in old cathedrals, lighting up the beauty of a saintly face. A light which the poet tells was never seen on land or sea. I thought of this beautiful and defenseless girl adrift in the power of a reckless man, who, with all the advantages of wealth and education, had trailed his manhood in the dust, and she, with simple, childlike faith in the Unseen, seemed to be so good and pure that she commanded my respect and won my heart. In her presence every base and unholy passion died, subdued by the supremacy of her virtue."

"Why, Eugene, what has come over you? Talking of the virtue of these quadroon girls! You have lived so long in the North and abroad, that you seem to have lost the cue of our Southern life. Don't you know that these beautiful girls have been the curse of our homes? You have no idea of the hearts which are wrung by their presence."

"But, Alfred, suppose it is so. Are they to blame for it? What can any woman do when she is placed in the hands of an irresponsible master; when she knows that resistance is vain? Yes, Alfred, I agree with you, these women are the bane of our Southern civilization; but they are the victims and we are the criminals."

"I think from the airs that some of them put on when they get a chance, that they are very willing victims."

"So much the worse for our institution. If it is cruel to debase a hapless victim, it is an increase of cruelty to make her contented with her degradation. Let me tell you, Alf, you cannot wrong or degrade a woman without wronging or degrading yourself."

"What is the matter with you, Eugene? Are you thinking of taking priest's orders?"

"No, Alf," said Eugene, rising and rapidly pacing the floor, "you may defend the system as much as you please, but you cannot deny that the circumstances it creates, and the temptations it affords, are sapping our strength and undermining our character."

"That may be true," said Lorraine, somewhat irritably, "but you had better be careful how you air your Northern notions in public."

"Why so?"

"Because public opinion is too sensitive to tolerate any such discussions."

"And is not that a proof that we are at fault with respect to our institutions?"

"I don't know. I only know we are living in the midst of a magazine of powder, and it is not safe to enter it with a lighted candle."

"Let me proceed with my story," continued Eugene. "During the long months in which I was convalescing, I was left almost entirely to the companionship of Marie. In my library I found a Bible, which I began to read from curiosity, but my curiosity deepened into interest when I saw the rapt expression on Marie's face. I saw in it a loving response to sentiments to which I was a stranger. In the meantime my conscience was awakened, and I scorned to take advantage of her defenselessness. I felt that I owed my life to her faithful care, and I resolved to take her North, manumit, educate, and marry her. I sent her to a Northern academy, but as soon as some of the pupils found that she was colored, objections were raised, and the principal was compelled to dismiss her. During my search for a school I heard of one where three girls of mixed blood were pursuing their studies, every one of whom would have been ignominiously dismissed had their connection with the negro race been known. But I determined to run no risks. I found a school where her connection with the negro race would be no bar to her advancement. She graduates next week, and I intend to marry her before I return home. She was faithful when others were faithless, stood by me when others deserted me to die in loneliness and neglect, and now I am about to reward her care with all the love and devotion it is in my power to bestow. That is why I am about to marry my faithful and devoted nurse, who snatched me from the jaws of death. Now that I have told you my story, what say you?"

"Madness and folly inconceivable!" exclaimed Lorraine.

"What to you is madness and folly is perfect sanity with me. After all, Alf, is there not an amount of unreason in our prejudices?"

"That may be true; but I wasn't reasoned into it, and I do not expect to be reasoned out of it."

"Will you accompany me North?"

"No; except to put you in an insane asylum. You are the greatest crank out," said Lorraine, thoroughly disgusted.

"No, thank you; I'm all right. I expect to start North tomorrow. You had better come and go."

"I would rather follow you to your grave," replied Lorraine, hotly, while an expression of ineffable scorn passed over his cold, proud face.

# X

## Shadows in the Home

On the next morning after this conversation Leroy left for the North, to attend the commencement and witness the graduation of his ward. Arriving in Ohio, he immediately repaired to the academy and inquired for the principal. He was shown into the reception-room, and in a few moments the principal entered.

"Good morning," said Leroy, rising and advancing towards him; "how is my ward this morning?"

"She is well, and has been expecting you. I am glad you came in time for the commencement. She stands among the foremost in her class."

"I am glad to hear it. Will you send her this?" said Leroy, handing the principal a card. The principal took the card and immediately left the room.

Very soon Leroy heard a light step, and looking up he saw a radiantly beautiful woman approaching him.

"Good morning, Marie," he said, greeting her cordially, and gazing upon her with unfeigned admiration. "You are looking very handsome this morning."

"Do you think so?" she asked, smiling and blushing. "I am glad you are not disappointed; that you do not feel your money has been spent in vain."

"Oh, no, what I have spent on your education has been the best investment I ever made."

"I hope," said Marie, "you may always find it so. But Mas—"

"Hush!" said Leroy, laying his hand playfully on her lips; "you are free. I don't want the dialect of slavery to linger on your lips. You must not call me that name again."

"Why not?"

"Because I have a nearer and dearer one by which I wish to be called."

Leroy drew her nearer, and whispered in her ear a single word. She started, trembled with emotion, grew pale, and blushed painfully. An awkward silence ensued, when Leroy, pressing her hand, exclaimed: "This is the hand that plucked me from the grave, and I am going to retain it as mine; mine to guard with my care until death us do part."

Leroy looked earnestly into her eyes, which fell beneath his ardent gaze. With admirable self-control, while a great joy was thrilling her heart, she bowed her beautiful head and softly repeated, "Until death us do part."

Leroy knew Southern society too well to expect it to condone his offense against its social customs, or give the least recognition to his wife, however cultured, refined, and charming she might be, if it were known that she had the least infusion of negro blood in her veins. But he was brave enough to face the consequences of his alliance, and marry the woman who was the choice of his heart, and on whom his affections were centred.

After Leroy had left the room, Marie sat awhile thinking of the wonderful change that had come over her. Instead of being a lonely slave girl, with the fatal dower of beauty, liable to be bought and sold, exchanged, and bartered, she was to be the wife of a wealthy planter; a man in whose honor she could confide, and on whose love she could lean.

Very interesting and pleasant were the commencement exercises in which Marie bore an important part. To enlist sympathy for her enslaved race, and appear to advantage before Leroy, had aroused all of her energies. The stimulus of hope, the manly love which was environing her life, brightened her eye and lit up the wonderful beauty of her countenance. During her stay in the North she had constantly been brought in contact with anti-slavery people. She was not aware that there was so much kindness among the white people of the country until she had tested it in the North. From the anti-slavery people in private life she had learned some of the noblest lessons of freedom and justice, and had become imbued with their sentiments. Her theme was "American Civilization, its Lights and Shadows."

Graphically she portrayed the lights, faithfully she showed the shadows of our American civilization. Earnestly and feelingly she spoke of the blind Sampson in our land, who might yet shake the pillars of our great Commonwealth. Leroy listened attentively. At times a shadow of annoyance would overspread his face, but it was soon lost in the admiration her earnestness and zeal inspired. Like Esther pleading for the lives of her people in the Oriental courts of a despotic king, she stood before the audience, pleading for those whose lips were sealed, but whose condition appealed to the mercy and justice of the Nation. Strong men wiped the moisture from their eyes, and women's hearts throbbed in unison with the strong, brave words that were uttered in behalf of freedom for all and chains for none. Generous applause was freely bestowed, and beautiful bouquets were showered upon her. When it was known that she was to be the wife of her guardian, warm congratulations were given, and earnest hopes expressed for the welfare of the lonely girl, who, nearly all her life, had been deprived of a parent's love and care. On the eve of starting South Leroy procured a license, and united his destiny with the young lady whose devotion in the darkest hour had won his love and gratitude.

In a few days Marie returned as mistress to the plantation from which she had gone as a slave. But as unholy alliances were common in those days between masters and slaves, no one took especial notice that Marie shared Leroy's life as mistress of his home, and that the family silver and jewelry were in her possession. But Leroy, happy in his choice, attended to the interests of his plantation, and found companionship in his books and in the society of his wife. A few male companions visited him occasionally, admired the magnificent beauty of his wife, shook their heads, and spoke of him as being very eccentric, but thought his marriage the great mistake of his life. But none of his female friends ever entered his doors, when it became known that Marie held the position of mistress of his mansion, and presided at his table. But she, sheltered in the warm clasp of loving arms, found her life like a joyous dream.

Into that quiet and beautiful home three children were born, unconscious of the doom suspended over their heads.

"Oh, how glad I am," Marie would often say, "that these children are free. I could never understand how a cultured white man could have his own children enslaved. I can understand how savages, fighting with each other, could doom their vanquished foes to slavery, but it has always been a puzzle to me how a civilized man could drag his own children, bone of his bone, flesh of his flesh, down to the position of social outcasts, abject slaves, and political pariahs."

"But, Marie," said Eugene, "all men do not treat their illegitimate children in the manner you describe. The last time I was in New Orleans I met Henri Augustine at the depot, with two beautiful young girls. At first I thought that they were his own children, they resembled him so closely. But afterwards I noticed that they addressed him as 'Mister.' Before we parted he told me that his wife had taken such a dislike to their mother that she could not bear to see them on the place. At last, weary of her dissatisfaction, he had promised to bring them to New Orleans and sell them. Instead, he was going to Ohio to give them their freedom, and make provision for their future."

"What a wrong!" said Marie.

"Who was wronged?" said Leroy, in astonishment.

"Every one in the whole transaction," answered Marie. "Your friend wronged himself by sinning against his own soul. He wronged his wife by arousing her hatred and jealousy through his unfaithfulness. He wronged those children by giving them the *status* of slaves and outcasts. He wronged their mother by imposing upon her the burdens and cares of maternity without the rights and privileges of a wife. He made her crown of motherhood a circlet of shame. Under other circumstances she might have been an honored wife and happy mother. And I do think such men wrong their own legitimate children by transmitting to them a weakened moral fibre."

"Oh, Marie, you have such an uncomfortable way of putting things. You make me feel that we have done those things which we ought not to have done, and have left undone those things which we ought to have done."

"If it annoys you," said Marie, "I will stop talking."

"Oh, no, go on," said Leroy, carelessly; and then he continued more thoughtfully, "I know a number of men who have sent such children North, and manumitted, educated, and left them valuable legacies. We are all liable to err, and, having done wrong, all we can do is to make reparation."

"My dear husband, this is a wrong where reparation is impossible. Neither wealth nor education can repair the wrong of a dishonored birth. There are a number of slaves in this section who are servants to their own brothers and sisters; whose fathers have robbed them not simply of liberty but of the right of being well born. Do you think these things will last forever?"

"I suppose not. There are some prophets of evil who tell us that the Union is going to dissolve. But I know it would puzzle their brains to tell where the crack will begin. I reckon we'll continue to jog along as usual. 'Cotton fights, and cotton conquers for American slavery.'"

Even while Leroy dreamed of safety the earthquake was cradling its fire; the ground was growing hollow beneath his tread; but his ear was too dull to catch the sound; his vision too blurred to read the signs of the times.

"Marie," said Leroy, taking up the thread of the discourse, "slavery is a sword that cuts both ways. If it wrongs the negro, it also curses the white man. But we are in it, and what can we do?"

"Get out of it as quickly as possible."

"That is easier said than done. I would willingly free every slave on my plantation if I could do so without expatriating them. Some of them have wives and children on other plantations, and to free them is to separate them from their kith and kin. To let them remain here as a free people is out of the question. My hands are tied by law and custom."

"Who tied them?" asked Marie.

"A public opinion, whose meshes I cannot break. If the negro is the thrall of his master, we are just as much the thralls of public opinion."

"Why do you not battle against public opinion, if you think it is wrong?"

"Because I have neither the courage of a martyr, nor the faith of a saint; and so I drift along, trying to make the condition of our slaves as comfortable as I possibly can. I believe there are slaves on this plantation whom the most flattering offers of freedom would not entice away."

"I do not think," said Marie, "that some of you planters understand your own slaves. Lying is said to be the vice of slaves. The more intelligent of them have so learned to veil their feelings that you do not see the undercurrent of discontent beneath their apparent good humor and jollity. The more discontented they are, the more I respect them. To me a contented slave is an abject creature. I hope that I shall see the day when there will not be a slave in the land. I hate the whole thing from the bottom of my heart."

"Marie, your Northern education has unfitted you for Southern life. You are free, yourself, and so are our children. Why not let well enough alone?"

"Because I love liberty, not only for myself but for every human being. Think how dear these children are to me; and then for the thought to be forever haunting me, that if you were dead they could be turned out of doors and divided among your relatives. I sometimes lie awake at night thinking of how there might be a screw loose somewhere, and, after all, the children and I might be reduced to slavery."

"Marie, what in the world is the matter with you? Have you had a presentiment of my death, or, as Uncle Jack says, 'hab you seed it in a vision?'"

"No, but I have had such sad forebodings that they almost set me wild. One night I dreamt that you were dead; that the lawyers entered the house, seized our property, and remanded us to slavery. I never can be satisfied in the South with such a possibility hanging over my head."

"Marie, dear, you are growing nervous. Your imagination is too active. You are left too much alone on this plantation. I hope that for your own and the children's sake I will be enabled to arrange our affairs so as to find a home for you where you will not be doomed to the social isolation and ostracism that surround you here."

"I don't mind the isolation for myself, but the children. You have enjoined silence on me with respect to their connection with the negro race, but I do not think we can conceal it from them very long. It will not be long before Iola will notice the offishness of girls of her own age, and the scornful glances which, even now, I think, are leveled at her. Yesterday Harry came crying to me, and told me that one of the neighbor's boys had called him 'nigger.'"

A shadow flitted over Leroy's face, as he answered, somewhat soberly, "Oh, Marie, do not meet trouble half way. I have manumitted you, and the children will follow your condition. I have made you all legatees of my will. Except my cousin, Alfred Lorraine, I have only distant relatives, whom I scarcely know and who hardly know me."

"Your cousin Lorraine? Are you sure our interests would be safe in his hands?"

"I think so; I don't think Alfred would do anything dishonorable."

"He might not with his equals. But how many men would be bound by a sense of honor where the rights of a colored woman are in question? Your cousin was bitterly opposed to our marriage, and I would not trust any important interests in his hands. I do hope that in providing for our future you will make assurance doubly sure."

"I certainly will, and all that human foresight can do shall be done for you and our children."

"Oh," said Marie, pressing to her heart a beautiful child of six summers, "I think it would almost make me turn over in my grave to know that every grace and charm which this child possesses would only be so much added to her value as an article of merchandise."

As Marie released the child from her arms she looked wonderingly into her mother's face and clung closely to her, as if to find refuge from some unseen evil. Leroy noticed this, and sighed unconsciously, as an expression of pain flitted over his face.

"Now, Marie," he continued, "stop tormenting yourself with useless fears. Although, with all her faults, I still love the South, I will make arrangements either to live North or go to France. There life will be brighter for us all. Now, Marie, seat yourself at the piano and sing:—

> 'Sing me the songs that to me were so dear,
> Long, long ago.
> Sing me the songs I delighted to hear,
> Long, long ago."

As Marie sang the anxiety faded from her face, a sense of security stole over her, and she sat among her loved ones a happy wife and mother. What if no one recognized her on that lonely plantation! Her world was, nevertheless, there. The love and devotion of her husband brightened every avenue of her life, while her children filled her home with music, mirth, and sunshine.

Marie had undertaken their education, but she could not give them the culture which comes from the attrition of thought, and from contact with the ideas of others. Since her school-days she had read extensively and thought much, and in solitude her thoughts had ripened. But for her children there were no companions except the young slaves of the plantation, and she dreaded the effect of such intercourse upon their lives and characters.

Leroy had always been especially careful to conceal from his children the knowledge of their connection with the negro race. To Marie this silence was oppressive.

One day she said to him, "I see no other way of finishing the education of these children than by sending them to some Northern school."

"I have come," said Leroy, "to the same conclusion. We had better take Iola and Harry North and make arrangements for them to spend several years in being educated. Riches take wings to themselves and fly away, but a good education is an investment on which the law can place no attachment. As there is a possibility of their origin being discovered, I will find a teacher to whom I can confide our story, and upon whom I can enjoin secrecy. I want them well fitted for any emergency in life. When I discover for what they have the most aptitude I will give them especial training in that direction."

A troubled look passed over the face of Marie, as she hesitatingly

FRANCES ELLEN WATKINS HARPER

said: "I am so afraid that you will regret our marriage when you fully realize the complications it brings."

"No, no," said Leroy, tenderly, "it is not that I regret our marriage, or feel the least disdain for our children on account of the blood in their veins; but I do not wish them to grow up under the contracting influence of this race prejudice. I do not wish them to feel that they have been born under a proscription from which no valor can redeem them, nor that any social advancement or individual development can wipe off the ban which clings to them. No, Marie, let them go North, learn all they can, aspire all they may. The painful knowledge will come all too soon. Do not forestall it. I want them simply to grow up as other children; not being patronized by friends nor disdained by foes."

"My dear husband, you may be perfectly right, but are you not preparing our children for a fearful awakening? Are you not acting on the plan, 'After me the deluge?'"

"Not at all, Marie. I want our children to grow up without having their self-respect crushed in the bud. You know that the North is not free from racial prejudice."

"I know it," said Marie, sadly, "and I think one of the great mistakes of our civilization is that which makes color, and not character, a social test."

"I think so, too," said Leroy. "The strongest men and women of a down-trodden race may bare their bosoms to an adverse fate and develop courage in the midst of opposition, but we have no right to subject our children to such crucial tests before their characters are formed. For years, when I lived abroad, I had an opportunity to see and hear of men of African descent who had distinguished themselves and obtained a recognition in European circles, which they never could have gained in this country. I now recall the name of Ira Aldridge, a colored man from New York City, who was covered with princely honors as a successful tragedian. Alexander Dumas was not forced to conceal his origin to succeed as a novelist. When I was in St. Petersburg I was shown the works of Alexander Sergevitch, a Russian poet, who was spoken of as the Byron of Russian literature, and reckoned one of the finest poets that Russia has produced in this century. He was also a prominent figure in fashionable society, and yet he was of African lineage. One of his paternal ancestors was a negro who had been ennobled by Peter the Great. I can't help contrasting the recognition which these men had received with the treatment which has been given to Frederick

Douglass and other intelligent colored men in this country. With me the wonder is not that they have achieved so little, but that they have accomplished so much. No, Marie, we will have our children educated without being subjected to the depressing influences of caste feeling. Perhaps by the time their education is finished I will be ready to wind up my affairs and take them abroad, where merit and ability will give them entrance into the best circles of art, literature, and science."

After this conversation Leroy and his wife went North, and succeeded in finding a good school for their children. In a private interview he confided to the principal the story of the cross in their blood, and, finding him apparently free from racial prejudice, he gladly left the children in his care. Gracie, the youngest child, remained at home, and her mother spared no pains to fit her for the seminary against the time her sister should have finished her education.

# XI

## THE PLAGUE AND THE LAW

Years passed, bringing no special change to the life of Leroy and his wife. Shut out from the busy world, its social cares and anxieties, Marie's life flowed peacefully on. Although removed by the protecting care of Leroy from the condition of servitude, she still retained a deep sympathy for the enslaved, and was ever ready to devise plans to ameliorate their condition.

Leroy, although in the midst of slavery, did not believe in the rightfulness of the institution. He was in favor of gradual emancipation, which would prepare both master and slave for a moral adaptation to the new conditions of freedom. While he was willing to have the old rivets taken out of slavery, politicians and planters were devising plans to put in new screws. He was desirous of having it ended in the States; they were clamorous to have it established in the Territories.

But so strong was the force of habit, combined with the feebleness of his moral resistance and the nature of his environment, that instead of being an athlete, armed for a glorious strife, he had learned to drift where he should have steered, to float with the current instead of nobly breasting the tide. He conducted his plantation with as much lenity as it was possible to infuse into a system darkened with the shadow of a million crimes.

Leroy had always been especially careful not to allow his children to spend their vacations at home. He and Marie generally spent that time with them at some summer resort.

"I would like," said Marie, one day, "to have our children spend their vacations at home. Those summer resorts are pleasant, yet, after all, there is no place like home. But," and her voice became tremulous, "our children would now notice their social isolation and inquire the cause." A faint sigh arose to the lips of Leroy, as she added: "Man is a social being; I've known it to my sorrow."

There was a tone of sadness in Leroy's voice, as he replied: "Yes, Marie, let them stay North. We seem to be entering on a period fraught with great danger. I cannot help thinking and fearing that we are on the eve of a civil war."

"A civil war!" exclaimed Marie, with an air of astonishment. "A civil war about what?"

"Why, Marie, the thing looks to me so wild and foolish I hardly know how to explain. But some of our leading men have come to the conclusion that North and South had better separate, and instead of having one to have two independent governments. The spirit of secession is rampant in the land. I do not know what the result will be, and I fear it will bode no good to the country. Between the fire-eating Southerners and the meddling Abolitionists we are about to be plunged into a great deal of trouble. I fear there are breakers ahead. The South is dissatisfied with the state of public opinion in the North. We are realizing that we are two peoples in the midst of one nation. William H. Seward has proclaimed that the conflict between freedom and slavery is irrepressible, and that the country cannot remain half free and half slave."

"How will *you* go?" asked Marie.

"My heart is with the Union. I don't believe in secession. There has been no cause sufficient to justify a rupture. The North has met us time and again in the spirit of concession and compromise. When we wanted the continuance of the African slave trade the North conceded that we should have twenty years of slave-trading for the benefit of our plantations. When we wanted more territory she conceded to our desires and gave us land enough to carve out four States, and there yet remains enough for four more. When we wanted power to recapture our slaves when they fled North for refuge, Daniel Webster told Northerners to conquer their prejudices, and they gave us the whole Northern States as a hunting ground for our slaves. The Presidential chair has been filled the greater number of years by Southerners, and the majority of offices has been shared by our men. We wanted representation in Congress on a basis which would include our slaves, and the North, whose suffrage represents only men, gave us a three-fifths representation for our slaves, whom we count as property. I think the step will be suicidal. There are extremists in both sections, but I hope, between them both, wise counsels and measures will prevail."

Just then Alfred Lorraine was ushered into the room. Occasionally he visited Leroy, but he always came alone. His wife was the only daughter of an enterprising slave-trader, who had left her a large amount of property.

Her social training was deficient, her education limited, but she was too proud of being a pure white woman to enter the home of Leroy, with Marie as its presiding genius. Lorraine tolerated Marie's presence as a necessary evil, while to her he always seemed like a presentiment of trouble. With his coming a shadow fell upon her home, hushing its music and darkening its sunshine. A sense of dread oppressed her. There came into her soul an intuitive feeling that somehow his coming was fraught with danger. When not peering around she would often catch his eyes bent on her with a baleful expression.

Leroy and his cousin immediately fell into a discussion on the condition of the country. Lorraine was a rank Secessionist, ready to adopt the most extreme measures of the leaders of the movement, even to the reopening of the slave trade. Leroy thought a dissolution of the Union would involve a fearful expenditure of blood and treasure for which, before the eyes of the world, there could be no justification. The debate lasted late into the night, leaving both Lorraine and Leroy just as set in their opinions as they were before they began. Marie listened attentively awhile, then excused herself and withdrew.

After Lorraine had gone Marie said: "There is something about your cousin that fills me with nameless dread. I always feel when he enters the room as if some one were walking over my grave. I do wish he would stay at home."

"I wish so, too, since he disturbs you. But, Marie, you are growing nervous. How cold your hands are. Don't you feel well?"

"Oh, yes; I am only a little faint. I wish he would never come. But, as he does, I must make the best of it."

"Yes, Marie, treat him well for my sake. He is the only relative I have who ever darkens our doors."

"I have no faith in his friendship for either myself or my children. I feel that while he makes himself agreeable to you he hates me from the bottom of his heart, and would do anything to get me out of the way. Oh, I am *so* glad I am your lawful wife, and that you married me before you brought me back to this State! I believe that if you were gone he wouldn't have the least scruple against trying to prove our marriage invalid and remanding us to slavery."

Leroy looked anxiously and soberly at his wife, and said: "Marie, I do not think so. Your life is too lonely here. Write your orders to New Orleans, get what you need for the journey, and let us spend the summer somewhere in the North."

Just then Marie's attention was drawn to some household matters, and it was a short time before she returned.

"Tom," continued Leroy, "has just brought the mail, and here is a letter from Iola."

Marie noticed that he looked quite sober as he read, and that an expression of vexation was lingering on his lips.

"What is the matter?" asked Marie.

"Nothing much; only a tempest in a teapot. The presence of a colored girl in Mr. Galen's school has caused a breeze of excitement. You know Mr. Galen is quite an Abolitionist, and, being true to his principles, he could not consistently refuse when a colored woman applied for her daughter's admission. Of course, when he took her he was compelled to treat her as any other pupil. In so doing he has given mortal offense to the mother of two Southern boys. She has threatened to take them away if the colored girl remains."

"What will he do about it?" asked Marie, thoughtfully.

"Oh, it is a bitter pill, but I think he will have to swallow it. He is between two fires. He cannot dismiss her from the school and be true to his Abolition principles; yet if he retains her he will lose his Southern customers, and I know he cannot afford to do that."

"What does Iola say?"

"He has found another boarding place for her, but she is to remain in the school. He had to throw that sop to the whale."

"Does she take sides against the girl?"

"No, I don't think she does. She says she feels sorry for her, and that she would hate to be colored. 'It is so hard to be looked down on for what one can't help.'"

"Poor child! I wish we could leave the country. I never would consent to her marrying any one without first revealing to him her connection with the negro race. This is a subject on which I am not willing to run any risks."

"My dear Marie, when you shall have read Iola's letter you will see it is more than a figment of my imagination that has made me so loth to have our children know the paralyzing power of caste."

Leroy, always liberal with his wife and children, spared neither pains nor expense to have them prepared for their summer outing. Iola was to graduate in a few days. Harry was attending a school in the State of Maine, and his father had written to him, apprising him of his intention to come North that season. In a few days Leroy and his wife started North, but before they reached Vicksburg they were met by the intelligence that the yellow fever was spreading in the Delta, and that pestilence was breathing its bane upon the morning air and distilling its poison upon the midnight dews.

"Let us return home," said Marie.

"It is useless," answered Leroy. "It is nearly two days since we left home. The fever is spreading south of us with fearful rapidity. To return home is to walk into the jaws of death. It was my intention to have stopped at Vicksburg, but now I will go on as soon as I can make the connections."

Early next morning Leroy and his wife started again on their journey. The cars were filled with terror-stricken people who were fleeing from death, when death was everywhere. They fled from the city only to meet the dreaded apparition in the country. As they journeyed on Leroy grew restless and feverish. He tried to brace himself against the infection which was creeping slowly but insidiously into his life, dulling his brain, fevering his blood, and prostrating his strength. But vain were all his efforts. He had no armor strong enough to repel the invasion of death. They stopped at a small town on the way and obtained the best medical skill and most careful nursing, but neither skill nor art availed. On the third day death claimed Leroy as a victim, and Marie wept in hopeless agony over the grave of her devoted husband, whose sad lot it was to die from home and be buried among strangers.

But before he died he placed his will in Marie's hands, saying: "I have left you well provided for. Kiss the children for me and bid them good-bye."

He tried to say a parting word to Gracie, but his voice failed, and he fainted into the stillness of death. A mortal paleness overspread his countenance, on which had already gathered the shadows that never deceive. In speechless agony Marie held his hand until it released its pressure in death, and then she stood alone beside her dead, with all the bright sunshine of her life fading into the shadows of the grave. Heart-broken and full of fearful forebodings, Marie left her cherished dead in the quiet village of H—— and returned to her death-darkened home.

It was a lovely day in June, birds were singing their sweetest songs, flowers were breathing their fragrance on the air, when Mam Liza, sitting at her cabin-door, talking with some of the house servants, saw a carriage approaching, and wondered who was coming.

"I wonder," she said, excitedly, "whose comin' to de house when de folks is done gone."

But her surprise was soon changed to painful amazement, when she saw Marie, robed in black, alighting from the carriage, and holding Gracie by the hand. She caught sight of the drooping head and grief-stricken face, and rushed to her, exclaiming:—

"Whar's Marse Eugene?"

"Dead," said Marie, falling into Mammy Liza's arms, sobbing out, "dead! *died* of yellow fever."

A wild burst of sorrow came from the lips of the servants, who had drawn near.

"Where is he?" said Mam Liza, speaking like one suddenly bewildered.

"He is buried in H——. I could not bring him home," said Marie.

"My pore baby," said Mam Liza, with broken sobs. "I'se drefful sorry. My heart's most broke into two." Then, controlling herself, she dismissed the servants who stood around, weeping, and led Marie to her room.

"Come, honey, lie down an' lem'me git yer a cup ob tea."

"Oh, no; I don't want anything," said Marie, wringing her hands in bitter agony.

"Oh, honey," said Mam Liza, "yer musn't gib up. Yer knows whar to put yer trus'. Yer can't lean on de arm of flesh in dis tryin' time." Kneeling by the side of her mistress she breathed out a prayer full of tenderness, hope, and trust.

Marie grew calmer. It seemed as if that earnest, trustful prayer had breathed into her soul a feeling of resignation.

Gracie stood wonderingly by, vainly trying to comprehend the great sorrow which was overwhelming the life of her mother.

After the first great burst of sorrow was over, Marie sat down to her desk and wrote a letter to Iola, informing her of her father's death. By the time she had finished it she grew dizzy and faint, and fell into a swoon. Mammy Liza tenderly laid her on the bed, and helped restore her to consciousness.

Lorraine, having heard of his cousin's death, came immediately to see Marie. She was too ill to have an interview with him, but he picked up the letter she had written and obtained Iola's address.

Lorraine made a careful investigation of the case, to ascertain whether Marie's marriage was valid. To his delight he found there was a flaw in the marriage and an informality in the manumission. He then determined to invalidate Marie's claim, and divide the inheritance among Leroy's white relations. In a short time strangers, distant relatives of her husband, became frequent visitors at the plantation, and made themselves offensively familiar. At length the dreadful storm burst.

Alfred Lorraine entered suit for his cousin's estate, and for the remanding of his wife and children to slavery. In a short time he came armed with legal authority, and said to Marie:—

"I have come to take possession of these premises."

"By what authority?" she gasped, turning deathly pale. He hesitated a moment, as if his words were arrested by a sense of shame.

"By what authority?" she again demanded.

"By the authority of the law," answered Lorraine, "which has decided that Leroy's legal heirs are his white blood relations, and that your marriage is null and void."

"But," exclaimed Marie, "I have our marriage certificate. I was Leroy's lawful wife."

"Your marriage certificate is not worth the paper it is written on."

"Oh, you must be jesting, cruelly jesting. It can't be so."

"Yes; it is so. Judge Starkins has decided that your manumission is unlawful; your marriage a bad precedent, and inimical to the welfare of society; and that you and your children are remanded to slavery."

Marie stood as one petrified. She seemed a statue of fear and despair. She tried to speak, reached out her hand as if she were groping in the dark, turned pale as death as if all the blood in her veins had receded to her heart, and, with one heart-rending cry of bitter agony, she fell senseless to the floor. Her servants, to whom she had been so kind in her days of prosperity, bent pityingly over her, chafed her cold hands, and did what they could to restore her to consciousness. For awhile she was stricken with brain fever, and her life seemed trembling on its frailest cord.

Gracie was like one perfectly dazed. When not watching by her mother's bedside she wandered aimlessly about the house, growing thinner day by day. A slow fever was consuming her life. Faithfully and carefully Mammy Liza watched over her, and did all she could to bring smiles to her lips and light to her fading eyes, but all in vain. Her only interest in life was to sit where she could watch her mother as she tossed to and fro in delirium, and to wonder what had brought the change in her once happy home. Finally she, too, was stricken with brain fever, which intervened as a mercy between her and the great sorrow that was overshadowing her young life. Tears would fill the servants' eyes as they saw the dear child drifting from them like a lovely vision, too bright for earth's dull cares and weary, wasting pain.

# XII

## SCHOOL-GIRL NOTIONS

During Iola's stay in the North she found a strong tide of opposition against slavery. Arguments against the institution had entered the Church and made legislative halls the arenas of fierce debate. The subject had become part of the social converse of the fireside, and had enlisted the best brain and heart of the country. Anti-slavery discussions were pervading the strongest literature and claiming, a place on the most popular platforms.

Iola, being a Southern girl and a slave-holder's daughter, always defended slavery when it was under discussion.

"Slavery can't be wrong," she would say, "for my father is a slave-holder, and my mother is as good to our servants as she can be. My father often tells her that she spoils them, and lets them run over her. I never saw my father strike one of them. I love my mammy as much as I do my own mother, and I believe she loves us just as if we were her own children. When we are sick I am sure that she could not do anything more for us than she does."

"But, Iola," responded one of her school friends, "after all, they are not free. Would you be satisfied to have the most beautiful home, the costliest jewels, or the most elegant wardrobe if you were a slave?"

"Oh, the cases are not parallel. Our slaves do not want their freedom. They would not take it if we gave it to them."

"That is not the case with them all. My father has seen men who have encountered almost incredible hardships to get their freedom. Iola, did you ever attend an anti-slavery meeting?"

"No; I don't think these Abolitionists have any right to meddle in our affairs. I believe they are prejudiced against us, and want to get our property. I read about them in the papers when I was at home. I don't want to hear my part of the country run down. My father says the slaves would be very well contented if no one put wrong notions in their heads."

"I don't know," was the response of her friend, "but I do not think that that slave mother who took her four children, crossed the Ohio River on the ice, killed one of the children and attempted the lives of the other two, was a contented slave. And that other one, who, running away and finding herself pursued, threw herself over the Long Bridge into the Potomac, was evidently not satisfied. I do not think the numbers who are coming North on the Underground Railroad can be very contented. It is not natural for people to run away from happiness, and if they are so happy and contented, why did Congress pass the Fugitive Slave Bill?"

"Well, I don't think," answered Iola, "any of our slaves would run away. I know mamma don't like slavery very much. I have often heard her say that she hoped the time would come when there would not be a slave in the land. My father does not think as she does. He thinks slavery is not wrong if you treat them well and don't sell them from their families. I intend, after I have graduated, to persuade pa to buy a house in New Orleans, and spend the winter there. You know this will be my first season out, and I hope that you will come and spend the winter with me. We will have such gay times, and you will so fall in love with our sunny South that you will never want to come back to shiver amid the snows and cold of the North. I think one winter in the South would cure you of your Abolitionism."

"Have you seen her yet?"

This question was asked by Louis Bastine, an attorney who had come North in the interests of Lorraine. The scene was the New England village where Mr. Galen's academy was located, and which Iola was attending. This question was addressed to Camille Lecroix, Bastine's intimate friend, who had lately come North. He was the son of a planter who lived near Leroy's plantation, and was familiar with Iola's family history. Since his arrival North, Bastine had met him and communicated to him his intentions.

"Yes; just caught a glimpse of her this morning as she was going down the street," was Camille's reply.

"She is a most beautiful creature," said Louis Bastine. "She has the proud poise of Leroy, the most splendid eyes I ever saw in a woman's head, lovely complexion, and a glorious wealth of hair. She would bring $2000 any day in a New Orleans market."

"I always feel sorry," said Camille, "when I see one of those Creole girls brought to the auction block. I have known fathers who were deeply devoted to their daughters, but who through some reverse of fortune were forced to part with them, and I always think the blow has been equally terrible on both sides. I had a friend who had two beautiful daughters whom he had educated in the North. They were cultured, and really belles in society. They were entirely ignorant of their lineage, but when their father died it was discovered that their mother had been a slave. It was a fearful blow. They would have faced poverty, but the knowledge of their tainted blood was more than they could bear."

"What became of them?"

"They both died, poor girls. I believe they were as much killed by the blow as if they had been shot. To tell you the truth, Bastine, I feel sorry for this girl. I don't believe she has the least idea of her negro blood."

"No, Leroy has been careful to conceal it from her," replied Bastine.

"Is that so?" queried Camille. "Then he has made a great mistake."

"I can't help that," said Bastine; "business is business."

"How can you get her away?" asked Camille. "You will have to be very cautious, because if these pesky Abolitionists get an inkling of what you're doing they will balk your game double quick. And when you come to look at it, isn't it a shame to attempt to reduce that girl to slavery? She is just as white as we are, as good as any girl in the land, and better educated than thousands of white girls. A girl with her apparent refinement and magnificent beauty, were it not for the cross in her blood, I would be proud to introduce to our set. She would be the sensation of the season. I believe today it would be easier for me to go to the slums and take a young girl from there, and have her introduced as my wife, than to have society condone the offense if I married that lovely girl. There is not a social circle in the South that would not take it as a gross insult to have her introduced into it."

"Well," said Bastine, "my plan is settled. Leroy has never allowed her to spend her vacations at home. I understand she is now very anxious to get home, and, as Lorraine's attorney, I have come on his account to take her home."

"How will you do it?"

"I shall tell her her father is dangerously ill, and desires her to come as quickly as possible."

"And what then?"

"Have her inventoried with the rest of the property."

"Don't she know that her father is dead?"

"I think not," said Bastine. "She is not in mourning, but appeared very light-hearted this morning, laughing and talking with two other girls. I was struck with her great beauty, and asked a gentleman who she was. He said, 'Miss Leroy, of Mississippi.' I think Lorraine has managed the affair so as to keep her in perfect ignorance of her father's death. I don't like the job, but I never let sentiment interfere with my work."

Poor Iola! When she said slavery was not a bad thing, little did she think that she was destined to drink to its bitter dregs the cup she was so ready to press to the lips of others.

"How do you think she will take to her situation?" asked Camille.

"O, I guess," said Bastine, "she will sulk and take it pretty hard at first; but if she is managed right she will soon get over it. Give her plenty of jewelry, fine clothes, and an easy time."

"All this business must be conducted with the utmost secrecy and speed. Her mother could not have written to her, for she has been suffering with brain fever and nervous prostration since Leroy's death. Lorraine knows her market value too well, and is too shrewd to let so much property pass out of his hands without making an effort to retain it."

"Has she any brothers or sisters?"

"Yes, a brother," replied Bastine; "but he is at another school, and I have no orders from Lorraine in reference to him. If I can get the girl I am willing to let well enough alone. I dread the interview with the principal more than anything else. I am afraid he will hem and haw, and have his doubts. Perhaps, when he sees my letters and hears my story, I can pull the wool over his eyes."

"But, Louis, this is a pitiful piece of business. I should hate to be engaged in it."

A deep flush of shame overspread for a moment the face of Lorraine's attorney, as he replied: "I don't like the job, but I have undertaken it, and must go through with it."

"I see no '*must*' about it. Were I in your place I would wash my hands of the whole business."

"I can't afford it," was Bastine's hard, business-like reply. On the next morning after this conversation between these two young men, Louis Bastine presented himself to the principal of the academy, with the request that Iola be permitted to leave immediately to attend the sick-bed of her father, who was dangerously ill. The principal hesitated, but while he was deliberating, a telegram, purporting to come from Iola's mother, summoned Iola to her father's bedside without delay. The principal, set at rest in regard to the truthfulness of the dispatch, not only permitted but expedited her departure.

Iola and Bastine took the earliest train, and traveled without pausing until they reached a large hotel in a Southern city. There they were obliged to wait a few hours until they could resume their journey, the train having failed to make connection. Iola sat in a large, lonely parlor, waiting for the servant to show her to a private room. She had never known a great sorrow. Never before had the shadows of death mingled with the sunshine of her life.

Anxious, travel-worn, and heavy-hearted, she sat in an easy chair, with nothing to divert her from the grief and anxiety which rendered every delay a source of painful anxiety.

"Oh, I hope that he will be alive and growing better!" was the thought which kept constantly revolving in her mind, until she fell asleep. In her dreams she was at home, encircled in the warm clasp of her father's arms, feeling her mother's kisses lingering on her lips, and hearing the joyous greetings of the servants and Mammy Liza's glad welcome as she folded her to her heart. From this dream of bliss she was awakened by a burning kiss pressed on her lips, and a strong arm encircling her. Gazing around and taking in the whole situation, she sprang from her seat, her eyes flashing with rage and scorn, her face flushed to the roots of her hair, her voice shaken with excitement, and every nerve trembling with angry emotion.

"How dare you do such a thing! Don't you know if my father were here he would crush you to the earth?"

"Not so fast, my lovely tigress," said Bastine, "your father knew what he was doing when he placed you in my charge."

"My father made a great mistake, if he thought he had put me in charge of a gentleman."

"I am your guardian for the present," replied Bastine. "I am to see you safe home, and then my commission ends."

"I wish it were ended now," she exclaimed, trembling with anger and mortification. Her voice was choked by emotion, and broken by smothered sobs. Louis Bastine thought to himself, "she is a real spitfire, but beautiful even in her wrath."

During the rest of her journey Iola preserved a most freezing reserve towards Bastine. At length the journey was ended. Pale and anxious she rode up the avenue which led to her home.

A strange silence pervaded the place. The servants moved sadly from place to place, and spoke in subdued tones. The windows were heavily draped with crape, and a funeral air pervaded the house.

Mammy Liza met her at the door, and, with streaming eyes and convulsive sobs, folded her to her heart, as Iola exclaimed, in tones of hopeless anguish:—

"Oh, papa's dead!"

"Oh, my pore baby!" said mammy, "ain't you hearn tell 'bout it? Yore par's dead, an' your mar's bin drefful sick. She's better now."

Mam Liza stepped lightly into Mrs. Leroy's room, and gently apprised her of Iola's arrival. In a darkened room lay the stricken mother, almost distracted by her late bereavement.

"Oh, Iola," she exclaimed, as her daughter entered, "is this you? I am so sorry you came."

Then, burying her head in Iola's bosom, she wept convulsively. "Much as I love you," she continued, between her sobs, "and much as I longed to see you, I am sorry you came."

"Why, mother," replied Iola, astonished, "I received your telegram last Wednesday, and I took the earliest train I could get."

"My dear child, I never sent you a telegram. It was a trick to bring you down South and reduce you to slavery."

Iola eyed her mother curiously. What did she mean? Had grief dethroned her reason? Yet her eye was clear, her manner perfectly rational.

Marie saw the astounded look on Iola's face, and nerving herself to the task, said: "Iola, I must tell you what your father always enjoined me to be silent about. I did not think it was the wisest thing, but I yielded to his desires. I have negro blood in my veins. I was your father's slave before I married him. His relatives have set aside his will. The courts have declared our marriage null and void and my manumission illegal, and we are all to be remanded to slavery."

An expression of horror and anguish swept over Iola's face, and, turning deathly pale, she exclaimed, "Oh, mother, it can't be so! you must be dreaming!"

"No, my child; it is a terrible reality."

Almost wild with agony, Iola paced the floor, as the fearful truth broke in crushing anguish upon her mind. Then bursting into a paroxysm of tears succeeded by peals of hysterical laughter, said:—

"I used to say that slavery is right. I didn't know what I was talking about." Then growing calmer, she said, "Mother, who is at the bottom of this downright robbery?"

"Alfred Lorraine; I have always dreaded that man, and what I feared has come to pass. Your father had faith in him; I never had."

"But, mother, could we not contest his claim. You have your marriage certificate and papa's will."

"Yes, my dear child, but Judge Starkins has decided that we have no standing in the court, and no testimony according to law."

"Oh, mother, what can I do?"

"Nothing, my child, unless you can escape to the North."

"And leave you?"

"Yes."

"Mother, I will never desert you in your hour of trial. But can nothing be done? Had father no friends who would assist us?"

"None that I know of. I do not think he had an acquaintance who approved of our marriage. The neighboring planters have stood so aloof from me that I do not know where to turn for either help or sympathy. I believe it was Lorraine who sent the telegram. I wrote to you as soon as I could after your father's death, but fainted just as I finished directing the letter. I do not think he knows where your brother is, and, if possible, he must not know. If you can by any means, *do* send a letter to Harry and warn him not to attempt to come home. I don't know how you will succeed, for Lorraine has us all under surveillance. But it is according to law."

"What law, mother?"

"The law of the strong against the weak."

"Oh, mother, it seems like a dreadful dream, a fearful nightmare! But I cannot shake it off. Where is Gracie?"

"The dear child has been running down ever since her papa's death. She clung to me night and day while I had the brain fever, and could not be persuaded to leave me. She hardly ate anything for more than a week. She has been dangerously ill for several days, and the doctor says she cannot live. The fever has exhausted all her rallying power, and yet, dear as she is to me, I would rather consign her to the deepest grave than see her forced to be a slave."

"So would I. I wish I could die myself."

"Oh, Iola, do not talk so. Strive to be a Christian, to have faith in the darkest hour. Were it not for my hope of heaven I couldn't stand all this trouble."

"Mother, are these people Christians who made these laws which are robbing us of our inheritance and reducing us to slavery? If this is Christianity I hate and despise it. Would the most cruel heathen do worse?"

FRANCES ELLEN WATKINS HARPER

"My dear child, I have not learned my Christianity from them. I have learned it at the foot of the cross, and from this book," she said, placing a New Testament in Iola's hands. "Some of the most beautiful lessons of faith and trust I have ever learned were from among our lowly people in their humble cabins."

"Mamma!" called a faint voice from the adjoining room. Marie immediately arose and went to the bedside of her sick child, where Mammy Liza was holding her faithful vigils. The child had just awakened from a fitful sleep.

"I thought," she said, "that I heard Iola's voice. Has she come?"

"Yes, darling; do you want to see her?"

"Oh, yes," she said, as a bright smile broke over her dying features.

Iola passed quickly into the room. Gracie reached out her thin, bloodless hand, clasped Iola's palm in hers, and said: "I am so glad you have come. Dear Iola, stand by mother. You and Harry are all she has. It is not hard to die. You and mother and Harry must meet me in heaven."

Swiftly the tidings went through the house that Gracie was dying. The servants gathered around her with tearful eyes, as she bade them all good-bye. When she had finished, and Mammy had lowered the pillow, an unwonted radiance lit up her eye, and an expression of ineffable gladness overspread her face, as she murmured: "It is beautiful, so beautiful!" Fainter and fainter grew her voice, until, without a struggle or sigh, she passed away beyond the power of oppression and prejudice.

# XIII

## A Rejected Suitor

Very unexpected was Dr. Gresham's proposal to Iola. She had heartily enjoyed his society and highly valued his friendship, but he had never been associated in her mind with either love or marriage. As he held her hand in his a tell-tale flush rose to her cheek, a look of grateful surprise beamed from her eye, but it was almost immediately succeeded by an air of inexpressible sadness, a drooping of her eyelids, and an increasing pallor of her cheek. She withdrew her hand from his, shook her head sadly, and said:—

"No, Doctor; that can never be. I am very grateful to you for your kindness. I value your friendship, but neither gratitude nor friendship is love, and I have nothing more than those to give."

"Not at present," said Dr. Gresham; "but may I not hope your friendship will ripen into love?"

"Doctor, I could not promise. I do not think that I should. There are barriers between us that I cannot pass. Were you to know them I think you would say the same."

Just then the ambulance brought in a wounded scout, and Iola found relief from the wounds of her own heart in attending to his.

Dr. Gresham knew the barrier that lay between them. It was one which his love had surmounted. But he was too noble and generous to take advantage of her loneliness to press his suit. He had lived in a part of the country where he had scarcely ever seen a colored person, and around the race their misfortunes had thrown a halo of romance. To him the negro was a picturesque being, over whose woes he had wept when a child, and whose wrongs he was ready to redress when a man. But when he saw the lovely girl who had been rescued by the commander of the post from the clutches of slavery, all the manhood and chivalry in his nature arose in her behalf, and he was ready to lay on the altar of her heart his first grand and overmastering love. Not discouraged by her refusal, but determined to overcome her objections, Dr. Gresham resolved that he would abide his time.

Iola was not indifferent to Dr. Gresham. She admired his manliness and respected his character. He was tall and handsome, a fine specimen of the best brain and heart of New England. He had been nurtured under grand and ennobling influences. His father was a devoted Abolitionist. His mother was kind-hearted, but somewhat exclusive and aristocratic. She would have looked upon his marriage with Iola as a mistake and feared that such an alliance would hurt the prospects of her daughters.

During Iola's stay in the North, she had learned enough of the racial feeling to influence her decision in reference to Dr. Gresham's offer. Iola, like other girls, had had her beautiful day-dreams before she was rudely awakened by the fate which had dragged her into the depths of slavery. In the chambers of her imagery were pictures of noble deeds; of high, heroic men, knightly, tender, true, and brave. In Dr. Gresham she saw the ideal of her soul exemplified. But in her lonely condition, with all its background of terrible sorrow and deep abasement, she had never for a moment thought of giving or receiving love from one of that race who had been so lately associated in her mind with horror, aversion, and disgust. His kindness to her had been a new experience. His companionship was an unexpected pleasure. She had learned to enjoy his presence and to miss him when absent, and when she began to question her heart she found that unconsciously it was entwining around him.

"Yes," she said to herself, "I do like him; but I can never marry him. To the man I marry my heart must be as open as the flowers to the sun. I could not accept his hand and hide from him the secret of my birth; and I could not consent to choose the happiest lot on earth without first finding my poor heart-stricken and desolate mother. Perhaps some day I may have the courage to tell him my sad story, and then make my heart the sepulchre in which to bury all the love which might have gladdened and brightened my whole life."

During the sad and weary months which ensued while the war dragged its slow length along, Dr. Gresham and Iola often met by the bedsides of the wounded and dying, and sometimes he would drop a few words at which her heart would beat quicker and her cheek flush more vividly. But he was so kind, tender, and respectful, that Iola had no idea he knew her race affiliations. She knew from unmistakable signs that Dr. Gresham had learned to love her, and that he had power to call forth the warmest affection of her soul; but she fought with her own heart and repressed its rising love. She felt that it was best for his sake that they should not marry. When she saw the evidences of his increasing love she regretted that she had not informed him at the first of the barrier that lay between them; it might have saved him unnecessary suffering. Thinking thus, Iola resolved, at whatever cost of pain it might be to herself, to explain to Dr. Gresham what she meant by the insurmountable barrier. Iola, after a continuous strain upon her nervous system for months, began to suffer from general debility and nervous depression. Dr. Gresham saw the increasing pallor on Iola's cheek and the loss of buoyancy in her step. One morning, as she turned from the bed of a young soldier for whom she had just written a letter to his mother, there was such a look of pity and sorrow on her face that Dr. Gresham's whole heart went out in sympathy for her, and he resolved to break the silence he had imposed upon himself.

"Iola," he said, and there was a depth of passionate tenderness in his voice, a volume of unexpressed affection in his face, "you are wronging yourself. You are sinking beneath burdens too heavy for you to bear. It seems to me that besides the constant drain upon your sympathies there is some great sorrow preying upon your life; some burden that ought to be shared." He gazed upon her so ardently that each cord of her heart seemed to vibrate, and unbidden tears sprang to her lustrous eyes, as she said, sadly:—

"Doctor, you are right."

"Iola, my heart is longing to lift those burdens from your life. Love, like faith, laughs at impossibilities. I can conceive of no barrier too high for my love to surmount. Consent to be mine, as nothing else on earth is mine."

"Doctor, you know not what you ask," replied Iola. "Instead of coming into this hospital a self-sacrificing woman, laying her every gift and advantage upon the altar of her country, I came as a rescued slave, glad to find a refuge from a fate more cruel than death; a fate from which I was rescued by the intervention of my dear dead friend, Thomas Anderson. I was born on a lonely plantation on the Mississippi River, where the white population was very sparse. We had no neighbors who ever visited us; no young white girls with whom I ever played in my childhood; but, never having enjoyed such companionship, I was unconscious of any sense of privation. Our parents spared no pains to make the lives of their children (we were three) as bright and pleasant as they could. Our home was so happy. We had a large number of servants, who were devoted to us. I never had the faintest suspicion that there was any wrongfulness in slavery, and I never dreamed of the dreadful fate which broke in a storm of fearful anguish over our devoted heads. Papa used to take us to New Orleans to see the Mardi Gras, and while there we visited the theatres and other places of amusement and interest. At home we had books, papers, and magazines to beguile our time. Perfectly ignorant of my racial connection, I was sent to a Northern academy, and soon made many friends among my fellow-students. Companionship with girls of my own age was a new experience, which I thoroughly enjoyed. I spent several years in New England, and was busily preparing for my commencement exercises when my father was snatched away—died of yellow fever on his way North to witness my graduation. Through a stratagem, I was brought hurriedly from the North, and found that my father was dead; that his nearest kinsman had taken possession of our property; that my mother's marriage had been declared illegal, because of an imperceptible infusion of negro blood in her veins; and that she and her children had been remanded to slavery. I was torn from my mother, sold as a slave, and subjected to cruel indignities, from which I was rescued and a place given to me in this hospital. Doctor, I did not choose my lot in life, but I have no other alternative than to accept it. The intense horror and agony I felt when I was first told the story are over. Thoughts and purposes have come to me in the shadow I should never have learned in the sunshine. I am constantly rousing myself up to suffer and be strong. I intend, when this conflict is over, to cast my lot with the freed people as a helper, teacher, and friend. I have passed through a fiery ordeal, but this ministry of suffering will not be in vain. I feel that my mind has matured beyond my years. I am a wonder to myself. It seems as if years had been compressed into a few short months. In telling you this, do you not, can you not, see that there is an insurmountable barrier between us?"

"No, I do not," replied Dr. Gresham. "I love you for your own sake. And with this the disadvantages of birth have nothing to do."

"You say so now, and I believe that you are perfectly sincere. Today your friendship springs from compassion, but, when that subsides, might you not look on me as an inferior?"

"Iola, you do not understand me. You think too meanly of me. You must not judge me by the worst of my race. Surely our country has produced a higher type of manhood than the men by whom you were tried and tempted."

"Tried, but not tempted," said Iola, as a deep flush overspread her face; "I was never tempted. I was sold from State to State as an article of merchandise. I had outrages heaped on me which might well crimson the cheek of honest womanhood with shame, but I never fell into the clutches of an owner for whom I did not feel the utmost loathing and intensest horror. I have heard men talk glibly of the degradation of the negro, but there is a vast difference between abasement of condition and degradation of character. I was abased, but the men who trampled on me were the degraded ones."

"But, Iola, you must not blame all for what a few have done."

"A few have done? Did not the whole nation consent to our abasement?" asked Iola, bitterly.

"No, Miss Iola, we did not all consent to it. Slavery drew a line of cleavage in this country. Although we were under one government we were farther apart in our sentiments than if we had been divided by lofty mountains and separated by wide seas. And had not Northern sentiment been brought to bear against the institution, slavery would have been intact until today."

"But, Doctor, the negro is under a social ban both North and South. Our enemies have the ear of the world, and they can depict us just as they please."

"That is true; but the negro has no other alternative than to make friends of his calamities. Other men have plead his cause, but out of the race must come its own defenders. With them the pen must be mightier than the sword. It is the weapon of civilization, and they must use it in their own defense. We cannot tell what is in them until they express themselves."

"Yes, and I think there is a large amount of latent and undeveloped ability in the race, which they will learn to use for their own benefit. This my hospital experience has taught me."

"But," said Dr. Gresham, "they must learn to struggle, labor, and achieve. By facts, not theories, they will be judged in the future. The Anglo-Saxon race is proud, domineering, aggressive, and impatient of a rival, and, as I think, has more capacity for dragging down a weaker race than uplifting it. They have been a conquering and achieving people, marvelous in their triumphs of mind over matter. They have manifested the traits of character which are developed by success and victory."

"And yet," said Iola, earnestly, "I believe the time will come when the civilization of the negro will assume a better phase than you Anglo-Saxons possess. You will prove unworthy of your high vantage ground if you only use your superior ability to victimize feebler races and minister to a selfish greed of gold and a love of domination."

"But, Iola," said Dr. Gresham, a little impatiently, "what has all this to do with our marriage? Your complexion is as fair as mine. What is to hinder you from sharing my Northern home, from having my mother to be your mother?" The tones of his voice grew tender, as he raised his eyes to Iola's face and anxiously awaited her reply.

"Dr. Gresham," said Iola, sadly, "should the story of my life be revealed to your family, would they be willing to ignore all the traditions of my blood, forget all the terrible humiliations through which I have passed? I have too much self-respect to enter your home under a veil of concealment. I have lived in New England. I love the sunshine of her homes and the freedom of her institutions. But New England is not free from racial prejudice, and I would never enter a family where I would be an unwelcome member."

"Iola, dear, you have nothing to fear in that direction."

"Doctor," she said, and a faint flush rose to her cheek, "suppose we should marry, and little children in after years should nestle in our arms, and one of them show unmistakable signs of color, would you be satisfied?"

She looked steadfastly into his eyes, which fell beneath her truth-seeking gaze. His face flushed as if the question had suddenly perplexed him. Iola saw the irresolution on his face, and framed her answer accordingly.

"Ah, I see," she said, "that you are puzzled. You had not taken into account what might result from such a marriage. I will relieve you from all embarrassment by simply saying I cannot be your wife. When the war is over I intend to search the country for my mother. Doctor, were you to give me a palace-like home, with velvet carpets to hush my tread, and magnificence to surround my way, I should miss her voice amid all other tones, her presence amid every scene. Oh, you do not know how hungry my heart is for my mother! Were I to marry you I would carry an aching heart into your home and dim its brightness. I have resolved never to marry until I have found my mother. The hope of finding her has colored all my life since I regained my freedom. It has helped sustain me in the hour of fearful trial. When I see her I want to have the proud consciousness that I bring her back a heart just as loving, faithful, and devoted as the last hour we parted."

"And is this your final answer?"

"It is. I have pledged my life to that resolve, and I believe time and patience will reward me."

There was a deep shadow of sorrow and disappointment on the face of Dr. Gresham as he rose to leave. For a moment he held her hand as it lay limp in his own. If she wavered in her determination it was only for a moment. No quivering of her lip or paling of her cheek betrayed any struggle of her heart. Her resolve was made, and his words were powerless to swerve her from the purpose of her soul.

After Dr. Gresham had gone Iola went to her room and sat buried in thought. It seemed as if the fate of Tantalus was hers, without his crimes. Here she was lonely and heart-stricken, and unto her was presented the offer of love, home, happiness, and social position; the heart and hand of a man too noble and generous to refuse her companionship for life on account of the blood in her veins. Why should she refuse these desirable boons? But, mingling with these beautiful visions of manly love and protecting care she saw the anguish of her heart-stricken mother and the pale, sweet face of her dying sister, as with her latest breath she had said, "Iola, stand by mamma!"

"No, no," she said to herself; "I was right to refuse Dr. Gresham. How dare I dream of happiness when my poor mamma's heart may be slowly breaking? I should be ashamed to live and ashamed to die were I to choose a happy lot for myself and leave poor mamma to struggle alone. I will never be satisfied till I get tidings of her. And when I have found her I will do all I can to cheer and brighten the remnant of her life."

# XIV

## HARRY LEROY

It was several weeks after Iola had written to her brother that her letter reached him. The trusty servant to whom she delivered it watched his opportunity to mail it. At last he succeeded in slipping it into Lorraine's mail and dropping them all into the post office together. Harry was studying at a boys' academy in Maine. His father had given that State the preference because, while on a visit there, he had been favorably impressed with the kindness and hospitality of the people. He had sent his son a large sum of money, and given him permission to spend awhile with some school-chums till he was ready to bring the family North, where they could all spend the summer together. Harry had returned from his visit, and was looking for letters and remittances from home, when a letter, all crumpled, was handed him by the principal of the academy. He recognized his sister's handwriting and eagerly opened the letter. As he read, he turned very pale; then a deep flush overspread his face and an angry light flashed from his eyes. As he read on, his face became still paler; he gasped for breath and fell into a swoon. Appalled at the sudden change which had swept over him like a deadly sirocco, the principal rushed to the fallen boy, picked up the missive that lay beside him, and immediately rang for help and dispatched for the doctor. The doctor came at once and was greatly puzzled. Less than an hour before, he had seen him with a crowd of merry, laughter-loving boys, apparently as light-hearted and joyous as any of them; now he lay with features drawn and pinched, his face deadly pale, as if some terrible suffering had sent all the blood in his veins to stagnate around his heart. Harry opened his eyes, shuddered, and relapsed into silence. The doctor, all at sea in regard to the cause of the sudden attack, did all that he could to restore him to consciousness and quiet the perturbation of his spirit. He succeeded, but found he was strangely silent. A terrible shock had sent a tremor through every nerve, and the doctor watched with painful apprehension its effect upon his reason. Giving him an opiate and enjoining that he should be kept perfectly quiet, the doctor left the room, sought the principal, and said:—

"Mr. Bascom, here is a case that baffles my skill. I saw that boy pass by my window not more than half an hour ago, full of animation, and now he lies hovering between life and death. I have great apprehension for his reason. Can you throw any light on the subject?"

Mr. Bascom hesitated.

"I am not asking you as a matter of idle curiosity, but as a physician. I must have all the light I can get in making my diagnosis of the case."

The principal arose, went to his desk, took out the letter which he had picked up from the floor, and laid it in the physician's hand. As the doctor read, a look of indignant horror swept over his face. Then he said: "Can it be possible! I never suspected such a thing. It must be a cruel, senseless hoax."

"Doctor," said Mr. Bascom, "I have been a life-long Abolitionist and have often read of the cruelties and crimes of American slavery, but never before did I realize the low moral tone of the social life under which such shameless cruelties could be practiced on a defenseless widow and her orphaned children. Let me read the letter again. Just look at it, all tear-blotted and written with a trembling hand:—

Dear Brother

I have dreadful news for you and I hardly know how to tell it. Papa and Gracie are both dead. He died of yellow fever. Mamma is almost distracted. Papa's cousin has taken possession of our property, and instead of heirs we are chattels. Mamma has explained the whole situation to me. She was papa's slave before she married. He loved her, manumitted, educated, and married her. When he died Mr. Lorraine entered suit for his property and Judge Starkins has decided in his favor. The decree of the court has made their marriage invalid, robbed us of our inheritance, and remanded us all to slavery. Mamma is too wretched to attempt to write herself, but told me to entreat you not to attempt to come home. You can do us no good, and that mean, cruel Lorraine may do you much harm. Don't attempt, I beseech you, to come home. Show this letter to Mr. Bascom and let him advise you what to do. But don't, for our sake, attempt to come home.

Your heart-broken sister,
Iola Leroy

"This," said the doctor, "is a very awkward affair. The boy is too ill to be removed. It is doubtful if the nerves which have trembled with such fearful excitement will ever recover their normal condition. It is simply a work of mercy to watch over him with the tenderest care."

Fortunately for Harry he had fallen into good hands, and the most tender care and nursing were bestowed upon him. For awhile Harry was strangely silent, never referring to the terrible misfortune which had so suddenly overshadowed his life. It seemed as if the past were suddenly blotted out of his memory. But he was young and of an excellent constitution, and in a few months he was slowly recovering.

"Doctor," said he one day, as the physician sat at his bedside, "I seem to have had a dreadful dream, and to have dreamt that my father was dead, and my mother and sister were in terrible trouble, but I could not help them. Doctor, was it a dream, or was it a reality? It could not have been a dream, for when I fell asleep the grass was green and the birds were singing, but now the winds are howling and the frost is on the ground. Doctor, tell me how it is? How long have I been here?"

Sitting by his bedside, and taking his emaciated hand in his, the doctor said, in a kind, fatherly tone: "My dear boy, you have been very ill, and everything depends on your keeping quiet, very quiet."

As soon as he was strong enough the principal gave him his letter to read.

"But, Mr. Bascom," Harry said, "I do not understand this. It says my mother and father were legally married. How could her marriage be set aside and her children robbed of their inheritance? This is not a heathen country. I hardly think barbarians would have done any worse; yet this is called a Christian country."

"Christian in name," answered the principal. "When your father left you in my care, knowing that I was an Abolitionist, he confided his secret to me. He said that life was full of vicissitudes, and he wished you to have a good education. He wanted you and your sister to be prepared for any emergency. He did not wish you to know that you had negro blood in your veins. He knew that the spirit of caste pervaded the nation, North and South, and he was very anxious to have his children freed from its depressing influences. He did not intend to stay South after you had finished your education."

"But," said Harry, "I cannot understand. If my mother was lawfully married, how could they deprive her of her marital rights?"

"When Lorraine," continued Mr. Bascom, "knew your father was dead, all he had to do was to find a flaw in her manumission, and, of course, the marriage became illegal. She could not then inherit property nor maintain her freedom; and her children followed her condition."

Harry listened attentively. Things which had puzzled him once now became perfectly clear. He sighed heavily, and, turning to the principal, said: "I see things in a new light. Now I remember that none of the planters' wives ever visited my mother; and we never went to church except when my father took us to the Cathedral in New Orleans. My father was a Catholic, but I don't think mamma is."

"Now, Harry," said the principal, "life is before you. If you wish to stay North, I will interest friends in your behalf, and try to get you a situation. Going South is out of the question. It is probable that by this time your mother and sister are removed from their home. You are powerless to fight against the law that enslaved them. Should you fall into the clutches of Lorraine, he might give you a great deal of trouble. You would be pressed into the Confederate service to help them throw up barricades, dig trenches, and add to the strength of those who enslaved your mother and sister."

"Never! never!" cried Harry. "I would rather die than do it! I should despise myself forever if I did."

"Numbers of our young men," said Mr. Bascom, "have gone to the war which is now raging between North and South. You have been sick for several months, and much has taken place of which you are unaware. Would you like to enlist?"

"I certainly would; not so much for the sake of fighting for the Government, as with the hope of finding my mother and sister, and avenging their wrongs. I should like to meet Lorraine on the battle-field."

"What kind of a regiment would you prefer, white or colored?"

Harry winced when the question was asked. He felt the reality of his situation as he had not done before. It was as if two paths had suddenly opened before him, and he was forced to choose between them. On one side were strength, courage, enterprise, power of achievement, and memories of a wonderful past. On the other side were weakness, ignorance, poverty, and the proud world's social scorn. He knew nothing of colored people except as slaves, and his whole soul shrank from equalizing himself with them. He was fair enough to pass unchallenged among the fairest in the land, and yet a Christless prejudice had decreed that he should be a social pariah. He sat, thoughtful and undecided, as if a great struggle were going on in his mind. Finally the principal said, "I do not think that you should be assigned to a colored regiment because of the blood in your veins, but you will have, in such a regiment, better facilities for finding your mother and sister."

"You are right, Mr. Bascom. To find my mother and sister I call no task too heavy, no sacrifice too great."

Since Harry had come North he had learned to feel profound pity for the slave. But there is a difference between looking on a man as an object of pity and protecting him as such, and being identified with him and forced to share his lot. To take his place with them on the arena of life was the test of his life, but love was stronger than pride.

His father was dead. His mother and sister were enslaved by a mockery of justice. It was more than a matter of choice where he should stand on the racial question. He felt that he must stand where he could strike the most effective blow for their freedom. With that thought strong in his mind, and as soon as he recovered, he went westward to find a colored regiment. He told the recruiting officer that he wished to be assigned to a colored regiment.

"Why do you wish that," said the officer, looking at Harry with an air of astonishment.

"Because I am a colored man."

The officer look puzzled. It was a new experience. He had seen colored men with fair complexions anxious to lose their identity with the colored race and pose as white men, but here was a man in the flush of his early manhood, to whom could come dreams of promotion from a simple private to a successful general, deliberately turning his back upon every gilded hope and dazzling opportunity, to cast his lot with the despised and hated negro.

"I do not understand you," said the officer. "Surely you are a white man, and, as such, I will enlist you in a white regiment."

"No," said Harry, firmly, "I am a colored man, and unless I can be assigned to a colored regiment I am not willing to enter the army."

"Well," said the officer, "you are the d——d'st fool I ever saw—a man as white as you are turning his back upon his chances of promotion! But you can take your choice."

So Harry was permitted to enter the army. By his promptness and valor he soon won the hearts of his superior officers, and was made drill sergeant. Having nearly all of his life been used to colored people, and being taught by his mother to be kind and respectful to them, he was soon able to gain their esteem. He continued in the regiment until Grant began the task of opening the Mississippi. After weeks of fruitless effort, Grant marched his army down the west side of the river, while the gunboats undertook the perilous task of running the batteries. Men were found for the hour. The volunteers offered themselves in such numbers that lots were cast to determine who should have the opportunity to enlist in an enterprise so fraught with danger. Harry was one on whom the lot fell.

Grant crossed the river below, coiled his forces around Vicksburg like a boa-constrictor, and held it in his grasp. After forty-seven days of endurance the city surrendered to him. Port Hudson, after the surrender of Vicksburg, gave up the unequal contest, and the Mississippi was open to the Gulf.

# XV

## ROBERT AND HIS COMPANY

"Good morning, gentlemen," said Robert Johnson, as he approached Colonel Robinson, the commander of the post, who was standing at the door of his tent, talking with Captain Sybil.

"Good morning," responded Colonel Robinson, "I am glad you have come. I was just about to send for you. How is your company getting on?"

"First rate, sir," replied Robert.

"In good health?"

"Excellent. They are all in good health and spirits. Our boys are used to hardship and exposure, and the hope of getting their freedom puts new snap into them."

"I am glad of it," said Colonel Robinson. "They make good fighters and very useful allies. Last night we received very valuable intelligence from some fugitives who had escaped through the Rebel lines. I do not think many of the Northern people realize the service they have been to us in bringing information and helping our boys when escaping from Rebel prisons. I never knew a full-blooded negro to betray us. A month ago, when we were encamped near the Rebel lines, a colored woman managed admirably to keep us posted as to the intended movements of the enemy. She was engaged in laundry work, and by means of hanging her sheets in different ways gave us the right signals."

"I hope," said Captain Sybil, "that the time will come when some faithful historian will chronicle all the deeds of daring and-service these people have performed during this struggle, and give them due credit therefor."

"Our great mistake," said Colonel Robinson, "was our long delay in granting them their freedom, and even what we have done is only partial. The border States still retain their slaves. We ought to have made a clean sweep of the whole affair. Slavery is a serpent which we nourished in its weakness, and now it is stinging us in its strength."

"I think so, too," said Captain Sybil. "But in making his proclamation of freedom, perhaps Mr. Lincoln went as far as he thought public opinion would let him."

"It is remarkable," said Colonel Robinson, "how these Secesh hold out. It surprises me to see how poor white men, who, like the negroes, are victims of slavery, rally around the Stripes and Bars. These men, I believe, have been looked down on by the aristocratic slaveholders, and despised by the well-fed and comfortable slaves, yet they follow their leaders into the very jaws of death; face hunger, cold, disease, and danger; and all for what? What, under heaven, are they fighting for? Now, the negro, ignorant as he is, has learned to regard our flag as a banner of freedom, and to look forward to his deliverance as a consequence of the overthrow of the Rebellion."

"I think," said Captain Sybil "that these ignorant white men have been awfully deceived. They have had presented to their imaginations utterly false ideas of the results of Secession, and have been taught that its success would bring them advantages which they had never enjoyed in the Union."

"And I think," said Colonel Robinson, "that the women and ministers have largely fed and fanned the fires of this Rebellion, and have helped to create a public opinion which has swept numbers of benighted men into the conflict. Well might one of their own men say, 'This is a rich man's war and a poor man's fight.' They were led into it through their ignorance, and held in it by their fears."

"I think," said Captain Sybil, "that if the public school had been common through the South this war would never have occurred. Now things have reached such a pass that able-bodied men must report at headquarters, or be treated as deserters. Their leaders are desperate men, of whom it has been said: 'They have robbed the cradle and the grave.'"

"They are fighting against fearful odds," said Colonel Robinson, "and their defeat is only a question of time."

"As soon," said Robert, "as they fired on Fort Sumter, Uncle Daniel, a dear old father who had been praying and hoping for freedom, said to me: 'Dey's fired on Fort Sumter, an' mark my words, Bob, de Norf's boun' ter whip.'"

"Had we freed the slaves at the outset," said Captain Sybil, "we wouldn't have given the Rebels so much opportunity to strengthen themselves by means of slave labor in raising their crops, throwing up their entrenchments, and building their fortifications. Slavery was a deadly cancer eating into the life of the nation; but, somehow, it had cast such a glamour over us that we have acted somewhat as if our

FRANCES ELLEN WATKINS HARPER

national safety were better preserved by sparing the cancer than by cutting it out."

"Political and racial questions have sadly complicated this matter," said Colonel Robinson. "The North is not wholly made up of anti-slavery people. At the beginning of this war we were not permeated with justice, and so were not ripe for victory. The battle of Bull Run inaugurated the war by a failure. Instead of glory we gathered shame, and defeat in place of victory."

"We have been slow," said Captain Sybil, "to see our danger and to do our duty. Our delay has cost us thousands of lives and millions of dollars. Yet it may be it is all for the best. Our national wound was too deep to be lightly healed. When the President issued his Emancipation Proclamation my heart overflowed with joy, and I said: 'This is the first bright rift in the war cloud.'"

"And did you really think that they would accept the terms of freedom and lay down their arms?" asked Robert.

"I hardly thought they would," continued Captain Sybil. "I did not think that their leaders would permit it. I believe the rank and file of their army are largely composed of a mass of ignorance, led, manipulated, and moulded by educated and ambitious wickedness. In attempting to overthrow the Union, a despotism and reign of terror were created which encompassed them as fetters of iron, and they will not accept the conditions until they have reached the last extremity. I hardly think they are yet willing to confess that such extremity has been reached."

"Captain," said Robert, as they left Colonel Robinson's tent, "I have lived all my life where I have had a chance to hear the 'Secesh' talk, and when they left their papers around I used to read everything I could lay my hands on. It seemed to me that the big white men not only ruled over the poor whites and made laws for them, but over the whole nation."

"That was so," replied Captain Sybil. "The North was strong but forbearing. It was busy in trade and commerce, and permitted them to make the Northern States hunting-grounds for their slaves. When we sent back Simms and Burns from beneath the shadow of Bunker Hill Monument and Faneuil Hall, they mistook us; looked upon us as a lot of money-grabbers, who would be willing to purchase peace at any price. I do not believe when they fired on the 'Star of the West' that they had the least apprehension of the fearful results which were to follow their madness and folly."

"Well, Captain," asked Robert, "if the free North would submit to be called on to help them catch their slaves, what could be expected of us, who all our lives had known no other condition than that of slavery? How much braver would you have been, if your first recollections had been those of seeing your mother maltreated, your father cruelly beaten, or your fellow-servants brutally murdered? I wonder why they never enslaved the Indians!"

"You are mistaken, Robert, if you think the Indians were never enslaved. I have read that the Spaniards who visited the coasts of America kidnapped thousands of Indians, whom they sent to Europe and the West Indies as slaves. Columbus himself, we are informed, captured five hundred natives, and sent them to Spain. The Indian had the lesser power of endurance, and Las Cassas suggested the enslavement of the negro, because he seemed to possess greater breadth of physical organization and stronger power of endurance. Slavery was an old world's crime which, I have heard, the Indians never practiced among themselves. Perhaps it would have been harder to reduce them to slavery and hold them in bondage when they had a vast continent before them, where they could hide in the vastnesses of its mountains or the seclusion of its forests, than it was for white men to visit the coasts of Africa and, with their superior knowledge, obtain cargoes of slaves, bring them across the ocean, hem them in on the plantations, and surround them with a pall of dense ignorance."

"I remember," said Robert, "in reading a history I once came across at our house, that when the Africans first came to this country they did not all speak one language. Some had only met as mutual enemies. They were not all one color, their complexions ranging from tawny yellow to deep black."

"Yes," said Captain Sybil, "and in dealing with the negro we wanted his labor; in dealing with the Indian we wanted his lands. For one we had weapons of war; for the other we had real and invisible chains, the coercion of force, and the terror of the unseen world."

"That's exactly so, Captain! When I was a boy I used to hear the old folks tell what would happen to bad people in another world; about the devil pouring hot lead down people's throats and stirring them up with a pitch-fork; and I used to get so scared that I would be afraid to go to bed at night. I don't suppose the Indians ever heard of such things, or, if they had, I never heard of them being willing to give away all their lands on earth, and quietly wait for a home in heaven."

FRANCES ELLEN WATKINS HARPER

"But, surely, Robert, you do not think religion has degraded the negro?"

"Oh, I wouldn't say that. But a man is in a tight fix when he takes his part, like Nat Turner or Denmark Veasy, and is made to fear that he will be hanged in this world and be burned in the next. And, since I come to think of it, we colored folks used to get mightily mixed up about our religion. Mr. Gundover had on his plantation a real smart man. He was religious, but he would steal."

"Oh, Robert," queried Sybil, "how could he be religious and steal?"

"He didn't think," retorted Robert, "it was any harm to steal from his master. I guess he thought it was right to get from his master all he could. He would have thought it wrong to steal from his fellow-servants. He thought that downright mean, but I wouldn't have insured the lives of Gundover's pigs and chickens, if Uncle Jack got them in a tight place. One day there was a minister stopping with Mr. Gundover. As a matter of course, in speaking of his servants, he gave Jack's sins an airing. He would much rather confess Jack's sins than his own. Now Gundover wanted to do two things, save his pigs and poultry, and save Jack's soul. He told the minister that Jack was a liar and a thief, and gave the minister a chance to talk with Uncle Jack about the state of his soul. Uncle Jack listened very quietly, and when taxed with stealing his master's wheat he was ready with an answer. 'Now Massa Parker,' said Jack, 'lem'me tell yer jis' how it war 'bout dat wheat. Wen ole Jack com'd down yere, dis place war all growed up in woods. He go ter work, clared up de groun' an' plowed, an' planted, an' riz a crap, an' den wen it war all done, he hadn't a dollar to buy his ole woman a gown; an' he jis' took a bag ob wheat.'"

"What did Mr. Parker say?" asked Sybil.

"I don't know, though I reckon he didn't think it was a bad steal after all, but I don't suppose he told Jack so. When he came to the next point, about Jack's lying, I suppose he thought he had a clear case; but Jack was equal to the occasion."

"How did he clear up that charge?" interrogated Captain Sybil.

"Finely. I think if he had been educated he would have made a first-rate lawyer. He said, 'Marse Parker, dere's old Joe. His wife don't lib on dis plantation. Old Joe go ober ter see her, but he stayed too long, an' didn't git back in time fer his work. Massa's oberseer kotched him an' cut him all up. When de oberseer went inter de house, pore old Joe war all tired an' beat up, an' so he lay down by de fence corner and go ter sleep. Bimeby Massa oberseer com'd an' axed, "all bin a workin' libely?" I say "Yes, Massa."' Then said Mr. Parker, 'You were lying, Joe had been sleeping, not working.' 'I know's dat, but ef I tole on Joe, Massa oberseer cut him all up again, and Massa Jesus says, "Blessed am de Peacemaker."' I heard, continued Robert, that Mr. Parker said to Gundover, 'You seem to me like a man standing in a stream where the blood of Jesus can reach you, but you are standing between it and your slaves. How will you answer that in the Day of Judgment?'"

"What did Gundover say?" asked Captain Sybil.

"He turned pale, and said, 'For God's sake don't speak of the Day of Judgment in connection with slavery.'"

Just then a messenger brought a communication to Captain Sybil. He read it attentively, and, turning to Robert, said, "Here are orders for an engagement at Five Forks tomorrow. Oh, this wasting of life and scattering of treasure might have been saved had we only been wiser. But the time is passing. Look after your company, and see that everything is in readiness as soon as possible."

Carefully Robert superintended the arrangements for the coming battle of a strife which for years had thrown its crimson shadows over the land. The Rebels fought with a valor worthy of a better cause. The disaster of Bull Run had been retrieved. Sherman had made his famous march to the sea. Fighting Joe Hooker had scaled the stronghold of the storm king and won a victory in the palace chamber of the clouds; the Union soldiers had captured Columbia, replanted the Stars and Stripes in Charleston, and changed that old sepulchre of slavery into the cradle of a new-born freedom. Farragut had been as triumphant on water as the other generals had been victorious on land, and New Orleans had been wrenched from the hands of the Confederacy. The Rebel leaders were obstinate. Misguided hordes had followed them to defeat and death. Grant was firm and determined to fight it out if it took all summer. The closing battles were fought with desperate courage and firm resistance, but at last the South was forced to succumb. On the ninth day of April, 1865, General Lee surrendered to General Grant. The lost cause went down in blood and tears, and on the brows of a ransomed people God poured the chrism of a new era, and they stood a race newly anointed with freedom.

# XVI

## AFTER THE BATTLE

Very sad and heart-rending were the scenes with which Iola came in constant contact. Well may Christian men and women labor and pray for the time when nations shall learn war no more; when, instead of bloody conflicts, there shall be peaceful arbitration. The battle in which Robert fought, after his last conversation with Captain Sybil, was one of the decisive struggles of the closing conflict. The mills of doom and fate had ground out a fearful grist of agony and death,

> *"And lives of men and souls of States*
> *Were thrown like chaff beyond the gates."*

Numbers were taken prisoners. Pale, young corpses strewed the earth; manhood was stricken down in the flush of its energy and prime. The ambulances brought in the wounded and dying. Captain Sybil laid down his life on the altar of freedom. His prediction was fulfilled. Robert was brought into the hospital, wounded, but not dangerously. Iola remembered him as being the friend of Tom Anderson, and her heart was drawn instinctively towards him. For awhile he was delirious, but her presence had a soothing effect upon him. He sometimes imagined that she was his mother, and he would tell her how he had missed her; and then at times he would call her sister. Iola, tender and compassionate, humored his fancies, and would sing to him in low, sweet tones some of the hymns she had learned in her old home in Mississippi. One day she sang a few verses of the hymn beginning with the words—

> *"Drooping souls no longer grieve,*
> *Heaven is propitious;*
> *If on Christ you do believe,*
> *You will find Him precious."*

"That," said he, looking earnestly into Iola's face, "was my mother's hymn. I have not heard it for years. Where did you learn it?"

Iola gazed inquiringly upon the face of her patient, and saw, by his clear gaze and the expression of his face, that his reason had returned.

"In my home, in Mississippi, from my own dear mother," was Iola's reply.

"Do you know where she learned it?" asked Robert.

"When she was a little girl she heard her mother sing it. Years after, a Methodist preacher came to our house, sang this hymn, and left the book behind him. My father was a Catholic, but my mother never went to any church. I did not understand it then, but I do now. We used to sing together, and read the Bible when we were alone."

"Do you remember where she came from, and who was her mother?" asked Robert, anxiously.

"My dear friend, you must be quiet. The fever has left you, but I will not answer for the consequences if you get excited."

Robert lay quiet and thoughtful for awhile and, seeing he was wakeful, Iola said, "Have you any friends to whom you would like to send a letter?"

A pathetic expression flitted over his face, as he sadly replied, "I haven't, to my knowledge, a single relation in the world. When I was about ten years old my mother and sister were sold from me. It is more than twenty years since I have heard from them. But that hymn which you were singing reminded me so much of my mother! She used to sing it when I was a child. Please sing it again."

Iola's voice rose soft and clear by his bedside, till he fell into a quiet slumber. She remembered that her mother had spoken of her brother before they had parted, and her interest and curiosity were awakened by Robert's story. While he slept, she closely scrutinized Robert's features, and detected a striking resemblance between him and her mother.

"Oh, I *do* wonder if he can be my mother's brother, from whom she has been separated so many years!"

Anxious as she was to ascertain if there was any relationship between Robert and her mother, she forebore to question him on the subject which lay so near her heart. But one day, when he was so far recovered as to be able to walk around, he met Iola on the hospital grounds, and said to her:—

"Miss Iola, you remind me so much of my mother and sister that I cannot help wondering if you are the daughter of my long-lost sister."

"Do you think," asked Iola, "if you saw the likeness of your sister you would recognize her?"

"I am afraid not. But there is one thing I can remember about her: she used to have a mole on her cheek, which mother used to tell her was her beauty spot."

"Look at this," said Iola, handing him a locket which contained her mother's picture.

Robert grasped the locket eagerly, scanned the features attentively, then, handing it back, said: "I have only a faint remembrance of my sister's features; but I never could recognize in that beautiful woman the dear little sister with whom I used to play. Oh, the cruelty of slavery! How it wrenched and tore us apart! Where is *your* mother now?"

"Oh, I cannot tell," answered Iola. "I left her in Mississippi. My father was a wealthy Creole planter, who fell in love with my mother. She was his slave, but he educated her in the North, freed, and married her. My father was very careful to have the fact of our negro blood concealed from us. I had not the slightest suspicion of it. When he was dead the secret was revealed. His white relations set aside my father's will, had his marriage declared invalid, and my mother and her children were remanded to slavery." Iola shuddered as she pronounced the horrid word, and grew deadly pale; but, regaining her self-possession, continued: "Now, that freedom has come, I intend to search for my mother until I find her."

"I do not wonder," said Robert, "that we had this war. The nation had sinned enough to suffer."

"Yes," said Iola, "if national sins bring down national judgments, then the nation is only reaping what it sowed."

"What are your plans for the future, or have you any?" asked Robert.

"I intend offering myself as a teacher in one of the schools which are being opened in different parts of the country," replied Iola. "As soon as I am able I will begin my search for my dear mother. I will advertise for her in the papers, hunt for her in the churches, and use all the means in my power to get some tidings of her and my brother Harry. What a cruel thing it was to separate us!"

# XVII

## Flames in the School-Room

G ood morning," said Dr. Gresham, approaching Robert and Iola. "How are you both? You have mended rapidly," turning to Robert, "but then it was only a flesh wound. Your general health being good, and your blood in excellent condition, it was not hard for you to rally."

"Where have you been, Doctor? I have a faint recollection of having seen you on the morning I was brought in from the field, but not since."

"I have been on a furlough. I was running down through exhaustion and overwork, and I was compelled to go home for a few weeks' rest. But now, as they are about to close the hospital, I shall be permanently relieved. I am glad that this cruel strife is over. It seemed as if I had lived through ages during these last few years. In the early part of the war I lost my arm by a stray shot, and my armless sleeve is one of the mementos of battle I shall carry with me through life. Miss Leroy," he continued, turning respectfully to Iola, "would you permit me to ask you, as I would have someone ask my sister under the same circumstances, if you have matured any plans for the future, or if I can be of the least service to you? If so, I would be pleased to render you any service in my power."

"My purpose," replied Iola, "is to hunt for my mother, and to find her if she is alive. I am willing to go anywhere and do anything to find her. But I will need a standpoint from whence I can send out lines of inquiry. It must take time, in the disordered state of affairs, even to get a clue by which I may discover her whereabouts."

"How would you like to teach?" asked the Doctor. "Schools are being opened all around us. Numbers of excellent and superior women are coming from the North to engage as teachers of the freed people. Would you be willing to take a school among these people? I think it will be uphill work. I believe it will take generations to get over the duncery of slavery. Some of these poor fellows who came into our camp did not know their right hands from their left, nor their ages, nor even the days of the month. It took me some time, in a number of cases, to understand their language. It saddened my heart to see such ignorance. One day I asked one a question, and he answered, "I no shum'.""

FRANCES ELLEN WATKINS HARPER

"What did he mean?" asked Iola.

"That he did not see it," replied the doctor. "Of course, this does not apply to all of them. Some of them are wide-awake and sharp as steel traps. I think some of that class may be used in helping others."

"I should be very glad to have an opportunity to teach," said Iola. "I used to be a great favorite among the colored children on my father's plantation."

In a few days after this conversation the hospital was closed. The sick and convalescent were removed, and Iola obtained a position as a teacher. Very soon Iola realized that while she was heartily appreciated by the freedmen, she was an object of suspicion and dislike to their former owners. The North had conquered by the supremacy of the sword, and the South had bowed to the inevitable. But here was a new army that had come with an invasion of ideas, that had come to supplant ignorance with knowledge, and it was natural that its members should be unwelcome to those who had made it a crime to teach their slaves to read the name of the ever blessed Christ. But Iola had found her work, and the freed men their friend.

When Iola opened her school she took pains to get acquainted with the parents of the children, and she gained their confidence and co-operation. Her face was a passport to their hearts. Ignorant of books, human faces were the scrolls from which they had been reading for ages. They had been the sunshine and shadow of their lives.

Iola had found a school-room in the basement of a colored church, where the doors were willingly opened to her. Her pupils came from miles around, ready and anxious to get some "book larnin'." Some of the old folks were eager to learn, and it was touching to see the eyes which had grown dim under the shadows of slavery, donning spectacles and trying to make out the words. As Iola had nearly all of her life been accustomed to colored children she had no physical repulsions to overcome, no prejudices to conquer in dealing with parents and children. In their simple childish fashion they would bring her fruits and flowers, and gladden her lonely heart with little tokens of affection.

One day a gentleman came to the school and wished to address the children. Iola suspended the regular order of the school, and the gentleman essayed to talk to them on the achievements of the white race, such as building steamboats and carrying on business. Finally, he asked how they did it?

"They've got money," chorused the children.

"But how did they get it?"

"They took it from us," chimed the youngsters. Iola smiled, and the gentleman was nonplussed; but he could not deny that one of the powers of knowledge is the power of the strong to oppress the weak.

The school was soon overcrowded with applicants, and Iola was forced to refuse numbers, because their quarters were too cramped. The school was beginning to lift up the home, for Iola was not satisfied to teach her children only the rudiments of knowledge. She had tried to lay the foundation of good character. But the elements of evil burst upon her loved and cherished work. One night the heavens were lighted with lurid flames, and Iola beheld the school, the pride and joy of her pupils and their parents, a smouldering ruin. Iola gazed with sorrowful dismay on what seemed the cruel work of an incendiary's torch. While she sat, mournfully contemplating the work of destruction, her children formed a procession, and, passing by the wreck of their school, sang:—

> *"Oh, do not be discouraged,*
> *For Jesus is your friend."*

As they sang, the tears sprang to Iola's eyes, and she said to herself, "I am not despondent of the future of my people; there is too much elasticity in their spirits, too much hope in their hearts, to be crushed out by unreasoning malice."

# XVIII

## SEARCHING FOR LOST ONES

To bind anew the ties which slavery had broken and gather together the remnants of his scattered family became the earnest purpose of Robert's life. Iola, hopeful that in Robert she had found her mother's brother, was glad to know she was not alone in *her* search. Having sent out lines of inquiry in different directions, she was led to hope, from some of the replies she had received, that her mother was living somewhere in Georgia.

Hearing that a Methodist conference was to convene in that State, and being acquainted with the bishop of that district, she made arrangements to accompany him thither. She hoped to gather some tidings of her mother through the ministers gathered from different parts of that State.

From her brother she had heard nothing since her father's death. On his way to the conference, the bishop had an engagement to dedicate a church, near the city of C——, in North Carolina. Iola was quite willing to stop there a few days, hoping to hear something of Robert Johnson's mother. Soon after she had seated herself in the cars she was approached by a gentleman, who reached out his hand to her, and greeted her with great cordiality. Iola looked up, and recognized him immediately as one of her last patients at the hospital. It was none other than Robert Johnson.

"I am so glad to meet you," he said. "I am on my way to C—— in search of my mother. I want to see the person who sold her last, and, if possible, get some clew to the direction in which she went."

"And I," said Iola, "am in search of *my* mother. I am convinced that when we find those for whom we are searching they will prove to be very nearly related. Mamma said, before we were parted, that her brother had a red spot on his temple. If I could see that spot I should rest assured that my mother is your sister."

"Then," said Robert, "I can give you that assurance," and smilingly he lifted his hair from his temple, on which was a large, red spot.

"I am satisfied," exclaimed Iola, fixing her eyes, beaming with hope and confidence, on Robert. "Oh, I am so glad that I can, without the least hesitation, accept your services to join with me in the further search. What are your plans?"

"To stop for awhile in C——," said Robert, "and gather all the information possible from those who sold and bought my mother. I intend to leave no stone un-turned in searching for her."

"Oh, I *do* hope that you will succeed. I expect to stop over there a few days, and I shall be so glad if, before I leave, I hear your search has been crowned with success, or, a least, that you have been put on the right track. Although I was born and raised in the midst of slavery, I had not the least idea of its barbarous selfishness till I was forced to pass through it. But we lived so much alone I had no opportunity to study it, except on our own plantation. My father and mother were very kind to their slaves. But it was slavery, all the same, and I hate it, root and branch."

Just then the conductor called out the station.

"We stop here," said Robert. "I am going to see Mrs. Johnson, and hunt up some of my old acquaintances. Where do you stop?"

"I don't know," replied Iola. "I expect that friends will be here to meet us. Bishop B——, permit me to introduce you to Mr. Robert Johnson, whom I have every reason to believe is my mother's brother. Like myself, he is engaged in hunting up his lost relatives."

"And I," said Robert, "am very much pleased to know that we are not without favorable clues."

"Bishop," said Iola, "Mr. Johnson wishes to know where I am to stop. He is going on an exploring expedition, and wishes to let me know the result."

"We stop at Mrs. Allston's, 313 New Street," said the bishop. "If I can be of any use to you, I am at your service."

"Thank you," said Robert, lifting his hat, as he left them to pursue his inquiries about his long-lost mother.

Quickly he trod the old familiar streets which led to his former home. He found Mrs. Johnson, but she had aged very fast since the war. She was no longer the lithe, active woman, with her proud manner and resolute bearing. Her eye had lost its brightness, her step its elasticity, and her whole appearance indicated that she was slowly sinking beneath a weight of sorrow which was heavier far than her weight of years. When she heard that Robert had called to see her she was going to receive him in the hall, as she would have done any of her former slaves, but her mind immediately changed when she saw him. He was not

FRANCES ELLEN WATKINS HARPER

the light-hearted, careless, mischief-loving Robby of former days, but a handsome man, with heavy moustache, dark, earnest eyes, and proud military bearing. He smiled, and reached out his hand to her. She hardly knew how to address him. To her colored people were either boys and girls, or "aunties and uncles." She had never in her life addressed a colored person as "Mr. or Mrs." To do so now was to violate the social customs of the place. It would be like learning a new language in her old age. Robert immediately set her at ease by addressing her under the old familiar name of "Miss Nancy." This immediately relieved her of all embarrassment. She invited him into the sitting-room, and gave him a warm welcome.

"Well, Robby," she said, "I once thought that you would have been the last one to leave me. You know I never ill-treated you, and I gave you everything you needed. People said that I was spoiling you. I thought you were as happy as the days were long. When I heard of other people's servants leaving them I used to say to myself, 'I can trust my Bobby; he will stick to me to the last.' But I fooled myself that time. Soon as the Yankee soldiers got in sight you left me without saying a word. That morning I came down into the kitchen and asked Linda, 'Where's Robert? Why hasn't he set the table?' She said 'she hadn't seen you since the night before.' I thought maybe you were sick, and I went to see, but you were not in your room. I couldn't believe at first that you were gone. Wasn't I always good to you?"

"Oh, Miss Nancy," replied Robert; "you were good, but freedom was better."

"Yes," she said, musingly, "I suppose I would have done the same. But, Robby, it did go hard with me at first. However, I soon found out that my neighbors had been going through the same thing. But its all over now. Let by-gones be by-gones. What are you doing now, and where are you living?"

"I am living in the city of P——. I have opened a hardware store there. But just now I am in search of my mother and sister."

"I hope that you may find them."

"How long," asked Robert, "do you think it has been since they left here?"

"Let me see; it must have been nearly thirty years. You got my letter?"

"Yes, ma'am; thank you."

"There have been great changes since you left here," Mrs. Johnson said. "Gundover died, and a number of colored men have banded together, bought his plantation, and divided it among themselves. And I hear they have a very nice settlement out there. I hope, since the Government has set them free, that they will succeed."

After Robert's interview with Mrs. Johnson he thought he would visit the settlement and hunt up his old friends. He easily found the place. It was on a clearing in Gundover's woods, where Robert and Uncle Daniel had held their last prayer-meeting. Now the gloomy silence of those woods was broken by the hum of industry, the murmur of cheerful voices, and the merry laughter of happy children. Where they had trodden with fear and misgiving, freedmen walked with light and bounding hearts. The school-house had taken the place of the slave-pen and auction-block. "How is yer, ole boy?" asked one laborer of another.

"Everything is lobly," replied the other. The blue sky arching overhead and the beauty of the scenery justified the expression.

Gundover had died soon after the surrender. Frank Anderson had grown reckless and drank himself to death. His brother Tom had been killed in battle. Their mother, who was Gundover's daughter, had died insane. Their father had also passed away. The defeat of the Confederates, the loss of his sons, and the emancipation of his slaves, were blows from which he never recovered. As Robert passed leisurely along, delighted with the evidences of thrift and industry which constantly met his eye, he stopped to admire a garden filled with beautiful flowers, clambering vines, and rustic adornments.

On the porch sat an elderly woman, darning stockings, the very embodiment of content and good humor. Robert looked inquiringly at her. On seeing him, she almost immediately exclaimed, "Shore as I'se born, dat's Robert! Look yere, honey, whar did yer come from? I'll gib my head fer a choppin' block ef dat ain't Miss Nancy's Bob. Ain't yer our Bobby? Shore yer is."

"Of course I am," responded Robert. "It isn't anybody else. How did you know me?"

"How did I know yer? By dem mischeebous eyes, ob course. I'd a knowed yer if I had seed yer in Europe."

"In Europe, Aunt Linda? Where's that?"

"I don't know. I specs its some big city, somewhar. But yer looks jis' splendid. Yer looks good 'nuff ter kiss."

"Oh, Aunt Linda, don't say that. You make me blush."

"Oh you go 'long wid yer. I specs yer's got a nice little wife up dar whar yer comes from, dat kisses yer ebery day, an' Sunday, too."

"Is that the way your old man does you?"

"Oh, no, not a bit. He isn't one ob de kissin' kine. But sit down," she said, handing Robert a chair. "Won't yer hab a glass ob milk? Boy, I'se a libin' in clover. Neber 'spected ter see sich good times in all my born days."

"Well, Aunt Linda," said Robert, seating himself near her, and drinking the glass of milk which she had handed him, "how goes the battle? How have you been getting on since freedom?"

"Oh, fust rate, fust rate! Wen freedom com'd I jist lit out ob Miss Johnson's kitchen soon as I could. I wanted ter re'lize I war free, an' I couldn't, tell I got out er de sight and soun' ob ole Miss. When de war war ober an' de sogers war still stopping' yere, I made pies an' cakes, sole em to de sogers, an' jist made money han' ober fist. An' I kep' on a workin' an' a savin' till my ole man got back from de war wid his wages and his bounty money. I felt right set up an' mighty big wen we counted all dat money. We had neber seen so much money in our lives befo', let alone hab it fer ourselbs. An' I sez, 'John, you take dis money an' git a nice place wid it.' An' he sez, 'Dere's no use tryin', kase dey don't want ter sell us any lan'.' Ole Gundover said, 'fore he died, dat he would let de lan' grow up in trees 'fore he'd sell it to us. An' dere war Mr. Brayton; he buyed some lan' and sole it to some cullud folks, an' his ole frien's got so mad wid him dat dey wouldn't speak ter him, an' he war borned down yere. I tole ole Miss Anderson's daughter dat we wanted ter git some homes ob our ownselbs. She sez, 'Den you won't want ter work for us?' Jis' de same as ef we could eat an' drink our houses. I tell yer, Robby, dese white folks don't know eberything."

"That's a fact, Aunt Linda."

"Den I sez ter John, 'wen one door shuts anoder opens.' An' shore 'nough, ole Gundover died, an' his place war all in debt, an' had to be sole. Some Jews bought it, but dey didn't want to farm it, so dey gib us a chance to buy it. Dem Jews hez been right helpful to cullud people wen dey hab lan' to sell. I reckon dey don't keer who buys it so long as dey gits de money. Well, John didn't gib in at fust; didn't want to let on his wife knowed more dan he did, an' dat he war ruled ober by a woman. Yer know he is an' ole Firginian, an' some ob dem ole Firginians do so lub to rule a woman. But I kep' naggin at him, till I specs he got tired of my tongue, an' he went and buyed dis piece ob lan'. Dis house war on it, an' war all gwine to wrack. It used to belong to John's ole marster. His wife died right in dis house, an' arter dat her husband went right to de dorgs; an' now he's in de pore-house. My! but ain't dem tables turned. When we knowed it war our own, warn't my ole man proud! I seed it in him, but he wouldn't let on. Ain't you men powerful 'ceitful?"

"Oh, Aunt Linda, don't put me in with the rest!"

"I don't know 'bout dat. Put you all in de bag for 'ceitfulness, an' I don't know which would git out fust."

"Well, Aunt Linda, I suppose by this time you know how to read and write?"

"No, chile, sence freedom's com'd I'se bin scratchin' too hard to get a libin' to put my head down to de book."

"But, Aunt Linda, it would be such company when your husband is away, to take a book. Do you never get lonesome?"

"Chile, I ain't got no time ter get lonesome. Ef you had eber so many chickens to feed, an' pigs squealin' fer somethin' ter eat, an' yore ducks an' geese squakin' 'roun' yer, yer wouldn't hab time ter git lonesome."

"But, Aunt Linda, you might be sick for months, and think what a comfort it would be if you could read your Bible."

"Oh, I could hab prayin' and singin'. Dese people is mighty good 'bout prayin' by de sick. Why, Robby, I think it would gib me de hysterics ef I war to try to git book larnin' froo my pore ole head. How long is yer gwine to stay? An' whar is yer stoppin?"

"I got here today," said Robert, "but I expect to stay several days."

"Well, I wants yer to meet my ole man, an' talk 'bout ole times. Couldn't yer come an' stop wid me, or isn't my house sniptious 'nuff?"

"Yes, thank you; but there is a young lady in town whom I think is my niece, my sister's daughter, and I want to be with her all I can."

"Your niece! Whar did you git any niece from?"

"Don't you remember," asked Robert, "that my mother had a little daughter, when Mrs. Johnson sold her? Well, I believe this young lady is that daughter's child."

"Laws a marcy!" exclaimed Aunt Linda, "yer don't tell me so! Whar did yer ketch up wid her?"

"I met her first," said Robert, "at the hospital here, when our poor Tom was dying; and when I was wounded at Five Forks she attended me in the field hospital there. She was just as good as gold."

"Well, did I eber! You jis' fotch dat chile to see me, ef she ain't too fine. I'se pore, but I'se clean, an' I ain't forgot how ter git up good dinners. Now, I wants ter hab a good talk 'bout our feller-sarvants."

"Yes, and I," said Robert, "want to hear all about Uncle Daniel, and Jennie, and Uncle Ben Tunnel."

"Well, I'se got lots an' gobs ter tell yer. I'se kep' track ob dem all. Aunt Katie died an' went ter hebben in a blaze ob glory. Uncle Dan'el stayed on de place till Marse Robert com'd back. When de war war ober he war smashed all ter pieces. I did pity him from de bottom ob my heart. When he went ter de war he looked so brave an' han'some; an' wen he com'd back he looked orful. 'Fore he went he gib Uncle Dan'el a bag full ob money ter take kere ob. 'An wen he com'd back Uncle Dan'el gibed him ebery cent ob it. It warn't ebery white pusson he could hab trusted wid it. 'Cause yer know, Bobby, money's a mighty temptin' thing. Dey tells me dat Marster Robert los' a heap ob property by de war; but Marse Robert war always mighty good ter Uncle Dan'el and Aunt Katie. He war wid her wen she war dyin' an' she got holt his han' an' made him promise dat he would meet her in glory. I neber seed anybody so happy in my life. She singed an' prayed ter de last. I tell you dis ole time religion is good 'nuff fer me. Mr. Robert didn't stay yere long arter her, but I beliebs he went all right. But 'fore he went he looked out fer Uncle Dan'el. Did you see dat nice little cabin down dere wid de green shutters an' nice little garden in front? Well, 'fore Marse Robert died he gib Uncle Dan'el dat place, an' Miss Mary and de chillen looks arter him yet; an' he libs jis' as snug as a bug in a rug. I'se gwine ter axe him ter take supper wid you. He'll be powerful glad ter see you."

"Do you ever go to see old Miss?" asked Robert.

"Oh, yes; I goes ebery now and den. But she's jis' fell froo. Ole Johnson jis' drunk hisself to death. He war de biggest guzzler I eber seed in my life. Why, dat man he drunk up ebery thing he could lay his han's on. Sometimes he would go 'roun' tryin' to borrer money from pore cullud folks. 'Twas rale drefful de way dat pore feller did frow hisself away. But drink did it all. I tell you, Bobby, dat drink's a drefful thing wen it gits de upper han' ob you. You'd better steer clar ob it."

"That's so," assented Robert.

"I know'd Miss Nancy's fadder and mudder. Dey war mighty rich. Some ob de real big bugs. Marse Jim used to know dem, an' come ober ter de plantation, an' eat an' drink wen he got ready, an' stay as long as he choose. Ole Cousins used to have wine at dere table ebery day, an' Marse Jim war mighty fon' ob dat wine, an' sometimes he would drink till he got quite boozy. Ole Cousins liked him bery well, till he foun' out he wanted his darter, an' den he didn't want him fer rags nor patches.

But Miss Nancy war mighty headstrong, an' allers liked to hab her own way; an' dis time she got it. But didn't she step her foot inter it? Ole Johnson war mighty han'some, but when dat war said all war said. She run'd off an' got married, but wen she got down she war too spunkey to axe her pa for anything. Wen you war wid her, yer know she only took big bugs. But wen de war com'd 'roun' it tore her all ter pieces, an' now she's as pore as Job's turkey. I feel's right sorry fer her. Well, Robby, things is turned 'roun' mighty quare. Ole Mistus war up den, an' I war down; now, she's down, an' I'se up. But I pities her, 'cause she warn't so bad arter all. De wuss thing she eber did war ta sell your mudder, an' she wouldn't hab done dat but she snatched de whip out ob her han' an gib her a lickin'. Now I belieb in my heart she war 'fraid ob your mudder arter dat. But we women had ter keep 'em from whippin' us, er dey'd all de time been libin' on our bones. She had no man ter whip us 'cept dat ole drunken husband ob hern, an' he war allers too drunk ter whip hisself. He jis' wandered off, an' I reckon he died in somebody's pore-house. He warn't no 'count nohow you fix it. Weneber I goes to town I carries her some garden sass, er a little milk an' butter. An' she's mighty glad ter git it. I ain't got nothin' agin her. She neber struck me a lick in her life, an' I belieb in praising de bridge dat carries me ober. Dem Yankees set me free, an' I thinks a powerful heap ob dem. But it does rile me ter see dese mean white men comin' down yere an' settin' up dere grog-shops, tryin' to fedder dere nests sellin' licker to pore culled people. Deys de bery kine ob men dat used ter keep dorgs to ketch de runaways. I'd be chokin' fer a drink 'fore I'd eber spen' a cent wid dem, a spreadin' dere traps to git de black folks' money. You jis' go down town 'fore sun up to-morrer mornin' an' you see ef dey don't hab dem bars open to sell dere drams to dem hard workin' culled people 'fore dey goes ter work. I thinks some niggers is mighty big fools."

"Oh, Aunt Linda, don't run down your race. Leave that for the white people."

"I ain't runnin' down my people. But a fool's a fool, wether he's white or black. An' I think de nigger who will spen' his hard-earned money in dese yere new grog-shops is de biggest kine ob a fool, an' I sticks ter dat. You know we didn't hab all dese low places in slave times. An' what is dey fer, but to get de people's money. An' its a shame how dey do sling de licker 'bout 'lection times."

"But don't the temperance people want the colored people to vote the temperance ticket?"

"Yes, but some ob de culled people gits mighty skittish ef dey tries to git em to vote dare ticket 'lection time, an' keeps dem at a proper distance wen de 'lection's ober. Some ob dem say dere's a trick behine it, an' don't want to tech it. Dese white folks could do a heap wid de culled folks ef dey'd only treat em right."

"When our people say there is a trick behind it," said Robert, "I only wish they could see the trick before it—the trick of worse than wasting their money, and of keeping themselves and families poorer and more ignorant than there is any need for them to be."

"Well, Bobby, I beliebs we might be a people ef it warn't for dat mizzable drink. An' Robby, I jis' tells yer what I wants; I wants some libe man to come down yere an' splain things ter dese people. I don't mean a politic man, but a man who'll larn dese people how to bring up dere chillen, to keep our gals straight, an' our boys from runnin' in de saloons an' gamblin' dens."

"Don't your preachers do that?" asked Robert.

"Well, some ob dem does, an' some ob dem doesn't. An' wen dey preaches, I want dem to practice wat dey preach. Some ob dem says dey's called, but I jis' thinks laziness called some ob dem. An' I thinks since freedom come deres some mighty pore sticks set up for preachers. Now dere's John Anderson, Tom's brudder; you 'member Tom."

"Yes; as brave a fellow and as honest as ever stepped in shoe leather."

"Well, his brudder war mighty diffrent. He war down in de lower kentry wen de war war ober. He war mighty smart, an' had a good head-piece, an' a orful glib tongue. He set up store an' sole whisky, an' made a lot ob money. Den he wanted ter go to de legislatur. Now what should he do but make out he'd got 'ligion, an' war called to preach. He had no more 'ligion dan my ole dorg. But he had money an' built a meetin' house, whar he could hole meeting, an' hab funerals; an' you know cullud folks is mighty great on funerals. Well dat jis' tuck wid de people, an' he got 'lected to de legislatur. Den he got a fine house, an' his ole wife warn't good 'nuff for him. Den dere war a young school-teacher, an' he begun cuttin' his eyes at her. But she war as deep in de mud as he war in de mire, an' he jis' gib up his ole wife and married her, a fusty thing. He war a mean ole hypocrit, an' I wouldn't sen' fer him to bury my cat. Robby, I'se down on dese kine ob preachers like a thousand bricks."

"Well, Aunt Linda, all the preachers are not like him."

"No; I knows dat; not by a jug full. We's got some mighty good men down yere, an' we's glad when dey comes, an' orful sorry when dey goes 'way. De las preacher we had war a mighty good man. He didn't like too much hollerin'."

"Perhaps," said Robert, "he thought it were best for only one to speak at a time."

"I specs so. His wife war de nicest and sweetest lady dat eber I did see. None ob yer airish, stuck up folks, like a tarrapin carryin' eberything on its back. She used ter hab meetins fer de mudders, an' larn us how to raise our chillen, an' talk so putty to de chillen. I sartinly did lub dat woman."

"Where is she now?" asked Robert.

"De Conference moved dem 'bout thirty miles from yere. Deys gwine to hab a big meetin' ober dere next Sunday. Don't you 'member dem meetins we used to hab in de woods? We don't hab to hide like we did den. But it don't seem as ef de people had de same good 'ligion we had den. 'Pears like folks is took up wid makin' money an' politics."

"Well, Aunt Linda, don't you wish those good old days would come back?"

"No, chile; neber! neber! Wat fer you take me? I'd ruther lib in a corn-crib. Freedom needn't keep me outer heben; an' ef I'se sich a fool as ter lose my 'ligion cause I'se free, I oughtn' ter git dere."

"But, Aunt Linda, if old Miss were able to take care of you, wouldn't you just as leave be back again?"

There was a faint quiver of indignation in Aunt Linda's voice, as she replied:—

"Don't yer want yer freedom? Well I wants ter pat my free foot. Halleluyah! But, Robby, I wants yer ter go ter dat big meetin' de wuss kine."

"How will I get there?" asked Robert.

"Oh, dat's all right. My ole man's got two ob de nicest mules you eber set yer eyes on. It'll jis' do yer good ter look at dem. I 'spect you'll see some ob yer ole frens dere. Dere's a nice settlemen' of cullud folks ober dere, an' I wants yer to come an' bring dat young lady. I wants dem folks to see wat nice folks I kin bring to de meetin'. I hope's yer didn't lose all your 'ligion in de army."

"Oh, I hope not," replied Robert.

"Oh, chile, yer mus' be shore 'bout dat. I don't want yer to ride hope's hoss down to torment. Now be shore an' come to-morrer an' bring dat young lady, an' take supper wid me. I'se all on nettles to see dat chile."

# XIX

## Striking Contrasts

The next day, Robert, accompanied by Iola, went to the settlement to take supper with Aunt Linda, and a very luscious affair it was. Her fingers had not lost their skill since she had tasted the sweets of freedom. Her biscuits were just as light and flaky as ever. Her jelly was as bright as amber, and her preserves were perfectly delicious. After she had set the table she stood looking in silent admiration, chuckling to herself: "Ole Mistus can't set sich a table as dat. She ought'er be yere to see it. Specs 'twould make her mouf water. Well, I mus' let by-gones be by-gones. But dis yere freedom's mighty good."

Aunt Linda had invited Uncle Daniel, and, wishing to give him a pleasant surprise, she had refrained from telling him that Robert Johnson was the one she wished him to meet.

"Do you know dis gemmen?" said Aunt Linda to Uncle Daniel, when the latter arrived.

"Well, I can't say's I do. My eyes is gittin dim, an I disremembers him."

"Now jis' you look right good at him. Don't yer 'member him?"

Uncle Daniel looked puzzled and, slowly scanning Robert's features, said: "He do look like somebody I used ter know, but I can't make him out ter save my life. I don't know whar to place him. Who is de gemmen, ennyhow?"

"Why, Uncle Dan'el," replied Aunt Linda, "dis is Robby; Miss Nancy's bad, mischeebous Robby, dat war allers playin' tricks on me."

"Well, shore's I'se born, ef dis ain't our ole Bobby!" exclaimed Uncle Daniel, delightedly. "Why, chile, whar did yer come from? Thought you war dead an' buried long 'go."

"Why, Uncle Daniel, did you send anybody to kill me?" asked Robert, laughingly.

"Oh, no'n 'deed, chile! but I yeard dat you war killed in de battle, an' I never 'spected ter see you agin."

"Well, here I am," replied Robert, "large as life, and just as natural. And this young lady, Uncle Daniel, I believe is my niece." As he spoke he turned to Iola. "Do you remember my mother?"

"Oh, yes," said Uncle Daniel, looking intently at Iola as she stepped forward and cordially gave him her hand.

"Well, I firmly believe," continued Robert, "that this is the daughter of the little girl whom Miss Nancy sold away with my mother."

"Well, I'se rale glad ter see her. She puts me mighty much in mine ob dem days wen we war all young togedder; wen Miss Nancy sed, 'Harriet war too high fer her.' It jis' seems like yisterday wen I yeard Miss Nancy say, 'No house could flourish whar dere war two mistresses.' Well, Mr. Robert—"

"Oh, no, no, Uncle Daniel," interrupted Robert, "don't say that! Call me Robby or Bob, just as you used to."

"Well, Bobby, I'se glad klar from de bottom of my heart ter see yer."

"Even if you wouldn't go with us when we left?"

"Oh, Bobby, dem war mighty tryin' times. You boys didn't know it, but Marster Robert hab giben me a bag ob money ter take keer ob, an' I promised him I'd do it an' I had ter be ez good ez my word."

"Oh, Uncle Daniel, why didn't you tell us boys all about it? We could have helped you take care of it."

"Now, wouldn't dat hab bin smart ter let on ter you chaps, an' hab you huntin' fer it from Dan ter Barsheba? I specs some ob you would bin a rootin' fer it yit!"

"Well, Uncle Daniel, we were young then; I can't tell what we would have done if we had found it. But we are older now."

"Yes, yer older, but I wouldn't put it pas' yer eben now, ef yer foun' out whar it war."

"Yes," said Iola, laughing, "they say 'caution is the parent of safety.'"

"Money's a mighty tempting thing," said Robert, smiling.

"But, Robby, dere's nothin' like a klar conscience; a klar conscience, Robby!"

Just then Aunt Linda, who had been completing the preparations for her supper, entered the room with her husband, and said, "Salters, let me interdoos you ter my fren', Mr. Robert Johnson, an' his niece, Miss Leroy."

"Why, is it possible," exclaimed Robert, rising, and shaking hands, "that you are Aunt Linda's husband?"

"Dat's what de parson sed," replied Salters.

"I thought," pursued Robert, "that your name was John Andrews. It was such when you were in my company."

"All de use I'se got fer dat name is ter git my money wid it; an' wen dat's done, all's done. Got 'nuff ob my ole Marster in slave times, widout wearin' his name in freedom. Wen I got done wid him, I got done wid his name. Wen I 'listed, I war John Andrews; and wen I gits my pension, I'se John Andrews; but now Salters is my name, an' I likes it better."

"But how came you to be Aunt Linda's husband? Did you get married since the war?"

"Lindy an' me war married long 'fore de war. But my ole Marster sole me away from her an' our little gal, an' den sole her chile ter somebody else. Arter freedom, I hunted up our little gal, an' foun' her. She war a big woman den. Den I com'd right back ter dis place an' foun' Lindy. She hedn't married agin, nuther hed I; so we jis' let de parson marry us out er de book; an' we war mighty glad ter git togedder agin, an' feel hitched togedder fer life."

"Well, Uncle Daniel," said Robert, turning the conversation toward him, "you and Uncle Ben wouldn't go with us, but you came out all right at last."

"Yes, indeed," said Aunt Linda, "Ben got inter a stream of luck. Arter freedom com'd, de people had a heap of fath in Ben; an' wen dey wanted some one to go ter Congress dey jist voted for Ben ter go. An' he went, too. An' wen Salters went to Washin'ton to git his pension, who should he see dere wid dem big men but our Ben, lookin' jist as big as any ob dem."

"An' it did my ole eyes good jist ter see it," broke in Salters; "if I couldn't go dere myself, I war mighty glad to see some one ob my people dat could. I felt like de boy who, wen somebody said he war gwine to slap off his face, said, 'Yer kin slap off my face, but I'se got a big brudder, an' you can't slap off his face.' I went to see him 'fore I lef, and he war jist de same as he war wen we war boys togedder. He hadn't got de big head a bit."

"I reckon Mirandy war mighty sorry she didn't stay wid him. I know I should be," said Aunt Linda.

"Uncle Daniel," asked Robert, "are you still preaching?"

"Yes, chile, I'se still firing off de Gospel gun."

"I hear some of the Northern folks are down here teaching theology, that is, teaching young men how to preach. Why don't you study theology?"

"Look a yere, boy, I'se been a preachin' dese thirty years, an' you come yere a tellin' me 'bout studying yore ologies. I larn'd my 'ology at de foot ob de cross. You bin dar?"

"Dear Uncle Daniel," said Iola, "the moral aspect of the nation would be changed if it would learn at the same cross to subordinate the spirit of caste to the spirit of Christ."

"Does yer 'member Miss Nancy's Harriet," asked Aunt Linda, "dat she sole away kase she wouldn't let her whip her? Well, we think dis is Harriet's gran'chile. She war sole away from her mar, an' now she's a lookin' fer her."

"Well, I hopes she may fine her," replied Salters. "I war sole 'way from my mammy wen I war eighteen mont's ole, an' I wouldn't know her now from a bunch ob turnips."

"I," said Iola, "am on my way South seeking for my mother, and I shall not give up until I find her."

"Come," said Aunt Linda, "we mustn't stan' yer talkin', or de grub'll git cole. Come, frens, sit down, an' eat some ob my pore supper."

Aunt Linda sat at the table in such a flutter of excitement that she could hardly eat, but she gazed with intense satisfaction on her guests. Robert sat on her right hand, contrasting Aunt Linda's pleasant situation with the old days in Mrs. Johnson's kitchen, where he had played his pranks upon her, and told her the news of the war.

Over Iola there stole a spirit of restfulness. There was something so motherly in Aunt Linda's manner that it seemed to recall the bright, sunshiny days when she used to nestle in Mam Liza's arms, in her own happy home. The conversation was full of army reminiscences and recollections of the days of slavery. Uncle Daniel was much interested, and, as they rose from the table, exclaimed:—

"Robby, seein' yer an' hearin' yer talk, almos' puts new springs inter me. I feel 'mos' like I war gittin' younger."

After the supper, Salters and his guests returned to the front room, which Aunt Linda regarded with so much pride, and on which she bestowed so much care.

"Well, Captin," said Salters, "I neber 'spected ter see you agin. Do you know de las' time I seed yer? Well, you war on a stretcher, an' four ob us war carryin' you ter de hospital. War you much hurt?

"No," replied Robert, "it was only a flesh wound; and this young lady nursed me so carefully that I soon got over it."

"Is dat de way you foun' her?"

"Yes, Andrews,"—

"Salters, ef you please," interrupted Salters. "I'se only Andrews wen I gits my money."

"Well, Salters," continued Robert, "our freedom was a costly thing. Did you know that Captain Sybil was killed in one of the last battles of the war? These young chaps, who are taking it so easy, don't know the hardships through which we older ones passed. But all the battles are not fought, nor all the victories won. The colored man has escaped from one slavery, and I don't want him to fall into another. I want the young folks to keep their brains clear, and their right arms strong, to fight the battles of life manfully, and take their places alongside of every other people in this country. And I cannot see what is to hinder them if they get a chance."

"I don't nuther," said Salters. "I don't see dat dey drinks any more dan anybody else, nor dat dere is any meanness or debilment dat a black man kin do dat a white man can't keep step wid him."

"Yes," assented Robert, "but while a white man is stealing a thousand dollars, a black man is getting into trouble taking a few chickens."

"All that may be true," said Iola, "but there are some things a white man can do that we cannot afford to do."

"I beliebs eberybody, Norf and Souf, is lookin' at us; an' some ob dem ain't got no good blood fer us, nohow you fix it," said Salters.

"I specs cullud folks mus' hab done somethin'," interposed Aunt Linda.

"O, nonsense," said Robert. "I don't think they are any worse than the white people. I don't believe, if we had the power, we would do any more lynching, burning, and murdering than they do."

"Dat's so," said Aunt Linda, "it's ralely orful how our folks hab been murdered sence de war. But I don't think dese young folks is goin' ter take things as we's allers done."

"We war cowed down from the beginnin'," said Uncle Daniel, "but dese young folks ain't comin' up dat way."

"No," said Salters, "fer one night arter some ob our pore people had been killed, an' some ob our women had run'd away 'bout seventeen miles, my gran'son, looking me squar in de face, said: 'Ain't you got five fingers? Can't you pull a trigger as well as a white man?' I tell yer, Cap, dat jis' got to me, an' I made up my mine dat my boy should neber call me a coward."

"It is not to be expected," said Robert, "that these young people are going to put up with things as we did, when we weren't permitted to hold a meeting by ourselves, or to own a club or learn to read."

"I tried," said Salters, "to git a little out'er de book wen I war in de army. On Sundays I sometimes takes a book an' tries to make out de words, but my eyes is gittin' dim an' de letters all run togedder, an' I gits sleepy, an' ef yer wants to put me to sleep jis' put a book in my han'. But wen it comes to gittin' out a stan' ob cotton, an' plantin' corn, I'se dere all de time. But dat gran'son ob mine is smart as a steel trap. I specs he'll be a preacher."

Salters looked admiringly at his grandson, who sat grinning in the corner, munching a pear he had brought from the table.

"Yes," said Aunt Linda, "his fadder war killed by the Secesh, one night, comin' home from a politic meetin', an' his pore mudder died a few weeks arter, an' we mean to make a man ob him."

"He's got to larn to work fust," said Salters, "an' den ef he's right smart I'se gwine ter sen' him ter college. An' ef he can't get a libin' one way, he kin de oder."

"Yes," said Iola, "I hope he will turn out an excellent young man, for the greatest need of the race is noble, earnest men, and true women."

"Job," said Salters, turning to his grandson, "tell Jake ter hitch up de mules, an' you stay dere an' help him. We's all gwine ter de big meetin'. Yore grandma hab set her heart on goin', an' it'll be de same as a spell ob sickness ef she don't hab a chance to show her bes' bib an' tucker. That ole gal's as proud as a peacock."

"Now, John Salters," exclaimed Aunt Linda, "ain't you 'shamed ob yourself? Allers tryin' to poke fun at yer pore wife. Never mine; wait till I'se gone, an' you'll miss me."

"Ef I war single," said Salters, "I could git a putty young gal, but it wouldn't be so easy wid you."

"Why not?" said Iola, smiling.

"'Cause young men don't want ole hens, an' ole men want young pullets," was Salter's reply.

"Robby, honey," said Aunt Linda, "when you gits a wife, don't treat her like dat man treats me."

"Oh, his head's level," answered Robert; "at least it was in the army."

"Dat's jis' de way; you see dat, Miss Iola? One man takin' up for de oder. But I'll be eben wid you bof. I must go now an' git ready."

Iola laughed. The homely enjoyment of that evening was very welcome to her after the trying scenes through which she had passed. Further conversation was interrupted by the appearance of the wagon, drawn by two fine mules. John Salters stopped joking his wife to admire his mules.

"Jis' look at dem," he said. "Ain't dey beauties? I bought 'em out ob my bounty-money. Arter de war war ober I had a little money, an' I war gwine ter rent a plantation on sheers an' git out a good stan' ob cotton. Cotton war bringin' orful high prices den, but Lindy said to me, 'Now, John, you'se got a lot ob money, an' you'd better salt it down. I'd ruther lib on a little piece ob lan' ob my own dan a big piece ob somebody else's. Well, I says to Lindy, I dun know nuthin' 'bout buyin' lan', an' I'se 'fraid arter I'se done buyed it an' put all de marrer ob dese bones in it, dat somebody's far-off cousin will come an' say de title ain't good, an' I'll lose it all."

"You're right thar, John," said Uncle Daniel. "White man's so unsartin, black man's nebber safe."

"But somehow," continued Salters, "Lindy warn't satisfied wid rentin', so I buyed a piece ob lan', an' I'se glad now I'se got it. Lindy's got a lot ob gumption; knows most as much as a man. She ain't got dat long head fer nuffin. She's got lots ob sense, but I don't like to tell her so."

"Why not?" asked Iola. "Do you think it would make her feel too happy?"

"Well, it don't do ter tell you women how much we thinks ob you. It sets you up too much. Ole Gundover's overseer war my marster, an' he used ter lib in dis bery house. I'se fixed it up sence I'se got it. Now I'se better off dan he is, 'cause he tuck to drink, an' all his frens is gone, an' he's in de pore-house."

Just then Linda came to the door with her baskets.

"Now, Lindy, ain't you ready yet? Do hurry up."

"Yes, I'se ready, but things wouldn't go right ef you didn't hurry me."

"Well, put your chicken fixins an' cake right in yere. Captin, you'll ride wid me, an' de young lady an' my ole woman'll take de back seat. Uncle Dan'el, dere's room for you ef you'll go."

"No, I thank you. It's time fer ole folks to go to bed. Good night! An', Bobby, I hopes to see you agin'."

# XX

## A Revelation

I t was a lovely evening for the journey. The air was soft and balmy. The fields and hedges were redolent with flowers. Not a single cloud obscured the brightness of the moon or the splendor of the stars. The ancient trees were festooned with moss, which hung like graceful draperies. Ever and anon a startled hare glided over the path, and whip-poor-wills and crickets broke the restful silence of the night. Robert rode quietly along, quaffing the beauty of the scene and thinking of his boyish days, when he gathered nuts and wild plums in those woods; he also indulged pleasant reminiscences of later years, when, with Uncle Daniel and Tom Anderson, he attended the secret prayer-meetings. Iola rode along, conversing with Aunt Linda, amused and interested at the quaintness of her speech and the shrewdness of her intellect. To her the ride was delightful.

"Does yer know dis place, Robby," asked Aunt Linda, as they passed an old resort.

"I should think I did," replied Robert. "It is the place where we held our last prayer-meeting."

"An' dere's dat ole broken pot we used, ter tell 'bout de war. But warn't ole Miss hoppin' wen she foun' out you war goin' to de war! I thought she'd go almos' wile. Now, own up, Robby, didn't you feel kine ob mean to go off widout eben biddin' her good bye? An' I ralely think ole Miss war fon' ob yer. Now, own up, honey, didn't yer feel a little down in de mouf wen yer lef' her."

"Not much," responded Robert. "I only thought she was getting paid back for selling my mother."

"Dat's so, Robby! yore mudder war a likely gal, wid long black hair, an' kine ob ginger-bread color. An' you neber hearn tell ob her sence dey sole her to Georgia?"

"Never," replied Robert, "but I would give everything I have on earth to see her once more. I *do* hope, if she is living, that I may meet her before I die."

"You's right, boy, cause she lub'd you as she lub'd her own life. Many a time hes she set in my ole cabin an' cried 'bout yer wen you war fas' asleep. It's all ober now, but I'se gwine to hole up fer dem Yankees dat gib me my freedom, an' sent dem nice ladies from de Norf to gib us some sense. Some ob dese folks calls em nigger teachers, an' won't hab nuffin to do wid 'em, but I jis' thinks dey's splendid. But dere's some triflin' niggers down yere who'll sell der votes for almost nuffin. Does you 'member Jake Williams an' Gundover's Tom? Well dem two niggers is de las' ob pea-time. Dey's mighty small pertaters an' few in a hill."

"Oh, Aunt Linda," said Robert, "don't call them niggers. They are our own people."

"Dey ain't my kine ob people. I jis' calls em niggers, an' niggers I means; an' de bigges' kine ob niggers. An' if my John war sich a nigger I'd whip him an' leave him."

"An' what would I be a doin'," queried John, suddenly rousing up at the mention of his name.

"Standing still and taking it, I suppose," said Iola, who had been quietly listening to and enjoying the conversation.

"Yes, an' I'd ketch myself stan'in' still an' takin' it," was John's plucky response.

"Well, you oughter, ef you's mean enough to wote dat ticket ter put me back inter slavery," was Aunt Linda's parting shot. "Robby," she continued, "you 'member Miss Nancy's Jinnie?"

"Of course I do," said Robert.

"She married Mr. Gundover's Dick. Well, dere warn't much git up an' go 'bout him. So, wen 'lection time com'd, de man he war workin' fer tole him ef he woted de radical ticket he'd turn him off. Well, Jinnie war so 'fraid he'd do it, dat she jis' follered him fer days."

"Poor fellow!" exclaimed Robert. "How did he come out?"

"He certainly was between two fires," interposed Iola.

"Oh, Jinnie gained de day. She jis' got her back up, and said, 'Now ef yer wote dat ticket ter put me back inter slavery, you take yore rags an' go.' An' Dick jis' woted de radical ticket. Jake Williams went on de Secesh side, woted whar he thought he'd git his taters, but he got fooled es slick es greese."

"How was that?" asked Robert.

"Some ob dem folks, dat I 'spects buyed his wote, sent him some flour an' sugar. So one night his wife hab company ter tea. Dey made a big spread, an' put a lot ob sugar on de table fer supper, an' Tom jis' went fer dat sugar. He put a lot in his tea. But somehow it didn't tase right, an' wen dey come ter fine out what war de matter, dey hab sent him a barrel ob san' wid some sugar on top, an' wen de sugar war all gone de san' war dare. Wen I yeard it, I jis' split my sides a larfin. It war too good to keep; an' wen it got roun', Jake war as mad as a March hare. But it sarved him right."

"Well, Aunt Linda, you musn't be too hard on Uncle Jake; you know he's getting old."

"Well he ain't too ole ter do right. He ain't no older dan Uncle Dan'el. An' I yered dey offered him $500 ef he'd go on dere side. An' Uncle Dan'el wouldn't tech it. An' dere's Uncle Job's wife; why didn't she go dat way? She war down on Job's meanness."

"What did she do?"

"Wen 'lection time 'rived, he com'd home bringing some flour an' meat; an' he says ter Aunt Polly, 'Ole woman, I got dis fer de wote.' She jis' picked up dat meat an' flour an' sent it sailin' outer doors, an' den com'd back an' gib him a good tongue-lashin'. 'Oder people,' she said, 'a wotin' ter lib good, an' you a sellin' yore wote! Ain't you got 'nuff ob ole Marster, an' ole Marster bin cuttin' you up? It shan't stay yere.' An' so she wouldn't let de things stay in de house."

"What did Uncle Job do?"

"He jis' stood dere an' cried."

"And didn't you feel sorry for him?" asked Iola.

"Not a bit! he hedn't no business ter be so shabby."

"But, Aunt Linda," pursued Iola, "if it were shabby for an ignorant colored man to sell his vote, wasn't it shabbier for an intelligent white man to buy it?"

"You see," added Robert, "all the shabbiness is not on our side."

"I knows dat," said Aunt Linda, "but I can't help it. I wants my people to wote right, an' to think somethin' ob demselves."

"Well, Aunt Linda, they say in every flock of sheep there will be one that's scabby," observed Iola.

"Dat's so! But I ain't got no use fer scabby sheep."

"Lindy," cried John, "we's most dar! Don't you yere dat singin'? Dey's begun a'ready."

"Neber mine," said Aunt Linda, "sometimes de las' ob de wine is de bes'."

Thus discoursing they had beguiled the long hours of the night and made their long journey appear short.

Very soon they reached the church, a neat, commodious, frame building, with a blue ceiling, white walls within and without, and large windows with mahogany-colored facings. It was a sight full of pathetic interest to see that group which gathered from miles around. They had come to break bread with each other, relate their experiences, and tell of their hopes of heaven. In that meeting were remnants of broken families—mothers who had been separated from their children before the war, husbands who had not met their wives for years. After the bread had been distributed and the handshaking was nearly over, Robert raised the hymn which Iola had sung for him when he was recovering from his wounds, and Iola, with her clear, sweet tones, caught up the words and joined him in the strain. When the hymn was finished a dear old mother rose from her seat. Her voice was quite strong. With still a lingering light and fire in her eye, she said:—

"I rise, bredren an' sisters, to say I'm on my solemn march to glory."

"Amen!" "Glory!" came from a number of voices.

"I'se had my trials an' temptations, my ups an' downs; but I feels I'll soon be in one ob de many mansions. If it hadn't been for dat hope I 'spects I would have broken down long ago. I'se bin through de deep waters, but dey didn't overflow me; I'se bin in de fire, but de smell ob it isn't on my garments. Bredren an' sisters, it war a drefful time when I war tored away from my pore little chillen."

"Dat's so!" exclaimed a chorus of voices. Some of her hearers moaned, others rocked to and fro, as thoughts of similar scenes in their own lives arose before them.

"When my little girl," continued the speaker, "took hole ob my dress an' begged me ter let her go wid me, an' I couldn't do it, it mos' broke my heart. I had a little boy, an' wen my mistus sole me she kep' him. She carried on a boardin' house. Many's the time I hab stole out at night an' seen dat chile an' sleep'd wid him in my arms tell mos' day. Bimeby de people I libed wid got hard up fer money, an' dey sole me one way an' my pore little gal de oder; an' I neber laid my eyes on my pore chillen sence den. But, honeys, let de wind blow high or low, I 'spects to outwedder de storm an' anchor by'm bye in bright glory. But I'se bin a prayin' fer one thing, an' I beliebs I'll git it; an' dat is dat I may see my chillen 'fore I die. Pray fer me dat I may hole out an' hole on, an' neber make a shipwrack ob faith, an' at las' fine my way from earth to glory."

Having finished her speech, she sat down and wiped away the tears that flowed all the more copiously as she remembered her lost children. When she rose to speak her voice and manner instantly arrested Robert's attention. He found his mind reverting to the scenes of his childhood.

As she proceeded his attention became riveted on her. Unbidden tears filled his eyes and great sobs shook his frame. He trembled in every limb. Could it be possible that after years of patient search through churches, papers, and inquiring friends, he had accidentally stumbled on his mother—the mother who, long years ago, had pillowed his head upon her bosom and left her parting kiss upon his lips? How should he reveal himself to her? Might not sudden joy do what years of sorrow had failed to accomplish? Controlling his feelings as best he could, he rose to tell his experience. He referred to the days when they used to hold their meetings in the lonely woods and gloomy swamps. How they had prayed for freedom and plotted to desert to the Union army; and continuing, he said: "Since then, brethren and sisters, I have had my crosses and trials, but I try to look at the mercies. Just think what it was then and what it is now! How many of us, since freedom has come, have been looking up our scattered relatives. I have just been over to visit my old mistress, Nancy Johnson, and to see if I could get some clue to my long-lost mother, who was sold from me nearly thirty years ago."

Again there was a chorus of moans.

On resuming, Robert's voice was still fuller of pathos.

"When," he said, "I heard that dear old mother tell her experience it seemed as if some one had risen from the dead. She made me think of my own dear mother, who used to steal out at night to see me, fold me in her arms, and then steal back again to her work. After she was sold away I never saw her face again by daylight. I have been looking for her ever since the war, and I think at last I have got on the right track. If Mrs. Johnson, who kept the boarding-house in C——, is the one who sold that dear old mother from her son, then she is the one I am looking for, and I am the son she has been praying for."

The dear old mother raised her eyes. They were clear and tearless. An expression of wonder, hope, and love flitted over her face. It seemed as if her youth were suddenly renewed and, bounding from her seat, she rushed to the speaker in a paroxysm of joy. "Oh, Robby! Robby! is dis you? Is dat my pore, dear boy I'se been prayin' 'bout all dese years? Oh, glory! glory!" And overflowing with joyous excitement she threw her arms around him, looking the very impersonation of rapturous content. It was a happy time. Mothers whose children had been torn from them in the days of slavery knew how to rejoice in her joy. The young people caught the infection of the general happiness and rejoiced with them that rejoiced. There were songs of rejoicing and shouts of praise. The undertone of sadness which had so often mingled with their songs gave place to strains of exultation; and tears of tender sympathy flowed from eyes which had often been blurred by anguish. The child of many prayers and tears was restored to his mother.

Iola stood by the mother's side, smiling, and weeping tears of joy. When Robert's mother observed Iola, she said to Robert, "Is dis yore wife?"

"Oh, no," replied Robert, "but I believe she is your grandchild, the daughter of the little girl who was sold away from you so long ago. She is on her way to the farther South in search of her mother."

"Is she? Dear chile! I hope she'll fine her! She puts me in mine ob my pore little Marie. Well, I'se got one chile, an' I means to keep on prayin' tell I fine my daughter. I'm *so* happy! I feel's like a new woman!"

"My dear mother," said Robert, "now that I have found you, I mean to hold you fast just as long as you live. Ever since the war I have been trying to find out if you were living, but all efforts failed. At last, I thought I would come and hunt you myself and, now that I have found you, I am going to take you home to live with me, and to be as happy as the days are long. I am living in the North, and doing a good business there. I want you to see joy according to all the days wherein you have seen sorrow. I do hope this young lady will find *her* ma and that, when found, she will prove to be your daughter!"

"Yes, pore, dear chile! I specs her mudder's heart's mighty hungry fer her. I does hope she's my gran'chile."

Tenderly and caressingly Iola bent over the happy mother, with her heart filled with mournful memories of her own mother.

Aunt Linda was induced to stay until the next morning, and then gladly assisted Robert's mother in arranging for her journey northward. The friends who had given her a shelter in their hospitable home, learned to value her so much that it was with great reluctance they resigned her to the care of her son. Aunt Linda was full of bustling activity, and her spirits overflowed with good humor.

"Now, Harriet," she said, as they rode along on their return journey, "you mus' jis' thank me fer finin' yore chile, 'cause I got him to come to dat big meetin' wid me."

"Oh, Lindy," she cried, "I'se glad from de bottom ob my heart ter see you's all. I com'd out dere ter git a blessin', an' I'se got a double po'tion. De frens I war libin' wid war mighty good ter me. Dey lib'd wid me in de lower kentry, an' arter de war war ober I stopped wid 'em and helped take keer ob de chillen; an' when dey com'd up yere dey brought me wid 'em. I'se com'd a way I didn't know, but I'se mighty glad I'se com'd."

"Does you know dis place?" asked Aunt Linda, as they approached the settlement.

"No'n 'deed I don't. It's all new ter me."

"Well, dis is whar I libs. Ain't you mighty tired? I feels a little stiffish. Dese bones is gittin' ole."

"Dat's so! But I'se mighty glad I'se lib'd to see my boy 'fore I crossed ober de riber. An' now I feel like ole Simeon."

"But, mother," said Robert, "if you are ready to go, I am not willing to let you. I want you to stay ever so long where I can see you."

A bright smile overspread her face. Robert's words reassured and gladdened her heart. She was well satisfied to have a pleasant aftermath from life on this side of the river.

After arriving home Linda's first thought was to prepare dinner for her guests. But, before she began her work of preparation, she went to the cupboard to get a cup of home-made wine.

"Here," she said, filling three glasses, "is some wine I made myself from dat grape-vine out dere. Don't it look nice and clar? Jist taste it. It's fus'rate."

"No, thank you," said Robert. "I'm a temperance man, and never take anything which has alcohol in it."

"Oh, dis ain't got a bit ob alcohol in it. I made it myself."

"But, Aunt Linda, you didn't make the law which ferments grape-juice and makes it alcohol."

"But, Robby, ef alcohol's so bad, w'at made de Lord put it here?"

"Aunt Lindy," said Iola, "I heard a lady say that there were two things the Lord didn't make. One is sin, and the other alcohol."

"Why, Aunt Linda," said Robert, "there are numbers of things the Lord has made that I wouldn't touch with a pair of tongs."

"What are they?"

"Rattlesnakes, scorpions, and moccasins."

"Oh, sho!"

"Aunt Linda," said Iola, "the Bible says that the wine at last will bite like a serpent and sting like an adder."

"And, Aunt Linda," added Robert, "as I wouldn't wind a serpent around my throat, I don't want to put something inside of it which will bite like a serpent and sting as an adder."

"I reckon Robby's right," said his mother, setting down her glass and leaving the wine unfinished. "You young folks knows a heap more dan we ole folks." "Well," declared Aunt Linda, "you all is temp'rence to de backbone. But what could I do wid my wine ef we didn't drink it?"

"Let it turn to vinegar, and sign the temperance pledge," replied Robert.

"I don't keer 'bout it myself, but I don't 'spect John would be willin' ter let it go, 'cause he likes it a heap."

"Then you must give it up for his sake and Job's," said Robert. "They may learn to like it too well."

"You know, Aunt Linda," said Iola, "people don't get to be drunkards all at once. And you wouldn't like to feel, if Job should learn to drink, that you helped form his appetite."

"Dat' so! I beliebs I'll let dis turn to winegar, an' not make any more."

"That's right, Aunt Linda. I hope you'll hold to it," said Robert, encouragingly.

Very soon Aunt Linda had an excellent dinner prepared. After it was over Robert went with Iola to C——, where her friend, the bishop, was awaiting her return. She told him the wonderful story of Robert's finding his mother, and of her sweet, childlike faith.

The bishop, a kind, fatherly man, said, "Miss Iola, I hope that such happiness is in store for you. My dear child, still continue to pray and trust. I am old-fashioned enough to believe in prayer. I knew an old lady living in Illinois, who was a slave. Her son got a chance to come North and beg money to buy his mother. The mother was badly treated, and made up her mind to run away. But before she started she thought she would kneel down to pray. And something, she said, reasoned within her, and whispered, 'Stand still and see what I am going to do for you.' So real was it to her that she unpacked her bundle and desisted from her flight. Strange as it may appear to you, her son returned, bringing with him money enough to purchase her freedom, and she was redeemed from bondage. Had she persisted in running away she might have been lost in the woods and have died, exhausted by starvation. But she believed, she trusted, and was delivered. Her son took her North, where she could find a resting place for the soles of her feet."

That night Iola and the bishop left for the South.

# XXI

## A Home for Mother

After Iola had left the settlement, accompanied by Robert as far as the town, it was a pleasant satisfaction for the two old friends to settle themselves down, and talk of times past, departed friends, and long-forgotten scenes.

"What," said Mrs. Johnson, as we shall call Robert's mother, "hab become ob Miss Nancy's husband? Is he still a libin'?"

"Oh, he drunk hisself to death," responded Aunt Linda.

"He used ter be mighty handsome."

"Yes, but drink war his ruination."

"An' how's Miss Nancy?"

"Oh, she's com'd down migh'ly. She's pore as a church mouse. I thought 'twould com'd home ter her wen she sole yer 'way from yore chillen. Dere's nuffin goes ober de debil's back dat don't come under his belly. Do yo 'member Miss Nancy's fardder?"

"Ob course I does!"

"Well," said Aunt Linda, "he war a nice ole gemmen. Wen he died, I said de las' gemmen's dead, an' dere's noboddy ter step in his shoes."

"Pore Miss Nancy!" exclaimed Robert's mother. "I ain't nothin' agin her. But I wouldn't swap places wid her, 'cause I'se got my son; an' I beliebs he'll do a good part by me."

"Mother," said Robert, as he entered the room, "I've brought an old friend to see you. Do you remember Uncle Daniel?"

Uncle Daniel threw back his head, reached out his hand, and manifested his joy with "Well, Har'yet! is dis you? I neber 'spected to see you in dese lower grouns! How does yer do? an' whar hab you bin all dis time?"

"O, I'se been tossin' roun' 'bout; but it's all com'd right at las'. I'se lib'd to see my boy 'fore I died."

"My wife an' boys is in glory," said Uncle Daniel. "But I 'spects to see 'em 'fore long. 'Cause I'se tryin' to dig deep, build sure, an' make my way from earth ter glory."

"Dat's de right kine ob talk, Dan'el. We ole folks ain't got long ter stay yere."

They chatted together until Job and Salters came home for supper. After they had eaten, Uncle Daniel said:—

"We'll hab a word ob prayer."

There, in that peaceful habitation, they knelt down, and mingled their prayers together, as they had done in by-gone days, when they had met by stealth in lonely swamps or silent forests.

The next morning Robert and his mother started northward. They were well supplied with a bountiful luncheon by Aunt Linda, who had so thoroughly enjoyed their sojourn with her. On the next day he arrived in the city of P——, and took his mother to his boarding-house, until he could find a suitable home into which to install her. He soon came across one which just suited his taste, but when the agent discovered that Robert's mother was colored, he told him that the house had been previously engaged. In company with his mother he looked at several other houses in desirable neighborhoods, but they were constantly met with the answer, "The house is engaged," or, "We do not rent to colored people."

At length Robert went alone, and, finding a desirable house, engaged it, and moved into it. In a short time it was discovered that he was colored, and, at the behest of the local sentiment of the place, the landlord used his utmost endeavors to oust him, simply because he belonged to an unfashionable and unpopular race. At last he came across a landlord who was broad enough to rent him a good house, and he found a quiet resting place among a set of well-to-do and well-disposed people.

# XXII

## FURTHER LIFTING OF THE VEIL

In one of those fearful conflicts by which the Mississippi was freed from Rebel intrusion and opened to commerce Harry was severely wounded, and forced to leave his place in the ranks for a bed in the hospital.

One day, as he lay in his bed, thinking of his former home in Mississippi and wondering if the chances of war would ever restore him to his loved ones, he fell into a quiet slumber. When he awoke he found a lady bending over him, holding in her hands some fruit and flowers. As she tenderly bent over Harry's bed their eyes met, and with a thrill of gladness they recognized each other.

"Oh, my son, my son!" cried Marie, trying to repress her emotion, as she took his wasted hand in hers, and kissed the pale cheeks that sickness and suffering had blanched. Harry was very weak, but her presence was a call to life. He returned the pressure of her hand, kissed it, and his eyes grew full of sudden light, as he murmured faintly, but joyfully:—

"Mamma; oh, mamma! have I found you at last?"

The effort was too much, and he immediately became unconscious.

Anxious, yet hopeful, Marie sat by the bedside of her son till consciousness was restored. Caressingly she bent over his couch, murmuring in her happiness the tenderest, sweetest words of motherly love. In Harry's veins flowed new life and vigor, calming the restlessness of his nerves.

As soon as possible Harry was carried to his mother's home; a home brought into the light of freedom by the victories of General Grant. Nursed by his mother's tender, loving care, he rapidly recovered, but, being too disabled to re-enter the army, he was honorably discharged.

Lorraine had taken Marie to Vicksburg, and there allowed her to engage in confectionery and preserving for the wealthy ladies of the city. He had at first attempted to refugee with her in Texas, but, being foiled in the attempt, he was compelled to enlist in the Confederate Army, and met his fate by being killed just before the surrender of Vicksburg.

"My dear son," Marie would say, as she bent fondly over him, "I am deeply sorry that you are wounded, but I am glad that the fortunes of war have brought us together. Poor Iola! I *do* wonder what has become of her? Just as soon as this war is over I want you to search the country all over. Poor child! How my heart has ached for her!"

Time passed on. Harry and his mother searched and inquired for Iola, but no tidings of her reached them.

Having fully recovered his health, and seeing the great need of education for the colored people, Harry turned his attention toward them, and joined the new army of Northern teachers.

He still continued his inquiries for his sister, not knowing whether or not she had succumbed to the cruel change in her life. He thought she might have passed into the white basis for the sake of bettering her fortunes. Hope deferred, which had sickened his mother's heart, had only roused him to renewed diligence.

A school was offered him in Georgia, and thither he repaired, taking his mother with him. They were soon established in the city of A——. In hope of finding Iola he visited all the conferences of the Methodist Church, but for a long time his search was in vain.

"Mamma," said Harry, one day during his vacation, "there is to be a Methodist Conference in this State in the city of S——, about one hundred and fifty miles from here. I intend to go and renew my search for Iola."

"Poor child!" burst out Marie, as the tears gathered in her eyes, "I wonder if she is living."

"I think so," said Harry, kissing the pale cheek of his mother; "I don't feel that Iola is dead. I believe we will find her before long."

"It seems to me my heart would burst with joy to see my dear child just once more. I am glad that you are going. When will you leave?"

"Tomorrow morning."

"Well, my son, go, and my prayers will go with you," was Marie's tender parting wish.

Early next morning Harry started for the conference, and reached the church before the morning session was over. Near him sat two ladies, one fair, the other considerably darker. There was something in the fairer one that reminded him forcibly of his sister, but she was much older and graver than he imagined his sister to be. Instantly he dismissed the thought that had forced itself into his mind, and began to listen attentively to the proceedings of the conference.

When the regular business of the morning session was over the bishop arose and said:—

"I have an interesting duty to perform. I wish to introduce a young lady to the conference, who was the daughter of a Mississippi planter. She is now in search of her mother and brother, from whom she was sold a few months before the war. Her father married her mother in Ohio, where he had taken her to be educated. After his death they were robbed of their inheritance and enslaved by a distant relative named Lorraine. Miss Iola Leroy is the young lady's name. If any one can give the least information respecting the objects of her search it will be thankfully received."

"I can," exclaimed a young man, rising in the midst of the audience, and pressing eagerly, almost impetuously, forward. "I am her brother, and I came here to look for her."

Iola raised her eyes to his face, so flushed and bright with the glow of recognition, rushed to him, threw her arms around his neck, kissed him again and again, crying: "O, Harry!" Then she fainted from excitement. The women gathered around her with expressions of tender sympathy, and gave her all the care she needed. They called her the "dear child," for without any effort on her part she had slidden into their hearts and found a ready welcome in each sympathizing bosom.

Harry at once telegraphed the glad tidings to his mother, who waited their coming with joyful anticipation. Long before the cars reached the city, Mrs. Leroy was at the depot, restlessly walking the platform or eagerly peering into the darkness to catch the first glimpse of the train which was bearing her treasures.

At length the cars arrived, and, as Harry and Iola alighted, Marie rushed forward, clasped Iola in her arms and sobbed out her joy in broken words.

Very happy was the little family that sat together around the supper-table for the first time for years. They partook of that supper with thankful hearts and with eyes overflowing with tears of joy. Very touching were the prayers the mother uttered, when she knelt with her children that night to return thanks for their happy reunion, and to seek protection through the slumbers of the night.

The next morning, as they sat at the breakfast-table, Marie said:

"My dear child, you are so changed I do not think I would have known you if I had met you in the street!"

"And I," said Harry, "can hardly realize that you are our own Iola, whom I recognized as sister a half dozen years ago."

"Am I so changed?" asked Iola, as a faint sigh escaped her lips.

"Why, Iola," said Harry, "you used to be the most harum-scarum girl I ever knew, laughing, dancing, and singing from morning until night."

"Yes, I remember," said Iola. "It all comes back to me like a dream. Oh, mamma! I have passed through a fiery ordeal of suffering since then. But it is useless," and as she continued her face assumed a brighter look, "to brood over the past. Let us be happy in the present. Let me tell you something which will please you. Do you remember telling me about your mother and brother?"

"Yes," said Marie, in a questioning tone."

"Well," continued Iola, with eyes full of gladness, "I think I have found them."

"Can it be possible!" exclaimed Marie, in astonishment. "It is more than thirty years since we parted. I fear you are mistaken."

"No, mamma; I have drawn my conclusions from good circumstantial evidence. After I was taken from you, I passed through a fearful siege of suffering, which would only harrow up your soul to hear. I often shudder at the remembrance. The last man in whose clutches I found myself was mean, brutal, and cruel. I was in his power when the Union army came into C——, where I was living. A number of colored men stampeded to the Union ranks, with a gentleman as a leader, whom I think is your brother. A friend of his reported my case to the commander of the post, who instantly gave orders for my release. A place was given me as nurse in the hospital. I attended that friend in his last illness. Poor fellow! he was the best friend I had in all the time I have been tossing about. The gentleman whom I think is your brother appeared to be very anxious about his friend's recovery, and was deeply affected by his death. In one of the last terrible battles of the war, that of Five Forks, he was wounded and put into the hospital ward where I was an attendant. For awhile he was delirious, and in his delirium he would sometimes think that I was his mother and at other times his sister. I humored his fancies, would often sing to him when he was restless, and my voice almost invariably soothed him to sleep. One day I sang to him that old hymn we used to sing on the plantation:—

> "Drooping souls no longer grieve,
>     Heaven is propitious;
> If on Christ you do believe,
>     You will find Him precious."

"I remember," said Marie, with a sigh, as memories of the past swept over her.

"After I had finished the hymn," continued Iola, "he looked earnestly and inquiringly into my face, and asked, 'Where did you learn that hymn? I have heard my mother sing it when I was a boy, but I have never heard it since.' I think, mamma, the words, 'I was lost but now I'm found; glory! glory! glory!' had imprinted themselves on his memory, and that his mind was assuming a higher state of intellectuality. He asked me to sing it again, which I did, until he fell asleep. Then I noticed a marked resemblance between him and Harry, and I thought, 'Suppose he should prove to be your long-lost brother?' During his convalescence we found that we had a common ground of sympathy. We were anxious to be reunited to our severed relations. We had both been separated from our mothers. He told me of his little sister, with whom he used to play. She had a mole on her cheek which he called her beauty spot. He had the red spot on his forehead which you told me of."

# XXIII

## Delightful Reunions

Very bright and happy was the home where Marie and her children were gathered under one roof. Mrs. Leroy's neighbors said she looked ten years younger. Into that peaceful home came no fearful forebodings of cruel separations. Harry and Iola were passionately devoted to their mother, and did all they could to flood her life with sunshine.

"Iola, dear," said Harry, one morning at the breakfast-table, "I have a new pleasure in store for you."

"What is it, brother mine?" asked Iola, assuming an air of interest.

"There is a young lady living in this city to whom I wish to introduce you. She is one of the most remarkable women I have ever met."

"Do tell me all about her," said Iola. "Is she young and handsome, brilliant and witty?

"She," replied Harry, "is more than handsome, she is lovely; more than witty, she is wise; more than brilliant, she is excellent."

"Well, Harry," said Mrs. Leroy, smiling, "if you keep on that way I shall begin to fear that I shall soon be supplanted by a new daughter."

"Oh, no, mamma," replied Harry, looking slightly confused, "I did not mean that."

"Well, Harry," said Iola, amused, "go on with your description; I am becoming interested. Tax your powers of description to give me her likeness."

"Well, in the first place," continued Harry, "I suppose she is about twenty-five years old."

"Oh, the idea," interrupted Iola, "of a gentleman talking of a lady's age. That is a tabooed subject."

"Why, Iola, that adds to the interest of my picture. It is her combination of earnestness and youthfulness which enhances her in my estimation."

"Pardon the interruption," said Iola; "I am anxious to hear more about her."

"Well, she is of medium height, somewhat slender, and well formed, with dark, expressive eyes, full of thought and feeling. Neither hair nor complexion show the least hint of blood admixture."

"I am glad of it," said Iola. "Every person of unmixed blood who succeeds in any department of literature, art, or science is a living argument for the capability which is in the race."

"Yes," responded Harry, "for it is not the white blood which is on trial before the world. Well, I will bring her around this evening."

In the evening Harry brought Miss Delany to call on his sister and mother. They were much pleased with their visitor. Her manner was a combination of suavity and dignity. During the course of the evening they learned that she was a graduate of the University of A——. One day she saw in the newspapers that colored women were becoming unfit to be servants for white people. She then thought that if they are not fit to be servants for white people, they are unfit to be mothers to their own children, and she conceived the idea of opening a school to train future wives and mothers. She began on a small scale, in a humble building, and her work was soon crowned with gratifying success. She had enlarged her quarters, increased her teaching force, and had erected a large and commodious school-house through her own exertions and the help of others.

Marie cordially invited her to call again, saying, as she rose to go: "I am very glad to have met you. Young women like you always fill my heart with hope for the future of our race. In you I see reflected some of the blessed possibilities which lie within us."

"Thank you," said Miss Delany, "I want to be classed among those of whom it is said, 'She has done what she could.'"

Very pleasant was the acquaintance which sprang up between Miss Delany and Iola. Although she was older than Iola, their tastes were so congenial, their views of life and duty in such unison, that their acquaintance soon ripened into strong and lasting friendship. There were no foolish rivalries and jealousies between them. Their lives were too full of zeal and earnestness for them to waste in selfishness their power to be moral and spiritual forces among a people who so much needed their helping hands. Miss Delany gave Iola a situation in her school; but before the term was quite over she was force to resign, her health having been so undermined by the fearful strain through which she had passed, that she was quite unequal to the task. She remained at home, and did what her strength would allow in assisting her mother in the work of canning and preserving fruits.

In the meantime, Iola had been corresponding with Robert. She

FRANCES ELLEN WATKINS HARPER

had told him of her success in finding her mother and brother, and had received an answer congratulating her on the glad fruition of her hopes. He also said that his business was flourishing, that his mother was keeping house for him, and, to use her own expression, was as happy as the days are long. She was firmly persuaded that Marie was her daughter, and she wanted to see her before she died.

"There is one thing," continued the letter, "that your mother may remember her by. It was a little handkerchief on which were a number of cats' heads. She gave one to each of us."

"I remember it well," said Marie, "she must, indeed, be my mother. Now, all that is needed to complete my happiness is her presence, and my brother's. And I intend, if I live long enough, to see them both."

Iola wrote Robert that her mother remembered the incident of the handkerchief, and was anxious to see them.

In the early fall Robert started for the South in order to clear up all doubts with respect to their relationship. He found Iola, Harry, and their mother living cosily together. Harry was teaching and was a leader among the rising young men of the State. His Northern education and later experience had done much toward adapting him to the work of the new era which had dawned upon the South.

Marie was very glad to welcome Robert to her home, but it was almost impossible to recognize her brother in that tall, handsome man, with dark-brown eyes and wealth of chestnut-colored hair, which he readily lifted to show the crimson spot which lay beneath it.

But as they sat together, and recalled the long-forgotten scenes of their childhood, they concluded that they were brother and sister.

"Marie," said Robert, "how would you like to leave the South?"

"I should like to go North, but I hate to leave Harry. He's a splendid young fellow, although I say it myself. He is so fearless and outspoken that I am constantly anxious about him, especially at election time."

Harry then entered the room, and, being introduced to Robert, gave him a cordial welcome. He had just returned from school.

"We were talking of you, my son," said Marie.

"What were you saying? Nothing of the absent but good?" asked Harry.

"I was telling your uncle, who wants me to come North, that I would go, but I am afraid that you will get into trouble and be murdered, as many others have been."

"Oh, well, mother, I shall not die till my time comes. And if I die helping the poor and needy, I shall die at my post. Could a man choose a better place to die?"

"Were you aware of the virulence of caste prejudice and the disabilities which surround the colored people when you cast your lot with them?" asked Robert.

"Not fully," replied Harry; "but after I found out that I was colored, I consulted the principal of the school, where I was studying, in reference to the future. He said that if I stayed in the North, he had friends whom he believed would give me any situation I could fill, and I could simply take my place in the rank of workers, the same as any other man. Then he told me of the army, and I made up my mind to enter it, actuated by a desire to find my mother and sister; and at any rate I wanted to avenge their wrongs. I do not feel so now. Since I have seen the fearful ravages of war, I have learned to pity and forgive. The principal said he thought I would be more apt to find my family if I joined a colored regiment in the West than if I joined one of the Maine companies. I confess at first I felt a shrinking from taking the step, but love for my mother overcame all repugnance on my part. Now that I have linked my fortunes to the race I intend to do all I can for its elevation."

As he spoke Robert gazed admiringly on the young face, lit up by noble purposes and lofty enthusiasm.

"You are right, Harry. I think it would be treason, not only to the race, but to humanity, to have you ignoring your kindred and masquerading as a white man."

"I think so, too," said Marie.

"But, sister, I am anxious for you all to come North. If Harry feels that the place of danger is the post of duty, let him stay, and he can spend his vacations with us. I think both you and Iola need rest and change. Mother longs to see you before she dies. She feels that we have been the children of many prayers and tears, and I want to make her last days as happy as possible. The South has not been a paradise to you all the time, and I should think you would be willing to leave it."

"Yes, that is so. Iola needs rest and change, and she would be such a comfort to mother. I suppose, for her sake, I will consent to have her go back with you, at least for awhile."

In a few days, with many prayers and tears, Marie, half reluctantly, permitted Iola to start for the North in company with Robert Johnson, intending to follow as soon as she could settle her business and see Harry in a good boarding place.

Very joyful was the greeting of the dear grandmother. Iola soon nestled in her heart and lent additional sunshine to her once checkered life, and Robert, who had so long been robbed of kith and kin, was delighted with the new accession to his home life.

# XXIV

## Northern Experience

Uncle Robert," said Iola, after she had been North several weeks, "I have a theory that every woman ought to know how to earn her own living. I believe that a great amount of sin and misery springs from the weakness and inefficiency of women."

"Perhaps that's so, but what are you going to do about it?"

"I am going to join the great rank of bread-winners. Mr. Waterman has advertised for a number of saleswomen, and I intend to make application."

"When he advertises for help he means white women," said Robert.

"He said nothing about color," responded Iola.

"I don't suppose he did. He doesn't expect any colored girl to apply."

"Well, I think I could fill the place. At least I should like to try. And I do not think when I apply that I am in duty bound to tell him my great-grandmother was a negro."

"Well, child, there is no necessity for you to go out to work. You are perfectly welcome here, and I hope that you feel so."

"Oh, I certainly do. But still I would rather earn my own living."

That morning Iola applied for the situation, and, being prepossessing in her appearance, she obtained it.

For awhile everything went as pleasantly as a marriage bell. But one day a young colored lady, well-dressed and well-bred in her manner, entered the store. It was an acquaintance which Iola had formed in the colored church which she attended. Iola gave her a few words of cordial greeting, and spent a few moments chatting with her. The attention of the girls who sold at the same counter was attracted, and their suspicion awakened. Iola was a stranger in that city. Who was she, and who were her people? At last it was decided that one of the girls should act as a spy, and bring what information she could concerning Iola.

The spy was successful. She found out that Iola was living in a good neighborhood, but that none of the neighbors knew her. The man of the house was very fair, but there was an old woman whom Iola called "Grandma," and she was unmistakably colored. The story was sufficient. If that were true, Iola must be colored, and she should be treated accordingly.

Without knowing the cause, Iola noticed a chill in the social atmosphere of the store, which communicated itself to the cash-boys, and they treated her so insolently that her situation became very uncomfortable. She saw the proprietor, resigned her position, and asked for and obtained a letter of recommendation to another merchant who had advertised for a saleswoman.

In applying for the place, she took the precaution to inform her employer that she was colored. It made no difference to him; but he said:—

"Don't say anything about it to the girls. They might not be willing to work with you."

Iola smiled, did not promise, and accepted the situation. She entered upon her duties, and proved quite acceptable as a saleswoman.

One day, during an interval in business, the girls began to talk of their respective churches, and the question was put to Iola:—

"Where do you go to church?"

"I go," she replied, "to Rev. River's church, corner of Eighth and L Streets."

"Oh, no; you must be mistaken. There is no church there except a colored one."

"That is where I go."

"Why do you go there?"

"Because I liked it when I came here, and joined it."

"A member of a colored church? What under heaven possessed you to do such a thing?"

"Because I wished to be with my own people."

Here the interrogator stopped, and looked surprised and pained, and almost instinctively moved a little farther from her. After the store was closed, the girls had an animated discussion, which resulted in the information being sent to Mr. Cohen that Iola was a colored girl, and that they protested against her being continued in his employ. Mr. Cohen yielded to the pressure, and informed Iola that her services were no longer needed.

When Robert came home in the evening, he found that Iola had lost her situation, and was looking somewhat discouraged.

"Well, uncle," she said, "I feel out of heart. It seems as if the prejudice pursues us through every avenue of life, and assigns us the lowest places."

"That is so," replied Robert, thoughtfully.

"And yet I am determined," said Iola, "to win for myself a place in the fields of labor. I have heard of a place in New England, and I mean to try for it, even if I only stay a few months."

"Well, if you *will* go, say nothing about your color."

"Uncle Robert, I see no necessity for proclaiming that fact on the house-top. Yet I am resolved that nothing shall tempt me to deny it. The best blood in my veins is African blood, and I am not ashamed of it."

"Hurrah for you!" exclaimed Robert, laughing heartily.

As Iola wished to try the world for herself, and so be prepared for any emergency, her uncle and grandmother were content to have her go to New England. The town to which she journeyed was only a few hours' ride from the city of P——, and Robert, knowing that there is no teacher like experience, was willing that Iola should have the benefit of her teaching.

Iola, on arriving in H——, sought the firm, and was informed that her services were needed. She found it a pleasant and lucrative position. There was only one drawback—her boarding place was too far from her work. There was an institution conducted by professed Christian women, which was for the special use of respectable young working girls. This was in such a desirable location that she called at the house to engage board.

The matron conducted her over the house, and grew so friendly in the interview that she put her arm around her, and seemed to look upon Iola as a desirable accession to the home. But, just as Iola was leaving, she said to the matron: "I must be honest with you; I am a colored woman."

Swift as light a change passed over the face of the matron. She withdrew her arm from Iola, and said: "I must see the board of managers about it."

When the board met, Iola's case was put before them, but they decided not to receive her. And these women, professors of a religion which taught, "If ye have respect to persons ye commit sin," virtually shut the door in her face because of the outcast blood in her veins.

Considerable feeling was aroused by the action of these women, who, to say the least, had not put their religion in the most favorable light.

Iola continued to work for the firm until she received letters from her mother and uncle, which informed her that her mother, having arranged her affairs in the South, was ready to come North. She then resolved to return, to the city of P——, to be ready to welcome her mother on her arrival.

Iola arrived in time to see that everything was in order for her mother's reception. Her room was furnished neatly, but with those touches of beauty that womanly hands are such adepts in giving. A few charming pictures adorned the walls, and an easy chair stood waiting to receive the travel-worn mother. Robert and Iola met her at the depot; and grandma was on her feet at the first sound of the bell, opened the door, clasped Marie to her heart, and nearly fainted for joy.

"Can it be possible dat dis is my little Marie?" she exclaimed.

It did seem almost impossible to realize that this faded woman, with pale cheeks and prematurely whitened hair, was the rosy-cheeked child from whom she had been parted more than thirty years.

"Well," said Robert, after the first joyous greeting was over, "love is a very good thing, but Marie has had a long journey and needs something that will stick by the ribs. How about dinner, mother?"

"It's all ready," said Mrs. Johnson.

After Marie had gone to her room and changed her dress, she came down and partook of the delicious repast which her mother and Iola had prepared for her.

In a few days Marie was settled in the home, and was well pleased with the change. The only drawback to her happiness was the absence of her son, and she expected him to come North after the closing of his school.

"Uncle Robert," said Iola, after her mother had been with them several weeks, "I am tired of being idle."

"What's the matter now?" asked Robert. "You are surely not going East again, and leave your mother?"

"Oh, I hope not," said Marie, anxiously. "I have been so long without you."

"No, mamma, I am not going East. I can get suitable employment here in the city of P——."

"But, Iola," said Robert, "you have tried, and been defeated. Why subject yourself to the same experience again?"

"Uncle Robert, I think that every woman should have some skill or art which would insure her at least a comfortable support. I believe there would be less unhappy marriages if labor were more honored among women."

"Well, Iola," said her mother, "what is your skill?"

"Nursing. I was very young when I went into the hospital, but I succeeded so well that the doctor said I must have been a born nurse. Now, I see by the papers, that a gentleman who has an invalid daughter wants some one who can be a nurse and companion for her, and I mean to apply for the situation. I do not think, if I do my part well in that position, that the blood in my veins will be any bar to my success."

A troubled look stole over Marie's face. She sighed faintly, but made no remonstrance. And so it was decided that Iola should apply for the situation.

Iola made application, and was readily accepted. Her patient was a frail girl of fifteen summers, who was ill with a low fever. Iola nursed her carefully, and soon had the satisfaction of seeing her restored to health. During her stay, Mr. Cloten, the father of the invalid, had learned some of the particulars of Iola's Northern experience as a bread-winner, and he resolved to give her employment in his store when her services were no longer needed in the house. As soon as a vacancy occurred he gave Iola a place in his store.

The morning she entered on her work he called his employés together, and told them that Miss Iola had colored blood in her veins, but that he was going to employ her and give her a desk. If any one objected to working with her, he or she could step to the cashier's desk and receive what was due. Not a man remonstrated, not a woman demurred; and Iola at last found a place in the great army of bread-winners, which the traditions of her blood could not affect.

"How did you succeed?" asked Mrs. Cloten of her husband, when he returned to dinner.

"Admirably! 'Everything is lovely and the goose hangs high.' I gave my employés to understand that they could leave if they did not wish to work with Miss Leroy. Not one of them left, or showed any disposition to rebel."

"I am very glad," said Mrs. Cloten. "I am ashamed of the way she has been treated in our city, when seeking to do her share in the world's work. I am glad that you were brave enough to face this cruel prejudice, and give her a situation."

"Well, my dear, do not make me a hero for a single act. I am grateful for the care Miss Leroy gave our Daisy. Money can buy services, but it cannot purchase tender, loving sympathy. I was also determined to let my employés know that I, not they, commanded my business. So, do not crown me a hero until I have won a niche in the temple of fame.

In dealing with Southern prejudice against the negro, we Northerners could do it with better grace if we divested ourselves of our own. We irritate the South by our criticisms, and, while I confess that there is much that is reprehensible in their treatment of colored people, yet if our Northern civilization is higher than theirs we should 'criticise by creation.' We should stamp ourselves on the South, and not let the South stamp itself on us. When we have learned to treat men according to the complexion of their souls, and not the color of their skins, we will have given our best contribution towards the solution of the negro problem."

"I feel, my dear," said Mrs. Cloten, "that what you have done is a right step in the right direction, and I hope that other merchants will do the same. We have numbers of business men, rich enough to afford themselves the luxury of a good conscience."

# XXV

## An Old Friend

"Good-morning, Miss Leroy," said a cheery voice in tones of glad surprise, and, intercepting her path, Dr. Gresham stood before Iola, smiling, and reaching out his hand.

"Why, Dr. Gresham, is this you?" said Iola, lifting her eyes to that well-remembered face. "It has been several years since we met. How have you been all this time, and where?"

"I have been sick, and am just now recovering from malaria and nervous prostration. I am attending a medical convention in this city, and hope that I shall have the pleasure of seeing you again."

Iola hesitated, and then replied: "I should be pleased to have you call."

"It would give me great pleasure. Where shall I call?"

"My home is 1006 South Street, but I am only at home in the evenings."

They walked together a short distance till they reached Mr. Cloten's store; then, bidding the doctor good morning, Iola left him repeating to himself the words of his favorite poet:—

> "Thou art too lovely and precious a gem
> To be bound to their burdens and sullied by them."

No one noticed the deep flush on Iola's face as she entered the store, nor the subdued, quiet manner with which she applied herself to her tasks. She was living over again the past, with its tender, sad, and thrilling reminiscences.

In the evening Dr. Gresham called on Iola. She met him with a pleasant welcome. Dr. Gresham gazed upon her with unfeigned admiration, and thought that the years, instead of detracting from, had only intensified, her loveliness. He had thought her very beautiful in the hospital, in her gray dress and white collar, with her glorious wealth of hair drawn over her ears. But now, when he saw her with that hair artistically arranged, and her finely-proportioned form arrayed in a dark crimson dress, relieved by a shimmer of lace and a bow of white ribbon at her throat, he thought her superbly handsome. The lines which care had written upon her young face had faded away. There was no undertone of sorrow in her voice as she stood up before him in the calm loveliness of her ripened womanhood, radiant in beauty and gifted in intellect. Time and failing health had left their traces upon Dr. Gresham. His step was less bounding, his cheek a trifle paler, his manner somewhat graver than it was when he had parted from Iola in the hospital, but his meeting with her had thrilled his heart with unexpected pleasure. Hopes and sentiments which long had slept awoke at the touch of her hand and the tones of her voice, and Dr. Gresham found himself turning to the past, with its sad memories and disappointed hopes. No other face had displaced her image in his mind; no other love had woven itself around every tendril of his soul. His heart and hand were just as free as they were the hour they had parted.

"To see you again," said Dr. Gresham, "is a great and unexpected pleasure."

"You had not forgotten me, then?" said Iola, smiling.

"Forget you! I would just as soon forget my own existence. I do not think that time will ever efface the impressions of those days in which we met so often. When last we met you were intending to search for your mother. Have you been successful?"

"More than successful," said Iola, with a joyous ring in her voice. "I have found my mother, brother, grandmother, and uncle, and, except my brother, we are all living together, and we are so happy. Excuse me a few minutes," she said, and left the room. Iola soon returned, bringing with her her mother and grandmother.

"These," said Iola, introducing her mother and grandmother, "are the once-severed branches of our family; and this gentleman you have seen before," continued Iola, as Robert entered the room.

Dr. Gresham looked scrutinizingly at him and said: "Your face looks familiar, but I saw so many faces at the hospital that I cannot just now recall your name."

"Doctor," said Robert Johnson, "I was one of your last patients, and I was with Tom Anderson when he died."

"Oh, yes," replied Dr. Gresham; "it all comes back to me. You were wounded at the battle of Five Forks, were you not?"

"Yes," said Robert.

"I saw you when you were recovering. You told me that you thought you had a clue to your lost relatives, from whom you had been so long separated. How have you succeeded?"

"Admirably! I have been fortunate in finding my mother, my sister, and her children."

"Ah, indeed! I am delighted to hear it. Where are they?"

"They are right here. This is my mother," said Robert, bending fondly over her, as she returned his recognition with an expression of intense satisfaction; "and this," he continued, "is my sister, and Miss Leroy is my niece."

"Is it possible? I am very glad to hear it. It has been said that every cloud has its silver lining, and the silver lining of our war cloud is the redemption of a race and the reunion of severed hearts. War is a dreadful thing; but worse than the war was the slavery which preceded it."

"Slavery," said Iola, "was a fearful cancer eating into the nation's heart, sapping its vitality, and undermining its life."

"And war," said Dr. Gresham, "was the dreadful surgery by which the disease was eradicated. The cancer has been removed, but for years to come I fear that we will have to deal with the effects of the disease. But I believe that we have vitality enough to outgrow those effects."

"I think, Doctor," said Iola, "that there is but one remedy by which our nation can recover from the evil entailed upon her by slavery."

"What is that?" asked Robert.

"A fuller comprehension of the claims of the Gospel of Jesus Christ, and their application to our national life."

"Yes," said Robert; "while politicians are stumbling on the barren mountains of fretful controversy and asking what shall we do with the negro? I hold that Jesus answered that question nearly two thousand years ago when he said, 'Whatsoever ye would that men should do to you, do ye even so to them.'"

"Yes," said Dr. Gresham; "the application of that rule in dealing with the negro would solve the whole problem."

"Slavery," said Mrs. Leroy, "is dead, but the spirit which animated it still lives; and I think that a reckless disregard for human life is more the outgrowth of slavery than any actual hatred of the negro."

"The problem of the nation," continued Dr. Gresham, "is not what men will do with the negro, but what will they do with the reckless, lawless white men who murder, lynch and burn their fellow-citizens. To me these lynchings and burnings are perfectly alarming. Both races have reacted on each other—men fettered the slave and cramped their own souls; denied him knowledge, and darkened their spiritual insight; subdued him to the pliancy of submission, and in their turn became the thralls of public opinion. The negro came here from the heathenism of Africa; but the young colonies could not take into their early civilization a stream of barbaric blood without being affected by its influence and the negro, poor and despised as he is, has laid his hands on our Southern civilization and helped mould its character."

"Yes," said Mrs. Leroy; "the colored nurse could not nestle her master's child in her arms, hold up his baby footsteps on their floors, and walk with him through the impressible and formative period of his young life without leaving upon him the impress of her hand."

"I am glad," said Robert, "for the whole nation's sake, that slavery has been destroyed."

"And our work," said Dr. Gresham, "is to build over the desolations of the past a better and brighter future. The great distinction between savagery and civilization is the creation and maintenance of law. A people cannot habitually trample on law and justice without retrograding toward barbarism. But I am hopeful that time will bring us changes for the better; that, as we get farther away from the war, we will outgrow the animosities and prejudices engendered by slavery. The short-sightedness of our fathers linked the negro's destiny to ours. We are feeling the friction of the ligatures which bind us together, but I hope that the time will speedily come when the best members of both races will unite for the maintenance of law and order and the progress and prosperity of the country, and that the intelligence and virtue of the South will be strong to grapple effectually with its ignorance and vice."

"I hope that time will speedily come," said Marie. "My son is in the South, and I am always anxious for his safety. He is not only a teacher, but a leading young man in the community where he lives."

"Yes," said Robert, "and when I see the splendid work he is doing in the South, I am glad that, instead of trying to pass for a white man, he has cast his lot with us."

"But," answered Dr. Gresham, "he would possess advantages as a white man which he could not if he were known to be colored."

"Doctor," said Iola, decidedly, "he has greater advantages as a colored man."

"I do not understand you," said Dr. Gresham, looking somewhat puzzled.

"Doctor," continued Iola, "I do not think life's highest advantages are those that we can see with our eyes or grasp with our hands. To whom today is the world most indebted—to its millionaires or to its martyrs?"

"Taking it from the ideal standpoint," replied the doctor, "I should say its martyrs."

"To be," continued Iola, "the leader of a race to higher planes of thought and action, to teach men clearer views of life and duty, and to inspire their souls with loftier aims, is a far greater privilege than it is to open the gates of material prosperity and fill every home with sensuous enjoyment."

"And I," said Mrs. Leroy, her face aglow with fervid feeling, "would rather—ten thousand times rather—see Harry the friend and helper of the poor and ignorant than the companion of men who, under the cover of night, mask their faces and ride the country on lawless raids."

"Dr. Gresham," said Robert, "we ought to be the leading nation of the earth, whose influence and example should give light to the world."

"Not simply," said Iola, "a nation building up a great material prosperity, founding magnificent cities, grasping the commerce of the world, or excelling in literature, art, and science, but a nation wearing sobriety as a crown and righteousness as the girdle of her loins."

Dr. Gresham gazed admiringly upon Iola. A glow of enthusiasm overspread her beautiful, expressive face. There was a rapt and far-off look in her eye, as if she were looking beyond the present pain to a brighter future for the race with which she was identified, and felt the grandeur of a divine commission to labor for its uplifting.

As Dr. Gresham was parting with Robert, he said: "This meeting has been a very unexpected pleasure. I have spent a delightful evening. I only regret that I had not others to share it with me. A doctor from the South, a regular Bourbon, is stopping at the hotel. I wish he could have been here tonight. Come down to the Concordia, Mr. Johnson, tomorrow night. If you know any colored man who is a strong champion of equal rights, bring him along. Good-night. I shall look for you," said the doctor, as he left the door.

When Robert returned to the parlor he said to Iola: "Dr. Gresham has invited me to come to his hotel tomorrow night, and to bring some wide-awake colored man with me. There is a Southerner whom he wishes me to meet. I suppose he wants to discuss the negro problem, as they call it. He wants some one who can do justice to the subject. I wonder whom I can take with me?"

"I will tell you who, I think, will be a capital one to take with you, and I believe he would go," said Iola.

"Who?" asked Robert.

FRANCES ELLEN WATKINS HARPER

"Rev. Carmicle, your pastor."

"He is just the one," said Robert, "courteous in his manner and very scholarly in his attainments. He is a man whom if everybody hated him no one could despise him."

# XXVI

## Open Questions

In the evening Robert and Rev. Carmicle called on Dr. Gresham, and found Dr. Latrobe, the Southerner, and a young doctor by the name of Latimer, already there. Dr. Gresham introduced Dr. Latrobe, but it was a new experience to receive colored men socially. His wits, however, did not forsake him, and he received the introduction and survived it.

"Permit me, now," said Dr. Gresham, "to introduce you to my friend, Dr. Latimer, who is attending our convention. He expects to go South and labor among the colored people. Don't you think that there is a large field of usefulness before him?"

"Yes," replied Dr. Latrobe, "if he will let politics alone."

"And why let politics alone?" asked Dr. Gresham.

"Because," replied Dr. Latrobe, "we Southerners will never submit to negro supremacy. We will never abandon our Caucasian civilization to an inferior race."

"Have you any reason," inquired Rev. Carmicle, "to dread that a race which has behind it the heathenism of Africa and the slavery of America, with its inheritance of ignorance and poverty, will be able, in less than one generation, to domineer over a race which has behind it ages of dominion, freedom, education, and Christianity?"

A slight shade of vexation and astonishment passed over the face of Dr. Latrobe. He hesitated a moment, then replied:—

"I am not afraid of the negro as he stands alone, but what I dread is that in some closely-contested election ambitious men will use him to hold the balance of power and make him an element of danger. He is ignorant, poor, and clannish, and they may impact him as their policy would direct."

"Any more," asked Robert, "than the leaders of the Rebellion did the ignorant, poor whites during our late conflict?"

"Ignorance, poverty, and clannishness," said Dr. Gresham, "are more social than racial conditions, which may be outgrown."

"And I think," said Rev. Carmicle, "that we are outgrowing them as fast as any other people would have done under the same conditions."

FRANCES ELLEN WATKINS HARPER

"The negro," replied Dr. Latrobe, "always has been and always will be an element of discord in our country."

"What, then, is your remedy?" asked Dr. Gresham.

"I would eliminate him from the politics of the country."

"As disfranchisement is a punishment for crime, is it just to punish a man before he transgresses the law?" asked Dr. Gresham.

"If," said Dr. Latimer, "the negro is ignorant, poor, and clannish, let us remember that in part of our land it was once a crime to teach him to read. If he is poor, for ages he was forced to bend to unrequited toil. If he is clannish, society has segregated him to himself."

"And even," said Robert, "has given him a negro pew in your churches and a negro seat at your communion table."

"Wisely, or unwisely," said Dr. Gresham, "the Government has put the ballot in his hands. It is better to teach him to use that ballot aright than to intimidate him by violence or vitiate his vote by fraud."

"Today," said Dr. Latimer, "the negro is not plotting in beer-saloons against the peace and order of society. His fingers are not dripping with dynamite, neither is he spitting upon your flag, nor flaunting the red banner of anarchy in your face."

"Power," said Dr. Gresham, "naturally gravitates into the strongest hands. The class who have the best brain and most wealth can strike with the heaviest hand. I have too much faith in the inherent power of the white race to dread the competition of any other people under heaven."

"I think you Northerners fail to do us justice," said Dr. Latrobe. "The men into whose hands you put the ballot were our slaves, and we would rather die than submit to them. Look at the carpet-bag governments the wicked policy of the Government inflicted upon us. It was only done to humiliate us."

"Oh, no!" said Dr. Gresham, flushing, and rising to his feet. "We had no other alternative than putting the ballot in their hands."

"I will not deny," said Rev. Carmicle, "that we have made woeful mistakes, but with our antecedents it would have been miraculous if we had never committed any mistakes or made any blunders."

"They were allies in war," continued Dr. Gresham, "and I am sorry that we have not done more to protect them in peace."

"Protect them in peace!" said Robert, bitterly. "What protection does the colored man receive from the hands of the Government? I know of no civilized country outside of America where men are still burned for real or supposed crimes."

"Johnson," said Dr. Gresham, compassionately, "it is impossible to have a policeman at the back of each colored man's chair, and a squad of soldiers at each crossroad, to detect with certainty, and punish with celerity, each invasion of his rights. We tried provisional governments and found them a failure. It seemed like leaving our former allies to be mocked with the name of freedom and tortured with the essence of slavery. The ballot is our weapon of defense, and we gave it to them for theirs."

"And there," said Dr. Latrobe, emphatically, "is where you signally failed. We are numerically stronger in Congress today than when we went out. You made the law, but the administration of it is in our hands, and we are a unit."

"But, Doctor," said Rev. Carmicle, "you cannot willfully deprive the negro of a single right as a citizen without sending demoralization through your own ranks."

"I think," said Dr. Latrobe, "that we are right in suppressing the negro's vote. This is a white man's government, and a white man's country. We own nineteen-twentieths of the land, and have about the same ratio of intelligence. I am a white man, and, right or wrong, I go with my race."

"But, Doctor," said Rev. Carmicle, "there are rights more sacred than the rights of property and superior intelligence."

"What are they?" asked Dr. Latrobe.

"The rights of life and liberty," replied Rev. Carmicle.

"That is true," said Dr. Gresham; "and your Southern civilization will be inferior until you shall have placed protection to those rights at its base, not in theory but in fact."

"But, Dr. Gresham, we have to live with these people, and the North is constantly irritating us by its criticisms."

"The world," said Dr. Gresham, "is fast becoming a vast whispering gallery, and lips once sealed can now state their own grievances and appeal to the conscience of the nation, and, as long as a sense of justice and mercy retains a hold upon the heart of our nation, you cannot practice violence and injustice without rousing a spirit of remonstrance. And if it were not so I would be ashamed of my country and of my race."

"You speak," said Dr. Latrobe, "as if we had wronged the negro by enslaving him and being unwilling to share citizenship with him. I think that slavery has been of incalculable value to the negro. It has lifted him out of barbarism and fetich worship, given him a language of civilization, and introduced him to the world's best religion. Think what he was in Africa and what he is in America!"

"The negro," said Dr. Gresham, thoughtfully, "is not the only branch of the human race which has been low down in the scale of civilization and freedom, and which has outgrown the measure of his chains. Slavery, polygamy, and human sacrifices have been practiced among Europeans in by-gone days; and when Tyndall tells us that out of savages unable to count to the number of their fingers and speaking only a language of nouns and verbs, arise at length our Newtons and Shakspeares, I do not see that the negro could not have learned our language and received our religion without the intervention of ages of slavery."

"If," said Rev. Carmicle, "Mohammedanism, with its imperfect creed, is successful in gathering large numbers of negroes beneath the Crescent, could not a legitimate commerce and the teachings of a pure Christianity have done as much to plant the standard of the Cross over the ramparts of sin and idolatry in Africa? Surely we cannot concede that the light of the Crescent is greater than the glory of the Cross, that there is less constraining power in the Christ of Calvary than in the Prophet of Arabia? I do not think that I underrate the difficulties in your way when I say that you young men are holding in your hands golden opportunities which it would be madness and folly to throw away. It is your grand opportunity to help build up a new South, not on the shifting sands of policy and expediency, but on the broad basis of equal justice and universal freedom. Do this and you will be blessed, and will make your life a blessing."

After Robert and Rev. Carmicle had left the hotel, Drs. Latimer, Gresham, and Latrobe sat silent and thoughtful awhile, when Dr. Gresham broke the silence by asking Dr. Latrobe how he had enjoyed the evening.

"Very pleasantly," he replied. "I was quite interested in that parson. Where was he educated?"

"In Oxford, I believe. I was pleased to hear him say that he had no white blood in his veins."

"I should think not," replied Dr. Latrobe, "from his looks. But one swallow does not make a summer. It is the exceptions which prove the rule."

"Don't you think," asked Dr. Gresham, "that we have been too hasty in our judgment of the negro? He has come handicapped into life, and is now on trial before the world. But it is not fair to subject him to the same tests that you would a white man. I believe that there are possibilities of growth in the race which we have never comprehended."

"The negro," said Dr. Latrobe, "is perfectly comprehensible to me. The only way to get along with him is to let him know his place, and make him keep it."

"I think," replied Dr. Gresham, "every man's place is the one he is best fitted for."

"Why," asked Dr. Latimer, "should any place be assigned to the negro more than to the French, Irish, or German?"

"Oh," replied Dr. Latrobe, "they are all Caucasians."

"Well," said Dr. Gresham, "is all excellence summed up in that branch of the human race?"

"I think," said Dr. Latrobe, proudly, "that we belong to the highest race on earth and the negro to the lowest."

"And yet," said Dr. Latimer, "you have consorted with them till you have bleached their faces to the whiteness of your own. Your children nestle in their bosoms; they are around you as body servants, and yet if one of them should attempt to associate with you your bitterest scorn and indignation would be visited upon them."

"I think," said Dr. Latrobe, "that feeling grows out of our Anglo-Saxon regard for the marriage relation. These white negroes are of illegitimate origin, and we would scorn to share our social life with them. Their blood is tainted."

"Who tainted it?" asked Dr. Latimer, bitterly. "You give absolution to the fathers, and visit the misfortunes of the mothers upon the children."

"But, Doctor, what kind of society would we have if we put down the bars and admitted everybody to social equality?"

"This idea of social equality," said Dr. Latimer, "is only a bugbear which frightens well-meaning people from dealing justly with the negro. I know of no place on earth where there is perfect social equality, and I doubt if there is such a thing in heaven. The sinner who repents on his death-bed cannot be the equal of St. Paul or the Beloved Disciple."

"Doctor," said Dr. Gresham, "I sometimes think that the final solution of this question will be the absorption of the negro into our race."

"Never! never!" exclaimed Dr. Latrobe, vehemently. "It would be a death blow to American civilization."

"Why, Doctor," said Dr. Latimer, "you Southerners began this absorption before the war. I understand that in one decade the mixed bloods rose from one-ninth to one-eighth of the population, and that as early as 1663 a law was passed in Maryland to prevent English women from intermarrying with slaves; and, even now, your laws against miscegenation presuppose that you apprehend danger from that source."

"Doctor, it is no use talking," replied Dr. Latrobe, wearily. "There are niggers who are as white as I am, but the taint of blood is there and we always exclude it."

"How do you know it is there?" asked Dr. Gresham.

"Oh, there are tricks of blood which always betray them. My eyes are more practiced than yours. I can always tell them. Now, that Johnson is as white as any man; but I knew he was a nigger the moment I saw him. I saw it in his eye."

Dr. Latimer smiled at Dr. Latrobe's assertion, but did not attempt to refute it; and bade him good-night.

"I think," said Dr. Latrobe, "that our war was the great mistake of the nineteenth century. It has left us very serious complications. We cannot amalgamate with the negroes. We cannot expatriate them. Now, what are we to do with them?"

"Deal justly with them," said Dr. Gresham, "and let them alone. Try to create a moral sentiment in the nation, which will consider a wrong done to the weakest of them as a wrong done to the whole community. Whenever you find ministers too righteous to be faithless, cowardly, and time serving; women too Christly to be scornful; and public men too noble to be tricky and too honest to pander to the prejudices of the people, stand by them and give them your moral support."

"Doctor," said Latrobe, "with your views you ought to be a preacher striving to usher in the millennium."

"It can't come too soon," replied Dr. Gresham.

# XXVII

## Diverging Paths

On the eve of his departure from the city of P——, Dr. Gresham called on Iola, and found her alone. They talked awhile of reminiscences of the war and hospital life, when Dr. Gresham, approaching Iola, said:—

"Miss Leroy, I am glad the great object of your life is accomplished, and that you have found all your relatives. Years have passed since we parted, years in which I have vainly tried to get a trace of you and have been baffled, but I have found you at last!" Clasping her hand in his, he continued, "I would it were so that I should never lose you again! Iola, will you not grant me the privilege of holding this hand as mine all through the future of our lives? Your search for your mother is ended. She is well cared for. Are you not free at last to share with me my Northern home, free to be mine as nothing else on earth is mine." Dr. Gresham looked eagerly on Iola's face, and tried to read its varying expression. "Iola, I learned to love you in the hospital. I have tried to forget you, but it has been all in vain. Your image is just as deeply engraven on my heart as it was the day we parted."

"Doctor," she replied, sadly, but firmly, as she withdrew her hand from his, "I feel now as I felt then, that there is an insurmountable barrier between us."

"What is it, Iola?" asked Dr. Gresham, anxiously.

"It is the public opinion which assigns me a place with the colored people."

"But what right has public opinion to interfere with our marriage relations? Why should we yield to its behests?"

"Because it is stronger than we are, and we cannot run counter to it without suffering its penalties."

"And what are they, Iola? Shadows that you merely dread?"

"No! no! the penalties of social ostracism North and South, except here and there some grand and noble exceptions. I do not think that you fully realize how much prejudice against colored people permeates society, lowers the tone of our religion, and reacts upon the life of the nation. After freedom came, mamma was living in the city of A——, and wanted to unite with a Christian church there. She made application for membership. She passed her examination as a candidate, and was received as a church member. When she was about to make her first communion, she unintentionally took her seat at the head of the column. The elder who was administering the communion gave her the bread in the order in which she sat, but before he gave her the wine some one touched him on the shoulder and whispered a word in his ear. He then passed mamma by, gave the cup to others, and then returned to her. From that rite connected with the holiest memories of earth, my poor mother returned humiliated and depressed."

"What a shame!" exclaimed Dr. Gresham, indignantly.

"I have seen," continued Iola, "the same spirit manifested in the North. Mamma once attempted to do missionary work in this city. One day she found an outcast colored girl, whom she wished to rescue. She took her to an asylum for fallen women and made an application for her, but was refused. Colored girls were not received there. Soon after mamma found among the colored people an outcast white girl. Mamma's sympathies, unfettered by class distinction, were aroused in her behalf, and, in company with two white ladies, she went with the girl to that same refuge. For her the door was freely opened and admittance readily granted. It was as if two women were sinking in the quicksands, and on the solid land stood other women with life-lines in their hands, seeing the deadly sands slowly creeping up around the hapless victims. To one they readily threw the lines of deliverance, but for the other there was not one strand of salvation. Sometime since, to the same asylum, came a poor fallen girl who had escaped from the clutches of a wicked woman. For her the door would have been opened, had not the vile woman from whom she was escaping followed her to that place of refuge and revealed the fact that she belonged to the colored race. That fact was enough to close the door upon her, and to send her back to sin and to suffer, and perhaps to die as a wretched outcast. And yet in this city where a number of charities are advertised, I do not think there is one of them which, in appealing to the public, talks more religion than the managers of this asylum. This prejudice against the colored race environs our lives and mocks our aspirations."

"Iola, I see no use in your persisting that you are colored when your eyes are as blue and complexion as white as mine."

"Doctor, were I your wife, are there not people who would caress me as a white woman who would shrink from me in scorn if they knew I had one drop of negro blood in my veins? When mistaken for a white woman, I should hear things alleged against the race at which my blood would boil. No, Doctor, I am not willing to live under a shadow of concealment which I thoroughly hate as if the blood in my veins were an undetected crime of my soul."

"Iola, dear, surely you paint the picture too darkly."

"Doctor, I have painted it with my heart's blood. It is easier to outgrow the dishonor of crime than the disabilities of color. You have created in this country an aristocracy of color wide enough to include the South with its treason and Utah with its abominations, but too narrow to include the best and bravest colored man who bared his breast to the bullets of the enemy during your fratricidal strife. Is not the most arrant Rebel today more acceptable to you than the most faithful colored man?"

"No! no!" exclaimed Dr. Gresham, vehemently. "You are wrong. I belong to the Grand Army of the Republic. We have no separate State Posts for the colored people, and, were such a thing proposed, the majority of our members, I believe, would be against it. In Congress colored men have the same seats as white men, and the color line is slowly fading out in our public institutions."

"But how is it in the Church?" asked Iola.

"The Church is naturally conservative. It preserves old truths, even if it is somewhat slow in embracing new ideas. It has its social as well as its spiritual side. Society is woman's realm. The majority of church members are women, who are said to be the aristocratic element of our country. I fear that one of the last strongholds of this racial prejudice will be found beneath the shadow of some of our churches. I think, on account of this social question, that large bodies of Christian temperance women and other reformers, in trying to reach the colored people even for their own good, will be quicker to form separate associations than our National Grand Army, whose ranks are open to black and white, liberals and conservatives, saints and agnostics. But, Iola, we have drifted far away from the question. No one has a right to interfere with our marriage if we do not infringe on the rights of others."

"Doctor," she replied, gently, "I feel that our paths must diverge. My life-work is planned. I intend spending my future among the colored people of the South."

"My dear friend," he replied, anxiously, "I am afraid that you are destined to sad disappointment. When the novelty wears off you will be disillusioned, and, I fear, when the time comes that you can no longer serve them they will forget your services and remember only your failings."

"But, Doctor, they need me; and I am sure when I taught among them they were very grateful for my services."

"I think," he replied, "these people are more thankful than grateful."

"I do not think so; and if I did it would not hinder me from doing all in my power to help them. I do not expect all the finest traits of character to spring from the hot-beds of slavery and caste. What matters it if they do forget the singer, so they don't forget the song? No, Doctor, I don't think that I could best serve my race by forsaking them and marrying you."

"Iola," he exclaimed, passionately, "if you love your race, as you call it, work for it, live for it, suffer for it, and, if need be, die for it; but don't marry for it. Your education has unfitted you for social life among them."

"It was," replied Iola, "through their unrequited toil that I was educated, while they were compelled to live in ignorance. I am indebted to them for the power I have to serve them. I wish other Southern women felt as I do. I think they could do so much to help the colored people at their doors if they would look at their opportunities in the light of the face of Jesus Christ. Nor am I wholly unselfish in allying myself with the colored people. All the rest of my family have done so. My dear grandmother is one of the excellent of the earth, and we all love her too much to ignore our relationship with her. I did not choose my lot in life, and the simplest thing I can do is to accept the situation and do the best I can."

"And is this your settled purpose?" he asked, sadly.

"It is, Doctor," she replied, tenderly but firmly. "I see no other. I must serve the race which needs me most."

"Perhaps you are right," he replied; "but I cannot help feeling sad that our paths, which met so pleasantly, should diverge so painfully. And yet, not only the freedmen, but the whole country, need such helpful, self-sacrificing teachers as you will prove; and if earnest prayers and holy wishes can brighten your path, your lines will fall in the pleasantest places."

As he rose to go, sympathy, love, and admiration were blended in the parting look he gave her; but he felt it was useless to attempt to divert her from her purpose. He knew that for the true reconstruction of the country something more was needed than bayonets and bullets, or the schemes of selfish politicians or plotting demagogues. He knew that the South needed the surrender of the best brain and heart of the country to build, above the wastes of war, more stately temples of thought and action.

# XXVIII

## Dr. Latrobe's Mistake

O n the morning previous to their departure for their respective homes, Dr. Gresham met Dr. Latrobe in the parlor of the Concordia.

"How," asked Dr. Gresham, "did you like Dr. Latimer's paper?"

"Very much, indeed. It was excellent. He is a very talented young man. He sits next to me at lunch and I have conversed with him several times. He is very genial and attractive, only he seems to be rather cranky on the negro question. I hope if he comes South that he will not make the mistake of mixing up with the negroes. It would be throwing away his influence and ruining his prospects. He seems to be well versed in science and literature and would make a very delightful accession to our social life."

"I think," replied Dr. Gresham, "that he is an honor to our profession. He is one of the finest specimens of our young manhood."

Just then Dr. Latimer entered the room. Dr. Latrobe arose and, greeting him cordially, said: "I was delighted with your paper; it was full of thought and suggestion."

"Thank you," answered Dr. Latimer, "it was my aim to make it so."

"And you succeeded admirably," replied Dr. Latrobe. "I could not help thinking how much we owe to heredity and environment."

"Yes," said Dr. Gresham. "Continental Europe yearly sends to our shores subjects to be developed into citizens. Emancipation has given us millions of new citizens, and to them our influence and example should be a blessing and not a curse."

"Well," said Dr. Latimer, "I intend to go South, and help those who so much need helpers from their own ranks."

"I hope," answered Dr. Latrobe, "that if you go South you will only sustain business relations with the negroes, and not commit the folly of equalizing yourself with them."

"Why not?" asked Dr. Latimer, steadily looking him in the eye.

"Because in equalizing yourself with them you drag us down; and our social customs must be kept intact."

"You have been associating with me at the convention for several days; I do not see that the contact has dragged you down, has it?"

"You! What has that got to do with associating with niggers?" asked Dr. Latrobe, curtly.

"The blood of that race is coursing through my veins. I am one of them," replied Dr. Latimer, proudly raising his head.

"You!" exclaimed Dr. Latrobe, with an air of profound astonishment and crimsoning face.

"Yes;" interposed Dr. Gresham, laughing heartily at Dr. Latrobe's discomfiture. "He belongs to that negro race both by blood and choice. His father's mother made overtures to receive him as her grandson and heir, but he has nobly refused to forsake his mother's people and has cast his lot with them."

"And I," said Dr. Latimer, "would have despised myself if I had done otherwise."

"Well, well," said Dr. Latrobe, rising, "I was never so deceived before. Good morning!"

Dr. Latrobe had thought he was clear-sighted enough to detect the presence of negro blood when all physical traces had disappeared. But he had associated with Dr. Latimer for several days, and admired his talent, without suspecting for one moment his racial connection. He could not help feeling a sense of vexation at the signal mistake he had made.

Dr. Frank Latimer was the natural grandson of a Southern lady, in whose family his mother had been a slave. The blood of a proud aristocratic ancestry was flowing through his veins, and generations of blood admixture had effaced all trace of his negro lineage. His complexion was blonde, his eye bright and piercing, his lips firm and well moulded; his manner very affable; his intellect active and well stored with information. He was a man capable of winning in life through his rich gifts of inheritance and acquirements. When freedom came, his mother, like Hagar of old, went out into the wide world to seek a living for herself and child. Through years of poverty she labored to educate her child, and saw the glad fruition of her hopes when her son graduated as an M.D. from the University of P——.

After his graduation he met his father's mother, who recognized him by his resemblance to her dear, departed son. All the mother love in her lonely heart awoke, and she was willing to overlook "the missing link of matrimony," and adopt him as her heir, if he would ignore his identity with the colored race.

Before him loomed all the possibilities which only birth and blood can give a white man in our Democratic country. But he was a man of too much sterling worth of character to be willing to forsake his mother's race for the richest advantages his grandmother could bestow.

Dr. Gresham had met Dr. Latimer at the beginning of the convention, and had been attracted to him by his frank and genial manner. One morning, when conversing with him, Dr. Gresham had learned some of the salient points of his history, which, instead of repelling him, had only deepened his admiration for the young doctor. He was much amused when he saw the pleasant acquaintanceship between him and Dr. Latrobe, but they agreed to be silent about his racial connection until the time came when they were ready to divulge it; and they were hugely delighted at his signal blunder.

# XXIX

## Visitors from the South

"M amma is not well," said Iola to Robert. "I spoke to her about sending for a doctor, but she objected and I did not insist."

"I will ask Dr. Latimer, whom I met at the Concordia, to step in. He is a splendid young fellow. I wish we had thousands like him."

In the evening the doctor called. Without appearing to make a professional visit he engaged Marie in conversation, watched her carefully, and came to the conclusion that her failing health proceeded more from mental than physical causes.

"I am so uneasy about Harry," said Mrs. Leroy. "He is so fearless and outspoken. I do wish the attention of the whole nation could be turned to the cruel barbarisms which are a national disgrace. I think the term 'bloody shirt' is one of the most heartless phrases ever invented to divert attention from cruel wrongs and dreadful outrages."

Just then Iola came in and was introduced by her uncle to Dr. Latimer, to whom the introduction was a sudden and unexpected pleasure.

After an interchange of courtesies, Marie resumed the conversation, saying: "Harry wrote me only last week that a young friend of his had lost his situation because he refused to have his pupils strew flowers on the streets through which Jefferson Davis was to pass."

"I think," said Dr. Latimer, indignantly, "that the Israelites had just as much right to scatter flowers over the bodies of the Egyptians, when the waves threw back their corpses on the shores of the Red Sea, as these children had to strew the path of Jefferson Davis with flowers. We want our boys to grow up manly citizens, and not cringing sycophants. When do you expect your son, Mrs. Leroy?"

"Some time next week," answered Marie.

"And his presence will do you more good than all the medicine in my chest."

"I hope, Doctor," said Mrs. Leroy, "that we will not lose sight of you, now that your professional visit is ended; for I believe your visit was the result of a conspiracy between Iola and her uncle."

Dr. Latimer laughed, as he answered, "Ah, Mrs. Leroy, I see you have found us all out."

FRANCES ELLEN WATKINS HARPER

"Oh, Doctor," exclaimed Iola, with pleasing excitement, "there is a young lady coming here to visit me next week. Her name is Miss Lucille Delany, and she is my ideal woman. She is grand, brave, intellectual, and religious."

"Is that so? She would make some man an excellent wife," replied Dr. Latimer.

"Now isn't that perfectly manlike," answered Iola, smiling. "Mamma, what do you think of that? Did any of you gentlemen ever see a young woman of much ability that you did not look upon as a flotsam all adrift until some man had appropriated her?"

"I think, Miss Leroy, that the world's work, if shared, is better done than when it is performed alone. Don't you think your life-work will be better done if some one shares it with you?" asked Dr. Latimer, slowly, and with a smile in his eyes.

"That would depend on the person who shared it," said Iola, faintly blushing.

"Here," said Robert, a few evenings after this conversation, as he handed Iola a couple of letters, "is something which will please you."

Iola took the letters, and, after reading one of them, said: "Miss Delany and Harry will be here on Wednesday; and this one is an invitation which also adds to my enjoyment."

"What is it?" asked Marie; "an invitation to a hop or a german?"

"No; but something which I value far more. We are all invited to Mr. Stillman's to a *conversazione*."

"What is the object?"

"His object is to gather some of the thinkers and leaders of the race to consult on subjects of vital interest to our welfare. He has invited Dr. Latimer, Professor Gradnor, of North Carolina, Mr. Forest, of New York, Hon. Dugdale, Revs. Carmicle, Cantnor, Tunster, Professor Langhorne, of Georgia, and a few ladies, Mrs. Watson, Miss Brown, and others."

"I am glad that it is neither a hop nor a german," said Iola, "but something for which I have been longing."

"Why, Iola," asked Robert, "don't you believe in young people having a good time?"

"Oh, yes," answered Iola, seriously, "I believe in young people having amusements and recreations; but the times are too serious for us to attempt to make our lives a long holiday."

"Well, Iola," answered Robert, "this is the first holiday we have had in two hundred and fifty years, and you shouldn't be too exacting."

"Yes," replied Marie, "human beings naturally crave enjoyment, and if not furnished with good amusements they are apt to gravitate to low pleasures."

"Some one," said Robert, "has said that the Indian belongs to an old race and looks gloomily back to the past, and that the negro belongs to a young race and looks hopefully towards the future."

"If that be so," replied Marie, "our race-life corresponds more to the follies of youth than the faults of maturer years."

On Dr. Latimer's next visit he was much pleased to see a great change in Marie's appearance. Her eye had grown brighter, her step more elastic, and the anxiety had faded from her face. Harry had arrived, and with him came Miss Delany.

"Good evening, Dr. Latimer," said Iola, cheerily, as she entered the room with Miss Lucille Delany. "This is my friend, Miss Delany, from Georgia. Were she not present I would say she is one of the grandest women in America."

"I am very much pleased to meet you," said Dr. Latimer, cordially; "I have heard Miss Leroy speak of you. We were expecting you," he added, with a smile.

Just then Harry entered the room, and Iola presented him to Dr. Latimer, saying, "This is my brother, about whom mamma was so anxious."

"Had you a pleasant journey?" asked Dr. Latimer, after the first greetings were over.

"Not especially," answered Miss Delany. "Southern roads are not always very pleasant to travel. When Mr. Leroy entered the cars at A——, where he was known, had he taken his seat among the white people he would have been remanded to the colored."

"But after awhile," said Harry, "as Miss Delany and myself were sitting together, laughing and chatting, a colored man entered the car, and, mistaking me for a white man, asked the conductor to have me removed, and I had to insist that I was colored in order to be permitted to remain. It would be ludicrous, if it were not vexatious, to be too white to be black, and too black to be white."

"Caste plays such fantastic tricks in this country," said Dr. Latimer.

"I tell Mr. Leroy," said Miss Delany, "that when he returns he must put a label on himself, saying, 'I am a colored man,' to prevent annoyance."

FRANCES ELLEN WATKINS HARPER

# XXX

## Friends in Council

On the following Friday evening, Mr. Stillman's pleasant, spacious parlors were filled to overflowing with a select company of earnest men and women deeply interested in the welfare of the race.

Bishop Tunster had prepared a paper on "Negro Emigration." Dr. Latimer opened the discussion by speaking favorably of some of the salient points, but said:—

"I do not believe self-exilement is the true remedy for the wrongs of the negro. Where should he go if he left this country?"

"Go to Africa," replied Bishop Tunster, in his bluff, hearty tones. "I believe that Africa is to be redeemed to civilization, and that the negro is to be gathered into the family of nations and recognized as a man and a brother."

"Go to Africa?" repeated Professor Langhorne, of Georgia. "Does the United States own one foot of African soil? And have we not been investing our blood in the country for ages?"

"I am in favor of missionary efforts," said Professor Gradnor, of North Carolina, "for the redemption of Africa, but I see no reason for expatriating ourselves because some persons do not admire the color of our skins."

"I do not believe," said Mr. Stillman, "in emptying on the shores of Africa a horde of ignorant, poverty-stricken people, as missionaries of civilization or Christianity. And while I am in favor of missionary efforts, there is need here for the best heart and brain to work in unison for justice and righteousness."

"America," said Miss Delany, "is the best field for human development. God has not heaped up our mountains with such grandeur, flooded our rivers with such majesty, crowned our valleys with such fertility, enriched our mines with such wealth, that they should only minister to grasping greed and sensuous enjoyment."

"Climate, soil, and physical environments," said Professor Gradnor, "have much to do with shaping national characteristics. If in Africa, under a tropical sun, the negro has lagged behind other races in the march of civilization, at least for once in his history he has, in this country, the privilege of using climatic advantages and developing under new conditions."

"Yes," replied Dr. Latimer, "and I do not wish our people to become restless and unsettled before they have tried one generation of freedom."

"I am always glad," said Mr. Forest, a tall, distinguished-looking gentleman from New York, "when I hear of people who are ill treated in one section of the country emigrating to another. Men who are deaf to the claims of mercy, and oblivious to the demands of justice, can feel when money is slipping from their pockets."

"The negro," said Hon. Dugdale, "does not present to my mind the picture of an effete and exhausted people, destined to die out before a stronger race. Gilbert Haven once saw a statue which suggested this thought, 'I am black, but comely; the sun has looked down upon me, but I will teach you who despise me to feel that I am your superior.' The men who are acquiring property and building up homes in the South show us what energy and determination may do even in that part of the country. I believe such men can do more to conquer prejudice than if they spent all their lives in shouting for their rights and ignoring their duties. No! as there are millions of us in this country, I think it best to settle down and work out our own salvation here."

"How many of us today," asked Professor Langhorne, "would be teaching in the South, if every field of labor in the North was as accessible to us as to the whites? It has been estimated that a million young white men have left the South since the war, and, had our chances been equal to theirs, would we have been any more willing to stay in the South with those who need us than they? But this prejudice, by impacting us together, gives us a common cause and brings our intellect in contact with the less favored of our race."

"I do not believe," said Miss Delany, "that the Southern white people themselves desire any wholesale exodus of the colored from their labor fields. It would be suicidal to attempt their expatriation."

"History," said Professor Langhorne, "tells that Spain was once the place where barbarian Europe came to light her lamp. Seven hundred years before there was a public lamp in London you might have gone through the streets of Cordova amid ten miles of lighted lamps, and stood there on solidly paved land, when hundreds of years afterwards, in Paris, on a rainy day you would have sunk to your ankles in the mud. But she who bore the name of the 'Terror of Nations,' and the 'Queen of the Ocean,' was not strong enough to dash herself against

FRANCES ELLEN WATKINS HARPER

God's law of retribution and escape unscathed. She inaugurated a crusade of horror against a million of her best laborers and artisans. Vainly she expected the blessing of God to crown her work of violence. Instead of seeing the fruition of her hopes in the increased prosperity of her land, depression and paralysis settled on her trade and business. A fearful blow was struck at her agriculture; decay settled on her manufactories; money became too scarce to pay the necessary expenses of the king's exchequer; and that once mighty empire became a fallen kingdom, pierced by her crimes and dragged down by her transgressions."

"We did not," said Iola, "place the bounds of our habitation. And I believe we are to be fixtures in this country. But beyond the shadows I see the coruscation of a brighter day; and we can help usher it in, not by answering hate with hate, or giving scorn for scorn, but by striving to be more generous, noble, and just. It seems as if all creation travels to respond to the song of the Herald angels, 'Peace on earth, good-will toward men.'"

The next paper was on "Patriotism," by Rev. Cantnor. It was a paper in which the white man was extolled as the master race, and spoke as if it were a privilege for the colored man to be linked to his destiny and to live beneath the shadow of his power. He asserted that the white race of this country is the broadest, most Christian, and humane of that branch of the human family.

Dr. Latimer took exception to his position. "Law," he said, "is the pivot on which the whole universe turns; and obedience to law is the gauge by which a nation's strength or weakness is tried. We have had two evils by which our obedience to law has been tested—slavery and the liquor traffic. How have we dealt with them both? We have been weighed in the balance and found wanting. Millions of slaves and serfs have been liberated during this century, but not even in semi-barbaric Russia, heathen Japan, or Catholic Spain has slavery been abolished through such a fearful conflict as it was in the United States. The liquor traffic still sends its floods of ruin and shame to the habitations of men, and no political party has been found with enough moral power and numerical strength to stay the tide of death."

"I think," said Professor Gradnor, "that what our country needs is truth more than flattery. I do not think that our moral life keeps pace with our mental development and material progress. I know of no civilized country on the globe, Catholic, Protestant, or Mohammedan, where life is less secure than it is in the South. Nearly eighteen hundred years ago the life of a Roman citizen in Palestine was in danger from mob violence. That pagan government threw around him a wall of living clay, consisting of four hundred and seventy men, when more than forty Jews had bound themselves with an oath that they would neither eat nor drink until they had taken the life of the Apostle Paul. Does not true patriotism demand that citizenship should be as much protected in Christian America as it was in heathen Rome?"

"I would have our people," said Miss Delany, "more interested in politics. Instead of forgetting the past, I would have them hold in everlasting remembrance our great deliverance. Hitherto we have never had a country with tender, precious memories to fill our eyes with tears, or glad reminiscences to thrill our hearts with pride and joy. We have been aliens and outcasts in the land of our birth. But I want my pupils to do all in their power to make this country worthy of their deepest devotion and loftiest patriotism. I want them to feel that its glory is their glory, its dishonor their shame."

"Our esteemed friend, Mrs. Watson," said Iola, "sends regrets that she cannot come, but has kindly favored us with a poem, called the "Rallying Cry." In her letter she says that, although she is no longer young, she feels that in the conflict for the right there's room for young as well as old. She hopes that we will here unite the enthusiasm of youth with the experience of age, and that we will have a pleasant and profitable conference. Is it your pleasure that the poem be read at this stage of our proceedings, or later on?"

"Let us have it now," answered Harry, "and I move that Miss Delany be chosen to lend to the poem the charm of her voice."

"I second the motion," said Iola, smiling, and handing the poem to Miss Delany.

Miss Delany took the poem and read it with fine effect. The spirit of the poem had entered her soul.

## A Rallying Cry

*Oh, children of the tropics,*
*Amid our pain and wrong*
*Have you no other mission*
*Than music, dance, and song?*

FRANCES ELLEN WATKINS HARPER

When through the weary ages
Our dripping tears still fall,
Is this a time to dally
With pleasure's silken thrall?

Go, muffle all your viols;
As heroes learn to stand,
With faith in God's great justice
Nerve every heart and hand.

Dream not of ease nor pleasure,
Nor honor, wealth, nor fame,
Till from the dust you've lifted
Our long-dishonored name;

And crowned that name with glory
By deeds of holy worth,
To shine with light emblazoned,
The noblest name on earth.

Count life a dismal failure,
Unblessing and unblest,
That seeks 'mid ease inglorious
For pleasure or for rest.

With courage, strength, and valor
Your lives and actions brace;
Shrink not from toil or hardship,
And dangers bravely face.

Engrave upon your banners,
In words of golden light,
That honor, truth, and justice
Are more than godless might.

Above earth's pain and sorrow
Christ's dying face I see;
I hear the cry of anguish:—
"Why hast thou forsaken me?"

*In the pallor of that anguish*
*I see the only light,*
*To flood with peace and gladness*
*Earth's sorrow, pain, and night.*

*Arrayed in Christly armor*
*'Gainst error, crime, and sin,*
*The victory can't be doubtful,*
*For God is sure to win.*

The next paper was by Miss Iola Leroy, on the "Education of Mothers."

"I agree," said Rev. Eustace, of St. Mary's parish, "with the paper. The great need of the race is enlightened mothers."

"And enlightened fathers, too," added Miss Delany, quickly. "If there is anything I chafe to see it is a strong, hearty man shirking his burdens, putting them on the shoulders of his wife, and taking life easy for himself."

"I always pity such mothers," interposed Iola, tenderly.

"I think," said Miss Delany, with a flash in her eye and a ring of decision in her voice, "that such men ought to be drummed out of town!" As she spoke, there was an expression which seemed to say, "And I would like to help do it!"

Harry smiled, and gave her a quick glance of admiration.

"I do not think," said Mrs. Stillman, "that we can begin too early to teach our boys to be manly and self-respecting, and our girls to be useful and self-reliant."

"You know," said Mrs. Leroy, "that after the war we were thrown upon the nation a homeless race to be gathered into homes, and a legally unmarried race to be taught the sacredness of the marriage relation. We must instill into our young people that the true strength of a race means purity in women and uprightness in men; who can say, with Sir Galahad:—

*'My strength is the strength of ten,*
*Because my heart is pure.'*

And where this is wanting neither wealth nor culture can make up the deficiency."

"There is a field of Christian endeavor which lies between the school-house and the pulpit, which needs the hand of a woman more in private than in public," said Miss Delany.

"Yes, I have often felt the need of such work in my own parish. We need a union of women with the warmest hearts and clearest brains to help in the moral education of the race," said Rev. Eustace.

"Yes," said Iola, "if we would have the prisons empty we must make the homes more attractive."

"In civilized society," replied Dr. Latimer, "there must be restraint either within or without. If parents fail to teach restraint within, society has her check-reins without in the form of chain-gangs, prisons, and the gallows."

The closing paper was on the "Moral Progress of the Race," by Hon. Dugdale. He said: "The moral progress of the race was not all he could desire, yet he could not help feeling that, compared with other races, the outlook was not hopeless. I am so sorry to see, however, that in some States there is an undue proportion of colored people in prisons."

"I think," answered Professor Langhorne, of Georgia, "that this is owing to a partial administration of law in meting out punishment to colored offenders. I know red-handed murderers who walk in this Republic unwhipped of justice, and I have seen a colored woman sentenced to prison for weeks for stealing twenty-five cents. I knew a colored girl who was executed for murder when only a child in years. And it was through the intervention of a friend of mine, one of the bravest young men of the South, that a boy of fifteen was saved from the gallows."

"When I look," said Mr. Forest, "at the slow growth of modern civilization—the ages which have been consumed in reaching our present altitude, and see how we have outgrown slavery, feudalism, and religious persecutions, I cannot despair of the future of the race."

"Just now," said Dr. Latimer, "we have the fearful grinding and friction which comes in the course of an adjustment of the new machinery of freedom in the old ruts of slavery. But I am optimistic enough to believe that there will yet be a far higher and better Christian civilization than our country has ever known."

"And in that civilization I believe the negro is to be an important factor," said Rev. Cantnor.

"I believe it also," said Miss Delany, hopefully, "and this thought has been a blessed inspiration to my life. When I come in contact with

Christless prejudices, I feel that my life is too much a part of the Divine plan, and invested with too much intrinsic worth, for me to be the least humiliated by indignities that beggarly souls can inflict. I feel more pitiful than resentful to those who do not know how much they miss by living mean, ignoble lives."

"My heart," said Iola, "is full of hope for the future. Pain and suffering are the crucibles out of which come gold more fine than the pavements of heaven, and gems more precious than the foundations of the Holy City."

"If," said Mrs. Leroy, "pain and suffering are factors in human development, surely we have not been counted too worthless to suffer."

"And is there," continued Iola, "a path which we have trodden in this country, unless it be the path of sin, into which Jesus Christ has not put His feet and left it luminous with the light of His steps? Has the negro been poor and homeless? The birds of the air had nests and the foxes had holes, but the Son of man had not where to lay His head. Has our name been a synonym for contempt? 'He shall be called a Nazarene.' Have we been despised and trodden under foot? Christ was despised and rejected of men. Have we been ignorant and unlearned? It was said of Jesus Christ, 'How knoweth this man letters, never having learned?' Have we been beaten and bruised in the prison-house of bondage? 'They took Jesus and scourged Him.' Have we been slaughtered, our bones scattered at the graves' mouth? He was spit upon by the mob, smitten and mocked by the rabble, and died as died Rome's meanest criminal slave. Today that cross of shame is a throne of power. Those robes of scorn have changed to habiliments of light, and that crown of mockery to a diadem of glory. And never, while the agony of Gethsemane and the sufferings of Calvary have their hold upon my heart, will I recognize any religion as His which despises the least of His brethren."

As Iola finished, there was a ring of triumph in her voice, as if she were reviewing a path she had trodden with bleeding feet, and seen it change to lines of living light. Her soul seemed to be flashing through the rare loveliness of her face and etherealizing its beauty.

Every one was spell-bound. Dr. Latimer was entranced, and, turning to Hon. Dugdale, said, in a low voice and with deep-drawn breath, "She is angelic!"

Hon. Dugdale turned, gave a questioning look, then replied, "She is strangely beautiful! Do you know her?"

"Yes; I have met her several times. I accompanied her here tonight.

The tones of her voice are like benedictions of peace; her words a call to higher service and nobler life."

Just then Rev. Carmicle was announced. He had been on a Southern tour, and had just returned.

"Oh, Doctor," exclaimed Mrs. Stillman, "I am delighted to see you. We were about to adjourn, but we will postpone action to hear from you."

"Thank you," replied Rev. Carmicle. "I have not the cue to the meeting, and will listen while I take breath."

"Pardon me," answered Mrs. Stillman. "I should have been more thoughtful than to press so welcome a guest into service before I had given him time for rest and refreshment; but if the courtesy failed on my lips it did not fail in my heart. I wanted our young folks to see one of our thinkers who had won distinction before the war."

"My dear friend," said Rev. Carmicle, smiling, "some of these young folks will look on me as a back number. You know the cry has already gone forth, 'Young men to the front.'"

"But we need old men for counsel," interposed Mr. Forest, of New York.

"Of course," said Rev. Carmicle, "we older men would rather retire gracefully than be relegated or hustled to a back seat. But I am pleased to see doors open to you which were closed to us, and opportunities which were denied us embraced by you."

"How," asked Hon. Dugdale, "do you feel in reference to our people's condition in the South?"

"Very hopeful, although at times I cannot help feeling anxious about their future. I was delighted with my visits to various institutions of learning, and surprised at the desire manifested among the young people to obtain an education. Where toil-worn mothers bent beneath their heavy burdens their more favored daughters are enjoying the privileges of education. Young people are making recitations in Greek and Latin where it was once a crime to teach their parents to read. I also became acquainted with colored professors and presidents of colleges. Saw young ladies who had graduated as doctors. Comfortable homes have succeeded old cabins of slavery. Vast crops have been raised by free labor. I read with interest and pleasure a number of papers edited by colored men. I saw it estimated that two millions of our people had learned to read, and I feel deeply grateful to the people who have supplied us with teachers who have stood their ground so nobly among our people."

"But," asked Mr. Forest, "you expressed fears about the future of our race. From whence do your fears arise?"

"From the unfortunate conditions which slavery has entailed upon that section of our country. I dread the results of that racial feeling which ever and anon breaks out into restlessness and crime. Also, I am concerned about the lack of home training for those for whom the discipline of the plantation has been exchanged for the penalties of prisons and chain-gangs. I am sorry to see numbers of our young men growing away from the influence of the church and drifting into prisons. I also fear that in some sections, as colored men increase in wealth and intelligence, there will be an increase of race rivalry and jealousy. It is said that savages, by putting their ears to the ground, can hear a far-off tread. So, today, I fear that there are savage elements in our civilization which hear the advancing tread of the negro and would retard his coming. It is the incarnation of these elements that I dread. It is their elimination I do so earnestly desire. Whether it be outgrown or not is our unsolved problem. Time alone will tell whether or not the virus of slavery and injustice has too fully permeated our Southern civilization for a complete recovery. Nations, honey-combed by vice, have fallen beneath the weight of their iniquities. Justice is always uncompromising in its claims and inexorable in its demands. The laws of the universe are never repealed to accommodate our follies."

"Surely," said Bishop Tunster, "the negro has a higher mission than that of aimlessly drifting through life and patiently waiting for death."

"We may not," answered Rev. Carmicle, "have the same dash, courage, and aggressiveness of other races, accustomed to struggle, achievement, and dominion, but surely the world needs something better than the results of arrogance, aggressiveness, and indomitable power. For the evils of society there are no solvents as potent as love and justice, and our greatest need is not more wealth and learning, but a religion replete with life and glowing with love. Let this be the impelling force in the race and it cannot fail to rise in the scale of character and condition."

"And," said Dr. Latimer, "instead of narrowing our sympathies to mere racial questions, let us broaden them to humanity's wider issues."

"Let us," replied Rev. Carmicle, "pass it along the lines, that to be willfully ignorant is to be shamefully criminal. Let us teach our people not to love pleasure or to fear death, but to learn the true value of life, and to do their part to eliminate the paganism of caste from our holy religion and the lawlessness of savagery from our civilization."

"How DID YOU ENJOY THE evening, Marie?" asked Robert, as they walked homeward.

"I was interested and deeply pleased," answered Marie.

"I," said Robert, "was thinking of the wonderful changes that have come to us since the war. When I sat in those well-lighted, beautifully-furnished rooms, I was thinking of the meetings we used to have in by-gone days. How we used to go by stealth into lonely woods and gloomy swamps, to tell of our hopes and fears, sorrows and trials. I hope that we will have many more of these gatherings. Let us have the next one here."

"I am sure," said Marie, "I would gladly welcome such a conference at any time. I think such meetings would be so helpful to our young people."

# XXXI

## Dawning Affections

"D octor," said Iola, as they walked home from the *conversazione*, "I wish I could do something more for our people than I am doing. I taught in the South till failing health compelled me to change my employment. But, now that I am well and strong, I would like to do something of lasting service for the race."

"Why not," asked Dr. Latimer, "write a good, strong book which would be helpful to them? I think there is an amount of dormant talent among us, and a large field from which to gather materials for such a book."

"I would do it, willingly, if I could; but one needs both leisure and money to make a successful book. There is material among us for the broadest comedies and the deepest tragedies, but, besides money and leisure, it needs patience, perseverance, courage, and the hand of an artist to weave it into the literature of the country."

"Miss Leroy, you have a large and rich experience; you possess a vivid imagination and glowing fancy. Write, out of the fullness of your heart, a book to inspire men and women with a deeper sense of justice and humanity."

"Doctor," replied Iola, "I would do it if I could, not for the money it might bring, but for the good it might do. But who believes any good can come out of the black Nazareth?"

"Miss Leroy, out of the race must come its own thinkers and writers. Authors belonging to the white race have written good racial books, for which I am deeply grateful, but it seems to be almost impossible for a white man to put himself completely in our place. No man can feel the iron which enters another man's soul."

"Well, Doctor, when I write a book I shall take you for the hero of my story."

"Why, what have I done," asked Dr. Latimer, in a surprised tone, "that you should impale me on your pen?"

"You have done nobly," answered Iola, "in refusing your grandmother's offer."

"I only did my duty," he modestly replied.

"But," said Iola, "when others are trying to slip out from the race and pass into the white basis, I cannot help admiring one who acts as if he felt that the weaker the race is the closer he would cling to it."

"My mother," replied Dr. Latimer, "faithful and true, belongs to that race. Where else should I be? But I know a young lady who could have cast her lot with the favored race, yet chose to take her place with the freed people, as their teacher, friend, and adviser. This young lady was alone in the world. She had been fearfully wronged, and to her stricken heart came a brilliant offer of love, home, and social position. But she bound her heart to the mast of duty, closed her ears to the syren song, and could not be lured from her purpose."

A startled look stole over Iola's face, and, lifting her eyes to his, she faltered:—

"Do you know her?"

"Yes, I know her and admire her; and she ought to be made the subject of a soul-inspiring story. Do you know of whom I speak?"

"How should I, Doctor? I am sure you have not made me your confidante," she responded, demurely; then she quickly turned and tripped up the steps of her home, which she had just reached.

After this conversation Dr. Latimer became a frequent visitor at Iola's home, and a firm friend of her brother. Harry was at that age when, for the young and inexperienced, vice puts on her fairest guise and most seductive smiles. Dr. Latimer's wider knowledge and larger experience made his friendship for Harry very valuable, and the service he rendered him made him a favorite and ever-welcome guest in the family.

"Are you all alone," asked Robert, one night, as he entered the cosy little parlor where Iola sat reading. "Where are the rest of the folks?"

"Mamma and grandma have gone to bed," answered Iola. "Harry and Lucille are at the concert. They are passionately fond of music, and find facilities here that they do not have in the South. They wouldn't go to hear a seraph where they must take a negro seat. I was too tired to go. Besides, 'two's company and three's a crowd,'" she added, significantly.

"I reckon you struck the nail on the head that time," said Robert, laughing. "But you have not been alone all the time. Just as I reached the corner I saw Dr. Latimer leaving the door. I see he still continues his visits. Who is his patient now?"

"Oh, Uncle Robert," said Iola, smiling and flushing, "he is out with Harry and Lucille part of the time, and drops in now and then to see us all."

"Well," said Robert, "I suppose the case is now an affair of the heart. But I cannot blame him for it," he added, looking fondly on the beautiful face of his niece, which sorrow had touched only to chisel into more loveliness. "How do you like him?"

"I must have within me," answered Iola, with unaffected truthfulness, "a large amount of hero worship. The characters of the Old Testament I most admire are Moses and Nehemiah. They were willing to put aside their own advantages for their race and country. Dr. Latimer comes up to my ideal of a high, heroic manhood."

"I think," answered Robert, smiling archly, "he would be delighted to hear your opinion of him."

"I tell him," continued Iola, "that he belongs to the days of chivalry. But he smiles and says, 'he only belongs to the days of hard-pan service.'"

"Some one," said Robert, "was saying today that he stood in his own light when he refused his grandmother's offer to receive him as her son."

"I think," said Iola, "it was the grandest hour of his life when he made that decision. I have admired him ever since I heard his story."

"But, Iola, think of the advantages he set aside. It was no sacrifice for me to remain colored, with my lack of education and race sympathies, but Dr. Latimer had doors open to him as a white man which are forever closed to a colored man. To be born white in this country is to be born to an inheritance of privileges, to hold in your hands the keys that open before you the doors of every occupation, advantage, opportunity, and achievement."

"I know that, uncle," answered Iola; "but even these advantages are too dearly bought if they mean loss of honor, true manliness, and self respect. He could not have retained these had he ignored his mother and lived under a veil of concealment, constantly haunted by a dread of detection. The gain would not have been worth the cost. It were better that he should walk the ruggedest paths of life a true man than tread the softest carpets a moral cripple."

"I am afraid," said Robert, laying his hand caressingly upon her head, "that we are destined to lose the light of our home."

"Oh, uncle, how you talk! I never dreamed of what you are thinking," answered Iola, half reproachfully.

"And how," asked Robert, "do you know what I am thinking about?"

"My dear uncle, I'm not blind."

"Neither am I," replied Robert, significantly, as he left the room.

Iola's admiration for Dr. Latimer was not a one-sided affair. Day after day she was filling a larger place in his heart. The touch of her hand thrilled him with emotion. Her lightest words were an entrancing melody to his ear. Her noblest sentiments found a response in his heart. In their desire to help the race their hearts beat in loving unison. One grand and noble purpose was giving tone and color to their lives and strengthening the bonds of affection between them.

# XXXII

## WOOING AND WEDDING

Harry's vacation had been very pleasant. Miss Delany, with her fine conversational powers and ready wit, had added much to his enjoyment. Robert had given his mother the pleasantest room in the house, and in the evening the family would gather around her, tell her the news of the day, read to her from the Bible, join with her in thanksgiving for mercies received and in prayer for protection through the night. Harry was very grateful to Dr. Latimer for the kindly interest he had shown in accompanying Miss Delany and himself to places of interest and amusement. He was grateful, too, that in the city of P—— doors were open to them which were barred against them in the South.

The bright, beautiful days of summer were gliding into autumn, with its glorious wealth of foliage, and the time was approaching for the departure of Harry and Miss Delany to their respective schools, when Dr. Latimer received several letters from North Carolina, urging him to come South, as physicians were greatly needed there. Although his practice was lucrative in the city of P——, he resolved he would go where his services were most needed.

A few evenings before he started he called at the house, and made an engagement to drive Iola to the park.

At the time appointed he drove up to the door in his fine equipage. Iola stepped gracefully in and sat quietly by his side to enjoy the loveliness of the scenery and the gorgeous grandeur of the setting sun.

"I expect to go South," said Dr. Latimer, as he drove slowly along.

"Ah, indeed," said Iola, assuming an air of interest, while a shadow flitted over her face. "Where do you expect to pitch your tent?"

"In the city of C——, North Carolina," he answered.

"Oh, I wish," she exclaimed, "that you were going to Georgia, where you could take care of that high-spirited brother of mine."

"I suppose if he were to hear you he would laugh, and say that he could take care of himself. But I know a better plan than that."

"What is it?" asked Iola, innocently.

"That you will commit yourself, instead of your brother, to my care."

FRANCES ELLEN WATKINS HARPER

"Oh, dear," replied Iola, drawing a long breath. "What would mamma say?"

"That she would willingly resign you, I hope."

"And what would grandma and Uncle Robert say?" again asked Iola.

"That they would cheerfully acquiesce. Now, what would I say if they all consent?"

"I don't know," modestly responded Iola.

"Well," replied Dr. Latimer, "I would say:—

> *"Could deeds my love discover,*
> *Could valor gain thy charms,*
> *To prove myself thy lover*
> *I'd face a world in arms."*

"And prove a good soldier," added Iola, smiling, "when there is no battle to fight."

"Iola, I am in earnest," said Dr. Latimer, passionately. "In the work to which I am devoted every burden will be lighter, every path smoother, if brightened and blessed with your companionship."

A sober expression swept over Iola's face, and, dropping her eyes, she said: "I must have time to think."

Quietly they rode along the river bank until Dr. Latimer broke the silence by saying:—

"Miss Iola, I think that you brood too much over the condition of our people."

"Perhaps I do," she replied, "but they never burn a man in the South that they do not kindle a fire around my soul."

"I am afraid," replied Dr. Latimer, "that you will grow morbid and nervous. Most of our people take life easily—why shouldn't you?"

"Because," she answered, "I can see breakers ahead which they do not."

"Oh, give yourself no uneasiness. They will catch the fret and fever of the nineteenth century soon enough. I have heard several of our ministers say that it is chiefly men of disreputable characters who are made the subjects of violence and lynch-law."

"Suppose it is so," responded Iola, feelingly. "If these men believe in eternal punishment they ought to feel a greater concern for the wretched sinner who is hurried out of time with all his sins upon his head, than for the godly man who passes through violence to endless rest."

"That is true; and I am not counseling you to be selfish; but, Miss Iola, had you not better look out for yourself?"

"Thank you, Doctor, I am feeling quite well."

"I know it, but your devotion to study and work is too intense," he replied.

"I am preparing to teach, and must spend my leisure time in study. Mr. Cloten is an excellent employer, and treats his employés as if they had hearts as well as hands. But to be an expert accountant is not the best use to which I can put my life."

"As a teacher you will need strong health and calm nerves. You had better let me prescribe for you. You need," he added, with a merry twinkle in his eyes, "change of air, change of scene, and change of name."

"Well, Doctor," said Iola, laughing, "that is the newest nostrum out. Had you not better apply for a patent?"

"Oh," replied Dr. Latimer, with affected gravity, "you know you must have unlimited faith in your physician."

"So you wish me to try the faith cure?" asked Iola, laughing.

"Yes, faith in me," responded Dr. Latimer, seriously.

"Oh, here we are at home!" exclaimed Iola. "This has been a glorious evening, Doctor. I am indebted to you for a great pleasure. I am extremely grateful."

"You are perfectly welcome," replied Dr. Latimer. "The pleasure has been mutual, I assure you."

"Will you not come in?" asked Iola.

Tying his horse, he accompanied Iola into the parlor. Seating himself near her, he poured into her ears words eloquent with love and tenderness.

"Iola," he said, "I am not an adept in courtly phrases. I am a plain man, who believes in love and truth. In asking you to share my lot, I am not inviting you to a life of ease and luxury, for year after year I may have to struggle to keep the wolf from the door, but your presence would make my home one of the brightest spots on earth, and one of the fairest types of heaven. Am I presumptuous in hoping that your love will become the crowning joy of my life?"

His words were more than a tender strain wooing her to love and happiness, they were a clarion call to a life of high and holy worth, a call which found a response in her heart. Her hand lay limp in his. She did not withdraw it, but, raising her lustrous eyes to his, she softly answered: "Frank, I love you."

FRANCES ELLEN WATKINS HARPER

After he had gone, Iola sat by the window, gazing at the splendid stars, her heart quietly throbbing with a delicious sense of joy and love. She had admired Dr. Gresham and, had there been no barrier in her way, she might have learned to love him; but Dr. Latimer had grown irresistibly upon her heart. There were depths in her nature that Dr. Gresham had never fathomed; aspirations in her soul with which he had never mingled. But as the waves leap up to the strand, so her soul went out to Dr. Latimer. Between their lives were no impeding barriers, no inclination impelling one way and duty compelling another. Kindred hopes and tastes had knit their hearts; grand and noble purposes were lighting up their lives; and they esteemed it a blessed privilege to stand on the threshold of a new era and labor for those who had passed from the old oligarchy of slavery into the new commonwealth of freedom.

On the next evening, Dr. Latimer rang the bell and was answered by Harry, who ushered him into the parlor, and then came back to the sitting-room, saying, "Iola, Dr. Latimer has called to see you."

"Has he?" answered Iola, a glad light coming into her eyes. "Come, Lucille, let us go into the parlor."

"Oh, no," interposed Harry, shrugging his shoulders and catching Lucille's hand. "He didn't ask for you. When we went to the concert we were told three's a crowd. And I say one good turn deserves another."

"Oh, Harry, you are so full of nonsense. Let Lucille go!" said Iola.

"Indeed I will not. I want to have a good time as well as you," said Harry.

"Oh, you're the most nonsensical man I know," interposed Miss Delany. Yet she stayed with Harry.

"You're looking very bright and happy," said Dr. Latimer to Iola, as she entered.

"My ride in the park was so refreshing! I enjoyed it so much! The day was so lovely, the air delicious, the birds sang so sweetly, and the sunset was so magnificent."

"I am glad of it. Why, Iola, your home is so happy your heart should be as light as a school-girl's."

"Doctor," she replied, "I must be prematurely old. I have scarcely known what it is to be light-hearted since my father's death."

"I know it, darling," he answered, seating himself beside her, and drawing her to him. "You have been tried in the fire, but are you not better for the crucial test?"

"Doctor," she replied, "as we rode along yesterday, mingling with the sunshine of the present came the shadows of the past. I was thinking of the bright, joyous days of my girlhood, when I defended slavery, and of how the cup that I would have pressed to the lips of others was forced to my own. Yet, in looking over the mournful past, I would not change the Iola of then for the Iola of now."

"Yes," responded Dr. Latimer, musingly,

> *"'Darkness shows us worlds of light*
> *We never saw by day.'"*

"Oh, Doctor, you cannot conceive what it must have been to be hurled from a home of love and light into the dark abyss of slavery; to be compelled to take your place among a people you have learned to look upon as inferiors and social outcasts; to be in the power of men whose presence would fill you with horror and loathing, and to know that there is no earthly power to protect you from the highest insults which brutal cowardice could shower upon you. I am so glad that no other woman of my race will suffer as I have done."

The flush deepened on her face, a mournful splendor beamed from her beautiful eyes, into which the tears had slowly gathered.

"Darling," he said, his voice vibrating with mingled feelings of tenderness and resentment, "you must forget the sad past. You are like a tender lamb snatched from the jaws of a hungry wolf, but who still needs protecting, loving care. But it must have been terrible," he added, in a painful tone.

"It was indeed! For awhile I was like one dazed. I tried to pray, but the heavens seemed brass over my head. I was wild with agony, and had I not been placed under conditions which roused all the resistance of my soul, I would have lost my reason."

"Was it not a mistake to have kept you ignorant of your colored blood?"

"It was the great mistake of my father's life, but dear papa knew something of the cruel, crushing power of caste; and he tried to shield us from it."

"Yes, yes," replied Dr. Latimer, thoughtfully, "in trying to shield you from pain he plunged you into deeper suffering."

"I never blame him, because I know he did it for the best. Had he lived he would have taken us to France, where I should have had a life of careless ease and pleasure. But now my life has a much grander significance than it would have had under such conditions. Fearful as the awakening was, it was better than to have slept through life."

"Best for you and best for me," said Dr. Latimer. "There are souls that never awaken; but if they miss the deepest pain they also lose the highest joy."

Dr. Latimer went South, after his engagement, and through his medical skill and agreeable manners became very successful in his practice. In the following summer, he built a cosy home for the reception of his bride, and came North, where, with Harry and Miss Delany as attendants, he was married to Iola, amid a pleasant gathering of friends, by Rev. Carmicle.

# XXXIII

## CONCLUSION

It was late in the summer when Dr. Latimer and his bride reached their home in North Carolina. Over the cottage porch were morning-glories to greet the first flushes of the rising day, and roses and jasmines to distill their fragrance on the evening air. Aunt Linda, who had been apprised of their coming, was patiently awaiting their arrival, and Uncle Daniel was pleased to know that "dat sweet young lady who had sich putty manners war comin' to lib wid dem."

As soon as they arrived, Aunt Linda rushed up to Iola, folded her in her arms, and joyfully exclaimed: "How'dy, honey! I'se so glad you's come. I seed it in a vision dat somebody fair war comin' to help us. An' wen I yered it war you, I larffed and jist rolled ober, and larffed and jist gib up."

"But, Aunt Linda, I am not very fair," replied Mrs. Latimer.

"Well, chile, you's fair to me. How's all yore folks in de up kentry?"

"All well. I expect them down soon to live here."

"What, Har'yet, and Robby, an' yer ma? Oh, dat is too good. I allers said Robby had san' in his craw, and war born for good luck. He war a mighty nice boy. Har'yet's in clover now. Well, ebery dorg has its day, and de cat has Sunday. I allers tole Har'yet ter keep a stiff upper lip; dat it war a long road dat had no turn."

Dr. Latimer was much gratified by the tender care Aunt Linda bestowed on Iola.

"I ain't goin' to let her do nuffin till she gits seasoned. She looks as sweet as a peach. I allers wanted some nice lady to come down yere and larn our gals some sense. I can't read myself, but I likes ter yere dem dat can."

"Well, Aunt Linda, I am going to teach in the Sunday-school, help in the church, hold mothers' meetings to help these boys and girls to grow up to be good men and women. Won't you get a pair of spectacles and learn to read?"

"Oh, yer can't git dat book froo my head, no way you fix it. I knows nuff to git to hebben, and dat's all I wants to know." Aunt Linda was kind and obliging, but there was one place where she drew the line, and that was at learning to read.

Harry and Miss Delany accompanied Iola as far as her new home, and remained several days. The evening before their departure, Harry took Miss Delany a drive of several miles through the pine barrens.

"This thing is getting very monotonous," Harry broke out, when they had gone some distance.

"Oh, I enjoy it!" replied Miss Delany. "These stately pines look so grand and solemn, they remind me of a procession of hooded monks."

"What in the world are you talking about, Lucille?" asked Harry, looking puzzled.

"About those pine-trees," replied Miss Delany, in a tone of surprise.

"Pshaw, I wasn't thinking about them. I'm thinking about Iola and Frank."

"What about them?" asked Lucille.

"Why, when I was in P——, Dr. Latimer used to be first-rate company, but now it is nothing but what Iola wants, and what Iola says, and what Iola likes. I don't believe that there is a subject I could name to him, from spinning a top to circumnavigating the globe, that he wouldn't somehow contrive to bring Iola in. And I don't believe you could talk ten minutes to Iola on any subject, from dressing a doll to the latest discovery in science, that she wouldn't manage to lug in Frank."

"Oh, you absurd creature!" responded Lucille, "this is their honeymoon, and they are deeply in love with each other. Wait till you get in love with some one."

"I am in love now," replied Harry, with a serious air.

"With whom?" asked Lucille, archly.

"With you," answered Harry, trying to take her hand.

"Oh, Harry!" she exclaimed, playfully resisting. "Don't be so nonsensical! Don't you think the bride looked lovely, with that dress of spotless white and with those orange blossoms in her hair?"

"Yes, she did; that's a fact," responded Harry. "But, Lucille, I think there is a great deal of misplaced sentiment at weddings," he added, more seriously.

"How so?"

"Oh, here are a couple just married, and who are as happy as happy can be; and people will crowd around them wishing much joy; but who thinks of wishing joy to the forlorn old bachelors and restless old maids?"

"Well, Harry, if you want people to wish you much happiness, why don't you do as the doctor has done, get yourself a wife?"

"I will," he replied, soberly, "when you say so."

"Oh, Harry, don't be so absurd."

"Indeed there isn't a bit of absurdity about what I say. I am in earnest."
There was something in the expression of Harry's face and the tone of
his voice which arrested the banter on Lucille's lips.

"I think it was Charles Lamb," replied Lucille, "who once said that
school-teachers are uncomfortable people, and, Harry, I would not like
to make you uncomfortable by marrying you."

"You will make me uncomfortable by not marrying me."

"But," replied Lucille, "your mother may not prefer me for a daughter.
You know, Harry, complexional prejudices are not confined to white
people."

"My mother," replied Harry, with an air of confidence, "is too noble
to indulge in such sentiments."

"And Iola, would she be satisfied?"

"Why, it would add to her satisfaction. She is not one who can't be
white and won't be black."

"Well, then," replied Lucille, "I will take the question of your comfort
into consideration."

The above promise was thoughtfully remembered by Lucille till a
bridal ring and happy marriage were the result.

Soon after Iola had settled in C—— she quietly took her place in
the Sunday-school as a teacher, and in the church as a helper. She was
welcomed by the young pastor, who found in her a strong and faithful
ally. Together they planned meetings for the especial benefit of mothers
and children. When the dens of vice are spreading their snares for the
feet of the tempted and inexperienced her doors are freely opened for
the instruction of the children before their feet have wandered and
gone far astray. She has no carpets too fine for the tread of their little
feet. She thinks it is better to have stains on her carpet than stains on
their souls through any neglect of hers. In lowly homes and windowless
cabins her visits are always welcome. Little children love her. Old age
turns to her for comfort, young girls for guidance, and mothers for
counsel. Her life is full of blessedness.

Doctor Latimer by his kindness and skill has won the name of
the "Good Doctor." But he is more than a successful doctor; he is a
true patriot and a good citizen. Honest, just, and discriminating, he
endeavors by precept and example to instill into the minds of others
sentiments of good citizenship. He is a leader in every reform movement
for the benefit of the community; but his patriotism is not confined to

race lines. "The world is his country, and mankind his countrymen." While he abhors their deeds of violence, he pities the short-sighted and besotted men who seem madly intent upon laying magazines of powder under the cradles of unborn generations. He has great faith in the possibilities of the negro, and believes that, enlightened and Christianized, he will sink the old animosities of slavery into the new community of interests arising from freedom; and that his influence upon the South will be as the influence of the sun upon the earth. As when the sun passes from Capricorn to Cancer, beauty, greenness, and harmony spring up in his path, so he hopes that the future career of the negro will be a greater influence for freedom and social advancement than it was in the days of yore for slavery and its inferior civilization.

Harry and Lucille are at the head of a large and flourishing school. Lucille gives her ripening experience to her chosen work, to which she was too devoted to resign. And through the school they are lifting up the homes of the people. Some have pitied, others blamed, Harry for casting his lot with the colored people, but he knows that life's highest and best advantages do not depend on the color of the skin or texture of the hair. He has his reward in the improved condition of his pupils and the superb manhood and noble life which he has developed in his much needed work.

Uncle Daniel still lingers on the shores of time, a cheery, lovable old man, loved and respected by all; a welcome guest in every home. Soon after Iola's marriage, Robert sold out his business and moved with his mother and sister to North Carolina. He bought a large plantation near C——, which he divided into small homesteads, and sold to poor but thrifty laborers, and his heart has been gladdened by their increased prosperity and progress. He has seen the one-roomed cabins change to comfortable cottages, in which cleanliness and order have supplanted the prolific causes of disease and death. Kind and generous, he often remembers Mrs. Johnson and sends her timely aid.

Marie's pale, spiritual face still bears traces of the beauty which was her youthful dower, but its bloom has been succeeded by an air of sweetness and dignity. Though frail in health, she is always ready to lend a helping hand wherever and whenever she can.

Grandmother Johnson was glad to return South and spend the remnant of her days with the remaining friends of her early life. Although feeble, she is in full sympathy with her children for the uplifting of the race. Marie and her mother are enjoying their aftermath of life, one by rendering to others all the service in her power, while the other, with her face turned toward the celestial city, is

> *"Only waiting till the angels*
> *Open wide the mystic gate."*

The shadows have been lifted from all their lives; and peace, like bright dew, has descended upon their paths. Blessed themselves, their lives are a blessing to others.

PROSE

# The Bible

Amid ancient lore and modern learning, the Word of God stands unique and preeminent. Wonderful in its construction, admirable in its adaptation, it contains truths that a child may comprehend, and mysteries into which angels desire to look. It is in harmony with that adaptation of ends to means which pervades creation, from the polypus tribes, elaborating their coral homes, to man, the wondrous work of God. It forms the brightest link of that glorious chain which unites the humblest work of creation with the throne of the infinite and eternal Jehovah. As light, with its infinite particles and curiously blended colors, is suited to an eye prepared for the alternations of day; as air, with its subtle and invisible essence, is fitted for the delicate organs of respiration; and, in a word, as this material world is adapted to man's physical nature, so the word of eternal truth is adapted to his moral nature and mental constitution. It finds him wounded, sick and suffering, and points him to the balm of Gilead and the Physician of souls. It finds him stained by transgression and defiled with guilt, and directs him to the "blood that cleanseth from all unrighteousness and sin." It finds him athirst and faint, pining amid the deserts of life, and shows him the wells of salvation and the rivers of life. It addresses itself to his moral and spiritual nature, makes provision for his wants and weaknesses, and meets his yearnings and aspirations. It is adapted to his mind in its earliest stages of progression, and its highest state of intellectuality. It provides light for his darkness, joy for his anguish, a solace for his woes, balm for his wounds, and heaven for his hopes. It unveils the unseen world and reveals. Him who is the light of creation and the joy of the universe, reconciled through the death of His Son. It promises the faithful a blessed reunion, in a land undimmed with tears, undarkened by sorrow. It affords a truth for the living, and a refuge for the dying. Aided by the Holy Spirit, it guides us through life, points out the shoals, the quicksands and hidden rocks which endanger our path, and at last leaves us with the eternal God for our refuge, and his everlasting arms for our protection.

# CHRISTIANITY

Christianity is a system claiming God for its author, and the welfare of man for its object. It is a system so uniform, exalted, and pure, that the loftiest intellects have acknowledged its influence, and acquiesced in the justness of its claims. Genius has bent from his erratic course to gather fire from her altars, and pathos from the agony of Gethsemane and the sufferings of Calvary. Philosophy and science have paused amid their speculative researches and wondrous revelations, to gain wisdom from her teachings and knowledge from her precepts. Poetry has culled her fairest flowers and wreathed her softest, to bind her Author's "bleeding brow." Music has strung her sweetest lyres and breathed her noblest strains to celebrate his fame; whilst Learning has brought her richest pearls and rarest gems to lay at her feet and has bent from her lofty heights to bow at the lowly cross. The constant friend of man, she has stood by him in his hour of greatest need. She has cheered the prisoner in his cell and strengthened the martyr at the stake. She has nerved the frail and shrinking heart of woman for high and holy deeds. The worn and weary have rested their fainting heads upon her bosom, and gathered strength from her words and courage from her counsels. She has been the staff of decrepit age, and the joy of manhood in its strength. She has bent over the form of lovely childhood and suffered it to have a place in the Redeemer's arms. She has stood by the bed of the dying and unveiled the glories of eternal life; gilding the darkness of the tomb with the glory of the resurrection.

Christianity has changed the moral aspect of nations. Idolatrous temples have crumbled at her touch, and Guilt 'owned its deformity in her presence. The darkest habitations of earth have been irradiated with heavenly light, and the death-shriek of immolated victims changed for ascriptions of praise to God and the Lamb. Envy and Malice have been rebuked by her contented look, and fretful Impatience by her gentle and resigned manner.

At her approach, fetters have been broken, and men have risen redeemed from dust, and freed from chains. Manhood has learned its dignity and worth; its kindred with angels, and alliance to God.

To man, guilty, fallen, and degraded man, she shows a fountain drawn from the Redeemer's veins; there she bids him wash and be clean. She points him to "Mount Zion, to the city of the living God, to an innumerable company of angels, to the spirits of just men made perfect, and to Jesus, the Mediator of the New Covenant," and urges him to rise from the degradation of sin, renew his nature, and join with them. She shows a pattern so spotless and holy, so elevated and pure, that he might shrink from it discouraged, did she not bring with her a promise from the lips of Jehovah, that he would give power to the faint and might to those who have no strength. Learning may bring her ample pages, and her ponderous records, rich with the spoils of every age, gathered from every land, and gleaned from every source. Philosophy and science may bring their abstruse researches and wondrous revelations—Literature her elegance, with the toils of the pen and the labors of the pencil—but they are idle tales, compared to the truths of Christianity. They may cultivate the intellect, enlighten the understanding, give scope to the imagination, and refine the sensibilities; but they open not, to our dim eyes and longing vision, the land of crystal founts and deathless flowers. Philosophy searches earth; Religion opens heaven. Philosophy doubts and tremble at the portals of eternity; Religion lifts the veil, and shows us golden streets, lit by the Redeemer's countenance, and irradiated by his smile. Philosophy strives to reconcile us to death; Religion triumphs over it.

Philosophy treads amid the pathway of stars and stands a delighted listener to the music of the spheres; but Religion gazes on the glorious palaces of. God, while the harpings of the bloodwashed, and the songs of the redeemed, fall upon her ravished ear. Philosophy has her place; Religion her important sphere; one is of importance here, the other of infinite and vital importance, both here and hereafter.

# THE COLORED PEOPLE IN AMERICA

Having been placed by a dominant race in circumstances over which we have had no control, we have been the butt of ridicule and the mark of oppression. Identified with a people over whom weary ages of degradation have passed, whatever concerns them, as a race, concerns me. I have noticed among our people a disposition to censure and upbraid each other,—a disposition which has its foundation rather, perhaps, in a want of common sympathy and consideration, than mutual hatred or other unholy passions. Born to an inheritance of misery, nurtured in degradation, and cradled in oppression, with the scorn of the white man upon their souls, his fetters upon their limbs, his scourge upon their flesh, what can be expected from their offspring, but a mournful reaction of that cursed system which spreads its baneful influence over body and soul; which dwarfs the intellect, stunts its development, debases the spirit, and degrades the soul? Place any nation in the same condition which has been our hapless lot, fetter their limbs and degrade their souls, debase their sons and corrupt their daughters; and, when the restless yearnings for liberty shall burn through heart and brain—when, tortured by wrong and goaded by oppression, the hearts that would madden with misery, or break in despair, resolve to break their thrall and escape from bondage, then let the bay of the bloodhound and the scent of the human tiger be upon their track;—let them feel that, from the ceaseless murmur of the Atlantic to the sullen roar of the Pacific, from the thunders of the rainbow-crowned Niagara to the swollen waters of the Mexican gulf, they have no shelter for their bleeding feet, or resting place for their defenceless heads;—let them, when nominally free, feel that they have only exchanged the iron yoke of oppression for the galling fetters of a vitiated public opinion;—let prejudice assign them the lowest places and the humblest positions, and make them "hewers of wood and drawers of water;"—let their income be so small that they must from necessity bequeath to their children an inheritance of poverty and a limited education,—and tell me, reviler of our race! censurer of our people! if there is a nation in whose veins runs the purest Caucasian blood, upon whom the same causes would not produce the same effects; whose social condition, intellectual and moral character, would present a more favorable aspect than ours? But there is hope; yes, "blessed be God!" for our downtrodden and despised race. Public and private schools accommodate our children; and in my own Southern home, I see women whose lot is unremitted labor, saving a pittance from their scanty wages to defray the expense of learning to read. We have papers edited by colored editors, which we may consider an honor to possess and a credit to sustain. We have a church that is extending itself from east to west, from north to south, through poverty and reproach, persecution, and pain. We have our faults, our want of union and concentration of purpose; but are there not extenuating circumstances around our darkest faults—palliating excuses for our most egregious errors? and shall we not hope, that the mental and moral aspect which we present is but the first step of a mighty advancement, the faintest coruscations of the day that will dawn with unclouded splendor upon our down-trodden and benighted race, and that ere long we may present to the admiring gaze of those who wish us well, a people to whom knowledge has given power, and righteousness exaltation?

# SHALMANEZER, PRINCE OF COSMAN

S halmanezer, Prince of Cosman, stood on the threshold of manly life, having just received a rich inheritance which had been left him by his father.

He was a magnificent-looking creature—the very incarnation of manly strength and beauty. The splendid poise of his limbs, the vigor and litheness of his motions, the glorious light that flashed from his splendid dark eyes, the bright joyous smiles that occasionally wreathed his fresh young lips, and the finely-erect carriage of his head, were enough to impress the beholder with the thought, "Here is an athlete armed for a glorious strife!"

While Shalmanezer was thinking upon his rich inheritance and how he should use it, he suddenly lifted his eyes and saw two strange-looking personages standing near him. They both advanced towards Shalmanezer when they saw their presence had attracted his attention.

The first one that approached the young man and addressed him, was named Desire. He was a pleasant-looking youth, with a flushed face, and eager, restless eyes. He looked as if he had been pursuing a journey, or had been grasping at an object he had failed to obtain. There was something in his manner that betrayed a want of rest—a look in his eyes which seemed to say, "I am not satisfied." But when he approached, he smiled in the most seductive manner, and, reaching out his hand to Shalmanezer said:

"I have come to welcome thee to man's estate, and for thy enjoyment, I have brought thee three friends who will lead thee into the brightest paths, and press to thy lips the sweetest elixirs."

Gladly the young man received the greeting of Desire, who immediately introduced his three companions, whose names were, Pleasure, Wealth, and Fame.—Pleasure was a most beautiful creature. Her lovely dark eyes flashed out a laughing light; upon her finely-carved lips hovered the brightest and sweetest smiles, which seemed ever ready to break into merry ripples of laughter; her robe was magnificently beautiful, as if it had imprisoned in its warp and woof the beauty of the rainbow and the glory of the setting sun; in her hand she held a richly wrought chalice in which sparkled and effervesced a ruby-colored liquid which was as beautiful to the eye as it was pleasant to the taste.

FRANCES ELLEN WATKINS HARPER

When Pleasure was presented to Shalmanezer, she held out to him her cup and said in the sweetest tones:

> *"Come, drink of my cup. It is sparkling and bright*
> *As rubies distilled in the morning light;*
> *A truce to sorrow and adieu to pain—*
> *Here's the cup to strengthen, soothe and sustain."*

Just as Shalmanezer was about to grasp the cup, the other personage approached him. Her name was Peace, and she was attended by a mild, earnest-looking young man called Self Denial. In the calm depths of her dark-blue eyes was a tender, loving light, and on her brow a majestic serenity which seemed to say, "The cares of earth are at my feet; in vain its tempests sweep around my path." There was also a look of calm, grand patience on the brow of her attendant, which gave him the aspect of one who had passed through suffering unto Peace. Shalmanezer was gazing eagerly on the fair young face of Pleasure, and about to quaff the sparkling nectar, when Peace suddenly arrested his hand and exclaimed:

> *"Beware of this cup! 'Neath its ruddy glow,*
> *Is an undercurrent of shame and woe;*
> *'Neath its sparkling sheen so fair and bright,*
> *Are serpents that hiss, and adders that bite."*

The young man paused a moment, looked on the plain garb of Peace and then on the enchanting loveliness of Pleasure, and, pushing aside the hand of Peace with a scornful gesture, he said proudly and defiantly:

"I will follow Pleasure!"

Peace, thus repulsed, turned sadly away; and Self-Denial, wounded by Shalmanezer's rude rejection, bowed his head in silent sorrow and disappeared from the scene.

As Peace departed, Shalmanezer eagerly grasped the cup of Pleasure and pressed it to his lips, while she clasped her hand in his and said in a most charming manner, "Follow me;" and then he went willingly to the place where she dwelt.

As Shalmanezer approached the palace of Pleasure he heard the sweetest music rising on the air in magnificent swells or sinking in ravishing cadences; at his feet were springing the brightest and fairest flowers; the sweetest perfumes were bathing the air with the most exquisite fragrance; beautiful girls moved like visions of loveliness through the mazy dance; rare old wines sparkled on the festal board; the richest viands and most luscious fruits tempted the taste; and laughter, dance and song filled the air with varied delights. For a while Shalmanezer was enraptured with the palace of Pleasure. But soon he became weary of its gay confusion. The merry ripples of laughter lost their glad freshness; the once delightful music seemed to faint into strange monotones—whether the defect was in his ear or in the music he could not tell, but somehow it had ceased to gratify him; the constant flow of merry talk grew strangely distasteful to him; the pleasant viands began to pall upon his taste; at times he thought he detected a bitterness in the rare old wines which Pleasure ever and anon presented to his lips, and he turned wearily away from everything that had pleased his taste or had charmed and entranced his senses.

Shalmanezer sat moodily wishing that Desire would return and bring with him another attendant to whom he had been introduced when he had first clasped hands with Pleasure, and whose name was Wealth. While he was musing, he lifted up his eyes and saw Wealth and Desire standing at the door of his Boudoir, and near them he saw the sweet loving face of Peace, who was attended by Self Denial. Peace was about to approach him, but he repulsed her with an impatient frown, and turning to Desire he said:

"I have grown weary of Pleasure, and I wish to be introduced to the halls of Wealth."

Taller, graver and less fair was Wealth, than her younger sister, Pleasure. If the beauty of Pleasure could be compared to the vernal freshness of Spring—that of Wealth suggested the maturity of golden harvests, and ripe autumnal fruits. Like Pleasure, she was very richly attired; a magnificent velvet robe fell in graceful folds around her well-proportioned form; like prisms of captured light, the most beautiful jewels gleamed and flashed in her hair; a girdle of the finest and most exquisitely wrought gold was clasped around her waist; her necklace and bracelets were formed of the purest jewels and finest diamonds.— But there was something in her face which betokened a want which all her wealth could not supply. There was a mournful restlessness in her eye that at times seemed to border on the deepest sadness; and yet, there was something so alluring in her manner, so dazzling in her attire,

FRANCES ELLEN WATKINS HARPER

and fascinating in her surroundings, that men would often sacrifice time, talent, energy, and even conscience and manhood, to secure her smiles and bask in her favor.

"Shalmanezer," said Desire to Wealth, "has grown weary of thy sister, Pleasure, and would fain dwell in thy stately halls. Is there aught to hinder him from being one of thy favored guests?"

"Nothing at all," said Wealth, smiling. "The rich inheritance left him by his father has been increasing in value, and I am glad that he was too wise to throw in Pleasure's cup life's richest gifts away."

With these words she reached out her jewelled hand to Shalmanezer and said, "Follow me!"

Weary of the halls of Pleasure, Shalmanezer gladly rose to follow Wealth. As he was leaving, he paused a moment to bid adieu to Pleasure. But she was so changed, that he did not recognize in the faded woman with the weary, listless manner, dull eyes and hollow cheeks, the enchanting girl, who, a few years before, had led him to her halls a welcome and delighted guest. All was so changed. It seemed more like a dream than a reality, that he had dwelt for years in what now seemed like a disenchanted palace. The banquet table was strewn with broken and tasteless fragments; the flowers had lost their fragrance and beauty, and lay in piles of scentless leaves; the soft sweet music had fainted into low breathed sighs, and silence reigned in the deserted halls where dance and revelry and song had wreathed with careless mirth the bright and fleeting hours.

"Come," said Wealth, "my Chariot waits thee at the door."

Without one pang of regret, Shalmanezer turned from the halls of Pleasure, to ride with Wealth in her magnificent chariot.

As they drove along, Wealth showed Shalmanezer the smoke rising from a thousand factories. Pausing a moment, she said:—"I superintend these works and here are my subjects."

Shalmanezer gazed on the colossal piles of brick and mortar, as those castles of industry met his eye. Just then the bell rang, and he saw issuing from amid the smoke and whir of machinery a sight that filled his soul with deep compassion.

There were pale, sad-looking women wending their way home to snatch some moment's rest, and an humble meal before returning to their tasks. There were weary-looking men, who seemed to be degenerating in mental strength and physical vigor. There were young children who looked as if the warm fresh currents of life in their veins had been touched with premature decay. And saddest of all—he saw young girls who looked as if they were rapidly changing from unsophisticated girlhood into over-ripe womanhood.

"Are these thy servants?" said Shalmanezer, sadly.

"These," said Wealth, "are my servants, but not my favorites. In dark mines—close factories—beneath low roofed huts—they dig the glittering jewels, and weave the webs of splendor and beauty with which I adorn my favorites. But I see that the sight pains thee. Let us pass on to fairer scenes."

Bending down to her finely-liveried coachman, she whispered in his ear, and in a few minutes the factories, with their smoke and din, were left behind. Beautiful lawns, lovely parks, and elegant residences rose before the pleased eyes of Shalmanezer; beautiful children sported on the lawns; lovely girls roamed in the parks; and the whole scene was a bright contrast to those he had left behind.

At length they rode up an avenue of stately trees, and stopped at the home of Wealth. "Here is my dwelling," she said, "enter and be my welcome guest."

Shalmanezer accepted the invitation, and entering, gazed with delighted wonder on the splendor and beauty of the place. On the walls hung most beautiful pictures surrounded by the richest frames—rare creations of the grand old masters; lovely statues suggested the idea of life strangely imprisoned in marble; velvet carpets sank pleasantly beneath his tread; elegant book cases, inlaid with ivory and pearl, held on the shelves the grand and noble productions of the monarchs of mind who still rule from their graves in the wide realms of thought and imagination. In her halls were sumptuous halls for feasting; delightful alcoves for thought and meditation; lovely little boudoirs for cozy chats with cherished friends. Even religion found costly bibles and splendidly embossed prayer books in the chambers of repose, where beneath the softened light of golden lamps, the children of Wealth sank to rest on beds of down.

"Surely," said Shalmanezer, "he must be a strangely restless creature, who cannot be satisfied in this home of beauty, grace and affluence." And yet, while he spake, he was conscious of a sense of unrest. He tried to shake it off, but still it would return. He would find himself sighing amid the fairest scenes—oppressed with a sense of longing for something he could not define. His eye was not satisfied with seeing, nor his ear with hearing. It seemed as if life had been presented to him as a luscious fruit, and he had eagerly extracted its richest juices, and was ready to throw away the bitter rind in hopeless disgust.

While he sat gloomily surveying the past, and feeling within his soul a hunger which neither Wealth nor Pleasure could appease, he lifted his eyes towards a distant mountain whose summit was crowned with perpetual snows, although a thousand sunbeams warmed and cheered the vale below. As he gazed, he saw a youth with a proud gait, buoyant step and flashing eye, climbing the mount. In his hand he held a beautifully embossed card, on which was written an invitation from Fame to climb her almost inaccessible heights and hear the sweetest music that ever ravished mortal ear. As the youth ascended the mount, Shalmanezer heard the shouts of applause which were wafted to the ears of the young man, who continued to climb with unabated ardor.

"Here," said Shalmanezer, "is a task worthy of my powers. I have wasted much of my time in the halls of Pleasure; I have grown weary of the stately palaces of Wealth; I will go forth and climb the heights of Fame, and find a welcome in the suncrowned palaces of Renown. O, the sight of that young man inspires my soul, and gives new tone and vigor to my life. I will not pause another moment to listen to the blandishments of Wealth. Instead of treading on these soft carpets, I will brace my soul to climb the rugged heights to gaze upon the fair face of Fame."

Just as he was making this resolve, he saw Peace and her attendant gazing anxiously and silently upon him. His face flushed with sudden anger; a wrathful light flashed from his eyes; and turning his face coldly from Peace, he said: "I do wish Peace would come without her unwelcome companion—Self-Denial I do utterly and bitterly hate." Peace again repulsed, turned sadly away, followed by Self-Denial. With eager haste Shalmanezer rose up and left the bowers of Ease and halls of Pride, to tread the rugged heights of Fame, with patient, ready feet. As he passed upwards, new vigor braced his nerves. He felt an exhilaration of spirits he had never enjoyed in the halls of Wealth or bowers of Pleasure. Onward and upward he proudly moved, as the multitude, who stood at the base, cheered him with rapturous applause, and no music was ever so sweet to his ear as the plaudits of the crowd; but, as he ascended higher and higher, the voices of the multitude grew fainter and fainter; some voices that cheered him at the beginning of his journey had melted into the stillness of death; others had harshened into the rough tones of disapprobation; others were vociferously applauding a new aspirant who had since started to climb the summit of Renown; but, with his eye upon the palace of Fame, he still climbed on, while the air grew rarer, and the atmosphere colder. The old elasticity departed from his limbs, and the buoyancy from his spirits, and it seemed as if the chills of death were slowly creeping around his heart. But still, with fainter step he kept climbing upward, until almost exhausted, he sank down at the palace-gate of Fame, exclaiming, "Is this all?"

Very stately and grand was the cloud-capped palace of Fame. The pillars of her lofty abode were engraven with the names of successful generals, mighty conquerors, great leaders, grand poets, illustrious men and celebrated women. There were statues on which the tooth of Time was slowly gnawing; the statues of men whose brows had once been surrounded by a halo of glory, but were now darkened by the shadow of their crimes. Those heights which had seemed so enchanting at a distance, now seemed more like barren mounds, around which the chills of Death were ever sweeping.

Fame heard the voice of her votary, and came out to place upon his brow her greenest bays and brightest laurels, and bid him welcome to her palace; but when she saw the deathly whiteness of his face, she shrank back in pity and fear. The light was fading from his eye; his limbs had lost their manly strength; and Fame feared that the torpor of Death would overtake him before she could crown him as her honored guest. She bent down her ear to the sufferer, and heard him whisper slowly, "Peace! Peace!"

Then said Fame to her servants, "Descend to the vale, bring the best medical skill ye can find, and search for Peace, and entreat her to come; tell her that one of my votaries lies near to death, and longs for her presence." The servants descended to the vale, and soon returned, bringing with them a celebrated physician.—Peace had heard the cry of Shalmanezer, and had entered the room with her companion before the doctor had come. When the physician saw Shalmanezer, he gazed anxiously upon him, felt the fluttering pulse, and chafed the pale cold hands to restore the warmth and circulation.

In the meantime, Pleasure and Wealth having heard the story of Shalmanezer's illness, entered the room. "There is but one thing," said the physician, "can save Shalmanezer's life: some one must take the warm healthy blood from his veins and inject it into Shalmanezer's veins before he can be restored to health."

Pleasure and Wealth looked aghast when they heard the doctor's prescription. Pleasure suddenly remembered that she had a pressing engagement; Wealth said "I am no longer young, nor even well, and am sure I have not one drop of blood to spare;" Fame pitied her faithful votary, but amid the cold blasts that swept around her home, was sure it would be very imprudent for her to attempt to part with so much blood. Just as Pleasure, Wealth and Fame had refused to give the needed aid, Desire entered the room, but when he heard the conditions for the restoration of Shalmanezer, shrank back in selfish dismay, and refused also.

As Shalmanezer lay gasping for breath, and looking wistfully at his old companions, Peace, attended by Self-Denial, drew near the sick man's couch. Shalmanezer opened his eyes languidly, and closed them wearily; when life was like a joyous dream, he had repulsed Peace and utterly hated Self Denial, and what could he dare hope from either in his hour of dire extremity. While he lay with his eyes half-closed, Self Denial approached the bedside, and baring his arm, said to the doctor:

"Here is thy needed remedy. Take the blood from these veins, and with it restore Shalmanezer to health and strength."

The doctor struck his lancet into Self-Denial's arm, and drawing from it the needed quantity of blood, injected it into Shalmanezer's veins. The remedy was effectual. Health flushed the cheeks of Shalmanezer, and braced each nerve with new vigor, and he soon recovered from his fearful exhaustion. Then his heart did cleave unto Self-Denial. He had won his heart by his lofty sacrifice. He had bought his love by the blood from his own veins. Clasping hands with Self-Denial, he trod with him the paths of Peace, and in so doing, received an amount of true happiness which neither Pleasure, Wealth nor Fame could give.

# The Two Offers

W hat is the matter with you, Laura, this morning? I have been watching you this hour, and in that time you have commenced a half dozen letters and torn them all up. What matter of such grave moment is puzzling your dear little head, that you do not know how to decide?"

"Well, it is an important matter: I have two offers for marriage, and I do not know which to choose."

"I should accept neither, or to say the least, not at present."

"Why not?"

"Because I think a woman who is undecided between two offers, has not love enough for either to make a choice; and in that very hesitation, indecision, she has a reason to pause and seriously reflect, lest her marriage, instead of being an affinity of souls or a union of hearts, should only be a mere matter of bargain and sale, or an affair of convenience and selfish interest."

"But I consider them both very good offers, just such as many a girl would gladly receive. But to tell you the truth, I do not think that I regard either as a woman should the man she chooses for her husband. But then if I refuse, there is the risk of being an old maid, and that is not to be thought of."

"Well, suppose there is, is that the most dreadful fate that can befall a woman? Is there not more intense wretchedness in an ill-assorted marriage—more utter loneliness in a loveless home, than in the lot of the old maid who accepts her earthly mission as a gift from God, and strives to walk the path of life with earnest and unfaltering steps?"

"Oh! what a little preacher you are. I really believe that you were cut out for an old maid; that when nature formed you, she put in a double portion of intellect to make up for a deficiency of love; and yet you are kind and affectionate. But I do not think that you know anything of the grand, over-mastering passion, or the deep necessity of woman's heart for loving."

"Do you think so?" resumed the first speaker; and bending over her work she quietly applied herself to the knitting that had lain neglected by her side, during this brief conversation; but as she did so, a shadow flitted over her pale and intellectual brow, a mist gathered in her eyes, and a slight quivering of the lips, revealed a depth of feeling to which her companion was a stranger.

But before I proceed with my story, let me give you a slight history of the speakers. They were cousins, who had met life under different auspices. Laura Lagrange, was the only daughter of rich and indulgent parents, who had spared no pains to make her an accomplished lady.

Her cousin, Janette Alston, was the child of parents, rich only in goodness and affection. Her father had been unfortunate in business, and dying before he could retrieve his fortunes, left his business in an embarrassed state.

His widow was unacquainted with his business affairs, and when the estate was settled, hungry creditors had brought their claims and the lawyers had received their fees, she found herself homeless and almost penniless, and she who had been sheltered in the warm clasp of loving arms, found them too powerless to shield her from the pitiless pelting storms of adversity.

Year after year she struggled with poverty and wrestled with want, till her toil-worn hands became too feeble to hold the shattered chords of existence, and her tear-dimmed eyes grew heavy with the slumber of death.

Her daughter had watched over her with untiring devotion, had closed her eyes in death, and gone out into the busy, restless world, missing a precious tone from the voices of earth, a beloved step from the paths of life.

Too self reliant to depend on the charity of relations, she endeavored to support herself by her own exertions, and she had succeeded. Her path for a while was marked with struggle and trial, but instead of uselessly repining, she met them bravely, and her life became not a thing of ease and indulgence, but of conquest, victory, and accomplishments.

At the time when this conversation took place, the deep trials of her life had passed away. The achievements of her genius had won her a position in the literary world, where she shone as one of its bright particular stars. And with her fame came a competence of worldly means, which gave her leisure for improvement, and the riper development of her rare talents.

And she, that pale intellectual woman, whose genius gave life and vivacity to the social circle, and whose presence threw a halo of beauty and grace around the charmed atmosphere in which she moved, had at one period of her life, known the mystic and solemn strength of an all-absorbing love. Years faded into the misty past, had seen the kindling of her eye, the quick flushing of her cheek, and the wild throbbing of her heart, at tones of a voice long since hushed to the stillness of death.

Deeply, wildly, passionately, she had loved. Her whole life seemed like the pouring out of rich, warm and gushing affections. This love quickened her talents, inspired her genius, and threw over her life a tender and spiritual earnestness. And then came a fearful shock, a mournful waking from that "dream of beauty and delight."

A shadow fell around her path; it came between her and the object of her heart's worship; first a few cold words, estrangement, and then a painful separation; the old story of woman's pride—digging the sepulchre of her happiness, and then a new-made grave, and her path over it to the spirit world; and thus faded out from that young heart her bright, brief and saddened dream of life.

Faint and spirit-broken, she turned from the scenes associated with the memory of the loved and lost. She tried to break the chain of sad associations that bound her to the mournful past; and so, pressing back the bitter sobs from her almost breaking heart, like the dying dolphin, whose beauty is born of its death anguish, her genius gathered strength from suffering and wondrous power and brilliancy from the agony she hid within the desolate chambers of her soul.

Men hailed her as one of earth's strangely gifted children, and wreathed the garlands of fame for her brow, when it was throbbing with a wild and fearful unrest. They breathed her name with applause, when through the lonely halls of her stricken spirit, was an earnest cry for peace, a deep yearning for sympathy and heart-support.

But life, with its stern realities, met her; its solemn responsibilities confronted her, and turning, with an earnest and shattered spirit, to life's duties and trials, she found a calmness and strength that she had only imagined in her dreams of poetry and song.

We will now pass over a period of ten years, and the cousins have met again. In that calm and lovely woman, in whose eyes is a depth of tenderness, tempering the flashes of her genius, whose looks and tones are full of sympathy and love, we recognize the once smitten and stricken Janette Alston.

The bloom of her girlhood had given way to a higher type of spiritual beauty, as if some unseen hand had been polishing and refining the temple in which her lovely spirit found its habitation; and this had been the fact. Her inner life had grown beautiful, and it was this that was constantly developing the outer.

Never, in the early flush of womanhood, when an absorbing love had lit up her eyes and glowed in her life, had she appeared so interesting as when, with a countenance which seemed overshadowed with a spiritual light, she bent over the death-bed of a young woman, just lingering at the shadowy gates of the unseen land.

"Has he come?" faintly but eagerly exclaimed the dying woman. "Oh! how I have longed for his coming, and even in death he forgets me."

"Oh, do not say so, dear Laura, some accident may have detained him," said Janette to her cousin; for on that bed, from whence she will never rise, lies the once-beautiful and lighthearted Laura Lagrange, the brightness of whose eyes has long since been dimmed with tears, and whose voice had become like a harp whose every chord is turned to sadness—whose faintest thrill and loudest vibrations are but the variations of agony.

A heavy hand was laid upon her once warm and bounding heart, and a voice came whispering through her soul, that she must die. But, to her, the tidings was a message of deliverance—a voice, hushing her wild sorrows to the calmness of resignation and hope. Life had grown so weary upon her head—the future looked so hopeless—she had no wish to tread again the track where thorns had pierced her feet, and clouds overcast her sky; and she hailed the coming of death's angel as the footsteps of a welcome friend.

And yet, earth had one object so very dear to her weary heart. It was her absent and recreant husband; for, since that conversation, she had accepted one of her offers, and become a wife. But, before she married, she learned that great lesson of human experience and woman's life, to love the man who bowed at her shrine, a willing worshipper.

He had a pleasing address, raven hair, flashing eyes, a voice of thrilling sweetness, and lips of persuasive eloquence; and being well versed in the ways of the world, he won his way to her heart, and she became his bride, and he was proud of his prize.

Vain and superficial in his character, he looked upon marriage not as a divine sacrament for the soul's development and human progression, but as the title-deed that gave him possession of the woman he thought he loved.

But alas for her, the laxity of his principles had rendered him unworthy of the deep and undying devotion of a pure-hearted woman;

but, for awhile, he hid from her his true character, and she blindly loved him, and for a short period was happy in the consciousness of being beloved; though sometimes a vague unrest would fill her soul, when, overflowing with a sense of the good, the beautiful, and the true, she would turn to him, but find no response to the deep yearnings of her soul—no appreciation of life's highest realities—its solemn grandeur and significant importance.

Their souls never met, and soon she found a void in her bosom, that his earth-born love could not fill. He did not satisfy the wants of her mental and moral nature—between him and her there was no affinity of minds, no intercommunion of souls.

Talk as you will of woman's deep capacity for loving, of the strength of her affectional nature. I do not deny it; but will the mere possession of any human love, fully satisfy all the demands of her whole being? You may paint her in poetry or fiction, as a frail vine, clinging to her brother man for support, and dying when deprived of it; and all this may sound well enough to please the imaginations of school-girls, or love-lorn maidens.

But woman—the true woman—if you would render her happy, it needs more than the mere development of her affectional nature. Her conscience should be enlightened, her faith in the true and right established, scope given to her Heaven-endowed and God-given faculties.

The true aim of female education should be not a development of one or two, but all the faculties of the human soul, because no perfect womanhood is developed by imperfect culture. Intense love is often akin to intense suffering, and to trust the whole wealth of a woman's nature on the frail bark of human love, may often be like trusting a cargo of gold and precious gems, to a bark that has never battled with the storm, or buffeted the waves.

Is it any wonder, then, that so many life-barks go down, paving the ocean of time with precious hearts and wasted hopes? that so many float around us, shattered and dismasted wrecks? that so many are stranded on the shoals of existence, mournful beacons and solemn warnings for the thoughtless, to whom marriage is a careless and hasty rushing together of the affections?

Alas that an institution so fraught with good for humanity should be so perverted, and that state of life, which should be filled with happiness, become so replete with misery.

And this was the fate of Laura Lagrange. For a brief period after her marriage her life seemed like a bright and beautiful dream, full of hope and radiant with joy. And then there came a change—he found other attractions that lay beyond the pale of home influences.

The gambling saloon had power to win him from her side, he had lived in an element of unhealthy and unhallowed excitements, and the society of a loving wife, the pleasures of a well-regulated home, were enjoyments too tame for one who had vitiated his tastes by the pleasures of sin.

There were charmed houses of vice, built upon dead men's loves, where, amid the flow of song, laughter, wine, and careless mirth, he would spend hour after hour, forgetting the cheek that was paling through his neglect, heedless of the tear-dimmed eyes, peering anxiously into the darkness, waiting, or watching his return.

The influence of old associations was upon him. In early life, home had been to him a place of ceilings and walls, not a true home, built upon goodness, love and truth. It was a place where velvet carpets hushed its tread, where images of loveliness and beauty invoked into being by painter's art and sculptor's skill, pleased the eye and gratified the taste, where magnificence surrounded his way and costly clothing adorned his person; but it was not the place for the true culture and right development of his soul.

His father had been too much engrossed in making money, and his mother in spending it, in striving to maintain a fashionable position in society, and shining in the eyes of the world, to give the proper direction to the character of their wayward and impulsive son. His mother put beautiful robes upon his body, but left ugly scars upon his soul; she pampered his appetite, but starved his spirit.

Every mother should be a true artist, who knows how to weave into her child's life images of grace and beauty, the true poet capable of writing on the soul of childhood the harmony of love and truth, and teaching it how to produce the grandest of all poems—the poetry of a true and noble life.

But in his home, a love for the good, the true and right, had been sacrificed at the shrine of frivolity and fashion. That parental authority which should have been preserved as a string of precious pearls, unbroken and unscattered, was simply the administration of chance.

At one time obedience was enforced by authority, at another time by flattery and promises, and just as often it was not enforced at all. His early associations were formed as chance directed, and from his want of home-training, his character received a bias, his life a shade, which ran through every avenue of his existence, and darkened all his future hours.

Oh, if we would trace the history of all the crimes that have o'ershadowed this sin-shrouded and sorrow-darkened world of ours, how many might be seen arising from the wrong home influences, or the weakening of the home ties.

Home should always be the best school for the affections, the birthplace of high resolves, and the altar upon which lofty aspirations are kindled, from whence the soul may go forth strengthened, to act its part aright in the great drama of life with conscience enlightened, affections cultivated, and reason and judgment dominant.

But alas for the young wife. Her husband had not been blessed with such a home. When he entered the arena of life, the voices from home did not linger around his path as angels of guidance about his steps; they were not like so many messages to invite him to deeds of high and holy worth.

The memory of no sainted mother arose between him and deeds of darkness; the earnest prayers of no father arrested him in his downward course: and before a year of his married life had waned, his young wife had learned to wait and mourn his frequent and uncalled-for absence.

More than once had she seen him come home from his midnight haunts, the bright intelligence of his eye displaced by the drunkard's stare, and his manly gait changed to the inebriate's stagger; and she was beginning to know the bitter agony that is compressed in the mournful words, a drunkard's wife.

And then there came a bright but brief episode in her experience; the angel of life gave to her existence a deeper meaning and loftier significance; she sheltered in the warm clasp of her loving arms, a dear babe, a precious child, whose love filled every chamber of her heart, and felt the fount of maternal love gushing so new within her soul. That child was hers.

How overshadowing was the love with which she bent over its helplessness, how much it helped to fill the void and chasms in her soul. How many lonely hours were beguiled by its winsome ways, its answering smiles and fond caresses. How exquisite and solemn was the feeling that thrilled her heart when she clasped the tiny hands together and taught her dear child to call God "Our Father."

FRANCES ELLEN WATKINS HARPER

What a blessing was that child. The father paused in his headlong career, awed by the strange beauty and precocious intellect of his child; and the mother's life had a better expression through her ministrations of love. And then there came hours of bitter anguish, shading the sunlight of her home and hushing the music of her heart.

The angel of death bent over the couch of her child and beaconed it away. Closer and closer the mother strained her child to her wildly heaving breast, and struggled with the heavy hand that lay upon its heart. Love and agony contended with death, and the language of the mother's heart was,

> *"Oh, Death, away! that innocent is mine;*
> *I cannot spare him from my arms*
> *To lay him, Death, in thine.*
> *I am a mother, Death; I gave that darling birth*
> *I could not bear his lifeless limbs*
> *Should moulder in the earth."*

But death was stronger than love and mightier than agony and won the child for the land of crystal founts and deathless flowers, and the poor, stricken mother sat down beneath the shadow of her mighty grief, feeling as if a great light had gone out from her soul, and that the sunshine had suddenly faded around her path. She turned in her deep anguish to the father of her child, the loved and cherished dead.

For awhile his words were kind and tender, his heart seemed subdued, and his tenderness fell upon her worn and weary heart like rain on perishing flowers, or cooling waters to lips all parched with thirst and scorched with fever; but the change was evanescent, the influence of unhallowed associations and evil habits had vitiated and poisoned the springs of his existence.

They had bound him in their meshes, and he lacked the moral strength to break his fetters, and stand erect in all the strength and dignity of a true manhood, making life's highest excellence his ideal, and striving to gain it.

And yet moments of deep contrition would sweep over him, when he would resolve to abandon the wine-cup forever, when he was ready to forswear the handling of another card, and he would try to break away from the associations that he felt were working his ruin; but when the hour of temptation came his strength was weakness, his earnest purposes were cobwebs, his well meant resolutions ropes of sand, and thus passed year after year of the married life of Laura Lagrange.

She tried to hide her agony from the public gaze, to smile when her heart was almost breaking. But year after year her voice grew fainter and sadder, her once light and bounding step grew slower and faltering. Year after year she wrestled with agony, and strove with despair, till the quick eyes of her brother read, in the paling of her cheek and the dimming eye, the secret anguish of her worn and weary spirit. On that wan, sad face, he saw the death-tokens, and he knew the dark wing of the mystic angel swept coldly around her path.

"Laura," said her brother to her one day, "you are not well, and I think you need our mother's tender care and nursing. You are daily losing strength, and if you will go I will accompany you." At first, she hesitated, she shrank almost instinctively from presenting that pale sad face to the loved ones at home. That face was such a telltale; it told of heart-sickness, of hope deferred, and the mournful story of unrequited love.

But then a deep yearning for home sympathy woke within her a passionate longing for love's kind words, for tenderness and heart support, and she resolved to seek the home of her childhood and lay her weary head upon her mother's bosom, to be folded again in her loving arms, to lay that poor, bruised and aching heart where it might beat and throb closely to the loved ones at home.

A kind welcome awaited her. All that love and tenderness could devise was done to bring the bloom to her cheek and the light to her eye; but it was all in vain; her's was a disease that no medicine could cure, no earthly balm would heal. It was a slow wasting of the vital forces, the sickness of the soul. The unkindness and neglect of her husband, lay like a leaden weight upon her heart, and slowly oozed way its life-drops.

And where was he that had won her love, and then cast it aside as a useless thing, who rifled her heart of its wealth and spread bitter ashes upon its broken altars? He was lingering away from her when the death-damps were gathering on her brow, when his name was trembling on her lips! lingering away! when she was watching his coming, though the death films were gathering before her eyes, and earthly things were fading from her vision.

"I think I hear him now," said the dying woman, "surely that is his step;" but the sound died away in the distance. Again she started from an uneasy slumber, "that is his voice! I am so glad he has come."

　　　　　FRANCES ELLEN WATKINS HARPER

Tears gathered in the eyes of the sad watchers by that dying bed, for they knew that she was deceived. He had not returned. For her sake they wished his coming. Slowly the hours waned away, and then came the sad, soul-sickening thought that she was forgotten, forgotten in the last hour of human need, forgotten when the spirit, about to be dissolved, paused for the last time on the threshold of existence, a weary watcher at the gates of death.

"He has forgotten me," again she faintly murmured, and the last tears she would ever shed on earth sprung to her mournful eyes, and clasping her hands together in silent anguish, a few broken sentences issued from her pale and quivering lips. They were prayers for strength and earnest pleading for him who had desolated her young life, by turning its sunshine to shadows, its smiles to tears.

"He has forgotten me," she murmured again, "but I can bear it, the bitterness of death is passed, and soon I hope to exchange the shadows of death for the brightness of eternity, the rugged paths of life for the golden streets of glory, and the care and turmoils of earth for the peace and rest of heaven."

Her voice grew fainter and fainter, they saw the shadows that never deceive flit over her pale and faded face, and knew that the death angel waited to soothe their weary one to rest, to calm the throbbing of her bosom and cool the fever of her brain.

And amid the silent hush of their grief the freed spirit, refined through suffering, and brought into divine harmony through the spirit of the living Christ, passed over the dark waters of death as on a bridge of light, over whose radiant arches hovering angels bent. They parted the dark locks from her marble brow, closed the waxen lids over the once bright and laughing eye, and left her to the dreamless slumber of the grave.

Her cousin turned from that death-bed a sadder and wiser woman. She resolved more earnestly than ever to make the world better by her example, gladder by her presence, and to kindle the fires of her genius on the altars of universal love and truth. She had a higher and better object in all her writings than the mere acquisition of gold, or acquirement of fame.

She felt that she had a high and holy mission on the battle-field of existence, that life was not given her to be frittered away in nonsense, or wasted away in trifling pursuits. She would willingly espouse an unpopular cause but not an unrighteous one. In her the down-trodden slave found an earnest advocate; the flying fugitive remembered her kindness as he stepped cautiously through our Republic, to gain his freedom in a monarchial land, having broken the chains on which the rust of centuries had gathered.

Little children learned to name her with affection, the poor called her blessed, as she broke her bread to the pale lips of hunger. Her life was like a beautiful story, only it was clothed with the dignity of reality and invested with the sublimity of truth. True, she was an old maid.

No husband brightened her life with his love, or shaded it with his neglect. No children nestling lovingly in her arms called her mother. No one appended Mrs. to her name; she was indeed an old maid, not vainly striving to keep up an appearance of girlishness, when departed was written on her youth.

Not vainly pining at her loneliness and isolation: the world was full of warm, loving hearts, and her own beat in unison with them. Neither was she always sentimentally sighing for something to love, objects of affection were all around her, and the world was not so wealthy in love that it had no use for her's; in blessing others she made a life and benediction, and as old age descended peacefully and gently upon her, she had learned one of life's most precious lessons, that true happiness consists not so much in the fruition of our wishes as in the regulation of desires and the full development and right culture of our whole statures.

# bookfinity™

## Discover more of your favorite classics with Bookfinity™.

- Track your reading with custom book lists.
- Get great book recommendations for your personalized Reader Type.
- Add reviews for your favorite books.
- AND MUCH MORE!

Visit **bookfinity.com** and take the fun Reader Type quiz to get started.

Enjoy our classic and modern companion pairings!